Mallee Country

Mallee Country

Land, People, History

by

Richard Broome, Charles Fahey,
Andrea Gaynor & Katie Holmes

Mallee Country: Land, People, History

© Copyright 2020 Richard Broome, Charles Fahey, Andrea Gaynor and Katie Holmes
All rights reserved. Apart from any uses permitted by Australia's Copyright Act 1968, no part of this book may be reproduced by any process without prior written permission from the copyright owners. Inquiries should be directed to the publisher.

Monash University Publishing
Matheson Library Annexe
40 Exhibition Walk
Monash University
Clayton, Victoria 3800, Australia
www.publishing.monash.edu

Monash University Publishing brings to the world publications which advance the best traditions of humane and enlightened thought.

Monash University Publishing titles pass through a rigorous process of independent peer review.

ISBN: 9781925523126 (paperback)
ISBN: 9781925523133 (pdf)
ISBN: 9781925523140 (epub)

www.publishing.monash.edu/books/mc-9781925523126.html

Series: Australian History

Series Editor: Sean Scalmer

Design: Les Thomas

Cover image: Farm Gate near Manangatang (Courtesy Judy Irvin)

A catalogue record for this book is available from the National Library of Australia.

Printed in Australia by Griffin Press an Accredited ISO AS/NZS 14001:2004 Environmental Management System printer.

The paper this book is printed on is certified against the Forest Stewardship Council ® Standards. Griffin Press holds FSC chain of custody certification SGS-COC-005088. FSC promotes environmentally responsible, socially beneficial and economically viable management of the world's forests.

CONTENTS

Prologue: Mallee Country vii

Part One: Mallee Aborigines and European Intruders to 1880 1
Chapter 1: Deep Time 3
Chapter 2: Aboriginal Homelands 11
Chapter 3: An Impracticable Country 46
Chapter 4: Pastoral Adventurers 65

Part Two: Transforming the Mallee 1880–1945 101
Chapter 5: A Land for Farmers 103
Chapter 6: Developing Mallee Farms 1914–1925 129
Chapter 7: Troubled Times 1926–1945 158
Chapter 8: Camping and Working on Country 190

Part Three: The State and Mallee Lands 1945–1983 207
Chapter 9: Modernising Mallee Farms 209
Chapter 10: New Mallee Farms 242
Chapter 11: Conserving the Mallee 271

Part Four: Living with the Mallee 1983 to the Present 309
Chapter 12: Sustaining Mallee Farms 1983–2018 311
Chapter 13: Reinventing the Mallee 346

Epilogue 378
Appendix 385
Note on Measurements 387
Acknowledgements 388
Select Published Sources 392
Index 399
About the Authors 417

In memory of

*Janette Bailey
(1964–2016)*

*environmental historian
&
and a researcher for this book*

PROLOGUE

Mallee Country

Despite wheat's centrality to mallee country today, these lands were not always planted to wheat or grazed by sheep. They have an ecological and human history that stretches back to Deep Time, creating unique and startling landscapes. This history, therefore, begins with the land: its flora, fauna, climate and location in southern Australia; and why it is called mallee, sometimes with a capital letter, sometimes not.

* * *

Mallee lands are wondrous, producing a great diversity of flora as plants develop attributes to survive in semi-arid conditions with patchy and low-nutrient soils. The Victorian and South Australian mallee is home to 311 indigenous flora species: including eucalypts, acacia, casuarina, hakeas, grevilleas, melaleucas, boronia, many types of daisy, eight salt-tolerant saltbush varieties, and the spiky porcupine grass, *Triodia scariosa*.[1] This diversity is dwarfed by mallee country in south-western Australia, which hosts a staggering 3,559 kinds of indigenous plants, including 192 mallee-form eucalypts, few of them found elsewhere.[2]

The brilliant sunshine over mallee country and most of the Australian continent encourages trees and shrubs to produce more carbohydrate than the depleted soils of this ancient continent allow them to convert into plant fibre and seeds.[3] The excess sugars are donated to guests in return for pollination duties. Winged visitors—birds, bats, bees—and climbing guests, such as

---

1 Jocelyn Lindner, *Flora and Fauna of the Victorian and South Australian Mallee* (Ouyen: Jocelyn Lindner, 2015).
2 Western Australian Department of Parks and Wildlife, *Florabase: Database of the Western Australian Flora*, accessed 27 March 2017, https://florabase.dpaw.wa.gov.au.
3 Tim Low makes use of recent work done by Orians and Milewski on sugars and nutrient poor soils. G.H. Orians and A.V. Milewski, 'Ecology of Australia: The Effects of Nutrient-poor Soils and Intense Fires', *Biological Review* 82 (2007): 393–423, discussed in Tim Low, *Where Song Began: Australia's Birds and how they Changed the World* (Melbourne: Penguin, 2017), chap. 1.

possums and sugar gliders, luxuriate in blossoms and sugary exudates—manna, honeydew and, particularly in the eastern mallee, lerp. Lerp is a sugary covering excreted by psyllids and coccids that suck on eucalyptus leaves. They produce white excretions two to four millimetres long that often combine to form small clumps of snowy sweetness on countless leaves. Honeyeaters enter into fierce battles to protect such licking utopias from competitors. Parrots also gnaw at sweet sap oozing from bark, and small birds peck at aphids, which feast on eucalyptus leaves. Sugar is a powerhouse of mallee wildlife.

Mallee woodlands and shrublands are lands of plenty for honeyeaters such as the yellow-throated miners and noisy miners, and for many varieties of parrot including the Regent and Australian Ringneck. Each buries its beak and tongue into the nectar-bearing blossom of scores of different eucalypts, bottlebrush, banksias and other flowering plants. Countless billions of individual blossoms produce nectar for days on end. Different eucalypts flower at different times, making for a generous feast staggered over many months, while insects, aphids and fruits provide a year-round supplement to this sugary excess. Native bees also comb these trees and the myriad of small wildflowers. Each flying species in its own way pollinates the landscape, increasing biodiversity with hybrid plant species adapted to this environment.[4]

Sugars also attract others, including ants in their countless billions running in zig-zag lines up the abundant mallees to take the sweetness exuded by aphids. In 2006, forty-eight different types of ant were identified in the paddocks and remnant vegetation of just five Murray Mallee farms.[5] Ant trails traverse mallee landscapes, forming paths half a metre wide between low dome nests. Echidnas and lizards dine out on these ants. Spectacular jewel beetles, abundant in Western Australian and Murray Mallee country, feast on sugars, their larvae boring into the sapwood of mallees or shrubs and later emerging as adults to feed on mallee nectar or leaves. Pygmy possums, too, feed on nectar, as well as insects, while a range of other marsupials make do with the shoots, seeds and leaves found on and among the mallees.

Insects of all varieties—flies, wasps, crickets and beetles—provide extra food, adding to the diversity. Alec Chisholm observed thirty species of birds at Victoria's Wyperfeld National Park in 1934, most of them found only in mallee or dry country.[6] The iconic lowan or malleefowl scratch around the

---

4 Low, *Where Song Began*, chaps 1 and 2.
5 Mallee Region Biodiversity in Grain & Graze [poster, *c.* 2007], Centre for Environment, University of Tasmania, accessed 27 March 2017, http://www.utas.edu.au/__data/assets/pdf_file/0016/23245/Mallee_biodiversity_poster.pdf.
6 Alec H. Chisholm, 'Mallee National Park', *Argus*, 24 November 1934.

understorey for seeds and insects and build large mounds into which eggs are deposited to hatch amid the decaying humus. Overhead, wrens, pardalotes, honeyeaters, western warblers or flycatchers, thornbills (tits), swallows, wagtails, whistlers, wood swallows and birds of many kinds devour a plethora of aphids, moths, spiders, beetles and other insects. Major Mitchell (pink) and sulphur-crested cockatoos, galahs and corellas feed on seeds and the nuts of Murray Pines growing on sandy ridges. Above them soar crows, owls, hawks, ravens and, atop the avifaunal food chain, wedge-tailed eagles.[7]

In some mallee country, such as the Lake Grace region of Western Australia or the Hattah Lakes in Victoria, the periodic inundation of salt lakes draws vast numbers of darts, native hens, grebes, cormorants, ducks and other water birds. Breeding occurs if the waters are sufficiently deep to resist evaporation for over four months. The Murray River–edged mallee lands in Victoria and South Australia also provide year-round living for dozens of species of water birds, including ibis, herons, egrets, swans, varieties of duck, terns, coots and cormorants.

* * *

Mallee country is found in three large bands of land across the southern part of Australia (see Map 1).[8] These tracts of country were named by settlers after an Aboriginal word of the Wemba Wemba people from the north-west region of Victoria, '*mali*', for a form of eucalyptus.[9] Its spelling was finally settled as 'mallee' in Ham's 1846 map of Victoria.[10] The word 'mallee' is not

---

7   Chisholm, 'Mallee National Park'.
8   This project focuses on certain ecological sub-bioregions of the 403 defined by the federal Department of Environment and Heritage from 2005 onwards, according to climate, minerals, land forms, vegetation, flora and fauna. These bioregions were defined using various iterations of Interim Biogeographic Regionalisation of Australia data (IBRA). Because of the large extent of the mallee regions, our project is confined to a study of certain of these bioregions and local areas within them, governed by the availability of sources. Parts of the following sub-bioregions were chosen for study: the Murray–Darling Depression (MDD1-4, RIV5-6 and DR8-9); the lower Murray and lower Darling rivers and their Mallee hinterlands; the Eyre–Yorke Block (EYB 1-5); and in Western Australia the Eastern and Western Mallee (MAL1-2).
9   *Macquarie Encyclopedic Dictionary. The Signature Edition* (Sydney: Australia's Heritage Publishing, 2011), 754.
10 Alfred S. Kenyon, *The Story of the Mallee: A History of The Victorian Mallee Read before the Historical Society of Victoria, 18 March 1912* (reprinted Melbourne: Wilke & Co., 1982), 2.

MAP 1:
MALLEE COUNTRY OF SOUTHERN AUSTRALIA

commonly or uniformly used in all the regions shown on Map 1, and the term is particularly rare in Western Australia, where mallee country forms part of—and stretches beyond—the 'Wheatbelt'. Mallee is used to describe country in South Australia, New South Wales and Victoria, but only in South Australia between the Murray River and the Victorian border is it reified by a capital letter as in 'Murray Mallee', and only in Victoria does it become, 'the Mallee'.

To an ecologist, mallee country is the semi-arid zone in which mallee eucalypts predominate, or where they grew in the past before the radical transformation of their habitat into dry-farmed wheat lands. Mallees thrive in a Mediterranean climate of hot summers and mild winters, and grow in most soils except very heavy clays and deep siliceous sands with few nutrients. They are the frontier members of the eucalypt family, inhabiting very marginal ecologies. Beyond their range, the land is dominated by the even more drought-tolerant acacia and casuarina species or, in the west, the hardy eucalypt trees and saltbush of the Great Western Woodlands. It is estimated that before European settlement mallee woodlands ranged over the semi-arid Murray–Darling Basin, extending into south-western NSW, and westwards to the Eyre Peninsula and south-western Western Australia.[11] Stretching across large sections of the southern part of the continent, mallee country is one of Australia's main ecological systems, yet about three-quarters of it has now been cleared for agriculture.

Commissioners into Victorian land settlement in 1879 struggled to describe the unusual physiology of the mallee eucalypt, commenting: 'a most strange product of nature which is difficult to figure accurately to the mind of one who has never seen it … The figure it represents resembles that of a skeleton umbrella reversed without the central staff, and showing the ribs rising and radiating from the bottom'.[12] Characterised by multiple stems arising from a lignotuber (or 'mallee root'), mallees are usually less than ten metres in height, with the crown forming mainly at the end of the branchlets (see Figures 2.3 and 3.2). Some mallees, however, have a shrubbier habit. The lignotuber allows the trees to grow close together and regenerate quickly after fire or drought. As colonists soon discovered, this type of root also gives mallees a startling resilience; the lignotuber and root system bound the tree fast to the soil, they observed, and, if the tree was cut down or burned, new shoots soon shot out from the lignotuber. In 1880 a special reporter for the Melbourne-based *Argus* commented that 'the mallee tree is the most tenacious of life. If it is cut down or burned it springs up again with renewed vigour'.[13]

Mallee is a form rather than a species of eucalypt; it is both a verb and a noun. Not all species will mallee, that is grow with multiple stems, and sometimes species that typically mallee in the wild may form single-stemmed specimens. Over fifteen varieties of eucalypt typically taking on mallee form exist in Victoria, but the quintessential mallee in the Victorian Mallee is *Eucalyptus dumosa*.[14] Western Australia is home to by far the greatest concentration of mallee-form eucalypts—388 species and rising—with many of them found nowhere else.

---

11   Matt D. White, 'The Mallee Vegetation of North Western Victoria', *Proceedings of the Royal Society of Victoria* 118, no. 2 (2006): 239–40.

12   Victoria, Crown Lands Commission of Inquiry, Royal Commission Appointed to Inquire into the Progress of Settlement under the Land Act of 1869, Final Report, *Victorian Parliamentary Papers*, 1879, vol. 3, 601.

13   'In the Mallee Coutry', *Argus*, 18 May 1880.

14   White, 'The Mallee Vegetation of North Western Victoria', 231.

Mallee country across the continent is diverse and varied even in one region. Alfred Kenyon, an engineer and historian, identified four different areas in the Victorian Mallee: scrub country, which includes sandy ridges in places topped, surprisingly, with belts of pine trees; broken country with mixed mallee vegetation; heath country consisting of infertile sands and stunted mallee trees; and frontage country along the Murray River containing grass, red gums and box forest.[15] The country is similar in the adjoining South Australian Murray Mallee, while the Eyre Peninsula forms part of a transition zone between western and eastern mallee lands. In undulating Western Australian mallee country, the stately salmon gums occupying the shallow loamy valleys give way to differing types of mallee woodland, and the shy but remarkable biodiversity of the heath sandplains or kwongan. Shimmering salt pans and granite domes weathered over aeons punctuate the whole mallee country in the West.

Mallee country is extremely hot in summer, with temperatures regularly topping 40° Celsius for days on end, driven by proximity to the arid interior. Average rainfall is between three hundred and four hundred millilitres, less in some areas, and exacerbated in the eastern mallee lands by extreme variability from year to year. There the land is frequently plunged into dry spells that can become long-remembered drought years, often broken by damaging flooding rains.

The dryness is not uniform. Victoria's Mallee and South Australia's Murray Mallee country are fringed on the north and west by permanent water, the Murray River. The Victorian Mallee is intersected by the uncertain Wimmera River and sprinkled with occasionally filled salt lakes and depressions. The country straddling the Victorian–South Australian border is very dry, but, surprisingly, several ancient aquifers exist deep under the Pinnaroo–Murrayville region, and these were developed sustainably in the 1980s, incongruously for irrigating turf and a large share of Australia's potato crop.[16] On the Eyre Peninsula, salt lakes exist on the south-west coast, for instance lakes Hamilton, Greenly and Malata, and inland west of Whyalla lies vast Lake Gillies. Lake Grace in Western Australia's mallee country, about 175 square kilometres in extent, is one of the biggest salt lakes in the state. It is part of

---

15   Kenyon, *The Story of the Mallee*, 3.

16   *Managing the Ground Water Resources across the South Australian–Victorian Border: The Tertiary Limestone Aquifer: Information Sheet 2 of 4* (Adelaide: South Australian Department of Environment, Water and Natural Resources, 2014), accessed 27 March 2017, https://www.environment.sa.gov.au/files/sharedassets/public/water/groundwaters-agreement-tertiary-limestone-aquifer-fact.pdf.

a hundred-kilometre chain of salt lakes stretching from Pingrup to north of Kondinin that host a great variety of fauna.[17] But, in the remainder of mallee lands, there is little or no permanent water, only that found in depressions, wells, soaks and rocky crevices, before they are robbed of moisture by the sun. The soils are generally poor and in parts salty, a product of the land's ancient history, told in the first chapter below. Mallee country seems vast, eternal, challenging.

* * *

Nature, with its harsh climate, low rainfall and low-nutrient soils, is a mighty force shaping this story of the human occupation of mallee country. However, human ingenuity and culture play a massive part too. These two enormous influences acted on each other in an entwined manner to transform both mallee country and the humans who occupied it. This history explores the long and enduring Aboriginal custodianship of mallee country; its European discovery and transition into vast but struggling pastoral runs; and its eventual and seemingly irreversible transformation into wheat and cereal crop lands. Because mallee country is so vast in extent and type, this book focuses on dryland farming (not irrigation) and omits from its purview mallee country on the Yorke Peninsula, south-western New South Wales, and the northern wheatbelt of Western Australia.

The difficulty of farming in mallee regions over generations has fostered a belief in mallee exceptionalism: that mallee farmers faced and triumphed over the toughest farming conditions in Australia, surviving only through human resilience and innovation. This may be myth, but it is widely believed by mallee people to be true. Certainly, this history will reveal that mallee dry-farming country was extremely difficult, being distant from markets, and being hot and dry, much of it unfavourable for crops until fertilisers and other treatments were applied. The fragility of mallee soils once disturbed created further problems. Mallee farmers cleared the land with great ingenuity and brought it rapidly into production, but this often created problems of soil drift that needed further painful and expensive solutions.

Mallee country in the late nineteenth century was heavily influenced by policy-makers' vision of a continent populated and developed through closer

---

17 Sarah Allen, *Lake Grace Salt Lake* (Lake Grace: Shire of Lake Grace, 2010).

settlement schemes. Their dreams envisaged a fertile land, which, placed under the plough, would forge the hard-working, morally robust families that made for a strong citizenry. Politicians were slow to investigate whether mallee land was suitable for this kind of farming, and how closer settlement might work there. Later efforts to develop mallee country were sometimes carried on in spite of cautionary tales from earlier schemes and inconvenient evidence from those who suffered them.

The reality of mallee country meant that farming needed significant state intervention to make it work. Land schemes, government loans to settlers, railways to connect to markets, water projects, scientific advice and experimentation, wheat-handling and marketing infrastructure, pest control and more, were all needed to make mallee farming possible, and sometimes successful. Farmers' fortunes were also subject to the whim of prices on world markets and the success or failure of farmers competing with them in other regions of the world. Where the land was considered 'useless' for the plough, parks and reserves were instituted, fulfilling other human desires. All these issues—land and climate, visions, policy and global trends, human ideas, technologies and cultures—acted and interacted to shape the drama of European colonisation of mallee country.

This book, unlike many other studies of mallee areas, takes an approach that pushes beyond the frameworks of local history and the history of farming. In doing so it ranges from Deep Time to the present, covering all human land uses on mallee country, and spanning a continent (see Map 1). It focuses on semi-arid regions with similar flora and fauna, soils and land uses, but also recognises that they developed as wheat lands under different jurisdictions at somewhat different times and under different influences.

We must first investigate how these mallee lands were formed.

Part One

Mallee Aborigines and European Intruders to 1880

Aboriginal people enjoyed a long occupation of mallee lands. They adapted to the land and, over millennia, evolved a sustainable living from mallee country. They also shaped the land to their needs and purposes in various ways by fostering foods, making water, and especially by using fire. Humans and land were in a symbiosis, and Aboriginal people made culture about that relationship—what we might call a Great Tradition of being at one with the land. We know of this relationship, and of the traditions created in response to mallee lands, through glimpses recorded by early (and unwelcome) European witnesses. From the 1830s, Europeans also observed mallee country, overwhelmingly deeming it 'impracticable' to the project of colonisation, which demanded water, grasses for sheep and cattle, and fertile land for farming. They saw little of these in the mallee lands they skirted and sometimes traversed. However, sheep eventually proved to be the 'golden fleece' that drew pastoralists into the mallee country, where they sought profits from the land by tapping into a global market economy of wool for fabrics. These moves challenged and eventually ruptured Aboriginal societies across mallee lands. The pastoral economy used the same land as Aboriginal people but in a different and often inefficient manner. Pastoralists only sought grass and water and could not use country devoid of them. They confined their activities to stocking the land with sheep and sometimes cattle, so their understanding of mallee country's possibilities was narrow and not diverse like that of Aboriginal people. Through this constricted land use, in which sheep foraged intensively over particular stretches of country, pastoralism exhausted and permanently changed mallee country.

Chapter 1

DEEP TIME

We live in a fleeting moment of geological time, often oblivious to the stupendous layers of the Earth's history beneath. But we can only effectively comprehend our present by knowing something of the past behind and beneath us. Current mallee landforms and ecologies must be understood in the context of several millions of years, still a mere instant in the long geological history of the Earth.

Our planet Earth was, and still is, shaped by forces deep within, the actions of air and water at its surface, and outside cosmic energies from our Sun, as well as collisions with meteors, and ultimately from the 'big bang' and its residue thirteen billion years ago. The Earth's molten core, created at its fiery birth 4.54 billion years ago, supports huge floating tectonic plates of solid crust. The shifting continents rooted on these plates inch across the globe in a slow dance that has continued throughout this time. Each continent has been buffeted by tectonic lift and subsidence, volcanic action, and the winds and rains of ancient storms, whose waters carved the land. Gargantuan oceans also continually laid siege to the shores of these primeval continents.[1]

It is very difficult to conceive of the Earth's vast age, as geological time is so immense. However, if we equate the 4.54-billion-year age of the Earth to one earth day and focus on just the last thirty minutes of that imagined day, we initially find ourselves in a world dating back a hundred million years. It featured a primeval supercontinent, Gondwana, that was made up of today's Africa, South America, India, Arabia, Australia and Antarctica. Fifty million years ago, at the last fifteen-minute mark of our model day, Gondwana was being slowly torn into smaller pieces by tectonic plates on which it rested parting ways, seemingly from this distance in time like flotsam mildly disturbed on a pond. Australia and Antarctica were the last

---

1   'Age of the Earth', United States Geological Survey, last updated 9 July 2007, accessed 19 October 2018, http://pubs.usgs.gov/gip/geotime/age.html; James Lawrence Powell, *Mysteries of Terra Firma: The Age and Evolution of the Earth* (New York: Simon & Schuster, 2001).

segments of Gondwana to separate. Australia slowly drifted north, as it still does, at a rate of six centimetres per year, leaving Antarctica stranded at the 'bottom' of the world.[2]

At seven and a half minutes to twelve midnight, or twenty-five million years ago, the Miocene geological period heralded a world that would have looked vaguely familiar to us if we could time travel. Continents had assumed roughly their present shape. A warm but gradually cooling climate fifteen million years ago led to reduced rainfall, the expansion of grasslands and the contraction of forests across the globe, changing the balance of plants and species. At the end of the Miocene period five million years ago, most living species and seed plant families were like today. Ancestors of humans formed a separate evolutionary branch from chimpanzees at this time. 'Lucy' (*Australopithecus afarensis*), the famous hominid whose remains were found in Ethiopia in 1974 and dated at 3.2 million years, walked erect. Since then, 'Ardi' (*Ardipithicus ramidis*), another female hominid, has been found also in Ethiopia dating to 4.4 million years.[3] Over the Miocene period and indeed later periods, there were countless temperature and sea-level oscillations. Glacial periods locked a portion of the oceans' waters in ice, causing sea levels to fall. Warming released water back into the oceans raising their levels. Rising seas inundated vast tracts of global continental shelves.[4]

At the end of the Miocene about five million years ago, or just one and a half minutes from the end of our imagined earth day, the area of south-eastern Australia known as mallee country in Victoria, South Australia and New South Wales lay under the sea. This inundation by the ocean, called the Murray Gulf, stretched five hundred kilometres inland over the present-day south-eastern Australian mallee, its northern shoreline arcing from Menindee near Broken Hill to Kerang in central Victoria. The body of water was 200 thousand square kilometres in size at its maximum, an immense sea almost the size of modern-day Victoria. The Eyre Peninsula,

---

2   Tim Flannery, *The Future Eaters: An Ecological History of the Australasian Lands and People* (Sydney: Reed New Holland, 1994), chap. 1.

3   Christopher Joyce, 'Move Over Lucy; Ardi May be Oldest Human Ancestor', 1 October 2009, accessed 19 October 2018, https://www.npr.org/2009/10/01/113387960/move-over-lucy-ardi-may-be-oldest-human-ancestor.

4   'The Miocene Epoch', University of California Museum of Paleontology, accessed 25 September 2013, http://www.ucmp.berkeley.edu/tertiary/miocene.php; Cédric M. John, Garry D. Karner, Emily Browning, R. Mark Leckie, Zenon Mateo, Brooke Carson and Chris Lowery, 'Timing and Magnitude of Miocene Eustasy Derived from the Mixed Siliciclastic-carbonate Stratigraphic Record of the Northeastern Australian Margin', *Earth and Planetary Science Letters* 304 (2011): 455–67.

part of South Australia's mallee today, also lay submerged at this time, but not Western Australia's mallee country, which remained above the waters for 600 million years.

This 'inland' sea covering parts of south-east Australia expanded and contracted over about four million years with sea-level changes of up to sixty metres, each movement leaving an indelible imprint on the land still evident today. The ancient beach and dune systems known as the Parilla Sands, some of which are heavily mineralised, are now subject to mineral sand mining. About 170 ridges or ancient beachheads, each about three kilometres apart and two to twenty metres high, can still be detected in the Victorian–South Australia Mallee, arcing north-east like ripples spreading relentlessly out from a stone dropped into water. Geologists Bowler, Kotsonis and Lawrence, describe them as 'perhaps the finest sequence in the world' of ancient shorelines from the Pliocene period (5 million to 1.6 million years ago).[5]

As renewed glacial activity led to falling ocean levels and the continued retreat of the sea, tectonic movements became the dominant force shaping the land, with uplifts in the region from Pinnaroo to Bordertown in South Australia ending the sea's inundations and disrupting the ancient drainage flows now called the Murray–Darling system. The ancient Murray drainage brought water from the eastern highlands and the Darling brought monsoon waters from over a thousand kilometres to the north-east. Almost four million years ago, in warmer and wetter conditions, the back-up of water into depressions created by subsidence formed lakes. One of these, called Lake Bungunnia by geologists, was two hundred kilometres across at its greatest expanse a million years ago, sufficient to straddle three modern state borders. Over several million years, it laid down grey-green and red clays over marine sands, from a few metres to fifty metres in depth.

Wetter times also created a fast-flowing ancient Murray River between five and seven hundred thousand years ago, with a flow rate eight times that of the Murray River now. At the present-day site of Morgan in South Australia, the ancient Murray River veered dead south and gouged a uniquely deep and straight channel for seventy kilometres along a fault line in the Earth's surface. So deep was this channel that the lower flows of the river in later times meekly followed this early course. These prehistoric Murray journeys produced a flood plain far more fertile than the adjoining ancient seabeds.

---

5   J.M. Bowler, A. Kotsonis and C.R. Lawrence, 'Environmental Evolution of the Mallee Region, Western Murray Basin', *Proceedings of the Royal Society of Victoria* 118, no. 2 (2006): 166.

The modern Victorian Mallee and Murray Mallee landscape emerged half a million years ago, a mere ten seconds from the end of our model day. Arid conditions finally dried Lake Bungunnia, exposing a lake floor over an ancient seabed. During this drying time, dunes and dust became characteristic of mallee landscapes in this region. Three huge fingers of sand country, each over two hundred kilometres long, straddled the Victorian–South Australian border to form north to south: the Sunset Desert, Big Desert and the Little Desert. Some dunes in this sand country were formed from the older Parilla Sands laid down by early ocean retreat, but other dunes emerge from younger shoreline formations, or sands blown eastwards for tens of kilometres from the ancient Murray River channel south of Morgan. The deepest depressions of the now defunct Lake Bungunnia, such as Willandra Lakes, Lake Tyrrell, Wirrengren, and Buloke, developed distinctive Mallee gypsum-rich dunes, formed by salt water being discharged into depressions from the then higher water tables.

The colour of these Mallee dunes varied, with the deepest red being found in the Sunset Desert and the palest, almost white, sand appearing in the Little Desert just beyond the southern edge of the Victorian Mallee. The red colour of these eroded quartz sands in the north is due to staining from ferric iron in the clay deposits. This staining occurred when microscopic clay particles became airborne and coated each quartz grain. In turn, these clay-coated grains of quartz were mobilised by winds, making dust storms in the Victorian Mallee frequent in the last 500 thousand years, the last ten seconds of our geological day.[6]

In Western Australia, mallee country had a very different geological history, characterised by long periods of stability and weathering. Western Australia's mallee lands are part of one of the oldest exposed landscapes on Earth: a 600-million-year-old plateau formed three hours before the end of our model day. This plateau, part of the supercontinent Gondwana, remained above sea level where over eons it was slowly eroded by wind and rain and its soils leached of minerals over eons.[7] Minor uplift events created the Stirling and Ravensthorpe ranges, but most of the landscape remained relatively flat, with subtle variations in topography creating intricate soil mosaics. By sixty-six million years ago, rainforest was common on the plateau. But, in

---

6   Bowler, Kotsonis and Lawrence, 'Environmental Evolution of the Mallee Region', 183–5.

7   W.M. McArthur, 'History of Landscape Development', in *Reintegrating Fragmented Landscapes: Towards Sustainable Production and Nature Conservation*, eds R.J. Hobbs and D.A. Saunders (New York: Springer-Verlag, 1993), 11.

the face of increasing aridity, by 2.6 million years ago it was all gone, leaving a surface of sands, granite gravels and other weathered materials, in which an arid-adapted sclerophyll vegetation thrived.

The long period without inundation or glaciation gave the western flora time to evolve diverse strategies for coping with climatic change and nutrient-poor soils. Furthermore, south-western Australia was more climatically stable than many other parts of the world, enabling the persistence and diversification of older plant lineages.[8] By around forty million years ago, the western Australian flora was already more diverse that the eastern flora and had begun to develop unique characteristics, including rare features to help restrict water loss. When climatic changes established the Australian deserts around thirty million years ago, the Nullarbor Plain cut off the vegetation of the less arid south west from its eastern counterparts, ensuring that many of the plants evolving in the south west would be found nowhere else. In this context, the area's mosaic soils and features such as the modest Stirling and Ravensthorpe ranges provided opportunities for a remarkably rich and diverse flora to evolve.[9] The mallee landscapes in Western Australia assumed their present character about a million years ago, resting on soils of sand, gravels and yellow clay.

Mallee lands in all areas are pockmarked with salt country. This is a product of natural processes that created vast underground salt stores. The origin of the salt varies. All dryland areas in Australia, and indeed elsewhere in the world, accumulate salt naturally from wind-driven sea spray and from rainfall, which has some salt, although a thousand times less salt than seawater. Mallee lands in Western Australia have experienced these natural processes for 600 million years, leading to massive salt reserves deep in the underground soil and water table. In the South Australian, NSW and Victorian mallee country, salt deposits exist in the vast Parilla Sands aquifer, a legacy of the inland sea in the Murray Gulf five million years ago. The underground salt in mallee country is carried to the surface by aquifers that break the surface at numerous places, creating salt lakes and pans. This natural process was kept in check by Australia's deep-rooted native vegetation, especially mallee eucalypts, which harvest ground water and transfer it to the atmosphere though transpiration.

---

8 R.M. Cowling, A.J. Potts, P.L. Bradshaw, J. Colville, M. Arianoutsou, S. Ferrier, F. Forest, N.M. Fyllas, S.D. Hopper, F. Ojeda, Ş. Proches, R.J. Smith, P.W. Rundel, E. Vassilakis, and B.R. Zutta, 'Variation in Plant Diversity in Mediterranean-climate Ecosystems: The Role of Climatic and Topographical Stability', *Journal of Biogeography* 42 (2015): 552–64.

9 S.D. Hopper and P. Gioia, 'The Southwest Australian Floristic Region: Evolution and Conservation of a Global Hot Spot of Biodiversity', *Annual Review of Ecology, Evolution and Systematics* 35, no. 1, (2004): 623–50.

About fifty thousand years ago in the Pleistocene period—the astonishing last second of our day—it was becoming cooler but remained wet, with strong stream flows and lake formation. Sea levels were eighty metres below the levels of today. Scientific evidence suggests that, some time before this, humans had left Africa. How much earlier is in dispute. Recent studies of the human genome estimate that this migration occurred between sixty thousand and 120 thousand years ago.[10] An international team of archaeologists recently found finger bones in Saudi Arabia's Nefud Desert and have dated them back eighty-five thousand years.[11] People found their way to Australia from Asia via land bridges and watercraft about sixty thousand years ago. Of course, some Aboriginal people believe their ancestors always lived here, for that is what tradition states. Whatever the truth of these two competing knowledge claims, people have probably resided in the mallee lands of southern Australia for the past six millennia. Current evidence clearly reveals that the Willandra Lakes were occupied over forty-two thousand years ago.[12]

These first people had much to contend with, as climates oscillated. At first, conditions were cooler than today but favourable, with plentiful food supplies from bounteous wetlands and rivers. But with further cooling, lakes dried, and stream flows weakened. Glacial formation peaked again twenty thousand years ago, called the Last Glacial Maximum, dropping average temperatures to six degrees below today's level, reducing precipitation and increasing aridity. These were trying times for humans and may have caused retreat to more benign areas. Temperatures rose in the Holocene, the most recent geological period, which began 11,700 years ago. This was just 0.2 seconds from the end of our fictional earth day. Ice retreated, sea levels rose, and in the mid-Holocene conditions became warmer and wetter, creating lakes and revegetating dunes. This made mallee lands more habitable. About four thousand years ago somewhat drier conditions, like those of today, emerged.

The ancient Western Australian mallee landscape and the much younger south-east Australian mallee country were both shaped to a large degree by humans in the last second of our model day, or from fifty thousand years

---

10 George Busby, 'Genetic Studies Reveal Diversity of Early Human Populations—and Pin Down When We Left Africa', *The Conversation*, 22 September 2016, accessed 19 October 2018, http://theconversation.com/genetic-studies-reveal-diversity-of-early-human-populations-and-pin-down-when-we-left-africa-65745#republish.

11 'Arabian Finger Bones', ABC News, 10 April 2018, accessed 19 October 2018, http://www.abc.net.au/news/2018-04-10/finger-bone-fossil-found-in-saudi-arabia/9636058.

12 *Australian Story: Long Journey Home*, ABC television, viewed 12 February 2018.

ago. Since then, the natural world has been shaped by the human use of fire, which accelerated changes to the land through natural sources of ignition to be discussed in the next chapter. Then, in the last three thousandths of a second of our model day, Europeans arrived with sheep and then wheat, disturbing and eradicating the existing ecologies on a vast scale. This enormous transformation of mallee lands through clearing and dryland farming occurred in the blink of an eye in geological time. Such immense changes, which together amounted to a revolution, had not been experienced in eastern mallee lands since they became a watery world, through inundation by ocean and fresh-water run-off, three to five million years ago. This European settler transformation of mallee lands took just decades, whereas nature took millennia to transform the Victorian and Murray Mallee into the watery world of the Murray Gulf and Lake Bungunnia and many more millennia to make it into semi-arid mallee scrubland.[13] The ancient mallee landscapes of Western Australia had not experienced such rapid change in the last 600 million years, even though subjected to an ancestral Aboriginal regime of fire, albeit one experienced over millennia.

This recent time of human influence, powerful enough to shape Earth's natural systems, was dubbed the 'Anthropocene' by Paul Crutzen, an atmospheric scientist. Some place the Anthropocene from ten thousand years ago, when the farming revolution in the Fertile Crescent centred on modern-day Iraq created rising carbon dioxide and methane levels from forest clearing, agriculture and animal husbandry. Environmental historian J.R. McNeil emphasised the shift in global production around 1500 AD, driven by new shipping and trade technologies, which enlarged populations and energy uses to unprecedented levels. Others nominate 1784, the year when the wood- (later coal-)fired steam engine was invented by James Watt. Thereafter, human ingenuity ramped up consumption of the world's resources and CO_2 production to create a new force in global systems.[14] However, environmental historian

---

13   'Salinity and the Murray River', accessed 21 September 2018, http://www.murrayriver.com.au/about-the-murray/salinity/; Mallee Catchment Management Authority, *Mallee Salinity Workshop, May 30, 2012*, April 2013, accessed 19 October 2018, http://www.malleecma.vic.gov.au/resources/salinity/executive-summary; 'Salinity and Land Management on Western Australian Farms', Australian Bureau of Statistics, *Western Australian Statistical Indicators*, 1367.5 (June 2003), accessed 19 October 2018, http://www.abs.gov.au/ausstats/abs@.nsf/0/f59529c371a21f55ca256db800783a4f/$FILE/ATT34B9V/Salinity%20and%20land%20management%20on%20Western%20Australian%20farms_1.pdf.

14   J.R. McNeil, *Something New Under the Sun: An Environmental History of the Twentieth-Century World* (New York: W.W. Norton & Co., 2000), chap. 1.

Libby Robin, giving a less Eurocentric view, argued that the Anthropocene began in Australia with Aboriginal use of fire.[15]

This book relates the story of mallee country's Anthropocene, from original Aboriginal ownership stretching back two thousand human generations to the six or seven generations of European usurpation of mallee country, as pastoralists and farmers penetrated and reshaped the region. In terms of Deep Time, nature is the protagonist of this mallee story, shaping country over many eons, while humans are but recent bit players. However, in that final blink of time, less than one second in our model 24-hour earth day, humans and their associates—fire, animals, plants, technology—transformed the entire mallee stage and, in doing so, performed and delivered some extraordinary actions and dramatic lines.

---

15   Libby Robin, 'Histories for Changing Times: Entering the Anthropocene?', in 'Forum: Historians, the Anthropocene and Climate Change', *Australian Historical Studies* 44, no. 3 (September 2013): 329–40. See also, in the same forum, Alison Bashford, 'The Anthropocene is Modern History: Reflections on Climate and Australian Deep Time', 341–9.

Chapter 2

ABORIGINAL HOMELANDS

Under Big Skies

Each night for two thousand generations, Aboriginal people observed the starry universe as they gathered round campfires. The southern sky hosts the wondrous haze of the Milky Way, the Southern Cross circling the south celestial pole, a myriad of constellations and the wandering planets. They pondered this glorious canopy, naming each celestial body visible to the naked eye, forming creation stories about the over-arching night sky. This knowledge was emblematic of their deep relationship with nature.

Stories were widely shared but sometimes unique to a locale. Many groups detected a massive emu in the dark patches of the Milky Way extending from Scorpius to the Southern Cross, its head being what Europeans call the 'Coalsack'.[1] In 1857 a pastoralist, William Edward Stanbridge, declared that the people of Lake Tyrrell in the Victorian Mallee, whom he called the Booroung, had a deep knowledge of the heavens. He related their story of the lighting up of *tyrille* (space) by a small bird, which propelled an emu's egg into the sky and so created the Sun. The Booroung told Stanbridge the names and stories for twenty-six stars familiar to many stargazers today, as well as those for the Sun, Moon, Venus and Jupiter.[2]

Some, including CSIRO astrophysicist Ray Norris, have argued strongly for an Aboriginal astronomy. Norris maintained their knowledge went beyond stories to celestial calendars and possibly stone arrangements to mark celestial movements.[3] To the Booroung, the appearance of *Marpeankurrk* (Arcturus)

---

1   'Australian Aboriginal Astronomy: The Emu in the Sky', Australian Telescope National Facility, accessed 27 February 2017, http://www.atnf.csiro.au/research/AboriginalAstronomy/Examples/emu.htm.

2   William Edward Stanbridge, 'On the Astronomy and Mythology of the Aborigines of Victoria', *Transactions of the Philosophical Institute of Victoria* 2 (1858): 137–40.

3   See the website 'Australian Aboriginal Astronomy'. See also Ray Norris, 'Emu Dreaming', *Australasian Science* 29, no. 4 (May 2008): 16–19; Ray P. Norris and Duane W. Hamacher, 'The Astronomy of Aboriginal Australia', in *The Role of Astronomy in Society and Culture*, special issue of *Proceedings of the International*

heralded the season of the delicious larvae of the wood ant (*bittur*), and *Neilloan* (Lyra) the laying of malleefowl (*loan*) eggs.[4] At Ngaut Ngaut (Devon Downs) near Mannum in the South Australian Murray Mallee, the Nganguraki people created rock art depicting sun and moon people amidst a series of dots, which their descendants claim are phases of the moon. Scientific affirmation of this may follow if the markings yield to decoding.[5]

The Human Presence on Mallee Lands

Aboriginal people colonised parts of mallee lands across the southern parts of the continent over fifty thousand years ago. During this time, they responded to significant climatic changes and in turn shaped the land by their presence and their creative imagination.

In Western Australia, evidence of human occupation of the south west has been found at 38,000 BP on the upper Swan River.[6] At Devil's Lair, a cave just north of Cape Leeuwin, the presence of Nyungar people is dated at 48,000 BP, this site also providing evidence of ornamentation in the form of beads made from animal bone.[7] On the Nullarbor Plain, research at Koonalda and Allen's caves has dated human occupation there as at least 22,000 BP, although it may have been small in scale and transient depending on the climate.[8]

The nature of the climate determined the human use of many parts of the continent. The mallee region of Australia's south east was wetter than today prior to 35,000 BP, and its lakes and depressions were filled with life-giving water. But, with a global cooling phase known as the Last Glacial Maximum

---

Astronomical Union 5, issue S260 (2009): 10–17; Ray and Cilla Norris, *Emu Dreaming: An Introduction to Australian Aboriginal Astronomy* (Sydney: Emu Dreaming, 2008).

4   Stanbridge, 'On the Astronomy', 138–9.

5   Ray Norris, 'In Search of Aboriginal Astronomy', *Australian Sky and Telescope* (March–April, 2008): 24. See also Amy Roberts and the Mannum Aboriginal Community Association Inc., *Ngaut Ngaut: An Interpretative Guide* (Mannum: Mannum Aboriginal Community Association Inc., 2012), 23–4.

6   R.H. Pearce and Mike Barbetti, 'A 38,000-year-old Archaeological Site at Upper Swan, Western Australia', *Archaeology in Oceania* 16, issue 3 (October 1981): 173–8; John Mulvaney and Johan Kamminga, *Prehistory of Australia* (Sydney: Allen & Unwin, 1990), 201–03. BP (Before the Present) is the abbreviation used by archaeologists and geologists to refer to dates often obtained through radiocarbon dating technology.

7   C.S.M. Turney, Michael Ian Bird, L.K. Fifield, R.G. Roberts, M.A. Smith, C.E. Dortch, R. Grun, E. Lawson, J. Dortch, R.G. Cresswell, 'Early Human Occupation at Devil's Lair, Southwestern Australia 50,000 Years Ago', *Quaternary Research* 55, issue 1 (January 2001): 3–13.

8   Mulvaney and Kamminga, *Prehistory of Australia*, 201–03.

(LGM) around 25,000 to 18,000 BP, the climate dried. By 15,000 BP lake systems and surface waters in the region were mostly dry. A short wet phase emerged from 12,000 BP but petered out around 7,000 BP producing the semi-arid Victorian and Murray Mallee country of today.

During their long occupation, Aboriginal people in the south east responded to wetter and drier periods by expanding their living areas in wet periods and retreating to permanent waters in dry periods. Lake Mungo in the Willandra Lakes region north of the Murray River was occupied between 60,000 and 50,000 BP until 15,000 BP, when the stream feeding Willandra Creek changed course eastward to become the modern Lachlan River. People in the Willandra Lakes lived on wetland resources of fish and molluscs and also plants and small animals from the surrounding country. The oldest human remains yet found in Australia were discovered at Lake Mungo in 1968 by Jim Bowler, or more accurately uncovered by prevailing winds over the dunes in the Willandra Lakes region—now a World Heritage Site. The remains of Mungo Man found by Bowler in 1974 were dated at 42,000 BP. Those of Mungo Woman, thought to be the world's oldest cremation, were given a similar dating.[9] Their remains and those of 104 other individuals of the ancestors of the Paakantji, Ngyiampaa and Muthi Muthi people are highly significant.[10]

These people, whose living was derived from both the lake and the surrounding country, also left a remarkable legacy of a family's footprints embedded in hardened clay; these were found in 2003 and are believed to be twenty thousand years old. Mungo people practised cremations, mortuary rites and ornamentation, clear evidence of a conception of spirituality. Also, at Lake Nitchie a hundred kilometres to the west of Lake Mungo, the 7,000-year-old remains of a 188-centimetres-tall man were unearthed in 1970. Around the man's neck was a long double-stringed necklace of 162 Tasmanian devil teeth, each one with a finely drilled hole for stringing. Both the burial and the necklace suggest the Paakantji practised social hierarchy and possessed a complex culture.[11]

Through wet and drier periods people lived along the permanent waters of the ancient Murray River and its thin strip of well-resourced land with

---

9   Mungo National Park, 'Share Mungo Culture', http://www.visitmungo.com.au/share-culture.
10 Mulvaney and Kamminga, *Prehistory of Australia*, 194–9.
11 N.W.G. Macintosh, K.N. Smith and A.B. Bailey, 'Lake Nitchie Skeleton—Unique Aboriginal Burial', *Archaeology and Physical Anthropology in Oceania* 5, no. 2 (July 1970): 85–101.

semi-arid country beyond. Over time the Murray River changed and became more fertile, fostering greater cultural dynamism in the process. Colin Pardoe, who has worked on this region for over thirty years, remarked that in the period of the Last Glacial Maximum the Murray was 'faster, colder, bigger and altogether dangerous'. After 14,000 BP it became more like its modern self—'smaller, more sinuous, slower, warmer'. This led to greater levels of resources as the river, tamed by drying conditions, began to meander and became fringed with wetlands and swamps.[12]

Skeletal remains older than 16,000 BP have not been found along the river, possibly because of problems of preservation and exposure arising from shifts in the river's course over time. Human remains along the Murray become more prevalent from 10,000 BP, when Aboriginal cemeteries first appear in the archaeological record, increasing in frequency as we move closer to the present. A recent study of a lunette at Lake Victoria alone has produced a firm estimate of ten thousand individuals buried in the vicinity. Shell middens dating to 15,000 BP have been found along the river, some of them a thin line of shell four hundred metres in length.[13] Cooking mounds for tubers become numerous after 7,000 BP. Greater resources sustained greater populations. As populations grew they became more exclusionary in the battle to control resources and country. Tribal identities formed and gene pools became distinctive as river people intermarried with neighbours.[14]

South of the Murray River conditions were less promising for human occupation. However, Lake Tyrrell, a large saline lake that occasionally received fresh water from the Avoca River, was filled at similar times to the Willandra Lakes to the north. People at Lake Tyrrell lived off small fauna, birds and their eggs, and other plant and ground fauna, using soaks in surrounding country to obtain fresh water. Archaeological research at Box Gully on the lake's northern end has revealed human occupation from 32,000 to 26,000 BP when the drying forced most inhabitants to the permanent waters of the Murray. People returned to the region in more recent times.[15]

---

12   Colin Pardoe, 'Riverine, Biological and Cultural Evolution in Southeastern Australia', *Antiquity* 69, issue 265 (September 1995): 696–713.
13   Jillian Garvey, 'Australian Aboriginal Freshwater Shell Middens from Late Quaternary Northwest Victoria: Prey Choice, Economic Variability and Exploitation', *Quaternary International* 427, part A (January 2017): 85–102.
14   Pardoe, 'Riverine, Biological and Cultural Evolution'.
15   Thomas Richards, Christina Pavlides, Keryn Walshe, Harry Webber and Rochelle Johnston, 'Box Gully: New Evidence for Aboriginal Occupation of Australia South of the Murray River Prior to the Last Glacial Maximum', *Archaeology in Oceania* 42, no. 1 (April 2007): 1–11.

The driest parts of the Victorian Mallee were then as now between the Murray River and lakes Hindmarsh and Tyrrell west to the South Australian border. Aboriginal people from the Murray River penetrated south of the Murray in favourable climatic eras to utilise resources. There is evidence of Aboriginal occupation of the Raak Plains west of Hattah Lakes about 8,000 BP, at the end of the wet period that lasted from 12,000 to 7,000 BP. Wetter conditions in this area provided living water in salinas and wells, and this would also have supported flora, fauna and avifauna. These small populations, living in what was still difficult country, probably retreated to the Murray River once drying occurred around 7,000 BP, thereafter making yearly seasonal visits to the Raak Plains instead.[16]

The drier southern Mallee country around Wyperfeld Lakes and Pine Plains and to their west was occupied later, although evidence of earlier occupation may yet emerge. It is likely that people to the south rather than the north moved into this area. There is evidence of intensification about 3,000 BP due to hydraulic engineering and eel farming at Mt William and Budj Bim near Mt Eccles. This new technology was either encouraged by or followed population increases. Such pressures perhaps caused a migration northward.[17] These people travelled from the Grampians region along the Wimmera River where there was food and water, staying close to Lake Hindmarsh and Outlet Creek, and to the Wirrengren Plain when it occasionally received run-off during wet years. Travel to the west from the Pine Plains region and north to the Murray River for trade was also possible owing to the presence of soaks and wells.

Over hundreds of generations, local groups developed in mallee country forming their own distinctive languages and weaving their unique cultural canvases and traditions of knowledge. There are currently twenty-five different Aboriginal cultural groupings in mallee country: six in Western Australia; nine in South Australia; and ten in Victoria, some of which straddle the Victorian–NSW border (see Map 2).[18] Only the Ngargad (Ngarkat) in South Australia

---

16   Anne Ross, 'Holocene Environments and Prehistoric Site Patterning in the Victorian Mallee', *Archaeology in Oceania* 16, no. 3 (October 1981): 145–55.

17   Ross, 'Holocene Environments', 151–3; Harry Lourandos, 'Change or Stability? Hydraulics, Hunter-Gathers and Population, in Temperate Australia', *World Archaeology* 11, no. 3 (February 1980): 245–64.

18   Map 2 is based on the work of Norman Tindale in the 1930s. It is followed by *The Encyclopaedia of Aboriginal Australia: Aboriginal and Torres Strait Islander History, Society and Culture*, gen. ed. David Horton (Canberra: Aboriginal Studies Press, 1994), 2, 946, 1011, 1016; and also *Macquarie Atlas of Indigenous Australia*, eds Bill Arthur and Frances Morphy (Sydney: Macquarie, 2005), 259–61. Thanks also to advice from Ted Ryan a Victorian researcher, Tom Gara a South Australian historian, and Nicole Chalmer a Western Australian PhD candidate.

appear to have no descendants. The Wergia, a group of Wotjobaluk around Lake Hindmarsh in Victoria, take their name and identity directly from the land. 'Wergia' in their language means 'people of the mallee scrubs'.[19] The Tjaltjraak Native Title Corporation at Esperance today takes its name from the Nyungar word for a significant mallee eucalypt in the area, *tallerack*.[20]

Each mallee group held custodianship over specific lands by right of descent from the Great Ancestors of the locale, human–animal composites that lived in formative times before human society. In the late nineteenth century the Wotjobaluk people in north-western Victoria told ethnographer A.W. Howitt that a bat–human, Ngunung-ngunnut, who was feeling lonely, created opposite-gendered beings by altering himself into a man and another bat–human into a woman. He then made fire by rubbing pieces of wood together. Also, in heroic times, the Bram-bram-gal brothers travelled across the land of the Wotjobaluk and Wergia, naming things and places.[21]

Ownership of mallee country was mutually agreed upon with neighbours and verified by creation stories, not by invasion, conquest or purchase. People saw little sense in coveting the land of others, as it had no specific spiritual meaning to them. Local 'estates' were owned by clans of several hundred people. But clan members had rights through marriage or other arrangements to larger living areas of land, which have been called 'ranges'. They foraged over these estates and ranges according to the seasonality of foods. Rights to clan lands were jealously upheld, but boundaries were porous, made fluid by access arrangements. One person's estate was another's range, used only by agreement.[22]

Ideas of over-arching Great Ancestors and overlapping languages and dialects bound neighbouring groups together. People in south-east Australia believed in an all-Father who was the creator of all things, shaping the land, breathing life into beings, and laying down the laws of human society. The Wotjobaluk called him *Bunjil* the eaglehawk, as did the Kulin people of central Victoria, but the Wadi Wadi and Dadi Dadi people downstream of Swan Hill

---

19   Ian D. Clark, *Aboriginal Languages and Clans: An Historical Atlas of Western and Central Victoria, 1800–1900*, Monash Publications in Geography 37 (Melbourne: Monash University, 1990), 336.

20   'Tjaltjraak Esperance', Esperance Tjaltjraak Native Title Aboriginal Corporation website, accessed 21 September 2018, www.etntac.com.au.

21   A.W. Howitt, *The Native Tribes of South-East Australia* (Canberra: Aboriginal Studies Press, 1996), 484.

22   W.E.H. Stanner, 'Estate, Range, Domain and Regime', *Oceania* 36, no. 1 (September 1965): 1–26. See also Nicholas Peterson (ed.), *Tribes and Boundaries in Australia* (Canberra: AIATSIS, 1976).

on the Murray River used the terms *Tha-tha-pulli* and *Tulong* respectively.[23] The Murray River peoples believed the all-Father *Tulong* speared a giant Murray cod, *Ban-dyal*, which, although wounded, carved out the Murray River as it fled.[24] After his creative acts, *Bunjil* travelled to the sky to become a star. Some groups held that Fomalhaut was *Bunjil*, but others believed it was Altair.[25] Fomalhaut, a triple star and the eighteenth brightest, is in *Piscis Austrinus* and clearly seen, especially in spring. Altair, the twelfth brightest star, is in the constellation, *Aquila* the eagle, and is visible from spring to summer. It is flanked by two stars said to be *Bunjil*'s sisters—the black swans.[26]

Aboriginal attachment to country, based on clan ownership, was made vibrant by individual and intimate connections to natural species, which underpinned a person's identity. Ethel Hassell, who owned Jarramongup station with her husband Albert in the Western Australian mallee from 1878 to 1886, developed a sound knowledge of Aboriginal life in the region from conversations with station workers.[27] Hassell learnt that moieties existed amongst the local group she called the Wheelman, one being black crow (*wording*), the other *nunnich* (probably meaning eaglehawk).[28] Victorian clan members were also divided into moieties, being either *bunjil* (eaglehawk) or *waa* (crow). Everyone in Aboriginal society had their own birth totem, and usually one from their initiation as well. Totems—animals, birds or plants—carried obligations to husband and replenish these species by regularly performing ritual.

Humans and nature were in a symbiotic relationship through totemic relations, which (along with gender and age status) carried food restrictions, adding further nuances to their use of country. Hassell wrote that young people were forbidden to eat wild dog or eaglehawk, and 'certain meats were

---

23 Howitt, *Native Tribes*, 484–5.
24 Mudrooroo, *Aboriginal Mythology: An A–Z Spanning the History of Aboriginal Mythology from the Earliest Legends to the Present Day* (London: HarperCollins, 1994), 115. See also R.G. Kimber, 'The Ngarkat', typescript (Pinnaroo Historical Society, undated), 1.
25 Howitt, *Native Tribes*, 471–94.
26 Larry Sessions and Deborah Byrd, 'Fomalhaut Had First Visible Exoplanet', *Earthsky* (22 September 2017), http://earthsky.org/brightest-stars/solitary-fomalhaut-guards-the-southern-sky; Elizabeth Howell, 'Altair: One of the Summer Triangle Stars' (26 June 2013), https://www.space.com/21746-altair.html. Both accessed 27 July 2019.
27 See this relationship from Hassell's perspective in Ethel Hassell, *My Dusky Friends: Aboriginal Life, Customs and Legends and Glimpses of Station Life at Jarramungup in the 1880's* (East Fremantle: C.W. Hassell, 1975).
28 Ethel Hassell, 'Notes on the Ethnology of the Wheelman Tribe of Southwestern Australia', ed. D.S. Davidson, *Anthropos* 31 (1 September 1936): 684.

only eaten by men. Other meats were restricted to married folk'.²⁹ A.W. Howitt was informed that, in Victoria, a 'Wotjobaluk would not harm his totem if he could avoid it, but at a pinch he would eat it in default of other food. In order to injure another person he would, however, kill that person's totem'. The Wotjobaluk's neighbours, the Buandik of Mt Gambier, informed Howitt that, if a man had to eat his totem, he expressed 'sorrow for having to eat his *Wingong* (friend), or *Tumung* (his flesh). When using the latter word; the Buandik touch their breast to indicate the close relationship, meaning almost a part of themselves'.³⁰

Totemic relationships, being symbiotic, revealed there was no divide between humans and nature in Aboriginal societies. Each day, as small groups of related families traversed their land, hunting and gathering, their movements replicated that of the Great Ancestors. Each visit to a sacred site, or rehearsal of their ritual in song and dance to care for country and to make it productive, bound them more tightly to it. Each landform had a name and a story.

It is little wonder that Aboriginal people lived in semi-arid mallee country for millennia with aplomb, keeping most hardships at bay through skilful adaptations to country. Thomas Mitchell, when exploring the Murray River in 1836, watched unnoticed an Aboriginal man on the other side of the river. Mitchell remarked:

> his hands were ready to seize any living thing; his step, light and noiseless as that of a shadow, gave no intimation of his approach … Every little track or impression left on the earth by the lower animals caught his keen eye, but the trees overhead chiefly engaged his attention; for deep in the heart of some of the upper branches he probably hoped to find the opossum on which he was to dine.³¹

From their first moments on country, Aboriginal people changed the land by fire. Their presence added abundant sources of ignition to natural but infrequent lightning strikes. They made fire efficiently, but it was still far easier to carry a firestick as they travelled, sometimes firing country discretely along the way. Stephen Pyne remarked that, while lightning

---

29   Hassell, 'Notes on the Ethnology of the Wheelman Tribe of Southwestern Australia', 688.
30   Howitt, *Native Tribes*, 145–6.
31   T.L. Mitchell, *Three Expeditions into the Interior of Eastern Australia; with Descriptions of the Recently Explored Region of Australia Felix, and of the Present Colony of New South Wales* (London: T. & W. Boone, 1839), vol. 2, entry 4 June 1836, Project Gutenberg Australia, http://gutenberg.net.au/ebooks/e00036.html.

was an 'episodic ignition source; the Aboriginal firestick was an eternal flame'.[32] Each night campfires glowed, and surrounding clumps of vegetation might be fired to provide extra light. Pyne added: 'the constant interaction between firestick and landscape replenished both'.[33] The precise nature of these changes is difficult to gauge even as recently as a millennium ago.[34] However, Sylvia Hallam argued in her careful study of ethnographic material left by European explorers of south-west Western Australia that Aboriginal people at the time of contact with Europeans used fire extensively for ritual and economic purposes—and changed the land. Hallam concluded that 'Aboriginal groups *did* modify the structure and distribution of floral and faunal communities'.[35]

Aboriginal people fired the land to clear and maintain pathways through difficult country, to create grazing pastures for kangaroo, and to drive smaller animals from the bush. They used fire to increase species such as yams (*warran* in Western Australia), to maintain diversity of species, and to care for and 'clean' country.[36] Their burning was not indiscriminate or fickle. Some country was burnt, other parts left unburnt. Scholars, from Rhys Jones in 1969 onwards, argued from evidence provided by European colonists, and by Aboriginal people in contemporary times, that corridors and mosaics of country were burnt to shape hunting and gathering terrains. Ludwig Leichhardt observed 'the natives seem to have burnt the grass systematically along every watercourse and around every waterhole in order to have them surrounded with young grass as soon as the rain sets in'.[37] Sylvia Hallam called these managed spaces 'patches'.[38] Bill Gammage, in *The Biggest Estate on Earth: How Aborigines Made Australia* (2011), termed them 'mosaics', as do ecologists. Gammage argued Aboriginal people were

---

32 S.J. Pyne, *Burning Bush: A Fire History of Australia* (Sydney: Allen & Unwin, 1992), 85.

33 Pyne, *Burning Bush*, 88.

34 D.M.J.S. Bowman, 'The Impact of Aboriginal Landscape Burning on the Australian Biota', *New Phytologist* 140, no. 3 (November 1998): 400–04.

35 S.J. Hallam, *Fire and Hearth: A Study of Aboriginal Usage and European Usurpation in South-western Australia* (Canberra: Australian Institute of Aboriginal Studies, 1975), 111.

36 Sylvia. J. Hallam, 'Peopled Landscapes in Southwestern Australia in the Early 1800s: Aboriginal Burning off in the Light of Western Australian Historical Documents', *Early Days* 12, no. 2 (2012): 177–91; Fred Cahir, Sarah McMaster, Ian Clark, Rani Kerin and Wendy Wright, 'Winda Lingo Parugoneit or Why Set the Bush [on] Fire? Fire and Victorian Aboriginal People on the Colonial Frontier', *Australian Historical Studies* 47, no. 2 (June 2016): 225–40.

37 Quoted in Hallam, *Fire and Hearth*, 75.

38 Hallam, *Fire and Hearth*, 17, 64–5.

land managers making resources 'not merely sustainable, but abundant, convenient and predictable'.[39]

Burning was a process regulated by authority. Country set for burning was fired in late summer in southern Australia on a regular and controlled basis and in small sections, each perhaps every few years. This created controlled, cool burns, never the huge ones stemming from fuel stockpiles that were more likely to occur as a result of lightning strikes igniting long unburnt areas. Controlled burns were managed by experienced fire-managers, elders who built on eons of trial and error. They burnt when the wind and season were ideal, watched the fire closely, then controlled and guided it where necessary. Ethel Hassell, who lived on Jarramongup station in the late 1870s, recalled that one day in late summer two girls told her their people were going to start *man carls* (bush fires) and, significantly, that a corroboree for this event would be held that night. Hassell explained that burning was done annually 'to ensure the grass and herbage [came] up green and sweet at the first rains', but the land was fired only after the ground birds had hatched and 'the young ground rats were running about'.[40] Aboriginal people worked the land through fire, transforming it and transforming themselves by becoming managers of their lands and making knowledge about the origins and use of fire.

The edges of permanent water in mallee country such as the Murray River, which hosted *typha* reed beds, together with other semi-permanent waters in mallee country that spawned stands of bulrushes across southern Australia, were often fired. Botanist Beth Gott, who studied *typha*'s use for food and fibre, observed that burning returned fertilising ash to the earth, while the digging of tubers loosened and aerated the soil and 'provided space for new growth and seed germination'.[41] It took many years for Europeans to begin to understand Aboriginal management of fire instead of just fearing it as a destroyer of property and stock. European cultural memory, often being town centred, knew fire could raze whole cities as it did London in September 1666. For the last few decades researchers have discussed Aboriginal fire practices, gaining many insights into the purposes, methods and intentions of fire usage.[42] That they are still fiercely debating

---

39 Bill Gammage, *The Biggest Estate on Earth: How Aborigines Made Australia* (Sydney: Allen & Unwin, 2011), 3.
40 Hassell, *My Dusky Friends*, 110–11.
41 Beth Gott, 'Cumbungi, *Typha* Species: A Staple Aboriginal Food in Southern Australia', *Australian Aboriginal Studies*, no. 1 (1999): 42.
42 See Bowman, 'The Impact of Aboriginal Landscape Burning on the Australian Biota', for a literature review of most of the important research until the late 1990s.

fire management is testimony to the depth of knowledge about the subject that Aboriginal people had developed over eons.

The evidence that mallee country was burnt often is not extensive, even in Gammage's far-ranging *The Biggest Estate on Earth*. That it did occur is evident from early observations of mosaics of country and pathways, many of which were not natural. However, evidence is generally slim for mallee lands; numerous accounts by early Europeans emphasised that much of the country was impenetrable (see Chapter 3). John Wood Beilby trekked extensively through the Victorian Mallee in October 1849. Beilby travelled from the coast along the border to present-day Pinnaroo, east to present-day Ouyen, then south to Lake Hindmarsh (see Figure 3.3). He wore heavy clothing which was ripped to shreds by mallee scrub. Despite searching for pastoral land and continually seeking vistas from high ground, he seldom recorded burnt country. Near the South Australia border close to present-day Pinnaroo, Beilby saw 'a tract of mallay which had been burnt two or three years ago', and days later from a ridge near Cow Plains observed 'slopes of the hills which had been burnt last year'. There is, however, no information as to how it was burnt.[43]

Aboriginal people avoided John Septimus Roe, who often hacked his way through dense mallee country west of Esperance in late 1848 and early 1849. He knew they were nearby as he 'passed over tracts of country in which their fires were burning'. But these were obviously campfires, as he saw their 'signal fires rise up' after he had travelled a mile or so further on.[44] He commented that their campfire 'is invariably small and without flame'.[45] Only when heading from Cape Cheyne to Kojunup, via the Stirling Ranges, did he remark on seeing several stretches of country 'extensively burnt by the natives'.[46] Ecologists have recently affirmed that Nyungar people of this region ensured 'particular resources and habitats were protected by fire'.[47]

---

43 Beilby's account in Alfred S. Kenyon, *The Story of the Mallee: A History of The Victorian Mallee Read before the Historical Society of Victoria, 18 March 1912* (reprinted Melbourne: Wilke & Co., 1982), 22, 25.

44 'Report of J.S. Roe, Esq., Surveyor General of His Expedition to Explore the Interior Country South Eastward from York, between September 1848 and February 1849', typescript, J.S. Battye Library of West Australian History, 919.412 ROE, 154–5.

45 Roe, 'Report ... of His Expedition', 189.

46 Roe, 'Report ... of His Expedition', 211, 213.

47 Alison Lullfitz, Joe Dortch, Stephen D. Hopper, Carol Pettersen, Ron (Doc) Reynolds, and David Guilfoyle, 'Human Niche Construction: Noongar Evidence in Pre-colonial Southwestern Australia', *Conservation & Society*.15, no. 2 (2017): 210–11.

Other research also suggests the mallee was not extensively burnt. Many mallee birds prefer landscapes that have not been burnt for some time. Zoologist Michael F. Clarke proved the black-eared miner (*Manorina melanotis*) breeds only in large patches of long-unburnt mallee, requiring about thirty square kilometres to maintain a viable population. The malleefowl (*Leipoa ocellata*) requires a thick layer of leaf litter to make its nest building viable. And Clarke reported mallee eucalypts suffer significant nectar reduction for many years following fires.[48] Clarke and a team of landscape ecologists, in a study of mallee landscapes and fire management, found that of the twenty-eight species of mallee birds examined none positively benefitted from landscapes burnt in the previous ten years. Some species favoured landscapes that had not experienced fire for eleven to thirty-five years, and some species like the black-eared miner preferred older mallee not burnt for more than thirty-five years. The researchers opposed burning even 5 per cent of landscape per annum, as that would mean the whole country would be burnt every twenty years, thus becoming detrimental to many bird species. They also reported nectar-bearing blossom was absent for a decade after stem-replacing fire in mallee vegetation.[49] The preference of many mallee bird species for long-unburnt mallee vegetation thus suggests infrequent burning was the norm for many centuries.

Aboriginal people also chopped, carved and dug their lands to shape them to their needs. In the late 1830s, George Grey saw extensive turned-over yam (*warran*) grounds north of Perth, commenting with surprise: 'more had here been done to secure a provision from the ground by hard manual labour than I could have believed it in the power of uncivilised man to accomplish'.[50] Yet such industry was a common occurrence on mallee country. The American historian Richard White argued that 'all our work—inevitably embeds us in nature', by hunting or tending animals, gathering or cultivating seeds, digging,

---

48 Michael F Clarke, 'Catering for the Needs of Fauna in Fire Management: Science or Just Wishful thinking?', *Wildlife Research* 35, no. 5 (August 2008): 385–94.

49 Rick S. Taylor, Simon J. Watson, Andrew F. Bennett, Michael F. Clarke, 'Which Fire Management Strategies Benefit Biodiversity? A Landscape Perspective Case Study Using Birds in Mallee Ecosystems of South-eastern Australia', *Biological Conservation* 159 (March 2013): 248–56.

50 George Grey, *Journals of Two Expeditions of Discovery in North-West and Western Australia, During the Years 1837, 38, and 39: Describing many Newly Discovered, Important, and Fertile Districts, With Observations of the Moral and Physical Condition of the Aboriginal Inhabitants, &c. &c.* (London: T. & W. Boone, 1841), 2, 12.

cutting, and shaping wood.⁵¹ Understanding how Aboriginal people worked the land and its waters takes us to the heart of how they lived on, and with, mallee country.⁵²

Mallee countries reveal a spectrum of ecologies based on the availability of water. The focus here is on two main living areas: rich riverine ecologies along the Murray River and to a lesser extent the Wimmera River and other Victorian Mallee permanent lakes and waters; and dry country, which predominates in mallee lands across southern Australia. It is no coincidence that the Murray's rich and meandering river frontage, especially in Victoria, was crowded with many different tribal groups, whereas the drier lake areas and mallee back country sustained fewer cultural groupings, each one spread across vast areas (see Map 2 over page).

River and Lake Mallee Country

The Murray–Darling Basin, fed by monsoonal rains a thousand miles to the north flowing down the Darling River, and by snowmelt from highlands far to the east flowing down the Murray, appears from space like the far-reaching root system of some gargantuan tree. Charles Fenner, the eminent Australian geographer, estimated it covered one seventh of the area of Australia.⁵³ The Murray River has flowed more consistently since European settlement than the Darling, which can resemble a chain of ponds. The Murray has dried up in this way only in extreme droughts, notably the Federation Drought around 1902 and in 1913–1914.⁵⁴ The Wimmera River has its source in the Pyrenees and was always a smaller and less consistent river than the Murray.

---

51   Richard White, '"Are You an Environmentalist or Do You Work for a Living?" Work and Nature', in *Uncommon Ground: Rethinking the Human Place in Nature*, ed. William Cronon (New York: W.W. Norton & Co., 1996), 185.

52   The Canadian historian Gunther Peck, who used the theme of work to explore environmental history, has called regional sites where humans work 'geographies of labor'. In these places, he said, the 'spatial, material, and cultural connections between nature and labor' were enacted. Gunther Peck, 'The Nature of Labor: Fault Lines and Common Ground in Environmental and Labor History', *Environmental History* 11, no. 2 (April 2006): 214.

53   Charles Fenner, 'The Murray River Basin', *Geographical Review: American Geographical Society of New York* 24, no. 1 (January 1934): 79–91.

54   'Discover Murray Australia's Greatest River: Murray River Locks, Weirs, Dams & Barrages', http://www.murrayriver.com.au/about-the-murray/locks-weirs-dams-barrages/; and the Australian Emergency Management Knowledge Hub, 'Federation Drought', https://knowledge.aidr.org.au/resources/environment-federation-drought/. Both accessed 21 September 2018.

MAP 2:
ABORIGINAL GROUPS OF MALLEE COUNTRY AFTER NORMAN TINDALE (1940)

See David Horton (ed.) Encyclopedia of Aboriginal Australia (Canberra, ASP, 1994)
and Bill Arthur and Frances Morphy (eds), *Macquarie Atlas of Indigenous Australia* (Sydney, Macquarie, 2005).

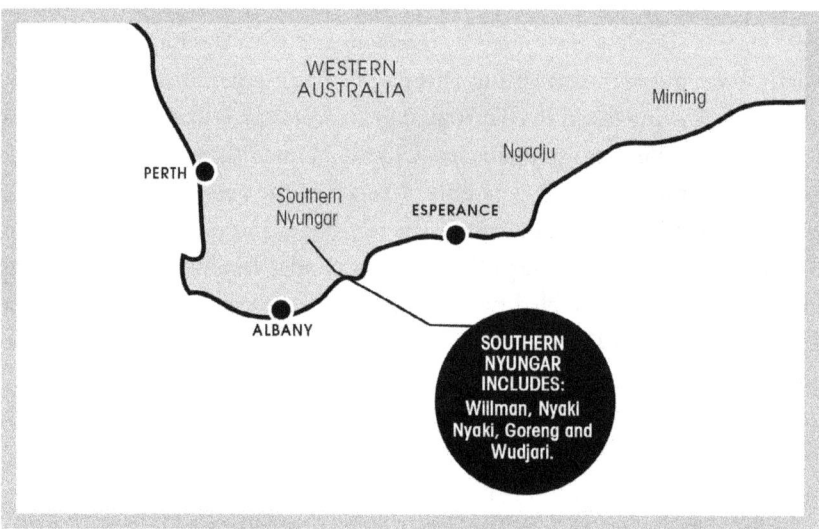

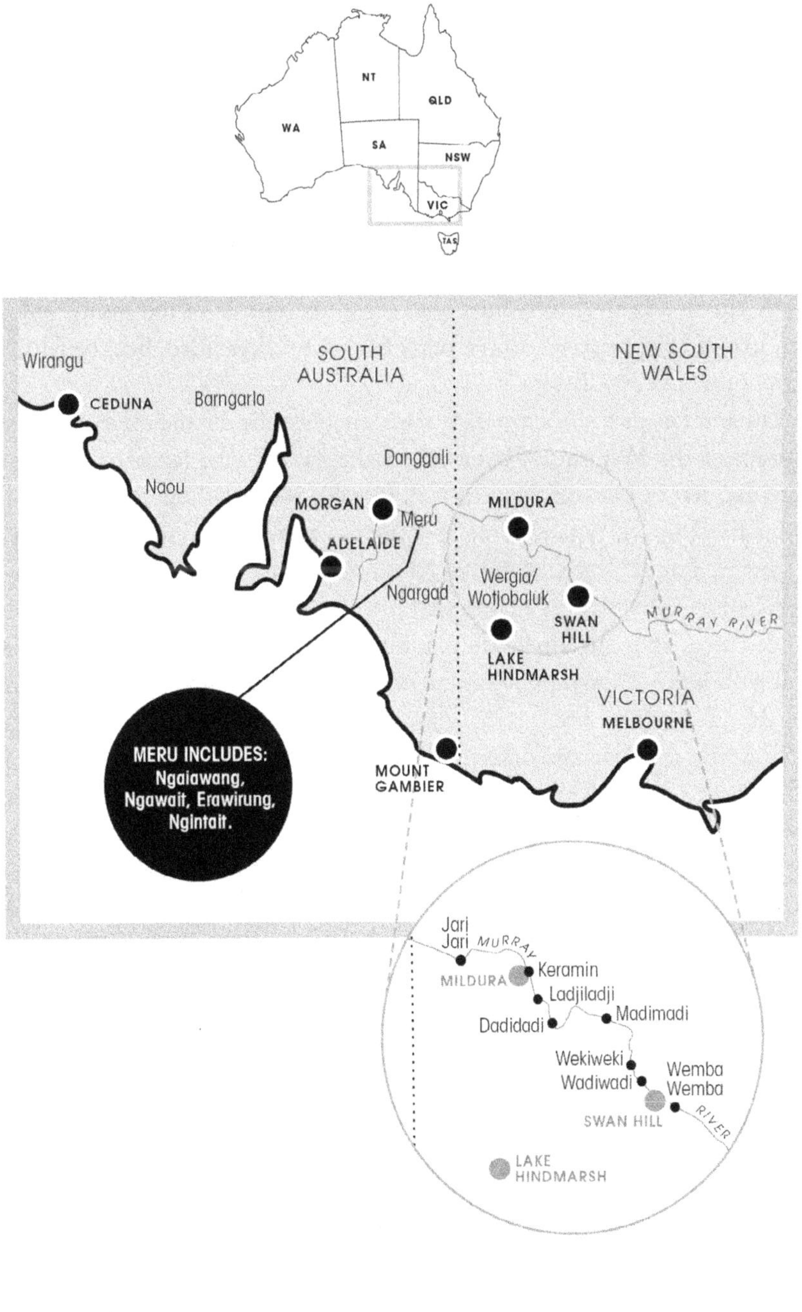

NT
QLD
WA
SA
NSW
VIC
TAS
SOUTH AUSTRALIA
NEW SOUTH WALES
Wirangu
CEDUNA
Barngarla
Naou
Danggali
MORGAN
Meru
ADELAIDE
Ngargad
MILDURA
Wergia/ Wotjobaluk
SWAN HILL
MURRAY RIVER
LAKE HINDMARSH
VICTORIA
MELBOURNE
MOUNT GAMBIER
MERU INCLUDES:
Ngaiawang, Ngawait, Erawirung, Ngintait.
Jari Jari
MURRAY
Keramin
MILDURA
Ladjiladji
Madimadi
Dadidadi
Wekiweki
Wadiwadi
Wemba Wemba
SWAN HILL
RIVER
LAKE HINDMARSH

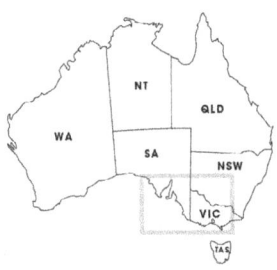

These rivers, particularly the Murray, unsurprisingly proved far more reliable than other surface waters. Some ancillary river waters, like Lake Boga near Swan Hill, which was connected to the Murray, acted as a safety valve for the Wemba Wemba people. In 1836 Thomas Mitchell saw 'vast' numbers of people at Lake Boga, which was 'a fine lake covered with black swans, ducks and other waterfowl'.[55] A.C. Stone, a settler at Lake Boga in the late nineteenth century, collected evidence of a long and intense occupation of the lake by people who called themselves Gourrmjanyuk. He observed large middens or cooking ovens 'containing hundreds of yards of burnt earth and ashes, and freely mixed with it are the remains of mussel shells and bones, with a very occasional chisel, tomahawk or grinding stone'.[56] Chalka Creek, fifty kilometres south of Mildura, also received the Murray's snowmelt and rain-fuelled floodwaters most years, feeding them into seven lakes including Lake Hattah. This provided a supply of fish and water birds for the people while the floodwaters remained, and sustained forests of red gums, buloke and non-eucalypt species. Some years few or no lakes filled, but the Murray River provided a backstop.[57]

Other lakes in the Victorian Mallee, such as Hindmarsh and Albacutya (outlets of the Wimmera River) and Lake Tyrrell (the largest salt lake in Victoria, fed by run-off from Tyrrell Creek), were shallow, unreliable and often dry. This was typical of mallee country across the continent. In Western Australia, Lakes Grace, Magenta, King and Dundas are notable examples of the shallow ephemeral salt lakes that run in long strings through the mallee lands there. They sustained animal, bird and reptile species but only small and mobile Aboriginal populations, who in dry times retreated to the more reliable granite country.

The Murray River was observed by Charles Sturt, who navigated it by whale boat in 1830, seeking an outlet to the Southern Ocean. After leaving the 'gloomy and contracted banks' of the Murrumbidgee, clogged with fallen trees, Sturt marvelled at 'a broad and noble river' he entered downstream from present-day Swan Hill. He named it the Murray and hoped it would be the 'high road' to the sea. It appeared to be flood prone, its southern bank being in parts low and swampy, revealing reed beds and evidence of inundation. Its width was over a hundred metres, and its depth three to six metres. Its reaches from bend to bend were up to eight hundred metres, giving 'splendid' views.

---

55   Mitchell, *Three Expeditions*, 21 June 1836.
56   A.C. Stone, 'The Aborigines of Lake Boga, Victoria', *Proceedings of the Royal Society of Victoria* XXIII (new series), part 2 (March 1911): 434.
57   John Burch, *Returning the Kulkyne* (Melbourne: John Burch, 2017), 12–14.

As Sturt's party rowed on, borne by a gentle current, the Murray 'improved upon us at every mile. Its reaches were of noble breadth, and splendid appearance'. Its current soon strengthened, 'fed by numerous springs'.[58]

Local Indigenous people knew all this, as the Murray along its entire length formed home countries to numerous Aboriginal groups (see Map 2). Indeed, the river's astonishing meanderings across flat country, until it abruptly turned south at Morgan, created a river frontage two to three times that of the in-line distance between two places.[59] Sturt found the zig zag tiresome as his party rowed the river.[60] He encountered numerous groups along the Murray, especially a body of six hundred warriors that threatened his party at the Murray–Darling junction.[61] Below this point he 'seldom communicated with fewer than 200 daily' and 'found the interior to be more populous than we had any reason to expect'.[62] In 1836 Thomas Mitchell surveyed the land along the Murray in this area and continually made contact with Aboriginal people, sometimes in large numbers.[63] In pre-contact times populations were even more numerous—perhaps double or more—for smallpox had twice devastated the river people by the early 1830s, possibly halving the populations each time.[64]

The Murray's riverine resources were abundant save for wintertime. In 1856, naturalist William Blandowski surveyed at Mondellimin, the Jari Jari name for Chaffey's Landing opposite the Murray–Darling junction. The Jari Jari, who were paid £200 in rations and presents, supplied Blandowski with sixteen thousand specimens: 19 species of fish, 3 species of turtles, 2 of crayfish and 1 lobster, 26 species of quadrupeds, 24 of snakes, 17 of lizards, and 3,000 of

---

58   Charles Sturt, *Two Expeditions into the Interior of Southern Australia: During the Years 1828, 1829, 1830 and 1831: With Observations on the Soil, Climate and General Resources of the Colony of New South Wales* (London: Smith, Elder and Co., 1833), vol. 2, 86–7, 88, 86–7, 91–2 respectively. See also Norman Mackay and David Eastburn (eds), *The Murray* (Canberra: Murray–Darling Basin Commission, 1990).

59   J.M. Bowler, A. Kotsonis, C.R. Lawrence 'Environmental Evolution of the Mallee Region, Western Murray Basin', *Proceedings of the Royal Society of Victoria* 118, no. 2 (2006): 35–62. Meander distance calculated from paddling distances on the Murray over four hundred kilometres upstream of Swan Hill, see 'Massive Murray Paddle', accessed 5 June 2017, http://www.massivemurraypaddle.org.au/.

60   Sturt, *Two Expeditions*, 138.

61   Sturt, *Two Expeditions*, 99.

62   Sturt, *Two Expeditions*, 126 and 124 respectively.

63   Mitchell, *Three Expeditions*, see entries for May and June 1836.

64   Noel Butlin, *Our Original Aggression* (London: Allen & Unwin, 1983). See also James Kirby, *Old Times in the Bush of Australia: Trials and Experiences of Early Bush Life in Victoria during the Forties* (Melbourne: Geo. Robertson and Co., n.d.), 78.

insects.⁶⁵ Each fish was drawn and given its 'yerree yarree' name. The large 60-centimetre *kenaru* (*Plotosus tandanus*) and 30-centimetre *manur* (*Megalope caillentassart*) were the finest eating, and 'prohibited to their young men'.⁶⁶

Peter Beveridge, a pastoralist at Tyntynder station (1846–68), just downstream from Swan Hill, reported that the Wadi Wadi dined on an abundance of fish for most of the year—Murray cod, silver perch, catfish and manor. The supply was so large that 'quite a moiety is allowed to go to waste'. Duck and other eggs were consumed 'by the thousand', and many varieties of plant foods.⁶⁷ Mussels were found in countless numbers. The zoologist Johann Krefft, who worked alongside Blandowski, affirmed there were 'large mounds of [their discarded shells] which may be traced upon the river banks at intervals for hundreds of miles'.⁶⁸

Foodstuffs on the river's edge were also profuse. James Kirby, a Swan Hill squatter resident there in 1846, observed 'footpaths which they made going up and down the riverside; and … about a mile apart large mounds of earth thrown up'. Kirby examined these and detected steam emanating from them, and, 'on looking further into them, discovered they were ovens for cooking the *compung* (the root of the bulrush which grows in the reed beds)'. These beds extended 'on an average from a half to a mile on both sides of the river'.⁶⁹ Beyond the river, which was lined with red gums replete with possum nests, were patches of grassland where emu and kangaroo were hunted. Beyond that, mallee scrub stretched to the horizon, harbouring reptiles, small game and other edible creatures as well as plants.⁷⁰

The river sustained semi-sedentary Indigenous populations of fish farmers, who supplemented marine resources with other meat and plant foods from the river frontage and the adjoining back country. But how arduous or easy was it to win a living on the Murray?

---

65 William Blandowski, 'Recent Discoveries in Natural History on the Lower Murray', *Transactions of the Philosophical Institute of Victoria* 2 (1858): 124–37.

66 Blandowski, 'Recent Discoveries in Natural History on the Lower Murray', 131.

67 Peter Beveridge, *The Aborigines of Victoria and Riverine as Seen by Peter Beveridge*, first published 1889 (Melbourne: Lowden Publishing, 2008), 16.

68 Johann Krefft, 'On the Manners and Customs of the Aborigines of the Lower Darling and Murray', *Transactions of the Philosophical Society of NSW* (1862–65), read 2 August 1865, 369. See also 368–9.

69 Kirby, *Old Times in the Bush of Australia*, 28.

70 For a description of these five biotas, see Jan Penney, 'The Death of Queen Aggie: Culture Contact in the Mid-Murray Region' (BA Hons thesis, La Trobe University, 1979), 10–27.

Fishing was the least difficult food-generating activity. Beveridge described a Wadi Wadi fishing expedition of fifty people who set out one autumnal dawn, half in canoes and half on foot. After travelling six kilometres the party paused, the men smoking while the women dived for mussels and giant lobsters to use as bait. Enough gathered, the party moved to a deep pool and fished with both lines and spears. By midday huge fish cutlets were 'frizzling and seething on the glowing coals' and were straightway consumed between pieces of 'pigface' (*carpobrotus glaucescens*), the bright pink salty fruit of which was used as 'bread'. They later drifted homeward down river, catching a large Murray cod by trawling. Beveridge listed the day's catch as 'ninety-three fish, besides those demolished at our midday meal, and a few lobsters'.[71]

Fishing extended beyond the river with even more success, by corralling and trapping strategies. During the spring flood caused by snowmelt, the Murray regularly breeched its banks, carrying fish inland. Blandowski described the ease with which large numbers of fish were speared in these shallow overflows.[72] Beveridge, too, wrote that fish were trapped behind lattice weirs as flood waters receded, providing abundant food; yet still 'behind every weir, fish of all kinds are left by thousands to rot and fester in the sun, or to be devoured by crows and other carrion-feeding creatures which are attracted to those points in countless numbers'.[73] James Kirby described a fisherman's long springy rod fixed in the ground behind him, with a fibre noose on the other end. The noose was attached to a peg under the water in a gap left in a weir. As the fish wriggled through, pushed by the receding floodwaters, the noose tightened freeing it from the peg. The stick was released and the silvery fish was flicked over the catcher's shoulder. Once the fish was extracted the trap was easily reset and the process repeated.[74]

Yet fish were sparse in the colder months. Beveridge observed that, during *myangie* (winter), the people were in a 'state of semi-starvation as regards both food and warmth'.[75] Stephen Webb, an archaeologist who examined skeletal remains of ancient Aboriginal populations, found those from the central Murray River area revealed markers of stress in surviving teeth, leg and cranium bones. Webb wrote that the evidence suggested 'large numbers

---

71   Beveridge, *The Aborigines*, 96, 98, 102 respectively.
72   Blandowski, 'Recent Discoveries in Natural History on the Lower Murray', 133.
73   Beveridge, *The Aborigines*, 90.
74   Kirby, *Old Times in the Bush of Australia*, 36.
75   Beveridge, *The Aborigines*, 140–1.

of sedentary, or at least semi-sedentary people living in close proximity to one another and sharing plentiful, but heavily exploited, food resources which, when less abundant, causes serious hardship for the whole population already under some stress'.[76]

Food gathering on river banks and adjoining lands was more difficult, requiring considerable labour. Possums, a key source of clothing and meat, favoured towering river red gums. Krefft watched a man ascend twenty metres up a gum to extract a possum from a tree hollow. After the substantial effort of climbing and cutting into a large limb with a stone axe, the hunter watched the hapless creature leap into the river where it was retrieved by a member of the axeman's family.[77] Once its flesh was eaten, the possum's skin was prepared for use with a stone or shell scraper, tanned, and then pegged out to cure, before being sewn with about fifty other prepared skins into a fur cloak. It was arduous work, and it is not surprising that the steel axe, with its superior cutting ability for wood and skin, was an instant object of admiration and wonderment among Aboriginal people.[78]

Catching ground creatures such as bandicoots, kangaroo rats and wombats required similar strenuous work. Krefft described how a wombat burrow was located by probing the ground with sticks, then dug out with wooden scoops and kangaroo skins fashioned into buckets. Blandowski recorded this mining operation clearly in a drawing made at Mondellimin in 1856–57 (see Figure 2.1).[79] Krefft wrote, they 'sink a shaft, which sometimes requires to be from ten to twelve feet deep; when they labour, they work with a will, and more than once I have noticed a couple of natives to sink three such shafts in a day'.[80] Sometimes their quarry dug as fast as they did, eluding them.

It was, however, the humble fibrous water plant, so ubiquitous along the Murray and other mallee permanent waters, that was at the centre of the Aboriginal work effort. Beveridge named three main fibre sources: *typha muellera* known as *kumpung or cumpung*, fibre rush, and the giant mallow.

---

[76] Stephen Webb, 'Intensification, Population and Social Change in South-eastern Australia: The Skeletal Evidence', *Aboriginal History* 8, part 2 (1984): 170.

[77] Krefft, 'On the Manners and Customs', 74.

[78] Kirby, *Old Times in the Bush of Australia*, 46; Beveridge, *The Aborigines*, 76.

[79] Harry Allen (ed.), *Australia: William Blandowski's Illustrated Encyclopaedia of Aboriginal Australia*, first published by Blandowski in 1862 under the title *Australien* (Canberra: Aboriginal Studies Press, 2010), 82.

[80] Krefft, 'On the Manners and Customs', 74.

Figure 2.1: William Blandoswki, Image 63 ('Wombat Digging'), from Wilhelm Blandowski, *Australien in 142 photographischen Abbildungen nach zehnjährigen Erfahrungen zusammengestellt* (Gleiwitz, 1862).
(Courtesy Haddon Library of Archaeology and Anthropology, Cambridge)

The botanist Beth Gott has identified many more.[81] These provided both food and the fibre so necessary to the making of twine for the manufacture of essential articles. The new shoots of *kumpung* made a fine salad, while its roots contained a potato-like starch, a rich source of carbohydrate for energy. The collection and steaming of the roots in an excavated earth oven instigated a chain of exertion. The fibrous skins were peeled off and the roots eaten. The skins were diced and chewed after a meal, a process Krefft termed 'strenuous' and performed with 'perseverance', to extract the remaining carbohydrate. The raw fibre was stored as 'beautiful white tows' in twine bags, and used as pillows, until teased into hanks.[82] Twine was made by twisting fibre from these hanks. Beveridge wrote: 'the ends were held with the left hand as the other hand worked the fibre across the thigh and as the hand is drawn back from twisting them, the retrograde action twines them together into the finished cord'.[83] Kirby remarked patronisingly: 'they were quite adept at this work', but the explorer Thomas Mitchell, when presented with a net in 1836 just west of Echuca, pronounced that 'in quality, as well as the mode of knotting, [it] can scarcely be distinguished from those made in Europe'.[84]

Fibre was made for fishing line, for weaving bags, belts and headbands, for binding axe heads and other implements, and for ritual purposes. It was also knotted into nets, large and small, for fishing and catching emu, ducks or small animals. Beveridge carefully recorded the mesh size and dimensions of each type of net, some of which were a hundred metres long and had a life of several years unless damaged. From Beveridge's careful measurements it can be calculated that each Aboriginal group needed about thirty-five kilometres of raw twine to have a set of nets. Taking the average lifespan of a net as three years, this meant that about twelve kilometres of twine had to be manufactured by hand each year. The work effort of net making, from tuber harvest through the steaming, chewing, twining and knotting processes, was enormous and estimated to take about two thousand hours, equal in current terms to a year of 35-hour weeks.[85]

---

81   Beth Gott and John Conran, *Victorian Koorie Plants*, 2nd ed. (Hamilton: Yangennanock Women's Group, 1998), 54–7; Nelly Zola and Beth Gott, *Koorie Plants, Koorie People: Traditional Aboriginal Food, Fibre and Healing Plants of Victoria* (Melbourne: Koorie Heritage Trust, 1996), 57–64.

82   Krefft, 'On the Manners and Customs', 361.

83   Beveridge, *The Aborigines*, 78.

84   Kirby, *Old Times in the Bush of Australia*, 34; Mitchell, *Three Expeditions*, 26 June 1836.

85   See Richard Broome, 'Murray Mallee: A Riverine Geography of Aboriginal Labor', *Agricultural History* 91, no. 2 (Spring 2017): 160–1.

Work in Aboriginal society was largely gendered, although both men and women fished and had the knowledge of how, when and where to hook, spear or corral a fish. Men hunted larger meat sources—emu, kangaroo and duck—and climbed high after possum, while women foraged for plant foods, small game and fibres or dived for mussels and crayfish. The flax or raw fibre for cordage was prepared by women, who also made the smaller and finer nets, the large ones being knotted by men. Workers were so highly skilled as to appear nonchalant.

Work was also often cooperative. To capture ducks, a large net was suspended at one end of a lagoon or pond, and men were stationed at intervals up to a kilometre or more along the waterway. A flock of ducks, after being frightened into flight, flew along the river seeking safer haven. As the birds approached the lagoon, men took up positions in the trees in case they flew too high. A whistle-sound, like that of a hawk, and a wooden disc thrown in the air caused the ducks to dip and finally crash into the net suspended between two trees. The net bearers then collapsed it, trapping part of the flock. In similar manner, fleeing emu were chased and herded into a taut net, which was then released, the trapped flightless birds being dispatched with clubs.[86]

The work effort reinforced social bonds. In 1858 Krefft visited two hundred Jari Jari camped near Yelta, their fires in a semi-circle and, in their midst, an elder 'old Jacob' telling stories. '[A]ll were busy' as they listened—heating and fashioning myall shoots into spears, carving waddies, fashioning nets, preparing possum skins for rugs, and cooking fish caught that day. Krefft added: 'all this time the sonorous voice of old Jacob could be distinctly heard, and shouts of laughter testified how well the old man's tales were appreciated'.[87] Blandowski remarked of possum-skin cloak manufacture: 'the fur skins are treated late into the night and it is very lively in the camp'.[88] Aboriginal workplaces resemble family-based cottage industries in pre-industrial England before time–work discipline took hold (see Figure 2.2).[89] Inter-clan or tribal exchange cycles connected these workplaces to other Aboriginal workshops, moving products of the land to places far removed from their source.[90]

---

86   Beveridge, *The Aborigines*, 80–8.
87   Krefft, 'On the Manners and Customs', 367.
88   Allen (ed.), *Australia: William Blandowski's Illustrated Encyclopaedia of Aboriginal Australia*, 83.
89   E.P. Thompson, 'Time, Work-Discipline, and Industrial Capitalism', *Past & Present* 38 (1967): 693.
90   Isabel McBryde, 'Exchange in South Eastern Australia: An Ethnohistorical Perspective', *Aboriginal History* 8, pt 2 (1984): 132–54; John Mulvaney, 'The Chain

Figure 2.2: William Blandowski, Image 41 ('Domestic Occupations of the Summer Season on the Lower Murray River'), from Wilhelm Blandowski, *Australien in 142 photographischen Abbildungen nach zehnjährigen Erfahrungen zusammengestellt* (Gleiwitz, 1862).
(Courtesy Haddon Library of Archaeology and Anthropology, Cambridge)

Great trade meetings were held on the Murray or by lakes in Victoria where and when food stocks were most plentiful. The people of Lake Boga near Swan Hill had names in their language for Aboriginal groups along the Murray River and for those at Lake Albacutya, Lake Hindmarsh, and Dimboola on the Wimmera River and its outlets, suggesting they traded with them all.[91] Near present-day Yelta on the Murray, people gathered to trade, exchange ritual and feast on fish while doing so. They exchanged myall spears from deep in the mallee scrub for riverine reeds, wongal twine and nets. Stone axe heads were probably traded as well, because Krefft observed that natural stone 'the size of a man's fist' was not found in the area. He reported 'green stone, serpentine, or jade tomahawks used by the natives, were obtained at Mount Macedon' near Melbourne, almost five hundred kilometres away, an observation confirmed by Isabel McBryde over a century

of Connection: The Material Evidence', in *Tribes and Boundaries in Australia*, ed. Nicolas Peterson (Canberra: AIAS, 1976), 72–94.
91   Stone, 'The Aborigines of Lake Boga, Victoria', 437.

later.[92] These products travelled north through the Victorian Mallee along the Wimmera River, into Lake Hindmarsh and on to Wirrengren, then across difficult country to Kulkyne and on to the Murray.[93]

Reciprocity and the power of giving drove much work effort. The anthropologist Marshall Sahlins pithily remarked: 'If friends make gifts, gifts make friends'.[94] The work effort required to create gifts to maintain prestige and good relations was made clear by Donald Thomson's classic study of exchange cycles in Arnhem Land. Thomson identified twenty-seven items moving in five directions up to 450 kilometres. Isabel McBryde found similar trading systems existed in south-eastern Australia.[95] Thomson observed: 'everybody, man or woman, works hard, and that the work is well organised and runs smoothly'. In camp no one is idle for long, as they pick up a net, basket or spear 'and work at this as they talk ... yet there is no feeling of haste, but rather of method of system and order'.[96] Blandowski's sketches at Mondellimin reveal similar unhurried, but constant, work amidst much talk and sociality.[97]

The Wimmera River, which rose in the Pyrenees, was home to the Wotjobaluk. Its flow, not being fed by snowmelt or other significant watercourses, was far less reliable than that of the Murray. The Wimmera regularly lapsed into a trickle and muddy waterholes in dry weather. It drained unreliably into Lake Hindmarsh. Only in wetter years did its waters flow beyond Hindmarsh via Outlet Creek into Lake Albacutya and on to Lake Agnes, in rare cases also inundating the plain at Wirrengren. In the 1960s Aldo Massola investigated the use of this impermanent lakes area, where he found many artefacts and noted the variability of water. Lake Hindmarsh had dried completely in 1902, 1906, between 1929 and 1932 and from 1945 to 1951. In 1918 the Wimmera's waters reached Wirrengren Plain, although the plain had not been inundated since 1853 when the water covering it was

---

92 Krefft, 'On the Manners and Customs', 366. See Isabel McBryde, 'Wil-im-ee Moor-ring: Or, Where Do Axes Come From?' *Mankind* 11 (1978): 354–82.

93 John Burch, 'The Wirrengren–Kulkyne Pathway: Locating a Cultural Icon', *Victorian Historical Journal* 87, no. 2 (December 2016): 261–77.

94 Marshall Sahlins, 'The Spirit of the Gift', *Stone Age Economics*, first pub. 1974 (London: Routledge, 2004), 186. See Sahlins' helpful discussion (149–84) of Marcel Mauss's 1923 seminal essay, *The Gift*.

95 McBryde, 'Exchange in South-eastern Australia', 132–54.

96 Donald Thomson, *Economic Structure and the Ceremonial Exchange Cycle in Arnhem Land* (Melbourne: Macmillan, 1949), 28, 26, 33 and 34 respectively.

97 Allen (ed.), *Australia: William Blandowski's Ilustrated Encyclopaedia of Aboriginal Australia*, passim.

metres deep.⁹⁸ During the times the Wimmera's waters reached these distant depressions, the Wotjobaluk and Wergia took full advantage. Wirrengren in Wergia means 'noise as made by many people', indicating that the area occasionally sustained enough people to hold meetings and ceremony over several days.

The Aboriginal fishing economy was intermittent on these impermanent lakes. However, in wet years the Wotjobaluk travelled 150 kilometres along the lake system as far as Wirrengren. The lakes region provided fish, crustaceans and mussels, birds and their eggs, reptiles, kangaroo and other game. The Wergia camped for months while the lakes were in flood and replenished from winter rains. To wade through the shallow lakes to new campsites or to gather food, the people made small canoes for carrying their children and possessions. The canoes were made from the bark of box trees, which was first cut with stone axes and then prised off with sharp sticks. Adrian Meehan, former co-owner with Suzanne O'Sullivan of 'Pine Plains' in Wyperfeld National Park, has studied the scarred trees for years, counting 450 of them. The box trees thrived with occasional watering, but changing hydrology and catchment patterns mean that Lake Agnes in Wyperfeld has not flooded since 1927.⁹⁹

People of the Dry Scrub Country

The mallee scrub or 'waterless' back country beyond the Murray and Wimmera rivers was not permanently occupied, but Aboriginal people travelled through it and used it on a seasonal, temporary basis. This is evident from the smatterings of material culture found by archaeologists over the years: scarred trees, stone scatters indicating small workshops, stone blades, grindstones and hearths of ancient campfires. Early overviews of Victorian Mallee prehistory in the 1960s by Aldo Massola, curator of anthropology at the National Museum of Victoria, and by archaeologists P. May and R.L.K. Fullagar in the 1980s, found evidence of widespread occupation. May and Fullagar remarked, 'wherever there was water or the likelihood of finding water (at such places as soaks or wells etc.) archaeological evidence will be found'.¹⁰⁰

---

98   Aldo Massola, 'Aboriginal Campsites on Wyperfeld National Park and Pine Plains Station', *Victorian Naturalist* 86 (March1969): 71.
99   Richard Broome, record of discussions with Adrian Meehan, on field trip to Pine Plains, 26–27 March 2014.
100 Massola, 'Aboriginal Campsites', 71–6; P. May and R.L.K. Fullagar, 'Aboriginal Exploitation of the Southern Mallee', *Records of the Victorian Archaeological Survey* 10 (June 1980): 169.

The river peoples journeyed seasonally into the arid mallee scrub for specific products: tough mallee wood for clubs, spears and axe handles; ochres for ceremonies; and foods such as kangaroo, emu and malleefowl or *lowan* eggs. The eggs were sought after, but John Beilby, an early traveller through the Victorian mallee, described how Aboriginal people would check the number present in a nest and refuse to take those from an early laying, preferring instead to return once more were laid. Nicholas Chevalier depicted a malleefowl mound being examined (see Figure 2.3).

Taarp was also considered a great delicacy.[101] Coccids, psyllids and aphids, which are phytophagus or plant-eating insects and can be found on eucalypt leaves, secrete a substance about 60 per cent sugar while in their nymphal stages. *Taarp* (lerp) is the carbohydrate they extrude, as they extract protein from the leaves.[102] Honey-eating birds as well as small marsupial sugar gliders and malleefowl feed on lerp.[103] It is ubiquitous on eucalypts and often found on leaves in suburban and country-town gardens, usually unnoticed by those below but sought out by birds and the trails of ants that scale tree trunks to feast on its sugary sweetness.

Humans sup on it too. A stockman, Robert Cay, who was lost in the Mallee in 1845, fed on lerp, pronouncing it 'very sweet … in size and appearance like a flake of snow, it feels like matted wool, and tastes like the ice on a wedding cake'.[104] The Wadi Wadi on the Murray near Swan Hill mixed *taarp* with water to make a 'sweet and luscious beverage', according to Peter Beveridge. He added that those on pastoral stations with access to European sugar in the post-contact world would still down tools to seek *taarp*, 'although there may be a chance of their forfeiting wages already earned by so doing'.[105]

Taarp collection was hard work as it was gathered in mallee country that was often over twenty kilometres from the river. It was plentiful in mid-summer when temperatures soared above 40° Celsius. Beveridge reported: 'every member of the tribe who could crawl, including children, start off to the *taarp* field in the jolliest of spirits' carrying containers to bring back

---

101 Beveridge, *The Aborigines*, 142.
102 W. Wooster, 'How the Lerp Crystal Palace is Built', *Microscopical Society of Victoria* (1880), quoted in Tim Low, 'Exuding Abundance', *Birdlife Australia* (December 2012), accessed 21 September 2018, http://www.birdlife.org.au/australian-birdlife/detail/exuding-abundance.
103 David C. Paton, 'The Importance of Manna, Honeydew and Lerp in the Diets of Honeyeaters', *Emu* 80, no. 4 (1980): 213–26, accessed 21 September 2018, http://www.publish.csiro.au/MU/pdf/MU9800213.
104 Quoted in Low, 'Exuding Abundance'.
105 Beveridge, *The Aborigines*, 143.

the precious cargo. So prolific were the deposits that 'an aboriginal can easily gather forty or fifty pounds weight of it in one day'.[106] However, many in the party soon flagged, leaving only the strongest to continue. The victors struggled back to camp many hours later 'surly as they could be'. However, after rest, and once the *taarp* was consumed, they headed back into the mallee heat again and again. Beveridge concluded: 'should the *taarp* harvest extend over six or eight weeks, as it does frequently, the blacks become quite fat and sleek, though they partake of very little other food all the time, thus showing how great must be the nutrient contained in this saccharine substance'.[107]

Careful strategies were devised for difficult journeys through mallee lands to obtain resources or to meet with other groups. Charley Thompson, the manager of Kulkyne pastoral station in the 1870s, recorded how the Jari Jari people negotiated a trip from their Murray River home base through harsh scrub country to Raak Plain, ninety kilometres south of Mildura. The men left first, travelling fifteen kilometres a day, hunting as they went. Emu, kangaroo or other sources of meat were killed, cleaned and cooked on a bed of coals in an earthen oven: 'The whole fire-hole or oven would be covered with earth, well-beaten down to prevent escape of heat and to exclude air'. Food caches were created at each camp. The elderly, together with the women and children, followed along the same route, digging up the cooked food at each campsite, complementing it with other food they gathered along the way. Aboriginal soaks and wells were also carefully placed to allow a country without surface water to be safely traversed.[108] Water was carried between soaks or wells in possum-skin bags, the fur turned inwards to strain and purify the water as they walked.[109]

Some Aboriginal groups lived continually in mallee country that was without permanent water, and did so for eons, suggesting a mastery of their environment. This was the case in the Western Australian mallee, the Eyre Peninsula and for groups living in the South Australian Murray Mallee adjoining the border with Victoria. These people occupied challenging environments at the other end of the mallee spectrum, areas quite

---

106 Beveridge, *The Aborigines*, 142.
107 Beveridge, *The Aborigines*, 145.
108 'From Kulnine to Kulkyne—Reminiscences of "Charley" Thompson of Kulkyne—1850s to 1920s', Nangiloc Community Website, accessed 21 September 2018, http://nangiloc.vic.au/history/reminiscences-charley-thompson-kulkyne-1850s-1920s/.
109 Aldo Massola, 'Aborigines of the Mallee', *Proceedings of the Royal Society of Victoria* 79 (new series), part 2 (1966): 269.

Figure 2.3: 'Mallee Scrub, River Murray', by Nicholas Chevalier, William Forrest engraver, from Edwin Carton Booth, *Australia* (London: Virtue & Co., c. 1874–76).
(Courtesy Pictures Collection, State Library Victoria)

different from those enjoyed by groups living along the Murray and near other permanent waters.

In Western Australia's mallee, the lake systems extending from Lake Grace to Lake Dundas were remnants of an ancient river system, now reduced to salty lakes. While these areas provided bird, animal and reptile food sources, fresh water was scarce. Aboriginal people countered this by moving to adjoining country containing granite outcrops. These outcrops—such as Hyden Rock, one of four granite protrusions in the area around Hyden—were formed about 120 million years ago and exposed sixty million years ago as the ancient plateau of the region weathered. They formed islands of abundance, and still do, in a semi-arid region dotted with salt pans and lakes. Rain falling on granite outcrops collects in *gnamma* holes, providing life-giving supplies of water. Aboriginal people covered those that were small and deep enough in order to extend their usefulness. Some holes were particularly valuable as their openings, often small, widened as they deepened. Ethel Hassell of Jarramongup station reported these '*yamma* holes' held water all summer. Such water supplies 'were greatly prized by the natives for usually there were great numbers of birds and game around them. They vary in size considerably, some holding only a few hundred gallons, others several thousand'.[110]

The run-off from the 325 millilitres of average rainfall per year (on current averages at least) created a woodlands ecology that sustained Nyungar people. Their calendar contained six seasons, indicating a nuanced understanding of the land, its climate and the rhythms of nature. The woodlands around the granite outcrops boasted salmon and york gums, she oaks, tea tree and a host of smaller plants. Sandalwood trees also grew, their seeds ground into damper by Nyungar people. This treed canopy attracted birds such as galahs, parrots and wattlebirds, while the outcrops themselves attracted sun-loving reptiles such as dragons, geckos and skinks, carpet pythons and other snake varieties. Rock wallabies leapt about. A thin but vital band of bush and grasses ringing these outcrops produced by the run-off also attracted kangaroo, echidnas and malleefowl.

Nyungar people were able to live well from these granite outcrops in an otherwise difficult terrain. The outcrops provided the raw materials and work sites to make tools, and some were special places. Mulka's Cave, a wondrous natural cavern some kilometres from Wave Rock at Hyden, is part of a massive granite outcrop of particular significance. The cave's Nyungar story focuses on the son of a tribally 'wrong' marriage. Mulka was left cross-eyed by this transgression, and was thus a poor hunter. He ate children instead, a further transgression. After stooping to enter the low and narrow mouth of this cave and adjusting their eyes to the dim light, today's visitors are rewarded with the revelation of 450 hand stencils and other motifs that attest to the rich culture and endurance over thousands of years of the Nyungar of this area. It is the largest rock art site in the south west of Western Australia.[111]

Trade routes threaded the Western Australian mallee country—indeed all mallee countries.[112] Nyungar people informed Ethel Hassell of great ceremonial meetings in past times, invariably involving trade, that were carried out 'from group to group at all times'. One of the important trade centres was Jerramungup (in Nyungar, *yarra-mo-up*, a special place of

---

110 Hassell, 'Notes on the Ethnology of the Wheelman Tribe of Southwestern Australia', 688.
111 Information gathered on a field trip to Lake Grace and Hyden Rock region 17–18 September 2015, including excellent and numerous information boards supplied by the Granite and Woodlands Discovery Trail and the Wave Rock Management Pty Ltd. 'Mulka's Cave', The Gold Region Tourism Organisation Inc. website, accessed 21 September 2018, http://www.australiasgoldenoutback.com/Listing/Mulka's_Cave.
112 Burch, *Returning the Kulkyne*, 20–1; Burch, 'The Wirrengren–Kulkyne Pathway', 261–77.

gathering). People came from as far away as Balladonia over five hundred kilometres to the east.[113] Hassell added that: 'the Wheelman tribe secured their unburned *wilgie* [red and yellow ochre] from inland tribes and pods of *mungite* honey from the coastal people, giving in return spear sticks, prepared stone flakes, throwing-sticks and foods. Articles were often traded for hundreds of miles'.[114]

The Naou living in 'waterless' country on the Eyre Peninsula in South Australia also survived through exploitation of soaks, wells and rock waterholes, which also attracted the game they hunted. The Reverend C.W. Schürmann, a Lutheran missionary based at Port Lincoln, wrote that, apart from these water sources, 'for thirty or more miles around there may not be a drop to be found'.[115] The Naou covered themselves with damp mud from failing soaks when parched for a drink, relieving their symptoms. Schürmann articulated an early environmental cultural determinism, arguing in 1846 that 'the numbers and condition of the Natives of Australia, are in general, dependent upon the nature of the country they inhabit'. Compared to the people of Adelaide, and particularly the Murray, he found the Naou, 'upon the whole, fewer, smaller, and thinner, less skilful, and less united in a social point of view'.[116]

Provisions and water were certainly less abundant on the Eyre Peninsula than were the fish stocks and waters on the Murray, but they were still sufficient to sustain the Naou, who, as Schürmann observed, lived a 'roving life … particularly so in a country which yields its scanty natural products in different localities, and at different seasons of the year'. His descriptions of their travelling nevertheless stressed their leisured mastery of their country. He remarked: 'they seem never in a hurry to start in the morning' and arrived in camp well before sunset. They might remain in one place for a fortnight, depending on the availability of food and water.[117] Food seemed always sufficient for their needs despite the semi-arid nature of the country. Schürmann listed an abundance of game, smaller animals, birds and reptiles, as well as vegetables the Naou gathered. Most root vegetables were roasted,

---

113 R. Forrest, and S. Crowe, *Yarra-mo-up, a Place of the Tall Yate Trees: A Report on the Noongar Social History of the Jerramungup Region* (Canberra: Australian Government Publication Service, 1996), 2.

114 Hassell, 'Notes on the Ethnology of the Wheelman Tribe of Southwestern Australia', 685.

115 C.W. Schürmann, *The Aboriginal Tribes of Port Lincoln in South Australia: Their Mode of Life, Manners, Customs, etc.* (Adelaide: George Dehane, 1846), 9.

116 Schürmann, *The Aboriginal Tribes of Port Lincoln*, 1.

117 Schürmann, *The Aboriginal Tribes of Port Lincoln*, 9.

but the roots of the grass tree, 'which grows in great abundance on the barren hills and plains of Port Lincoln', were eaten raw and 'in prodigious quantities at different seasons of the year'. Pigface, a succulent plant the Naou called *karkalla*, grew 'all over the grassy part of the country' and was abundant during late summer, during which time 'they never tire of it' and 'hunger can never assail them'.[118]

The Ngargad, who lived permanently way east of the Murray River in South Australia, near the Ninety Mile Desert south of Wilkawatt and Lameroo, also sustained life in a country without permanent surface water. They survived by digging 'soaks' into depressions resting on impervious clays that collected subterranean water. Permanent wells giving access to deeper waters were rarer. Colin R. Harris, who studied this region, mapped about fifteen soaks. Some were quite close together, while others were up to twenty kilometres apart, suggesting the Ngargad were able to move quite freely between them with the help of possum-skin water bags. Harris's survey found these soaks were cleared of surrounding vegetation, the result of gathering firewood over eons—the bigger the soak, the further the clearing extended. The surrounds were scattered with animal bones, some artefacts, and evidence of burials, suggesting a long and continuous occupation. When soaks dried in severe drought conditions, the Ngargad moved a hundred kilometres to the north west on the Murray River, near Nildottie, where they were hosted by a neighbouring people.[119]

Water finding was of course a serious business in dry country if wells, soaks or water-filled crevices were not available. Edward John Eyre, who crossed Naou and later Mirning country in the Eyre Peninsula and on the coastal plain of the Great Australian Bight in 1840–41, survived only because of his Aboriginal guides. Eyre, who occasionally saw Aboriginal people, but only from a distance, remarked: 'natives who, from infancy, have been accustomed to travel through arid regions, can remain any length of time out in a country where there are no indications of water'. He dug for soaks but often without success as his young guides were from country far to the east. However, they produced water by hauling a lateral root of a mallee eucalypt from the ground, cutting out a six-metre section, and chopping it into shorter lengths. These were stood end-on-end on a bark collection dish while the water seeped out. Eyre observed: 'I saw my own boys get one-third of a pint [almost a cup] out

---

118 Schürmann, *The Aboriginal Tribes of Port Lincoln*, 6.
119 Colin R. Harris, 'A Brief History of the Ninety Mile Desert', typescript report for the Nature Conservation Society of South Australia, *c.* 1977, 7–12.

in this way in about a quarter of an hour'. Being brought up around whites, they 'were by no means adept at the practice'.[120] This was not enough for Eyre's horses, but it could sustain human life, especially if more roots were cut and more time taken.

Water could be found in a myriad of ways.[121] A variety of trees provided water from their roots; beside mallee eucalyptus, they included casuarina, kurrajong, needlebush, mulga and acacia. Those most productive of water were trees growing in depressions. The South Australian explorer, Alexander Magarey, stated in 1895 that 'water trees' enabled Aborigines 'to go far away out into the arid wilds, there to roam and hunt and gather food with the utmost liberty and confidence'.[122] Magarey listed other water-finding techniques as well, including seeking recesses in hollow trees and brushing the dew from bushes on cold mallee mornings. Observing the presence of flocks of finches, the ubiquitous top-knot or bronze-winged pigeons, and cockatoos 'is an infallible warning in dry country of the nearness of water'. Their absence warns that the country is probably waterless. Animals and insects were less reliable indicators but useful nonetheless. Finding a water frog (*Cyclorana platycephala*) in earth under the base of a dry clay pan and squeezing it dry could provide a life-saving drink.[123] Aldo Massola stated that the people of the Victorian Mallee knew every place likely to hold water, and each was 'given a distinguishing name by them'.[124]

Food as well, even in the most marginal mallee country, was generally sufficient—even plentiful. Schürmann pointed to the abundant food sources of the Naou on the Eyre Peninsula. The explorer Edward John Eyre, who became an Aboriginal protector at Moorundie on the Murray River near Blanchetown, recognised that 'the very regions, which, in the eyes of the European, are most barren and worthless, are to the native the most valuable

---

120   Edward John Eyre, *Journals of Expeditions of Discovery into Central Australia and Overland from Adelaide to King George's Sound* (London: T. & W. Boone, 1845), vol. 1, 350.

121   Kimber, 'The Ngarkat', 10; Schürmann, *The Aboriginal Tribes of Port Lincoln in South Australia*, 9; Alexander Thomas Magarey, 'Aboriginal Water-Quest', *Proceedings of the Royal Geographical Society of Australasia South Australian Branch*, session 1895, reprinted as *Australian Aboriginal Tracking, Water Finding and Smoke Signalling* (Perth: Hesperian Press, 2015), 6–16. Also, I.A.E. Bayly, 'Review of How Indigenous People Managed for Water in Desert Regions of Australia', *Journal of the Royal Society of Western Australia* 82 (1999): 17–25, 21 September 2018, http://www.rswa.org.au/publications/Journal/82(1)/82(1)bayly.pdf.

122   Magarey, 'Aboriginal Water-Quest', 7.

123   Magarey, 'Aboriginal Water-Quest', 10.

124   Aldo Massola, 'Aborigines of the Mallee', *Proceedings of the Royal Society of Victoria* 79 (new series), part 2 (1966): 269.

and productive'.[125] If all else failed, mallee roots provided food sustenance. Eyre's youthful guides peeled bark from young roots of *Eucalyptus dumosa* and roasted them in hot ashes until crisp. They were beaten with stones and then chewed to extract a farinaceous powder between the fibres. Eyre commented that it was 'by no means unpleasant in flavour, but rather sweet, and resembling the taste of malt; how far a person could live upon this diet alone, I have no means of judging, but it certainly appeases the appetite, and is, I should suppose, nutritious'.[126]

The Ngargad lived in very marginal semi-arid scrub country from Peake to Pinnaroo in the South Australian mallee. The anthropologist Dick Kimber, who wrote about them in 1974 using a variation of their name, Ngarkat, admitted he could find little hard evidence of their way of life. Their country was devoid of any permanent surface water, and they relied on soaks, as noted by Harris above. Kimber speculated that the lack of water meant their living groups might have been small bands of about fifteen people. The whole group perhaps numbered less than a hundred individuals, probably the smallest population of any mallee people. Stone suitable for tool making did not occur in their country, so they traded stone from the Wotjobaluk far to their east, who in turn received axe-head blanks from the Mount William quarry of the Kulin. It is unclear what the Ngarkat traded in return—perhaps, speculated Kimber, gypsum, wood for weapons, or access to their country for hunting emu.[127]

Little else is known of Ngarkat culture owing to a lack of early European observers in this region. Some glimmers of their worldview and life style survive. Kimber wrote in the 1960s that six small and low rectangular stone arrangements about three by four metres in dimension existed near Coonalpyn in the south west of their country. These structures were erased when the land was cleared around 1960, but a resident of Jabuk took photographs that Kimber fortunately viewed.[128]

The Ngarkat did not survive invasion and settlement. One reason was a smallpox epidemic that raged along the Lower Murray and its hinterlands in the 1790s, fifty years before Europeans reached the area. It was most likely spread unintentionally by Macassan fishermen on the north coast of Australia, although some have argued for a Sydney source. A chain of infection travelled

---

125 Eyre, *Journals*, vol. 1, 351.
126 Eyre, *Journals*, vol. 1, 371.
127 Kimber, 'The Ngarkat', 1–33.
128 Kimber, 'The Ngarkat', 25–6.

south via the river systems of Queensland and NSW to the British settlement at Sydney in 1789, and on to the Murray, spreading havoc. The aetiology of this disease in hitherto untouched populations suggests it constituted a biological disaster that halved all Aboriginal populations it touched.[129] Peter Beveridge recalled seeing many pock-marked faces among older men on the Murray in the 1840s, the tell-tale sign of smallpox survivors. Beveridge wrote that people visiting his pastoral station outside Swan Hill remembered, with 'loathing horror', that 'the whole country became perfectly decimated' by the disease. As the death toll mounted the people fled 'leaving the sick behind to die, and the dead to fester in the sun, or as food for the wild dogs, and the carrion loving birds to fatten upon'.[130] Kimber speculated that the Ngarkat, who traded with river people, were most likely infected as well. The need to replenish their population then may have led to theft of women from neighbours and a violent retribution in which many Ngarkat were killed.

Whatever the circumstances of their decline, the Ngarkat never recovered and vanished. Their extinction is appalling, and close to being forgotten. The Ngarkat deserve to be remembered as a people who prevailed in the most difficult mallee country, though they could not survive the onslaught of colonisation.[131] In 1954 their desert country succumbed too, being levelled, burnt and shaped into farms in a reclamation project led by the Australian Mutual Provident Society (see Chapter 10). A film documenting this, and featuring the South Australian Symphony Orchestra, was a rhapsody to the conquest of 'desert scrub' and Aboriginal country. It makes for salutary viewing.[132] The European penetration of mallee country made such devastation possible.

---

129 For smallpox in Australia, see Judy Campbell, *Invisible Invaders: Smallpox and Other Diseases in Aboriginal Australia 1780–1880* (Melbourne: Melbourne University Press, 2002); Noel Butlin, *Our Original Aggression* (London: Allen & Unwin, 1983). For the disease, see 'Smallpox', in A.S. Benenson (ed.), *Control of Communicable Diseases in Man*, 15th ed. (Washington D.C.: American Public Health Association, 1990).

130 Beveridge, *The Aborigines*, 15.

131 Kimber, 'The Ngarkat', 28–31.

132 *Desert Conquest* directed by Lex Halliday, produced by Australian Mutual Provident Society (Australian Instructional Films, 1954),via the Sate Library of South Australia, accessed 30 January 2017, http://www.slsa.sa.gov.au/site/page.cfm?u=991&c=44290.

Chapter 3

AN IMPRACTICABLE COUNTRY

Mallee country lay hidden from European eyes for decades. Its semi-arid and vast nature resisted easy exploration, and its immense distance from the coastal bridgeheads of Sydney founded in 1788, Perth (1829), Melbourne (1835) and Adelaide (1836) kept it concealed. Settlers became aware of mallee country after 1830, but it remained mysterious and daunting for another two decades. These lands finally yielded some of their secrets to European explorers, who left accounts of their heroic deeds in country they described as 'impracticable'. This characterisation typecast mallee lands for two generations. Aboriginal guides were vital to the early explorers, as were the stamina of their horses and the sweat of unsung convicts and manservants in their parties. Aboriginal landowners generally met these exploration parties with wariness and, sometimes, resistance.

The Murray River itself led Charles Sturt into mallee country as he searched for a 'high road' to the southern coast. On 7 January 1830, Sturt led a small party of seven, including several convicts, from Gundagai on the Murrumbidgee River, rowing in a south-westerly direction downstream before entering a 'broad and noble river' on 14 January.[1] Sturt named it the Murray, erasing the Wemba Wemba's name Milloo, which Aboriginal people further downstream called Millewa. The river had kilometre-long reaches but meandered across flat mallee country, its frontage being two to three times the in-line distance, thus slowing Sturt's progress. He went where the river directed him, tied as he was to a boat. At each bend, he took compass readings, 'so that not a single winding or curve of the Murray is omitted in the large chart'.[2] The map promised to be useful on his return journey and served also to assert possession of the country. With each notation he made, Sturt described in European and appraising terms the adjoining mallee country of what later became Victoria and South Australia. For example, on

---

1   Charles Sturt, *Two Expeditions into the Interior of Southern Australia: During the Years 1828, 1829, 1830 and 1831: With Observations on the Soil, Climate and General Resources of the Colony of New South Wales* (London: Smith, Elder and Co., 1833), vol. 2, 86.
2   Sturt, *Two Expeditions*, 146.

approaching present-day Mildura, he described the sandy soil and low scrub, with occasional sand ridges crowned by cypress trees. Altogether it was 'barren and unpromising', he wrote. Downstream of the junction with the Rufus River, named after the red-headed George McLeay, his second in charge, some of the party climbed a sandy ridge. Their vista was also scrubby, 'barren' and 'most unpromising'. Across the modern-day border into South Australia, Sturt again wrote that the country was 'inhospitable; and unprofitable'. The 'barren and sandy interior', covered in brush with occasional cypress belts on sandy ridges, was altogether 'unsatisfactory'.[3]

It was only as the party reached the lower Murray around Mannum that the country assumed a useful and productive appearance for pastoral and agricultural pursuits. On the west bank the landscape changed to 'woody' with distant hills beyond, although mallee country to the east of the river remained 'scrubby and low'. Further downstream the country matched Sturt's European sensibilities of good and fertile land, graced by undulating hills planted by nature with trees to make a 'pleasure ground' to the eye.[4] He spied large oat-grass pastures beneath the trees, probably evidence of Aboriginal burning to create kangaroo grounds.

Sturt's party contacted many Aboriginal groups, but relations, at first curious, became increasingly wary and then tense. His preconception of a sparsely populated country was totally disrupted, at least along the river, Sturt recording he 'communicated with fewer than 200 daily'. He identified several from each group as 'ambassadors', who accompanied him, cutting across country to negate the river's meander, before passing him on to the next group. Most 'ambassadors' slept in Sturt's camp. The two peoples exchanged food, goods and experiences as best they could across the language and cultural divide. Sturt and Macleay continually sought information from the land owners, asking about the river and surrounding country. Both parties drew marks in the sand to make their point. Good relations were promoted with the 'ambassadors' by gift exchanges, combined singing, and on one occasion by shaving a man, to his apparent delight.

What Aboriginal people made of these encounters is largely unknowable. They certainly watched Sturt's every move, for the 'ambassadors', like most emissaries, were spies as well. They tried to fathom why Sturt's party had intruded on country and were keen to move them down river. Feeling very vulnerable, leading just one boat party on a not very broad river and

---

3   Sturt, *Two Expeditions*, 92, 129–30, 136–7.
4   Sturt, *Two Expeditions*, 148 and 152.

surrounded by new peoples each day, Sturt fostered this Aboriginal 'chain of communication to ensure our own safety'. He believed good relations with one group influenced the next meeting.[5] From his superfluous provision barrels, Sturt distributed metal axes and iron hoop, which were highly prized by the recipients. In what is now South Australia, he allowed an old man to ride in the boat for several days, and was informed by him of a big change in the direction of the river southward at present-day Morgan. The man then left, but still beat the party to the next camp by cutting across country.

Rather than improving, relations soured, and trouble brewed with each meeting. At the Murray–Darling junction six hundred painted and armed warriors stood on a long sand spit on the north-east side, threatening Sturt's progress. Sturt quickly issued guns to his men. At this moment of high tension, an 'ambassador' recently met, whom Sturt called 'the remarkable savage', leapt into the water from the southern bank and swam to the sand spit. The man, in what Sturt deemed an act of Providence and courage, remonstrated with and quietened the large body of warriors, many of whom 'came swimming over to us like a parcel of seals'.[6]

What Sturt believed was due to Divine intervention or the fickleness of 'savages' was a matter of local politics, confirmed by Mitchell's observations six years later. The 'remarkable savage' and his people believed it better to move the party on. To kill them would have been easy, but the 'remarkable savage' chose diplomacy. He and his people, being connected by trade and kin networks to peoples to the north, were well aware of the threat posed by white faces intruding on country. The Wiradjuri of the Bathurst Plains, whose country stretched south to mallee country, no doubt spread stories of their war with Europeans in 1824.[7] Oblivious to all this, Sturt rewarded 'the remarkable savage'. He then explored the Darling River a few kilometres, before stopping to raise the British flag. Sturt later wrote: 'the eye of every native had been fixed upon that noble flag, at all times a beautiful object, and to them a novel one, as it waved over us in the heart of a desert'. While he believed they were 'still lost in astonishment', he hoisted a small sail and escaped downstream.[8]

---

5   Sturt, *Two Expeditions*, 127 and 131.

6   Sturt, *Two Expeditions*, 107.

7   Ken Fry, *Beyond the Barrier: Class Formation in a Pastoral Society: Bathurst 1818–1848* (Bathurst: Crawford House Press, 1993), chap. 2. On advancing news, see Henry Reynolds, *The Other Side of the Frontier: An Interpretation of the Aboriginal Response to the Invasion and Settlement of Australia* (Townsville: James Cook University, 1981), chap. 1.

8   Sturt, *Two Expeditions*, 103–08.

As the 'chain of communication' lengthened, news spread down river that these intruders were curiosities and possessed metal. At times, Sturt's party was mobbed. Around the future South Australian border high tension prevailed in the face of continual inspections. George McLeay, who had revelled in these interactions, grew weary of them. Sturt wrote that, at each meeting, 'we were, in some measure, obliged to submit to an examination, and to be pulled about, and fingered all over. They generally measured our hands and feet with their own, counted our fingers, felt our faces, and besmeared our shirts all over with grease and dirt'.[9] Some groups resisted their departure, holding fast to the boat, leading to much pushing and shoving. The Murray south of Morgan, where it widened and flowed more directly, provided some relief. George French Angas fifteen years later painted the Murray at Moorundi, south of Blanchetown, showing its less threatening aspect (see Figure 3.1). Sturt's party reached Lake Alexandrina after thirty-three days of rowing. Shoals blocked their access to the ocean at Encounter Bay, but the party walked to the seashore to bathe.

Figure 3.1: 'The River Murray above Moorundi', by George French Angas, 1846, James William Giles engraver.
(Courtesy National Library of Australia, nla.obj-135640230)

---

9   Sturt, *Two Expeditions*, 132.

The party was in a state of high anxiety during the return journey of 3,200 kilometres as they continually rowed against the current. No 'ambassadors' were offered, but they met 'sufficient bodies to be troublesome' and we 'were rarely without a party of them, who followed us in spite of our efforts to tire them out'.[10] Trouble beckoned on several occasions, spurring the party to row harder. Exhaustion mounted as they rowed from dawn till after seven at night, with only an hour's break at midday to take bread and water. They relished the meagre flesh of an occasional bird they shot but caught few fish, not wanting to heave to. Near the junction with the Darling they hauled the boat over shallow rapids and were surprised by Aborigines while standing defenceless in the water. Astonishingly, the group included 'the remarkable savage', who again offered help. The party finally reached the Murrumbidgee and left mallee country after seventy-seven days straight at the oars, Sturt taking his turn. They reached their depot in poor condition, only to find it deserted. They rowed for a further two weeks then rested, exhausted, starving and thankful to be free of 'inhospitable' country. Relief arrived a week later.[11]

From 1831, Major Thomas Mitchell, the Surveyor General of NSW, charted NSW's inland river systems including the Darling River. He followed the Darling downstream to Menindee, clashing with Aborigines and killing several. In March 1836, Mitchell set out again with twenty-four European men and two Aboriginal male guides, Piper and Burnett, the latter proving vital to his success. He traced the Darling south from Menindee, but, being barred by difficult country, he followed three rivers—the Lachlan, which flowed into the Murrumbidgee and then into the Murray. From May to June 1836 Mitchell and his party explored the Murray west to the Murray–Darling junction and up the Darling till it became a 'chain of ponds', making it impossible to return to Menindee. He backtracked eastward beside the Murray, renaming Swan Hill, Lake Boga and many other places that already had Aboriginal names. Mitchell's party left the Murray beyond present-day Robinvale. While on the Murray he was told of Sturt's party by two families: 'they had some years before seen white men go down and return up the river in a large canoe'.[12] Mitchell then trekked south west in a rough line through Pyramid Hill to

---

10   Sturt, *Two Expeditions*, 196 and 203.

11   H.J. Gibbney, 'Sturt, Charles (1795–1869)', *Australian Dictionary of Biography* (Melbourne: Melbourne University Press, 1967), vol. 2, 495–98.

12   T.L. Mitchell, *Three Expeditions into the Interior of Eastern Australia; with Descriptions of the Recently Explored Region of Australia Felix, and of the Present Colony of New South Wales*, (London: T. & W. Boone, 1839), vol. 2, 4 June 1836, Project Gutenberg Australia, http://gutenberg.net.au/ebooks/e00036.html.

Wedderburn, Horsham, Casterton and Portland Bay, skirting the southern parts of the Victorian Mallee.

Mitchell echoed Sturt's view of mallee lands. Near present-day Balranald, Mitchell tracked through 'unpromising' sand-ridge country, covered with 'that most unpleasing of shrubs to a traveller, the Eucalyptus dumosa, and the prickly grass mentioned by Mr Oxley'. *Eucalyptus dumosa* is not a tree, Mitchell continued, 'but a lofty bush with a great number of stems, each two or three inches in diameter, and the bushes grow thickly together, having between them nothing but the prickly grass in large tufts'. Traversing scrubby country just west of present-day Robinvale, he described it as 'one of the most barren regions in the world'. But eleven days later, when opposite present-day Red Cliffs, and while travelling across very sandy ground where nothing seemed to grow but mallee trees and prickly grass, Mitchell had an insight about sand drift. He remarked: 'Nature appears to have provided curiously against that evil here by the abundant distribution of two plants so singularly adapted to such a soil'. However, this did not quell his annoyance at the prickly grass (probably *Triodia scariosa*), which from a distance appeared to be an overgrown lavender but had 'blades consisting of sharp spikes which shoot out in all directions'.[13]

Mitchell continually recorded landforms and vegetation in his journal, but these observations were punctuated by ongoing expressions of anxiety about Aboriginal attacks, given his experience and trouble on the Darling the previous year. Just east of Lake Benanee, on 23 May 1836, Mitchell split his party in two, leaving Granville Stapylton, his second in command, with eight men at a depot. Mitchell then pushed west with fifteen men, including his guides Burnett and Piper. He arrived at Lake Benanee the next day, just north east of present-day Euston and Robinvale, and found it 'swarming with natives on both the beach and in canoes'. He recognised them as being those from the lower Darling River (possibly Paakantji) several hundred miles away, the very men with whom he had clashed a year earlier. Mitchell recalled that while on the Lachlan River he had heard 'that these people were coming down to fight us'.

This meeting began several days of high anxiety and ritual aggression. In one parley, Mitchell bid his blacksmith flex his muscles and assume a fighting pose. Piper's Aboriginal woman friend told Piper that the Darling River people meant to attack them all. Mitchell's men fired a rocket to intimidate them, but the Darling people threatened the camp and set fire to the bush. Mitchell

---

13 Mitchell, *Three Expeditions*, 17, 25 and 28 May 1836.

ordered his men to draw their guns and advance, forcing the Aborigines to retire.[14] On 26 May Mitchell, advancing to the Murray–Darling junction, met some local people who reiterated that those at Lake Benanee 'did not belong to that part of the country, but had come there to fight us, on hearing of our approach'. A local man added they were the same ones who had wanted 'to kill another white man [Captain Sturt] in a canoe, at the junction of the rivers lower down'.[15] So the 'remarkable savage' of Sturt's account, who stopped the imminent attack on Sturt's party, was asserting the rights of local land owners to determine policy on country.

On 27 May, Mitchell heard the 'voices of a vast body of blacks following our track' as he made for the river junction. Feeling vulnerable in a strange country, and with his party split in two, Mitchell determined to make a stand. While his men hid in the bush, Mitchell sent Burnett and Piper on reconnaissance to determine if these were the Darling people, which was quickly confirmed. Mitchell later composed a self-interested account to inform posterity of what happened next. He wrote that, once the Darling people realised Mitchell's party lay in ambush, they raised their spears. This caused a man in Mitchell's party, named King, to fire his carbine. A general fusillade erupted as the Aborigines fled to the river. Mitchell's men chased them, firing continuously and killing seven.

Mitchell stressed that he had not ordered this attack but that his men fired 'in their own defence'. The Darling people would have replied, if asked, that they were defending themselves against white men who laid an ambush. Mitchell added that the Darling people were the aggressors, having come here 'for the avowed purpose of meeting and attacking us' and 'had persisted in following us with such bundles of spears as we had never seen on other occasions'.[16] The Darling people would have replied again, if asked, that they only sought revenge for wrongs done to them in their own country the previous year, and that Mitchell had continually entering Aboriginal country uninvited and unsanctioned. Mitchell euphemistically called the attack site Mount Dispersion. The NSW Legislative Council investigated his actions and his inadequate report, delaying his knighthood by several years and sparking a new policy requiring every Aboriginal death to be subject to an official inquest.[17]

---

14   Mitchell, *Three Expeditions*, 24 and 25 May.
15   Mitchell, *Three Expeditions*, 26 May 1836.
16   Mitchell, *Three Expeditions*, 27 May 1836.
17   R.H.W. Reece, *Aborigines and Colonists: Aborigines and Colonial Society in New South Wales in the 1830s and 1840s* (Sydney: Sydney University Press, 1974), 119–21,

The local Murray people also saw Mitchell as a transgressor. Following the party's arrival at Lake Boga near Swan Hill, his guide Piper was accosted by some local men. When Piper asked the name of this lake, they refused to answer, repeating 'too much ask'. They blamed Piper for bringing the white fellows there and launched two spears at him. Piper fended them off with his carbine and shot one man in the jaw as the others fled. He then shot the wounded man again, killing him. Piper informed Mitchell of this with much satisfaction, for this slain Aboriginal man was no friend or kin to Piper.[18]

There is one Aboriginal account of the aggression of Mitchell's party, that by Tilki from the Murray near Kulkyne Station. His evidence was recorded by the 1859 select committee on the 'Present Condition of the Aborigines'. Tilki recalled being 'a child on my mother's back' when his mother and other women were gathering mussels at the Murray River near Mount Dispersion: 'There some men belonging to Mitchell's exploring expedition fired upon us, and a musket ball carried off part of my thumb, which never grew afterwards so well as the one I have here on my right hand'.[19] It is a convincing yet curious statement. If Tilki was on his mother's back, then arguably he would have been too young to remember this event, but, because it was such a traumatic incident, some recollection may have been retained. Moreover, his memory could have been shaped and reinforced by his mother's storytelling. He was fortunate, for a 19 mm musket ball hitting part of his thumb would most likely have shattered the bone. Further, he and his mother were not Darling people. So did Mitchell's men also attack local people near Mount Dispersion, or were Tilki and the Murray people inadvertently caught up in the line of fire?

In late June 1836 Mitchell and his party left the 'unpromising' mallee country and its assertive people via the Murray River. On 30 June, he ascended a granite outcrop a hundred metres high, which he called Pyramid Hill, and viewed the surrounding plains to the south 'shining fresh and green in the light of a fine morning'. It was a novel scene for him in his explorations of the arid interior, and it moved him to call this vista 'Australia Felix.' He surveyed the scene and, without irony, declared it: 'A land so inviting and still without inhabitants!'. Buoyed by the moment, he continued:

135–36. See also D.W.A. Baker, 'Mitchell, Sir Thomas Livingstone (1792–1855)', *Australian Dictionary of Biography* (Melbourne: Melbourne University Press, 1967), vol. 2, 238–42.

18   Mitchell, *Three Expeditions*, 21 June 1836.

19   Quoted in John Burch, *Returning the Kulkyne* (Melbourne: John Burch, 2017), 105.

> As I stood, the first European intruder on the sublime solitude of these verdant plains as yet untouched by flocks or herds, I felt conscious of being the harbinger of mighty changes, and that our steps would soon be followed by the men and the animals for which it seemed to have been prepared.[20]

He tracked south west, found and followed the Wimmera River, which he named, to present-day Horsham. He then continued south west and reached Portland on the southern coast, where, to his astonishment, the Henty brothers were busily forming a sheep empire. Thomas (later Sir Thomas) Mitchell's characterisation of western Victoria as *Australia Felix* prompted a squatting rush to the Port Phillip District (later Victoria) soon after.

One of the first to overland sheep and cattle from NSW was Edward John Eyre in 1836. He then drove stock from Port Phillip to Adelaide in July 1838. Seeking a westward route that was far south of the one along the Murray River, Eyre encountered the Wimmera River, following it north to Lake Hindmarsh, which he named. For three weeks, Eyre's party tried to penetrate the mallee to the north and to the west of Lake Hindmarsh, but was driven back each time by thick scrub and the lack of usable grass or water. Duncan Cooper represented this country in a sketch of 1850 revealing its close wooded and parched nature, complete with cattle bones (see Figure 3.2). One sortie gained a hundred miles north before its members abandoned their horses after four days without water. Eyre and two men struggled back to Lake Hindmarsh on foot. Two horses were later found, but the others vanished. The entire party retreated east, then headed north to link with the existing Murray River route to Adelaide. Eyre reported that there was no permanent water between Lake Hindmarsh and the Murray River, dismissing any hope of a more southern route to Adelaide. The Victorian Mallee was avoided by European settlers for a decade.[21] The 1847 survey of the Victorian–South Australian border by Henry Wade, who trekked northward from the coast, was abandoned near the Little Desert on the southern edge of mallee country.[22]

---

20   Mitchell, *Three Expeditions*, 30 June 1836.
21   Eyre, in *South Australian Gazette*, 14 July 1838, reprinted in Alfred S. Kenyon, *The Story of the Mallee: A History of the Victorian Mallee Read before the Historical Society of Victoria, 18 March 1912* (Melbourne: Wilke & Co., 1982), 7–10.
22   Kenyon, *The Story of the Mallee*, 12.

Figure 3.2: 'Mallee Scrub North of Wimmera River', by Duncan Cooper (1850), brush and pen and sepia ink and wash over pencil 14.2 x 22.5 cm (image and sheet). (Courtesy National Gallery of Victoria, Melbourne. Purchased 1956, accession no. 3335.4-4)

In 1839, Eyre, now based in South Australia, set out in search of new pastoral country. He surveyed parts of the Flinders Ranges and the next year surveyed north of Spencers Gulf with a party led by three Aboriginal men. The vast dry lake, Lake Torrens, formed an impenetrable barrier further north, so he retreated from 'so inhospitable and impracticable a country'.[23] He then turned to the peninsula that later bore his name, exploring west from Port Lincoln to Streaky Bay. He also transported stock by sea to Albany and overlanded them to Perth, which sparked his interest in overlanding across the continent from east to west through mallee country. He returned from his trip to the West with an Aboriginal man named Wylie from King George Sound.[24]

Eyre made a series of expeditions on the Eyre Peninsula in preparation for the push across a continent. In September 1839, he left Streaky Bay leading a small party, heading due east and tracking under the Gawler Ranges, which he named. He continued east, just north of the 60-kilometre salt pan, Lake Gillies. Eyre described the country as covered in low scrub, sandy ridges

---

23 Edward John Eyre, *Journals of Expeditions of Discovery into Central Australia and Overland from Adelaide to King George's Sound* (London: T. & W. Boone, 1845), vol. 1, 15 August 1840.

24 Wendy Birman, 'Wylie', *Australian Dictionary of Biography* (Melbourne: Melbourne University Press, 1967), vol. 2, 629–30.

or stony rises, with very little grass for the horses and no permanent water. The party found water in rocky crevices beneath the Gawler Ranges, but 'we never found a drop of permanent fresh-water nor a single spring near them. There are no watercourses, and no timber; all is barren rocky and naked in the extreme'.[25] His trek succeeded owing to recent rain, but Eyre realised the sun would soon dry these precious rockhole supplies. Armed with this knowledge, in September 1840 he sent his overseer and half the party westwards along this very route direct to Streaky Bay. Rain had recently fallen and the overseer, who had taken the route with Eyre in 1839, knew where water was to be found. Besides, 'our former dray tracks of 1839, which were still distinctly visible, would be a sufficient guide to prevent him getting off the line of route'.[26]

While half of his party moved directly to Streaky Bay, Eyre journeyed over 350 kilometres from Mount Arden along the east coast of the Eyre Peninsula to Port Lincoln to organise supplies for the future push across the continent. It was a very difficult journey across scrubby plains devoid of permanent surface waters and without much grass for the horses. Native soaks and natural water in the crevices of granite outcrops kept them alive. In places the country was extremely scrubby. Near Mount Hill, eighty kilometres north east of Port Lincoln, they passed through the 'strongest' scrub yet. So dense was it that 'the drays were tearing down the brush with loud crashes, at every step which the horses took'. It was like a clearing party; 'the brush rapidly disappearing before the wheels, and leaving almost an open road as if it had been cut away by axes'.[27]

After purchasing supplies at Port Lincoln, including sheep and kangaroo dogs, Eyre trekked north west along the coast to Streaky Bay. He encountered numerous salt lakes and much scrub country, some of which had 'a singularly wild and deserted aspect'.[28] Yet there were many Indigenous people here. Eyre observed several Aboriginal fires and at Mount Hall numerous huts, which were deserted by their owners in order to avoid contact with Eyre's party. Near Venus Bay, eighty kilometres from Streaky Bay, he saw about thirty paths leading to a large deep hole in the limestone, carefully blocked with stones and mud. After his men cleared it, a spring bubbled forth 'and we got an abundant supply'.[29]

---

25 Eyre, *Journals*, chap. 10, 27 September 1839.
26 Eyre, *Journals*. His comment is found in vol. 1, immediately after the entry dated 27 September 1839.
27 Eyre, *Journals*, vol. 1, 30 September 1840.
28 Eyre, *Journals*, vol. 1, 28 October 1840.
29 Eyre, *Journals*, vol. 1, 1 November 1840.

In just one year, Eyre had surveyed all three sides of this large triangular peninsula of southern mallee lands, travelling over a thousand kilometres in the process. He concluded rather grimly: 'the great mass of the peninsula is barren, arid and worthless'. Some good land around Port Lincoln was already occupied by several pastoralists but further development was hampered by isolation from both labour and markets.[30]

At Streaky Bay the forward party was refreshed and well fed on oysters. This respite, together with the supplies sent from Adelaide by sea and those brought by Eyre from Port Lincoln, readied his party for the trek west. Initially they headed to Fowlers Bay to establish a base, and here Eyre employed an Aboriginal guide, Wilguldy, through whom he interacted peacefully with local Aboriginal groups. Wilguldy and others 'learnt to drink tea, and eat meat and damper, with which we supplied them liberally, in return for the valuable services they rendered us'.[31] Three arduous journeys were made to the Bight in late 1840, across what was now desert not mallee country, but each time the party was forced back owing to lack of water. Eyre retired most of his men to Adelaide and then determined to make the 850 miles trek to King George Sound with only his trusted overseer John Baxter, two Aboriginal youths, and Wylie.

On 25 February 1841 the five pushed on from Fowlers Bay, facing many privations as their rations dwindled. Water was a constant problem forcing many backtracks to a known supply. The expedition was in tatters once Baxter was killed by the Aboriginal youths on 29 April, while Eyre was away from camp in search of water. They absconded with most of the supplies, leaving Eyre and Wylie to struggle on. Wylie's bushcraft saved them numerous times from thirst and starvation, enabling them to stagger into Esperance on 2 June where they encountered a French whaler refreshing. The two reached King George Sound on 7 July after one of the most astonishing and horrific adventures of any party in the history of Australian exploration. Eyre prefaced his gripping journal of the 1839–41 expeditions with a description of the land he had traversed as 'sterile and worthless', adding: 'a very large portion of this land had never before been trodden by the foot of civilized man, and from its nature is never likely to be so invaded again'.[32]

---

30   Eyre, *Journals*, vol. 1, 2 October 1840.
31   Eyre, *Journals*, vol. 1, 16 November 1840.
32   Eyre, *Journals*, vol. 1, vi; Geoffrey Dutton, 'Eyre, Edward John (1815–1901)', *Australian Dictionary of Biography* (Melbourne: Melbourne University Press, 1966), vol. 1, 362–4.

Mallee country in three directions beyond Esperance remained largely unknown until the end of the 1840s. In September 1848, the Western Australian Surveyor General, John Septimus Roe, was instructed to survey land and look for coal in the far south west of the colony for the purpose of supplying fuel to steamers now travelling to the east coast along the Bight. He journeyed from Cape Riche, eighty kilometres east of Albany, to the Russell Ranges on the edge of the Great Australian Bight, 150 kilometres east of present-day Esperance. Roe and five European companions effectively traversed most of the span of Western Australia's mallee lands. Bob, a Ngadju man from the Cape Riche area, acted as guide. He and twelve horses underpinned the party's success over very difficult terrain.

Roe was an experienced explorer, having surveyed Western Australian lands for the previous twenty years, but he and his party suffered much hardship on this trip. The party left Cape Riche on 12 October and trekked north east into the interior via the Pallinup River. Experiencing good grassy country and sufficient surface water all the way to Jerramungup, about ninety kilometres from the coast, they continued north east, soon striking less favourable 'poor and scubby' country marked by 'a chain of salt and brackish pools'. Sandy plains gave way to 'very dense thickets, through which the axe was in frequent requisition to clear the way for the horses'. Storms temporarily relieved the October heat and provided some surface water. The party passed to the south east of Lake Magenta through salt country of 'poor quality, covered with dense scrub and dense thickets without trees'. Trekking to the south of Lake King, Roe observed granite peaks eighty kilometres to the north east, but these were surrounded by 'sand plains and thickets'. The country (probably around Lake Sharpe) now resembled 'one extensive salt basin or low depressed plain' with no grass or water for the horses for two days. Finally, a half a bucket of reddish fresh liquid for the horses was dug from a drying watercourse, but there was no grass, it being burnt except for a thicket. This suggested an Aboriginal mosaic burn, to encourage new grass while leaving shelter for game.[33]

Deeply anxious about water supplies, Roe headed for granite peaks over forty kilometres away. The party reached Peak Charles and Peak Eleanora

---

33   'Report of J.S. Roe, Esq., Surveyor General of His Expedition to Explore the Interior Country South Eastward from York, between September 1848 and February 1849', typescript, J.S. Battye Library of West Australian History, 919.412 ROE, 140, 141, 143, 146. This report is also available in Mason Hercock (ed.), *The Western Australian Explorations of John Septimus Roe 1829–1849* (Perth: Hesperian Press, 2014), 419–65.

after two days of endeavour, led by Bob's unerring capacity to stay on a straight line while the party was deeply immersed in scrub over their heads. The horses followed along in great distress, literally staggering into camp. Granite outcrops promised water supplies in crevices and *gnamma* holes and some grass at their base, and this fortunately was the case with Peak Charles. Roe surveyed the country next day with his telescope from its 300-metre summit. Besides some distant peaks he spied sixty kilometres of 'dark scrub and thicket, intersected by broad sheets of salt lakes and samphire marshes'. After three days' rest, the party continued east through a 'frowning sea of scrub'.[34] With no water and the horses already weakened, one mount had to be abandoned. Another horse called 'Ney' was guided slowly along behind the party to a camp at Mount Ridley. However, en route to the next camp, Ney again lost strength and struggled to keep his feet. With great difficulty the horse was brought to a granite outcrop, which might contain refreshment. It was named after Ney, as the party was forced to leave him to his fate. Ney's saddle was left suspended from a tree. From Mount Ney they struck east heading for the Russell Ranges.

The last eighty-kilometre trek was the hardest of the whole journey. Despite the prevalence of granite sheets, which usually provided some water and grass, the horses weakened, staggered and frequently fell. Loads were lightened, repacked and redistributed. The party then encountered 'sapling thickets 12 to 15 feet high, so closely packed that axes only could have opened a passage'. They changed course but met with thickets so dense that 'at the distance of 3 or 4 feet no part of a horse could be seen'. Care had to be taken to keep them in line. The work was so laborious that the horses eventually broke into cold sweats 'always the forerunner of a complete and fatal break up', forcing a halt. The party finally struggled to the Russell Ranges. After a desperate search they found good water and grass and rested there for four days. Roe contemplated going further east into the country of the Ngadju and Mirning, whose mastery of mallee land enabled them to live there comfortably. He had seen Aboriginal fires on his journey, but the original owners had avoided making contact despite Bob's best efforts. In any case, Roe had by now reached his set goal and decided against further exploration in light of the vista his glass revealed of 'so fearful and impracticable a country'.[35]

Roe's party returned via a coastal route, hoping for easier travel. When south of Mount Ney, two of the party travelled on their best horses seeking Ney

---

34   Roe, 'Report ... of His Expedition', 147, 148.
35   Roe, 'Report ... of His Expedition', 157, 159.

and miraculously brought him back after two days, much to Roe's joy. They passed through Esperance Bay, and were told by Aboriginal people that scrub and salt lakes covered the interior to the north. At various points the party searched for coal seams. They were assisted by Bob, who knew the country, or stories about it, and, finally, between Seal Island and East Mount Barren, they found coal ten kilometres from the coast. More seams were discovered inland from Fitzgerald Inlet, a pit was dug, and a test burn carried out, the coal producing a 'good flame'.[36]

The country that Roe surveyed was not vacant. Aboriginal land owners had lived here for eons, although Roe failed to make contact. His party did, however, detect old tracks of three horses and a pony belonging to James Drummond, a celebrated botanist, who first collected plants in the region around Cape Riche in 1840 and was back in the neighbourhood in 1848.[37] It was Drummond who later made the link between poisonous plants and stock deaths. Roe saw cattle tracks as well. European ships heading east occasionally stopped to refresh. Bob, the Aboriginal guide, confirmed a French whaler had loaded some coal from this very inlet. Traversing the 'dreary waste' bordering the coast, Roe's party discovered a skeleton on a limestone rock shelf dressed in remnants of European clothing that were somewhat in disarray due to wild dogs. Bob told of three men who a year or so earlier had left a whaling vessel to walk to Albany. Though kitted out with arms and provisions, they soon became distressed for water and split up, only one man surviving. Nyungar people had offered the man whose body Roe found some assistance, but the fearful seaman had threatened his would-be saviours with a gun. Roe's party buried the skeletal remains under a cairn of limestone.[38]

Roe reached Mr and Mrs Cheyne's station at Cape Riche, eighty-six days after setting out from that spot. He concluded that, while coal deposits had been found and much geographical knowledge formed of unknown country, 'no great addition has been made to the amount of good land available to the Colony'.[39] Roe and his men sorely needed refreshment, and their foot-sore horses needed rest, re-shoeing and their saddles and harnesses repaired. Bob returned to his people, refusing to guide them any further north. Roe's

---

36   Roe, 'Report ... of His Expedition', 186–7.

37   Roe, 'Report ... of His Expedition', 184. See Rica Erickson, 'Drummond, James (1787–1863)', *Australian Dictionary of Biography*, National Centre of Biography, Australian National University, http://adb.anu.edu.au/biography/drummond-james-1995/text2433, published first in hardcopy 1966, accessed online 21 October 2018.

38   Roe, 'Report ... of His Expedition', 204–05.

39   Roe, 'Report ... of His Expedition', 215.

party left after four days for Perth, heading north with a new and unnamed Aboriginal guide, bound for the military outpost at Kojunup, then on to Bunbury and Perth. North of the Stirling Ranges they passed through fine grassy land, some of it fired recently by Nyungar people; kangaroo and emu were evident, and nearby was a fine fresh water lake, well stocked with duck. Their guide's people, who welcomed them, were affected by whooping cough, but Roe observed 'the disorder had visited them but mildly'.[40]

Roe left Cape Riche along the 'beaten sandal wood track' and soon met four teams taking their precious cargo to Cheyne's station for transshipment to China. That 'beaten track' followed a much older track, for, as Sylvia Hallam argued, 'sandalwood trails followed Aboriginal trails from soak to soak and camp to camp'.[41] After four days' travel, Roe's party stopped at Myerup where Mr Maxwell had a sandalwood station 'at a good spring, and amongst good grass'.[42] Sandalwood has been used in Asia for centuries to make incense sticks or perfumed carvings. A local Western Australian variety, *Santalum spicatum*, was discovered in 1844, and its range was soon confirmed as stretching in a band from Perth to Esperance. A trial shipment overseas in 1844 brought high prices, which led to a rush to gather the precious wood at a time when the colony was in an economic slump. By 1848 it challenged wheat and wool as the West's leading export. However, the logging of most supplies near Perth, and a global oversupply, led to a crash in the industry. Western Australian exports slumped from 1,335 tons in 1848 to 219 tons by 1851. The onslaught on the trees all but ceased, only to revive in the 1890s as an adjunct to the gold rushes.[43]

In early August 1849, the surveyor Edward Riggs White once again challenged the Victorian Mallee, only two years after his colleague Henry Wade had been forced to abandon his survey of the Victorian–South Australian border. By late October White had extended the official border line 150 kilometres, supported by access to the limited water of four Aboriginal wells he discovered along that distance. He covered more extensive country than required by a straight border line in his search for water, finding more wells and criss-crossing country thirty kilometres either side of the present Ouyen

---

40 Roe, 'Report ... of His Expedition', 212.
41 S.J. Hallam, *Fire and Hearth: A Study of Aboriginal Usage and European Usurpation in South-western Australia* (Canberra: Australian Institute of Aboriginal Studies, 1975), 75–6.
42 Roe, 'Report ... of His Expedition', 211.
43 Pamela Statham Drew, 'Sandalwood: Western Australia's Sometime Saviour', *Journal of the Fremantle Historical Society* 5 (2007): 87–105.

Highway, which travels west from Ouyen to Pinnaroo. But, with four bullocks dead from thirst, and water failing in the last known well, White's party was forced to retreat to a pastoral station to the south (Baird and Hodkinson's) at the end of October 1849. But White remained determined to push to the Murray River. He set out alone, not surveying the line along the way, but checking for water in mallee country. With just two horses, he headed north from Pine Plains but, on the sixth day, one of the horses, which had been without water for four days, could not go on. He led the other, but it too soon lay down. White bled the horse and 'drank about half a pint of his blood, which was black, thick, and unhealthy-looking, and had the same bad smell as his breath'. White staggered on and reached the Murray, tragically for his horse only two kilometres away, near a pastoral station west of the Murray–Darling junction.[44]

In 1849 John Wood Beilby explored the Mallee for pastoral country. He had run sheep on the Gardiners Creek in Melbourne, then at the Glenelg River where he lost money as a result of sheep diseases, wild dogs and Aboriginal attacks.[45] Following surveyor White's dray line along the boundary, Beilby encountered White's party on 2 October, near where the Ouyen Highway crosses the border today. He was astonished at the toll the Mallee had extracted. The men, who were arduously cutting a track for the surveying dray through the mallee scrub, looked 'lean, careworn, dusty and thirsty'. When Beilby reached the main party, he remarked on their clothing: 'all were more or less tattered', torn by the mallee scrub. He added that 'all appeared a very seedy lot of long bearded ragamuffins'.[46] Beilby and his companion K. were dressed much the same, as the mallee scrub and porcupine grass had lacerated their clothing too, as well as the legs of their horses. The surveyor did not offer Beilby so much as a cup of water, so careful was he of his resources. East of the border Beilby himself ran into trouble but fortunately found water in an Aboriginal well on the mail track between Kow Plains and Pine Plains stations.[47]

Edward White finally completed the survey in 1850. Although he found evidence of many Aboriginal wells and soaks, which he utilised in his continued criss-crossing of the Mallee, he never encountered any Aboriginal people nor used them as guides, so sparsely utilised was this area and so uninterested were the people in making contact. Beilby also found evidence of Aboriginal

---

44   Kenyon, *The Story of the Mallee*, see 12–18 for excerpts from White's diary.
45   R.V.B. and A.S.K., 'Pastoral Pioneers. John Beilby, No. 129', *Australasian*, 6 June 1936, 4.
46   Kenyon, *The Story of the Mallee*, 22–3.
47   *Australasian*, 6 June 1936, 4.

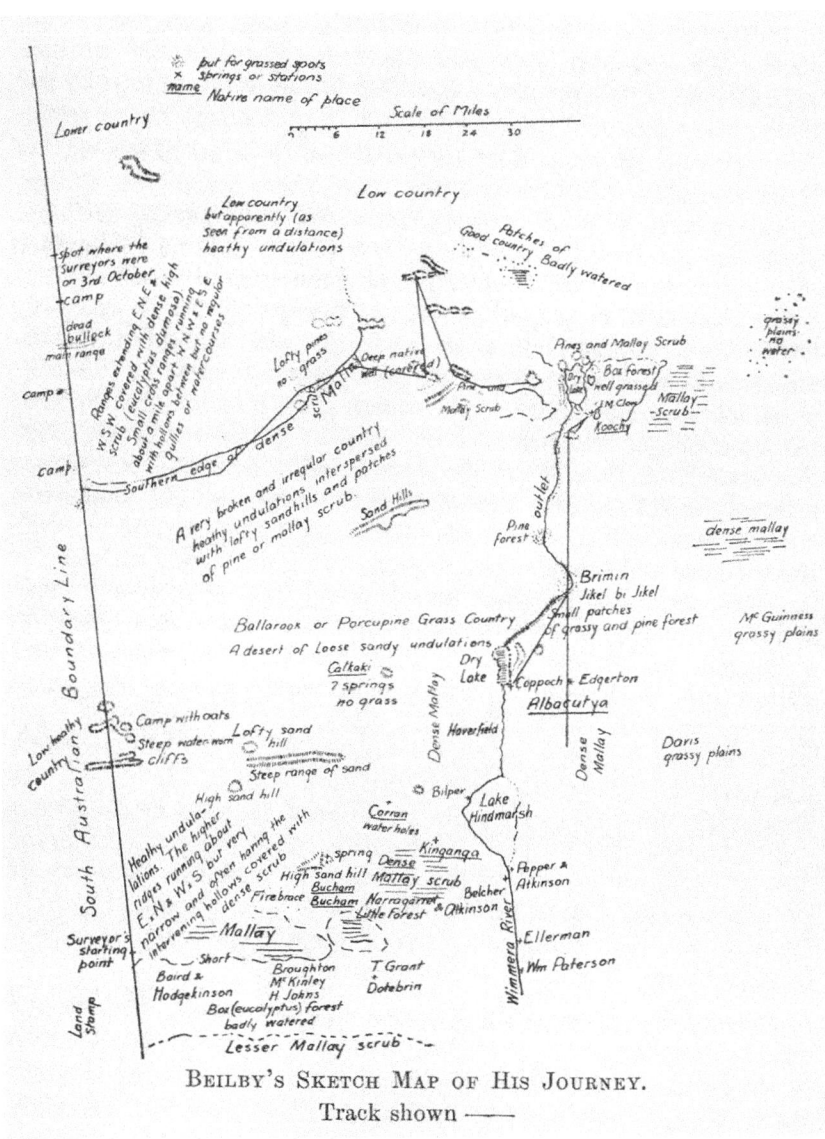

Figure 3.3: Beilby map, c. 1849, first published in A.S. Kenyon, *The Story of the Mallee* (1916), 46.

occupation: wells in good order and empty camps by soaks, which he believed were used in the season of emu and *lowan* eggs. Beilby wrote:

> the natives make yearly visits to localities furnishing ample supply of eggs, which they eat in all stages of incubation; but when, on examining a nest, they find only a small numbers of eggs, they carefully cover them over, and abstain from molestation, until the full number are deposited, and the nest completed.[48]

John Beilby left the surveyor's boundary path and struck east, then south to Pine Plains and on to Lake Hindmarsh. He left a remarkably well-annotated map of his journey in the south-east section of the Victorian Mallee in 1849 (see Figure 3.3). Beilby did find some modestly sized patches of grass, one six hundred acres in extent, and the Wirrengren Plain near Pine Plains station, seven miles long. But, overall, the country was sandy or scrubby and punctuated by sandy ridges with pines, and he judged it to be generally 'bleak, barren and desolate' or 'dreary', no place for a pastoral enterprise. His constant search for water and grass for his horses evoked the comment that 'riding a hard-mouthed and fiery horse, and dragging a sluggish pack-horse through the thick scrub, fallen, twisted and twined into each other in every conceivable and inconceivable way, requires the temperament and equanimity of an angel'. Beilby concluded of Victoria's mallee region that 'it was a disgusting country throughout, in which it would require uncommon inducements, in the way of prospective advantage, to encourage any but a misanthrope to a permanent residence'. When he reached James Clow's Pine Plains station he found it deserted owing to lack of water, but those running sheep at Outlet Creek and Lake Hindmarsh were surviving despite the distance from markets and high labour costs. Beilby applied for a lease near Brim but seems to have thought better of it, perhaps reminding himself that he considered the Mallee 'a disgusting country'.[49] However, others were less damning and thought enough of the region to gamble on its future with sheep.

---

48 B.J. B[eilby],'Wanderings in the Wider World with Rough Notes of a Journey in Search of a Run', *Port Phillip Gazette*, 1 December 1849.

49 B.J. B[eilby],'Wanderings', *Port Phillip Gazette*, 29 November and 1 December 1849. See an abridged version in Kenyon, *The Story of the Mallee*, 19–36.

Chapter 4

PASTORAL ADVENTURERS

Pastoralism spread out from Australia's southern coastal beachheads in the 1830s, driven by the demand for fine wool in the United Kingdom, the finding of new land by explorers, and the fact that wool growing was ideally suited to the grasslands of the newly founded colonies in the south. Mallee country was the last area to experience pastoral interest because of its distant and marginal nature: 'impracticable' it was called. But, from the 1840s, the Murray Mallee and the mallee lands in the Eyre Peninsula were subjected to pastoral exploitation.

The pastoral story on mallee country told of a tussle between a difficult land, an inexperienced people and unwilling stock, each having an impact on the other. The land, covered as it was by a sea of mallee scrub with occasional islands of grass, forced human endeavour into a pastoral use. Wool might work in mallee country where other economic operations might not. Wool was light and valuable enough to be clipped and carried out, and still make some profit, or it could be walked out on the sheep's back at a pinch. But the mallee scrub, together with the region's soils, predators, climate, lack of water and vast distance from ports, set limits on the extent to which pastoralists could make sheep profitable. Sheep had to adapt to eating other than sweet grass, given its scarcity, and learn to make do with saltbush and the mallee scrub. Nature and sheep became entwined as sheep munched their way across mallee country, adapting to it but also pounding it where they flocked together and thus changing its face. People were forced to adapt as well to this marginal pastoral sphere, especially in the way they lived on and worked the land, often becoming as nomadic and as minimalist as the people they displaced.

Alfred Crosby, the great historian of ecological transfers, suggested that settler triumph was inevitable: 'the success of Europeans as colonists was automatic as soon as they put their tough, fast, fertile and intelligent animals ashore'.[1] Yet, because of the nature of mallee country and its limitations, sheep

---

1   Alfred W. Crosby, *Germs, Seeds and Animals: Studies in New Ecological History* (York: M.E. Sharpe, 1994), 34.

raising on some mallee runs was in crisis to the point of collapse by the 1870s, prompting subsequent generations to pursue different economic endeavours.

The Struggle for Country

Overlanding of stock from NSW to Port Phillip began in 1836–1837, and in 1838 stock was also driven from Melbourne to grazing lands around Adelaide. Edward John Eyre tried to pioneer a shorter southern route from Melbourne to Adelaide, but, as we have seen, was blocked by mallee country north of Lake Hindmarsh and forced back to the Murray River route.[2] In 1839 pastoralists ferried sheep across Spencer Gulf to Port Lincoln on the southern tip of the Eyre Peninsula. Speculators then shipped them further from Port Lincoln to King George Sound for overlanding to the Swan River (Perth). In 1841 Eyre even considered overlanding sheep from the Eyre Peninsula to the West, but again found mallee country and the desert beyond a barrier.

George Grey, governor of South Australia, lauded such overlanders as 'remarkable' men. He declared that, once overlanders introduced stock to new country, it was like 'the Nile upon the thirsty land of Egypt; then does the country bear fruit, and the land give forth her increase'.[3] The thousand-kilometre journey with stock was risky but offered high profits. In 1840, seventy thousand stock, mostly sheep, were overlanded to South Australia. Evelyn Pitfield Stirling Sturt, an overlander in 1840, later recorded that the Murray River flats in summer 'afford fine feed for stock, and famous camping places at night'. He recalled the camp roused each day at 2 am, 'breakfast was then cooked, drays loaded, bullocks yoked, and the stock moved off' until 10 am, when they rested in the heat until 4 pm before completing a few more miles for the day. Difficult river crossings were made at the Darling and Rufus, but overcoming them added 'zest to our labours'.[4] S.T. Gill's laconic depiction of overlanding twenty years later understated the dangers (see Figure 4.1)

---

2 A.G.L. Shaw, *A History of the Port Phillip District: Victoria before Separation* (Melbourne: The Miegunyah Press, 1996), 63–4.

3 George Grey, *Journals of Two Expeditions of Discovery in North-West and Western Australia: During the Years 1837, 38, and 39, under the Authority of Her Majesty's Government: Describing many Newly Discovered, Important, and Fertile Districts, With Observations of the Moral and Physical Condition of the Aboriginal Inhabitants, &c. &c.* (London: T. & W. Boone, 1841), vol. 2, 184, 190.

4 Evelyn Sturt in Thomas Francis Bride (ed.), *Letters from Victorian Pioneers* (Melbourne: Curry O'Neil, 1983, originally published 1898), 369–70.

Figure 4.1: 'Overlanders', by S.T. Gill (c. 1864).
(Courtesy Pictures Collection, H17157, State Library Victoria)

The penetration of Aboriginal country by overland parties, each with hundreds or thousands of sheep and cattle, caused dismay and eventual cultural rupture for Aboriginal landowners. People had witnessed or knew of Sturt and Mitchell's journeys through the Murray–Darling region. They also gained experience of new objects and materials such as metal, leather and cloth as they filtered down the trade routes. But to see a slow-moving tide of sheep and cattle, and to hear the crack of stockmen's whips above the cacophony of bleats, barks and shouts, must have been astounding. Astonishment quickly turned to anger and violence.

The worst clash was at Rufus River in 1840, one of two crossing points for all parties travelling the north bank of the Murray. Old pioneers told stories of this massacre up to eighty years later. John George Coombs, who worked along the Murray in South Australia, recalled 'I was only a lad' when the massacre was perpetrated (in reality he was born twelve years after the event). He actually heard of it from an Aboriginal station worker with the racialised name of 'Monkey'. Men, women and children, Coombs declared, were shot down 'like dogs', and the event was plain 'murder'. Monkey, a small boy at the time, survived by pretending to be dead in the water as his parents were fatally shot beside him.⁵ Edmund Morey also wrote of the massacre, although he did not arrive at the Murray till three years after the event. He reminisced much later that forty Aboriginal people were killed by vigilantes. The bloodied waters of the creek gave the Rufus River its name, he claimed. Morey was unaware Mitchell had named it after his red-headed overseer McLeay.⁶

The Rufus River clash was really a series of related events. In April 1841, overlanders led by Henry Field and Henry Inman clashed at Lake Bonney with Maraura people from Lake Victoria. An Aboriginal man was killed and a flock of five thousand sheep and eight hundred cattle scattered. A government party was sent to retrieve property but was recalled before reaching Lake Bonney, owing to a change of governor. A vigilante party led by Henry Field stepped in to exact revenge instead, allegedly shooting six to eight people but failing to retrieve any property. The new governor, George Grey, was disinclined to use government forces to protect settlers' private interests. He also doubted Aboriginal people were the aggressors. Besides, he believed they had the same rights as settlers and should not be regarded 'as aliens, with whom a war can exist and against Whom Her Majesty's troops may exercise belligerent rights'.⁷

Grey sent a party to investigate, with orders not to fire unless necessary. The Aboriginal protector Matthew Moorhouse went along as an observer. Before they arrived at Lake Victoria, the Maraura and another overlanding party had clashed, causing deaths on both sides. A fourth expedition under Moorhouse was sent to protect the next overlanding party of Robinson, but, when Moorhouse arrived, the overlanders had already clashed with the Maraura, killing five and wounding others. Moorhouse abandoned mediation and passed command to Police Inspector Shaw. Later that day the official party and the overlanders caught the Maraura in a cross fire. Moorhouse reported that thirty Maraura men, women and children were killed and more wounded. Maraura defence of country at a cost of at least thirty deaths, possibly a fifth of their population, was ended.⁸

Resistance to overlanders mostly came from those most able, namely the denser Aboriginal populations along the Murray and its connected lakes and billabongs. However, the population densities among these river peoples had

---

5   John George Coombs, 'Seventy Years in the Murray Country', *Murray Pioneer and Australian River Recorder*, 21 December 1923.

6   Edmund Morey, 'Reminiscences of a Pioneer', no. VI, *Sydney Mail and New South Wales Advertiser*, 4 December 1907.

7   George Grey to Lord John Russell, in Robert Foster, Rick Hosking, and Amanda Nettelbeck, *Fatal Collisions: The South Australian Frontier and the Violence of Memory* (Adelaide: Wakefield Press, 2000), 32.

8   For the Rufus Massacre, see Foster, Hosking and Nettelbeck, *Fatal Collisions*, 29–44.

been reduced, perhaps by half, from smallpox, which raged down the river around 1830.⁹ Charles Sturt avoided violence in 1830, but Mitchell clashed with the Darling people at Mount Dispersion in 1836. Overlanders and early pastoralists who followed did not always experience problems, but misunderstandings often emerged over stolen sheep, the abuse of Aboriginal women, and especially the unnegotiated presence of stock on Aboriginal land. These were moral problems between two different groups—invaders and landowners—both believing they had rights. Pastoralists were given licences by the government to be there, while the river people's ownership was sanctioned by the Great Ancestors. The killing of Andrew Beveridge of Piangil (and Tyntynder) near Swan Hill in August 1846 led to heightened tension and violence. John Hawdon of Murray Downs station wrote in November 1846: 'There have been a great number of blacks shot because of this [Beveridge] murder. The blacks do not come much now to the station, although we see them every day in the reeds'.¹⁰

What might be the tally of deaths through violence in the battle for the land along the Murray? John Lay listed twenty-six known collisions from Gunbower to Kulkyne between 1836 and 1852. He believes a dozen Europeans were killed in that time, but avoids estimating total Aboriginal deaths.¹¹ A massacre map produced by Lyndall Ryan and others at the University of Newcastle, which lists collisions involving six or more Aboriginal deaths, has identified eight massacres in the Victorian Mallee along the Murray to the South Australian border causing at least seventy-seven Aboriginal deaths.¹² Other deaths occurred in dry mallee country but in lower numbers, given the sparser population, although evidence is slim in such isolated areas. The University of Newcastle massacre map currently has no listings for the interior Victorian Mallee. Violence, wherever it occurred, thinned Aboriginal numbers, and this was compounded by disease and cultural dislocation, leading to erasure of some groups.

It was ironic that mallee country was penetrated with the assistance of Aboriginal people, either willingly as guides or unwittingly as the original

---

9 Richard Broome, *Aboriginal Victorians: A History since 1800* (Sydney: Allen & Unwin, 2015), 6–10, 90–1; John Burch, *Returning the Kulkyne* (Melbourne: John Burch, 2017), 102–03.

10 Quoted in *Swan Hill Guardian*, 19 November 1946, in John Lay, *Boodgery: First Contact in the Mid Murray 1820–1860* (Ballan: Not So Shabby Books, 2016), 71.

11 Lay, *Boodgery*, 86–7.

12 The Centre for 21st Century Humanities, 'Colonial Frontier Massacres in Central and Eastern Australia 1788–1932', accessed 12 November 2018, https://c21ch.newcastle.edu.au/colonialmassacres/.

land managers. Archaeologist Sylvia Hallam observed a generation ago that 'in south-western Australia, as elsewhere on the continent, European distributions and lines of communications followed Aboriginal distributions and lines of movement, and both owed much to the opening-up of the landscape by Aboriginal usage and particularly firing'.[13]

Such willing or unwitting assistance occurred in mallee country as well. John Burch has recently revealed the route of the Wirrengren–Kulkyne pathway used by Wotjobaluk people and their neighbours to travel north–south across the Victorian Mallee for trade and rituals. Aboriginal people sometimes shared knowledge of it with early Europeans. John Wood Beilby, who was looking for a run in the Victorian Mallee in 1849, met an Aboriginal shepherd at Lake Hindmarsh station where he worked. This 'intelligent fellow ... gave me a clear account of all the belts of mallay [sic] to be passed through and the wells to be found on the country I had now determined to explore to the westward and the north west'.[14] Europeans also stumbled across these pathways marked by wells and soaks, as did the surveyor Edward White.[15] The Wirrengren–Kulkyne path soon became a sheep and bullock stock route. Its occasional patches of grass, used by famished stock, were perhaps products of Aboriginal firing.

Laying Down Pastoral Runs

By 1840, pastoralists could appreciate the boundlessness of mallee country across southern Australia, but naturally favoured fertile sheep country closer to the wool stores of Melbourne and Adelaide. However, once better country was totally occupied, they began to speculate on new possibilities in hitherto 'impracticable' mallee lands. In 1839, on the Eyre Peninsula, Captain Henry Hawson and Charles Smith settled a special survey of four thousand acres and founded Port Lincoln at the Peninsula's southern tip. Hawson created a run at Little Swamp, where his thirteen-year-old son was fatally speared by Nauo people in 1840. Despite this unnerving tragedy, settlers pushed east and west along the coast from Port Lincoln in the early 1840s, and some more clashes occurred. The University of Newcastle massacre map lists

---

13   S.J. Hallam, *Fire and Hearth: A Study of Aboriginal Usage and European Usurpation in South-western Australia* (Canberra: Australian Institute of Aboriginal Studies, 1975), 76.

14   B.L. B[eilby], 'Wanderings in the Western Wilds Being Rough Notes of a Journey in Search of a Run', *Port Phillip Gazette*, 1 December 1849.

15   John Burch, 'The Wirrengren–Kulkyne Pathway: Locating a Cultural Icon', *Victorian Historical Journal* 87, no. 2 (December 2016): 261–77.

three collisions on the Eyre Peninsula in the 1840s: Arno Bay, Yeelanna and Waterloo Bay, with at least twenty-four Aboriginal deaths.[16] Pastoralists took up runs where there was grass, water and harbour access to markets, at sites such as Lake Hamilton, Elliston, Venus Bay, Streaky Bay and Fowlers Bay on the Great West Coast.[17]

By the late 1840s, Murray River frontages on both sides of the river from Swan Hill to North-West Bend (Morgan) and further downstream were occupied. The country along the Wimmera River to Pine Plains, and the Yarriambiack Creek to Lake Coorong, was also taken. Frontages on the Richardson and Avoca rivers, which flowed from the Pyrenees Range, were occupied, and, within a few years, country around Lake Tyrrell and Ouyen was under sheep too.[18] Mallee country around Esperance in Western Australia had to wait another ten years or more before it was first settled by pastoralists. Map 3 reveals mallee country being opened up and the major place names being laid down by ensuing waves of settlers.

Pastoral licences in mallee country were generally insecure and vast. Licences under the Waste Lands Act Orders in Council (1847), legislated by the British government, for using lands distant from the colonial capitals were only issued for one year. Runs were huge even in the best mallee country because grassed patches were small and infrequent, although scrub sustained sheep. In the 1850s, there were only fifteen stations along the seven hundred kilometres of river frontage on the southern bank of the Murray from Swan Hill west to the South Australian border, averaging forty-six kilometres of river frontage each.[19] These stations mostly penetrated only five kilometres inland and few stockmen ventured even twenty-five kilometres from the river.[20] In the same decade there were a further twenty-six runs in the rest of the Victorian Mallee, almost all near watercourses.

---

16 'Colonial Frontier Massacres', accessed 12 November 2018, https://c21ch.newcastle.edu.au/colonialmassacres/.
17 Unohoo [pseud.], 'Eyre Peninsula in the 'Sixties', *Port Lincoln Times*, 13 November 1931.
18 Alfred S. Kenyon, *The Story of the Mallee: A History of the Victorian Mallee Read before the Historical Society of Victoria, 18 March 1912* (Melbourne: Wilke & Co., 1982), 55–84.
19 Peter Phillips, 'Murray River Kayak [Blog]', accessed 23 September 2018, http://echuca-murraymouthkayakjourney.blogspot.com.au/2012/11/update-from-peter-phillips.html, entries day 8 and 20 for river distances.
20 J.T. Schell, as told to Walter Ogilvy, 'Early Days on the Murray and Darling: The Life Story of Pioneer', *Murray Pioneer and Australian River Record*, 19 December 1924.

MAP 3:
AUSTRALIAN MALLEE COUNTRY PLACE NAMES

EYRE PENINSULA

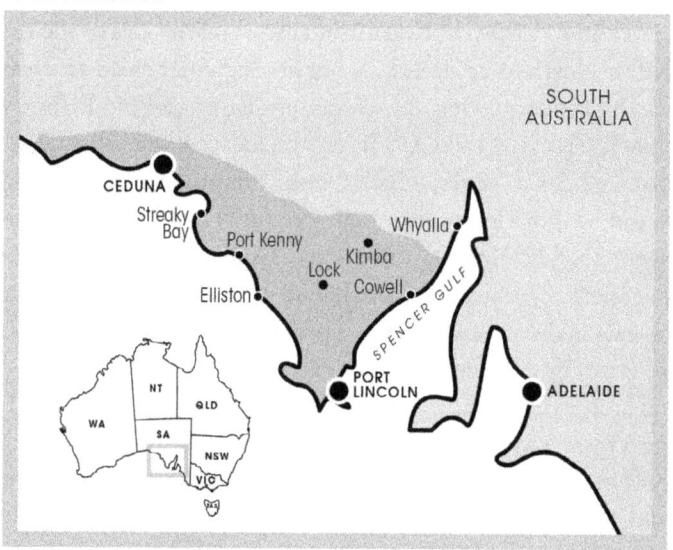

WESTERN AUSTRALIAN MALLEE

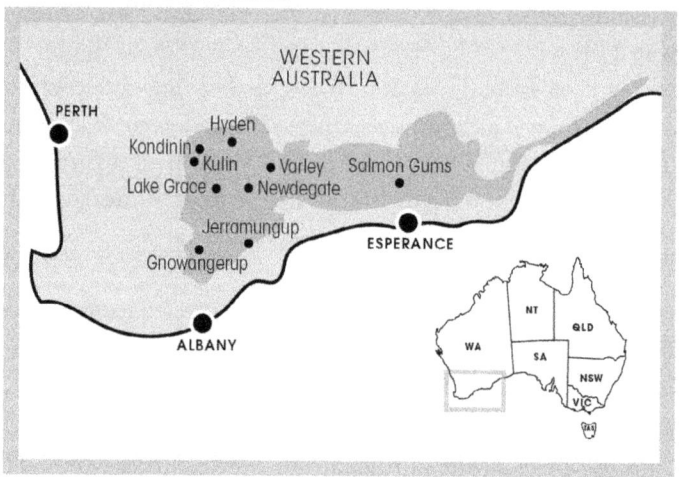

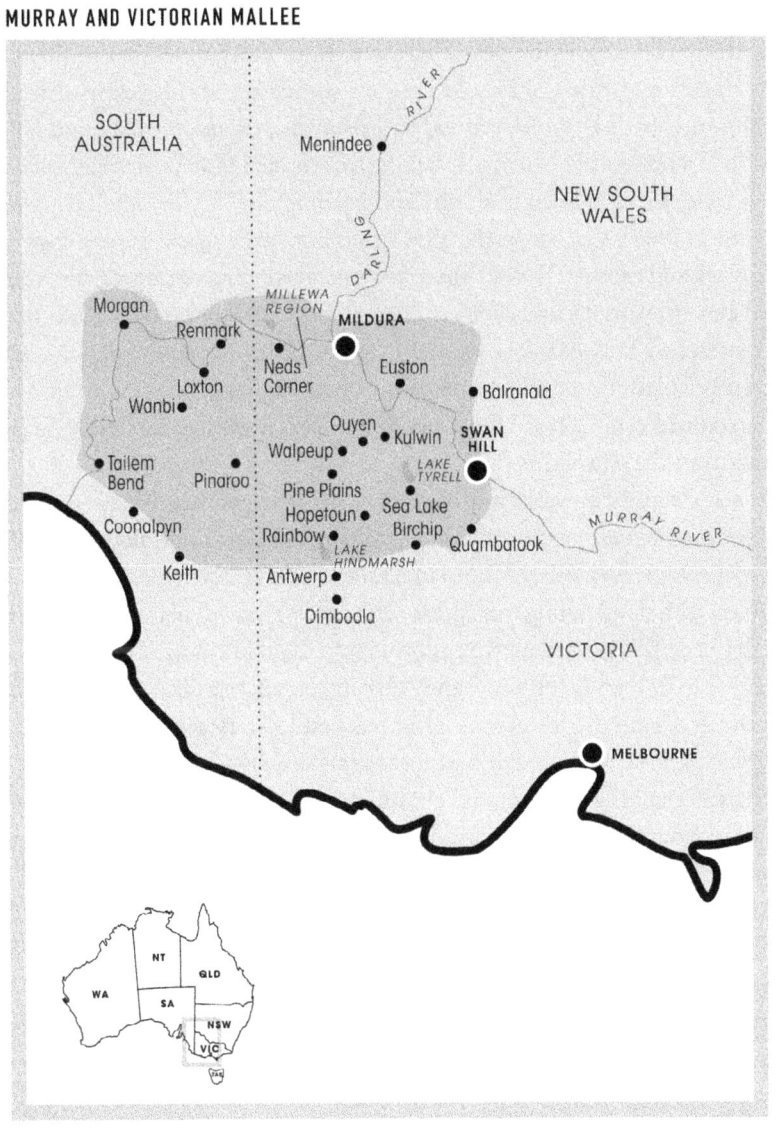

Stock returns for 1861 recorded that twenty-six huge stations carried only 240,228 sheep and 7,845 cattle.[21]

Many runs were initially very marginal owing to a series of challenges. John Frederick Haigh arrived from Yorkshire in 1849 and leased Sheringa, west of Port Lincoln on the Eyre Peninsula. In May 1850 he wrote to his partner 'that sheep farming won't pay. Therefore, I am determined to stop before I am completely ruined'. He soldiered on somehow, and his sons inherited the run in 1867.[22] Poor returns led to a primitive existence. Edmund Morey described a hut on the Murray as having a curtained four-poster bed, a couch, a slab table, a rough form to sit on, 'and nothing else'.[23] J.T. Schell recalled of his time at Ned's Corner in the 1850s that huts were made of pine logs with bark roofs and earthen floors: 'There were no glass windows along the Murray then'. Bosses, workers and even family members all slept on beds made of cow hide stretched between forked sticks, sat on boxes for chairs and ate salted or freshly killed meat and damper from tin plates. Vegetables were rare until some stations established kitchen gardens. Tea, however, was plentiful, and drunk from tin pannikins.[24]

The availability of water was perhaps of greatest concern. Water was not of course a problem on the Murray River, although its flow could slow markedly in dry spells. However, other Victorian Mallee waters often experienced reduced volumes, with flows falling to a trickle, leaving a series of unconnected billabongs or a dry bed. The Wimmera River flowed into Lake Hindmarsh intermittently, seldom into Outlet Creek and Lake Albacutya, and very rarely to Lake Wonga and the Wirrengren. The Avoca River reached Lake Boga, itself connected to the Murray, only twice in the first forty years of white settlement.

In the remaining Murray Mallee, and mallee lands in general, there was no permanent surface water, so pastoralists had to 'make' water. James Maxwell Clow took up Pine Plains in 1847 but, with insufficient water, was unable to graze sheep there until a seven-metre well was sunk at considerable cost in 1848. The surrounding country contained many depressions, and the pasturage on their beds and slopes was salsolaceous (or soda-yielding) herbage of 'the best description'. Many of these depressions had clay bases but needed rain or an inundation from the Wimmera River to fill them. To his chagrin, Clow was

---

21   Kenyon, *The Story of the Mallee*, 84.
22   John Haigh to William Mortlock, 3 May 1850, reprinted in *West Coast Sentinel*, 6 May 1927.
23   Edmund Morey, 'Reminiscences of a Pioneer in New South Wales', no. XI, *Sydney Mail and New South Wales Advertiser*, 8 January 1908.
24   Schell, 'Early Days on the Murray and Darling'.

forced by continued dryness to give up the lease for a meagre £15 the next year. The run was abandoned by the time John Beilby visited it in Spring 1849.[25] However, shortly afterwards, the Wimmera River inundated Pine Plains and surrounding country to such an extent that it was unusable for a time.[26]

If good sub-surface water was found, it took much labour to bring it to the surface. On the Eyre Peninsula's west coast, shepherds hauled water from wells for their flocks. If the well was shallow they used an ancient device, a lever whip. It comprised a long pole with a rope and bucket on one end and a weight on the other end, the pole resting on a forked branch acting as a fulcrum.[27] In the 1860s, during lambing down, the boss of Pine Plains station had to cart water thirty kilometres through the scrub for weeks to shepherd George Everard. In the 1870s at the same station, Everard pumped water morning and night to supply stock with enough to slake their thirst.[28] Stations in dry country early on lacked sufficient water to wash fleeces, forcing owners to walk sheep with heavy and greasy coats southwards.[29] Pastoralists dug wells, but some yielded only salt water. Robert Woods at Swan Hill dug three wells to twenty-five metres in the 1870s, but all were salty.[30] John Miller of Jerrejee station near Kulkyne similarly sank wells sixty metres, to find only salty water.

Feed for stock was the other vital problem. Initially the grass seemed promising, at least in some areas along the rivers and in small patches elsewhere. Port Phillip Aboriginal Protector George Augustus Robinson knew a thing or two about pastoral country, having seen much of it in his travels in the 1840s. In April 1845 he journeyed up the Wimmera River deeming the country 'well grassed … plains country' although the 'malli [sic] famous for spears grew half mile from the river'. At Lake Hindmarsh 'the kangaroo grass in places up to saddle flap'.[31] These mallee native grasses were hardy, being attuned to

---

25   B.L. B[eilby], 'Wanderings', 1 December 1849.
26   William Maxwell Clow, in Bride (ed.), *Letters from Victorian Pioneers*, 355–6.
27   Unohoo [psued.], *Port Lincoln Times*, 13 November 1931.
28   George Everard, 'Pioneering Days: Journal of George Everard' (Horsham, Victoria: *Horsham Times* Print, 1892, reprinted April 1977), 27, 44.
29   B.L. B[eilby], 'Wanderings', 1 December 1849.
30   Evidence of Robert Woods, in Victoria. Crown Lands Commission of Inquiry, 'Evidence of Report of the Crown Lands Commission of Inquiry on Both the Agricultural and Pastoral Occupation of the Public Lands to be Instituted on the Expiration of the Present Land Act at the Close of 1880 (September 1879)', *Victorian Parliamentary Papers*, 1879–80, vol. 3, paper no. 73, Q. 9955–57.
31   Ian D. Clark (ed.), *The Journals of George Augustus Robinson, Chief Protector, Port Phillip Aboriginal Protectorate, Volume 4: 1 January 1844 – 24 October 1845* (Melbourne: Heritage Matters, 1998), 10 and 13 April 1845.

a semi-arid climate. They grew in tufts among patches of sandy or clay mallee soils but generally were not sustainable under the onslaught of many sheep.

Stockowners seeking profits from their annual licences often overgrazed their runs, wearing away native grasses. These were replaced by 'perennial ryegrass, cocksfoot, Timothy grass, Yorkshire fog grass, white clover, red clover, Lucerne and many other species', either by design or accident. However, these were not sufficient to sustain high numbers of sheep as 'soil phosphate levels were too low and summer rainfall too meagre for these plants to flourish over a wide area'.[32] Mallee pastoralists later complained the hot wind quickly burnt these new grasses off.

Overstocking transformed the land as well as changing the grasses. Despite runs being large, sheep were forced to congregate around water. Thousands of hooves pounded the same ground day after day. Samuel Dixon was a jackaroo on the hundred-square-mile Maryvale station at Streaky Bay on the Eyre Peninsula in the 1860s. He recalled the country as replete with limestone outcrops and ridges of she oaks with grass in between, but 'heavy stocking not only prevented any fresh growth, but wore off the scanty soil, leaving wide areas of bare rock'.[33] Mallee country saved many pastoralists for it did sustain sheep, but it also had limits, as scrub around water sources was eaten out.

Predators took their toll at the margins. At night, the bleating of sheep was punctuated by the howl of dingoes, called 'wild dogs' by most pastoralists and shepherds. Losses from wild dogs could be heavy. J.T. Schell and his fellow drovers lost fifty sheep to wild dogs while driving them along the Murray from stations on the Murrumbidgee to North West Bend (Morgan) in South Australia.[34] Samuel Dixon recalled wild dogs at Streaky Bay could worry sixty sheep a night, most of which died. Others were scattered. Losses amounted to 10 per cent in bad years.[35] Edmund Morey, who took up the Boomiaricool run near Euston on the NSW side of the Murray, recalled that around 1850, 'the Murray swarmed with wild dogs', and in those days there was no recourse to poisoning them with strychnine. Mallee fences, built 1.5 metres high with mallee brushwood to make a sheep yard for night-time, were the only defence. Station dogs would sometimes rush the dingoes, but only a big fighting dog would go into battle alone, and, on occasions, remembered

---

32   'Settlement', *Victorian Year Book 1973, Centenary Edition* (Melbourne: Commonwealth Bureau of Census and Statistics, 1973), no. 87, 106.

33   Samuel Dixon, 'Jackerooing Fifty Years Ago: A Pioneer's Reminiscences', *Register* (Adelaide), 19 July 1912.

34   Schell, 'Early Days on the Murray and Darling'.

35   Dixon, 'Jackerooing Fifty Years Ago'.

Morey, 'the dingoes hunted back the shepherd's dogs'. He recalled that on an adjoining run a station dog chained inadvertently to a fence was 'torn to pieces' by wild dogs.[36]

Transport to markets was as vital to profits as feed and water. Although wool was light and valuable enough to haul long distances, it was still a costly and slow business. From Murray Mallee stations it took three months to send wool by bullock team to Melbourne and return with supplies. Each team of ten bullocks conveyed a load of twenty bails, piled three high, a load of almost three tonnes. Haulage prices doubled during the gold rushes, from the usual £10 a tonne.[37] Salvation came for Murray–Darling pastoralists in the form of steamers, although shipping was always the norm for those on the Eyre Peninsula and at Esperance.

In 1851 the South Australian governor, Sir Henry Young, inspired the colony's Legislative Assembly to offer a £4,000 prize (equal to the annual wages of eighty shepherds), to the first and second iron steamboats to navigate the Murray to at least the junction of the Darling. Success would funnel wool and goods through South Australia. In late August 1853, the *Lady Augusta* under Captain Francis Cadell, and with the governor, his wife and an official party on board, left Goolwa and travelled 2,400 kilometres to Swan Hill. It was powered by free wood, cut along the riverbank. Another smaller steamer, the *Mary Anne* captained by William Randell made the same trip, but was beaten into Swan Hill. The *Lady Augusta*, towing a barge the *Eureka*, returned just eight weeks later carrying 440 bales of wool, twenty times that of a bullock wagon, and a thousand sheepskins and tallow. Sir John Young declared 'steamers will henceforth never leave these waters, to the great benefit of all the colonies, and the speedy exploration of the rest of the continent'.[38]

A correspondent to the *South Australian Register* on that first trip recorded the bright prospects of the river trade. The Murray's levels rose owing to snowmelt and rains from October to April, coincidentally and conveniently the shearing and transhipping season. The Darling, although less reliable, was still navigable for a hundred kilometres above the Murray junction. The party reached the junction on 7 September 1853 and was welcomed by pastoralists from along the Darling in NSW, who expressed their eagerness to ship wool to Adelaide via steamer. They claimed the lower Darling mallee country was good, their sheep were free of scab, footrot and catarrh, and their

---

36   Morey, 'Reminiscences', no. XI.
37   *South Australian Register*, 8 October 1853.
38   Sir John Young in Bride (ed.), *Letters from Victorian Pioneers*, 353.

fleeces averaged a kilogram in weight. Settlement stretched up the Darling as far as Lake Menindee, but distant stations had been abandoned because of Aboriginal attacks and the cost of haulage. A large body of Aboriginal people led by an Elder named Jacob, aged in his fifties, also gathered to greet the *Lady Augusta* and help load wood fuel. About ten Aboriginal men left with the steamer bound for Jamieson's Yerre Yerre station at Mildura to wash sheep.

The Murray pastoralists, confident of the quality of their wool, expressed concern to Captain Cadell that wool shipped via Adelaide would be classed as South Australian and not Port Phillip wool, thus affecting prices. However, South Australia's collector of customs assured them the 'Port Phillip' brand would remain.[39] The *Register*'s correspondent listed forty stations on *both* sides of the Murray from the Darling Junction east to Swan Hill, and estimated there were now 450,000 sheep on these stations alone, which would produce annually just over four thousand bales of wool, potentially all going to Adelaide by steamer. This equalled a third of South Australia's total wool clip. The amount of wool to be transported would increase as stations were 'properly' stocked, he predicted, and the wool from backcountry stations would be shipped by river as well. There was a possibility this might increase productivity, as Murray River stations had the pick of the Murray Mallee lands. The pastoralists learnt that their backcountry could carry sheep in winter, leaving the river frontage for the hot summer months, thus extending their runs' potential. With the coming of new grasses to improve pasture, sheep were brought from inland NSW to fatten on the Murray for the Melbourne market.

Initially labour was a problem, being scarce or inappropriately skilled because of the isolation of early mallee pastoral runs. George Everard, who worked at Lake Albacutya station in the southern Victorian Mallee in 1857, later recalled that the station cook 'made our lives a misery'. The boss had no alternative 'as there were no travellers passing. During my six months there was only one passed with his swag, but he would not take on cooking'.[40] Not all workers hired as shearers were expert or diligent. At Pine Plains in the 1850s a team of shearers, most of them ex-convicts from Tasmania, took to a keg of whisky after a hawker arrived with some for sale. They were drunk for a week and took several days to sober up before getting back to shearing.[41]

---

39 *South Australian Register*, 8 October 1853.
40 Everard, 'Pioneering Days', 18.
41 Everard, 'Pioneering Days', 21.

Working Mallee Runs

Pastoralism created unique patterns and rhythms of work, depending on a seasonal and mobile workforce. London-born George Everard emigrated to Port Phillip in 1851, aged fifteen. Fifty years later he wrote a remarkable biography of his working life. Everard first worked across southern Victoria until 1857 when he gained employment dipping sheep at North Brighton station, north of Horsham on the southern rim of Victoria's Mallee. His boss told Everard and his brother to buy blue shirts and moleskin trousers, work attire more acceptable to mallee pastoralists. From 1857 he was rarely out of work, freely tramping the country as there was 'not a fence between North Brighton and the Murray' except for homestead horse paddocks, a distance of 250 kilometres.[42]

George Everard initially obtained six months' work shepherding at John Coppock's Lake Albacutya run for the standard wage of £1 per week with rations—4.5 kilograms of flour, 5.5 kilograms of meat, 1 kilogram of sugar and 100 grams of tea, with salt *ad infinitum*—a rate unchanged for years. Some bosses found ways to cut or withhold wages, but Coppock paid fairly. So did Hugh Jamieson of Yerre Yerre station at Mildura, whose station 'was the best managed on the Murray': everything 'near perfect'.[43] Everard worked as a mallee shepherd, shearer, drover, fencer, water pumper, cook, and dogger (wild-dog hunter) until about 1900, when he settled in a hut near Lake Albacutya and lived by rabbiting until his death in 1925, aged ninety-five.

Over the years the Mallee enchanted Everard. He first gazed upon it in a wet phase during the 1850s when the Wimmera River flooded lakes Hindmarsh and Albacutya, as well as the surrounding low-lying country to Pine Plains and beyond to Wirrengren. Such an inundation also occurred about 1830.[44] Everard recalled his experience five decades later: it 'was one of the most beautiful places I had ever seen' with plains of bulloak, quandong and currant bush, and hills covered with pines and pigface at their base. Drying country was covered with 'marsh-mallows' two metres high, and 'sow thistles' (*Sonchus oleraceus*). The latter, an annual native to Europe and Asia, had taken hold in the Mallee, carried on the wind or the sheep's back.[45] Everard never

---

42 Everard, 'Pioneering Days', 15.
43 Everard, 'Pioneering Days', 42–3.
44 B.L. [B]eilby, 'Wanderings', *Port Phillip Gazette*, 29 November, 1 December 1849.
45 Victorian Resources Online, 'Common Sow-thistle', accessed 16 April 2017, http://vro.agriculture.vic.gov.au/dpi/vro/vrosite.nsf/pages/sip_salt_common_sow_thistle.

witnessed another such inundation, except for sporadic filling of Hindmarsh and Albacutya.[46]

Ironically, Everard and other workers in the pastoral industry that displaced the original owners followed a beat along the outlets of the Wimmera River similar to those used by the Wotjobaluk, driven not by a Great Tradition but the promise of paid work. Everard spent his life roving between stations such as Lake Hindmarsh, Lake Albacutya, Pine Plains, Kow Plains, Lake Coorong, and Kulkyne, with occasional forays to runs at Mount Gambier and along the Murray–Darling. He moved where he was known and always gained work. Everard drew two pastoral maps—for 1859 and 1865—to accompany his reminiscences; both were of stations on his beat from Lake Hindmarsh to Pine Plains and east around Lake Corrong. His Mallee love affair was interrupted by occasional trips to Melbourne, Geelong or Mount Gambier to blow his savings at the theatre.

Mallee lands, like other inland areas of Australia, were then only suited to pastoralism. This industry in turn shaped the workforce and its culture. Many bachelors like Everard tramped the country seeking work. They worked hard, then spent their savings fast in the theatres and pubs of Melbourne, Adelaide, Port Lincoln or other regional towns. Two years' wages could vanish in two weeks, sometimes lavished as well on a horse or spring cart to save their feet while seeking work. They were sustained by bush hospitality, which provided a feed and a bed, while yarning and singing about sheep and mallee country built a camaraderie called mateship, with fireplaces producing tea and damper and, on cool nights, warmth for men to toast their feet.

But hospitality added to station costs. While Everard was shepherding at Lake Hindmarsh in the 1860s, his hut, being close to the road, was visited nightly in shearing season by workers heading to the Darling on horseback: 'We often had six or eight of them, and our rations went at a rare rate'. After a month's tucker was eaten in a matter of days by constant visitors, the boss fixed the problem. He did not deny travellers, so strong was the ethic of hospitality, but moved Everard's hut further from the road behind some sand hills, after which 'we never saw a traveller'.[47]

While shearers worked in groups, shepherds' work was lonely. Runs had several shepherds each placed at one of many outstations and able to manage a thousand sheep at best. Shepherds saw the boss weekly or fortnightly during a brief supply drop. The Everard brothers when lambing down at Pine Plains

---

46 Everard, 'Pioneering Days', 18–24.
47 Everard, 'Pioneering Days', 31.

had no one else within thirty kilometres: 'it was a lonely job'.[48] George Everard worked with his brother Joseph for a decade until Joseph committed suicide by jumping down a well at Pine Plains in 1866, rendering George bereft for months. Dogs and books were shepherds' only friends and the country their only solace, leading in Everard's case to a deep affection for the Mallee.

Shepherding in the Mallee was not generally idle work. Water had to be hauled from wells twice daily, feed cut from scrub in hard times, and sheep moved to find the precious small patches of good grass while still being within reach of water. Drafting sheep according to age and gender was a difficult and slow business, with recalcitrants being manhandled over a fence if they ran amongst the wrong lot. This task was only relieved by technology. William Lockhart Morton, later a mallee pastoralist near Birchip, in 1848 invented a swing gate (and a sheep dip) that revolutionised the work of drafting and dipping worldwide. Morton claimed two men and a shepherd could draft four thousand sheep in a 'short time'. His invention preceded colonial patent protection, but in 1886 he gained parliamentary recognition for his creation.[49] Post-and-wire fences finally replaced shepherds in the 1870s.

Aboriginal Workers

Some Aboriginal people avoided early settlers. George Everard, shepherding for Pine Plains, pushed his flock north beyond Wirrengren and Underbool into salt-lake country at Tolongawank, about sixty kilometres west of Ouyen on the fringe of sunset country. There he met two Wotjobaluk youths, Nero and Blucher, who spoke little English and were part of a family headed by a man named Charlie. Everard never saw them again but often encountered their campsites, with hakea roots 'piled up like small hay stacks at all their camps; in the summer they had little else to depend on [for water]'.[50] The family finally retreated to Bordertown, then Ebenezer Mission at Antwerp.

Most Wotjobaluk and river peoples in the Victorian Mallee attached themselves to pastoralists who had usurped their home country. The same applied to the Eyre Peninsula and other mallee country. A careful look at the image of shearers at Hillsea Station near Lake Hamilton (see Figure 4.2)

---

48 Everard, 'Pioneering Days', 27.
49 Victoria, Parliament, Legislative Assembly, 'Final Report from the Select Committee upon the Claim of William Lockhart Morton, together with the Proceedings of Committee and Minutes of Evidence, 30 September 1886', *Victorian Parliamentary Papers*, 1886, D no. 4. Morton's letter to the *Argus*, 1 January 1848, is reprinted on 5.
50 Everard, 'Pioneering Days', 29.

reveals a man holding a broom, the trademark of a roustabout in the shearing shed, who appears to be an Aboriginal worker. The man with a hat and beard, four along to his left holding a fleece, may be Indigenous too. Many pastoral photographs of the late nineteenth century in mallee country (and elsewhere) reveal the presence of Aboriginal people in the sheep industry.

Figure 4.2: Shearers at Hillsea Station, Near Lake Hamilton, Eyre Peninsula, c. 1900.
(Courtesy State Library of South Australia)

A two-way paternal relationship developed within pastoralism; most sheep owners realised they owed something to the original owners, and Aboriginal people believed that pastoralists, as usurpers, owed them sustenance and protection.[51] Some pastoralists in Victoria were local guardians of Aborigines under the 1869 Aborigines Act, and their power to issue government rations compounded this mutual relationship of stewardship and dependence. Many Aboriginal workers requested European names and sought kinship relations with pastoralists, the better to enmesh them. These relationships were functional—pastoralists needed labour, while Aboriginal people needed or wanted sustenance and liked pastoral work. Some historians have seen Aboriginal people as an exploited and poorly paid reserve labour force. Yet there is much

---

51 Richard Broome, '"There Were Vegetables Every Year Mr Green Was Here": Right Behaviour and the Struggle for Autonomy at Coranderrk Aboriginal Reserve', *History Australia* 3, no. 2 (December 2006): 43.1–43.16.

evidence that they worked on their own terms. They remained uninterested in European work values but anxious to form close ties to individual pastoralists on their home country.[52]

When not at work, Aboriginal people were sustained by the waterways of the Victorian Mallee as before. In 1854 Hugh Jamieson of Yerre Yerre station estimated that, even though the population was 'dying off', fifteen hundred people still lived along the Murray's banks from Swan Hill to the South Australian border and along the Darling north to Fort Bourke eight hundred kilometres upstream.[53] In 1877 there were 437 Aboriginal people in north-west Victoria, 377 of them living off Ebenezer Mission. This mallee population represented 41 per cent of the total Victorian Aboriginal population at the time, revealing the importance of the river and lakes to those who chose to stay off reserves and missions.[54] By 1885 the Aboriginal Protection Board estimated 250 remained along the Murray from Swan Hill to Ned's Corner near the border.[55] These river people could choose whether to work on stations or live off traditional country.

Aboriginal men and women did a variety of pastoral work, guiding and showing country, shepherding, fencing, washing and shearing, punching bullocks and riding horses—all with skill. Edmund Morey, who settled near Euston in NSW in 1846, aged twenty, 'had to depend largely on the natives for labour, especially when sheep had taken the place of cattle on our runs'.[56] He developed good relations with the people, stemming from the initial mutual hilarity of Morey cutting their hair and naming them. John Beilby, searching for a run in 1849 near Lake Albacutya, met an Aboriginal shepherd named 'Nobby', who was hunting for possum while his wife watched the sheep. 'Nobby' quizzed Beilby about the sheep season further south, asking: 'all gone nip-nip in your one country'? Beilby commented of Aboriginal workers: 'I have had occasion to employ and see them employed by nearly all my neighbours

---

52 For the reserve labour ideas, see Peggy Brock, 'Pastoral Stations and Reserves in South and Central Australia, 1850s–1950s', in *Aboriginal Workers*, eds Ann McGrath and Kay Saunders, with Jackie Huggins, special issue of *Labour History*, no. 69 (November 1995): 102–14. For the alternative view see Richard Broome, 'Aboriginal Workers on South-eastern Frontiers', *Australian Historical Studies* 26, no. 103 (October 1994): 202–20.

53 Hugh Jamieson, in Bride (ed.), *Letters from Victorian Pioneers*, 381.

54 Census of Victoria, 1877, tabulated in Richard Broome, *Aboriginal Victorians: A History since 1800* (Sydney: Allen & Unwin, 2005), 147.

55 Burch, *Returning the Kulkyne*, 126.

56 Edmund Morey, 'Reminiscences of a Pioneer in New South Wales', no. IX, *Sydney Mail and New South Wales Advertiser*, 25 December 2007.

in every department of pastoral servitude in a remote district, where from the scarcity of European labour their services had been most valuable during several years past'.[57] Hugh Jamieson, owner of Yerre Yerre station at Mildura for twenty years from 1847, rejected stereotypes of his Aboriginal workers as 'savage', 'lazy' and of 'limited ability'. Rather, the Jarijari or Ladjiladji people were 'possessed of a considerable amount of intelligence, observation, quickness of apprehension, [and] an aptitude for instruction in both reading and writing'. He used them 'exclusively' in shepherding, sheep washing and to a degree shearing. During the gold-rush labour crisis, he and others along the Murray–Darling stations found them 'of great value'. However, Jamieson still considered European labour more dependable. Each summer his Aboriginal workers and families 'have the greatest desire to abandon every employment and indulge in the roving life of naked savages', leaving him short of labour at shearing time. His Aboriginal workers followed traditional rhythms, not those of the European work ethic and calendar, the Murray's food supplies underpinning their independence.[58]

As the pastoral occupation intensified, Aboriginal numbers fell in mallee country. When the scientist George Neumayer travelled through the Victorian Mallee conducting his magnetic survey, he arrived a Lake Corrong station on 22 October 1861 (which he recorded as 'Lake Corong', and then spelt 'Coorong'). He recorded 'Mr Bell has now resided seventeen years at this place and he tells me there were hundreds of blacks here at the time when he first came'. Only one remained by 1861—a boy who became the local identity 'Jowley' and survived to 1912.[59] John George Coombs, manager at Moorna station near the South Australian border, recalled that after 1870 Aboriginal people in his district 'perished quickly. By this time most all of their country had gone, and sometimes they were even hunted out of the river bends, not being allowed to camp there. No slice of country anywhere was reserved for them'.[60] John Burch in his history of the huge Kulkyne station estimated there were seven people remaining there in the 1890s.[61] In Victoria the Aboriginal population declined by 80 per cent in the first two decades of contact owing to disease and violence, and by 90 per cent by 1877 as a result of poor nutrition,

---

57   J.W. Beilby, in Kenyon, *The Story of the Mallee*, 34.
58   Jamieson, in Bride (ed.), *Letters from Victorian Pioneers*, 379–80.
59   George Neumayer, in Kenyon, *The Story of the Mallee*, 47.
60   'Seventy Years in Murray Country', *Murray Pioneer and Australian River Record*, 21 December 1923.
61   Burch, *Returning the Kulkyne*, 127. For his discussion of the Aboriginal population decline at the Kulkyne, see 129–41.

alcohol abuse and settler indifference.[62] Aboriginal missions, however, provided safer havens in mallee country.

Aboriginal Missions

Poonindie Mission was established by Archdeacon Mathew Hale in Pangkala and Nauo country near Port Lincoln on the Eyre Peninsula in 1850 to train Aboriginal youths from Adelaide and the Murray Mallee as good Christian farmers. Aboriginal boys moved voluntarily to this isolated place, where Hale encouraged autonomy. Some became shepherds, ploughmen and bullock drivers. An engraving of the mission in 1853 reveals a dozen cabins for living quarters, several substantial fenced cottages, a barn and various farm buildings, a substantial paddock fenced with rubble, and people working another field (see Figure 4.3). However, the workers' enthusiasm declined once Hale left and was replaced by more dictatorial managers who directed jobs to white workers. Death rates among Aboriginal residents soared to 50 per cent. Fortunately, nearby landholders still valued and employed Aboriginal workers. In 1880, Poonindie resident John Solomon came second in a Port Lincoln district ploughing match, inspiring him to enter the National Ploughing Championships in Ballarat; but he failed to gain a place. The Poonindie women maintained the houses and communal areas of the mission and also worked as domestics for the white mission staff.[63]

Some local settlers coveting more land initially resented Poonindie's presence, sentiments that later resurfaced. In 1895 Poonindie's trustees were pressured to relinquish the land. Several former residents petitioned for three thousand acres 'of the poorest land on the whole run' on the south side of the Tod River, adding: 'we propose to live on it and cultivate and work the land among ourselves. With this and what we can earn by shearing, fishing and getting guano, we can support ourselves and our families'.[64] Their pleas were ignored, although Emanuel Solomon received some land, and a portion became an Aboriginal reserve. Sixty remaining Poonindie people were scattered to Point Pearce (York Peninsula) and Point McLeay (Lake Alexandrina) missions to live among strangers, their dream of farming mallee lands extinguished.

---

62   Richard Broome, *Aboriginal Victorians: A History since 1800* (Sydney: Allen & Unwin, 2005), 90–3, 147.
63   Peggy Brock and Doreen Kartinyeri, *Poonindie: The Rise and Destruction of an Aboriginal Community* (Adelaide: South Australian Government Printer and Aboriginal Heritage Branch, Department of Environment and Planning South Australia, 1989), chaps 2 and 3.
64   Brock and Kartinyeri, *Poonindie*, 70.

Figure. 4.3: 'Poonindie Mission Station, 1853', by William Dickes.
(Courtesy Rex Nan Kivell Collection, National Library of Australia, nla.obj-136100653)

The Lutherans formed a farming community at Koonibba in 1899, forty kilometres west of Ceduna, where the Wirangu learned pastoral and farming skills over ensuing generations.[65]

In the 1850s, two missions opened in mallee country in Victoria. In 1851, the Reverends Taeger and Spieseke established a Moravian one among the Wemba Wemba at Lake Boga, just south east of Swan Hill. Their efforts went unrewarded and they retreated to Germany.[66] In 1854, J.H. Goodwin, a lay preacher, surveyed the rivers for the Anglican Church and found fertile mission ground. Along the Murray River from the Murrumbidgee to the South Australian border he encountered six tribes totalling six hundred people, another four hundred residing along Lake Victoria and the Rufus River, and distinct groups of seventy people every fifteen miles along the Darling. Goodwin formed an Anglican mission named Yelta at the Murray–Darling junction; it soon contained buildings, a school and gardens. However, few Aboriginal people visited or showed much interest in Christianity, and fewer stayed, preferring casual work on local pastoral stations. In 1863, four

---

65 W.H. Edwards and R. Winderlich, 'Koonibba', in *The Encyclopaedia of Aboriginal Australia*, gen. ed. David Horton (Canberra: Aboriginal Studies Press, 1994), vol. 1, 558–9.

66 Robert Kenny, *The Lamb Enters the Dreaming: Nathanael Pepper & the Ruptured World* (Melbourne: Scribe, 2007), chap. 6.

Aboriginal families built huts at Yelta, and one man requested a pump to irrigate his garden, but interest soon waned. Goodwin reported that only Fred Wowinda 'has remained very constantly to us', on occasion 'reading the Testament to a black from a neighbouring station'.[67] The mission closed in 1869.[68]

In 1859 the Moravians tried again. The Reverends Hagenauer and Spieseke founded Ebenezer at Antwerp on donated land beside the Wimmera, south of Lake Hindmarsh. There they claimed one of the first successful Aboriginal conversions in Australia, of a youth named Nathanael Pepper. However, Pepper's conversion in 1860 was of his own making in the face of mission scepticism, a story told by Robert Kenny.[69] The Wotjobaluk and missionaries built a Christian farming community at Ebenezer, but it struggled on mallee soil. In 1871 it almost doubled in size to 3,600 acres but was still unable to carry sufficient stock to supply the meat and milk needs of sixty residents. In 1875 a neighbour donated another thousand acres, but more land still was needed once the population reached a hundred in 1877 following an inflow from Ramahyuck mission in Gippsland.

Drought in the late 1870s caused the hay crop to fail, reducing fodder. Sheep numbers fell on the mission as rabbits ate pasture and dingoes harassed the sheep. Fencing reduced losses. But pressures on food production increased when some Aboriginal male farm workers left with their families to work on the rail line being built from Dimboola to South Australia. Able-bodied worker numbers fell further owing to the Victorian Aborigines Protection Act of 1886, which excluded those between fourteen and thirty-four deemed 'half caste' from living on missions. Ebenezer's population slumped to under thirty. In 1901 some residents left voluntarily, declaring: 'as free British subjects they may go where they please'.[70] The government closed Ebenezer in 1904, pushing the remaining residents into the wider world. The Lake Hindmarsh Land Act 1904 then opened the mission's land to selection, except for that deemed a reserve and containing the church and its burial ground. The community's fate is examined in Chapter 8.[71]

---

67   Quoted in Aldo Massola, *Aboriginal Mission Stations in Victoria* (Melbourne: Hawthorn Press, 1970), 28.
68   Aldo Massola, 'The History of the Yelta Mission Station', *Victorian Historical Magazine* 33, no. 1 (August 1962): 251–61.
69   Kenny, *The Lamb Enters the Dreaming*.
70   Victoria, Board for the Protection of the Aborigines, *Thirty-seventh Report*, 1901, *Victorian Parliamentary Papers*, 1901, paper no. 42, 11.
71   Aldo Massola, *Aboriginal Mission Stations in Victoria*, 31–62.

Despite their authoritarian atmosphere, missions provided refuge, work and family life, often on home country. They were the birthplace of the next generation and ensured Aboriginal survival; genealogical analysis has revealed that Aboriginal Victorians today are descended from mission families, not those who lived off missions and on pastoral stations.[72] Similarly, many descendants of Poonindie's residents remain today, although the Pangkala/Nauo people of the Eyre Peninsula who were not residents of Poonindie have few known surviving descendants.[73]

Murray Mallee Runs in Crisis

Reality hit Murray Mallee pastoralists in the mid-1860s. In the 1850s, pioneers experienced very wet years and inundations, but, in the sixties, climate variation led to drought. Harry Brand, who pioneered the Murray Mallee around Chowilla in the 1850s and took up a run in the Renmark area, lost £4,000 in this drought, in which thousands of sheep died, feed prices soared, and river transport ceased. Many were ruined before the rains came in 1864.[74] More woes followed. When heading for work at a mining rush in the Barrier Ranges (Broken Hill), probably in 1867, George Everard forded the Murray River, then at its lowest level in his long experience. He waded across, only swimming a chain in the middle. Both banks were strewn with dead and dying sheep 'bogged in mud ... the poor creatures still alive with their eyes torn out by the cursed crows'. Up the Darling the cattle were being served in the same way, which gave Everard 'the horrors'.[75] J. Macfarlane depicted just such a grisly end in a stark line drawing (see Figure 4.4).

Such shocks altered Murray Mallee pastoralism. Alfred Kenyon prepared a map of pastoral properties existing in 1865, 'the zenith of pastoral occupation'. It contained 119 properties, with only small portions of sand country unoccupied, although many apparent runs were actually unoccupied paper speculations. However, Kenyon's 1873 map showed only forty-five runs, the

---

72   Len Smith, Janet McCalman, Ian Anderson, Sandra Smith. Joanne Evans, Gavan McCarthy, and Jane Beer, 'Fractional Identities: The Political Arithmetic of Aboriginal Victorians', *Journal of Interdisciplinary History* 38, no. 4 (Spring 2008): 533–51.
73   Brock and Kartinyeri, *Poonindie*, 78.
74   Harry Brand, 'Reminiscences of a Pioneer as Told to Walter Ogilvy', typescript, *c.* 1911, Loxton Library.
75   Everard, 'Pioneering Days', 33–4. The first Barrier Ranges rush was in 1867—see George Farwell, 'Broken Hill', *The Australian Encyclopaedia* (Sydney: The Grolier Society of Australia, 1963), 2, 158–60.

result of consolidations following the 1869 Land Act and speculations caused by annual licences. In the later map, the waterless runs in the western and central Victorian Mallee region had vanished, many only ever existing on paper at the Melbourne Titles Office.[76] To read Kenyon is to appreciate the mobility of licences as properties changed hands or suffered amalgamations.

Difficult times continued into the 1870s, pushing runs to expand to keep afloat financially. Lake Corrong, incorporating Minapree and Wilhelmina, expanded to 400 thousand acres. Brim station, now combined with Nullan and Davis Plains, grew to 300 thousand acres. Piangil, leased with Burra, Stratford and Lowan Flats, was now 220 thousand acres. Henry 'Money' Miller's consolidation was the most spectacular, as revealed by John Burch's forensic historical investigations.[77] In 1867 he leased 300 thousand acres, centred on Kulkyne station, but in a series of takeovers by 1877 his leases increased tenfold, totalling three million acres or an astonishing one-quarter of the Victorian Mallee. 'Money' Miller's empire revolved around the Kulkyne and Bumbang on the Murray, and his winter pastures centred on Pine Plains. Thomas McCredie, who leased L'Albert and Titybong, remained viable by also leasing Pental Island in the Murray River, which was well grassed from snowmelt inundations. In 1879 he crowded twenty-five thousand sheep on it 'because of the back country being so dry'.[78] However, the size of runs could not alter carrying capacity—one sheep to twenty acres being common.

As deeper pockets prevailed, leaseholds were fenced, and water was made by scooping out earth for tanks and sometimes covering them, all to increase viability. 'Tank' was the common nineteenth-century English word for a dam, derived from the Gujerati word *tankh*, itself from the Sanskrit *tadaga*, pond or lake. Creating a tank was tricky in mallee country. Leaseholders might have small grass patches and land replete with scrub feed, but the sandy soil was unable to hold water. Where clay existed for a tank base, it might be too far from good feed. John Miller, one of Henry Miller's managers, explained: 'there are paddocks 25 miles square in which we cannot find any clay suitable for making tanks'.[79] In 1879 Thomas McCredie explained that tanks ranged in size from seven hundred to three thousand cubic yards, and often took two years to fill once scooped out. Once 'the sheep get into the way of making roads

---

76   See maps in Kenyon, *The Story of the Mallee*, 68, 71.
77   Burch, *Returning the Kulkyne*, 34–8.
78   Thomas McCredie, Crown Lands Commission of Inquiry, 'Evidence', 1879, Q. 9920.
79   Henry Miller, Crown Lands Commission of Inquiry, 'Evidence', 1879, Q. 10343.

to them, they fill more easily, the water draining in more readily'. Tanking had doubled the capacity of his four runs, Piangil on the Murray downstream from Swan Hill, and the much larger backcountry runs: Burra, Stratford and Lowan Flats.[80] Henry Miller built tanks by enlarging Aboriginal soaks and wells on the Wirrengren–Kulkyne pathway to facilitate cattle movements between his properties.[81]

Figure 4.4: 'A Cruel Death', by J. Macfarlane (1889).
(Courtesy Pictures Collection, State Library Victoria)

Poor seasons caused sheep numbers to plummet in the late 1870s, a decline revealed by leaseholders' evidence before a 'Crown Lands Commission of Inquiry on Both the Agricultural and Pastoral Occupation of the Public Lands' in 1879. Arthur Mandeville of Lake Corrong station stated that in late 1878 he had twenty-five thousand sheep, but six months later he had only fifteen thousand. Ten to fifteen dead sheep were skinned daily. Others perished in the scrub, their carcasses a complete loss. With the drought killing grass, station holders used the scrub to sustain their flocks. Thomas McCredie declared he valued scrub more than ephemeral grass, and it formed 95 per

---

80   McCredie, Crown Lands Commission of Inquiry, 'Evidence', 1879, Q. 10137–8.
81   Burch, *The Wirrengren–Kulkyne Pathway*, 270–1.

cent 'of what the sheep are supported by now'.[82] At Lake Corrong station the manager Arthur Mandeville testified of his sheep: 'you see them standing on their hind legs, eating all they can'. He added: 'the sheep would die now if we did not cut the scrub'. Leaseholders cut dogwood, bull oak, but not wild hop as 'the sheep do not care for it'. They would eat quandong, but 'we have so few you would require a black fellow to find one for you'. They pushed the scrub over 'so that the bark is not broken, and it grows again next season'.[83]

The Mallee was in crisis. John Miller, manager of Kulkyne station, declared to the commissioners that the land was 'deteriorating' and 'the country has been overstocked and destroyed to a great extent'. He added: 'the rabbits are the present cause'.[84] John McLennon, manager of Brim, Nullan and Davis Plains stations, reported that these three runs of 300 thousand acres used to carry thirty thousand sheep but now had only 5,200. The land was in poor shape and the scrub was dead because of rabbits. The runs would need seven years to recover, three of those without sheep.[85]

The woes of mallee pastoralists were elaborated by Thomas McCredie, who handed the commissioners his pamphlet, 'The Mallee Country and Rabbits', setting out the case for tax relief. Early runs had carried one sheep per fifteen acres in winter, but fewer in summer. Pastoralists had spent big on fencing and establishing tanks, but other factors limited profits, including: continued scanty rainfall, the difficulty of fattening stock on such poor country, the Melbourne market being a distant three hundred miles away, the financial drain of providing bush hospitality in sparsely settled country (sometimes fifteen strangers sat down to a free meal), and stock tax amounting to 25 per cent of gross income. The shilling per head of stock tax was the same for all pastoralists regardless of the country, and: 'As if all these evils were not enough ... there are wild dogs and rabbits'.[86]

Edward Lascelles, leaseholder at Lake Corrong station, recalled that rabbits appeared at Morton Plains on the south-east edge of the Mallee in 1866 but were not a problem until the mid-1870s. Their rise coincided with severe drought. Grass being unavailable, the rabbits ate the bark and killed large amounts of scrub, the staple food for sheep especially in hard times.

---

82 McCredie, Crown Lands Commission of Inquiry, 'Evidence', 1879, Q. 10213–15.
83 Arthur Mandeville, Crown Lands Commission of Inquiry, 'Evidence', 1879, Q. 10399–408.
84 John Miller, Crown Lands Commission of Inquiry, 'Evidence', 1879, Q. 10328.
85 John McLennon, Crown Lands Commission of Inquiry, 'Evidence', 1879, Q.10465–6.
86 Thomas McCredie, 'The Mallee Country and Rabbits', Crown Lands Commission of Inquiry, 'Evidence', 1879, 411–12.

A better season in 1878 saw rabbit numbers explode.[87] Rabbits also depleted the food sources of smaller marsupials, which reduced traditional bush foods for Aboriginal station workers.

At first few discussed the issue or took action for fear of devaluing their licences. Besides, eradication efforts were extremely expensive and made little economic sense, given that all land leases in Victoria were due to expire in 1880 and renewal depended on the findings of the 1879 inquiry. Thomas McCredie estimated it would take six men two months to distribute three hundred pounds of poisoned wheat at a cost of over £1,100, and yet his income after tax for the previous year was only £1,450.[88] John Miller concurred: 'I do not think the profits of the station would pay for the exterminating of the rabbits'.[89] John McLennon whose sheep fell from thirty thousand to 5,200 in two years, blamed rabbits, dingoes and poor seasons: 'The rabbits were in myriads, despite poisoning them with phosphorous and wheat. They invaded the kitchen garden, destroying the vegetables and fruit trees'. They 'were actually running under the verandah ... so that we could shoot them from the doors, four or five at a time'.[90]

Wild dogs remained a constant threat to pastoral holdings, some owners considering them the greatest problem. John Miller told the 1879 Inquiry that at Jerrejee station at Kulkyne, wild dogs were thriving, even after he had killed a hundred in eighteen months. Baiting and trapping were rendered less effective because the dogs could catch rabbits so easily. Only one man on the station was skilful enough to trap wild dogs, which sometimes escaped leaving a foot behind and survived with the support of a mate. Some 'quite fat' three-legged wild dogs had been killed recently.[91] Arthur Mandeville from Lake Corrong station claimed eighty wild dogs had been killed there in the past year by shooting, baiting and trapping, while others escaped to die in the scrub.[92] John McLennon, the manager of Brim station, gave ten shillings for each dingo tail or skin, paying out on twenty-two dogs in ten months. He added: 'one dog each night will destroy, between what it will kill and what

---

87 Kenyon, *The Story of the Mallee*, 73.
88 McCredie, 'The Mallee Country and Rabbits', Crown Lands Commission of Inquiry, 'Evidence', 1879, Q. 10205. For his income see Q. 10140.
89 John Miller, Crown Lands Commission of Inquiry, 'Evidence', 1879, Q. 10328.
90 McLennon, Crown Lands Commission of Inquiry, 'Evidence', 1879, Q. 10534.
91 John Miller, Crown Lands Commission of Inquiry, 'Evidence', 1879, Q. 10336–10341.
92 Mandeville, Crown Lands Commission of Inquiry, 'Evidence', 1879, Q. 10362–10366.

will die afterwards, something like three or four sheep. They do not eat them after they kill them; they just kill them, as it were, for amusement'.[93]

By 1879, four things had crushed Mallee pastoral runs: drought, overstocking, rabbits and wild dogs. Edward Lascelles claimed licences to run after run were surrendered, Lake Hindmarsh being the first, the annual rental of which plummeted from £705 to £36 in one year.[94] George Everard, who was in work continuously for two decades, was now without a job and desperate. He recalled the country was in a 'deplorable condition with rabbits and dingoes. Some of the stations had no one but a caretaker at the homestead. The sheep were all removed or dead, slaughtered by wild dogs'. Seeking work, he walked from Nhill to Pine Plains and on to the Murray River, then to Swan Hill, Morton Plains, Lake Corrong, Kow Plains and on to Pinnaroo, then back to Lake Hindmarsh and on to the Murray–Darling junction, where he finally gained casual work. He had criss-crossed the Murray Mallee several times, walking over a thousand kilometres, 'the longest time and the biggest tramp and loneliest I ever made'.[95]

Pastoralists in 1879 faced a fifth factor, an ideological assault on them by middle- and working-class Victorians professing a different and utopian vision of rural life dating back to the gold rush: free selection of small farms. The 1879 Crown Lands Commission Inquiry into pastoral leases due to expire in 1880 gave this vision renewed life. Pastoralists telling tales of woe pushed for long leases, low rentals and compensation for improvements when leases expired, but their pleas fell on deaf ears. The inquiry recommended an end to leases in their current form in order to foster free selection 'as the leading feature of the land system of this country', and thus end the 'monopoly in few hands of the sources of wealth derivable from pastoral pursuits'. Pastoralism locked up land 'capable of yielding millions of tons of breadstuffs annually, of sustaining in comfort thousands of husbandmen with their families, of employing all the available labour of the country, and of increasing the general wealth of the entire community'.[96]

The commissioners acknowledged that the Mallee was exceptional, declaring it a 'scorching wilderness' wracked with high costs and uncertain returns. When questioning the surveyor general A.J. Skene back in Melbourne, the commissioners stated they had followed Skene's suggested route. Now they wanted his

---

93   McLennon, Crown Lands Commission of Inquiry, 'Evidence', 1879, Q. 10476.
94   Kenyon, *The Story of the Mallee*, 73.
95   Everard, 'Pioneering Days', 51.
96   Crown Lands Commission of Inquiry, 'Report', 1879, iv.

confirmation of their observations of the country from the Murray River south to the middle of the Mallee. 'It appeared to us as a complete wilderness—the soil wretched, poor, and sandy, and the scrub very dense, and, in certain cases, almost impracticable?' Skene replied: 'That is the case'. They asked him about the country west of Pine Plains, which they had not visited. He replied it was all 'white sand ridges, with here and there a tree dotted over them, and in the valleys between dense mallee'.[97] The commissioners concluded that agriculture, and mixed wheat and sheep grazing, should be encouraged on the Mallee's fringes and more fertile parts, but the Mallee's interior should remain for bigger pastoral properties leased by people with deep pockets.[98]

The outcome was the *Mallee Pastoral Leases Act 1883*, which divided the Victorian Mallee into leased allotments up to twenty thousand acres on the southern and eastern fringe, and sixty-five huge leased 'blocks' over the rest of the Mallee. Each 'block' was divided into half, part A and part B. Successful bidders at auction nominated which half would be leased for five years and which for twenty years. Improvements were expected, especially the eradication of rabbits and dingoes, and compensation for money expended was due at the end of the lease. This Act was designed to end the land monopoly by returning five million acres of the Mallee 'blocks' to the government in five years, ready for closer settlement, the other half in twenty years. An amending Act in 1885 offered compensation of 10s per acre prepared for cultivation and provided for construction of a rabbit-proof fence.[99]

A wire-netting and vermin-proof fence 197 miles long was erected by the Victorian government in 1885. It ran along the 36th parallel from Tyntynder station near Swan Hill, then between Birchip and Brim to Lake Hindmarsh and on to the South Australian border. The fence aimed to stop invading rabbits from the south and dingoes from the north. The line from Tyntynder was paid for by lessees on both sides of the fence at £2 10s per mile. A further eighty-seven miles was erected north along the border line.[100] Parts are still visible, and many today consider it the boundary between the Wimmera and the Mallee.[101] Several wire netting trusts in South Australia also erected

---

97   Crown Lands Commission of Inquiry, 'Evidence', 1879, Q. 10807, 10814.
98   Crown Lands Commission of Inquiry, 'Report', 1879, xi–xii.
99   Kenyon, *The Story of the Mallee*, 58–60.
100 'Rabbit-Proof Fencing', return to an order of the House, 11 June 1889, *Victorian Parliamentary Papers*, C. no. 1, 1889.
101 Yarriambiack Shire Council & Wimmera Mallee Tourism, 'Explore … welcome … relax … Brim Victoria', accessed 23 September 2018, https://www.wimmeramalleetourism.com.au/images/Brimbrochureweb.pdf.

rabbit and dingo fences during the 1890s with government subsidies. The program proved cheaper than the £300,000 paid out by the South Australian government from 1880 to 1889 for rabbit scalps.[102]

Pastoralism's failure in mallee country was largely attributable to the forces of nature; it was semi-arid scrub territory, prone to drought with little grass or permanent water and with predatory wild dogs and rabbits that competed with sheep for feed. Of course, along the permanent waters of the Murray River substantial stations like Euston and Chowilla survived and later thrived, especially after fertilisers revolutionised pasture improvement in the 1920s. Their prosperity was marked by large homesteads with shady verandahs. Some of the new farmers who replaced pastoralists elsewhere later raised sheep along with wheat, an insurance policy against poor wheat seasons. A hundred years later there were over two million sheep in the Victorian Mallee, a marked increase though they comprised only 6 per cent of the state's flock.[103]

Before their demise in many mallee areas, sheep took their toll on the land. Concentrated as they were around water—creeks, billabongs, wells and soaks—their hard-cloven hooves pounded and compacted the soils, stultifying new growth in these vital areas. Sheep ate out some plant species such as yams and pigface, reducing biodiversity, and cropped scrub hard when drought made the scarce grass scarcer. Their competitor, the rabbit—another introduced species—finished what sheep began. They ate the grasses, then ring-barked and killed tea tree, hop bush and saltbush, leading to sand drift and desertification.[104]

With mallee country in crisis a new way of using the land was tried. Joseph Bosisto, inspired by his friend Ferdinand Von Mueller, the Victorian government botanist, had experimented with distilling eucalyptus oil in the Dandenongs in 1853. A small industry developed, boosted by the belief in the 1880s that eucalyptus oil constituted an alternative to carbolic acid in surgical infection control. It was also used in liniments, syrups, soaps and room deodorants. In 1882, Bosisto, with the backing of Melbourne chemists Alfred Felton and Frederick Grimwade and three other shareholders, turned his attention

---

102   Roland Breckwoldt, 'The Dingo Fences', in Sheen Coupe, *Frontier Country*, vol. 2 (Sydney: Weldon Russell Publishing, 1989), 148–51; John Pickard, 'The Victorian Mallee Fence: A Forgotten and Misunderstood Relic of Settling the Mallee Region of Victoria', *Victorian Historical Journal* 90, no. 1 (June 2019): 30–56.

103   *Victorian Year Book 1973, Centenary Edition* (Melbourne: Commonwealth Bureau of Census and Statistics, Victorian Office, 1973), 894.

104   Burch, *Returning the Kulkyne*, 198–200.

to the southern tip of the Mallee and its *Eucalyptus dumosa*, establishing a factory at Antwerp.[105] Their enterprise, operating as the Eucalyptus Mallee Company, began on 577 acres. It expanded in 1884 when the company leased ten thousand acres under the *Mallee Pastoral Leases Act 1883*, which allowed them to subdivide if needed as well as extract oil.[106] Labour was drawn at first from itinerant rural labourers and Aboriginal people from nearby Ebenezer Mission. Over time more of the workers resided in Antwerp township or in improved quarters on the station.[107]

In 1890 the company planned for 'a continuous and increasing supply of the raw material', by harvesting 2,000-acre plots on rotation every three years. Horses that powered the operation were fed from a seventy-acre hay field.[108] The company survived the Federation Drought and prospered. The oil from Antwerp, principally of *E. dumosa*, looked and smelled different from the more traditional *Eucalyptus globulus* oil that had dominated international markets. It gradually won acceptance, and by 1904 the factory was producing 35,020 kilograms of oil per annum for local and international consumption.[109] However, a press report in 1904 commented on 'the increasing distance that the teams have now to go for mallee leaves', suggesting the operation was unsustainable.[110] Production was clearly outpacing *Eucalyptus dumosa*'s famed regenerative capacity. In 1907 the increasing switch to agriculture gave the company an incentive to subdivide and convert the lease to cropping. The oil operation moved to Ki Downs, a 40,000-acre leasehold near Euston in the NSW mallee, but failed to compete with independent distillers and closed the following year.[111] The industry continued on a small scale. Family oil distilleries operated in mallee stands around Gerang Gerung, Kiata and Nhill, adding to farm income, particularly when oil was sold directly to local stores and users such as football clubs, which applied it liberally to injured and bruised players.[112]

---

105 'Visit to the Antwerp Mallee Oil Distilling Works', *Horsham Times*, 2 June 1882, 3.
106 D.J. Shiel, *Eucalyptus, Essence of Australia: The Story of the Eucalyptus Oil Industry—and of the "eucy" Men, and their Contribution to the Australian Bush Tradition* (Melbourne: Queensberry Hill Press, c. 1985), 88.
107 Shiel, *Eucalyptus*, 90–2.
108 'In the Mallee Country', *Australasian*, 4 October 1890, 6.
109 Shiel, *Eucalyptus*, 88, 95.
110 'Tillage and Pasture', *Leader*, 23 April 1904, 6.
111 Michael Pearson 'The Good Oil: Eucalyptus Oil Distilleries in Australia', *Australasian Historical Archaeology* 11 (1993): 101.
112 Shiel, *Eucalyptus*, 97, 103.

Pastoralism in the West

As many Murray Mallee pastoralists faced their demise, the industry in Western Australia's mallee was still in its infancy. Sheep breeding in Western Australia began slowly with initially high mortality rates. The Glenelg Land Regulations of 1837, which allowed poor quality land grants to be swapped for better grazing land on a ratio of three to one, boosted the industry. Sheep numbers climbed seven-fold from 1837 to 1843 reaching 76,191, aided by the discovery of James Drummond, a botanist, that sheep died from eating poison plants: Box poison (*Gastrolobium parviflorum*) and thickleaf poison (*Gastrolobium crassifolium*). Decades of culling by low-paid weed pickers followed. The south west's development was further boosted by new land regulations in 1864, which denied Aboriginal access to Crown lands for traditional purposes, to eighty kilometres west of Esperance.[113]

Sheep raising, most suited to mallee scrub country, remained in its infancy for a generation. Most woolgrowers remained close to the coastal fringe, while cattlemen focused on northern country leases. The Hassell family finally established an outstation at Jerramungup in 1849 and, by the 1880s, controlled 283,000 hectares in various leases from Bridgetown to Jerramungup. The Hassells, and woolgrowers who followed them, employed Aboriginal workers as shepherds, shearers, doggers and pickers of poisonous plants.[114] A report in 1903 listed six Aboriginal workers cutting chaff for wages and another eleven women, children and Elders being supported by rations of meat, flour, tea and sugar.[115] However, Western Australia's pastoral economy remained small, producing just 1 per cent of Australia's wool clip in 1880.[116]

Notable pastoral pioneers of the region were Andrew and Charles Dempster, who surveyed south east of Northam with an Aboriginal guide Correll in 1861, reaching Lake Grace.[117] In September 1865 Andrew Dempster turned

---

113   R. Forrest and S. Crowe, *Yarra-mo-up, a Place of the Tall Yate Trees: A Report on the Noongar Social History of the Jerramungup Region* (Canberra: Australian Government Publishing Service, 1996), 37.
114   Forrest and Crowe, *Yarra-mo-up*, 27–40.
115   G.S. Olivey, *Reports on Stations Visited by Travelling Inspector of Aborigines, 1903* (Perth: Government Printer, 1903), 47–8.
116   Pamela Statham, 'Swan River Colony, 1829–1850', in *A New History of Western Australia*, ed. C.T. Stannage (Perth: University of Western Australia Press, 1981), 190 and 194–6; Geoffrey Bolton, 'Pastoralism', in *Historical Encyclopedia of Western Australia*, eds Jenny Gregory and Jan Gothard (Perth: University of Western Australia Press, 2009), 665–7.
117   Andrew Dempster, Exploration Diaries 1827–1871, vol. 5, 28–43, typescript, J.S. Battye Library.

his attention north of Esperance. Over two weeks he journeyed to the Dundas Hills, north east of present-day Norseman, with another white man and an Aboriginal guide suffering the colonial epithet of 'Curly Wig'. Dempster concluded that, if tanks could be made in granite outcrops, there was 'an open course with sufficient grass for stock en route to a better country'.[118] By 1870, the four Dempster brothers had chosen substantial leaseholds at Esperance and in the Fraser Ranges, two hundred kilometres to the north east. When their station store came under the control of Benjamin Harnett and his wife in 1876, the inventory listed 270 items: from tools, prismatic compasses and all manner of station equipment, to pannikins, frying pans and clothing. Entries for the station store in 1876–77 listed a dozen Aboriginal workers on the station spending money on shirts, trousers, sugar and tobacco, suggesting they were paid wages.[119]

The surviving fragments of the Dempsters' station records remind us of the generic pastoral impact on mallee lands. Historian Geoffrey Bolton declared a generation ago that cattle and sheep transformed Australian land more than any other introduced or invasive species.[120] In June 1872, the Dempsters purchased 288 cattle to see if 'killing and salting on the Station will be more profitable than driving to market'. Cattle continued to be raised on their properties, changing the land with their hard hooves and pads of dung. Pigs, also destructive of land, were raised, killed and shipped out from Esperance. In October 1876, the 15,104 sheep shorn there also ate the native grasses, yams and bulbs, saltbush and scrub of the region. In 1891, 328 merino rams were imported from Canowie in South Australia, evidence of the Dempsters' successful improvement strategies.[121]

The Dempsters kept assiduous equine records. Horses were vital to station work and conquering the land but were far less destructive than stock, and a small fraction of stock numbers. In 1892 there were 217 horses on the Esperance property, forty of them with shepherds. In 1898, the station book listed 162 horses, mostly those broken in, recorded under the categories of draught, buggy, packhorse and hack, suggesting their roles in changing mallee

---

118 'Journal of A. Dempster on a Trip North of Esperance Bay', typescript, J.S. Battye Library; Dempster, Exploration Diaries 1827–1871, vol. 5, 400–04; *Perth Gazette and Western Australian Times*, 10 November 1865.
119 Dempster Brothers, 'Day Book 1873–1878', MN 558, J.S. Battye Library.
120 Geoffrey Bolton, *Spoils and Spoilers, Australians Make their Environment, 1788–1980* (Sydney: Allen & Unwin, 1981), 90–5.
121 Dempster Brothers, Station Records, MN 558, J.S. Battye Library.

country.[122] Horse deaths were not inconsiderable, with eighty-eight named working horses listed as dying from 1891 to 1898, about one a month. Of these many died from unknown causes, which implies they were worn out by the mallee heat and constant work in hard country. Others died from broken legs, becoming bogged in salt country, eating poison [plants?] and snakebite.

In the late 1890s, the rabbit, defying all predictions to the contrary, crossed the Nullarbor Plain. Two rabbit-proof fences were erected in 1903–04, both running from the coast between Esperance and Albany and heading northwards, devouring forests for their fence posts. Would they work? Westralians held their breath. The fences were not impervious, but they did slow the rabbits, which only reached plague proportions in the 1920s and 1930s, coincidently feeding mallee families in the Depression. However, rabbits made working the land harder, a task that increasingly fell to wheat farmers after 1900.[123]

---

122 Dempster Brothers, 'Horse and Cattle Book Esperance', 1870–1898, MN 558, J.S. Battye Library.
123 Bolton, *Spoils and Spoilers*, 81.

Part Two

Transforming the Mallee 1880–1945

Closer settlement brought dramatic changes to the environment of mallee lands. Sheep and rabbits had wreaked much havoc, but humans, with their machines and horses, inflicted irreversible change on this vast but fragile landscape.

Victoria led the way in the opening of mallee lands to closer settlement. Confident that populating this final frontier with white families would bring civilisation to a much-maligned landscape, successive colonial and state governments subdivided the Victorian Mallee. South Australian governments followed suit in the adjoining Murray Mallee, where local inventions such as the mallee roller and the stump-jump plough enabled economical clearing. The 'howling wilderness' was transformed into fields of wheat. But the removal of the vegetation holding fine ancient soils together left paddocks exposed to the powerful mallee winds, creating the red dust storms that distinguished the region for more than a century.

In the rush to settle eastern mallee lands, little thought was given to the susceptibility of the region to recurring dry periods. The Indigenous owners and the unique ecosystems of the mallee lands were well adapted to the absence of water, but, for many settlers who experienced the Federation Drought, the Mallee seemed to be willing them to fail. Closer settlement eventually forced settlers and governments to come to terms with mallee lands, developing strategies to farm it more productively. Amongst the settlers who survived, there developed an understanding about the personal qualities needed to live and farm in this challenging environment: resilience, tenacity, forbearance, adaptability. Mallee lands were transforming their residents just as the lands themselves were being transformed. However, lessons were not learned at equal pace across mallee lands. Mistakes made in the east would be repeated in the west.

Indigenous people developed strategies in this period to hold or regain small pieces of mallee land and in various ways to stay connected to country.

Chapter 5

A LAND FOR FARMERS

By the end of the nineteenth century pastoralism had generally proved a failure on eastern mallee country, and new visions of wheat farming challenged and soon supplanted that of raising sheep as the main pursuit. The shift to wheat happened a generation earlier in eastern mallee country than in the West. The experience of settlers in the eastern mallee could have prepared those in Western Australia for some of the challenges they might encounter, but it did not always work out that way. It took settlers in the eastern mallee many years to understand the nature of this challenging country. No matter how bold and visionary individual dreams or schemes for settlement might have been, the realities of climate, soil, the absence of a secure water supply and the fickleness of markets would see the hopes of many reduced to dust.

In 1865 the surveyor general of South Australia, George Goyder, published a map of South Australia illustrating an imaginary line running roughly east to west and joining places with a rainfall of ten inches (twenty-five centimetres). North of this line, Goyder warned, wheat growing was an unsafe occupation. But legislative changes in South Australia in the form of the Strangways Act in 1869 meant that settlers with enough cash for a 20 per cent deposit on land could bid for up to 320 acres, regardless of location. Settlers mythologised good seasons through the folklore 'rain follows the plough'; good seasons fuelled optimism and increased agricultural activity and expansion. Farmers recklessly crossed Goyder's line of rainfall. Settlement also took place in the mallee-covered central plains of the Yorke Peninsula and the eastern side of St Vincent Gulf. The old Scrub Lands Act was revived in 1877, and nearly a million acres were taken up over the next four years, much of it mallee.[1]

Technological innovations in the form of the mallee roller, the stump-jump plough and the stripper propelled this settlement from the 1870s. A team of horses or oxen pulled the roller—often an old steam boiler but sometimes a cruder construction made from a large log—over the mallee scrub, reducing it to broken stems. Unbroken stems were cut by axe. After drying, the splintered

---

1   For Goyder's line see, Janis Sheldrick, *Nature's Line: George Goyder, Surveyor, Environmentalist, Visionary* (Adelaide: Wakefield Press, 2015).

mallee was burnt to the spiky lignotuber. The stump-jump plough, designed to hurdle the remaining stumps and the submerged and vigorously sprouting mallee roots, made possible the cultivation of the soil. These two innovations enabled the economic conversion of mallee scrub to wheat fields, shaping the pattern of mallee settlement. Another South Australian invention, the stripper, harvested the grain by removing the heads of wheat from the stalks and left the straw standing, boosting the capacity to farm more efficiently.

While South Australian wheat growing advanced, the Victorian government vacillated on plans for the future of the Mallee, its furthest frontier. A lands commission bent on the triumph of closer settlement recognised the distinguishing feature of the Victorian Mallee—its unique vegetation—and ushered in a policy approach to the region based on this environmental understanding.[2] This 'desolate' country, covered with 'dismal scrub', achieved a special distinction: tailor-made land legislation. The *Mallee Pastoral Leases Act 1883* attempted to advance closer settlement in all but the most 'desolate' of mallee country. The Act divided the Mallee into 10,000-acre blocks and 20,000-acre allotments, with the aim of controlling vermin and ultimately returning control of the land to the Crown once all leases had expired in 1903.[3]

The agrarian ideals of the 1850s resurfaced to play a role in new imaginings of the Victorian Mallee enabled by the 1883 Act. The mallee roller and the stump-jump plough did the rest. Revised understandings of mallee soils also fuelled this vision. Formerly they were derided for their inability to retain moisture. In the 1880s, however, the view changed completely, and it was believed—drawing on anecdote rather than science—that the lighter mallee soils were more suited to wheat than the heavier soils of the Wimmera. The *Weekly Times* declared the Mallee 'splendidly adapted for agriculture'.[4] An agricultural Mallee, settled by small-scale white yeoman farmers—farmers were then conceived to be men and of British descent—would underpin the prosperity of the colony. Aboriginal people after 1860 were being moved onto reserves in Victoria and virtually ineligible for closer settlement. Although after 1886 those of mixed descent were being moved into the wider community, they never seemed white enough to qualify for land. Their continued presence on mallee country as outsiders is the subject of Chapter 8.

---

2   J.M. Powell, *The Public Lands of Australia Felix: Settlement and Land Appraisal in Victoria 1834–91 with Special Reference to the Western Plains* (Melbourne: Oxford University Press, 1970), 204.

3   *Mallee Pastoral Leases Act 1883* (Colony of Victoria), accessed 12 November 2018, http://www8.austlii.edu.au/cgi-bin/viewdb//au/legis/vic/hist_act/tmpla1883242/.

4   *Weekly Times*, 7 April 1888.

The Victorian Mallee was surveyed, mapped, and divided into blocks with some 1.2 million hectares deemed agriculturally viable. An 1883 map shows the initial subdivision with straight lines running at ten-mile intervals, ignoring any natural contours of the land. The demand for land, bolstered by the success of farming on the Wimmera and northern plains of north-central Victoria, and the perceived need to settle farmers' sons, encouraged leaseholders to subdivide allotments for agriculture and turn blocks into allotments for subsequent subdivision. Many unscrupulous leaseholders subdivided mallee land, which they did not own, and sold it off to settlers at tidy profits. In 1889 legislators, trying to catch up with an existing practice, permitted selection of 320 acres for agriculture. Closer settlement could begin in earnest.[5]

As surveyors graded the land, they assigned a classification regarding its suitability for cereal production: first, second, third or fourth–class land. Wide-ranging pastoral holdings, whose size made vermin control difficult, were reduced to multiple bureaucratic bundles. Small landholders were to rescue the land from vermin and reclaim it for intensive agricultural yield.[6] A profound shift in thinking about what the Mallee could be used for became possible. Flora Shaw, writing in 1883 for *The Times* of London, noted that the combined effect of the mallee roller and the stump-jump plough was 'to convert a vermin-infested desert of impenetrable scrub into one vast granary'.[7] Good seasons encouraged optimism. George Everard, a former itinerant worker who had spent many years working on sheep runs in the Mallee, imagined the country transformed: 'In a very few years the whole of the north-western portion of Victoria will be one vast wheat field, affording homes to thousands of prosperous families'.[8]

The idea of the yeoman farmer was central to the vision of a settled, agricultural society. It underpinned closer settlement across Australia and the settlement of mallee lands in particular. This idea migrated with English settlers and drew upon a belief that rural life encompassed true prosperity.

---

5   *An Act to further amend 'The Mallee Pastoral Leases Act 1883' and for other purposes* (Colony of Victoria), accessed 12 November 2018, http://www.austlii.edu.au/au/legis/vic/hist_act/tmaa1885152.pdf.

6   James Mann believed that the shift in responsibility for rabbit control from the government to the settler was central to the government's plan in allowing closer settlement. See James Mann, *Mallee Pioneer: The Recollections of James Barrett Mann, Founder of Morningquest* (Swan Hill: B.R. Mann, 1981).

7   Flora Shaw, 'Victoria: The Mallee Country, "Letters from Australia"', *The Times*, 5 April 1893, 13.

8   George Everard, *Pioneering Days in the Wimmera and Mallee* (Horsham: *Horsham Times* Print, *c.* 1892, reprinted April 1977), 37.

Land should be made productive, and unused land was 'wasted'. The yeoman ideal also embodied the cultural understanding that agriculture was a virtuous, civilising endeavour. This belief in the inherent value of agriculture buttressed the enormous state investment that successive Victorian governments poured into maintaining small-scale farmers on the land. It helps explain why governments later sought to protect farmers from the vicissitudes of the market. Historian David Goodman observed that the market was perceived 'as a threat to be curbed, above all, a threat to a just and natural relationship to the land'.[9]

Flora Shaw, seeking to attract young Englishmen to the Victorian Mallee, observed the difference between Mallee farmers with their civilised conversation and those encountered on the pastoral frontiers where a man might spend weeks on end with only sheep for company. Such isolation had a 'roughening, even brutalizing effect which not ten in one hundred men are able to resist'. A young Englishman could rest assured that in the Mallee he would find 'intelligent relaxation and the society of men of his own standard of development'.[10]

Not everyone shared this vision of a civilised, civilising Mallee. Echoes of the desolation and despair voiced by early white settlers remained. James Mann observed in his recollections of settling in the Quambatook district that it was difficult to get a loan from the bank as the Mallee was viewed as a doubtful investment. Buildings were cheaply constructed in the belief 'that the Mallee land would fail to produce and turn out to be worthless ... It was spoken of as a land of flies and dust and lack of water and starvation'.[11] An account from *The Victorian Tourist's Railway Guide* in 1892 continued to represent the original vegetation as hostile to human habitation and cultivation:

> It is a country that people generally know very little about, that nobody has done much with, that has broken the banks of many men, the hearts of not a few; that contains the skeleton and the ugly ghosts of many a bright dawn. It is haunted by the spirit of the heritage of our desolation; it is endurable only to those who love the wilderness, or who dauntlessly labour for its redemption.[12]

---

9   David Goodman, *Gold Seeking: Victoria and California in the 1850s* (Sydney: Allen & Unwin, 1994), 126.

10 Shaw, 'Victoria', 13.

11 Mann, *Mallee Pioneer*, 48, 54. See also Katie Holmes and Kylie Mirmohamadi, 'Howling Wilderness and Promised Land: Imagining the Victorian Mallee, 1840–1914', *Australian Historical Studies* 46, no. 2 (2015): 191–213.

12 Francis Myers, *The Victorian Tourist's Railway Guide: Edited by 'Telemachus'* (Melbourne: Fergusson & Mitchell, 1892), 133.

Figure 5.1: 'Off to the Mallee Blocks', A.J. Campbell photographer, Echuca District, 1894. This party heads to futures unknown in the Victorian Mallee. They carry a tank, presumably for water, sacks of grain, and other goods. A child sits atop the second cart, and a woman drives a jinker at the back. The photographer, A.J. Campbell, became a well-known ornithologist and wrote about the impact of settlement and land clearing—the activities anticipated in this image—on the birds of the mallee lands.
(Courtesy Museums Victoria, MM 20522,
https://collections.museumvictoria.com.au/items/794683)

The enduring sense of the Mallee as a 'howling wilderness' competed with the new vision of a prosperous wheat belt and added weight to celebrations of the region's subsequent transformation.

One of the great believers in the agricultural transformation of the Victorian Mallee was Edward Lascelles. Lascelles was a pastoralist who had acquired the Lake Corrong sheep station near Hopetoun in 1876, just before rabbits devastated its carrying capacity. He became a passionate advocate for rabbit eradication and for the prospect of the Mallee as a wheat-growing area. The Victorian Lands Department gave Lascelles permission to subdivide a number of his Mallee blocks into 480-acre allotments, and he actively set about promoting the Hopetoun area as one suitable for agriculture.

Lascelles had convinced London *Times* correspondent Flora Shaw to visit Hopetoun and write a feature article for her 'Letters from Australia' series. He then used parts of this article in a prospectus published to promote the area's subdivision. In a triumph of the imagination, Lascelles' prospectus features stylised drawings of Hopetoun, wheat fields and the mallee roller at work and numerous illustrations of lakes and dams, conveying the strong impression of an area where water was plentiful, the lifestyle leisured and the landscape bucolic. The final image of the prospectus is of an imaginary 'Five-thousand acre Mallee wheat field'. A road cuts through its middle, up and over the distant gently undulating hills on the horizon. The unimaginable flat expanse of the Mallee in the Hopetoun area is here softened by a more familiar and appealing suggestion of gently rolling downs: 'the Mallee Roller and Stump-jump Plough have worked a change that can only be understood by a personal visit. Settlers' cottages now dot the undulating ridges of the vast clearings, and thousands of acres of golden grain gladden the eye where before was a vast solitude of dismal scrub'.[13]

In 1898, notwithstanding the evidence of severe drought, the Hon. Donald Melville MLC, a strong advocate of extending the railway to Mildura, claimed attitudes to the Mallee had changed: 'In the place of the mallee being a dreadful desert it is now one immense wheat-field from end to end … capable of yielding, within three years or the like, more than the entire output of our gold-fields'.[14] Lascelles' re-imagining of the Mallee had triumphed; the 'howling wilderness' now suggested opportunities for riches surpassing even the rivers of gold that had flowed from other Victorian regions.

It was not the whole Mallee district, however, that was seen as suitable for agriculture and opened for settlement. Soils across the Mallee varied, with an 1891 report judging one-third 'worthless', one-third suited only for grazing and one-third suited for agriculture.[15] The south-eastern Mallee and the Murray River fringe were the most sought-after areas, and settlers clamoured for them when land was released for settlement by the government or private landholders. Hundreds of hopeful applicants were turned away. Those who were successful soon realised that the government's eagerness to promote land settlement was not matched by its provision of adequate road, rail or water supply.

---

13 *The Mallee Country of Victoria and its Wonderful Resources with Maps and Illustrations* (Melbourne: Alfred Drakard, under instructions from E.H. Lascelles Esq., Prahran and St Kilda Chronicle Offices, 1893), 21.

14 *Mildura Cultivator*, 9 July 1898, 2.

15 Victorian Parliamentary Report, *Report from the Select Committee upon the Settlement of the Mallee Country* (Victoria: Government Printer, 1891), iv.

Figure 5.2: 'Reclaiming the Mallee Scrub', published in the *Illustrated Australian News*, 1892, depicts the process by which the mallee was rolled, burnt and ploughed, thereby making way, as the telescopic insert suggests, for agriculture. The 'useless' scrub was to be reclaimed for the redeeming activity of cultivating the soil.

From the early 1890s settlers led the assault on the Victorian Mallee. As Mallee novelist G.B. Eggleton put it, they 'bit savagely into the dense forest of mallee scrub with their "mallee rollers", driving it ever further from their make-shift homes'.[16] Transformation was rapid, and by 1897 Victoria had eclipsed South Australia as a wheat-producing region, a position it held for thirteen years. Many settlers moved from South Australia, bringing their experience of wheat farming with them. Significant numbers had previously made the journey from Germany. Others came from Ireland, both Protestants from the north and Catholics from the south, and from Scotland and England. Those from South Australia, the Victorian Wimmera and the northern plains were best placed to farm mallee lands, but the government leased land to any settler, regardless of experience or capital.

Settlers' aspirations to settle on the land at the lowest upfront cost melded with government ambitions to establish a white, settled yeomanry. Many arrived with just 'a wagonload of treasured possessions; and the will to win'. The Mallee-born G.B. Eggleton fictionalised the story of his parents' settlement, imagining their interactions with the mallee landscape: 'The threat of drought and shortage of water hung constantly over them. Their roads were bowls of choking dust throughout the dry months, and heart-breaking bogs when the rains came'. The landscape evoked mixed emotions, arousing their senses and causing them to curse the heat and flies while still admiring the 'dust-soaked sweat' produced. The sound of contented horses feeding was as satisfying as the 'roar of a "stripper" in a great quivering stretch of ripe brown wheat; [and] the sudden shock of cold water, gulped from a swinging canvas bag'.[17]

Jack Doran, son of a Beulah settler, had a less poetic memory: 'for sustained misery nothing compared with tramping in a cloud of dust behind a set of harrows from sunrise to sunset'. Winnowing, separating the chaff from the grain, was especially challenging. Early on a hand winnower was turned for days on end at the height of summer leaving you 'only dry hide and bone. Whenever the wind changed you had to drag the winnower around the heap to a new position. It was backbreaking, prickly work and pure slavery'.[18] A horse-driven treadmill could be used to replace hand winnowing. When fields had been sufficiently cleared of mallee roots, the harvester, which both

---

16   G.B. Eggleton, *These Bare Hands* (Mildura: Sunraysia Publishing Co., 1977), 5.
17   Eggleton, *These Bare Hands*, 5.
18   Keith C. Hofmaier, *Mallee Memories: Some Folk History of Beulah and District* (Warracknabeal: *Warracknabeal Herald*, 1976), 19.

stripped and winnowed the crop, replaced the stripper. The revolution in harvesting is described in Chapter six.

The key to the success of settlement in Victoria's Mallee was farming experience, gained sometimes over thirty years, and the willingness of families to work together. A.S. Kenyon, chief engineer of the State Rivers and Water Supply and the Mallee's first historian, believed it could be settled by men with little capital. Many such men did try their hand, but there is little doubt that calling up family capital and using family labour greatly assisted successful settlement. The Mann brothers from Quambatook—an area with good soil and climate—cleared land together and frequently took off-farm work to generate an income until their farm became established. The Coote and Pearse families also illustrate the importance of family labour and support.

Charles Coote, a Mallee farmer and diarist, was the first son of immigrants from Northern Ireland. He learnt farming skills on the family property near Glenloth, 190 kilometres north west of Bendigo. His father acquired an additional block at Narrewillock. When Charles's diary opens in his twenty-fourth year, he was an accomplished user of farm tools and machines—ploughs for cultivating, strippers for harvesting—and a handler of livestock. Growing up on a farm, he also learned a range of other skills such as building haystacks, grubbing trees, and fencing. As a young man, he was well equipped to turn his hand to pioneering. His father's farm of 240 acres offered limited opportunity for supporting three young men and their sister. The Mallee offered new hope.[19]

In 1890, Charles Coote and his younger brother David selected 780 acres on the southern fringe of the Mallee, later the parish of Quambatook. The Coote family developed their Mallee block while working their farm in Narrewillock. The sons moved back and forth between the two blocks in late spring, fallowing at Narrewillock and rolling mallee at Quambatook. Summer saw them harvest—first hay (in Narrewillock) and then grain, and in late summer they burnt the rolled mallee. The key to successful mallee settling was rapidly bringing newly rolled land into production. Within six years the Cootes were cultivating over six hundred acres. In 1896 they extended their operations by purchasing a partially cleared block of a thousand acres west of Quambatook in the parish of Kaniera, which was largely operated by younger brothers David and John. Stock and machinery moved in a triangle between

---

19   Charles Coote's diary spanned 1896 to 1953. Charles William Coote, Diaries and Papers, 1896–1955, 1964.0005, University of Melbourne Archives. A handful of various accounts and some photographs are in the possession of Rohan Walker.

the three properties. When the two mallee blocks were sufficiently cleared, the land at Narrewillock was sold, adding to their capital fund.[20]

William Pearse, from an established Wimmera farming family, selected land in 1891 on the eastern Mallee near Bulga, twenty-four kilometres south of the Murray in the County of Tatchera. Pearse initially made little effort to improve the block, and by July 1893 a mere thirty acres had been rolled. Conditions of leasehold stipulated that settlers needed to 'improve' their land by clearing the mallee scrub, fencing, and building dams and a dwelling. Threatened with forfeiture, Pearse became more active. In September 1893 he let a contract to roll 150 acres of his block, scooped out a dam and started the construction of a house. Over the next few years he developed a pattern of moving backwards and forwards between his father's developed Wimmera farm and his Mallee selection. By the season of 1895 he was cropping over three hundred acres. The allure of the Mallee was the ability to rapidly turn raw mallee into cropping land and obtain a quick return on investment. Pearse had the added advantage of capital support from his father's farm.[21]

Mallee farmers needed access to transport for their farms to be viable. The building of railways was one of the ways the Victorian and South Australian governments actively encouraged the process of settlement. Railways were essential for carting grain to markets, but in the Federation Drought they carted water into the Mallee. In 1890 the Melbourne–Kerang railway was linked to Swan Hill, providing access to markets for settlers on the eastern fringes of the Mallee. In the early 1890s most towns in the southern Mallee—Birchip (1893), Sea Lake (1895), Jeparit (1894), Quambatook (1894) and Rainbow (1898)—were also linked to Melbourne. The Victorian parliament's Standing Committee on Railways oversaw railway building, its members regularly hearing evidence from hopeful settlers. Charles Coote, who quickly developed a lifelong passion for rural politics, keenly attended hearings and gave evidence.

---

20 For the clearing of the Coote farms at Meering West, see Department of Conservation, Forests and Lands, VPRS 5357/P0 Land Selection and Correspondence Files, Unit 1773, 412/218K & P0/1846/413/218k, Public Record Office Victoria (PROV), and the Coote Diary, 1896. The progress of the Meering West and Kaniera farms, including cropping details and yields, is set out in Charles Coote Accounts, 1896–1917, within Coote, Diaries and Papers.

21 William Pearse's original selection was in the Parish of Nowie, VPRS 5357/P0, Unit 1918, 2786/218K, PROV. William Alfred Joseph Pearse, Diaries, 1892–1947, MS 12961, Box 1715/1–12, State Library Victoria. See 7 July 1893, 20 September 1893 and 1 February 1896.

In South Australia, over-extension of new farming lands in the 1870s and disastrous seasons in the early 1880s dampened the desire for continued mallee settlement. Politicians anxiously watched farmers cross the border to take up Victorian Mallee lands. By 1900, confidence in South Australian agriculture had revived with new farming techniques. Farming land was rested or fallowed every third year; its fertility was boosted by applying superphosphate every cropping year; and it was made more efficient with each advance in machinery. New strains of wheat were developed too. South Australians also pioneered the interior of the Eyre Peninsula and the Pinnaroo lands in the south-east corner of the Murray Mallee.

Throughout the Murray Mallee, rainfall is only just over ten inches (25.4 centimetres) per year, although it reaches twenty-five inches (63.5 centimetres) on the southern edge. Soils on the southern edge of the Ninety Mile Plain were similar to the pale sandy loam soils of the adjacent Victorian Mallee. A lack of surface streams and the porous soils covered by rugged mallee vegetation made the land 'uninviting, uncertain and unsought' to agricultural settlers until the 1890s.[22] The process of mullenising—clearing the land through rolling, cutting, heaping and burning—and the example of settlement in the adjoining Victorian Mallee encouraged official inspections and inquiries into the suitability of the Pinnaroo lands for wheat. Although an inspection party made a favourable report in 1893, financial depression and droughts from 1897 to 1902 meant little was done.

A change in South Australian land tenure and alienation was introduced in 1888 permitting leases with the right of purchase or perpetual lease, after land classification by local land boards. Boards assessed the land and set the price at a minimum of 2s 6d, up to a maximum of £1 per acre.[23] From 1908, advances of up to £400 were granted for improvements, £250 for living expenses and £200 for livestock. The size of the block was determined by its unimproved capital value. A settler could purchase land to the value of £5,000 and, in theory, purchase five thousand acres of First Class Land.

---

22 John Andrews, 'The Emergence of the Wheat Belt in Southeastern Australia to 1830', in *Frontiers and Men: A Volume in Memory of Griffith Taylor, 1880–1963*, ed. John Andrews (Melbourne: F.W. Cheshire, 1967), 17.

23 Under perpetual lease the settler paid 4 per cent per annum of the purchase price and this price was set for all time. A conditional purchaser made no payment for the first four years. From the beginning of the sixth year a low interest of 2 per cent was charged, which increased to 4 at the beginning of the eleventh year. At this point the settler began to pay down the capital at the rate of £5.64 in every £100 of purchase price. Settlers were required to ring fence the property in six years and generally reside for nine moths per year.

This permitted South Australian farmers to obtain larger farms than their contemporaries in Victoria.[24]

These measures, and the success of Victorian settlers, encouraged settlement along the northern fringe of the South Australian Murray Mallee, with land being selected at distances of forty kilometres from the Murray River. By 1902 the Pinnaroo country on the western fringe was also taken up. In the same year, a royal commission recommended, not without dissent, the construction of a railway from Pinnaroo to Tailem Bend on the Melbourne to Adelaide line. It opened in 1906 and by 1908 all the land within ten miles of the line crossing the southern fringe of the Murray Mallee was taken. The area sown to wheat in the counties of Chandos and Buccleugh grew from a mere seven thousand acres in 1905 to 180,000 acres in 1910.[25]

This success overcame official caution. Settlement in the more northern counties of Alfred and Albert was promoted by an 'orgy of railway construction'. Between 1910 and 1916 surveyors could barely keep pace with the demands of settlers. The government cleared land for roads, sunk bores and wells, and added the cost of these to the price of land. In less than twenty years the South Australian agricultural frontier was extended by five million acres and moved from areas where the rainfall was fifteen inches to only seven and a half inches. In the Murray Mallee the area sown to wheat grew from 57,317 acres in 1898 to 520,628 acres in 1916, an almost tenfold increase.[26]

The settlement of the Eyre Peninsula reflects a similar story of expansion. Before 1883 settlers moved into the coastal areas of the Eyre Peninsula—in the counties of Flinders, Musgrave and Jervois—where rainfall was sufficient to encourage agriculture and transport was available by ship. By 1883 30,729 acres were sown to wheat on the Eyre Peninsula. At this stage Eyre was a more important agricultural district than the Murray Mallee, a position it maintained until the early twentieth century. From 1907 railway construction pushed into the lower rainfall districts of the peninsula, and by 1915 the railway had opened up areas where the rainfall was ten inches or less. The government surveyed blocks ten miles either side of the rail and constructed

---

24   The conditions for settlement in South Australia are set out in: Western Australia, 'Report of the Royal Commission on the Mallee Belt and Esperance Lands', *Votes and Proceeding of the Parliament of Western Australia*, 1917, paper no. 5, Appendix no. 9, 137–8.

25   E. and L. Dunsdorfs, *Historical Statistics of the Australian Wheat Growing Industry* (Melbourne: University of Melbourne, 1956), 53–6.

26   Andrews, 'The Emergence of the Wheat Belt', 21.

underground tanks in several areas. By 1914 just over half a million acres was sown to wheat.[27]

By the outbreak of World War I settlement in both the Murray Mallee and the Eyre Peninsula had spread beyond Goyder's line. This agricultural expansion followed the Victorian practice of providing liberal terms for settlers. Most importantly South Australia offered larger areas than Victoria to settlers. In the long run this enabled South Australian farmers to make better use of new methods of mechanised farming.

Clearing and Farm Making

Among prospective farmers in Victoria in the 1890s and South Australia in the early twentieth century, the appeal of the Mallee was the speed with which a marketable crop could be obtained. In Victoria in the 1890s, prospective farmers could move into the forests of South Gippsland or the Otway Ranges, but they faced a lifetime's work clearing the towering mountain ash and its dense understorey of scrub. The Mallee was promoted as an area where a young man with little capital could gain a foothold on the agricultural ladder. The experiences of William Pearse and Charles Coote reveal the rapidity of their clearing and crop sales. Governments supported this by building railways, thereby allowing grains to be dispatched to Melbourne or Adelaide for export sales.

In 1918 John Gray, a South Australian settler, gave a practical account of what was involved in clearing the mallee to a Western Australian commission into settlement in the Esperance district. Gray purchased 1,566 acres from the South Australian government around 1907–08 (his first crop was in the season 1908–09) at a variable cost of 3s to 17s per acre. Government surveyors initially judged only half his block near Parilla, mid-way between Pinnaroo and Lameroo, to be arable. The existing vegetation consisted of mallee and broom, with scrub pine on the rises. The tallest mallee was five to seven metres, the rest low and stunted. It was all, nonetheless, 'good rolling stuff'. Gray seemed unaware of the importance mallee scrub played in binding the fine soil together, harbouring wildlife, and enabling a complex ecosystem to thrive. He explained that most settlers in his district rolled the scrub. A man with a team of seven horses and an iron roller three metres wide could roll about ninety acres a week. On his own block, he rolled seven hundred acres in the first year, besides carting a large amount of chaff and building materials.

---

27   Andrews, 'The Emergence of the Wheat Belt', 24–5; Dundsdorfs, *Historical Statistics of the Australian Wheat Growing Industry*, 56–7.

Figure 5.3: Mallee rollers could be crude in their construction, such as this one made from a tree trunk, but still devastating in their power. Here Bill Boyd (senior) is pictured with a team of bullocks attached to the roller. Photograph Bill Boyd, Nandaly, Bimbourie, Victoria, 1920.
(Courtesy Museums Victoria, MM 2224, https://collections.museumvictoria.com.au/items/771565)

Rolling was a winter job. Before summer, a firebreak was made by 'throwing all the heavy mallee back from the boundary about half a chain and burning all the smaller mallee and bushes'. The 'springbacks', which defied the roller, were cut by hand to assure a good burn.[28]

The burning season in South Australia was from 1 February to 15 October. A hot windy day was good for burning. Before the main burn, a firebreak of about fifty metres was burnt on the lee side of the paddock to prevent the fire running out of control. After a good burn, Gray explained, there would not be too much clearing to do. If the mallee was heavy there would be snags to cut, and probably some picking up to be done; any remaining sticks were raked into a heap.[29]

The distinct advantage of mallee over other forms of clearing was that cropping began before the roots were grubbed out. In the autumn and winter,

---

28   Western Australia, 'Report of the Royal Commission on the Mallee Belt and Esperance Lands', 150–11. This report contains valuable information from Murray Mallee settlers.

29   Western Australia, 'Report of the Royal Commission on the Mallee Belt and Esperance Lands', 150.

after the first burn, the soil was prepared with a stump-jump plough. As the crop grew in the field, shoots from the roots would be slashed. After harvest, when the grain was winnowed, bagged and carted to the railway sidings, the stubble was burnt. The burning, combined with the physical damage of the plough, eventually killed the roots. After the first few seasons of cropping, farmers started to fallow their fields. The ploughs and scarifiers used in fallowing also damaged surviving mallee roots. The ploughman and his team of horses were followed by a labourer—or family member—who painstakingly grubbed out, lifted and carted away the roots. Some were transported by rail to Melbourne and Adelaide as firewood, some used as fuel for heating and cooking, but most were simply piled up and burnt.[30]

Horses were 'the powerhouse of the farm' and before the advent of tractors were central to the activities of ploughing, seeding, cropping, travelling and carting water.[31] Farmers relied on them, and many took great pride in a team of well-cared-for horses. Charles Coote frequently made mention in his diary of the activities of his horses. On Sunday 4 June 1911, Coote reflected on the progress of his cropping work:

> We take manure, seed and horse feed—nose bags—to paddock in wagon and feed at dinner time in harness—no water. Harry works scarifier with 6 [horses] abreast and does about 18 acres a day with 69 cwt. I work 4 [horses] in new 15 foot Massey Harris drill and seed 20 acres putting about 48 lbs of federation wheat and 48 lbs of Wischer super per acre.

Careful horse management was essential. Coote's seeding commenced on 16 May 1911 and finished on 1 July. At its end, he observed that the horses were:

> Fairly poor considering they have eaten about 400 bushels of oats and about 20 tons of hay for 12 regularly fed. Bad shoulders and necks are common with them—the worst they have been yet. There were no colds or sickness of any kind among them though colds have been common in the district.

As a critical item of capital, farmers had to make sure they had an adequate horse team, and breeding new stock was important. Coote normally had his horses serviced with locally sourced stock and timed their births for the spring.

---

30   Western Australia, 'Report of the Royal Commission on the Mallee Belt and Esperance Lands', evidence of A.B. Thiele, A.J.A. Koch and H.H. Bettess on clearing, 149–50.

31   Rebecca Jones, *Slow Catastrophes: Living with Drought in Australia* (Melbourne: Monash University Publishing, 2017), 57.

Figure 5.4: The Holding Brothers outside their Mallee camp, c. 1910. Many early settlers spent years living in basic accommodation, sometimes little more than a tent, as they cleared their blocks and sought to establish themselves on firmer foundations.
(Courtesy Museums Victoria, MM 4284,
https://collections.museumvictoria.com.au/items/769682)

In 1911 three horses were pregnant, and their birthing caused much difficulty. In October 1911, Rose, a five-year-old mare in foal, fell in a muddy dam and could not get herself up. They tried to drag her out with two carts but she fell again after five minutes. In desperation, Coote sought advice from a vet, forty-one kilometres away in Kerang. His advice was to place her in a sling and not overfeed her. He gave Coote a 'drench', charged him £1 1s and said it would be £3 3s if he came to visit.[32]

Although Rose survived the birth of her foal, another mare, Judy, died within a week of giving birth. In an age without antibiotics, medicines were of little value. Judy was given '3 doses of aconite, 2 of laudanum and 2 injections each for bowels and womb'. These were of little use and she died 'in great agony'. As was common among farmers, Coote conducted an amateur autopsy on poor Judy.[33] A death of an old and loyal horse was a

---

32 Coote, Diary, 19 October and 2, 19, 21 November 1911.
33 Coote, Diary, 26 November 1911.

sad occasion. In December 1912 Bess died during the harvest, and Coote wrote: 'we pulled her to a stump heap near the hay stack and put [mallee] roots on her. She was 24 years old and had worked for 22 years faithfully and well and practically died in harness as I took the collar off her for the last time last night'.[34]

Horses helped transform mallee country as did machines. The National Archives of Australia contain many patents for mallee-killing machines, testament to both the ingenuity of farmers and implement makers and the resilience of mallee eucalypts. Several machines invented in the 1910s and 20s used a firebox or oil burners to scorch 'mallee shoots and other noxious growths'. One horse-drawn machine patented in 1921 was designed to lever mallee shoots out of the ground. In 1932, a farmer from Peake in the Murray Mallee, patented a formidable-looking machine that cut mallee shoots by means of a row of blades mounted so as to operate in scissor fashion.[35] Such machines presumably sought to speed up the process of exhausting the mallees' resilience by subjecting the lignotuber to repeated assaults on the shoots. However, none were sufficiently effective or economic to see them widely adopted. Even without such machines, men and horses, metal implements and fire transformed a semi-arid and complex ecosystem uniquely adapted to a variable climate into a monoculture of wheat. Some oats were grown as hay and grain for horse feed.

The human labour involved in clearing inflicted a heavy toll. Poet John Shaw Neilson's family took up a selection in the Mallee in 1895. Neilson's autobiography provides a rare insight into the physical and mental cost that work in the Mallee exacted. The Neilson family was desperately poor and frequently worked to clear scrub for money. A repeated thumb injury ultimately led Neilson himself to a breakdown. He spent five weeks in hospital, and it was eighteen months before he could work again. It became something of a pattern. His brothers fared no better. One brother developed 'dry pleurisy', which they attributed to the heavy axe work he had undertaken as a teenager. In 1915 another brother also had a nervous breakdown, caused, the family believed, by 'the strenuous life he had been leading. The hard work and worry brought about by the drought'.[36]

---

34 Coote, Diary, 14 December 1912.
35 '[Patent No. 1921001387]—An improved mallee stump lever plough', 16th April 1921, A13882, 1387/1921B0, National Archives of Australia (NAA); '[Patent No. 1932010355]—A machine for cutting mallee shoots', 29th November 1932, A13882, 10355/1932B0, NAA.
36 John Shaw Neilson, *The Autobiography of John Shaw Neilson* (Canberra: National Library of Australia, 1978), 85.

Drought

Plants, birds and animals evolved on the semi-arid southern mallee lands attuned to extended dry periods. Indigenous owners adapted to the highly variable climate by moving around the country as water availability and other resources dictated. In seeking permanent settlement, European settlers asked more of the land than it could reliably provide; without water, crops die, farm animals die, and people suffer. When settlers experienced an extended dry period in the 1890s, they initially called it a 'water famine', and then a 'drought'. The term implied that the normal condition was sufficient rainfall, whereas extended dry spells are natural in mallee country.

Drought is as much a human as an environmental event. The lack of rain associated with drought is not only a natural event that parches the land but a socio-economic one that dries up agricultural industry, and has emotional and cultural implications as well. The response of the Victorian government to this situation in the Mallee was to bring water from afar, making on-going settlement possible. The continuing agricultural productivity of the area and the desire to establish settlers on the land were seen as worth this cost. But many settlers fell victim to the ravages of drought before the state stepped in to alleviate their suffering.

One of the primary determinants of drought in eastern Australia is now known as the El Niño Southern Oscillation, or just El Niño for short.[37] When European settlers arrived in the eastern mallee lands from the 1840s onwards, they had no idea about the susceptibility of the region to prolonged dry periods, nor how variable the climate could be. Most came from areas where weather patterns were stable and predictable and severe drought unknown. But, by the time the Mallee and Murray Mallee were opened for closer settlement, pastoralists had experienced what drought could do, and knowledge of the susceptibility of the area to drought had become more widespread. The problem was actively discussed by the Victorian press in 1880 at the time the Victorian government was considering closer settlement there. But the vision of a settled agricultural population cultivating the vast

---

37 The scientific understanding of El Niño began in the 1920s and has grown rapidly in more recent years. Eastern Australia's weather patterns are shaped by complex ocean–atmosphere systems that determine the sea surface temperature across the Pacific Ocean. An El Niño event typically occurs every three to four years and results in hotter and drier years in eastern Australia, especially if they coincide with other variables such as a Pacific Decadal Oscillation. La Niña events, which usually follow El Niño, typically bring cooler temperatures and above-average rainfall. In the eastern mallee lands this means that rains vary from ample to non-existent. Dry years are frequent, and sometimes extended.

region was too enticing to resist. Those who voiced caution were disregarded in the enthusiasm for arable land and the desire to settle Australia's 'empty' spaces.

In a mood of optimism, and despite dry years in the early 1880s, the Victorian government opened up areas for settlement regardless of adequate water supply. It was not long before the dry years returned and what became known as the Federation Drought brought dust and desolation to the golden fields. The drought lasted from 1895 to 1903 across five states, driving communities to despair and governments to request prayers for rain. It was more severe in the east of the continent than in the west, NSW losing two-thirds of all its stock. In western NSW, north of mallee country, six million acres were abandoned to rabbits. The Federation Drought was particularly severe in the Mallee where the average rainfall dropped by two-thirds, exposing the environmental limits of farming in the eastern mallee lands. The *Argus*, which had long been sceptical of the agricultural potential of the region, voiced the despair:

> there is a province in Victoria from which almost all hope has gone and where famine conditions prevail. It is a land where food is scarce, and where water is so short that people have almost learned to do without it; it is a region that is without money, and from which credit has almost vanished. This country is the mallee.[38]

The Federation Drought was the first major drought experienced by a significant number of farmers in the Victorian and the less-developed South Australian Mallee. As the 'water famine' took hold in the late 1890s, local papers such as the *Sea Lake Times* called on the colonial government to provide water to those to whom it had readily leased land and not leave them 'without the helping hand of the State'.[39] Three months later the *Mildura Cultivator* ran a simple news item: 'The Sea Lake tank is dry. Water trains have been telegraphed for, but so far there has been no reply. Settlers are in great distress'.[40] The government eventually sent water trains, farmers sleeping with their carts along the sidings in order to be first to receive the precious fluid.

Metropolitan papers printed stories of the desperation that visitors encountered in the Mallee. 'Is the mallee worth saving?' the *Argus* asked in 1898.[41]

---

38   'The Thirsty Mallee', *Argus*, 8 March 1898.
39   *Sea Lake Times*, 18 December 1897.
40   *Mildura Cultivator*, 26 March 1898.
41   *Argus*, 17 March 1898.

Fig 5.5: The susceptibility of the mallee lands to drought made the search for underground water urgent. This South Australian image depicts the first artesian bore in mallee lands. The image appears to have been enhanced with additional detail drawn on the men, the bore-drilling equipment, the dog, the tank and even the spouting water. Only the background looks untouched. Bores began to be sunk in the South Australian and Victorian mallee lands in the 1890s when water was located within a sandstone aquifer, about thirty metres below ground. As this enhanced image makes clear, the successful sinking of a bore was worth recording!
(Courtesy State Library of South Australia, PRG 280/1/6/455)

In 1901, the same paper remarked that the Mallee was 'not a picturesque part of the country at any time', and described a land 'baked so hard that it is impossible to plough'. The reporter added that the Mallee farmer nevertheless kept 'battling away, against fate as it were, and struggling with a heroism which commands respect and admiration'.[42] About half of the mallee farmers walked off their farms, and the men from surviving families often left the farm in search of work. James and Bob Mann both went to Western Australia.

In 1902 most farms produced nothing at all as struggling crops could barely sustain any remaining sheep and horses. 'By the end of September',

---

42   *Argus*, 28 May 1901.

recalled James Mann, 'the whole countryside was eaten out as bare as a fallow paddock'.[43] Mann observed that it was difficult for people to believe the extent of the failure of the crop—nothing in their experience had prepared them for the harshness of this drought. The *Sea Lake Times* reported in disbelief: The fields were 'parched and bare' and there was 'nothing to sustain' livestock or farmer.[44] The idea that the Mallee actively willed farmers to fail, that the land periodically unleashed its own spirit against those who sought to tame it, appeared repeatedly around 1900. It was a perception reinforced by recurrent drought.

Drought is defined by lack of rain but is accompanied by high temperatures, searing winds and scorched hopes. Rebecca Jones argues in her book *Slow Catastrophes: Living with Drought in Australia* that drought confronts the senses. It can be seen, felt, heard and tasted. It 'stroked the skin of its subjects', while the dust it generated 'coated the body, seeped into the pores of the skin and filled ears, eyes and mouth'.[45] Early settlers in the Mallee were particularly ill equipped to protect themselves from the extremes drought inflicted. Houses were rudimentary at best, and most settlers had to cart water from distant sources. The Pearse family lived in a house made from native cypress and lined with calico bags. The floor was earthen and there was a square hole in the wall for a window, covered with a wheat bag. When the family upgraded their accommodation in 1908, they moved to a three-room hut made from corrugated iron. As Jones notes, it would have 'braised the occupants in their own sweat'.[46] Although Pearse had water tanks, they ran dry each summer, and he had to cart water from the public tanks at Bulga eight kilometres away, Waikerie, eleven kilometres away, or from the Murray River, twenty-two kilometres away. The round trip of sixteen to forty kilometres, hauling four hundred gallons of water through heat and sand, strained both horse and master.[47]

Adding to the physical strain of drought was the impact of watching valuable and loved animals die. Pearse lost nine horses in the drought, lamenting in 1896, 'it is a terror all my best horses are gone. I have not strength to pull

---

43 Mann, *Mallee Pioneer*, 57.
44 *Sea Lake Times*, November 1902, quoted in Jennifer A. McLennan, *Time, Tide and the Tyrrell: A History of the Shire of Wycheproof* (Melbourne: Hargreen Publishing, 1994), 121.
45 Jones, *Slow Catastrophes*, 280, 281.
46 Jones, *Slow Catastrophes*, 285.
47 Jones, *Slow Catastrophes*, 59.

wagon'.[48] Like many other horses, five of Pearse's died with bellies full of sand ingested while trying to scrounge feed from barren paddocks.

Legacies of Drought

Recognising that a more reliable water supply was crucial if settlement in the Mallee was to be viable, the Victorian government began a scheme to dig open channels that would carry water from the Grampians, the Murray and the Goulburn rivers. The scheme provided work for hundreds of unemployed men and local farmers ruined by drought. Once the channels were constructed, keeping them clear of sand drift would continue to employ many a Mallee man. What became an extensive 17,500-kilometre network of channels continued to provide water to the Victorian Mallee until the Wimmera–Mallee pipeline was opened in 2010.

The extension of the rail network also increased the state's ability to provide assistance to farmers in times of desperation and enabled further areas of the Mallee to be opened for settlement. The 1902 'Final Report from the Parliamentary Standing Committee on Railways' advised that rail needed to be in place before new areas were made available for lease and that settlement needed to be 'on soil which is likely to sustain families'. The committee also advised that land should not even be classified until provided with water.[49] Despite the severity of the Federation Drought, there seems to have been no consideration about whether closer settlement of the Mallee itself was a good idea. It was assumed that water and rail and the new science of 'Dry Farming' (see next chapter) would make future droughts manageable, and the government was prepared to invest in the infrastructure needed to enable settlement to happen.

The Federation Drought was the first of many major droughts of the twentieth century. The human response to the calamity established a way of talking about drought in the Mallee that has endured. It is a narrative of farmers being pushed to the limits of endurance but repaid tenfold if they had the stamina to withstand the trials of Mallee life. Farming in the Mallee 'entails one of the most strenuous and resolute battles with Nature', the *Mildura Cultivator* advised in 1912, and it required particular characteristics: 'the exercise of wise judgments, great fore-sight, boundless

---

48   Jones, *Slow Catastrophes*, 57.
49   Victoria, 'Final Report from the Parliamentary Standing Committee on Railways on the Question of Mallee Water Supply: Together with the Appendices and Minutes of Evidence' (Melbourne: Robt S. Brain, Government Printer, 1902).

resource, and infinite adaptability'.⁵⁰ The Mallee had enormous 'recuperative power'.⁵¹ After drought would come abundance, a story inflected with hints of a Christian resurrection narrative.

The Federation Drought was formative in other ways. It taught profound lessons to the farmers who lived through it and managed to stay on their land. The best farmers learnt to shape their practices to the conditions of the climate and the land. In *Slow Catastrophe*, Rebecca Jones draws on the diaries of a number of famers to explore the different strategies they used to cope with drought. Of William Pearse she notes that his family had support from extended family and a broad community network, which, along with very abstemious living and self-sufficiency in food, enabled the family to survive years when they had barely any farm income.⁵²

Charles Coote, like Neilson, took off-farm work to survive and keep his family fed. Coote became a highly successful farmer, and the Federation Drought was formative to his success. He learnt to expect a variable rainfall and plan for drought, taking advantage of the years of plenty to stockpile grain and fodder. He installed large ground-water tanks and ensured that he would 'keep excess as a buffer against years of scarcity'.⁵³ His methods reflect both years of learning and the biblical model of using the years of plenty to harbour resources for the lean years. With this strategy, when the 1914 drought hit, Coote had five ground tanks, plus large roof tanks, '220 bags of oats, 50 tons of hay and 1233 bags of wheat, some of which he sold at a price inflated by drought and war'.⁵⁴

The 1914 drought was short lived but brutal. It affected all the southern mallee lands. Large sections of the region received no winter or early spring rains, resulting in the lowest annual rainfall then on record. William Pearse broke his plough on the baked soil. Having learnt the toll drought took on his horses from 'sanding' during the Federation Drought, Pearse sent two of them away on agistment, likewise two cows and calves. The 1914 drought once again exposed the lack of a secure water supply for the Mallee, and many of the channels that had been built to carry water into the region filled with

---

50   *Mildura Cultivator*, 6 January 1912, 4. These motifs have developed into a discourse of resilience, especially in response to drought. See Deb Anderson, 'Drought, Endurance and "The Way Things Were": The Lived Experience of Climate and Climate Change in the Mallee', *Australian Humanities Review* 45 (November 2008), accessed 12 November 2018, http://australianhumanitiesreview.org/2008/11/01/drought-endurance-and-the-way-things-were-the-lived-experience-of-climate-and-climate-change-in-the-mallee/.
51   *Argus*, 9 February 1910.
52   Jones, *Slow Catastrophes*, 66–74.
53   Jones, *Slow Catastrophes*, 83.
54   Jones, *Slow Catastrophes*, 86.

sand, rendering them useless. Pearse found himself carting water in the spring of 1913 and continued to do so until the breaking of the drought in autumn 1915. He harvested nothing in 1914.[55]

In South Australia it was a similar story. Near Karoonda two settlers, 'J.B.' and his mate, simply 'left the property to look after itself, trucked [their] horses to Adelaide' and got carpentry work. The South Australian government provided drought relief including wheat seed, superphosphate, fodder and food. The Victorian government also stepped in with assistance in the form of seed and fodder. Such aid enabled some farmers to stay on their blocks and wait for the abundant rain that fell in June 1915. It also set in place a pattern of government intervention during drought years that effectively enabled farmers to remain on their land, revealing once again the enormous investment successive governments made to develop mallee lands for agriculture and maintain farmers on their leaseholds.

The 1914 drought is remembered for its severity and for its concurrence with the outbreak of World War I. The scarcity of work in country areas as a result of the drought led many young men to enlist and helped fuel the idea that the Anzacs' purported fighting prowess stemmed from the fit and healthy country men who swelled the ranks. Their remittances home may in turn have kept their families on the land. Another legacy of drought was that survivors capitalised on the misfortune of those forced to abandon the mallee and purchased blocks cheaply. Many leading farming families owed their accumulation of land to the early acquisition strategies of their forebears. Success bred success. Larger blocks enabled farmers to produce more in times of plenty, providing a buffer for the lean years.

Dust Storms

Land clearing and drought bred a new form of environmental catastrophe. The problem of dust was anticipated by the earliest European explorer to the region. When Major Thomas Mitchell travelled through the eastern mallee in 1836, he observed that the sand was so loose that 'but for this dwarf tree and prickly grass, the sand must have drifted so as to overwhelm the vegetation of adjacent districts'.[56] In 1883, in response to an *Argus* editorial encouraging the

---

55 Pearse, Diary, the entries for November and December simply do not mention harvesting.
56 Major Mitchell, quoted in Alfred S. Kenyon, *The Story of the Mallee: A History of the Victorian Mallee Read before the Historical Society of Victoria, 18 March 1912* (Melbourne: Wilke & Co., 1982), 27.

clearing of the Mallee, a correspondent argued the same point: 'what keeps the sand now within the mallee from being blown is the scrub upon it. Remove that, and you would have thousands upon thousands of acres of valuable land ... rendered utterly useless'.[57] The propensity of the mallee to 'blow' emerged from its ancient history. The sand ridges that run east–west across the eastern mallee were formed by wind activity. As our *Argus* correspondent realised, by the time Europeans arrived, these were being protected from erosion by the mallee scrub. Once that cover was removed and the soil cultivated, the sand ridges once again became mobile.

Stories abound of what it was like to experience a mallee dust storm: of the dark descending, of not being able to see more than a hand's width in front of you, of Christmas dinners ruined, fences disappearing, and the domestic clean-up needed once the dust had settled, only for it to start all over again.

To those who experienced the first major dust storm in the Victorian Mallee in November 1902, it seemed that the end of the world had come. Howling winds blew in early November carrying ash and soil from the South Australian Mallee. The whole land appeared to move, as James Mann recalled in his memoirs of his early experiences of farming near Quambatook:

> On the approach of the first storm the sky looked terrifying, rolling up in red, black and blue color in the west and the gust came on slowly without noise. A most peculiar stillness prevailed, the fowls went to roost, cattle turned their tails to the west and stood with their heads down.

As the dust blacked out all light, 'one could not see one's hand when placed before the eyes'. When the sun reappeared, the country was desolate: 'Dams and depressions were filled with sand, fences in some cases, especially wire netting ones were buried and drains filled up ... the havoc inside the houses was pitiful'.[58] In January 1903 the dust blew again, this time silting up tanks and smothering rail lines throughout the region.[59]

As settlement and clearing continued apace, dust storms became more frequent. A combination of factors added to the susceptibility of the soil to 'drift'. Clearing the vegetation was the first step in the process, and, for small farmers where every strip of land could contribute to an income, even timber previously left as wind breaks was cleared, accelerating the drift and dust

---

57 *Argus*, 13 September 1883.
58 Mann, *Mallee Pioneer*, 56.
59 McLennan, *Time, Tide and the Tyrrell*, 116.

storms.[60] Farmers were under pressure to clear as it was considered part of 'improving' the land and a condition of leasehold. The farming practices widely adopted in the early decades of the twentieth century added significantly to the problem. The chief culprit was the practice of fallowing, whereby some fields were kept free of crop to enable farmers to control for weeds, and to replenish the soil after the previous year's crops. Like clearing, fallowing was considered a feature of good farming, and farmers were strongly encouraged to practise bare fallowing. But fallowing deprived the fine ancient soil of any vegetation that would hold it in place, leaving it vulnerable to the harsh mallee winds.

As dust storms and 'drift' increased in their intensity and frequency, they came to be seen as part of Mallee life. Before 1900 the Victorian Mallee had been dubbed a 'howling wilderness'. In the twentieth century, the wind became another punishing feature of mallee life, as if trying to rid the land of those who dared to rest upon it. As settlers pushed north into sandier and drier country the propensity of soil to drift intensified, making these early dust storms a foretaste of things to come.

---

60   Carl Beer, *Amongst the Last of the Pioneers: A Story of the Pioneering Days of the Mallee and Millewa* (Mildura: Larena Media Services, 1986), 24.

Chapter 6

DEVELOPING MALLEE FARMS 1914–1925

The First World War and the Recovery from Drought

War brings both devastation and opportunities, and this was the case when Australia joined Britain in the war against Germany. It also revealed the vulnerability of mallee farmers to external forces such as markets and transport, both unpredictable like the weather, and prompted government interventions designed to temper these forces. As major pre-war suppliers of Britain's wheat, Australian producers were initially seen as crucial to the war effort. However, the 1914 drought stymied these plans, and the government was forced to import wheat for domestic consumption to cover the shortfall and provide seed for the 1915 season. To boost the war effort, the Commonwealth exhorted farmers to increase their planting for the 1915–16 season, but transport disruptions threatened any benefits.[1]

Charles Coote of Quambatook in the Victorian Mallee continued assiduously to maintain his 50-year long diary during this period. This allows us to track the thinking of a farmer who was in many ways typical of mallee experience and yet in other ways atypical because of his cautiousness and ultimate success. As a careful farmer, Charles Coote had cash reserves and a good supply of wheat to weather the 1914 drought.[2] He released his wheat on to the market in October 1914, selling at the price fixed by the government. In December he fulminated against 'Labour Socialist domination' and considered he had lost over £350, equivalent to three times the annual wage of an urban labourer or twice the wage of a skilled urban tradesman. This loss occurred because the government imported wheat in December 1914 at prices well above what he

---

1 Ernest Scott, *Australia during the War, Vol. XI, Official History of Australia in the War of 1914–18* (Sydney: Angus & Robertson, 1936), 582.
2 He held 3,900 bushels of wheat 1,200 bushels of oats and 45 tons of hay. Charles Coote, Diary, 13 October 1913, in Charles William Coote, Diaries and Papers, 1896–1955, 1964.0005, University of Melbourne Archives.

had received.[3] Coote, however, soon joined many other mallee wheat farmers in profiting from the federal government's intervention in the market and from generally good seasons in the years immediately after the drought, including an exceptional year in 1916. It happened this way (see Figures 6.1 and 6.2).

Figure 6.1: Charles and Ada Coote on their wedding day 28 July 1915.
Charles Coote worked his Mallee block for two decades before he was married at the late age of 43 to Ada Edwards, a music teacher aged 38.
By the time of his marriage his farm was a success.
(Courtesy Rohan Walker)

---

3   Coote, Diary, 28 November 1914 and 6 December 1914. Urban wages were published in *Victorian Statistical Register of the State of Victoria for the Year 1915*, Part VIII, 'Production'.

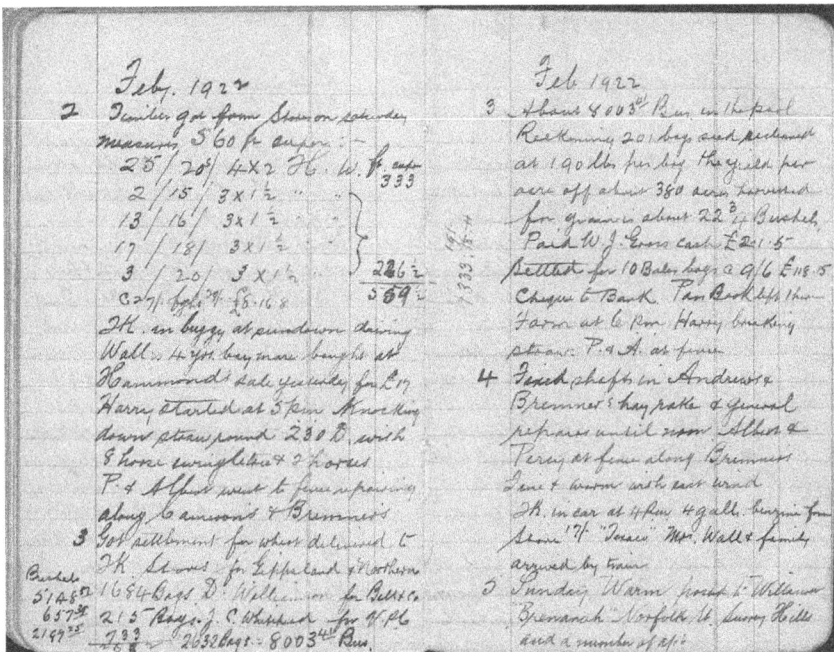

Figure 6.2: Charles Coote, Diary, February 1922. Charles Coote meticulously recorded the progress of his mallee farm at Quambatook from 1896 to 1954. Few entries were as important as the annual accounting of the wheat harvest. The return for the 1921–22 season of 22.75 bushels per acre was a very good one.
(Courtesy University of Melbourne Archives)

Made cautious by the loss from wheat in late 1914, Coote decided to take advantage of a shortage of feed, and in 1915 he planted over four hundred acres of oats and only 270 acres of wheat. Most of his peers in the Victorian Mallee, however, remained committed to wheat and increased their sowing by over a quarter in 1915. Alfred Pearse in Tyntynder, north of Coote, cropped twenty acres of oats and 225 acres of wheat in the 1913–14 season before the drought. In the following year, 1914–15, he optimistically put in a crop, only to have it fail. To recover losses, he decided to cut more mallee and increased his wheat acreage to 450 acres for the season 1915–16.[4]

On the Eyre Peninsula and in the Murray Mallee in South Australia, where the progress of settlement and clearing was less developed than in Victoria, farmers had less scope to increase their acreage. Here their response was to cultivate to the same level as before the drought. During the following season

---

4   William Alfred Joseph Pearse, Diaries, 1892–1947, MS 12961, Box 1715/1–12, State Library Victoria (SLV). See 16 January 1913 and 21 June 1915.

both Victorian and South Australian mallee farmers continued their 1915 plantings. While 1915–16 was an above-average season, record rains came in the winter of 1916. At the end of June 1916 Coote wrote, '253 points of rain for June, highest for 31 years'. The 1916–17 season was a bumper one. The season brought Coote the highest return he was to achieve in over fifty years of farming, thirty-eight bushels per acre.[5]

Australia was considered Britain's war granary. The loss of shipping ruptured this ideal and forced England to turn to the Atlantic trade. For every single shipment from Australia, three could be sent from the US and Canada and two from the Argentine. A fear that the North American crop would be below average in 1916 enabled Billy Hughes, Australia's prime minister, to convince the English government to buy the whole Australian crop. The North American harvest, however, was better than feared. The result was that the bumper Australia crop of 1916–17, fully paid for, was left standing at railway sidings.

In 1917 wheat siding storages were attacked first by mice, and then by weevils and other insects. It was the non-native variety of mouse that caused such havoc—*mus domesticus*. Unbeknownst to most settlers, this little rodent had accompanied them on their journeys from Europe and was as alien and invasive to the Mallee as Europeans. The environmental conditions that made the Mallee good land for growing wheat also made it a desirable home for *mus domesticus*. Indeed, south-eastern Australia proved itself one of the most desirable locations in the world for the house mouse, which settled in for an extensive breeding program. The fine sandy soils of the Mallee are perfect for mice as they drain easily and are thus less likely to flood in heavy rain. In clearing the Mallee and disturbing the habitats of indigenous marsupials, humans created a comfortable environment for *mus domesticus*. Humans have also provided food and shelter for mice—haystacks, farm buildings, piggeries, wheat stacks, vast fields of grain. The key ingredient required to send mouse breeding habits into overdrive is rain. The conditions required for a mouse plague begin up to eighteen months beforehand. Good rain—frequently drought-breaking rain—creates a bumper harvest and thus abundant food

---

5   Coote, Diary; for statistics on wheat crops and yields see E. and L. Dunsdorfs, *Historical Statistics of the Australian Wheat Growing Industry* (Melbourne: University of Melbourne, 1956), 56–7. In the Murray Mallee, 454,965 acres were planted in the drought season, 480,620 in the following season, and 520,628 in the bumper year of 1916. Thereafter crop planting declined due to wartime problems. In Victoria the mallee counties increased their acreage from 1,012,998 in 1914 to 1,275,122 in 1916. Victorian planting also fell away in the last two years of the war. See Coote, Diary, 10 January 1917, for yields in 1916.

residue left on the fields. A wet summer-to-autumn period extends the breeding season and increases the chance of the mice surviving the winter. Once an outbreak is in full swing, there is little humans can do to prevent the damage it will cause. Months later, the outbreak will rapidly and somewhat mysteriously cease, and within a few weeks the mice will be gone.

Large outbreaks of mice began occurring in the eastern mallee lands in the late nineteenth century. In 1917, following a good 1916 harvest, *mus domesticus* demonstrated its full potential. On 1 June 1917 an officer from the Victorian Vermin Destruction Department reported that thirteen tons of mice, 912,000 in all, had been destroyed in three days at eight railway sidings where grain was stored, namely: Lascelles, Woomelang, Birchip, Morton Plains, Donald, Nandaly, Berriwillock, Hopetoun, and Nullawil where the count was 130,000 (see Figure 6.3).[6] Farm seed stores also provided a target. In March 1917 Coote observed that his 'place was moving with mice now'. By June they were still in plague proportions, and on 6 June he took 'out of [the] oat bin five kerosene buckets full of mice poisoned last night with strychnine and flour each bucket weighing 35 or 36 lbs and said to contain about 1000 mice'. A month later he recorded that many of the farmers in his district were buying seed 'on account of mice destroying so much'.[7]

Discussion of this and recurring mouse plagues in the Mallee reveals a sense of human impotence in the face of millions of mice and their encroachment on the most intimate of domestic spaces. A letter to the *Sea Lake Times* told of mice 'running over beds, tearing mattresses and pulling out the kapock'. They chewed through the leather on boots and ate corks down to the tops of bottles. One man had his ear bitten.[8] The language used to describe these domestic incursions is striking. In April 1917 the *Horsham Times* reported on the mice 'invading homes' and the use of poison to control them: 'it is nothing to find it hardly possible to get out of bed in the morning without stepping on a kind of carpet of dead mice which litter the floor'. One house managed to poison a thousand to fifteen hundred in one night.[9] 'Mice at the Table', read a column in the same newspaper in June 1917. The 'plague' evoked 'general disgust', but the response to it was interpreted in gendered ways; men might boast about the size of their piles and count the dead, but 'Housewives [were] at their wits end to purge their homes of the unsavoury smell'. There

---

6   Scott, *Australia During the War*, 583–9.
7   Coote, Diary, 26 March, 6 June, 6 July, 11 July, and 9 August 1917.
8   Jennifer A. McLennan, *Time, Tide and the Tyrrell: A History of the Shire of Wycheproof* (Melbourne: Hargreen Publishing, 1994), 157.
9   *Horsham Times*, 17 April 1917, 4.

was no escape from the rodents; they were under your feet, running up your legs, in your bed, your shoes, running over your sleeping children, eating your clothes, and their smell infused everything. *En masse* the mice became more than mammal, mutating into an unnatural force that defied human understanding and action. One newspaper reported the plague had sent the men of the Wheat Board 'a little bit "piccadilly"' as they struggled to come up with an effective means of eradicating the pest.[10]

Figure 6.3: A night's catch of mice at Hopetoun (Vic.) June 1917.
The bountiful rains of 1916 and a bumper harvest in the summer of 1916–17 provided the ideal conditions for a mouse plague. Farmers such as Charles Coote recorded their properties 'moving with mice' in June and July 1917.
Wheat at railway sidings, its shipment delayed by wartime shipping restrictions, was destroyed by mice.
(Courtesy State Library Victoria)

The Wheat Board was popular amongst Australian farmers, who had long protested the power of wheat merchants.[11] In response to the war, the federal government, with the agreement of the states, set up a compulsory pool

---

10   *Beulah Standard and Mallee and Wimmera Advertiser*, 17 May 1917, 3.
11   See B.D. Graham, *The Formation of the Australian Country Parties* (Canberra: ANU Press, 1966), 36–7.

to purchase the wheat harvest and offered farmers a guaranteed minimum price each year of its operation. In January 1916 Coote overcame his former distaste for this socialist measure and noted that the pool 'system was working smoothly', even if the 'issue of certificates [was] slow'. For the duration of the war and into the early 1920s, the pool returned high prices to wheat farmers and prices that kept pace with wartime inflation.[12]

Overall, the war had a mixed impact on mallee farming, with pioneer farmers facing more difficulties. For those in the process of rolling new mallee, the disruption of markets and labour shortages hindered the work of bringing extra land under cultivation. In both the Eyre Peninsula and the Murray Mallee, settlers maintained the areas they seeded on the eve of the war through 1915–16 to 1916–17. Thereafter, plantings declined owing to labour shortages. In Victoria the boost in cropping during these years stalled towards the end of the war. However, for established farmers the pool was a boon. Ever the meticulous record keeper, Charles Coote started a new set of accounts with the arrival of the wheat pool. His 'Wheat Pool Book' recorded wheat returns for the next thirty years. In the prosperous war years, Coote took advantage of the misfortune of those who fell behind because of the 1914–15 drought, and in 1918 he took over the selections of two of his neighbours, bringing his total holdings to eighteen hundred acres.

Dry Farming and the Farming Year

The confidence among Australian farmers in the first two and a half decades of the twentieth century owed much to the discovery of 'dry farming'. This agricultural system was first developed in North America and later adapted to suit Australian conditions. Dry farming emphasised the importance of tilling or ploughing the land and had two variations. In the long fallow technique, land was ploughed in winter and early spring of the year before seeding to conserve a full fifteen months of winter rainfall. More common was normal fallow where the land was ploughed in winter or spring eight to eleven months prior to seeding. After summer rains the fallow was cultivated to kill weeds. Frequent cultivation became an essential feature of the system, and it was based on an erroneous notion that moisture was released from the soil by capillaries. Repeated cultivation cut these and stopped the loss of

---

12   Coote, Diary, 23 January 1916; C.W. Coote, 'Wheat Pools Since 1915–1916' (in the possession of Rohan Walker). The prices Coote listed for wheat kept pace with serious wartime inflation.

moisture.[13] In the long-term, excessive cultivation led to massive wind erosion, but in the short-term fallow had a dramatic impact on productivity by killing moisture-consuming weeds.

In wheat-growing areas of southern Australia, farmers' diaries indicate that fallow was experimented with as early as the late 1880s, before the science of dry farming was promoted. Moreover, Australian farmers made important local changes to their farming practices. As Lionel Frost has shown, experiments by the Correll brothers in South Australia in the late 1890s demonstrated that superphosphate could be applied during sowing to over-cropped soils by use of American seed drills, with an immediate increase in fertility. Sheep became an important part of this new farming system, leading to a rise again in sheep numbers in the eastern mallee.[14] Sheep fed off fallowed and stubble land. This reduced weeds and provided new sources of income through the sale of wool and, more importantly, lamb and mutton.[15]

In the early twentieth century farming benefitted from scientific and technological gains. Plant breeders produced new wheat varieties that were rust resistant and suitable for early ripening in hot Australian spring and early summer conditions. The Mallee Tourist and Heritage Centre at Pinnaroo contains the Wurfel Grain Collection, one of a number across the country displaying the enormous variety of wheat available for planting. By World War I most farmers were planting the famous Federation variety. Harvesting technology also improved. During the 1840s South Australian farmers had adopted Ridley's stripper and its refinements, which literally stripped the ears off ripe wheat. This left the arduous job of winnowing to separate the grains of wheat from the head to hand winnowing or the use of horses in treadmills. After 1900 Victorian manufacturers developed a stripper–harvester that stripped and winnowed the crop, and their Canadian competitors developed

---

13 The best account of dry farming is Lionel Frost, 'Victorian Agriculture and the Role of Government, 1880–1914' (PhD thesis, Monash University, 1982), 101–34. See also A.R. Callaghan and A.J. Millington, *The Wheat Industry in Australia* (Sydney: Angus & Robertson, 1956), 113–24.

14 The number of sheep in Victoria's mallee counties was 320,985 at the 1901 Census. By 1912 this had increased to 809,654. See *Victorian Statistical Register of the State of Victoria for the Year 1911*, Part VIII, 'Production'.

15 For the early use of fallowing, see the James Harris James Diaries 1889–1891. James farmed at Wanurp north of Bendigo and kept a dairy from 1888 to 1932. His journal is held by the East Loddon Historical Society. For the Corrells, see Lionel Frost, 'The Correll Family and Technological Change in Australian Agriculture', *Agricultural History* 75, no. 2 (Spring 2001): 217–41.

a more complex version of this, the stripper–thresher. This was locally copied and called the header.[16]

In the prosperous years of the early twentieth century, many farmers and lands administrators believed that a new model of dry farming had solved the problem of farming in low rainfall areas. By the eve of the Great War the practice of dry farming had imprinted on the established mallee block an annual pattern of work that changed little for the next two decades. For most of the first half of the twentieth century horsepower set the pace of work. Yet even as tractors replaced horses—quite slowly from the late 1920s—the seasonal pattern remained essentially the same. Mechanisation changed the scale of work rather than its pattern.

Always an acute observer of his world, Charles Coote depicted a working regime that was essentially the same from the Victorian Mallee, through the neighbouring Murray Mallee in South Australia, westward into the Eyre Peninsula and onto Esperance in Western Australia. By the outbreak of war in 1914, Coote had farmed for almost two decades and the process of clearing was almost, but not completely, finished. Sowing and fallowing still dug up roots that had to be picked up, carted and stacked. In newer regions, brought into production during the war and immediate post-war years, fallowing generally was delayed for several years until the mallee had been rolled down, cut and burnt. When fallowing was introduced its annual pace was, to a large extent, determined by the number of roots still in the fields. In the case of Charles Coote and his brothers, the early and difficult years of fallowing were handled by using strong bullocks as well as horses to pull ploughs through root-littered fields. With these under control, if not eliminated, the distinctive dry-farming year was visible.[17]

For Charles Coote, situated in the southern Victorian Mallee, the beginning of the year was the busiest. Although the timing of the harvest depended upon the season, January usually found his labour force busily cropping. In the season 1920–21, Coote's farm of 1,818 acres produced 585 acres of wheat. The harvest commenced on 21 December 1920 and continued to 21 January with two harvesting machines, each with a six-foot cut. Harvesting was delayed on several occasions with machinery breakdowns, and each machine stripped

---

16 For the development of agricultural machinery in Australia, see John Lack and Charles Fahey, 'Harvester Wars: The Global Struggle between H.V. McKay, Massey–Harris and International Harvester', *Ontario History* 46, no. 1 (Spring 2004): 9–40.

17 In 1905 Coote worked his fallow with fourteen bullocks pulling a 5-furrow plough and five horses pulling a 3-furrow plough. Coote, Diary, 17 August 1905.

just over seven acres per day. In the 1920s the only change in technology was a larger cut on the harvester, which made little difference to the time taken to bring the crop in. In 1926 three men using a new 8-foot harvester and two 6-foot harvesters cut six hundred acres of wheat in twenty-seven days with twenty horses (see Figure 6.4).[18]

Figure 6.4: A Sunshine Harvester with 5-horse team in the 1920s.
The success of mallee farming depended upon harvesting large areas and reducing labour costs. Initially farmers used a stripper to harvest as its light construction permitted it to be operated in sandy fields with submerged roots. When the roots had been removed the heavier harvester was employed. This machine both stripped and winnowed the grain.
(Courtesy Rohan Walker)

Carting was the next critical task. This started once the harvest was under way, or shortly after. From Charles Coote's farm at Quambatook, two dray loads of around fifty 3-bushel bags could be carted in a day. In 1921 Coote operated two drays, which were normally loaded late in the day. On 27 January he rose at 3.30 am and, after harnessing the horses, he left his Meering West farm at 6.00 am and arrived at the rail siding at 7.45. Much to his consternation he found he was tenth in line on the weighbridge. He returned to his farm by late morning, loaded once again and set off at 1.15 pm. Returning to the farm, he loaded the dray at sundown in readiness for the next morning's early start. In 1921, 1,939 bags from his farm were carted into Quambatook,

---

18   Coote, Diary, 21 December 1920, 21 January 1921, 2 and 31 December 1926.

representing nine full days of work for two men.[19] Only in the 1930s did he contract carting to lorry drivers.

With the harvest in, farmers often took holidays in late summer, Coote usually choosing Melbourne. In some years the carting had barely finished when preparations were made for the next season. As crops were harvested, sheep were fed on the stubble or, as in February 1921, Coote burnt his stubble to aid the coming sowing season. In preparation for sowing, seed wheat and oats were winnowed in March. Seed was exchanged between neighbours for biological diversity, and during the 1920s new varieties were tried on the Coote farm. In 1921 three varieties—Federation, Yandilla King and Penny—were sown. In autumn the fallowed land was scarified. In March 1921 Coote's fallow was infested with wild melons that were 'thick and vigorous' in some parts. Cultivating continued through March and April, usually with a team of eight horses. In these months hard-worked horses were also driven into Quambatook to pick up supplies of superphosphate. In 1921, workers on Coote's farm commenced drilling in the seed oats and superphosphate on 25 April. Two horse teams worked on this operation, one to disc the field and the other to drill the super and seed, and the planting was completed by 2 May.[20] This allowed a small window before wheat sowing commenced.

There was no shortage of other tasks. With horses hard at work in these months, chaff was essential. In May 1921 four horses drove the chaff cutter and two men laboured, one to hand up the sheaves and another to fed them into the cutter. Horses needed to be clipped, harnesses oiled, stables cleaned, sheep and lambs branded and, when it rained, drains to dams were cleaned. With sheep on his property in 1921, Coote had to mend fences and dig out rabbit burrows.[21] Rains in May 1921 delayed wheat sowing. As they waited for crab-holes to dry, workers on the farm pickled wheat to combat rust and cleaned the seed drill. On 4 June wheat sowing commenced with two teams, one to scarify and one to drill. The seeding of wheat continued until 18 July. Progress varied with the weather; on 4 June, when fields were sticky from rain, they could only do four and a half acres a day, while in July they could drill over twenty.[22]

Coote appears to have been a reluctant sheep farmer. Yet sheep were an essential part of weed eradication. With over 1,800 acres, Coote had sufficient

---

19   Coote, Diary, 27 January, 1 and 13 February 1921.
20   Coote, Diary, 4 February, 9, 22 March, 25 April and 2 May 1921.
21   Coote, Diary, 10, 20, 23, 27 and 30 May 1921.
22   Coote, Diary, 4 June, 9 and 18 July 1921.

land to run sheep. In 1921 he ran around three hundred of his own sheep, and he also contracted with a neighbour to agist seven hundred sheep in August. Letting out his land was Coote's preferred means of managing sheep. Lambs in his own flock had to be marked and branded in September and shorn and dipped in November.[23]

At the completion of wheat sowing, Coote turned his attention to fallowing. In 1921 he worked two ploughs on 320 acres with a team of eight horses each. Fallowing continued into mid-October. Although Coote had been working his land for almost three decades in 1921, fallowing dug up the inevitable load of roots. On 3 October Coote noted that his labourer, Parker, had finished 'heaping roots'. Ploughed fields were scarified. Throughout fallowing, hard-working horses required plenty of chaff, and chaff cutting kept men busy when they were not ploughing or scarifying. In 1921 Coote employed two men to do the hard work of sowing and fallowing, but he was not idle. He watched his men with an eagle eye while he undertook sheep management and other general maintenance tasks, such as cutting thistles, noted in his diary on 1 November as 'very thick in patches'.[24]

Every spring Coote kept an anxious eye on the weather in anticipation of the harvest. In early November 1921 he repaired the reaper and binder. On 10 November they started cutting oats, some of which were self-sown, off 270 acres. Cut oats were stooked to dry and then stacked in early December. Two stack builders were paid off on 12 December, the harvesters were overhauled, and a sample of the wheat was stripped and inspected. Two days later the harvest was in full swing, with two harvesters working until 11 January 1922. Hungry horses necessitated several stops for chaff cutting during those weeks. The 1921–22 harvest was particularly good, and, on 16 February 1922, Charles tallied up his returns: 'about 8003 Bus[hels] in the pool. Reckoning 201 bags retained, at 191 lbs per bag, the yield per acre off 380 acres harvested for grain [was] about 22 ¾ Bushels'.[25]

This busy calendar with its arduous and long hours was made more bearable and perhaps possible by a helpmate. During the war Charles Coote resumed his friendship with his old neighbour Ada Edwards. They were married in 1915 and moved into town, so the support she provided was away from the farm.[26] But other women—wives or daughters who lived on mallee farms—were

---

23 Coote, Diary, 9 July, 9, 15 August, 30 September, 2 and 22 November 1921.
24 Coote, Diary, 3 September, 3 October and 1 November 1921.
25 Coote, Diary, 9, 10, 23, 27 November, 5 and 10 December 1921 and 16 February 1922.
26 Charles Coote says very little about his courtship with Ada. More can be learnt from a memoir Ada wrote in the 1960s (in the possession of Rohan Walker).

critical to their operation. Calculating the historical contribution of women to Australian agriculture has been hindered by their deliberate exclusion from official counts of farming employment. At the census of 1891 the various colonial statisticians agreed that it reflected poorly on a young country such as Australia to record women working in the fields. By administrative fiat, they simply decided not to count women farm workers. The early Commonwealth parish statistics did not follow this path and clearly indicate the importance of women on mallee farms. Single women were not excluded from selecting properties, and many mallee women acquired land through transfer from neighbouring selectors or through inheritance. In the Meering West area, where Charles Coote farmed, the average number of hands per farm in 1911 was three, typically including, one female. In later years women were returned as working on farms only if they were proprietors. In 1930, for example, about 6 per cent of farms in Coote's district were operated by women; all other women were removed from the returns.[27]

Women were clearly mallee workers. Inside farm homes they performed household duties of washing, cleaning and cooking for the family; outside the house their domain might extend to the dairy and raising poultry. Farms in more favourable country with higher rainfall were likely to have dairy cattle and chooks and to own cream separators. In Charles Coote's district, women milked two to three cows twice daily and managed around fifty hens and other poultry. In the newer mallee and more marginal areas fewer cows were kept.[28] Even so, in the mid-1920s Maud and William Lane milked two cows on their soldier settlement farm at Wagant, providing dairy produce for their family of four. William considered the dairy Maud's job and, within three days of her sudden death in January 1928, sold off their dairy cattle. In September 1915 Alfred Pearse sold small amounts of butter and eggs at the Nyah Bazaar, and in July 1916 he sold one of his wife's cows for £12. This was a welcome cash input into the farm, long after most of the wheat harvest had been sold. His wife's skim milk, from the separator, was fed to pigs, which were regularly killed and consumed on the farm and sold to neighbours.[29]

---

27 *Census of Victoria, General Report, 1891*, 192. See also Parish Agricultural Statistics, 1911–12 and 1930–31, Commonwealth Bureau of Census and Statistics: MP570/1, Statistical Returns, Collector's Book—Agricultural, dairying and pastoral statistics—Victoria, National Archives of Australia (NAA). The 1911–12 Victorian returns are the most complete statistical account we have of the employment of women on farms. They also record production from dairies and poultry raising.

28 William Henry Lane, Diaries, 1923–1941, PA01/123, Australian Manuscripts Collection, SLV. See 3 February 1928.

29 Pearse, Diary, 22 September, 1 October 1915 and 18 July 1916.

Few diaries ever record women working at the heavier tasks of clearing, cultivation or harvesting operations. When Ada Coote first came to the farm in December 1916, she drove the harvester once round the field with Charles acting as 'consulting authority at [the] rear'. (In the 1930s their daughters had a similar drive of the new autoheader.)[30] This was simply a piece of fun. Yet women were vital to most farm operations. They fed both the family and hired labour. During carting, women rose during the night—before husbands, siblings and hired workers—to prepare breakfast. They had food ready when teams returned for lunch, and meals for those returning at sundown. When grain was threshed rather than stripped, they fed upwards of half a dozen workers. Women also provided a conduit to the outside world. Maud Lane at Kulwin in the mid-twenties regularly drove the buggy from the Wagant farm to Kulwin to collect mail, groceries and other provisions.

Over Expansion

The prosperity experienced by mallee farmers during the war years continued into the early 1920s. In 1936, Arthur Perkins, the director of agriculture in South Australia, labelled the twelve seasons from 1915–16 to 1926–27 as the 'finest 12-year period of which we have records'. Over these twelve seasons, the average yield for the whole state was twelve and a half bushels per acre. In the newly settled mallee districts of the Eyre Peninsula and the Murray Mallee the yields were, respectively, eight and nine bushels per acre. These good years encouraged a period of reckless expansion that was brought to a dramatic end by drought in the late 1920s and a collapse in wheat prices in the early 1930s. Recovery was drawn out and was not really accomplished until after 1945.[31]

The reckless expansion was particularly evident in the Western Australian mallee. Between 1887 and 1891, a royal commission examined the poor state of agriculture in Western Australia. Matthew Tonts has argued this commission was captivated by the ideal of a sturdy yeomanry intensely farming small properties.[32] Following from its deliberations, the government introduced the *Homesteads Act 1893*. This entitled any person not owning more than a hundred acres of agricultural land to a free homestead farm not exceeding 160 acres.

---

30   Coote, Diary, 7 December 1916.

31   A.J. Perkins, 'Ten Years of Progress in Wheat Growing', *Journal of the Department of Agriculture of South Australia* 31 (15 October 1927): 240.

32   Matthew Tonts, 'State Policy and the Yeoman Ideal: Agricultural Development in Western Australia, 1890–1914', *Landscape Research* 27, no. 1 (2002): 103–15, see 109–10.

The following year saw the establishment of the Agricultural Bank, which could loan settlers up to £400 at interest rates not exceeding 6 per cent and deferred payments for five years.

By the late 1890s, the Western Australian government faced severe economic disruption caused by precipitously declining gold production and thus needed to find alternative sources of employment. Under these economic imperatives, legislators passed the *Land Act 1898*, which established conditions for subsequent settlement. The Act offered up to a thousand acres at a minimum of 10s per acre, depending upon the quality of the land, and established four means of acquiring land: a free homestead of 160 acres as provided under the 1893 act; conditional purchase of up to a thousand acres with or without residence; and direct payment. Settlers in the second and third categories were given twenty years to purchase their properties. Resident-conditional purchasers had to provide within ten years improvements of 10s per acre, and non-residents 20s. Direct purchasers were given a year to pay, and had to provide 5s in improvements within seven years. The price of land above the 10s minimum was determined by farming conditions: the position of railways, annual rainfall and soil potential.[33]

In the first two decades after 1900, settlement in the Western Australian mallee proceeded very slowly. In 1912 the government allocated £50,000 to overcome the remoteness of the Esperance area and counter problems caused by drought in 1911. The scheme was a failure, and by 1914 less than four thousand acres were sown to wheat in the Eastern Goldfields Statistical Division. In 1917 a royal commission investigated the progress of settlement on the 'Mallee Belt and Esperance Lands' with the clear intention of promoting more rapid settlement. To bolster the potential of mallee lands, the commissioners took evidence from settlers and officials in South Australia and Victoria, and wilfully ignored the scientific evidence presented to the commission on problems with salinity. The commission declared:

> In other parts of Australia adverse professional opinion respecting mallee lands has been disregarded with advantage to the state, and the Commission having given the question close consideration strongly urges that scientific prejudice against our mallee lands be not permitted to stand in the way of their being opened for agricultural purposes.[34]

---

33   Tonts, 'State Policy and the Yeoman Ideal', 111–12, and Sean Glynn, *Government Policy and Agricultural Development: A Study of the Role of Government in the Development of the Western Australian Wheat Belt 1900–1930* (Perth: UWA Press, 1975), 88 and 109.

34   'Report of the Royal Commission on the Mallee Belt and Esperance Lands', *Votes and Proceeding of the Parliament of Western Australia, 1917*, Paper no. 5, xiv.

The commissioners recommended the extension of facilities and direct subsidisation of wheat growers.

While machinery and farming techniques were mostly transferable across mallee lands, the achievements in one mallee region were not always applicable elsewhere. Against its own best judgment, the Agricultural Bank was persuaded to make advances to settlers, and in the 1920s there was rapid development. A railway line was opened between Salmon Gums and Esperance in September 1925. Under these inducements settlement went ahead, and, despite earlier failures, the area under wheat expanded from less than two thousand acres to just over 59,000 acres in 1928. Low crop yields for most of the 1920s underscored the problems of the region, and disaster struck when prices collapsed in the early 1930s. By 1933 liabilities to the Agricultural Bank mounted to £674,527, and the government had invested a further £792,491 in the construction of railways, roads and dams. Capital had also been expended to establish an experimental farm and undertake soil surveys. By 1932 there were 219 abandoned farms in the area, and '282 settlers who were only kept there with the moneys of the bank'. From 1928 to 1930 the area planted to wheat dropped by almost a half in the Esperance Statistical Division.[35]

The same thing happened in South Australia. The early success of the first mallee settlers in the Pinnaroo district of the Mallee Murray and the coastal fringes of the Eyre Peninsula encouraged reckless expansion in South Australia. During the First World War, settlement in Pinnaroo and the Far West Coast stalled, largely due to a shortage in the supply of labour to clear farms. However, government controls on wheat marketing and guaranteed prices through a compulsory pool improved profitability for existing farmers. High wheat prices continued into 1919 and the early 1920s; this, together with the indefatigable promotion of South Australia's director of agriculture, Arthur Perkins, fuelled demand for new land. In the Murray Mallee, settlement pushed north of Goyder's line and into areas with less than eight inches of rain in the counties of Albert and Alfred. On the Eyre Peninsula, settlers were encouraged by railway construction to move from the coast to inland counties—Dufferin, Le Hunte and Buxton—north of the ten-inch rainfall line. In these places the area cropped to wheat doubled between 1921 and 1931.[36]

---

35 Glynn, *Government Policy*, 127–8. 'Report of the Royal Commission on the Agricultural Bank', *Votes and Proceedings of the Parliament of Western Australia*, vol. 11, 1932, 15. Dunsdorfs, 'Historical Statistics of the Australian Wheat Growing Industry', 80–1.

36 Dunsdorfs, 'Historical Statistics of the Australian Wheat Growing Industry', 57–8.

In boosting this settlement, Perkins called on farmers to adopt the new science of dry farming. Fallow was his major prescription, although it would be difficult in the initial years of settlement. He nevertheless exhorted farmers to raise the proportion of wheat sown on fallow to not less than 85 to 90 per cent. Fallowing should be done early and there should be no respite for horse teams between seeding and fallowing. Fallowing should be completed in August and 'thereafter teams should be kept busy until harvest time' for as 'much [time] as may be essential to the destruction of weeds, to the consolidation of the sub-surface layers, to the breaking up of surface crust, and to the gradual formation of a mellow but shallow seed bed'. He advised farmers: 'Tillage operations should be continued subsequent to harvest, and even during harvest should opportunity offer. On the whole probably from 50 to 60 per cent of the value of the crop can be said to depend upon adequate preparation of the seed bed'. In 1916 Perkins cautioned farmers against light dressing of superphosphate. By 1927 he was advising that the evidence for the benefits of heavy dressings of super was clear.[37]

In calling on farmers to fallow, Perkins had some words of caution. Farmers 'should avoid working sandy land dry', and particularly when it was 'liable to drift'. He warned settlers it was 'possible to over-work land light in texture'. On light lands he advised wheat should 'probably not be attempted more than once every three or four years'. In the intervening years land could be left to 'carry according to circumstances, Oats Barley, Grazing crops, or left out to grass'. Finally, he observed, sheep should be regarded as an integral part of any farm on which wheat cannot be grown to advantage in alternate years. Sheep increased the fertility of the soil and prepared the way for improved wheat yields. In his view 'no Mallee Farm should be without its flock of sheep, and preferably a flock of breeding ewes, and the sooner new farms are rendered sheep-proof, and adequate provision is made for water, the sooner these farms come into their own'.[38]

In South Australia, first-time settlers could acquire credit to purchase land to the value of £5,000, and land sizes were larger than in corresponding areas of the Victorian Mallee. By 1931, when figures first became available, the average farm in Albert and Alfred counties was about 1,300 acres. Nonetheless, where rain fell below ten inches annually, this was insufficient land for the mixed farming recommended by Perkins. As settlers moved onto their new

---

37   Perkins, 'Ten Years of Progress in Wheat Growing', 248–50.
38   Perkins, 'Ten Years of Progress in Wheat Growing', 251.

farms they engaged largely in a monoculture with extensive cropping of wheat. They ignored the strictures about fallowing sandy areas and they did not have sufficient land to become mixed wheat–sheep farmers. As dry years set in after 1927, crop yields dropped precipitously, and the region was on the verge of human and ecological tragedy.[39]

On established Victorian Mallee farms, in the fourteen to thirteen-inch rainfall band, sheep had become an essential part of the farm by the early 1920s. This was possible largely because of the consolidation of farms. In Charles Coote's parish of Meering West, all farms taken up in the 1890s and early twentieth century were less than seven hundred acres. Coote was able to extend the size of his property by selecting with his brothers. He eventually became the sole owner of these multiple selections, and at the end of the Great War he purchased additional land to further increase the size of his property to 1,818 acres, making it larger than the average farm in the district. Nonetheless, the average in his area in 1921 was twelve hundred acres and the typical farmer had seven hundred acres of pasture on which to graze 380 sheep. When the government sponsored settlement in the northern and north-western Mallee, which became known as the 'New Mallee', authorities ignored the experience of established settlers and offered properties of around seven hundred acres.[40] Settlement of this 'New Mallee' was destined to fail, and prominent among the newcomers to the region were soldier settlers.

Soldier Settlers

In the history of Australian land settlement few schemes have the notoriety of the soldier settlement schemes introduced to repay a 'debt of honour' to men who had served in the Great War. The state government was keen to populate Victoria with the 'right' sort of settlers, men with good 'moral fibre'. Such men would make good yeoman farmers, irrespective of whether they

---

39   Land sizes can be estimated from the *Statistical Register of South Australia, Production*, in 1931. In this year the average farmer in County Alfred held 1,316 acres. He cropped 410 acres with wheat. In the eight hundreds of this county, wheat yields fell below 1.5 bushels per acre in 1927–28. Low average flock sizes, 88 per farm for the whole county, suggests many farms without sheep. (Note, a 'hundred' is a cadastral unit deriving from English practice and adopted in South Australia; it measures 100 square miles or 162 square kilometres. See Michael Williams, *The Making of the South Australian Landscape: A Study in the Historical Geography of Australia* (London and New York: Academic Press, 1974), 90–5.)

40   Parish Agricultural Statistics, Meering West, 1921–22 Season, Series MP570, Box 20, NAA.

had any farming experience or not.[41] Unacknowledged assumptions were also at play; returned servicemen were seen as naturally suited to outdoor life and, just as they had proved themselves exemplary soldiers, so they would make successful settlers.[42] Thus many men with little or no farming experience were permitted to take up land. The plight of the soldier settler has become the symbol of the troubles faced by mallee settlers in the 1920s and 1930s.[43] Their situation was most precarious in the Victorian Mallee, although state-based schemes also operated in Western Australia and South Australia.

Under the *Discharged Soldiers Settlement Act 1917*, the Victorian government repurchased land and made this available to returned servicemen. Those returned men seeking land had to produce a qualifications certificate proving their length and location of service and their experience as farmers. Successful applicants were allotted blocks of repurchased land, either as dry land or as irrigation blocks. Land was sold at market rates leaving soldier settlers with heavy debts from the outset. This was soon compounded by the cost of clearing, improving and stocking their land with seed, implements and livestock. In the Mallee there was no need for government to repurchase blocks, as Crown land was available. The difficulty was that vacant Crown land, known as the 'New Mallee', was generally in areas where the rainfall was below twelve inches per year.[44]

In the Victorian Mallee, nearly 500,000 acres of Crown land, including in the Millewa, were 'opened up' for the soldier settlement scheme. Although the 1915 royal commission into the workings of the Closer Settlement Acts in Victoria found that, overall, such schemes had proved a failure,[45] the belief in the desirability of closer settlement remained strong. Progressive reformers

---

41 Richard Waterhouse, *The Vision Splendid: A Social and Cultural History of Rural Australia*, (Fremantle: Curtin University Books, 2005), 200, 201. He notes that by 1927, in the face of appalling failure rates, critics began to argue that 'soldier settlers did not have a moral right to be a permanent financial burden on the community' (202).

42 Marilyn Lake, *The Limits of Hope: Soldier Settlement in Victoria, 1915–38* (Melbourne: Oxford University Press, 1987), 3–9.

43 See Lake, *The Limits of Hope*, and Bruce Scates and Melanie Oppenheimer, *The Last Battle: Soldier Settlement in Australia, 1916–1939* (Melbourne: Cambridge University Press, 2017).

44 Some soldier settlers were placed on blocks abandoned in the southern Mallee region. For the various Acts and conditions governing soldier settlement, see: Victoria, 'Report of the Royal Commission on Soldier Settlement', *Victorian Parliamentary Papers*, vol. 2, no. 32, 1925: 5 and 8–9. For the geographical spread of soldier setters, see J.M. Powell, 'The Mapping of Soldier Settlement: A Note for Victoria 1917–29', *Journal of Australian Studies* 2, no. 3 (June 1978): 44–51.

45 Lake, *The Limits of Hope*, 3–9.

had faith in the 'moral superiority of rural life' and believed that the drift to the cities could be halted if amenities in rural areas were improved.[46] The 'welfare of the State rests upon a basis of land settlement' stressed Prime Minister W.M. Hughes. Land settlement also confronted the problem of what to do with the thousands of returned servicemen languishing on city streets boding trouble.[47] Cities were potentially corrupting influences on soldier heroes. The Victorian scheme saw approximately 11 per cent of returned servicemen take up allotments on dryland farms, with holdings of roughly seven to eight hundred acres.

Many of the returned men who took up holdings in the 'New Mallee' were inexperienced farmers. Melbourne University's professor of agriculture, who accompanied the Better Farming Train on its first tour of the Mallee in 1926, observed of many farmers in the area that they had 'never bought a sheep or a pig in their lives'. They had no knowledge of how or what to farm, especially in areas very different from the districts they may have come from.[48]

In establishing soldier settlers on farms, the government showed it had learnt almost nothing from the prior history of mallee settlement. Blocks were too small to permit mixed farming or safe crop rotations, and the possession of capital was simply not considered necessary. Generous loan advances to returned men were seen as an adequate substitute. Payment for blocks was on terms, spread over thirty-six and a half years, and deferred for three years. Soldier settlers also had access to loans or advances of 100 per cent of the cost of improvements. Civilian settlers took up similar blocks but were given less generous conditions. They required a deposit, their rental payments were not deferred, and advances were for only 80 per cent of improvements.[49]

The Closer Settlement Board files of soldier settlers often reveal an unfolding human tragedy. The Board's archive is divided into those settlers who succeeded and those who failed, the latter stamped with the words 'Deficiency Case'. The files contain the initial application for a settlement block, personal references regarding character and work habits, requests to the Board for financial

---

46 Graeme Davison, 'Country Life: The Rise and Decline of an Australian Ideal', in *Struggle Country: The Rural Ideal in Twentieth Century Australia*, eds Graeme Davison and Marc Brodie (Melbourne: Monash University ePress, 2005), 01.3–4.

47 Lake, *The Limits of Hope*, 34–5.

48 S.M. Wadham, 'Why the Better Farming Train is a Success', *Victorian Railways Magazine* 3, no. 11 (November 1926): 6.

49 *Closer Settlement Act 1912* (Victoria), http://www.austlii.edu.au/au/legis/vic/hist_act/csa1912210.pdf; and *Discharged Soldiers Settlement Act 1917* (Victoria), http://www.austlii.edu.au/au/legis/vic/hist_act/dssa1917305.pdf. Both accessed 12 November 2018.

advances, and reports from inspectors. The inspectors, who lived amongst the settlers, were regularly called upon to make moral judgments about farmers, including their sobriety, level of ambition, honesty, and desirability as settlers. Farmers' wives were also subject to surveillance. Reports judged whether blocks looked 'uncared for' or 'untidy' and assessed the likelihood of success. Some inspectors showed compassion and leniency, supporting repeated requests for advances. In doing so, they became complicit in the disaster that unfolded.

The problems encountered by soldier settlers can be illustrated through the story of settlement in the parishes of Kulwin and Wagant. Here the normal and voluminous records of land administrators can be supplemented with the diary of one settler, William Henry Lane. In distributing the public estate, Victorian land officials developed a detailed system of record keeping. This paper work expanded rapidly under soldier settlement, where considerable sums of public monies were being distributed. Long-term credit purchases drew out this record keeping, and some files extend from the 1920s to the 1960s. The impact of several droughts, and the collapse of wheat prices, led to rent arrears and rising debts. This in turn led to schemes of debt re-scheduling and more paper work. Although as a diarist William Lane was little given to introspection, he recorded working patterns in great detail, and his diary complements the official record. His diary also records his relationships with his fellow soldier settlers.[50]

Kulwin and Wagant were located at the margins of the twelve-inch rainfall line. The area had been occupied under grazing licences, and early subdivision plans suggest that graziers had burnt off the mallee. The land was undulating, with red loamy soils on the flats growing mallee and turpentine, and with sandy ridges supporting spinifex and wattle brush. The region was 240 miles from Melbourne, with connection to markets supplied by railway from Ouyen on the Melbourne to Mildura line. In 1920 the railway was extended to Kulwin from Mittyack.[51]

From the very beginning there were signs that settlement would be difficult for the inexperienced, or those without much capital. William Lane was not the first to occupy his block. In September 1921 Ernest William Watson, then residing in central Melbourne, applied to take up allotment 39 Section C

---

50 William Henry Lane, Diaries, 1926–1941, PA01/123, Australian Manuscripts Collection, SLV. There are two land selection files for William Lane: his initial selection at Wagant and later at Wemen. See VA 1034 Department of Crown Lands and Survey, VPRS 5714/P0, Land Selection Files Section 12 Closer Settlement Act 1938, Unit 2181, 570/12 and Unit 2408, 134/264B, PROV.

51 VPRS 5714/PO, Unit 2181, 570/12, PROV.

in the Parish of Wagant. At the time of his application, Watson was a single man, aged twenty-two, who had served 529 days abroad. Before the war he had worked as a farm labourer, first in Gippsland, then near Echuca. He had never owned farming land before, and his only property was a building block near Reservoir, on the outskirts of Melbourne. He believed that the whole block could be used for wheat and oat farming, and that it would carry one sheep to twenty-five acres. The block had no improvements in the form of fences, buildings, dams or permanent water supply, though there was a State Rivers and Water Supply channel within a mile of the block. His block was allocated to him by the Closer Settlement Board at a price of 8s per acre.[52]

Watson's tenure was short-lived. Within a year a note appeared on his file that he wished to surrender his block on the 'grounds of ill health & unsuitability to work a mallee farm'. A note from Dr Alfred Barrett observed that he was suffering 'from debility and melancholia', most likely shell shock. A file note ordered an inspection of the block to 'safeguard the stock, implements etc. that had been advanced to this settler, and it was very important that another settler be placed on the block at once'.

The Closer Settlement Board need not have worried. Demand for blocks was strong and in April 1922, after receiving approval from the Board, Lane occupied Watson's abandoned block. Within several years, about fifty settlers took up land in Wagant and thirty in the adjoining parish of Kulwin. Blocks ranged in size from 740 to about 840 acres. Like their predecessors in the Old Mallee, the soldier settlers first rolled and cut the mallee in the winter in preparation for a late summer burn and, all being well, for an autumn or early winter planting.[53]

Lane's first surviving diary covers 1923 while he was camping out and living a bachelor's life. He planted a crop, and much of February was spent stripping and carting. With the harvest in, work was done on his house in preparation for the arrival of his family. After seeding in April and May, he faced the unremitting task of grubbing mallee roots and cutting 'spring backs', or shoots that grew from mallee roots that had been rolled, cut and burnt. This task absorbed most of his time, and that of a hired labourer, from June through to November.[54] Despite the fact that many of the men who joined

---

52 Qualifications certificate of Watson, VPRS 5714/PO, Unit 2181, 570/12, PROV. This file includes details of three settlers—Watson, Lane and Arthur Roy Crook.

53 All files in the parishes of Kulwin and Wagant have been examined to draw up this picture.

54 Lane, Diary, January to November 1923, and improvements schedule, VPRS 5714/PO, Unit 2181, 570/12, PROV.

him in the Kulwin and Wagant districts carried the physical and emotional scars of the war, files show that they made significant strides in clearing their blocks in the first years of settlement.

Within five years Lane had cleared 680 acres of mallee and had cultivated all of this land. Off course not all of this was farmed each year. In 1926 he put in 350 acres of wheat and 30 acres of oats, an increase on 1925 when he cultivated 248 acres of wheat. He also began fallowing. After seeding in June 1926, he planned to fallow 150 acres. This did not quite replace the winter task of grubbing, as the fallow plough upturned dead roots. Despite such mammoth cultivating efforts, Lane was dilatory fencing his property, and still had not completely enclosed his selection after four years. His neighbour Arthur Roy Crook, who settled in October 1920, had by 1927 cleared 740 acres, all under cultivation. Unlike Lane, his land was totally enclosed with sheep-proof fencing. Without sheep, Lane had less inducement to complete fencing, although his horse management suffered—on 3 July 1926 he 'went looking for horses'.[55]

Undoubtedly the rapid strides made by soldier settlers in Kulwin and Wagant were aided by generous advances from the Closer Settlement Board. In the 1920s, Lane's diary includes multiple references to such advances and his negotiations with the Board's local inspector. On 1 June 1926 he wrote: '[I] went to Kulwin for stores. I received a cheque for £10 from C[loser] S[ettlement] B[oard]. Sowed in the afternoon'. Two weeks later on 15 June 1926 he recorded: 'Norm and Mrs Poole left to go home. I finished sowing. We [he and his wife, Maud] went down to Kulwin and I saw Mr Matthews about future advances on 50 acres of rolling, 150 acres of fallowing and 66 chains of fencing also shoot cutting'. During ten years of settling, William Lane had received £2,000 from the Board in advances, including basic subsistence costs. Lane was not unusual. In the 1920s his neighbour Roy Crook borrowed for housing, fencing, rolling and clearing, dam sinking and a vague category of 'advances on other improvements'. In all, he borrowed £1,526 for improvements, and further £300 on livestock and £731 for farming machinery, tanks and harness.[56]

Historians have probed the relationship between settlers and inspectors. Marilyn Lake has argued that the 1920s was an age that proclaimed the gospel of efficiency and inspectors challenged settlers to adopt this philosophy. While

---

55   Lane, Diary 15 June 1926 and 3 July 1926.
56   VA Closer Settlement Board, VPRS 749/P0 Advances Files—Mallee Division, Unit 188, 1497, PROV.

relations were testy at times, settlers nevertheless continued to receive advances, and the debts owed to the Closer Settlement Board quickly spiralled out of control. From a large sample of files of closer and soldier settlers, Jacqueline Coucill estimated that, by the early 1930s, the average debt across Victoria was £2,406, but for wheat farmers in the Mallee the figure was £3,363. This was seventeen times the average annual wage for males in manufacturing in 1931. When generally benign seasons turned dry in the late 1920s and wheat prices collapsed, soldier settlers faced ruin. All that saved them was a massive debt write off and the provision of extra land to surviving settlers.[57]

Mallee Towns and Urban Life

The task of subduing mallee country and planting and harvesting crops was enormous, and depended on urban services. Within a year of her husband settling on his block, Maud Lane and her two infant children, Jack and Dorothy, moved from the green of Monbulk to the harsh dryness of the Victorian Mallee. The farm the Lanes occupied was seven miles from the town of Ouyen and five miles from the little hamlet of Kulwin. In January 1926, Maud Lane (maybe with her children) made at least eight solo trips to Kulwin; William made four solo trips to Kulwin and two to Ouyen, and the family went to Kulwin as a group on two occasions. Yet this was not their only contact with town centres, and visitors to the Lane farm brought mail and other goods from town several times a week. January was always a busy month when the harvest was in full swing and produce had to be taken to the railhead, but trips to town occurred all year. In April 1926 Maud was in Kulwin on eight occasions, William on four, and he visited Ouyen on a further four occasions. The family was also visited three times by neighbours and went to neighbours' houses on six occasions.[58]

Charles Coote's farm in the parish of Meering West was seven miles from Quambatook. In his early days as a farmer, Coote used this and other towns for obvious agricultural reasons, such as disposing of wheat and buying supplies. However, town became a vital part of his life and, though a model farmer, he was also a prominent townsman. As a young man, Coote went to town to enjoy well-earned breaks from rolling and clearing mallee, and his diary records the occasional night spent at parties and other social events. On one occasion, this dour Presbyterian wrote, there was 'plenty of beer'. He very

---

57 Jacqueline Coucill, 'Back on Track: The Closer Settlement Scheme in Victoria and the Revaluation Process 1932–1938' (PhD thesis, La Trobe University, 2004), 194.
58 Calculated from William Lane's Diary.

quickly became involved in local affairs. Early on he helped settlers move the weatherboard Mechanics Institute building with their bullocks. From the 1890s, he attended a range of political meetings—to lobby for railways and water, to win better security for leaseholders, to vote for Federation, and then to debate the early laws of the Commonwealth, most importantly the tariff.[59] Coote joined with other local farmers to establish a grain store at the railway siding at Quambatook. This provided long-term grain storage, enabling harvested wheat to be held back until the price was right. He held shares in the Quambatook Stores, a community-owned joint-stock store. Despite bad debts in the 1930s, the store proved a good investment and the source of valuable off-farm income.[60]

When he and Ada married in 1915, Coote moved from his farm and set up in the town. Ever an early adopter of new technology, Coote purchased a car in 1915 and drove it daily to the farm. The town had luxuries, most importantly electricity, not available on farms before the Second World War. Ada Coote, and later their two daughters—Bessie and Marjorie—could participate in town affairs. Ada was a keen painter and accomplished musician. She directed local musical performances, and she judged painting exhibitions at the Quambatook agricultural show. Ada also played the organ at local churches. Living in Quambatook, Charles and Ada Coote's daughters could catch the train to the larger town of Boort, where they attended secondary school and boarded during the week.[61]

The location of towns was determined by two major factors: the siting of railway lines and the provision of rail sidings. When the South Australian government constructed the railway to Pinnaroo, sidings were built at ten-mile intervals. After representation from farmers, who had great difficulty carting grain over sandy tracks, sidings were located at five-mile intervals. In Victoria, sidings were generally at ten-mile intervals, and in Western Australia the distance was set at fifteen miles. A critical factor in the development of towns was the distance that horses could travel. On the Coote farm it was possible, as we have seen, to take two dray loads—each of about fifty bags of wheat—to the railway siding per day. Until the replacement of horses by trucks—which began in the 1930s—small hamlets could survive.

---

59   Coote, Diary, 18 December 1896, 4 September 1897, 2 October 1897, 27 July 1897, 27 July 1898, 1 September 1898, 22 January 1900, 19 March, 24 1902 and 27 November 1902.
60   Coote, Diary, 4 November 1916 and 18 April 1917.
61   Coote, Diary, 25 July 1925, 18 July 1925, 7 September 1931, and 10 September 1931.

In South Australia, the government surveyed towns, most of which never grew beyond a few buildings: a store, a hall, a church, a school and a few houses. Lowaldie in South Australia was surveyed into seventy-two township allotments, with half these offered for sale in 1914. Further allotments were offered for sale in 1916, and only one was sold. Only two buildings were ever constructed, a residence and a Mechanics' Institute. The residence operated as a post office, phone exchange, limited general store and grain buyer. The Institute was used for school and church services. In 1933 the hamlet of Kulwin had only two rated buildings: a shop and a bakery.[62]

Pinnaroo and Lameroo were the principal towns on the Murray Mallee railway. Lameroo was surveyed in 1904, and few buildings were built before the arrival of the railway in April 1906. Railways enabled imports of cheap building materials. Within a year Lameroo had a hotel, three general stores, two blacksmiths, a bank and a Methodist church, which doubled as a school. In 1907 further allotments were sold and the town boasted a saddler, a bootmaker, a tinsmith, a butcher, a greengrocer, a doctor, and a general agent. There was also a private hall, a boarding house and a billiard saloon. The following year, a policeman was stationed in the town, one of the stores built a bakehouse, a carpenter set up business, and a solicitor offered his services. The town also boasted a Mutual Improvement Society and a Literary Society. The town continued to expand until the end of the Great War. By this time, it had grown to three general stores, two butcher shops, a greengrocer, a furniture shop, two blacksmiths, two carpenters and builders, a saddler, a bootmaker, two banks, a post office, a police station, a school, a Mechanics' Institute, a masonic lodge and five churches. Pinnaroo, surveyed in 1904, also grew in its first decade, offering similar retail and commercial services. As well, a dentist, a doctor and a lawyer practised in the town.[63]

Victorian Mallee towns—such as Quambatook, Birchip, Hopetoun, and Ouyen—had a similar character and provided basic commercial and professional services. Recovering the character of mallee towns a hundred years on is difficult as the census did not distinguish towns from adjacent farming districts, and occupational classifications given by the census are too broad to make any serious observations on social structure. Rate books do give us some feel for social structure, as do photographs such as this one of the Quambatook Post Office. (see figure 6.5).

---

62   Swan Hill Shire Rate Books 1933, Greater Swan Hill Shire Offices.
63   For Murray Mallee towns, see A. & P. Kloeden, 'Murray Mallee Heritage Survey', unpublished report (Adelaide: Bruce Harry & Associates, 1998), 22–36.

Figure 6.5: The Post Office at Quambatook Vic, c. 1920.
Towns provided essential services for farms such as retail stores, legal services machinery repairs and sport and recreation. The railway siding connected farms to the world for the purchase of farm supplies—machinery and superphosphate—and to dispatch produce—grain, wool and livestock.
(Courtesy State Library Victoria)

At the beginning of the 1920s, the land around the town of Quambatook had been farmed for close on thirty years. In 1921, as best we can determine, almost fifty buildings were rated in the town. Around half of these were simple residences. The most common buildings in the main street were stores, of which there were ten (four operated by women including a postmistress), along with five offices for agents of various kinds (insurance, machinery brokers and wool and wheat buyers), and a hotel. There was a blacksmith's forge, a carpenter, a carrier, and the professionals included three clergymen, a solicitor, a doctor and a nurse. In the 1920s, some farmers, including Charles Coote, lived in the town—commuting to their farms. The remaining houses were occupied by unskilled workers (mainly labourers) and women, who were simply listed as engaged in home duties. Ten years on, in the depths of the Great Depression, the town had grown to just under eighty buildings. The most common occupation ascribed to the ratepayers' was home duties, accounting for some twenty-nine buildings. Labourers occupied a further six. The commercial structure of the town was similar to 1921, the major difference being the appearance of four garages and the disappearance of the doctor. As the diary of Charles Coote often lamented, securing a medical professional was an ongoing problem.[64]

In mallee towns, there was a clearly defined élite. In an economy dependent upon the unpredictable arrival of rain—in autumn to plant and in spring for crops to grow—incomes fluctuated from year to year. Farmers who did not set aside reserves from the good years had to seek accommodation from a range of creditors—the bank manager, the solicitor, shopkeepers and produce merchants, who formed the core of the local middle class. Well-to-do farmers were also stable members of the local élite. And, in areas with large numbers of soldier settlers, an important official was the Closer Settlement Board inspector, to whom applications for advances were made. Many among the town's professionals—teachers, bank managers, clergymen, doctors and solicitors—were sojourners, moving on as career opportunities arose.

In the Quambatook district, Charles Coote was joined by members of the Adamthwaite and Mann families as leading members of the local farming bourgeoisie. In the Mallee there was a streak of rural radicalism, and these families joined together to operate a wheat store—to hold wheat into the winter when prices increased—and they set up the Quambatook stores to free farmers from storekeepers. These same families were the leaders of rural politics. Charles Coote regularly travelled to conferences of the Country Party with Alfred Adamthwaite and James Mann. Coote, an honorary justice of the peace, also monitored the state of his town—who was using the tennis courts, what was the state of buildings on the agricultural reserve, and where swagmen were sleeping.[65]

Successful mallee farming was an outward-looking enterprise, and one that required significant amounts of capital. Charles Coote was a prolific reader of newspapers. He regularly monitored both equity and produce markets and kept his eye on the state of crops in North America and other competitor regions. As farms were developed, mallee farmers emerged as the major property holders in their districts. The typical householder in Quambatook occupied a house valued at less than £25 to £30 annually, and many were much humbler, being £12 to £15. In 1921, the local solicitor's residence was valued at £132 and the doctor's at £50. James B. Mann in the same year was rated at £422 and his wife at a further £185. Alfred Adamthwaite held farming land and a house and shop in Quambatook worth £194, while Charles Coote's farm and house in Quambatook were together valued at £357.

---

64 This picture of the social structure of Quambatook is drawn from VA 2447 Kerang Shire, VPRS 9576 Rate Books, Unit 34 (1921–22) and Unit 44 (1931–32), PROV. Houses were rated on their net annual value, i.e. their value if let for rental.
65 Coote, Diary, 25 January 1933.

At the bottom of the mallee urban ladder was the unskilled labourer. John Franke, a Quambatook labourer in 1921, was rated at only £12 for his house. Rural and town work was notoriously seasonal. Most farmers only took on extra labour during harvest time, and work around the town—stacking and carting wheat—was also governed by the seasons. Other work, such as weeding water channels or road culverts, depended upon council contracts and was short term. Of course, there was a certain amount of work provided by the railway for repairers and gangers or station staff.

By 1931, Quambatook, and most mallee towns had reached the limits of their growth before technology and other circumstances ruptured their expansion. The arrival of the car, symbolised by the town's garages, triggered the decline of many small hamlets. Cars permitted farmers to by-pass these hamlets and shop in larger towns. The tractor spelt the coming decline of saddlers and blacksmiths. Bad debts in the Great Depression forced many small storekeepers to the wall. Farmers gained through the Debt Adjustment Act at the expense of traders. Those town dwellers—proprietors and labourers—who limped through the low prices of the 1930s faced a run of dry years from 1938 to 1945. From 1939 young men enlisted in the services. One of the more common social events recorded in the Coote diary during the Second World War was the town send-off for servicemen. The census returns—inadequate as they are—show that there was little work for girls in mallee towns, so they too drifted off. The war opened new opportunities for women, but they were in the cities. Throughout the war, Coote regularly lamented that townsmen were drawn to Melbourne by high wages and plenty of work in war industries.

Chapter 7

TROUBLED TIMES
1926–1945

Optimism about closer settlement continued to fuel the expansion of farming on mallee lands in the first decades of the twentieth century. The superintendent of the Victorian Department of Agriculture A.E.V. Richardson observed in 1914: 'lands which, a decade ago, were regarded as beyond the limit of safe cultivation, are now producing millions of bushels of wheat annually, and the "unsafe" lands of today will undoubtedly be the granaries of tomorrow'. Modern methods of agriculture would underpin productivity not previously imagined, 'for with proper methods of culture, the soil must get richer and more productive and wealth-producing as the years roll by'.[1] A growing belief in scientific farming alongside continued faith in a yeomanry to people the vastness of Australia's interiors marked the 1920s. White families would feed the nation. However, ill-conceived land schemes, a failure to learn from the past, the environmental realities of mallee farming, and the vagaries of world wheat markets led to troubled times for mallee farmers that seriously dented the agrarian ideal.

Empire Settlement Scheme

One of the most ill-conceived and notorious attempts to settle the Victorian Mallee was the Empire Settlement Scheme. At the scheme's heart was the desire to populate Australia with white English settlers, strengthen the bonds of Empire and stimulate economic growth. Britain, conscious of its growing post-war unemployment rate and keen to support rural developments in its dominions, agreed to assist its citizens to join the scheme. The 1922 intergovernmental agreement saw the cost of passage for an immigrant split three ways between the Victorian government, the British government and the

---

[1] A.E.V. Richardson, 'Wheat and its Cultivation: Part I', *Journal of the Department of Agriculture of Victoria* 12 (1914): 715, quoted in Lionel Frost, 'Victorian Agriculture and the Role of Government, 1880–1914' (PhD thesis, Monash University, 1986), 281.

immigrant. The Commonwealth government agreed to provide an interest-free loan to the Victorian government of £166,000 and to guarantee bank advances for new immigrants. Dryland farms of 640 acres were to be sold to the new arrivals, with the promise of supervision, advice and an advance of £500 for stock and equipment.

The Victorian government vigorously promoted the scheme, with the state premier travelling to England to boast of the bright futures awaiting potential immigrants. The booklet *Victoria, the Speedway to Rural Prosperity* described the Mallee as ideal for farming. Success in wheat growing and animal husbandry was 'practically assured' for those with a reasonable amount of capital who made the journey. The pamphlet described the 'great vital emptiness' of Australia. Victoria, it stated, 'has much fertile space to spare, and needed a strong accession of British people to her rural population'. The British heritage was crucial for Victoria: 'its life will be renewed, and added to by the same class and type as those who established these Australian colonies not 100 years ago. Our population can be kept pure and unsullied'. The *Speedway* pamphlet, as it became known, noted that Victoria had seen a rapid increase in the area devoted to cultivation, a growth attributed to improved farming methods such as fallowing, fertilisers, suitable seeds and the increased attention to crop rotation. Thanks to these improved methods, 'the soil is becoming richer, more productive and wealth-producing each season'. The pamphlet's description of the climate clearly misconstrued the truth about the hot and dry Mallee. Northern Victoria had an 'average rainfall generally below 20 inches … The climate is wonderfully sunshiny and genial, and combined with the soil, has made this part the granary of Australia'.[2]

The area of the Mallee chosen for these uninitiated newcomers was the Millewa in the north-west corner of the Victorian Mallee. The rainfall there is lower than in the southern Mallee and the soil mostly lighter, although this was not widely known to would-be settlers. The area had previously been considered too marginal for agricultural settlement. However, the belief in new farming techniques, the promise of science, and the triumph of ideology saw it opened in 1925 as part of the Empire Settlement Scheme.

The Victorian government made a huge investment in the Millewa. It constructed rudimentary roads and a rail line to transport supplies needed to build houses, excavate dams, make and fertilise farms, and create the necessary

---

2   Victoria, Department of Crown Lands and Survey, *Victoria, the Speedway to Rural Prosperity: A Handbook for Intending Settlers, Showing Methods of Acquiring Farms from the Crown* … Rev. ed. (Melbourne: H.J. Green, Government Printer, 1926), 10, 11, 12, 15.

infrastructure for storing and carrying wheat. Work on the channel system to carry water from the Murray River began, with dams built at Willah and at intervals along the rail track as an interim measure for water storage, using rail transport, until the channels were complete.[3] About a hundred British families in search of land and prosperity journeyed in hope to the Millewa. Given the propaganda fed them, it is not surprising that these British settlers, many of them urban dwellers, arrived with little understanding of the Mallee or farming. A six-week training course at Camp Elcho near Geelong did little to equip them with the skills required to succeed in Australian conditions, although reports suggest it significantly fuelled their belief that the Mallee offered excellent prospects for would-be farmers.[4]

Like participants in other land schemes, British settlers were required to undertake 'improvements' to their blocks. They had to build homes, fences, stockyards and a dam, which would be filled each winter by water from the channel system—once it was operating. Like many of the settlers in the Millewa region, those migrating from England found the work demanding and relentless. They had the added challenge of an environment that was hot, dry and boundless, entirely foreign to their homeland. To top this off, wheat prices were falling as they were pioneering.[5]

Dissatisfactions inevitably arose. In 1927, about sixty British settlers in the Willah parish came together to form the British Settlers League. Their secretary wrote to the British government's representative for migration in Melbourne, Mr Amery, airing their concerns. Their major difficulty was the hold-up in paying advances to settlers. Contractors could not begin work, delaying by at least a year settlers' efforts to begin sowing. Amery forwarded this complaint to the Commonwealth, which was clearly sensitive about the matter as it 'involved the whole question of satisfactory settlement and the effect of complaints reaching London'. The national body established to administer the scheme was the Development and Migration Commission, which acknowledged that no school had been provided for the hundred British

---

3   Andrew McCormick, 'Closer Settlement in the Mallee: Dust Followed the Plough: The Millewa in the 1930s and 1940s' (MA thesis, La Trobe University, 2010), 51, accessed 12 November 2018, http://hdl.handle.net/1959.9/520929.

4   McCormick, 'Closer Settlement in the Mallee', 44–5.

5   In real terms the prices of wheat received by the farmer rose from a base of 100 in the season 1921–22 to 124 in 1924–25. The index dropped to 82 in 1929–30 and 43 in 1930–31. The five-year average from 1930–31 to 1935–36 was 62. Calculated from Commonwealth C-Series Cost of Living Index, and from Charles Coote, Wheat Pool Book, in Charles William Coote, Diaries and Papers, 1896–1955, 1964.0005, University of Melbourne Archives.

settlers, adding: 'obviously the Commission will need to give consideration as to what action it will take concerning Victoria'.[6]

A flashpoint for the settlers and the Victorian government came when Prime Minister Stanley Bruce publicly acknowledged in October 1928 that the extension of the Nowingi railway into the Millewa was unviable. It would involve the state in considerable economic loss and destine settlers to heartbreak and an income below a living wage. The secretary of the Overseas Mallee Settlers' Association, Mr Legge-Wilkinson, pointed out in a letter to Prime Minister Bruce that sixty British settlers in the Millewa were only a few miles north of this area. The assessment of the Nowingi area also applied to them. Legge-Wilkinson added that the booklet *Victoria, the Speedway to Rural Prosperity* had been their Bible with its promise that the Mallee offered the 'best chance of making good'. Settlers 'have since lost their entire capital and reaped to date crops of debt and mallee shoots'. The letter concluded by praising the prime minister for his candour: 'you are admired for the pluck which it must have required to say in public that there are limits to land settlement in Australia'.[7]

The prime minister's candid assessment of the fate awaiting settlers in the Nowingi area unwittingly caused something of a diplomatic incident. The Overseas Mallee Settlers from Willah were galvanised and lobbied hard and effectively. The British government sent a secret (coded) cable to Herbert Gepp, the chairman of the Development and Migration Commission: the 'highest political circles' in Britain and overseas were 'extremely disturbed' over the 'most damning' report on the Nowingi line and the government's refusal to sanction the scheme. Gepp was urged to use all his 'influence and powers' to engage an independent adjudicator and hold an inquiry into the matter.

For Britain, the Migration Agreement between the Commonwealth and British governments was at stake. Australia was failing to uphold its end of the bargain. One of the key issues that emerged in the 'Report on the Position of British Settlers in Millewa', which was compiled by the Mallee District Council, was the failure of the Victorian government to properly assess the suitability of the Millewa region as a wheat-producing area. The settlers were particularly aggrieved about the false premises on which they had come. They

---

6   Memorandum. Discussion with Mr Banks Amery—12 April 1927, Australia, Prime Minister's Department, Development Branch Correspondence Files, Series A786, Control H61/1, Barcode 168719, National Archives of Australia (NAA).

7   Mr Legge-Wilkinson to Prime Minister of Australia, 8 November 1928, Series A786, Control H61/1, Barcode 168719, NAA.

had been told that 'in return for their capital, personal energies and enterprise, they would be settled upon land of the right kind to return them a steady income'. But they found themselves in an area where 'not even the very best of farming methods can ensure success ... where the rainfall will always be an uncertain quantity'. The settlers were 'weary of the situation for they are without money or prospects, they are in a place far from the ordinary amenities of life and where, in the opinion of many, it is unfit for white women to live'.[8] Victoria may have wanted to attract Britons to help fill its empty land, but such space was not ready for that most civilising of influences, the white British woman.

One such white woman, Clarice Lampard, was more concerned about the impact of the Mallee on her husband's health. She wrote to Gepp at the Development and Migration Commission, commenting on the toll that clearing the 'thick dead Mallee with shoots mostly more than 12 ft high' had taken on her husband. He had 'worked here for five years without a break and this harvest has almost broken his health. He is a sick man and will need help this year'. Clarice Lampard wrote without her husband's knowledge; she could not 'stand back and see him worrying himself ill with hard work and financial trouble'.[9]

In 1930, pressure from the British government forced the Victorian government, which hitherto had blamed wheat prices and poor seasons for the trouble, to appoint a royal commission to investigate the plight of the British settlers. It reported in 1933, confirming the settlers' claims that neither 'the soil or the rainfall would enable farming to be carried on successfully even by experienced Australians upon the blocks [in the north-west Mallee] allocated to the complainants'. It found that only one year in three produced enough rainfall to maximise the potential of the soil. The royal commission was particularly critical of the *Speedway* publication and the impressions of farming in Victoria that it promoted. It stated the *Speedway* contained 'turgid panegyrics of farming conditions in Victoria—somewhat like the salesman's puffing generalities which most people have learned to discount largely when not uttered on behalf of Governments'.[10] The royal commission's report 'led to

---

8   'Report on Position of British Settlers in Millewa', compiled by the Mallee District Council of the Overseas Settlers' Association, 1–2, Series A786, Control H61/1, Barcode 168719, NAA.

9   Clarice Lampard to Mr Gepp of Migration Committee, 29 January 1929, Series A786, Control H61/1, Barcode 168719, NAA.

10   Victoria, 'Report of the Royal Commission on Migrant Land Settlement: Together with Schedule', *Victorian Parliamentary Papers*, 1933, paper no. 3, 7.

a demand for compensation that echoed to Britain and back'.[11] The Victorian government paid between £300 and £500 to each of those who had already walked off their blocks, and set aside £100,000 for compensation on top of £300,000 already lost on farmers' bad debts.

Victoria was not the only state to make use of the Empire Settlement Scheme to populate its 'empty lands'. Western Australia's endeavour took the form of the '3,500 Farms Scheme', a plan to establish wheat farms in the area south of Southern Cross and west of Salmon Gums. Early estimates for this ambitious scheme predicted twelve million bushels of wheat would be produced annually, with substantial advances in wool and sheep production. About 650 miles of railways were to be built at a cost of nearly £3,000,000. The program of work was to take five years and employ two thousand men.

But reservations were expressed early. The *Northern Times* newspaper reported in May 1930: 'The project was merging into the light of early practicability when disquieting reports came to hand disclosing unsatisfactory harvest returns by farmers already settled within certain of these areas, a paucity of yield attributed to the presence of salts in the soil'. The Western Australian government heeded the warnings from the fate of the Victorian Empire Settlement Scheme in the Victorian Mallee. Research commissioned by the state government 'was of such a disquieting nature that it was decided to suspend any further activity'. The scheme, boasted the *Northern Times*, was 'one of the mightiest agricultural projects ever conceived by a State Government in the British Dominions'.[12] But the venture was killed by doubts and a fall in global wheat prices.

The decision to abandon the scheme, however, came too late for two hundred settlers who had already taken up land in the area and found themselves between twenty and fifty miles from the nearest railway station. As a form of compensation 'the State Government paid them a transport subsidy of 4½d. per ton mile on wheat',[13] but there was widespread abandonment of blocks. At least the government and the might-have-been settlers were saved the expense and hardship that Victoria's Millewa settlers endured.

---

11   Richard Broome, *The Victorians: Arriving* (Melbourne: Fairfax, Syme & Weldon, 1984), 145.

12   *Northern Times* (Carnarvon, WA), 29 May 1930.

13   Sean Glynn, *Government Policy and Agricultural Development: A Study of the Role of Government in the Development of the Western Australian Wheat Belt, 1900–1930* (Perth: University of Western Australia Press, 1975), 130.

Soldier Settlement

While the agonies of the Empire Settlement Scheme were playing out, the returned servicemen established on the land under the 1917 soldier settlement scheme were still battling to make a go of mallee farming, especially in the Victorian Mallee. Their heroic efforts, and the commitment of the Victorian government to make the scheme work, again testified to the continuing power of the closer settlement ideal. Several case studies reveal the difficulties of all parties in the context of variable seasons and wheat prices.

William Abbott's case was typical of a settler's hopes and difficulties, soldier or not. Abbott had no wheat-farming experience, being either a clerk or a dairyman before his war service. He was discharged in 1919 as medically unfit from the effects of mustard gas. Despite his condition he applied in March 1920 for a block. He was then unemployed, married with one child, and living in Sandringham, Melbourne. Abbott gained 941 acres at Daytrap, near Chinkapook, twenty kilometres north east of Lake Tyrrell in the Victorian Mallee. Part of his block was cleared, although Abbott later described this cleared area as 'overgrown with rubbish and cropped out'. He lamented to Inspector Ellery that his wife 'went up to the block looked at the place & returned to Melbourne'.[14] Abbott continued alone.

By 1923 Abbott was in trouble and requested an advance from the Closer Settlement Board. He had sixty acres in fallow but noted, 'at present time I am pretty hard up against it as I cannot get any stores without the money'. Ellery considered Abbott a 'good settler' and recommended an advance of £25. By November 1923 Abbott had received £1,024 in advances. In October 1924 Abbott explained his need for these significant advances. He intended to run sheep as well as wheat, and his brother, soon to be married, would work the block with him: 'I am quite confident that I can succeed'. A new inspector was sceptical, recording, 'it is freely reported that lessee spends too much money at the hotels'. He recommended against any direct advances to Abbott, but the board paid £20 'against improvements' direct to the local storekeeper.

In May 1925 Abbott still expressed confidence in his ability to 'eventually meet all [his] obligations'. His letter suggested he had no sheep or a brother working with him but had a hundred acres in good fallow and 150 acres cleared, ploughed and 'ready for cropping'. Inspector Cloonan reported in June: the 'lessee appears not to understand the best method of farming he has this year seriously damaged his fallow by too deep working with a disc'. The

---

14 All correspondence relating to William Abbott found at VPRS 749/P0000/1, PROV.

inspector gave Abbott clear instructions. The board advanced a further £50, warning that Abbott in future must finance the farm himself. Nine months later Abbott was applying for sustenance. Benign seasons in the early twenties and the hope of making farms work encouraged the board to make advances. When the seasons turned against Abbott and other settlers and wheat prices remained low, debts mounted to dangerous levels, and compound interest on loans placed many farmers in a parlous position.

The very dry year of 1927 marked the turning point. Inspector Cloonan declared that year that Abbott was unlikely to succeed: 'He appears to be very indifferent'. The fencing was 'in very bad order' and the 'farm seems uncared for'. Abbott's situation prompted a visit from the supervisor, who thought him in a 'hopeless position' and that the best solution, for the board and for Abbott, was to find a purchaser for the block. Abbott resisted and instead applied for, and was granted, drought relief. He was even advanced another £196.

In 1929 he sought a further nine months sustenance and manure. Inspector Ellery thought he was 'improving in his farming' and that he was 'endeavouring to make a success'. He advised six tons of manure and £8 a month sustenance for nine months. A few months later, however, Ellery observed that Abbott's likelihood of success was 'doubtful'. There was a 'general air of neglect about the holding, fences down, no outbuildings, machinery poor & uncared for. Lessee lacks ability & experience' and, although the block had 'good soil', it was 'badly cut with roads making working of [it] difficult and detracting from value'. Abbott's total liabilities were assessed at a massive £5,855.

Abbott's fortunes spiralled down. He requested advances, and the board complied. The final inspector's report in March 1934 noted that Abbott considered 'himself in a hopeless position and appears to have lost heart. States he has sufficient land but has never been granted adequate plant [horses] to work it properly … This block bears a neglected appearance indicating lack of ambition to succeed'. Abbott agreed to relinquish his lease. He was paid £75 by the Closer Settlement Board for 'improvements' and walked away from his block owing a staggering £7,118, nearly seventy times the basic annual wage of an Australian farm labourer.[15]

The Baird family provides another revealing case study of farmer difficulties and Board complicity in their ineptitude. In November 1918 Frank Baird applied for two allotments of land totalling 959 acres near the Victorian town of Hopetoun. He was twenty-four, had served on the Western Front, and like Abbott was discharged as medically unfit. His application refers

---

15 *Victorian Year Book, 1934–35*, 431.

Figure 7.1: The task of grubbing mallee roots could continue for many years after the initial work of rolling and clearing the mallee scrub. This *c.* 1935 photo of 'Kulwin Park Farm', Kulwin, Victoria, shows the protruding mallee roots and the challenging work of extracting them from the ground. The extent of clearing and landscape transformation is evident in the denuded landscape.
(Courtesy Museums Victoria, MM2532, https://collections.museumvictoria.com.au/items/773725)

to rheumatism and aching joints but did not disclose he was discharged for a bayonet wound to the hip; Baird repeated the view of the army's medical officer, that he needed 'open air and warm climate'.[16] Baird had experience of farming wheat and sheep on his father's farm. His correspondence with the Closer Settlement Board reveals a sense of entitlement. 'I need the following advances at once', he wrote in November 1919, and the next April requested money to pay a workman, warning the board that to go slow 'will mean no return next season'. Inspector Redding reported 'this settler is doing good work', and within two years the board had advanced Frank Baird £1,120.

Colin Baird, a returned soldier and brother of Frank, was allocated a 480-acre block next door to Frank's in 1920. Colin's application noted that his 'future wife [was] used to country'.[17] Mary Welfare was a teacher at Hopetoun

---

16   All correspondence relating to Frank Baird found in VPRS 749/P0000/000010, PROV.
17   All correspondence relating to Colin Baird found in VPRS 749/P0000/000010, PROV.

West primary school when they met; she was one of many teachers posted to the Mallee who would prove to be attractive marriage prospects for farmers. She had been born on the Western Australia goldfields and was a graduate of the University of Western Australia. They married in 1921 and had eight children by the end of the decade. In 1922 Colin requested a freeze on his repayments and permission to hold back more seed and more hay 'for horse feed as hay crops are so uncertain on average years here, we make provision when the good seasons occur'. He also requested £40 to pay his account at the local store, noting that he had 'managed to pay up all liabilities but have no money left to pay this account'. The board declined his request noting his advances 'considerably exceed the amount you were entitled to under the Act'.

By 1923 Frank Baird was in dire straits, being incapacitated and in Caulfield military hospital for a second treatment of his hip wound. A visitor sent by the board reported he was a 'cot case'. Frank pleaded for leniency. He did not return to his block for two years and could not work it for another year after that, although his brother Colin and their father worked it for him. By April 1925 Frank owed the board £4,180. He thought his 'position hopeless'. Both brothers tried to sell their blocks, without success. Both took bank loans to pay debts to local creditors and brought share farmers onto their blocks. Frank's letters to the board became desperate. By January 1928 all sense of entitlement had vanished, and he wondered if the board considered him 'an outsider'. He pleaded that four years of 'complete incapacitation, followed by a dry year & a drought' had ruined his efforts and requested some help. Frank Baird struggled on before being declared bankrupt in May 1933. Another returned soldier was transferred to the land.

Colin and Mary Baird tried to expand their way out of trouble. In May 1929 Mary applied in her name for a 1,600-acre block at Dattuck, now bordering the Wyperfield National Park. It is a highly variable landscape with soils ranging from too much clay to too much sand. They cleared the land and built a small house for their large family. The inspector thought Mary a 'good type' and recommended an advance of £60. The board declined until Colin had sold his own block. In March 1930 Mary again requested an advance, the inspector reporting their 'excellent progress', but the board again declined, stating it did not grant advances 'to husbands and also to wives who both hold blocks of land'.[18]

The tone of the board's letters to Mary is subtly different from those addressed to male settlers, and minor issues took on major significance. In July

---

18   All correspondence relating to Mary Baird found in VPRS 749/P0000/000010, PROV.

1932 Mary requested an advance for wire netting to erect a rabbit-proof fence as her land was surrounded by Crown land that was 'infested with rabbits': 'I have poisoned and fumigated on my holding but find it impossible to cope with the rabbits, swarming in from the crown lands which are overgrown with dense scrub. Unless this fencing material can be made available to me I will lose the whole of my crop'. The board declined her request. The local inspector reminded the board that the neighbouring settler was given an advance to purchase rabbit traps, and that the rabbits were now being driven onto Mary's property. The board remained unmoved.

Mary then informed the board that she would herself act against rabbits on Crown land. The board supplied two tins of poison, along with a bill for £3 18s 4d. Mary refused to pay to kill rabbits on Crown land. The board sought payment for two years, but Mary refused. The final inspector's report in Mary's file of 4 February 1935 noted she had gone to Queensland for several months, but 'I will endeavour to collect installment when she returns'. Her sixth son Bob noted in his memoirs: 'Of course we hadn't gone to Queensland. We'd done the MIDNIGHT FLIGHT!'[19] In 1997, sixty-four years after their escape, Mary and Colin's eight children erected a plaque to their parents on the Dattuck block. The inscription concluded that they 'settled this place in hope in the 1920s, and left in despair in the 1930s'.

Experiences such as those of the Bairds and Abbotts were played out by the hundreds across the Victorian Mallee. They may have differed in the kinds of relations settlers had with inspectors, the size of the debt or the speed with which settlers came to grief. But settlers continued to receive advances, and the debts owed to the Closer Settlement Board quickly spiralled out of control. The board seemed reluctant to remove settlers from their blocks, even in the face of overwhelming evidence that continued assistance was compounding the problem. Foreclosing on settlers who had endured the trials of the war and were often, like Frank Baird, carrying significant wartime injuries would have been politically fraught. Poor seasons after 1927 compounded the problem, and a collapse in the world price of wheat after 1930 added to settlers' woes.

Eventually the board removed some settlers. In 1932 the Victorian parliament legislated on a process of adjustment for Mallee settlers to be taken in two steps: first, by adjusting land areas; and, second, by the radical step of writing off debts. Although the Act was passed in the early 1930s, the process of adjustment was not completed until 1937 and beyond.

---

19 Bob Baird, 'The Bairds in the Mallee, 1919–1934' (unpublished manuscript in the author's possession, 2007), 9.

Figure 7.2: Leaving the Mallee was a common experience for settlers. Many decided, through choice or because their blocks proved unviable, that farming in the Mallee was not for them. This photograph captures a sense of defeat as Les Cocking and Fred Roberts leave the Mallee in 1929.
(Courtesy Museums Victoria, MM2371, https://collections.museumvictoria.com.au/items/769179)

To counter the difficulties of the Great Depression, the state government also introduced a bill to alleviate hardship arising from rents owed by Crown leaseholders, and granted a moratorium on debts for farmers.

Between 1933 and 1938, 1,127 Mallee holdings were deemed unsuitable and withdrawn. The Victorian government paid farmers to leave their blocks and restructured the debts of those remaining. It encouraged farmers to diversify into sheep production so as to ensure an income in the face of droughts and the failure of wheat crops. The soldier settlement and Empire Settlement schemes cost governments and people dearly. Economist W.D. Forsyth estimated in 1942 that about half of the increase in Australia's national debt from £135 to £171 per head in the 1920s was due to the Empire Settlement Scheme alone. The desire to people the land with British stock, he added, led to wasteful spending and increased overseas debt, contributing 'to the severity of the depression in Australia'.[20] The process of financial adjustment initiated in 1932 was continued through the 1940s and into the 1950s with drought relief for Crown leaseholders. To the settlers who walked off with nothing, or who were removed from their leaseholds with a mere £100 in compensation, the system appeared punitive. Those who remained to fight on against land and climate were given very generous financial support. It came too late for many like William Abbott or the Baird family.

Underpinning government land policy and the endless loans given in the interwar years by the Closer Settlement Board was a continued if less assured belief in the yeoman ideal. The Victorian government placed its hope in the selection of the right 'type' of settler, Australian or British, despite the lessons learned from earlier schemes about the importance of the suitability of the land as well as the skills and capital needed by prospective farmers. Government-designed farmer education schemes reveal an ongoing commitment to the farmer rather than the farm.

Farmer Education: The Better Farming Train

In Western Australia, the Department of Agriculture recognised the need for farmer education on improved methods of cultivation and animal husbandry. The distances involved in reaching mallee farmers, together with a limited budget, made this difficult. Strategies such as the publication of the *Agricultural Journal*, special bulletins, lectures, regionally based experimental farms, and wheat yield competitions all helped drive an improvement in the standard

---

20   W.D. Forsyth, *The Myth of Open Spaces: Australian, British and World Trends of Population and Migration* (Melbourne: Melbourne University Press, 1942), 179.

of farming. The use of fertilisers, fallowing and new wheat seed increased in the 1920s. In South Australia a similar approach was adopted. The Waite Agricultural Research Centre near Loxton was established in 1924, and the *Journal of the Department of Agriculture of South Australia* produced research for farmers. As in Victoria, field days and annual cropping competitions provided other opportunities for farmers to learn from fellow farmers and experts alike, and agricultural shows and parish competitions gave farmers the chance to display their skills in animal husbandry and agriculture.[21]

For Victorian farmers, the Better Farming Train complemented these activities with particular attention to the scientific nature of modern farming. This enterprise was a joint endeavour between the Victorian government and the Department of Railways. The train travelled across Victoria on a mission to educate the state's farmers in modern scientific farming methods, as well as moral improvement. It was modelled on similar strategies in North America, and the Canadian prototype was particularly influential in the development of the scheme in Victoria.[22] Between 1925 and 1935 the Better Farming Train made a total of seven visits to different regions in the Mallee. The push to educate the Mallee farmer marked a desire to spread the 'doctrine of better farming' and a recognition that farmers in challenging regions needed useful knowledge and support. Like its North American predecessors, the train incorporated a women's car to spread the principles of scientific living to the domestic sphere.[23]

The Better Farming Train's tours through the Mallee were amongst the most successful undertaken in Victoria. In 1928, seven thousand people turned out to view the exhibitions, listen to lectures, attend demonstrations and lantern slide shows, and speak with the much-touted 'expert' staff.[24] A South Australian newspaper reported in January 1926 that 'at two small towns in the [Victorian] mallee every member of every household, including

---

21   McCormick, 'Closer Settlement in the Mallee', 64; Kate Darian-Smith, 'Histories of Agricultural Shows and Rural Festivals in Australia', in *Festival Places: Revitalising Rural Australia*, eds Chris Gibson and John Connell (Bristol: Channel View Publications, 2011), 25–43.

22   For an extended discussion of the Better Farming Train in Victoria, see Katie Holmes and Kylie Mirmohamadi, 'All Aboard for Modernity: The Better Farming Train', *Journal of Agricultural History* 91, no. 2 (Spring 2017): 215–38.

23   Richard J. Orsi, *Sunset Limited: The Southern Pacific Railroad and the Development of the American West, 1850–1930* (Berkeley: University of California Press, 2005), 305.

24   The population of the Mallee in 1928 was 44,928. *Victorian Year Book 1928–29* (Melbourne: H.J. Green, Government Printer, 1929), 50. It increased by 51.8 per cent between 1921 and 1933.

babies, came along'.²⁵ As images of its visits to the Mallee reveal, there was something of a country fair atmosphere when the Better Farming Train came to town. It was a family event and offered longed-for contact with the outside world. Women donned hats and their Sunday best clothes, men dressed in suits, and children came along for the entertainment.

One of the key techniques in the 'doctrine of better farming' that the train carried to the Mallee was the system of bare fallowing. Arguably adopted in the late nineteenth century from a system developed in America's semi-arid farming districts, fallowing involved disc ploughing the soil after rain, thereby trapping the moisture below the surface. The scientific justification of this system at the time was that moisture rose to the surface through capillary tubes in the soil. If those tubes were broken, evaporation would be limited.²⁶ In Australia the 'scientific' system of fallowing, accompanied by the use of superphosphate, was believed to protect grain yields against low rainfall.

The Department of Agriculture was very clear that bare fallowing was the 'outstanding factor in making for success in wheat growing' in the Mallee. Officers from the department accompanied the train to explain the 'good' methods of fallowing. Exhibits demonstrated how 'fallowing conserves moisture in the soil, as well as … how the soil bacteria are more active in fallowed land than in non-fallow'.²⁷ Pamphlets marrying scientific authority with practical information were distributed. Only science enabled the experts to know that the 'minute organisms' active in Mallee soils played 'a very important part in wheat growing'. They were essential to the formation of nitrates, 'a fact that explains why the wheat grower here finds it unnecessary to purchase nitrogenous fertilisers'.²⁸ Amongst the key exhibits on the train were 'actual sods' brought from the department's experimental Mallee farms. The 1934 train displayed the differences in types of fallowing and the ensuing results.

The Better Farming Train and accompanying literature assumed that, as the farmer improved his land, so too he was improving himself and his family. The moral education the train aimed to inculcate was particularly clear in the descriptive text accompanying exhibits and the slogans displayed on the walls. 'Good Fallow' was the product of a hard-working, industrious farmer; 'Poor

---

25 *News* [South Australia], 22 January 1926.
26 L.E. Frost, 'Victorian Agriculture and the Role of Government, 1880–1914' (PhD thesis, Monash University, 1982), 256–7.
27 'Better Farming Train Pamphlet, Tour No. 22, North Western Lines, 30 July to 11 August 1928', 3, Department of Agriculture Correspondence Files, VPRS 3477/P/0002, unit 32, folder 1, PROV.
28 'Better Farming Train Pamphlet, Tour No. 22, North Western Lines, 30 July to 11 August 1928'.

Fallow' reflected sloth and a lack of care.[29] Farmers were exhorted to 'Feed your fields and flourish', 'Wage war on weeds', 'Use phosphates and enlarge your bank account', 'Farm with your head', and 'Keep the plough going'. And they were assured that 'Healthy crops make wealthy owners', 'Diminishing yields denote bad farming', 'Feed your land and it will feed you'. Within the language of the train's walls, farming was understood as a predictable enterprise where simple rules could be followed with success assured. Success was about the right approach, the right attitude, and the right additives. The variables of climate, soil quality, and size of holdings did not feature in this inventory of qualities that would ensure fortune.

Ironically the farming methods promoted by the train, the Department of Agriculture and the inspectors of the Closer Settlement Board had a devastating impact on the Mallee. The system of bare fallowing was widely adopted across the Victorian Mallee, but we now know that its basic premise—trapping the moisture within the soil by breaking capillary action—is false. Indeed, excessive tillage destroys the soil structure, depletes soil fertility and causes erosion, although the destruction of weeds prevented loss of moisture.

However, farmers had absorbed the message and made it their own. When the Better Farming Train returned to the Mallee for its final visit in 1935 and problems with dust storms and drift were 'very bad', farmers were reported as voicing 'much opposition to the proposal to restrict fallowing near roads and channels'.[30] The problem of 'drifting sand' was raised with the 'experts' on board the train, who advised that 'the drift would be mitigated by cutting out the burning-off of stubble and following up with oats for grazing—with the roots remaining in the soil it would be less liable to drift', a practice that also proved ineffective.[31]

One of the most popular of all the Better Farming Train's attractions was the women's section. Female experts from the city promoted both 'scientific' and 'modern' management of (largely domestic) female labour carried out on farms, and these methods were tethered to the notion of moral improvement based on the influence of the family and home. They instructed country women in 'domestic hygiene', needlecraft, cookery and infant health and welfare, insisting that 'modern research' and technology could render the 'country home ... much easier of management',

---

29 In Australian English, the aural association between 'Good/ Poor Fallow' and 'Good/ Poor Fellow' (meaning man) would have been unavoidable.

30 VPRS 3477/P/2, Unit 32, Folder 1, PROV. Note in file, n.d. *c.* 1935.

31 *Argus*, 20 March 1935.

and enhance the comfort of its 'housewife'.[32] On board the train, domestic instruction was represented as an extension of the scientific management of the farm. Parallels between the farmer's work in the paddock and his wife's in the (rationalised) farmhouse were explicitly drawn. Truby King, the exponent of systematic childcare, whose work created 'model modern babies', suggested that a child welfare nurse might give occasional addresses to farmers.[33] This should take place:

> after [the farmers] have been impressed with the supreme importance of sound knowledge, science, and system in the rearing of crops and stock, as men ought to understand the equally practical, equally scientific, and equally intellectual nature of the problem of how to do the very best for mother and child.

The farmer would then realise that his wife's work in the care and rearing of the family was on par with 'the difficulties that confront him in the rearing of first class calves'.[34]

The rationalisation of farm work was closely aligned with the modernisation of housework and the organisation of the farmhouse. In the pamphlet handed out on the 1928 tour of the north-western Mallee district, the 'rural housewife' was informed that the 'highly developed equipment' available could ease the management of the country home. Additionally, she could be assisted by 'what modern research has to tell her in regard to domestic practices, health principles, etc.'. If this 'highly developed equipment' ran on electricity, however, it would have been of limited use to the Mallee housewife; home generators supplied power in the 1950s with mains electricity not widely adopted through the Mallee until the 1960s. The alignment of farm work with housework suggests a gendered cultural imagining of how land could be transformed through settlement. Married women were cast as agents of settlement through their child-rearing and homemaking. They were a key element of 'correct' yeoman settlement, embodied in the family farm. The Better Farming Train was one of the few places, like country fairs, where women's labour and contribution to the rural economy was actually visible, and at least partially acknowledged.

---

32 'Better Farming Train Pamphlet, Tour No. 22, North Western Lines, 30 July to 11 August 1928', 12.

33 Heather Sheard, *All the Little Children: The Story of Victoria's Baby Health Centres* (Melbourne: Municipal Association of Victoria, 2007), 32.

34 *Argus*, 23 November 1925, 18.

Mallee Life

While the Better Farming Train was attentive to Mallee women's participation in the settlement endeavour, evidence of how women themselves experienced their Mallee lives is harder to find. With notable exceptions such as that of Mary Baird, the Closer Settlement files predominantly reflect the voices of men, albeit refracted through a highly bureaucratic archive. One place we do hear women's voices is in their letters to 'The Women's Bureau' page of the *Weekly Times*. Ruth Ford has observed that the 130 letters from Mallee women printed between 1931 and 1940 reflected the urge to correspond as in part 'a response to their physical isolation'.[35]

The women's letters challenged the popular perception of the Mallee as desolate and drought ravaged, and show more complex emotions. They reveal women's intense immersion in their landscape and the love/hate relationship many had with it. One correspondent, writing under the nickname 'Hop-Bush', described the 'gorgeous skyscapes—beautiful and varying sunrises and sunsets—an ever-changing sea of bronze and gold as the wind ruffles the tips of the Mallee on sunny days'. Although hard work was part of Mallee life, for 'Hop-Bush' the 'vast open spaces bring good health, and add zest to the joy of living'.[36] For many writers spring was a season to treasure with its abundant wildflowers and 'pure fresh air' full of birdsong. One writer told of the six varieties of wattles in the surrounding bush. In 1948 Hazel Hogan wrote *The Story of Kulwin*, an account of her experiences as a settler in the small district near Sea Lake. She recalled the 'lovely wild Mallee birds ... Mallee birds which have been a joy to us from dawn to sunset throughout the long, past years'. But the Major Mitchell cockatoo was becoming rare, and 'the wildflowers retreat each year as cultivation and soil erosion advances'. As paddocks were cleared of the mallee trees, with them went the 'inviting, shady places for luncheon baskets and a picnic'.[37]

Mallee women's letters to the *Weekly Times* also reveal the anguish many women experienced as they faced years of bad seasons or low wheat prices. While spring usually brought hopes of a good harvest, six weeks without rain would see hopes fade and despair encroach. Repeated crop failures left

---

35   Ruth Ford, '"The Wattles Are in Bloom ... Crops Are Looking Wonderfully Well": Settler Women in the Victorian Mallee, 1920–30s', in *Outside Country: Histories of Inland Australia*, eds Alan Mayne and Stephen Atkinson (Adelaide: Wakefield Press, 2011), 65.
36   Quoted in Ford, '"The Wattles Are in Bloom ..."', 72.
37   Hazel V. Hogan, *The Story of Kulwin* (Kulwin: CWA of Victoria, Kulwin Branch, 1948), 8.

many women such as 'Blue Bonnet Also' desperate. After twenty-one years of living in the Mallee, in June 1935 she reflected, 'we're worse off this year than when we started. The flies, mosquitoes and dust would drive any housekeeper grey'. Her isolation echoed the parched landscape: 'I never see sports, dances or picture shows. As for rain, it has forgotten how ... the paddocks are brown, excepting on the sand hills, where oats are sown ... We don't live in the Mallee, we just exist'.[38]

Women wrote eloquently about the searing summer heat and, as the 1930s progressed, the increasing frequency of dust storms. One correspondent recalled a night-time dust storm that made the house rock, and the work that awaited her in the morning: 'Every floor, shelf, ornament had to be scrubbed—sweeping and dusting made no effect. The noise of the sand hitting the window was like rain'.[39] The letters reflect the environmental disaster unfolding in the Mallee. They also reveal the differences in experience between those who had settled in the 1890s in the 'old Mallee', where rainfall was higher and farms established, and those in the more marginal areas of the 'new Mallee', on farms too small to be viable and where farming practices designed to extract greater productivity from the soil led to increased degradation.

Just as women acknowledged the harshness of the surrounding landscape, many also learnt to love it, their pen names often selected from native wildflowers. Some sought to soften the area around their home with a garden that would provide essential food for the family and respite from the heat. In *A Woman's Work*, Florence Beaton recalls the garden her mother Clara established on their block near Carwarp, where she planted citrus, mulberry and fig trees, a currant vine, wisteria and bougainvillea. She also transplanted wildflowers from the surrounding bush, and her husband built a fence from mallee roots to protect the garden from rabbits. Like many others in the Mallee, she grew peppercorn trees, which provided a haven of shade outside the garden.[40] While Mallee women writing to the *Weekly Times* certainly recounted hardship and unrelenting work, many, as Ruth Ford observes, also registered pride in sustaining their families by growing vegetables, keeping chooks, milking, baking and bottling. Especially during the Depression, when those in the city had limited access to such life-sustaining necessities, life in the Mallee seemed preferable to that in the city.

---

38   *Weekly Times*, 15 June 1935, quoted in Ford, '"The Wattles Are in Bloom ..."', 75.
39   *Weekly Times*, 8 June 1935, quoted in Ford, '"The Wattles Are in Bloom ..."', 79.
40   Florence Beaton, *A Woman's Work: The Story of a Mallee Farmer's Wife from 1913* (Red Cliffs, Vic.: Sunnyland Press, 1985), 35–6.

Figure 7.3: Mallee roots were often used for firewood, but here they formed a wall for Clara Beaton's garden near Carwarp, Victoria, 1934. (Courtesy Museums Victoria, MM5321, https://collections.museumvictoria.com.au/items/770366)

Ford concluded: 'Their letters construct an oasis of abundance and tranquillity despite their own continuing hardships'.[41]

Established Farmers

Although the financial crisis of the early 1930s hit both recently settled and earlier settled mallee regions, farmers in the older settled districts were better placed to deal with its effects. By the mid-1920s many in districts such as Pinnaroo, Lameroo, Hopetoun, Birchip or Quambatook had over a quarter of a century of experience in mallee farming, and many, like Charles Coote, had come from family farming backgrounds. After several decades of crop growing, they had dug up and carted most of the roots from their fields. Having lived through the drought years of 1902–03 and 1914–15, they appreciated the need for broad acres, and the cautious among them realised the importance of off-farm investments to carry them over dry years.[42] Australian wheat farmers were price takers on international markets, but they had agency in their farming methods. One way to express this agency was the sharing of

---

41 Ford, '"The Wattles Are in Bloom ..."', 84.
42 Charles Coote's taxation accounts reveal that by the 1930s earlier off-farm investments had become a significant proportion of his total income. See Charles Coote, Taxation Journal, 1917–1953, in Coote, Diaries and Papers.

information on farming methods, and local cropping competitions were an important means of doing this.

In the Murray Mallee, the Chandos District Wheat Crop Competition commenced in 1924. By 1936 over eight hundred crops, including a category for juniors, had been judged. Local committees in the major centres—Pinnaroo, Parilla, Lameroo, Parrakie, Geranium and Jabuk—organised the competitions, and prizes were awarded for the best local and district crops. Out of these competitions important information was disseminated, and better farming practices encouraged and tried. By the mid-1930s, these competitions demonstrated that progressive farmers had modified dry-farming practices. Chandos farmers demonstrated a willingness to experiment with new seed varieties. Currawa and Joffre—a disease-resistant variety—dominated the early years of the competitions. They were replaced by Gallipoli and Free Gallipoli in the early 1930s, and Ranee, Nabawa and Waratah were the favoured varieties by the mid-30s. Very importantly, these progressive farmers experimented with alternative farming techniques such as reducing cultivation of fallow, particularly during summer. With larger acreages than the recent settlers in the Millewa or the New Mallee, they could use sheep to graze on fallow as a weed-control measure and have longer rotation cycles: fallow, wheat, oats, and grazing. They experimented too with the timing of seeding, opting where the season permitted for an earlier sowing, and ploughed the fallow immediately this was finished. Attention was paid to best cultivation implements, the optimum amount of superphosphate required, and how best to pickle seed wheat to control disease.[43]

Despite the collapse of wheat prices in the early 1930s, these techniques permitted farmers who practised them to ride out the difficult years more successfully than their newer colleagues. But overall the collapse had devastating effects. Farmers in the old mallee fell deeply into debt and were often only kept on the land through schemes of government debt protection and rescheduling of loans.[44] In Charles Coote's immediate district the number

---

43 For the Chandos District Wheat Competitions, see 'Wheat Growing in the Mallee', *Journal of the Department of Agriculture of South Australia* (June 1937): 844–53 and 926–34. Director of Agriculture Arthur J. Perkins also analysed areas that were safe to grow wheat. See 'Our Wheat Growing Areas—Profitable and Unprofitable', *Journal of the Department of Agriculture of South Australia* (May 1936): 1199–221. Note that most entries from the County of Chandos were from its south (846).

44 The generous debt relief given to Victorian Mallee farms can be seen in the surviving files of the Farmers' Debt Adjustment Board, VPRS 10192, PROV. Unfortunately, only a sample of these has been retained. For settlers in the Mallee, see also Schedules of Revaluation and Adjustment of Settlers Liabilities under Section 32 Closer Settlement Act 1932, VPRS 14485/P01/units 19 and 20, PROV.

of farms declined by just under a quarter between 1921 and 1941. In the new Mallee district around Kulwin the decline was almost two-thirds, and in the Millewa it was over half.[45] However, part of the decline in farm numbers was due to eventual acceptance by land officials that the concept of a yeomanry had little place in dry regions.

Between 1932 and 1937, Victorian land administrators undertook a process of placing closer and soldier settlers on what it termed 'living areas'. William Lane, for example, was moved from his Wagant farm of 794 acres to a farm almost double this area in the parish of Wemen in 1934.[46] This started a process of farm consolidation that was eventually taken up by the federal government and given more urgency during the war and post-war years. Outside help was clearly needed even by established farmers. The travails of the 1930s took their toll on the successful Chandos farmers in South Australia, for example, and attendance at crop competitions fell away in the mid-1930s. Farm reclamation was clearly a national problem, and this is examined in Chapter 9.

Locusts

The dominant mallee settler narratives were of a harsh and alienating climate and vegetation. Metaphors of war were commonly used to describe the process of clearing land and establishing farms: 'Always remember, if you do not kill the bushes, they will soon kill you', South Australian mallee farmer A.W. Kelly told a 1917 royal commission.[47] The Melbourne *Argus* characterised a soldier settler's struggle with the Mallee in similarly combatant terms: 'It is the story of a warfare, no less exacting, no less fierce, not a whit less decisive, than the war from which most of the settlers have come. It is a war for the safety of democracy—mankind is vindicating his right to occupy the strongholds of Nature'.[48] Sometimes, the isolation and hardship saw such metaphors materialise through accidental deaths and suicide. In dealings with locusts, war was waged against nature using the same strategies, techniques, and even vehicles, deployed in war against humans.

---

45 For the turnover of farms in the Victorian Mallee, see Charles Fahey, 'Agricultural Settlement in Victoria's Last Frontier: The Mallee, 1890–1951, *Agricultural History* 91, no. 2 (Spring 2017): 187–214, see Table 4, 204.

46 William Lane's files are in VPRS 5714/P0/2408/134/264B and VPRS 5714/P0/2181/570/12, PROV.

47 Western Australia, 'Report of the Royal Commission on the Mallee Belt and Esperance Lands', *Votes and Proceeding of the Parliament of Western Australia*, 1917, Paper no. 5, 148.

48 P.C. Morrison, 'Battle of the Mallee', *Argus*, 14 April 1928, 8.

The linguistic entanglement of locusts and warfare goes right back to (and perhaps beyond) biblical times, when locusts were the Lord's army and a potent symbol of His power.[49] In Australia, white settlers ignored Aboriginal people's locust traditions and imposed their own ideas about these native insects. Though they mostly did not regard locusts as a symbol of God's power, many settlers retained the military associations learned from the Bible, perhaps reinforced in some minds by the locust's armour-like exoskeleton.

Locusts in the Victorian Mallee seem to be a product of wheat farming, at least when in plague proportions. In November 1934 an early locust plague there evoked the language of war. Newspapers provided a blow-by-blow account of the distribution of the swarms and the damage incurred, as well as the success of counter-measures. Early in the outbreak, locusts in the Colignan district devoured twenty tons of a green wheat crop in two hours. At Red Cliffs, about sixty men laboured to distribute forty-five tons of arsenic bran baits from a mixing depot to protect the £1,000,000 grape crop. Later, preventive spraying with lead arsenate was carried out throughout all settlements around Mildura.[50]

Even with this arsenal at hand, the insects' enigmatic habits were unsettling. While surveillance of the invaders on farmland seemed adequate, the *Argus* reported that 'some anxiety is felt about the extent of the plague in the unsettled areas of the Mallee from which no reports have been received'.[51] The following day, the director of agriculture was moved to refute 'alarming suggestions that the grasshoppers were advancing from the northern Mallee as an invading horde'.[52] However, a week into the plague, the swarming insects were indeed moving southward in large numbers, and twenty tons of bait had been distributed from Ouyen alone.[53] A month after the outbreak began, flying locusts 'invaded the township' of Nullawil, while canvas used for covering wheat stacks, along with 'all available tarpaulins', served to protect Rainbow's bowling and croquet greens from the menace.[54]

Some farmers believed that arsenic baiting was 'the most successful form of attack' on the locusts,[55] but Alec Chisholm cautioned against the widespread use of poisons, as this also killed birds that preyed on the grasshoppers.

---

49 See Exodus 10 and the Book of Joel.
50 *Argus*, 9 November 1934, 3; 24 November 1934, 19.
51 *Argus*, 9 November 1934, 3.
52 *Argus*, 10 November 1934, 19.
53 *Argus*, 15 November 1934, 18.
54 *Argus*, 13 December 1934, 3.
55 *Argus*, 15 November 1934, 18.

Instead, Chisholm suggested the need for more research into where, why and how plague-scale outbreaks occurred.[56] Similarly, James Barrett pointed out that 'locust plagues can be checked by insectivorous birds' and called for more national parks to preserve the 'balance of nature'.[57] These advocates, who saw nature as something to work with rather than against, were in the minority.

The Second World War played a key role in consolidating linkages between war on humans and war on insects. In spring 1945 an RAAF aircraft equipped for DDT anti-mosquito spraying was used to treat a Rutherglen insect outbreak that threatened to destroy the stone fruit crop in northern Victoria. Attention then turned to the locusts, which were unusually prevalent in the Victorian Mallee that season.

In Australia in the 1940s, the insecticide of choice for locust control was BHC or benzene hexachloride, otherwise known as Gammexane or Lindane. Gammexane was one of the new organochlorine insecticides developed during World War II, inspired by the example of DDT. Gammexane is a potent neurotoxin and likely carcinogen. It is also persistent in the environment, though, with a half-life of fifteen months in soil, it is less so than DDT. It is highly toxic to fish and bees and causes eggshell thinning in birds. An international ban on its agricultural use was finally implemented in 2009 under the Stockholm Convention on Persistent Organic Pollutants.

In 1946 further testing of aerial application of insecticides was contemplated, but plans were overtaken by the discovery of a concentration of locust egg beds in the Mallee, and the Victorian Department of Agriculture approached the Royal Australian Air Force (RAAF) to see whether three aircraft and a suitable number of crew from Laverton air base could assist in preventive spraying.[58] The RAAF immediately set about reconditioning and modifying more planes, and anti-grasshopper operations in the Mallee using four aircraft commenced in October 1946. The RAAF, happy to be in action again, committed to assisting with the operation for as long as possible. The Air Force also proposed the use of Mustang aircraft for spraying as part of pilot training exercises.[59] Locust control had become thoroughly entangled with military objectives.

---

56 Alec H. Chisholm, 'The Locust Plague', *Argus*, 9 November 1934, 3.
57 James W. Barrett, 'Value of Birds and Animals', *Argus*, 10 November 1934, 19.
58 153/1/1304, Directorate of Operations—Department of Agriculture, Victoria—request for planes to spray mallee area with Gammexane, 1946–1951, in A705 Department of Air, Central Office, Correspondence files, multiple number (Melbourne) series, 1922–1960, NAA.
59 A705, 153/1/1304, NAA.

In 1950, as another locust plague emerged in the Mallee, the Victorian Department of Agriculture again sought the assistance of the RAAF. When the request was declined, Premier Jack McDonald wrote to Prime Minister Robert Menzies to ask for Air Force cooperation. Unable to spare the three Dakotas requested, the RAAF assisted by providing two sets of spraying equipment as well as a tanker for insecticide, a radio vehicle to communicate with aircraft pilots, and associated personnel.[60] A similar approach was taken to a major locust outbreak in the summer of 1952–53, which started in western New South Wales and proceeded south. The Victorian Department of Agriculture assisted by 'attacking' swarms in southern NSW 'to prevent the invasion of Victoria over the Murray River'.[61] The campaign involved twenty-nine days of constant aerial spraying with organochlorine insecticides by RAAF and commercial TAA planes, both charging the states for their services.[62]

Dust Storms and Drought

As settlement extended into the Mallee and more acreage was cleared, planted and fallowed, dust storms and soil drift increased in regularity and intensity and became identified with life across mallee lands. Recalling life on a South Australian farm at Paruna, Milton Edwards noted, 'to live in the Mallee is to watch the weather and understand the wind'.[63] Wind from the north 'carried a mixture of promises'—the suggestion of rain or alternatively a dust storm. 'North winds could be so destructive and overbearing … The bad days became horrid because farmers at that time worked the soil until it was as smooth as a sandy beach. On a really dreadful day, the sheer brutality of the wind showed no apparent feeling for living things'. In Western Australia, as the pioneer farmers cleared the trees and replaced them with crops, so the land was left 'dry, timberless and without any sort of cover'. Around Kondinin 'the strong winds regularly blew thick dust into the township, billowing through the streets and into houses and stores covering everything with a layer of dirt'.[64]

---

60   A705, 153/1/1304, NAA.

61   Grasshopper Control Conference and CSIRO, *Grasshopper Control Conference Held at Canberra, A.C.T., May 1954* (Melbourne: Commonwealth Scientific and Industrial Research Organisation, 1954), preface 2.

62   Grasshopper Control Conference and CSIRO, *Grasshopper Control Conference*, 3. TAA is the abbreviation for Trans Australian Airlines, which operated from 1946 to 1994 (rebranded Australian Airlines in 1986).

63   Milton Edwards, *To the Mallee Born* (Adelaide: M. Edwards, 1993), 14.

64   Deryck J. Eggleston, *Kondinin, Page by Page: Frank Eggleston's Letters 1925–1932* (Perth: Deryck J. Eggleston, 2010), 24–5.

The effects of dust storms were devastating and carried mallee topsoil as far as New Zealand's glaciers. Soil drift—less dramatic but equally challenging—filled the water channels, buried fences and houses, made roads impassable and brought trains to a standstill. Denuded sand ridges exposed vast areas of limestone boulders or heavier subsoil. Problems of soil drift were particularly intense in the light soil areas such as the Millewa. Carl Beer, in his memoirs of the Millewa, wrote of over-cultivation and over-cropping, which contributed to desertification.

Figure 7.4: The clearing of the mallee scrub, and the removal of the roots that held the fine mallee soils together, led to widespread dust storms across the mallee lands. In this image a dust storm rolls down Langley Avenue, Mildura, Victoria c. 1936. (Courtesy Museums Victoria, MM4914, https://collections.museumvictoria.com.au/items/773844)

The collapse of commodity prices in the early 1930s left farmers desperate to make as much money as they could on their too-small blocks. They cropped as much land as possible, encouraged by the government's 'Grow more wheat' campaign. Their desperation compounded the problem of land degradation. Conditions similar to those of dust bowl Oklahoma in the 1930s were replicated in the Victorian Mallee. Some walked off their farms. Carl Beer wrote: 'Farms were abandoned to the wind and the rabbits and as the latter ate any trace of green herbage, so the wind increased its devastation till the country itself literally fled'. Beer conjured a ghostly landscape, inhabited only by vermin:

> Trees with the earth blown out from under the roots stood either balanced precariously on a few stray roots or fallen over to make a shelter for more rabbits moving in from even more drought-stricken areas. Houses abandoned gradually banked up with sand on the windward side until overwhelmed under the force of the drifts.[65]

Photographic evidence from the 1930s and 1940s shows the extent of the problem. Images of contorted Mallee roots perched above the ground suggest that more than a metre of top soil had blown away in some areas. *Mallee Country Facing Drought*, a film released in 1944 at the peak of a new and severe drought and with the war in Europe and the Pacific still raging, showed confronting images of the impact of soil drift. The camera panned over starving sheep, channels full of sand, rail tracks completely buried by sand, and houses abandoned and left to the encroaching dunes. The narrator forewarned of an impending apocalypse in the Mallee if the situation was not dealt with. As the camera focused on the main road to Mildura buried in sand, the deep voice of the male narrator warned: 'this part of the land will be dead and buried as ancient cities were buried in the sand unless we do something about it … if the roads go and the railways go, then the farmer must go too'. The film continued with increasingly distressing images of a desolate landscape, dead horses and sheep skulls, and sand dunes rising to engulf a home.

The film focused on the settlement of Kiamal near Ouyen where in 1925 1,100 settlers lived. In 1944 only 180 remained, causing the narrator to bemoan the town's fate:

> The desert has come up from under the good earth and stands at the settlers' door. Death is in the air. Horses die under the shade of the only trees. Where there are no trees there can be no life for very long. And soon only the bobtail lizard leaves his tracks in the sand.

The soil being blown away was 'more precious than gold or silver'. The narrator's voice rose to a crescendo, increasingly urgent and full of doom. This was not just dust blowing away, 'call it earth. The good earth. That's somebody's farm up there in the sky. Part of our land, part of Australia blowing away to be irrevocably lost in the Pacific Ocean'.[66]

---

65 Carl Beer, *Amongst the Last of the Pioneers: A Story of the Pioneering Days of the Mallee and Millewa* (Mildura: Larena Media Services, 1986), 31.
66 *Cinesound Review No. 0682: Mallee Country Facing Drought* (Cinesound Productions, 1944).

Such apocalyptic scenarios were part of a broader narrative about the dust bowl phenomenon that had its origins in the United States. As Janette Bailey has shown, in the late 1930s and 1940s Australians began to integrate 'dust bowl imagery into their own national story to treat it not only as an American story but also as an Australian reality'. Central to the dust bowl imagery 'was the narrative of once-mighty civilisations fallen to soil neglect, now buried under desert sands'.[67] Like the 'ancient cities', Australia too could be either buried or blown away if stewardship of the soil was neglected. The idea was dramatised as a 'world where human existence was dominated by desert'.[68] The sensationalist newspaper *Truth* made the direct connection between the US dust bowl and Australia, where a 'creeping death' was 'gradually increasing its strangulating grip on our fertile lands'.[69] *Truth* was not alone in sending this message, and it was repeated by all the major daily newspapers of NSW, Victoria and South Australia. It was a problem of national proportions requiring a national solution.

Anxiety about the viability of the Victorian Mallee and its drifting and blowing soil was intensified by dry years from the late 1930s, which slid into severe drought by the mid-1940s. Years of significantly below-average rainfall, relentlessly blowing dust, dying sheep, and another world war conflagration all compounded feeling about the 1944–45 drought as unparalleled. To add to the widespread misery, Victorian government debt adjustments continued unabated, and significant numbers of farmers left the region, generating a sense of foreboding among those who remained. The viability of the Mallee as a wheat-growing area was once again in question. These troubled years marked the death knell of the belief in the yeoman farmer and his family unit as the foundation of closer settlement. In the Victorian Mallee the population fell by 34 per cent between 1933 and 1939, and further again during the 1940s.[70]

Charles Coote, the Quambatook farmer who kept a diary throughout his farming life, recorded his growing concern as the drought tightened its grip. In September 1944 he noted: 'drought becoming intensified. Crops which looked fairly 5 or 6 weeks ago have died or been eaten off. The worst prospect I can recall at this time of the year. Paddocks are as bare as if swept where

---

67   Janette-Susan Bailey, *Dust Bowl: Depression America to World War Two Australia* (New York: Palgrave Macmillan, 2016), 60.
68   Bailey, *Dust Bowl*, 156.
69   Quoted in Bailey, *Dust Bowl*, 166.
70   Alan J. Holt, *Wheat Farms of Victoria: A Sociological Survey* (Melbourne: School of Agriculture, University of Melbourne, 1946), 40.

normal stocking has been practiced [*sic*]'. Drawing on hard experience, Coote had stored plenty of fodder to enable him to keep feeding his sheep and to provide grain for the next year's sowing. But other farmers were not so well placed. On 22 October 1944 Coote recorded: 'harvest prospects are nil. All fodder has to be imported. Seed grains for another cropping are not available in the north except in silos for wheat. Australia may have to import oats from New Zealand & some think fodder from America'. By November 1944 the combination of drought and war led Coote to fear a 'famine previously unknown in Australia'.

As summer arrived, and with it more heat and dust, Coote was concerned for the future of the Mallee. He set the scene with a description of the 'longest dust black out' he could recall. His diary entry for 8 December 1944 read:

> about 2.30 or 3.00 pm a dense dust storm came from west & NW. In patches it was quite black in others dusty brown or red. It was a magnificent spectacle as it came billowing on a living moving mass of many hues and towering height apparently intending to crush all that stood in its path.

Coote was sitting in his car opposite the sheep yard: 'The storm settled down with a cool moderate breeze until utter blackness or darkness enveloped all'. The 'eerie feeling' prompted Coote to turn on the dash light so he could see something. 'The wind gradually increased in strength and dust decreased in intensity for a few seconds and the bonnet of the car gradually became visible but only for a brief space of time when complete darkness again returned and lasted a further 5 to 10 minutes'. The night was cool and calm, but the wind and dust returned the following day, prompting Coote to ask: 'Is the dry central plain of Australia extending?'

Those who had no stockpile of feed suffered badly. The George family, farmers in the Millewa who had come to Victoria through the Empire Settlement Scheme, had applied for additional land in 1936 as part of the scheme to compensate settlers for the failure of the imperial venture. The family had two leases totalling 16,600 acres, with 5,500 acres cleared for grazing. In 1944 the drought dried up the channels carrying water for stock, and they filled with sand. Sheep, weak from lack of food, became bogged in rapidly drying dams. The Georges lost 1,071 sheep in the drought.[71]

---

71 Ivan George, *From London to Willah 1926–49* (Mildura: Ivan George, 1990), 59.

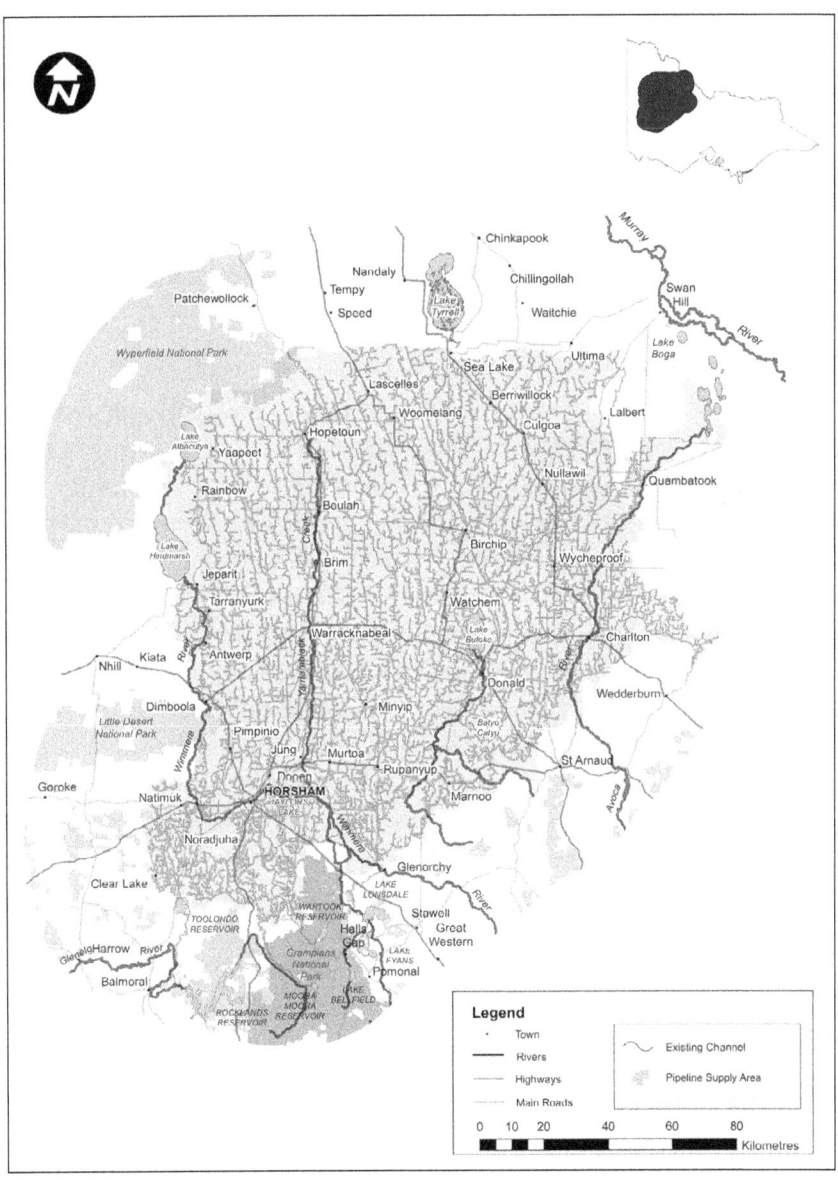

Figure 7.5 This map shows the southern section of the Wimmera-Mallee open channel system. The full system ran from the Grampians ranges near Horsham to north of Ouyen and east to the Murray River, covering 17,000 kms, and suppling water to 36 towns and 22,000 farms. Its scale reflects the state's enormous commitment to supplying water to this landscape. As an open channel system however it had high levels of evaporation and seepage. The Wimmera-Mallee pipeline replaced the open channel system in 2010.
(Courtesy GWM Water, https://www.gwmwater.org.au/2-uncategorised/58-historic-information-about-water-supply-in-the-wimmera-and-mallee)

Hazel Hogan wrote of the impact of the drought across the Mallee, conveying a sense of widespread desolation:

> Dams dried up. Water tanks became rusty. Stock died. Were sold. Agisted south, and died eventually from starvation and exhaustion. The Mallee resembled a "sandy sea". Soil erosion blotted our paddocks and water holes. Spilled over fences and railway lines. Buried machinery and wood heaps. Damaged roads. Formed sand hills which are a menace still.[72]

Hogan lamented that there was an exodus from the Mallee to Melbourne. Women went in search of war jobs and an off-farm income. Children were sent to seaside holiday camps to give them some relief from the heat and despair.

The 1944–45 drought extended to Western Australia, which was often spared the impact of El Niño events. Dams dried, leaving sheep without water, and forcing farmers to cart water up to eighty miles from distant township supplies. Lake Grace relied on water brought eastward by steam train from Collie, farmers anxiously lining up to collect it from the railway siding. The Kondinin Reticulation Scheme constructed before the war failed. By March 1945, three thousand gallons a week were being carted from outside the district. The Board of the Reticulation Scheme took the desperate step of hiring a water diviner to search for the precious fluid, to no avail.[73] When the drought passed and the war ended, now wiser farmers across the region set about constructing dams—a job made much easier with bulldozers in place of horses. State government agencies also developed plans for a more permanent solution to the problem of a reliable water supply. At Kulin, a 4,000,000-gallon dam with a graded water catchment area was built in 1951.[74]

After drought inevitably comes some relief for the survivors: those resilient or wise enough to hang on, and those not 'let go' by the Closer Settlement Board as it restructured debt and amalgamated blocks. When rain eventually came, it re-confirmed the capacity of mallee lands for resurrection. In 1948 Hazel Hogan wrote of the changed landscape: 'Green was the Mallee now. Far and wide, from horizon to horizon, the paddocks and roadsides were gorged with green. Weeds and thistles with stalks so tall as to remind one of miniature "trees" … grass that was a joy to behold … wildflowers at the

---

72 Hogan, *The Story of Kulwin*, 15.
73 William E. Greble, *A Bold Yeomanry: Social Change in a Wheat Belt District: Kulin 1848–1970* (Perth: Creative Research, 1979), 164.
74 Greble, *A Bold Yeomanry*, 184.

wayside'.[75] Years of remarkable prosperity and comparatively abundant rain marked the decades following the Second Word War, but much work remained to be done to solve the problem of 'drift' and the propensity of the mallee lands to 'blow'. The situation prompted an anonymous poet to pen the lines:

> So when our sons assume the mortgage,
> Of the land that's had our toil
> They'll not have to ask the question—
> Here's the farm—but where's the soil?[76]

---

75 Hogan, *The Story of Kulwin*, 16.
76 Quoted in George T. Thompson, *A Brief History of Soil Conservation in Victoria 1834–1961* (Melbourne: Soil Conservation Authority, 1979), 89.

Chapter 8

CAMPING AND WORKING ON COUNTRY

The desire to erase the Aboriginal presence was as strong in Australia's wheat lands as elsewhere on the continent. In the decades around Federation, when wheat growers were taking up mallee lands through closer settlement in southern Australia, Aboriginal people continued to be displaced from traditional lands. By the late twentieth century some settler Australians doubted that Aboriginal people had ever resided on mallee lands. This was an ill-informed view, for farmers over the years continually uncovered stone tools, grinding stones and axes as they ploughed the mallee lands.[1] Indeed, in the early twentieth century A.S. Kenyon and other collectors removed truckloads of stone tools from the Victorian Mallee, part of the hundred thousand or more from across the state now in the Museums Victoria stone artefacts collection.[2]

Despite this attempted erasure of their presence, Aboriginal people clung tenaciously to their land across mallee country, camped and worked on it, considered it theirs and continued to derive their identity as a people from their connections to land. This is revealed by case studies of the Dimboola–Antwerp region in the Victorian Mallee and the country around Gnowangerup in Western Australian mallee country. Eventually Aboriginal claims to an enduring connection to mallee lands were vindicated by a long overdue recognition of native title.

Antwerp in Victoria

By the 1880s approximately 450 Aboriginal people lived in the Victorian Mallee, about sixty at Ebenezer Mission and almost four hundred along the Murray and in other lake areas.[3] Aboriginal people in Victoria experienced

---

1   Ken Stewart (Wamba Wamba man and Living Murray Indigenous Facilitator with the Mallee Catchment Management Authority), interviewed by Karen Twigg, 23 September 2015, Mildura.
2   Tom Griffiths, *Hunters and Collectors: The Antiquarian Imagination in Australia* (Melbourne: Cambridge University Press, 1996), 67–71.
3   Richard Broome, *Aboriginal Victorians: A History since 1800* (Sydney: Allen & Unwin, 2005), 147.

a second dispossession when the Aborigines Protection Act of 1886 shifted policy from protection to assimilation. Those considered of 'mixed descent' and between the ages of fourteen and thirty-four were pushed into the community to fend for themselves. This weakened reserves and mission communities by depriving them of their younger workers. However, those over thirty-four and considered of 'mixed descent' ('half caste' under the actual wording of the Act) could stay. Several family men over the age of thirty-four were allowed 'temporary permissive occupancy' to farm individual blocks on reserves: three at Framlingham near Warrnambool, and two at Ebenezer near Antwerp. Albert Coombes's occupancy of his block was, however, threatened in 1894 by P. Boglish, Ebenezer's manager, as Coombes neglected to attend church, served wine to his friends on Sunday afternoons, and his wife allegedly was not a good housekeeper.[4]

The Board for the Protection of the Aborigines in Victoria successively closed reserves and missions after the 1890s for fear of them becoming permanent Aboriginal places.[5] The board removed Wotjobaluk residents from Ebenezer Mission near Antwerp in 1904, and most of the mission's land was leased out to local white farmers. Many residents were sent to Lake Tyers. Some later drifted back home and joined other former Ebenezer residents and their descendants camping by the Wimmera River at Antwerp and Dimboola.

Two men held land from 1891: Albert Coombes, and the other was either Pelham Cameron or Richard Kennedy. All three had leases of Ebenezer land at some stage in the 1890s. Aboriginal Elder Auntie Nancy Harrison, great granddaughter of Richard Kennedy, confirmed this and that all continued on their land once Ebenezer closed in 1904.[6] Pelham Cameron then aged fifty-one years, his wife Blanche, and their four children—Clara, Archibald, Catherine and Elizabeth (Lizzie)—fenced and farmed thirty acres of land. It was the worst possible time to farm, given the depression of the 1890s, and at the end of that decade they faced the horrendous Federation drought. Their pioneering efforts were admirable.

Pelham Cameron worked his land until 1912, when he turned sixty. He transferred his leasehold to Carl Nitschke and secured a small house block in Antwerp. He and Blanche moved to Dimboola in the early 1920s. They became caretakers for the Dimboola Park and Rowing Club and were given comfortable accommodation under the tall grandstand. The park was beside

---

4   P. Boglish to Hagenauer, 8 May 1894, Albert Coombes (Snr) file, B337, item 171, National Archives of Australia (NAA).
5   Broome, *Aboriginal Victorians*, 185–95.
6   Nancy Harrison, interviewed by Richard Broome, Dimboola, 25 October 2016.

their beloved Wimmera River, and directly opposite was a canoe tree, further linking them to country. Blanche passed away in 1929 and Pelham three years later.[7]

During the Ebenezer years, while the people transformed themselves into Christian farmers, they never lost their love of country or their Wotjobaluk identity. This is clear from their subsequent actions. Most camped on country along the Wimmera River after being pushed off Ebenezer. This patriotism or love of land was acknowledged by Europeans. In the Victorian parliament, James Menzies, MLA for Lowan, observed that those who went away to find work invariably came back to the original settlement, as 'they have the same strong instinct for the place of their birth as we inherit ourselves'.[8] However, those campers were often in poor circumstances, a matter drawn to the attention of parliament as early as 1905, just one year after their removal from Ebenezer. In 1913, Menzies referred to forty Aboriginal people camped at Antwerp and Dimboola in 'primitive structures under insanitary conditions' that encouraged disease. The men were generally of 'good behaviour' and undertook casual rural work when it was available, but Menzies believed they suffered discrimination in employment. Some of their children attended school in these two towns, but 'many white parents object to those children attending the schools in such a condition'. William Hutchinson, MLA for the adjoining electorate of Borung, also wanted action to help these campers, though largely because their camps along the river were considered by white Australians as a 'public nuisance' and 'dangerous to the public welfare'.[9]

Menzies quizzed these men on their aspirations for land when he met them at the Dimboola Agricultural Show. Half of them wanted land at Antwerp where they obtained some work as shearers and farm labourers, while the other half wanted some Crown land on a river frontage. But Menzies reported that the second group would agree to settle at Antwerp with the others if land was made available. He hoped the government could find some land for them. Chief Secretary Jack Murray promised to investigate the situation; the state had a duty to these people, he believed,

---

7   Gail Harradine, interviewed by Richard Broome, Horsham, 26 October 2016. Obituaries in *Dimboola Banner*, 5 July 1929 and 11 August 1932.

8   James Menzies, *Victorian Parliamentary Debates (VPD)* 1913–14, vol. 134, Legislative Assembly, 2614. Menzies was the father of Australia's longest serving prime minister, Robert Gordon Menzies.

9   Menzies and William Hutchinson, *VPD*, 1913–14, vol. 134, Legislative Assembly, 2613–14 and 2615 respectively.

for 'in a Higher Court, the black fellow would be able to establish a much stronger moral right to the land than any of our white friends who own it today'.[10] But Murray failed to provide land for them, and Victoria's Central Board for the Protection of the Aborigines always opposed policies that might undermine assimilation.

A generation later, during the 1930s Great Depression, Aboriginal people continued to camp on Crown land by the Wimmera River. Despite their makeshift accommodation, many led respectable lives. They dressed as well as most mallee farming families, as revealed in a surviving photograph of the Marks and Harrison families taken in 1920.[11] Some people held jobs in the district from a young age. Young Lester Marks Harradine worked at Norton's market garden in Dimboola with at least one family member, Uncle Eric Clarke. His dirt-filled work clothes and stance place him as a full and independent member of the team (see Figure 8.1).

Figure 8.1: Work team at Norton's Market Garden, Dimboola, c. 1935.
Lester Marks Harradine is in the front row kneeling on both knees.
His uncle Eric Clarke is in the back row second from left.
(Lester Marks Harradine Collection. Courtesy Leila Harradine)

10   Menzies, Hutchinson and John Murray, *VPD*, 1913–14, vol. 134, Legislative Assembly, 2613–17.
11   See Broome, *Aboriginal Victorians*, 215.

In October 1938 it was reported that the Antwerp school teacher said of his Aboriginal students, that he 'could wish for nothing better', while the local shopkeeper stated several of the men 'were in good demand during the busy season, but out of season there was a good deal of privation', there being little work.[12] The Aboriginal campers attended Salvation Army services at Antwerp under an old gum on the reserve adjoining the river and the Antwerp cemetery, singing their favourite hymns, 'In the Sweet Bye and Bye' and 'Shall We Gather at the River'.[13] The Reverend Schulz, the Anglican minister of Jeparit, ministered and cared for them too, pronouncing some of them 'honest, upright, and firm believers in Christ', while others had 'copied the lowest principles from their white fathers or their contact with the whites'. He distributed food and clothing and called for the government to provide a dozen houses for them.[14]

In 1938 the Aboriginal Fellowship Group also lobbied for assistance. George Hamilton Lamb, elected to Lowan in 1935, informed them he had supplied Aboriginal people in the district with blankets and coils of wire for fencing the Antwerp reserve. He also gained agreement from the Lands Department not to lease to any whites the reserve on which Aboriginal people camped.[15] Later the same year, Arthur Burdeu of the Aborigines Uplift Society championed the Antwerp–Dimboola people. They were in no man's land, he claimed, neither under the protection of an Aboriginal Act nor enjoying the rights of other Victorians to receive the dole. They also suffered an economic and social colour bar.[16]

In 1940, Burdeu approached the secretary of lands requesting a permit of occupancy to build houses for Aboriginal people on Crown land in the Parish of Katyil at Antwerp. The lands inspector for Dimboola, F.J.H. Newtown, reported that eight Aboriginal families occupied about forty acres of Crown land on the west side of the Antwerp Cemetery adjoining the Wimmera River. The families were the Harrison, Kennedy, Kinnear, Moore, Bull and three groups of Marks families. There were 48 people in all—27 males and

---

12   John R. Williamson to Miss Brown, Victorian Aboriginal Group, 4 October 1938, Papers of Amy Brown and Valentine Leeper *c.* 1920 – *c.* 1969, MS Box 3651–3657, State Library Victoria.

13   Anon. manuscript, 'Re Robert (Bobby) Kinnear', Dimboola Historical Society Archives.

14   Pastor Schulz, 'Aborigines at Antwerp, Victoria', *Uplift: The Official Organ of the Aborigines Uplift Society* 1, no. 5 (1938).

15   H. Lamb to Helen Baillie, 21 May 1938, in Papers of Amy Brown and Valentine Leeper.

16   *Uplift* 1 (November 1938).

21 females, half of them under twelve years of age. Athol Harrison, his wife Margaret and son Robert indicated they would return from Dimboola if land was given. Antwerp storekeeper W.H. Bond informed Newton that the land was part of the old Ebenezer Mission and the land had been fenced by the people themselves. There was no local opposition to the plan.

Burdeu met with the Department of Lands in December 1940 and indicated he wished to begin with one one-acre block, on which he proposed to erect a three-roomed house, and provide land for a vegetable garden and to keep a cow. Alf King for the department drew up a plan for nine allotments on the higher ground near the cemetery, with the lower, wetter ground being set aside for gardening and grazing. Arthur Burdeu paid 10s in February 1941 for the permissive occupancy of one block to start the scheme. In 1947 when the scheme lapsed, the rent was £2 10s suggesting four more blocks had been set aside.[17]

Some of the history of these Antwerp blocks is recalled by Wotjobaluk Elder, Auntie Nancy Harrison, daughter of Athol Harrison and Margaret Harrison (née Kennedy). She is also the great, great granddaughter of Jungingininyook (Richard Kennedy), one of the Aboriginal men who found the three lost Duff children after nine days in the Wimmera in 1864, and who later farmed at Ebenezer. He was also one of the most skilled of the Aboriginal cricketers (then called 'Dick-a-Dick') who toured England in 1867.[18]

Athol and Margaret Harrison moved to the Antwerp reserve in 1941, the year Nancy was born. Athol built a two-roomed weatherboard house, probably with materials supplied by the Aborigines Uplift Society. He made a garden and a chicken house, and grazed three cows and two horses. Athol Harrison provided for his growing family of eight children by rabbiting, shovelling salt at the Pink Lakes, and labouring on nearby farms, while Margaret sewed the children's clothes, managed the house and helped in the kitchen garden. Harrison later worked on the railways. Other families built similar houses and kitchen gardens. In the early 1950s the Railways Department transferred Athol Harrison to Burrumbeet, and the family left the Antwerp reserve.

Traditional ideas remained strong among these camper families. They maintained deep kinship ties and identities as Aboriginal people, reinforced by their close living and their outsider status in the region. In doing so they

---

17 F.J.H. Newton to Carey, 26 November 1940; memo on Burdeu discussions, 17 December 1940; memo Alf King, 15 January 1941; Burdeu to Secretary of Lands, 16 February 1941, C 55663. Copies held in Dimboola Historical Society Archives.

18 D.J. Mulvaney, *Cricket Walkabout: The Australian Aboriginal Cricketers on Tour 1867–8* (Melbourne: Melbourne University Press, 1967).

preserved strong connections to Wimmera and Mallee country, consolidated by the presence of their forebears in the shape of Aboriginal shell middens along the riverbank, especially from Horseshoe Bend to Dimboola. Bush foods were gathered to supplement the larder and provide variety. Nancy Harrison's grand uncles, Walter, Lance and Eddie, caught possums they cooked in hot ashes and ate with damper. The skins were sold to the 'rabbito'. The menfolk also caught kangaroo in the Little Desert, and their families gathered pigface, quandong, mistletoe and saltbush berries, and yams while driving along the Wimmera River. Redfin and trout were caught in the billabong.

Many people connected to country through foraging expeditions. Those with cars drove further north to Lake Hindmarsh, Lake Albacutya and east to the Little Desert. Wotjobaluk country stretched further north still, towards Ouyen. Stories about country remained strong. The Wimmera River was both a source of life and a potential danger, so children had to be accompanied by adults. Nancy Harrison recalled a belief in the Goollum Goollum, wild men from across the border who kidnapped children. We were told that some 'Goollum Goollum bodies are buried along the river, who had been killed by our old people'. There were Ngutcha Ngutcha by the river too, hairy men who lived in hollow trees and would 'lead you into the river and drown you'.[19]

Ron Marks, a Wotjobaluk man born in 1951 and descended from Norman Marks (his great, great grandfather), recalled similar stories: 'We weren't allowed to fish or swim on the northern side of the river … we wouldn't swim over halfway, because on the other side there is deep water'. But on 'our side it was a sandy bank, and we always used to say that, when you catch a lot of fish there, our ancestors are putting them on the hook for you'.[20]

The Wotjobaluk believed the irrigation weir placed in the river ruined country. Ron Marks commented:

> The Weir mucked up everything. Mucked up the flow of the water, and threatened the stories that were created around that area, because Antwerp was a place where people regularly got together, to sit around the campfire and yarn, but the language wasn't continued, because no one was speaking it fluently, since the Mish [Ebenezer].

Farming changed the land too. But Marks argued that the Wotjobaluk adapted to farming, 'using it in its new form' by gaining work in dairying and with

---

19   Harrison, interview.
20   Ron Marks, interviewed by Richard Broome, Horsham, 26 October 2016.

cereal crops and on the railways that transferred the wheat, and by hunting quail in the stubble after the harvest.[21]

From the 1940s other families lived at nearby Dimboola, just out of town near the Wimmera River, in three contiguous areas called the 'Old Sale Yards', the 'Old Common' and the 'Ranch'. These names were also claims on country. Indeed, a few individuals who refused to live at Ebenezer in the late nineteenth century probably stayed at the Old Common for two generations. Those who continued to reside there in the 1940s constructed dwellings from local materials. Tom and Eric Clarke built a mud brick house for their mother Emma Clarke on the Old Common. Ron Marks also recalled that 'we got all our materials that we needed from the tip, so if we needed corrugated iron, roof replacement, we'd go there'. In 1946 a photograph of families on the Old Common shows thirty-one members of the Harrison, Marks and Kennedy families standing before a particularly large, but nonetheless typical, makeshift house occupied by Aboriginal campers (see Figure 8.2). Ron Marks remembered that in the 1950s there were about ten huts and tents scattered about this area.

Figure 8.2: Members of the Harrison, Marks and Kennedy families at the Common, Dimboola. Photograph by Elsie Dicker, 1946.
(Courtesy Dimboola Historical Society)

These Wotjobaluk people survived by working in the new economy. Men worked in the nearby Chinese market gardens or in Norton's gardens and orchards, which exported produce from Dimboola to Melbourne by rail. Some humped massive wheat bags onto freight trains at the railhead. Others

---

21   Marks, interview.

travelled further to find work, Nancy Harrison recalling of the Old Common, 'a lot of people would come and go'.[22] Some bagged salt in arduous conditions at the Pink Lakes saltworks fifty kilometres west of Ouyen. Athol Harrison did such work in his holidays from his railways job. Gail Harradine's mother, Leila, relates stories of her brother Thomas Clarke working there too:

> he talked of the heat, the exposure to the sun, the sun's reflection on the salt, making it twice as bad … if you got a cut or something, the salt would get right in, and be quite painful. Mum [Leila] recalls him coming home very tired, from the heavy, physical shovelling.[23]

He was of course digging into the bed of an ancient sea that had covered the Murray Mallee five million years before. Others worked in the Railways Department, as Dimboola was a significant large rail centre on the main line to Adelaide. Track workers lived away from their families for weeks on end, bunking in rail carriages converted to sleeping accommodation.

Aboriginal women also participated in paid work, either produce picking or domestic service. Their workplace relationships with employers were often complex, given the prevailing racial attitudes towards Aboriginal people. Pelham Cameron, the landholder at Ebenezer, who was 'well known and highly respected', had a daughter, Clara. She married Alf Marks Senior. In the inter-war years Clara Marks worked for the Martindale family, which owned an emporium in Dimboola, Martindale & Sons. Judging by surviving photographs, Clara and the Martindale family shared a friendship. One image depicts a well-dressed Clara arm-in-arm with Mrs Martindale, and another shows Clara sitting resplendent between the Martindale sons (see Figure 8.3). A third image reveals Clara in work attire assiduously plucking a bird (see Figure 8.4). The Martindales arranged the funeral of her father Pelham Cameron in 1932. These relations of paternalism revealed in three images, two being reproduced here, were mutually beneficial and marked by loyalty, care and genuine affection between boss and domestic worker.[24]

Figures 8.3 and 8.4, facing page.
Above: Clara Marks (née Cameron) with sons of the Martindale family, Dimboola, 1930s.
Below: Clara Marks (née Cameron) at work for the Martindale family, Dimboola, 1930s.
(Both photographs from the Lester Marks Harradine Collection. Courtesy Leila Harradine)

---

22   Harrison, interview.
23   Gail Harradine, interview.
24   *Dimboola Banner*, 11 August 1932.

While the men were away working, their women carried the family burden. Families on the Dimboola Old Common and adjoining country supplemented their income by living off the land as before. Often boys and older men hunted and fished for bush tucker. Ron Marks knew of techniques passed down from his great grandfather, William Thomas (Fisher) Marks, who stunned fish by placing certain berries in water or caught them in weirs, then cooked them in clay or leaves, all in the traditional way. Ron Marks and other boys inherited some of Fisher Marks's tactics: 'we as kids would run through the dammed water, stir up the silt, and then the fish would have to come to the surface to breathe, and we'd just grabbed what we wanted'. Ron became expert with a hook and line from his favourite log in the nearby billabong and supplied the family with fish, mostly non-native and increasingly invasive redfin perch (*Perca fluviatilis*) and tench (*Tinca tinca*). Redfin was good eating, and, if tench was steamed with onion, as his grandfather taught, it too become edible.

The men went rabbiting or hunted kangaroo in the Little Desert. Ron Marks's uncles took him hunting as a small boy, as long as he behaved: 'I had to be so respectful of the laws, and the laws were plain and simple: "You muck up, you don't come"'. They hunted rabbits with snares made of wire clothesline, which were illegal but effective. They also hunted kangaroo, foxes for a bounty, and water rats for their pelts. 'They'd look for roo, but rabbits were prolific. So if you got a feed of rabbit you really didn't want to taste roos, or emus'.[25]

Part of the joy of bush tucker was the chase and being on country. Gail Harradine recalls trips in her youth onto country that she now visits to paint. Her family spent much time fishing at Gridgigal (Adam's Waterhole). She also recalled visiting desert country: 'You go out in the Little Desert and the colour just shimmers, and changes over the day, and it is pretty hard to capture. It is just a very different landscape. Even though it is so dry, it has amazing vegetation, birds, and animals'. Gail Harradine always uses the symbol of the mussel shell in her paintings and did so before discovering, eerily, that Pelham Cameron's totem was the mussel shell. That is appropriate, for 'the river is like a backbone of country'. This recognised an old truth, that rivers, lakes and billabongs tied people to this semi-arid mallee country. Harradine mused: 'by feeling close to country there is a certainty as things don't change', adding: 'I am part of two cultures, but I've grown up with the values of my family, and that's Wotjobaluk'. Gail Harradine cherished the stories of Elders and their commitment to country: 'I appreciate people like Uncle Patrick Kennedy and Uncle "Rocky" [Samuel Harrison] who kept the connections

---

25 Marks, interview.

going by continuing to live on country at the Antwerp Reserve beside the cemetery until a decade ago. Without people living there we wouldn't have even got the Native Title'.[26]

Gnowangerup in the West

Far to the west, around 1900, about twelve hundred Nyungar people lived in the Great Southern Region of Western Australia, ranging from Geraldton to Esperance.[27] Perhaps less than half this number lived in, or were connected to, mallee country. Many worked on pastoral properties, while others followed a more traditional life. Some eked out a living collecting kangaroo and other animal skins, which became quite fashionable in the late nineteenth century.[28] The trade slowed after the *Game Act 1892* sought to protect kangaroo. After that, brushtail possum skins underpinned a booming trade for black and white hunters. By 1904 possum pelts constituted Western Australia's fifth-most valuable export commodity. In 1906 four million skins were exported. This rate could not last, and possum hunting was banned in 1910 except by strictly controlled licence, although Aboriginal people could still hunt possum for meat.[29]

The expansion of the wheat frontier brought significant changes to Aboriginal livelihoods and land use. A few dozen Aboriginal people sought land to farm. One applicant from Norseman said he was 'tired of white men who forgot to pay him wages'.[30] Most were from the New Norcia Mission a hundred kilometres north of Perth, where they had learned farming. Anna Haebich found that at least sixteen men were granted one or two hundred acres in the Midlands, Avon and Great Southern districts. The grants required that a house be built within two years, and a certain amount of land was to be cleared, cropped and fenced within five years. Besides having to deal with the problems of developing and financing a pioneering farm, Aboriginal farmers found their grants could be revoked at any time. Most Aboriginal families lost their farms by 1910, which was not atypical for any new farmers in pioneering conditions and with a rudimentary market infrastructure. Another

---

26   Harradine, interview.
27   Anna Haebich, *For Their Own Good: Aborigines and Government in the Southwest of Western Australia, 1900–1940* (Perth: University of Western Australia Press, 1988), 1.
28   Geoffrey Bolton, *Spoils and Spoilers: Australians Make their Environment 1788–1980* (Sydney: George Allen & Unwin, 1981), 102–03.
29   Haebich, *For Their Own Good*, 20–8.
30   Quoted in Haebich, *For Their Own Good*, 28.

dozen who purchased land under conditional purchase and homestead block schemes did better, although some did not survive the drought and financial problems of the immediate pre-war years.[31]

Those who did not try farming worked as rural labourers in a diversity of jobs through which they earned monetary wages, unlike Aboriginal workers in the northern cattle industry of Western Australia. Land clearing, wood cutting and burning, stone and stump removal, fencing and ploughing, and eradicating poisonous plants were some of the many tasks undertaken by Aboriginal people, often working as family groups. Other men did shearing, for parts of the old pastoral economy still survived, and some wheat farmers were turning to mixed sheep and wheat production.

Aboriginal workers generally operated in their home country creating a beat of farmers who employed them year after year. Being on home country allowed them to connect to family and tradition. It also allowed them to supplement their wages with known bush foods and make up for the seasonal nature of most of their work, which inevitably left them under-employed. Anna Haebich identified one group that worked between Katanning and Bremer Bay, the home country of the Goreng tribe.[32] In the early years of the twentieth century many Aboriginal workers, despite having few or no assets, were comparatively successful at meeting their daily needs. A police officer in the York District reported Aboriginal workers 'were more frugal than the white labourers and certainly more comfortable'.[33]

However, work became more elusive as labour competition increased with immigration, land clearing tailed off, hunting for cash was phased out, and drought bit hard in 1911 and 1914. On top of this, white labourism saw unions try to exclude Aboriginal people from the workforce. This was predicated on fear of competition from unpaid workers in the north, and racial attitudes to black workers across the state. Anna Haebich concluded that, while agricultural development brought prosperity to white settlers, it pauperised Aboriginal people.[34]

Their conditions forced many Aboriginal people into towns where those without work could obtain rations. Katanning, a burgeoning wheat centre on the western edge of the mallee, drew large numbers. It was a traditional meeting place for people of the South West and had been gazetted as an Aboriginal

---

31   Haebich, *For Their Own Good*, 28–35.
32   Haebich, *For Their Own Good*, 36.
33   Quoted in Haebich, *For Their Own Good*, 41.
34   Haebich, *For Their Own Good*, 46.

reserve since 1900. Annie Lock of the Australian Aborigines Mission held meetings at Katanning from 1912 and encouraged Aboriginal parents to send their children to school there. In 1911 there were thirty Aboriginal people at Katanning, and, by 1913, two hundred resided there. Similar numbers collected to the north of Perth at Moora. This Aboriginal population, about 10 per cent of Katanning, caused anxiety. There was resistance also to the presence of Aboriginal children in schools. Eventually they were expelled by authorities to the Carrolup River, thirty kilometres west of the town.[35]

When A.O. Neville became Chief Protector of Aborigines in Western Australia in 1915, he introduced a settlement policy in the south of the state, hoping to centralise the Aboriginal population at Carrolup and Moore River. Carrolup on the western edge of mallee country was a 10,000-acre reserve, which Neville hoped would become an agricultural settlement. Neville forcibly moved five hundred children and those dependent on rations to these two settlements, which comprised a quarter of the Aboriginal population of the Great Southern region. However, some refused to leave their home country or kin and live under government control. Carrolup progressed for a few years but was closed in 1922 for reasons of economy while Neville was overseas, and to his personal fury.[36] Many residents were forcibly removed to Moore River. Those who refused to go by escaping the round-up faced having no reserves to camp on in between periods of farm work.[37]

Work was scarce, but the proliferation of rabbits supplemented available sources of bush food. Camping places were also limited, so families used town reserves or patches of unalienated land. These camping places needed access to water and firewood, but to be far enough out of town so as not to cause offence, while close enough to provide a casual labour pool. The Gnowangerup Reserve was between the rubbish dump and the sewerage farm. The people lived in makeshift housing made from wheat bags and materials from the local dump. Some were permanent residents, while others used it as a base in between working around the region. A vibrant community life emerged in most reserve camps, a mix between traditional ways and the entertainments of being near town with its agricultural shows and travelling boxing troupes. It must be remembered, however, that segregation always shaped those interactions.[38]

---

35 Haebich, *For Their Own Good*, 131–47.
36 Pat Jacobs, *Mr Neville: A Biography* (Fremantle: Fremantle Arts Centre Press, 1990), 106–09.
37 Haebich, *For Their Own Good*, 169–78, 194–99.
38 Haebich, *For Their Own Good*, 222–42.

The Australian Aborigines Mission (later the United Aborigines Mission) began work in the late 1920s at Gnowangerup. Gnowangerup was a traditional place for Nyungar people, and a number were already living in the area. Brother and Sister Wright ran the mission in a relatively benign way. They sought conversions and discouraged language use and other traditional practices amongst the young but tolerated traditional practices among the older residents, who kept their distance from the missionaries. By 1928 a hundred people lived at the mission and this number increased in the Depression years. The mission was not institutionalised, unlike the government mission at Moore River. Families continued to live together, people came and went as they pleased, and 'the Aborigines remained in control of their lives'.[39] It is little wonder the reserve was fondly remembered years later.

Leonard (Jack) Williams was born on the Tambellup–Gnowangerup Road in 1933 and moved with his parents to the Gnowangerup Mission in 1935. They lived in a house supplied by the mission and made of boughs with a tin roof. Larger families had houses with verandahs as well. The sides were open, so they filled them in with wheat bags. The Williams family numbered eleven, so they had to squeeze into their two-bedroomed house, but, despite the stresses involved, living at close quarters helped solidify their caring and sharing attitude to each other. The men worked off the mission on local farms and the women as domestics in town. Jack Williams recalls 'they were good workers and they used to go out in the paddocks and clear and burn all the timber. Heap it up and burn it and then they ploughed all the paddocks. They used to pick up all the mallee roots too'.[40]

The old people identified most closely with Aboriginal culture and tradition, but the younger residents were also strongly in touch with tradition. Jack Williams' family went bush all school holidays and roamed around as 'there were no boundaries, nothing was fenced off, there were only small farms here and there, spread around over small areas'.[41] They travelled annually for fifteen years to a traditional camping ground at Pallenup River in search of wild ducks and black swans. The river was salty so they always camped near a fresh-water spring. The young ones learned how to catch bush tucker and use bush medicine 'because it was part of our culture and our survival'.[42] For

---

39   Haebich, *For Their Own Good*, 243.
40   Leonard (Jack) Williams, in *Ngulak ngarnk nidja boodja = Our mother, this land*, project manager Tjalaminu Mia, photography Victor France, Warren Belletti (Perth: Centre for Indigenous History & the Arts, 2000), 24.
41   Williams, in *Ngulak ngarnk nidja boodja*, 25.
42   Williams, in *Ngulak ngarnk nidja boodja*, 27.

instance, young Jack knew the white flower that bloomed when the malleefowl eggs were ready to harvest. His grandfather, Eddie Williams, and his father, Leonard (Len), were both good bushmen. His grandfather used to tell traditional stories 'in song'.

Alma Woods, another resident of Gnowangerup Mission, also remembers eating bush foods, wild berries (*cummock*) and bush carrots (*coorjing*), emu and kangaroos. These foods supplemented damper, now made from milled flour, and new foods: lamb, rabbits and chicken eggs.[43] Alma Woods, who was born at Borden in 1926, lived on a mallee farm where her father worked before the family moved to the Gnowangerup Mission. She recalled watching the old people perform corroborees there. They painted themselves and were adorned with leaves and feathers. Men and women performed dances with chants. It 'makes me sad to think about it as it has all gone now'.[44]

Both Alma Woods and Jack Williams saw the last corroboree of the Nyungar of the South West region held at Gnowangerup in 1938 or 1939. People came from as far away as Kalgoorlie, Ravensthorpe and Esperance, and Geraldton too. There were Wongi, Yamaji and Pitinjarra people, as well as Nyungar. Jack Williams recalled:

> we had a big fire there and the dancers used to come out from the thick clumps of mallee thicket and perform their corroboree. It gave me quite a scare because they were all painted up. I can still feel it now, it used to make the hair on my back stand on end and on my head too … I will never forget the last Noongar corroboree.[45]

The Williams family left the mission and spent a year working on a farm. When the boss decided to move to a farm in Quairading, he offered to apply for some land for Leonard Williams Sr on the Tambellup–Gnowangerup Road. We began to peg out five hundred acres, recalled Jack, but then word came 'that because we were Aboriginal people we weren't entitled to hold land rights so we couldn't have a title deed. So we ended up just clearing land for farmers and later for soldier settlers, instead of for ourselves and our families'.[46] What Jack Williams remembered was not strictly correct, for Aboriginal people could hold land, but in practice they were the last in line behind returned men, British settlers and local white Australians. Besides,

---

43 Alma Woods, in *Ngulak ngarnk nidja boodja*, 31.
44 Woods, in *Ngulak ngarnk nidja boodja*, 31.
45 Williams, in *Ngulak ngarnk nidja boodja*, 27.
46 Williams, in *Ngulak ngarnk nidja boodja*, 29.

there were objections raised to any Aboriginal application for land, including that they would not use the land properly, and it would become a 'black's camp'. Anna Haebich found that 'only three reserve blocks totalling 500 acres were granted to Aboriginal farmers between 1915 and 1936'.[47] Williams recalled that Aboriginal servicemen after the Second World War were again not offered land or houses under schemes enjoyed by their white fellow soldiers.

Jack Williams ended up living in the Tambellup area for the next forty years, staying close to the country of his birth. His father Leonard Sr always said: 'This is white man's country now, it is no longer ours and you can't go backwards you have to go forward' and earn their respect to be equal. There was an immense feeling of loss in his family and many other Aboriginal families of the region about stolen land and vanishing tradition. Jack Williams in his old age believed 'there had been far too much land cleared. Now it is all dried up with a lot of salt erosion … It makes me feel sad because of how I used to be able to see these places in their natural state'.[48] In 1973, when Williams was a mature man in his early forties, the Nyungar population in the South West had grown to almost eleven thousand. They had survived as a people despite great cultural and material losses.[49] But Williams concluded in his mid-sixties in 2000: 'It was heartbreaking not being able to really run free and have your own land. Just heartbreak'.[50]

From the late twentieth century, action under Native Title legislation was to expand access to country for many Aboriginal people across mallee lands, and this is discussed in Chapter 13.

---

47 Haebich, *For Their Own Good*, 225.
48 Williams, in *Ngulak ngarnk nidja boodja*, 29.
49 Neville Green, 'Aborigines and Settlers in the Nineteenth Century', in *A New History of Western Australia*, ed. Tom Stannage (Perth: University of Western Australian Press, 1991), 122.
50 Williams, in *Ngulak ngarnk nidja boodja*, 25.

Part Three

The State and Mallee Lands 1945–1983

Farmers faced crises in the 1930s as wheat prices collapsed and a long drought followed. To shore up their position many intensified their cropping, resulting in new problems of significant sand drift. Governments introduced adjustment schemes, buying out failing farmers and increasing the farm size of the remainder. Government scientists experimented with ways to arrest sand drift and to improve pastures and seed varieties as well as introducing the myxomatosis virus to reduce rabbit numbers. Tractors and, later, self-propelled headers increased the productivity of farmers. These developments ushered in a golden age for mallee farmers.

Good prices in the post-war years encouraged massive new mallee land schemes in South Australia and Western Australia. Diesel tractors and anchor chains ripped up areas with an efficiency unimaginable to earlier settlers. In South Australia the Australian Mutual Provident Society introduced private enterprise into mallee settlement for the first time, transforming so-called useless scrub into productive farmland and recording this triumph over nature on film. In the West, large-scale clearing continued under government schemes for soldier settlement and the massive 'A Million Acres a Year' scheme. The optimism driving this expansion was arrested by drought and wheat quotas in the late 1960s, and followed by attempts to reverse environmental degradation with new farming techniques, such as no-till farming. In 1985 the West Australian government ceased the policy of large-scale release of Crown land for agriculture.

Mallee lands always attracted a few visionaries seeking to protect their fauna and flora. Wyperfeld National Park in Victoria and the Stirling Range National Park in Western Australia were gazetted over a hundred years ago but faced continued threats of resumption by farmers. In the second half of the twentieth century public attitudes slowly changed to accept the inherent value of native flora and fauna promoted by such bodies as Victoria's Land Conservation Council. More national parks were gazetted across all mallee lands. By the 1980s, farmers had begun to conserve fauna and flora on their private holdings, ending, finally, a century of relentless onslaught on nature.

Chapter 9

MODERNISING MALLEE FARMS

The immediate post-war years were both difficult and promising for mallee farmers. The previous few decades had seen these farmers pushed to the brink. Many carried debts from low commodity prices in the 1930s. Their farms had suffered from environmental damage, drought, and being unviably small. War had disrupted wheat exports and fertiliser and machinery imports. However, state and federal governments from the 1930s provided funds for farm debt adjustment and stabilisation schemes. Also, scientific efforts by state government research bodies were now directed to soil drift and erosion problems, crop types and growing cycles, and pest eradication. The efforts of the Rural Reconstruction Commission from 1943 gave governments necessary information for action. Rising commodity prices from the late 1940s led to a welcome post-war farm boom.

Rural Reconstruction

In 1941, John Curtin's new federal Labor government began to plan for post-war reconstruction and a better, more equitable Australia.[1] The plight of rural Australia looked stark, and a Rural Reconstruction Commission was established in March 1943. Its four members—the Hon. Frank Wise, James F. Murphy, Professor Samuel Macmahon Wadham and Cecil Ralph Lambert— had two terms of reference.[2] The first was to foster a rural economy geared to 'the effectual prosecution of the war', the second to re-organise and rehabilitate this rural economy for the post-war period.[3] The commission recognised and documented problems created by the overly optimistic agricultural expansion of the 1920s, the collapse of prices in the Depression, wartime needs, and a

---

1   For post-war reconstruction see, Stuart Macintyre, *Australia's Boldest Experiment: War and Reconstruction in the 1940s* (Sydney: NewSouth Publishing, 2015).

2   Frank Wise (1897–1986) was a Labor politician and premier of Western Australia; James Francis Murphy (1893–1949) was a civil servant; Samuel Wadham (1891–1972) was professor of agriculture at Melbourne University; and Cecil Ralph Lambert (1899–1971) was a banker and civil servant.

3   Commonwealth of Australia, *Gazette*, No. 51, 4 March 1943.

dry period, most critically the 1944–45 drought. These problems were acute across mallee lands in three states.

Wadham and Lambert drove the commission. Wadham's investigations continued his long-standing contribution to understanding rural life and developing rural policy. Professor of agriculture at Melbourne University from 1926 and an ex-soldier, Wadham represented Victorian soldier settlers in 1929 on a state government board dealing with settlement in the Mallee region, arguing successfully for an increase in farm sizes. He then served on the royal commission into the wheat industry in 1934, and he was well known in country districts for his radio broadcasts. With Lambert, Wadham wrote the commission's analysis of the history and place of rural industries in Australia and the factors that influenced costs of production such as soils, rainfall, technical services, credit, transport and labour. They criticised irrigation policy and management and the ongoing commitment of governments to farms that were too small.[4]

Wadham believed success in post-war rural life demanded access to health services, comfortable housing, community centres, education and electricity. He commissioned several path-breaking studies of Victorian country towns, wheat farms, and orchards in the Sunraysia district. He also mentored a student undertaking a doctorate in rural sociology at the University of North Carolina on the Victorian dairy industry. These studies pioneered statistical sampling to elicit information from farm households, survey techniques that informed the empirical methods of the Bureau of Agricultural Economics, created from recommendations of the Rural Reconstruction Commission. From the late 1940s, the bureau, and its successor bodies (today ABARES) surveyed farms to determine the costs of production and to analyse farming life.[5]

---

4   L.R. Humphreys, 'Wadham, Sir Samuel Macmahon (1891–1972)', *Australian Dictionary of Biography*, National Centre of Biography, Australian National University, accessed online 1 June 2018, published first in hardcopy 2002, http://adb.anu.edu.au/biography/wadham-sir-samuel-macmahon-11930/text21375; and Peter C. Grundy, 'Lambert, Cecil Ralph (Eski) (1899–1971)', *Australian Dictionary of National Biography*, National Centre of Biography, Australian National University, accessed on line 1 June 2018, published first in hardcopy 2000, http://adb.anu.edu.au/biography/lambert-cecil-ralph-eski-10774/text19105.

5   Maurice Rothberg, 'Victorian Dairy Farming: A Social Survey' (PhD thesis, University of North Carolina, 1948); A.J. McIntyre, *Sunraysia: A Social Survey of a Dried Fruits Area* (Melbourne: Melbourne University Press, 1948); A.J. & J.J. McIntyre, *Country Towns of Victoria: A Social Survey* (Melbourne: Melbourne University Press, 1944). ABARES stands for Australian Bureau of Agricultural and Resource Economics and Sciences.

Wadham recruited the services of a young public servant, Alan J. Holt, to study Victorian wheat farms. His slim volume, *Wheat Farms of Victoria*, laid bare the rudimentary nature of domestic farm life compared to that of urban Australia, the disparity in part a result of the long period of declining prices of farm produce and drought.[6] In the metropolitan areas of Victoria, sewerage, fresh water, town gas and electricity had from 1900 become a normal part of domestic life for most. In the bush, and most particularly in the Mallee, the farmers' standard of living had fallen far behind that of their city contemporaries. Holt's survey revealed that most farmers took the radio for granted (battery operated), and they generally owned cars. However, their houses were basic, typically four rooms, including two bedrooms, and a verandah. Just over 40 per cent were habitable but in need of attention, and 10 per cent were dilapidated. Sixty per cent were weatherboard and one-fifth were galvanised iron. Inside they were generally lined with hessian and paper, and oven-like in summer. Iron roofs, a necessity for catching drinking water, added to the summer heat. In Melbourne in the late 1930s, the average consumption of water per head per day was eighteen to twenty gallons. Allowing three to five gallons for sewer flushing, Holt estimated that the average Melburnian consumed twelve gallons for drinking, kitchen and washing purposes. In the Mallee, with its soaring summer heat, the average water tank provided only a third of this amount. In drought years, the deficiency was even worse.[7]

Kitchens and bathrooms were basic as well. Less than 40 per cent of kitchens had sinks and it was common for the housewife to pour waste water into tins that were periodically emptied. Every farm had a one-fire wooden stove, which was kept burning on the hottest summer days. Three quarters of households had bathrooms under the main roof, and about a fifth were detached. Only half of the Victorian wheat farms had water laid onto the bathroom. Water was generally heated in a kettle on the kitchen stove or in a laundry copper. For this reason, the bathroom and the laundry were often combined. Lighting was almost universally by kerosene lamp, and electricity was only available on farms near towns. Charles Coote lived in Quambatook and travelled daily to his farm, so his wife Ada could enjoy electricity. In the 1940s they owned a refrigerator, a luxury beyond the dreams of most farm

---

6   Charles Fahey interviewed Alan Holt at his Melbourne house in the early 1980s. He was very reticent about his part in the wheat survey. Holt was secretary for lands, Department of Crown Lands and Survey, during the 1969 battle to stop agricultural settlement in the Little Desert. See Chapter 11.

7   Alan J. Holt, *Wheat Farms of Victoria: A Sociological Survey* (Melbourne: School of Agriculture, University of Melbourne, 1945), 64–79.

housewives, who made do with a Coolgardie safe in which food was kept cool by water evaporation from a hessian covering.

Holt's greatest concern was for 'sanitary arrangements'. Although most farms had channel water laid onto the garden, only 5 per cent of farms had septic tanks. The majority used pan latrines, which, as the urbanite Holt observed, many of the menfolk bypassed, 'being content to go "down the paddock"'. He thought they were a lot better off than the women, as the majority of latrines were, 'to say the least unpleasant'.[8]

Holt identified many other disadvantages. Medical facilities were poor, with doctors, hospitals and ambulances remote from farms. Primary education appeared adequate in terms of numbers of schools, but Holt called for more research. Secondary education, on the other hand, was clearly inadequate. Food too was problematic. While wheat farmers killed most of their meat on the farm—usually poultry and mutton, as lamb was sold—dairy supply was not 'always continuous nor adequate in quantity and quality'. The dairy was generally the responsibility of the farmer's wife and other female household members. Holt recorded that, although vegetables and fruit were grown on some farms, the supply of both was generally inadequate. The farming community, he found, was inward looking, and it was common for husbands and wives to have grown up on local farms. One could not be 'other than impressed by the isolation which smudges with a dirty finger almost all the fabric of the social organisation of the wheat areas'. Women, Holt emphasised, were the chief victims of this rural isolation.[9]

Holt's survey, and other investigations into rural life, made a deep impression on the members of the Rural Reconstruction Commission. Wadham was convinced that the future of rural Australia depended on improved conditions for rural women. In its seventh report, 'Rural Amenities', the commission recommended a major overhaul of rural services and extensive reforms, including better-quality housing, education, water supply and health services and ready access to telephone services and electricity. In an 'Afterword' the commissioners argued that a high tariff policy increased farm costs, creating a case 'for government action in providing at least some of the initial cost of the amenities and in some instances, perhaps, part of the running cost as well'.[10]

---

8   Holt, *Wheat Farms of Victoria*, 79.
9   Holt, *Wheat Farms of Victoria*, 123–30.
10 Australia, Rural Reconstruction Commission, *Seventh Report, Rural Amenities* (Canberra: Commonwealth Government Printer, 18 May 1945), 91.

The Impact of the War on Agriculture

During wartime, wheat farmers and those working mallee country faced particular difficulties. War disrupted shipping and access to markets. A large wheat crop was expected in the summer harvest of 1939–40, and there were extensive stocks already on hand. Faced with a sizeable wheat surplus, the Commonwealth government established the Australian Wheat Board, and all deliveries were siphoned through licensed traders. The board determined local prices and negotiated export sales. In November 1940 a wheat stabilisation scheme was established. This gave a guaranteed price for wheat but restricted the amount farmers could grow, based on the average acreage sown in the four years prior to the 1940–41 harvest. In Western Australia, growers were restricted to two-thirds of their basic acreages, and a subsidy was paid for their reduced areas.[11] Each year Victoria's Charles Coote requested authority to plant. In 1944 he requested 648 acres, slightly more than the six hundred he was normally permitted. That year he desperately sought superphosphate, visiting manufacturers to argue his case.[12]

Although mallee farmers were pioneers in using labour-saving machinery, the labour of sons and contract workers remained crucial at peak times, most importantly during the harvest. From September 1939, Charles Coote frequently recorded his attendance at farewells for young men enlisting in the services. He faced the grim prospect that his ever-reliable farm manager and worker, Frank Farr, would volunteer. Farr stayed behind, but, as the war came closer to Australia, Coote lamented that military and industrial demands continued to draw population from the Quambatook district to the armed services and to Melbourne. Since the nineteenth century, rural labourers had earned less than urban workers, and the growth of war industries worsened this disparity. Labour shortages increased after Japan entered the war in December 1941, and its thrust deep into the Pacific cut off superphosphate supplies from Nauru. As Sir John Crawford observed in his history of agriculture during the war, Australian farmers would 'no more think of sowing a wheat crop without superphosphate than of sowing without grain'. The war also disrupted agricultural machinery supplies. These

---

11 J.G. Crawford, C.M. Donald, C.P. Dowsett, D.B. Williams and A.A. Ross, *Wartime Agriculture in Australia and New Zealand, 1939–1950* (Stanford: Stanford University Press, 1954), 52–61.

12 Charles Coote, Diary, 15 and 27 January 1944, in Charles William Coote, *Diaries and Papers*, 1896–1955, 1964.0005, University of Melbourne Archives. In 1941 Coote left forty-five acres cultivated above his licence unharvested (note at the beginning of 1941 Diary).

factors led to a decline in the planting of wheat and favoured a transfer to sheep and wool production.[13]

Increased wartime demand revived the small eucalyptus oil extraction industry. Although the industry had ceased to operate in Victoria and NSW mallee country in 1907–08, distilleries existed on Kangaroo Island from 1912, where producers showed that 'it would be more profitable to conserve the "Mallee" for oil, than to work the land for grain'.[14] When the industry on the island also faltered due to overharvesting of mallee,[15] much of the land abandoned in the Victorian Mallee in the late 1930s came back into contention. Mallee regrowth there was judged suitable for oil production, leading to applications for eucalypt harvesting from South Australian farmers working for Adelaide-based pharmaceutical company F.H. Faulding. Faulding had established ten basic stills in the Pinnaroo–Peebinga region in the early 1930s, operated seasonally by farmers.[16] However, the consequences of clearing vast tracts of mallee land slowed expansion. In the 1930s, as we have seen, sand drift and regular dust storms in the Victorian Mallee decreased agricultural productivity and increased the cost of maintaining channels, roads and railway lines. By the 1940s, mallees were considered important allies in the fight against erosion. Some applications for oil harvesting were therefore denied because they might increase the risk of drift.[17] Harvesting where applications were granted was monitored, and it was recommended in at least one case that 'all cutting should cease immediately the Mallee shows any loss of vigor in coppicing'.[18] Land managers were awake at last to the limits of mallee resilience.

In 1950, four distillers still operated at irregular intervals on abandoned farming areas in the Victorian Mallee, supplying Fauldings and Thurleys of Sydney, and boosting some farmers' incomes.[19] The peak year of production in

---

13 Coote, Diary, 19 February 1941, 9 November 1941, and 15 January 1941; Crawford et al., *Wartime Agriculture in Australia and New Zealand*, 53–4.

14 Richard T. Baker and Henry G. Smith, *Research on the Eucalypts, especially in Regard to their Essential Oils* (Sydney: Government Printer, 1920), 437.

15 'Eucalyptus Oil Produced in Mallee', *Pinnaroo and Border Times*, 27 November 1941.

16 D.J. Shiel, *Eucalyptus, Essence of Australia: The Story of the Eucalyptus Oil Industry— and of the 'Eucy' Men, and their Contribution to the Australian Bush Tradition* (Melbourne: Queensberry Hill Press, c. 1985), 129.

17 VA 1034 Department of Conservation Forests and Lands, VPRS 11563 General Correspondence Files, Annual Single Number System 1 VPRS 11563/P1, Unit 845, 66/1555, J.H. Simon, Manya, Public Record Office Victoria (PROV).

18 VPRS 11563/P1, Unit 845, 66/1555, 8 May 1946, Report (standard form) from R. Jones, Forest Officer, J.H. Simon, Manya, 1945, PROV.

19 VPRS 11563/P1, Unit 265, 47/882, 19 June 1950, Mildura District, List of Eucalyptus Distilleries, 1933–46, PROV.

Australia was 1947, when around a thousand tonnes of oil was produced, 70 per cent of it exported.[20] A new round of post-war agricultural development reduced production with eucalyptus-producing areas turned over to cropping. In 1966, F.H. Faulding complained to the Forests Commission about this loss of eucalyptus areas, given the challenges of cheap imported oil.[21] In the mid-1970s, only one distillery was still operating in the Victorian Mallee, north of Murrayville.[22]

Reconstructing Marginal Farms

The Rural Reconstruction Commissioners argued that settlement of marginal wheat areas in the 1920s was 'an outstanding example of the huge cost in wasted capital, in human effort, in land depreciation and in public relief that can come from faulty settlement planning and from delay in applying fundamental reconstruction measures'. They reported on the measures put in place to salvage marginal lands, now made more urgent by war.[23]

The problems of marginal lands were laid bare by dry years in the late 1920s and the collapse of prices in the 1930s. Nationally, the 1934 royal commission into the wheat industry recommended the re-organisation of uneconomic holdings. Little action followed in the 1930s, possibly for fear of adding to unemployment. Indeed 'drought relief payments continued to irrigate the hopes of settlers', and moratoria on debt collection shifted much of the financial burden from farmers to their creditors.[24] Where land was held on purchase lease from governments, authorities could take action, and the Victorian government led the way by devising methods of salvaging closer and soldier settlers. This problem was not confined to the marginal wheat lands of the Mallee for there were hundreds of indebted closer settlers on irrigation and dry blocks too.

---

20   B.E.J. Small, 'Assessing the Australian *Eucalyptus* Oil Industry,' *Forest and Timber* 13 (1977): 13–16.

21   VPRS 11563/P1, Unit 845, 66/1555, A.J. Farrow, Chief Buying Officer for F.H. Faulding, Wholesale Druggists and Manufacturing Chemists to Forests Commission, J.H. Simon, 7 September 1966, Manya, 1945, PROV.

22   Land Conservation Council (Vic.), *Final Recommendations: Mallee Study Area* (Melbourne: Land Conservation Council (Vic.), 1977), 74.

23   Australia, Rural Reconstruction Commission, *Financial and Economic Reconstruction of Farms, Fourth Report* (Canberra: Commonwealth Government Printer, 28 August 1944), 10.

24   Australia, Rural Reconstruction Commission, *Fourth Report*, for debt adjustment, 27–37.

The sheer scale of the problem undoubtedly forced the Victorian government to act first. From simple schemes of reallocating settlers onto larger properties, the lands administrators turned to the massive problem of assessing the viability of farms, inventorying assets and liabilities, and rescheduling debt for farmers considered 'efficient'. Under this program, settlers in large areas of the 'New Mallee' in the north and north west of the Victorian Mallee were essentially given a second chance. The Victorian government wrote off Mallee debts in excess of £10,000,000.[25] The Western Australian government was forced to adopt a four-pronged policy: writing off debts, creating changes in land tenure with annual leaseholds on reduced rents, replacing conditional purchase, and amalgamating holdings to make viable farms.[26]

A national solution emerged during the drought of 1938 after a conference between state and federal governments to consider the distribution of proceeds of the tax on flour. Victoria requested payment for drought relief, while South Australia opposed using the money as a dole and argued that a long-term plan was required to amalgamate small holdings. The Commonwealth agreed to set aside £500,000 each year for five years to rehabilitate marginal areas.[27]

Financial assistance enabled South Australia, Victoria and Western Australia to tackle the reclamation of marginal lands. The South Australian government established the Marginal Lands Committee to map marginal lands and the number of settlers involved, devise remedies and calculate their cost. The plan envisaged the removal of 617 settlers and the reconstruction of 659 properties on the 1,695,000 acres affected. The larger part of the fund, £821,000, was set aside for purchasing properties of farmers willing to sell, and the remainder, £152,900, was for improved fencing and water supply to make these properties suitable for sheep. Settlers in the Murray Mallee and Eyre Peninsula were encouraged to engage in mixed farming with sheep as livestock, and cropping was to extend over wide rotations. In parts of the northern areas, settlers were to engage in sheep farming only. Low rentals were offered on 'make up areas' under perpetual lease or pastoral lease, on

---

25   Australia, Rural Reconstruction Commission, *Fourth Report*, 40. For the process of saving Victorian settlers, see Jacqueline Coucill, 'Back on Track: The Closer Settlement Scheme in Victoria and the Revaluation Process 1932–1938' (PhD thesis, La Trobe University, 2004).

26   David Murray, 'Land Settlement and Farming Systems', in *Yilgarn: Good Country for Hardy People: The Landscape and People of the Yilgarn Shire, Western Australia*, ed. Lyall Hunt (Southern Cross: Yilgarn Shire & WA College of Advanced Education, 1988), 294–5.

27   A.R. Callaghan and A.J. Millington *The Wheat Industry in Australia* (Sydney: Angus & Robertson, 1956), 162.

condition that these lands remained uncultivated. Financial support was given for clearing mallee vegetation. There was no provision for moving farmers to higher rainfall areas or compulsory resumptions. Vacating settlers were to be paid their equity, and those without equity were to be paid a small gratuity to tide them over.[28]

In Western Australia, a plan was approved in 1940 to reduce the number of farms in designated districts, including halving them in the Esperance and Salmon Gums area from 2,202 to 1,082. It was estimated that on average £430 was needed to provide living areas of 2,000 to 3,000 acres, of which 1,200 to 1,400 acres would be cleared land. Like the South Australian plan, it envisaged a partial or complete transfer from wheat to sheep farming, with the provision of superphosphate for oat crops, finance for essential machinery, additional horses, at least two hundred ewes per farm, and fencing and water supplies. Where settlers had a debt for stock to private finance companies, this was taken over by the Agricultural Bank.[29]

Between 1933 and 1938, the Victoria government oversaw the vacation of 1,127 farms in the Mallee and granted additional land to 867. In June 1941, the Commonwealth approved a plan to deal with the remaining 530 settlers considered marginal. Three hundred farmers would be removed with a cash payment of £320 each, and reconstructed holdings would have a minimum of 2,500 acres, principally for grazing. A limited amount of cropping would be permitted to provide fodder for stock and to promote the growth of natural grasses. Provision was also to be made through the State Rivers and Water Supply Commission to provide water. The cost of this was estimated to be £750 per farm.[30]

Rabbits

From the early 1920s, William Lane detailed in his diary the seemingly never-ending task of turning mallee scrub into farm land. As the interminable round of picking up, carting and burning roots eased off in the 1930s, another task emerged: the eradication of rabbits. The sand ridges of mallee farms created an ideal place for rabbits to breed, and by the early 1930s rabbits had infested Lane's farm. In ploughing the fallows each winter, he unearthed rabbit burrows. Between July and October 1932, for example, he spent a part of at least twenty-four days digging them out. In the summer of 1933, as he

---

28 Australia, Rural Reconstruction Commission, *Fourth Report*, 72–4.
29 Australia, Rural Reconstruction Commission, *Fourth Report*, 74–5.
30 Australia, Rural Reconstruction Commission, *Fourth Report*, 68–72.

scarified and harrowed the fallow to prepare for seeding, he spent another fortnight on the rabbits.[31]

From 1918 use of the myxoma virus to control rabbits was mooted but rejected for fear of harm to other animals or humans. Efforts to release the virus in the semi-arid areas of South Australia in the 1930s failed. In the war years, labour scarcity hindered efforts to control rabbits, and dry years also robbed farmers of the financial means to combat the rabbit. As a result, rabbit numbers escalated in the 1940s.[32] In the winter of 1949, Charles Coote of Quambatook regularly recorded digging out burrows while his farm manager Frank Farr ploughed the fallow. The sand drifts that characterised the dry years of 1938 to 1944 provided rabbits with new opportunities to establish burrows. In the early 1950s, three million rabbit carcases were exported from Western Australia alone, where it was estimated that rabbits cut stock carrying capacity by 50 per cent and crop losses were 10 per cent. In the early 1950s, the rabbit population in the Victorian Mallee was estimated at fifty million and across Australia at 500 million.[33]

After the war, rabbit eradication scientific work resumed. From May to December 1950, the Wild Life section of the CSIRO injected rabbits with the myxomatosis virus at three sites in the Murray Valley. These efforts appeared to fail. Indeed, rabbit counts increased following the inoculations. However, late in December 1950, myxomatosis took hold. By the end of March 1951, the disease had been recorded over 500 thousand square miles along the Murray and Darling Rivers. During the winter of 1951 it lay dormant but broke out again in the summer of 1952–53. A particularly wet summer helped the breeding of mosquitoes, the main vector of the disease's spread, and explains why earlier attempts in arid areas had failed. Myxomatosis initially spread over the whole of Victoria and the agricultural districts of South Australia, then into New South Wales and parts of Southern Queensland.[34] It reached Western Australia in the summer of 1952–53.

Farmers helped its spread. In March 1951 Charles Coote was visited by a neighbour who brought 'two (2) sick rabbits, maximatosis [sic]', which he released in Coote's paddocks. The initial mortality rates were exceptionally

---

31   Calculated from William Lane, Diary, July to October 1931 and January 1932, in William H. Lane, Diaries, 1926–1941, PA01/123, Australian Manuscripts Collection, State Library Victoria.
32   D.B. Williams, *Economic and Technical Problems of Australia's Rural Industries* (Melbourne: Melbourne University Press, 1957), 88–91.
33   See, for example, Coote, Diary, 27 and 30 July 1949; *Journal of Agriculture, Western Australia* 20, no. 3 (1979): 90–1.
34   Coote, Diary, 3 March 1951.

high, 99.8 per cent, and remained over 90 per cent from 1951 to 1956, reducing the population in Australia to fifty to a hundred million. Renewed campaigns were helped by the introduction of a new poison, 1080, which was more lethal than strychnine. Rabbit eradication improved farm productivity and increased the average fleece weight of sheep.[35] Although official publications did not break down the extent of eradication regionally, there is no doubt it had a significant impact on mallee landscapes. In 1960 one Murray Mallee farmer observed that is was a 'job to get enough rabbits to feed his dogs'.[36]

Soil Conservation and Pasture Improvement

In its sixth report, the Rural Reconstruction Commission stated that probably 'the most important change in southern Australia, wherever the rainfall between March and September or October is reliable enough for the introduction of subterranean clover, has been the introduction of "ley" farming'.[37] The Victorian Department of Agriculture led the introduction of ley farming, namely the growing of grass or legumes in rotation with other crops. As early as 1913, the department's superintendent A.E.V. Richardson had warned farmers that the greatest weakness with the system of fallowing wheat fields was that it deprived the soil of organic matter. He recommended crop rotation that included a year or two of pasture, and the planting of green manure crops, such as oats, that were later to be ploughed back into the soil. These measures, however, did not restore the equivalent organic matter removed by fallow and wheat, and the pasture that grew was largely disease-hosting grasses.[38]

Clover-ley farming was first undertaken in 1922 at the Rutherglen Research Station. In 1927 the first crop planted after clover was grown demonstrated the greatly improved fertility of the soil. Encouraged, scientists from 1931 conducted long-term experiments with subterranean clover at the Rutherglen Research Station. A paddock that had been over-cropped with wheat was sown to subterranean clover for five years and then sown to wheat in 1937. This dramatically improved the soil structure, and later experiments demonstrated

---

35 *Quarterly Review of Agricultural Economics* 6, no. 3 (1953): 93.
36 *Journal of Agriculture, South Australia* 64 (December 1960): 182.
37 Australia, Rural Reconstruction Commission, *Farm Efficiency and Costs and Factors Relating Thereto, Sixth Report* (Canberra: Commonwealth Government Printer, April 1945), 16.
38 J.A. Morrow, N.C. Killeen, and J.G. Bath, 'Development of Clover-Ley Farming at Rutherglen Research Station', *Journal of the Department of Agriculture of Victoria* 46, no. 1 (January 1948): 13–20; Neil Barr and John Carey, *Greening a Brown Land: The Australian Search for Sustainable Land Use* (Melbourne: Macmillan Education, 1992), 134–5.

that the process significantly improved the nitrogen content of the soil. Two years of wheat were grown after a paddock had been under subterranean clover for two or three years. Long fallow was abandoned, and the clover re-established itself after cropping without having to be re-sown. Under this system, the division of the farm into an area used for cropping and another of native pastures used for sheep could be abandoned and replaced by sheep and crops rotated across the whole farm. Although the system required the use of superphosphate, it was self-sustaining in terms of nitrogen.[39]

The initial experiments in clover-ley farming were better suited to wetter districts such as Rutherglen, but clover-ley farming in drier mallee districts was slowly adopted over the next two decades. Its introduction in the Victorian Mallee required further experimentation and the reconstruction of wheat farms following the crisis of the drought years of 1937–38 to 1945–46.

In mallee districts, a more serious problem than declining nitrogen levels was the control of erosion. Low nitrogen challenged farm productivity, but erosion challenged the very existence of farms. Research into mallee soil problems was institutionalised through the new Mallee Research Station at Walpeup set up in 1932, and scientists began a rigorous study of trial plots at Walpeup to experiment with ways of stabilising soils. These results were fed into the farming practice of progressive farmers. The peak drought years of 1944–45 gave added impetus to this. In the far north west, public meetings called on the department to expedite the research.[40]

Soil conservation was now a national problem. Each state had its own soil conservation board or authority with power to implement policy and responsibility to educate farmers about the benefits and strategies of soil conservation. In 1949 Henry Bolte, minister for water supply in Victoria, introduced the Soil Conservation and Land Utilisation Bill, observing: 'We could not have made a bigger mess of the soil of the country if its destruction had been carried out under supervision'.[41] In Victoria, departmental visits to farms to inspect erosion-control methods encouraged the development of further test plots at Walpeup in the late 1940s.

The collective efforts involved in this education strategy are striking, with different layers of government and local organisations involved in attempting

---

39 Morrow, Killeen, and Bath, 'Development of Clover-Ley Farming at Rutherglen Research Station', 13–20 and 39–40.

40 H.J. Sims, 'Wind Erosion Control: Comments on Methods Used in the Walpeup District', *Journal of the Department of Agriculture of Victoria* 46, no. 6 (June 1948): 241–8.

41 Quoted in George T. Thompson, *A Brief History of Soil Conservation in Victoria, 1834–1961* (Melbourne: Soil Conservation Authority, 1979), 45.

to deal with the pressing problem of soil conservation. In Victoria the Hanslow Cup competition encouraged soil drift solutions and promoted conservation. The 1958 Hanslow competition attracted 174 entries and about five hundred people turned out to the linked Mallee field day. Local banks, businesses and shire councils supported these competitions, and field days highlighted the strategies competition winners had implemented on their farms.[42]

Many farmers were proactive about seeking solutions to drift on their properties. In 1945 J.J. Trimble, an 'enthusiast for rye corn', sold his sheep and was using rye and the native everlastings to prevent wind erosion (see Figure 9.1). His farm looked like 'acres of rolling green, without a bare patch and no dust rising'. The *Argus* reporter who observed this claimed a local councillor told him soil drift could only be tackled by young men raised in the Mallee who knew the type of land it was.[43]

Figure 9.1: Wind Erosion in the Manangatang district. The severity of the problem of soil drift is frighteningly evident in this picture taken in 1941 by the Soil Conservation Board. The mallee root is exposed to chest height.

(Courtesy Victorian Public Record Office)

---

42 Thompson, *A Brief History of Soil Conservation in Victoria, 1834–1961*, 71.
43 Howard S. Palmer, 'Drift Checked in the Mallee: Value of Rye as a Remedy', *Argus*, 17 January 1945.

The historian of the Victorian Soil Conservation Authority has argued that the authority brought farmers and field officers together in an atmosphere of non-compulsion that built trust. The authority also encouraged farmers to develop a 'whole farm plan' and to see soil conservation as a broad social problem and not just about the 'repair of site damage or correction of strictly localized conditions'. The strategies implemented combined changes in fallowing, in particular the use of cereal rye and superphosphate to stabilise windblown areas, and in managing areas where sheep wore out country by increasing the number of 'water points' and the number of shady spots to prevent them congregating in just a few locations. Between 1948 and 1952 the Victorian government supplied free cereal rye and superphosphate to any farmer wanting to use them. After that time the government believed that the use of super and cereal rye 'as the first agent in the revegetation of wind-eroded land' had become so widespread and their advantages so well known that free supplies could no longer be justified.[44]

In South Australia authorities tended to blame the individual farmer. The Murray Mallee District Soil Conservation Board reported on the problem of drift in 1952. It sheeted home responsibility to those with smaller holdings who in the Great Depression had 'over-cropped and over-stocked, especially during the low price periods, in an attempt to keep them an economic farming proposition'. Insufficient capital to invest in drift control aggravated the problem: 'By this time the farmer was well into debt and he was hard put to provide the essentials for a bare living'. In these circumstances, the board believed that farmers' acceptance of, or indifference to, drift was now the main problem. 'The *idea* of controlling the drift simply did not occur to them as being a vital part of their farming methods in these dry areas.' The board's report added: 'They are men who have battled through the depression years and managed to hang on to their properties. Now they are growing old and have no son on the farm to carry on ... The tendency is to simply make enough to live on and let the drift go'.[45]

In Western Australia soil conservation focused on 'the salt problem'. The Rural and Industries Bank urged a study centred on Lake Grace, Newdegate and Pingrup. It found that around 250 thousand acres across 150 farms in those districts were affected and concluded, like the Victorian and South Australian authorities, that 'the rehabilitation of many farms will

---

44 Thompson, *A Brief History of Soil Conservation in Victoria, 1834–1961*, 73.
45 A.R. Birch and J.P. Blencowe, 'The Badly Drifting Farm: Report of the Murray Mallee District Soil Conservation Board, 1948–1952' (Murray Bridge: Murray Mallee District Soil Conservation Board, 1952), 5, 15–16.

require an increase in the size of the properties and altered methods of farm management'.[46] Some control was achieved using oats and Wimmera rye grass, but there was a danger that unrestricted grazing would compound the problem with erosion.

The Western Australian Soil Conservation Act of 1945 established the Soil Conservation Service, which counted 'the control of land clearing' among its main concerns.[47] In 1950 two Soil Conservation Districts were proclaimed, including the north-eastern part of the mallee lands, which mandated permits for clearing.[48] In 1951 farmers made application to clear 182,503 acres in the two districts, and all were approved, occasionally with a caveat to leave shelter belts.[49] By 1954, the permit system appears to have been regarded as a data-collection exercise rather than an opportunity for significant intervention. The intent to conserve was overwhelmed by the major expansion of agriculture then underway. By 1961 almost 1.3 million acres had been cleared in these two districts alone. Applications slowed only because very little vegetation remained.[50]

Farmers across mallee lands were responding to the soil conservation crisis. Neil McFarlane, the son of a soldier settler in Mirkoo, Victoria, became a full-time farmer at the age of sixteen in 1956. Remembering drought and dust storms in the 1940s, he declared: 'I can't express how deeply that experience of those years impacted on me … getting rid of those weeds, getting rid of rabbits, restoring hopelessly eroded hills … It took nearly a generation to retrieve that damage that was done by the drought and the blow-outs in the forties'.[51] This concern for the soil spread to all governments. From 1975 to 1977 the Commonwealth and state governments collaborated on a soil conservation study, which estimated that just over half of Australian farmland was degraded.[52] It laid the basis for the National Soil Conservation Program in 1983, which recognised the need to take account of relationships between ecological, economic and social factors in agriculture.[53]

---

46   Western Australia, *Annual Report of the Department of Agriculture*, 30 June 1946, 45.
47   Western Australia, *Annual Report of the Department of Agriculture*, 30 June 1948, 37.
48   Western Australia, *Annual Report of the Department of Agriculture*, 30 June 1949, 34.
49   Western Australia, *Annual Report of the Department of Agriculture*, 30 June 1950, 31.
50   Western Australia, *Annual Report of the Department of Agriculture*, 30 June 1954, 44.
51   Neil McFarlane, interviewed by Ruth Ford, Vinefera, 2014.
52   Australia, Department of Environment, Housing and Community Development, *A Basis for Soil Conservation Policy in Australia: Commonwealth and State Government Collaborative Soil Conservation Study 1975–77, Report 1* (Canberra: AGPS, 1978).
53   Helen Allison and R.J. Hobbs, *Science and Policy in Natural Resource Management: Understanding System Complexity* (Cambridge: Cambridge University Press, 2006), 28–30.

These investigations identified the traditional practice of bare fallowing as a major cause of erosion, although the importance of fallowing was recognised. In publications outlining the new evidence on cultivation practices, research officers reviewed the purpose of long fallow. These were: to prepare a good seed bed for the crop in the following year; conservation of moisture for the crop sown in the next autumn; control of weeds; the liberation of nitrates; and the control of diseases—take-all, root rots and flag smut. It was admitted that experimental work had shown the 'superiority in the yield of crops grown on well-prepared fallows'. However, 'clean, bare fallows drift to a greater extent than dirty fallows; and blown patches on fallows cause progressive reductions in yields'. Fallow, while not being eliminated, had to be modified in various ways.[54]

A critical problem identified was the burning of stubble after a wheat crop. This practice facilitated subsequent planting of oat crops after wheat by a combine machine and produced a cleaner oat crop. During wartime a shortage of new implements made it difficult for farmers to replace old combines. By the late 1940s machinery production had increased, and the Victorian Department of Agriculture recommended that farmers broadcast the oats with a seed drill and cover the crop with disc harrows used in tandem (see Figure 9.2). The replacement of horses by more powerful tractors facilitated this practice. Stubble could also be left out to grazing, and the straw was broken down before the ground was worked again. In some cases, part of the stubble was fallowed, and this could be worked with a twin-disc plough.[55]

Rotation regimens to lessen drift were developed. One of these was fallow—wheat—fallow—wheat, followed by several years of grazing. Trials were conducted at the Walpeup Research Station during the period 1939–42. These tests, disrupted by the war, did not give spectacular results in maintaining productivity. They did, importantly, demonstrate considerable benefit in arresting sand drift. More successful was the trial conducted at Walpeup over the period 1937–43 of using cover crops on fallows, which 'provide vegetative cover to protect the soil against erosion over the summer period'.[56] After the winter ploughing, a cereal crop—usually oats—was planted on the fallow land in early spring. After the crop had become firmly established, it was grazed down, and sufficient roots and stalks were left to protect the soil over

---

54   Allison and Hobbs, *Science and Policy in Natural Resource Management*, 242.
55   Allison and Hobbs, *Science and Policy in Natural Resource Management*, 242–3.
56   Allison and Hobbs, *Science and Policy in Natural Resource Management*, 246.

Figure 9.2 Disc drill and tandem-disc harrow. To combat soil erosion scientists advised farmers to alter their fallowing methods and to plant cover crops such as oats on wheat stubble. This was made possible by adoption of tractors to pull the drill and tandem disc harrow through the stubble. Farmers were advised not to burn the stubble.
Courtesy *Journal of Agriculture, Victoria*, 1949

the summer. Department guide books advised that grazing had to be handled judiciously, and sufficient cover had to be left to protect the soil. Many farmers had difficulty with this. Some allowed crops to be overgrazed, while others permitted too much growth. A dry spring made management of this new regimen hard, and difficulties were increased by the presence of young grasshoppers. While cover crops did have the disadvantage of reducing subsequent wheat yields, the upside was that they substantially reduced drift. On sand hills, the Walpeup scientists recommended the planting of rye corn. Under these new cropping regimes, rotations were of longer duration. One pattern was a three-year rotation: fallow—wheat—oats or fallow—wheat—grass or oats for grazing. More advantageous were still longer rotations: fallow, wheat, oats for hay or grain, and grass or oats for grazing.[57]

The Walpeup Research Station also conducted experiments on whether clover-ley farming could be adapted to the drier conditions of the Victorian Mallee. As early as 1938, barrel medic was identified as possible leguminous pasture. Barrel medic was first recorded in Victoria in 1907, and it probably spread from South Australia to the Mallee and Wimmera in the 1920s. Commercial production of the seed was commenced in Australia in 1938, the same year the research station at Walpeup commenced trials to determine if

---

57 Allison and Hobbs, *Science and Policy in Natural Resource Management*, 244–6.

Figure 9.3: Cover crop trials at Walpeup Research Station, 1945.
On the left oats have been drilled into wheat stubble.
On the right traditional bare fallowing was employed.
The latter practice was subject to wind erosion. Cover crops were more feasible
with the rapid adoption of tractors that could pull a heavy seed drill
and tandem disc harrow through the stubble.
Farmers were advised not to burn the stubble.
(Courtesy Victorian Public Record Office)

barrel medic would grow in the dry conditions of the north west (see Figure 9.3). Following these trials, it was adopted by farmers in the early 1940s and withstood the drought years of 1943–45. In 1955 the department's *Journal of Agriculture* reported that the original plantings at Walpeup were still extant. Readers were also advised that farmers with long experience of barrel medic had found that, even in seasons where winter and spring growth was disappointing, the dry burrs of the barrel medic supplied nutritious autumn feed. It was recommended that barrel medic should be planted on fallow, not stubble, with a cover crop of cereals—wheat, oats or barley.[58]

---

58 J. McCann, 'Pastures on Wheat Farms in Wimmera and Mallee', *Journal of the Department of Agriculture of Victoria* 53, no. 3 (March 1955): 97–104, see especially 100–01.

Trace Elements on Light Lands

By the late 1930s, much of mallee land regarded as suitable for agriculture had been developed—and sometimes abandoned, and perhaps redeveloped. There were, however, areas that had proven resistant to profitable agriculture, that produced good crops for a couple of years, then only stunted growth and pastures that caused sheep to sicken and die. These were the 'light' or 'desert' lands. Found in the Western Australian wheatbelt in both small patches and extensive sandplains, and occurring in large tracts called the Ninety Mile Desert, Big Desert and Little Desert of South Australia and Victoria, they are characterised by sandy nutrient-deficient soils. Some of these are deep sands; others have clay or ironstone subsoils. While some of these lands, especially in south-western Australia, carried substantial trees, most supported heath or a mixture of heath and low mallees. This 'scrub plain' was widely regarded as the poorest country, on which it was impossible to make a living. In Western Australia, turning it to profitable use was made more difficult by the presence of poison plants—*Gastrolobium* and *Oxylobium* species containing sodium fluoroacetate (1080) that is fatal to livestock.

A 1938 Western Australian honorary royal commission into the state's 'light lands and poison-infested lands' characterised over twelve million acres of such lands within twenty-five miles of existing railways as 'awaiting use'.[59] The commissioners were optimistic about the prospects for agriculture on the sandplains with suitable application of fertilisers, use of pasture legumes, and tree belts to guard against erosion, though they warned of the high cost of bringing such land into production, especially while overseas markets remained limited.[60] Curiously, they seemed to underplay the failures experienced by farmers attempting to work these lands: something was missing! A decade of scientific research and practical experimentation finally solved the mystery.

As early as 1928, researchers at the Waite Agricultural Research Institute at the University of Adelaide discovered that grey-speck disease of oats was cured by applying small amounts of manganese to the crop. In the mid-1930s, parallel work by researchers at the CSIR (later CSIRO) division of animal nutrition in South Australia, and Western Australian Department of Agriculture researchers E.J. Underwood and J.F. Filmer, found that wasting

---

59 Western Australia, *Report of the Honorary Royal Commission on Light Lands and Poison-Infested Lands* (Perth: Government Printer, 1938), 10.

60 Western Australia, *Report of the Honorary Royal Commission on Light Lands and Poison-Infested Lands*, 25.

of ruminants on coastal sands was due to a cobalt deficiency.[61] The significance of trace elements for crop and animal production was becoming clearer, and parallel investigations continued in Western Australia and South Australia. David Riceman, a researcher at CSIR's Robe station, studied trace elements for crop and pasture production and, in 1938, demonstrated the beneficial effects of copper supplementation for oats on the coastal sands at Robe.[62] Western Australian farmers were also experimenting with trace elements at this time, and their results were followed up by L.J.H. Teakle of the Western Australian Department of Agriculture.[63]

Experimentation was inhibited by the demands of war, but Riceman and colleagues continued their experiments from 1944 with farmers in the Keith district. This work unequivocally showed that soils in the area needed additional copper and zinc as well as phosphorus to grow pastures; later research demonstrated that some of the Ninety Mile Desert soils also required supplementary manganese.[64] Meanwhile, in Western Australia, some farmers took the initiative, with one northern wheatbelt farmer arranging in 1946 for the manufacture of twenty tonnes of a superphosphate–copper–zinc mixture to trial on his farm.[65] In 1947 Eric Smart began working sandplain country on his farm at Mingenew. He collaborated with the Department of Agriculture to develop systems using blue lupins and nitrogenous fertilisers to make such country highly productive. Smart became an outspoken advocate for the transformation of these 'wastelands'. Field days on his farm, Erregulla Springs, attracted up to a thousand people. He was knighted in 1966 for his efforts.[66]

In southern mallee country in Western Australia, science again helped bring light lands into agricultural productivity. In 1947 the shire councils of Gnowangerup and Lake Grace requested departmental experiments with various fertilisers, trace elements, cereal crops and legumes to enable development of their light lands. The following year attention turned to Esperance,

---

61 R.J. Moir, 'Underwood, Eric John (1905–1980)', *Australian Dictionary of Biography*, National Centre of Biography, Australian National University, accessed online 8 May 2017, published first in hardcopy 2002, http://adb.anu.edu.au/biography/underwood-eric-john-11900/text21315.

62 N.S. Tiver, *Desert Conquest: A Review of the Main Events Which Have Contributed to the Development of the Ninety-Mile Desert* (Adelaide: AMP Society, 1986), 2.

63 G.H. Burvill, 'The Last Fifty Years, 1929–1979', in *Agriculture in Western Australia: 150 Years of Development and Achievement 1829–1979*, ed. G.H. Burvill (Perth: University of Western Australia Press, 1979), 60.

64 Tiver, *Desert Conquest*, 2–3.

65 Burvill, 'The Last Fifty Years', 61.

66 Eric F. Smart, *Western Australian Wasteland Transformed* (Mingenew: E.F. Smart, 1960); Burvill, 'The Last Fifty Years', 64.

where a research station was established to further knowledge gained through the various farmers' and departmental experiments on sandplain country elsewhere in the state.[67] This was later complemented by the department's establishment of a trial plot between Newdegate and Lake Grace in 1951, which in 1955 became the Newdegate Research Station.[68]

Farm Mechanisation

The introduction of myxomatosis had an immediate impact on the productivity of pastoral and cropping lands, but the tractor's impact was less immediate and rather drawn out. Horses experienced a long twilight in rural Australia, but eventually tractors became dominant and transformed rural landscapes and rural life. In the USA, tractors were purchased in large numbers in the 1920s and thereafter to 1960, with a slight fall off in the early 1930s. In Australia the introduction of the tractor was slower. In 1935 only one in ten rural properties in Australia owned a tractor; by 1950 the proportion was almost six in every ten properties.[69]

Economic historians Alan Olmstead and Paul Rhode have argued that the introduction of the tractor in the USA was complex, and the early tractors were not simple replacements for horses. The first tractors 'were behemoths, patterned after the giant steam plows that preceded them'. They were useful for ploughing, harrowing and belt work, but not for cultivating fields of growing crops, nor powering farm equipment in tow. After 1910 a reduction in the machine's size and a consequent increase in its versatility made it more suited to a wider range of farm tasks. Mass production also reduced prices over time.[70] Important improvements included rubber tyres, which gave greater mobility, improved air and oil filters, and power-takeoff (PTO), which enabled tractors to pull and power harvesting machines.[71] Harry Ferguson's coupling of the tractor to the plough (and other cultivating tools) by the mid-1930s

---

67 G.H. Burvill, 'The Development of Light lands', in *Agriculture in Western Australia: 150 Years of Development and Achievement 1829-1979*, ed. G.H. Burvill, 165–6.
68 Burvill, 'The Development of Light Lands', 168–9.
69 'Tractors on Australian Farms', *Quarterly Review of Agricultural Economics* 6, no. 1 (January 1953): 11–13.
70 Alan L. Olmstead and Paul W. Rhode, 'Reshaping the Landscape: The Impact and Diffusion of the Tractor in American Agriculture, 1910–1960', *The Journal of Economic History* 61, no. 3 (September 2001): 663–98.
71 Olmstead and Rhode, 'Reshaping the Landscape', 668–9. For the Ferguson System, see Edward P. Neufeld, *A Global Corporation: A History of the International Development of Massey–Ferguson Limited* (Toronto: Toronto University Press, 1969), 94–100.

made the tractor and plough essentially one machine; the tractor no longer simply dragged the plough. The 'Ferguson System' removed the dangerous tendency of the tractor to pivot on its rear wheels and permitted penetration of the soil without excessive implement weight. And, in addition, hydraulic systems allowed the tractor driver to adjust the depth of plough shears.[72]

In the USA, Olmstead and Rhode found that tractor owners used mechanisation to increase the scale of their operations. In Australia, mallee farming was from its inception based on cultivating larger areas, so the tractor was a logical mechanised extension of horse-propelled farming. In 1930, farmers in Kulwin and Wagant in Victoria's 'New Mallee' in the north cultivated an average of 447 acres each on properties of 840 acres. By 1941, government reorganisation of properties increased the size of farms to 1,500 acres, and further consolidation by 1951 resulted in farms of 2,500 acres with 620 cultivated. The extra land gave greater scope for crop rotation and grazing. In 1930, just under a fifth of Kulwin–Wagant farmers used tractors, and this had doubled by 1941 (see Figure 9.4). In 1951 all of Kulwin's farmers employed tractors. High wool and wheat prices in the second half of the 1940s further encouraged their adoption, and in June 1952 half of all tractors were less than six years old.[73]

Once introduced, the progress of the tractor was ineluctable. In the mid-1950s, Bureau of Agricultural Economics' surveys of wheat farms reported a trend towards more powerful machines. In the bureau's 1954–56 survey of the wheat industry, 40 per cent of wheat farmers had two tractors, and there was a tendency to purchase units over forty horsepower, with farmers moving from kerosene to diesel.[74] In subsequent decades this trend to more powerful tractors gathered pace.

Post-war Boom

Across the Australian wheat belt, wheat acres declined in the 1940s. Although this was also the case in mallee lands, the area cropped by individual farmers increased (or in some areas remained stable), as marginal producers left the land and their properties were taken over by neighbouring farmers. In the late

---

72 Neufeld, *A Global Corporation*, 94–9.
73 Tractor numbers and details of Kulwin–Wagant were calculated from: Australian Bureau of Statistics; Parish Agricultural Statistics, WP 570, items 34–5, 48–9 and 65–6, National Archives of Australia; Australia, Bureau of Agricultural Economics, *The Australian Wheat Growing Industry: An Economic Survey* (Canberra: Bureau of Agricultural Economics, December 1960), 17.
74 Australia, Bureau of Agricultural Economics, *The Australian Wheat Growing Industry*, 17.

Figure 9.4: A tractor pulling a Sunshine Header with power-take-off. The mass adoption of the tractor in the late 1940s permitted farmers to harvest larger areas with headers driven with power-take-off (PTO) from the tractor. When the mallee was first settled the cut of stripper was six foot. By the late 1940s 10-foot cuts were common.
(Courtesy State Library Victoria)

1940s, the price of wheat increased dramatically; the average real price from 1947 to 1950 was double the price in 1941. For those who moved to wool, even more spectacular results were achieved from 1949 to 1952. In 1951 the real price of wool was almost seven times its price in 1941. Mallee farmers were able to take advantage of these years and clear off the debts incurred in the miserable 1930s and the dry early 1940s. In 1943–44 Charles Coote paid tax on a farm income of £416 and off-farm investments of £358; in 1951 his net return from his farm was £8,455 and off-farm investments £591. This was a massive real increase of seven times his 1943–44 income.[75]

Initially, mallee farmers reacted to these improved financial circumstances by making changes that could be quickly implemented. Charles Coote changed his patterns of rotation in the late 1940s by introducing oats planted in the

---

75   Charles Coote, Taxation Journal, 1917–1953, in Charles William Coote, Diaries and Papers, 1896–1955, 1964.0005, University of Melbourne Archives.

wheat stubble. This required the purchase of a new tractor and a tandem disc plough that could work with the combine in stubble fields. Self-sown oats also provided grazing land and arrested drift. In August 1949 he inspected a thin growth of two hundred acres of self-sown oats. Coote, unlike most of his neighbours, did not run sheep; rather he contracted out his stubble and self-sown oats to neighbours. By the early 1950s this provided a significant addition to his income. He also used the good times to renew his harvesting plant. In January 1951, he purchased a new A.L. Sunshine Harvester with a ten-foot cut and a power take off, which could be driven from his new John Deere tractor. Coote was well aware of the power of new machinery. In June 1949, he recorded that his farm manager Frank Farr had seeded 531 acres of wheat in seventeen days, 'say 32 ac[res] a day [for] one man'.[76] As a well-established farmer, Coote could afford to increase his water supply in 1949 with the construction of three new dams, and the deepening of existing dams. Most mallee farmers undertook capital changes through the 1950s. Undoubtedly the most important of these was the planting of barrel medic pastures. Throughout the decade fences were also renewed, and, like Coote, most landholders paid attention to water supply.[77]

In South Australia, capital improvements were aided by the Provisional Allotment Scheme of 1947, and the results were proudly described in the *Journal of Agriculture, South Australia*. In December 1960, the journal carried an extensive report on the rehabilitation of A.G. Woolridge's farm in the Murray Mallee at Karoonda. The scheme was essentially 'share farming between the government and the settler'. Rents were free while the property was in an eroded state, and the settler was promised permanent tenure after rehabilitation. The government provided seed and super to sow down all the sand drifts and eroded areas, but the work was to be done by the settler. Although the tasks of seeding and harvesting rye on the drifts were to take precedence, the settler was also permitted to graze stock and plant a cereal crop. Properties ranged from five hundred to four thousand acres, and the terms set allowed from two to six years to stabilise the drifts.

Woolridge was given a Provisional Allotment of 3,700 acres in 1952. His was considered one of the poorer blocks with six to seven hundred acres of active drift and a further seven hundred of bare and neglected land. In his first year Woolridge was hampered by a late start, and he only planted two hundred acres of rye. Over the next five years fourteen hundred acres of drifted and

---

76 Coote, Diary, 14 June 1949 and 26 August 1949.
77 Coote Diary, 6 May 1949.

eroded land were sown and stabilised, using cereal rye and super. In 1955 at the request of the Wanbi Research Centre, sulphate of ammonia was added to the super. Mallee scrub and regrowth had to be pulled out and areas cleared of projecting stumps. Bare land was ripped and rabbits were eradicated. The bulk of this work was done between 1952 and 1958.

In 1952 the property had no fences. Over time Woolridge fenced out eleven paddocks and intended to lay on a further six miles to bring the number of paddocks up to sixteen. Stock had initially to trek to a single bore. Woolridge put down another bore and planned in 1960 to lay on water to all paddocks and thus avoid stock trampling down pasture. From 1953 he put down sixty to eighty tons of superphosphate per year (in addition to the fertiliser used with the rye). Half was put in with the crop, and the other half was top dressed on the previous year's stubble. Each year barrel clover and Wimmera rye grass were sown with the crop. In the early days a 'single clover plant was an exciting find'. By 1960 the natural burr and barrel clovers could be seen as pasture in practically every paddock. No fallowing was carried out and the land was worked up with a combine after the opening rains. It was very seldom given more than one working before sowing to oats or barley.

These measures had greatly improved the productivity of the farm. Woolridge was only permitted to run four hundred sheep in 1953. By 1960 he considered that he could carry nine hundred grown sheep and six hundred lambs. The year before he had carried nine hundred sheep through a drought with little or no damage to his property. In 1953 barley yielded only two bags to the acre. By 1960 a fair crop was considered five or more bags. In the drought year of 1959 he reaped fourteen hundred bags of barley and cut thirty tons of oaten hay.[78]

Woolridge was not an unusual farmer in adopting this new farming regime, and one of the most profound changes in the history of Australian agriculture was the widespread, almost universal, acceptance of pasture improvement in the 1950s and 1960s. In both the South Australian and Victorian *Year Books* this change was proudly proclaimed.[79] By 1969 over a million acres was sown to pasture on the 2,360 cereal and grazing properties on the Eyre Peninsula. On Victorian Mallee farms, the number was even larger with 2,269,000 acres sown, or almost a third of privately owned land. Both the Eyre Peninsula and the Victorian Mallee also carried over two million sheep.[80] Such changes were also evident in other mallee regions but cannot be precisely isolated because

---

78 J.P. Blencowe, 'A Provisional Allotment in the Murray Mallee', *Journal of Agriculture, South Australia* 64 (December 1960).

79 *Year Book of Victoria*, 1963, Clover-Ley Farming, 517–19.

80 *Year Book of South Australia*, 1972, 363, and *Year Book of Victoria*, 1972, 275.

of the variability of boundaries used to report statistics.[81] By 1966 the area sown to pasture in Western Australia was four times the area in 1946.[82]

The financial impact of these changes was also dramatic. From the mid-1950s to the mid-1960s the Australian Bureau of Statistics reported favourably on the profitability of mallee wheat farms. Unfortunately, however, these pioneering studies in the use of sampling techniques employed geographical divisions that did not distinguish most mallee lands from other farming environments. They do, however, permit us to distinguish changes in the scale of farms moving east to west. In the Victorian Mallee (and by extension the South Australian Murray Mallee) the average farm in the mid-1960s was 2,776 acres, between four and six times larger than the original size of selections offered in the first three decades of settlement. In South Australia's Eyre Peninsula and Western Australia, properties were considerably larger. On the Eyre Peninsula the average size of farms, 5,874 acres, was twice that of Victoria. At this stage there was little difference in the area sown to the major cereal crops in these areas; farms in both the South Australian and Victorian Mallee cropped just over eight hundred acres.

Yields in the Victorian Mallee were greater than in other mallee areas to the westward, and productivity had increased significantly from the 1940s on. In the pioneering years between 1911 and 1951 the average yield per acre across the Victorian Mallee was less than ten bushels per acre, whereas the wheat survey of 1965 reported an average yield of 20.3 bushels per acre. On the Eyre Peninsula the yield in 1965 was lower at 16.2 bushels per acre and slightly lower again in Western Australia.[83] In all districts, farmers specialised in wheat, with barley the second crop. In both South Australia and Western Australia, lower yields in the mid-1960s compared to Victoria were compensated for by greater attention to grazing. On the Eyre Peninsula an average flock size was 1,214 sheep compared to 402 in Victoria. In Western Australia farmers carried a thousand more sheep than those on the Eyre Peninsula.[84]

The increase in yields to the 1960s was due to improvements in farm management, and the adoption of pasture improvement undoubtedly played a major part. New seed varieties were also important. In Victoria's Mallee

---

81 The Murray Mallee, for example, had extensive irrigation farming.
82 *Journal of Agriculture, Western Australia* 8, no. 9 (September 1967): 361.
83 Australia, Bureau of Agricultural Economics, *The Australian Wheat Growing Industry: An Economic Survey, 1964–65 to 1966–67* (Canberra: Bureau of Agricultural Economics, December 1969), 27.
84 Australia, Bureau of Agricultural Economics, *The Australian Wheat Growing Industry 1964–65 to 1966–67*, 20.

the seed of choice was Insignia. In both South and Western Australia, farmers chose from a wider variety. Insignia was rivalled in Western Australia by Gamenya, and Heron and Gabo were popular in South Australia. Each year the agricultural department of each state released recommendations for seed varieties. In Western Australia the state was divided into 'Early', 'Midseason' and 'Late-sowing' regions. Farmers there were advised in 1965 that Gabo and Gamenya, recommended for the Esperance district, were early maturing, of medium height with strong straw. While both were susceptible to flag-smut, Gabo was susceptible to rust, while Gamenya was rust resistant. Gamenya was particularly suited to clover-ley soils.[85]

By the mid-1960s, the use of weedicides was common in Victoria and South Australia. All areas used superphosphate. New nitrogenous fertilisers were applied by a minority of farmers, most commonly in Victoria, followed by South Australia. For such practices machinery was essential. On the Eyre Peninsula, a farmer could cultivate and seed a hundred acres in only seven 10-hour days and strip and cart the same area in just under three days. In Victoria cultivating took longer as fallow was more often used—the typical Victorian Mallee farm still had 668 acres of fallowed land compared to 220 on the Eyre Peninsula. This added about three days of work per hundred acres cultivated.[86]

Floods and Droughts

The 1950s and most of the 1960s were profitable on mallee farms, which were generally free of drought from 1944 to 1967, apart from 1956 and 1959. However, flooding periodically occurs in mallee country in the Murray–Darling Basin. The most dramatic of these—'the mother of all floods'—was 1956.[87] It brewed for three years, following soaking rains in 1954 and again in 1955, boosted by the swelling of the Darling River and its tributaries from rain in western Queensland. The Murray's catchment also experienced heavy rains. Over seven months these swollen rivers flowed inexorably to their confluence at Wentworth. The amount of water involved and the flat terrain of the Victorian and Murray Mallee lands meant that, once the water had broken

---

85 *Journal of Agriculture, Western Australia* 5, no. 12 (December 1964): 900–01.
86 Australia, Bureau of Agricultural Economics, *The Australian Wheat Growing Industry 1964–65 to 1966–67*, 19, 31, 34–40.
87 Bob Pollock speaking on *Landline—Flood, Sweat and Tears* (Ultimo: ABC TV, 2006), first broadcast 16 July 2006, accessed online 19 January 2018, http://www.abc.net.au/tv/programs/landline/old-site/content/2006/s1685568.htm.

the river banks and the levees, it spread out across the vast landscape and stayed for months.

Town after town faced a crisis. Red Cliffs in Victoria housed the district's State Rivers Pumping Station and the State Electricity Supply Power Station. Both sites faced water rising at the rate of one inch (2.5 centimetres) per hour, prompting weeks of frantic levee building, as any cut to electricity supply would end the work of pumps holding back water. Farmers drove their 'Fergies' (Ferguson tractors) to shore up the levee bank and cart sand bags. The Fergie 'could perch atop a levee bank while it was being built, [and was] light enough to ride over the sand bag heights and tough enough to survive the occasional dunking in the water'.[88] The Fergies defended Wentworth further downstream too; the town was exposed to rising waters on three sides, so three ring roads of levees were required. If one of the levees had broken, the town would have been lost. Farmers sat atop their Fergies 'holding back the water'; women helped fill sandbags and made sandwiches to support the effort. The town was saved—'an island in an inland sea'—and still hosts the 'Festival of the Flood' every five years in memory of the environmental and human drama that unfolded.

It was downstream in South Australia that the full impact of the flooded Murray was felt. It remains the worst natural disaster in South Australia's history, its waters spreading up to a hundred kilometres from the river's normal course. From June to August 1956 the waters rose, reaching a peak of 12.3 metres at Morgan, the highest flood recorded since white settlement. In Renmark the official gauge disappeared under water. Max Flatchen, an Adelaide journalist, recalled the way 'the remorseless Murray crept up the main street of Mannum to unimaginable heights. The river drove up drain pipes and exploded in geysers in streets'. It was a night that everybody dreaded because 'the river was sly and treacherous'. Flatchen likened the battle to 'an epic of human endeavor'.[89] Towns along the river were evacuated and farms inundated, destroying crops, flooding pastures and drowning livestock. Whole towns were submerged for up to six months. With a flow rate of 350,000 megalitres per day, the Murray could fill Adelaide's Mt Bold Reservoir seven times each day.

---

88   Glenn Miller, in Murray Darling Association, *1956 Murray Darling Floods—Part 1* (Mildura: Apricot Film & Television, 2006), accessed 19 January 2018, https://www.youtube.com/watch?time_continue=278&v=oLqAPICdvhc.

89   Max Flatchen, quoted in Murray Darling Association, *1956 Murray Darling Floods—Part 2* (Mildura: Apricot Film & Television, 2006), accessed 19 January 2018, https://www.youtube.com/watch?time_continue=527&v=BYaTZBzzRKU.

The impact of this flood on land, people and fauna was immense. Krista Eleftheriou recalled: it was not just the amount of water that was overwhelming, it was what it did, where it went, and the human and animal struggle to counter the 'wall of water'.[90] Gloria Wilson was fourteen and living on a house boat when her family was carried into a 60-mile expanse of water near Loxton in South Australia: 'We came across a little island nearly covered with stranded kangaroos, goats, goannas and birds and knew we were lost'. Alan Scown from Mildura remembers rabbits 'by the thousands' being washed out of warrens, seeking temporary refuge on fallen logs and timber: 'You would see them sitting in rows on tree limbs and logs'. Doss Wilson also remembers the rabbits, as well as the large number of snakes that were driven to higher ground.[91] In an attempt to bring a human perspective to the 1956 flood, scientists have classified it as a 'one-in-a-hundred-year' event and agree that, with the right confluence of weather events, it could happen again across this ancient floodplain.

At the other end of the spectrum, the season 1967–68 was for many young farmers their first confrontation with extreme drought. Russell Hilton, a young third-generation farmer from Hopetoun, recalled: 'If you hadn't been around in '38–'44 you didn't know what a drought was, and then '67 was brutal … I mean it just didn't rain'. But Russell's father had taught him well: 'all the messages that I'd had from my father, how important it was to get the crop in on time, sow, gauge the depth of the moisture before you sow, all those fine details which in a good year don't really count but in a dry year are really critical, became key to farming'. He added: 'we did quite well that year. There were two paddocks we grazed off to sheep. We sowed off 30 points [10.6 millimetres] of rain'.[92]

A special issue of the *Journal of Agriculture, Victoria* devoted to the drought recalled that the 1967 season started badly with below-average rainfall in the cereal districts in the first three months of the year. Normally dry, this period usually experienced summer thunderstorms to allow for cultivation of fallows and to provide some carry-over subsoil moisture. Rainfall failed in the next quarter, and winter-growing weeds on fallow land, which were normally killed by cultivation before seeding, did not germinate. In the key

---

90   Krista Eleftheriou, speaking on *Landline—Flood, Sweat and Tears*.
91   Gloria Wilson, Alan Scown and Doss Wilson, in Mary J. Chandler, *'56 Memories Flood Red Cliffs* (Red Cliffs, Vic.: Mary J. Chandler, 1996), 42, 46, 49.
92   Russell Hilton, interviewed by Katie Holmes, in Australia's southern mallee lands oral history project, 10 June 2014, National Library of Australia (NLA), https://nla.gov.au/nla.cat-vn6578387.

months of May and June only two rainfalls were recorded, both providing less than half an inch. Across the Mallee, farmers elected to allow weeds to germinate and abandoned planting. Only on the eastern edge of the Mallee were rains adequate. In the heavier soils of the southern Mallee, rains were inadequate, and sowing was delayed to July and August. Only in August did the total exceed one inch. For earlier sown crops these rains were satisfactory, although crops in drier areas were thin. Late-sown crops began to make some headway.

The critical factor, however, was the failure of spring rains. Without rain, ear formation was arrested, and a lack of moisture to keep plants cool destroyed green tissue, essential for the plant to form grain.[93] Bob Schilling, a third-generation farmer near Rainbow remembered:

> '67 was my first experience of drought. I was on my own then. Dad was gone and we planted crop, thought it was right, but a lot of it never came out of the ground. And I did still sell a bit of wheat that year, but it was pretty tough going. I had sheep. But we survived; that one wasn't too bad.[94]

Yet, despite the lack of rain, the season proved better than 1944, and Victoria produced six times the crops of that earlier disastrous year. C.T. Patton, an agronomist with the Victorian Department of Agriculture, put this improved position in the 1967 drought down to the use of Insignia wheat, which was able to withstand the dry conditions better than older varieties. Liberal use of superphosphate induced earlier heading of the crop. Well-fertilised crops made better use of the limited growing season and were well on the way to finishing when the season stalled. While science made a difference, old lessons in stock management had to be relearned. In the special issue of the journal, instructions were given on whether farmers should sell their sheep and how to hand feed sheep that were not placed on the market.[95]

Hungry sheep was one of Russell Hilton's key memories of the 1967 drought, along with dust and soil drift:

---

[93] C.T. Paton, 'Wheat Farmers Lose $50 million', *Journal of Agriculture, Victoria* 65, part 12 (1967): 507–09.

[94] Bob Schilling and Shirley Schilling, interviewed by Katie Holmes, in Australia's southern mallee lands oral history project, 9 June 2014, NLA, http://nla.gov.au/nla.cat-vn6578385.

[95] 'Which to Sell? Which to Feed', *Journal of Agriculture, Victoria* 65, part 12 (1967): 521–6 and 533–6.

you'd move a mob of sheep and put them in the paddock and they'd with great enthusiasm go around the paddock thinking there was feed, and then after two hours they'd be lined up at the gate again waiting to find another paddock ... you were feeding them along roads, any skerrick of feed you could find, and the sheep lost condition, they were skin 'n bone literally and dying in paddocks.[96]

Like many droughts in the eastern mallee, the 1967 drought was followed by good rain, and with it came mice. Indeed, what many mallee residents consider to be the worst mouse plague in living memory occurred in 1969. Like earlier mouse plagues, human activity played a significant part in its severity. The 1969 crop exceeded expectations, and, with limited storage, silo space was rationed. Farmers were forced to store grain on their farms, often in weld mesh silos lined with hessian. Mice simply ate through the hessian, and the grain provided a ready food supply for breeding mice. Their carcasses contaminated the wheat and had to be sieved out. They damaged vehicles, eating through the wires and upholstery.[97] In Berriwillock locals nick-named the 100-metre stretch of road leading to the silos the 'fur-lined highway' owing to the number of mice squashed on the road and their carcasses piled along its sides. The cost of the plague to grain growers across southern NSW, Victoria and South Australia was estimated to be in the order of $14,000,000.[98]

In the late 1960s over-production in most years created new problems and led to a build-up of wheat stocks by the Australian Wheat Board. World over-production led to a crisis in the wheat industry. In response, the Commonwealth government allocated wheat quotas to each state and left administration to state governments.[99] Quotas caused considerable anger among wheat growers. Backing the producers, economists argued that quotas did not react to price signals and, based on recent production, penalised the more efficient growers. In the long run they were overtaken by events on the world market. By the early 1970s demand for wheat from China and Russia was strong enough to render quotas unnecessary, and concern about them vanished by 1974.[100]

The trend of rising production picked up in the early 1970s and continued throughout the decade. To meet this demand, mallee farmers increased their

---

96 Hilton, interview.
97 Brendon Ledwich, in conversation with Karen Twigg, Berriwillock, June 2016.
98 J.A. Caughley, 'House Mouse (*Mus donesticus*) in Queensland' (Brisbane: Department of Natural Resources and Mines, October 1998), 7.
99 Greg Whitwell and Diane Sydenham, *A Shared Harvest: The Australian Wheat Industry, 1939–1989* (Melbourne: Macmillan, 1991), 180–4.
100 Whitwell and Sydenham, *A Shared Harvest*, 185–8.

use of machinery. Tractors became more powerful through the 1960s in order to drive larger cultivation and seeding machinery. The trend towards larger tractors gathered pace in the 1970s, and particularly in Western Australia. In 1971 only 3 per cent of tractors in the West were over seventy-five kilowatts; by 1976 the proportion was 36 per cent.[101] The old tractor-driven (PTO) harvester was replaced by auto-headers (see Figure 9.5), and the comfort of both tractors and headers was improved by enclosed cabins.

The environmental impact of rising demand for wheat and more powerful machinery was increased cultivation and a growth in the size of land holdings. In the older settled Victorian Mallee lands, properties were initially subdivided on a smaller scale than in both South and Western Australia. With increasing demand for wheat, farmers on the Eyre Peninsula brought a greater proportion of their land into cultivation. In the wheat survey of 1964–67, these farmers had an average of over 2,800 acres under native pasture. This was increasingly sown to crops in the 1970s. In 1964–67 an average of a little over eight hundred acres was sown to cereals on the Eyre Peninsula; by 1976 the area was almost thirteen hundred acres (523 hectares). The drive to bigger farms, however, came from the West. By the late 1970s the average Esperance and southern farm in Western Australia was over six thousand acres (2,561 hectares) with 1,464 acres (593 hectares) sown to cereals. [102] Through the 1970s and 1980s, Western Australia continued to lead this trend to large-scale cropping.

In the eastern mallee the hope that improved soil conservation methods had reduced drift and dust storms was shattered by the 1982 drought. Bob Schilling recalled:

> '82 was the worst one I've seen. Because we had sheep, if you didn't get rid of the sheep soon enough they pulverised the ground and then it started to blow and that was the biggest problem we had, paddocks that were sown and never grew. They became a problem. I'd end up making big furrows. That's all we could do to stop it blowing … We'd put them about 10, 15 feet apart. Eventually it would fill it up but then the next year when the rains came you had to level it all out again to try 'n grow a crop.[103]

---

101 *Journal of Agriculture, Western Australia* 20, no. 4 (1979): 99.
102 Australia, Bureau of Agricultural Economics, *The Australian Wheat Growing Industry 1964–65 to 1966–67*, 19; and 'Wheat Growing Industry', in *Australian Agricultural and Grazing Industries Survey, 1976–77* and *1977–78* (Canberra: Bureau of Agricultural Economics, n.d.), 2–3.
103 Bob Schilling, interview.

Figure 9.5: A Connor Shae self-propelled header at a heritage machinery rally in Quambatook 2018. In the late 1960s and early 1970s the PTO tractor-driven headers were replaced with self-propelled headers with enclosed cabins, the predecessor of the massive machines now used on mallee farms.
(Courtesy Graham Mann)

Russell Hilton believed one of the key differences between the 1967 and 1982 droughts was in the handling of sheep. In '82, as soon as farmers 'saw a drought was coming they sold the sheep that had any weight on them for food to be canned or sold as lambs. The sheep that you weren't going to carry through you shot and put in pits'.[104]

The 1982 drought, and the severe dust storms that it heralded, raised troubling questions for many Mallee farmers. If three decades of improved knowledge of soil management had not saved their farms from desolation, what would? How could they better protect their land against recurring drought and drift? As suggested later in Chapter 12, not until farmers ceased their long-held practice of cultivating the soil would the answers to those questions be forthcoming.

---

104   Hilton, interview.

Chapter 10

NEW MALLEE FARMS

In the muted shades of 1950s Eastman colour film, aerial footage shows vast swathes of mallees falling in a neat arc—as if by magic—as an invisible chain is drawn through the bush by crawler tractors. As the music reaches a triumphant climax, the narrator enthusiastically proclaims: 'Man and his machines changing the face of the age-old desert, soon to restore nature's balance of soil fertility!'[1] The 'desert' would be conquered using powerful modern technologies to make good nature's deficiencies. In its place virtuous and comfortable farming families, guided by science and enabled by technology, would feed a hungry world.

The short film *Desert Conquest* was produced in 1954 by life insurance and superannuation firm Australian Mutual Provident (AMP) to promote its vast land development scheme in the Ninety Mile Desert region of South Australia's lower south east. This was just one of several large post-war land development schemes undertaken by government and private enterprise. Some of the central themes in early mallee settlement were also evident in these schemes; the landscape was disparaged as useless scrub, even 'rubbish', while farming was regarded as the epitome of white manly independence, and civilised rural homes the basis of a stable and prosperous society. Established farming families looked to expand their holdings and urban workers sought a fresh start on the land, while local governments sought to expand their revenue bases. The massive post-war expansion of mallee farming was underpinned by faith—sometimes misplaced—in the power of modern science and technology to transform bush into farmland. While many successful farms were established in new mallee areas, the human and environmental cost was high.

Business, Government and New Mallee Farms

By 1948 individual farmers were already moving in to the Ninety Mile Desert, based on information yielded by David Riceman's trace element experiments

---

1 *Desert Conquest*, directed by Lex Halliday, produced by Australian Mutual Provident Society (Australian Instructional Films, 1954).

(see Chapter 9). In that year, Adelaide's *Advertiser* proclaimed that: 'A new generation of "landseekers", equipped with high-powered tractors, massive ploughs and a scientific formula for turning bad soil into good, is following closely in the wake of knowledge that the ill-named "90-Mile Desert" is potentially one of the most productive areas of South Australia'.[2] An urgent task facing the newcomers was to re-name the land to reflect the new vision of 'green pastures dotted with prosperous homesteads and townships and crossed by busy roads and railways'. Alternate names included the 'Ninety-Mile Plain', 'Ninety-Mile Downs' and 'Heath Downs of South Australia'.

An early enthusiast for the region was Hugh Robinson, pastoral manager for AMP. Robinson had been following the trace element research and, after flying over the area in a small plane with a friend, proposed an ambitious idea for large-scale agricultural development to AMP general manager Monty Buttfield. While Buttfield was aware of the problems encountered by the large-scale soldier settler schemes, he warmed to the idea of an entrepreneurial land development program to mark AMP's centenary. The company subsequently negotiated access to the land with the South Australian government, arguing that the scheme would exploit idle resources, provide opportunities for hard-working men and increase exports to Britain. South Australia's Land Settlement (Development Leases) Act passed in October 1949 enabled the scheme, providing 21-year leases to the developer. AMP would pay costs associated with establishing water supply, homesteads, fencing and pastures, and then sell subdivided blocks as perpetual leases financed on attractive terms by AMP. Returned soldiers would be given priority.[3] R.G. Casey, federal minister for national development, praised the way the plan brought together science and capital to provide for Australia's growing population and feed the world.[4]

AMP chose a group settlement model to implement the scheme. Male settlers selected in an interview process would be paid wages to work together for five years to clear and prepare the land, then enter a ballot to find out which 1,000 to 1,500-acre farm they could buy. Wives were not interviewed, and many found themselves taking care of babies and small children in huts with no electricity or hot water, isolated from family and

---

2   'Scientists Provide a Formula for Making Good Earth', *Advertiser*, 29 October 1948.

3   June Fergusson, *Bush Battalion: The AMP Society's Ninety Mile Desert Development in South Australia* (Sydney: Australian Mutual Provident Society, 1984), 17, 20–9; *Land Settlement (Development Leases) Act 1949*, South Australia.

4   'Huge A.M.P. Desert Scheme', *Age*, 14 April 1950.

medical care.[5] The men were motivated to work hard because lower development costs would reduce purchase prices. As the success of the scheme hung on the economic viability of the farms after subdivision, this similarly stimulated the use of more efficient equipment and techniques for turning bushland into farmland at minimal expense.

The 'uninviting' mallee and heath were cleared at first by dragging coupled 50-foot logs behind heavy diesel tractors. These pushed over and uprooted thirty acres of bushland per hour.[6] A breakthrough came with the idea of drawing heavy anchor chain between two crawler tractors, enabling two men to clear eight hundred acres per day.[7] Once the toppled vegetation had dried out, burning commenced. This was planned and carried out in military style using radio, maps, even ex-army Land Rovers (see figure 10.1). Still, burns sometimes escaped into surrounding bush. A 1984 history of the scheme reflected contemporary attitudes to such escapes: 'there was nothing to be done and not much need to worry. Little but wilderness stood in the way of flames'.[8] As the wind drove the flames through the smashed trunks and branches, smoke billowed into the air, darkening the sky in apocalyptic shades of grey and brown. The bush was annihilated—at least above the ground. Mallees, of course, were no strangers to fire, and their lignotubers lay under the ground ready to re-grow.

To prepare the soil for seeding, Shearer 'Majestic' disc ploughs were pulled through the sand, cutting and turning the roots and debris. Levellers— steel frames fabricated in the project workshop—were used instead of more delicate harrows for dislodging roots and smoothing the surface as much as possible. Still too much debris remained for conventional drills, so fertiliser and pasture seed—lucerne, subterranean clover, African veldt grass, ryegrass, phalaris—were broadcast together using spinners mounted in pairs on custom-made frames, trailed by various devices for covering the seed. In an era before widespread use of nitrogenous fertilisers, the aim was to establish pastures with nitrogen-fixing legumes that would both sustain sheep and build up soil fertility for grain cropping in rotation. However, even with the backing of science and diesel engines, human ascendency over the environment was neither easy nor assured. Sand caused tractor parts to wear and fail, and bog holes and rocks caused breakages.

---

5 Adair Dunsford (ed.), *The Desert Blooms: Stories of the Women of the AMP Society Land Development Scheme* (Adelaide: Wakefield Press, 1995).

6 John Redrup, 'Science Tames the Scrub and Desert Land', *Age*, 25 February 1952.

7 Fergusson, *Bush Battalion*, 48.

8 Fergusson, *Bush Battalion*, 48.

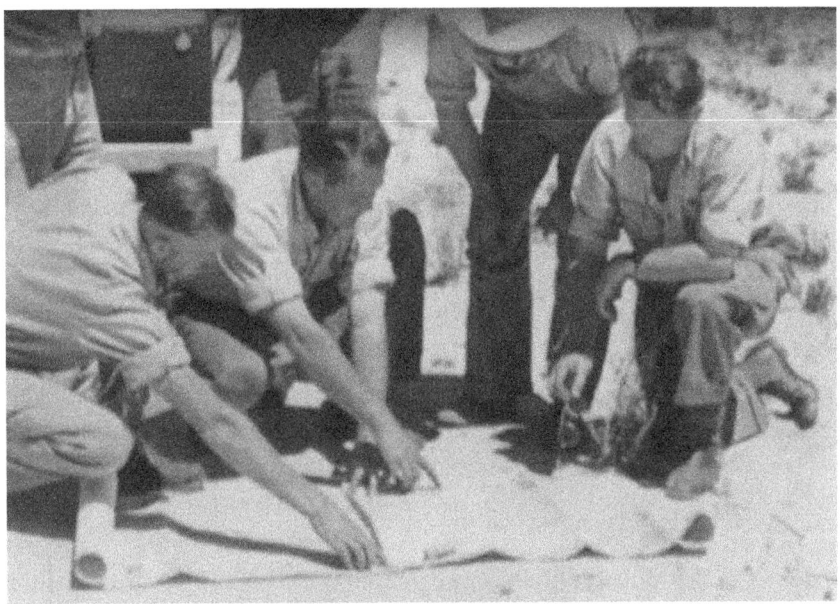

Figure 10.1: These stills from the film *Desert Conquest* (1954) show men associated with the AMP's South Australian agricultural development scheme undertaking a post-clearing burn, described by the narrator as 'firing operations on a grand scale, controlled with military precision... a job well done, planned and carried out by men who knew what they were doing'.
(Courtesy Australian Mutual Provident Society and State Library of South Australia)

The camp machinery workshop was continually improvising and repairing in order to keep equipment in the field.[9]

The scale of the work was such that it was best observed from the air. Project directors doubtless peered down through vibrating aircraft windows with fascination and pride at the green lines that emerged from the raw sand after rain: a record of the busy, threaded trail of the seeders. The film that captured this heroic story saw the signature of modernity in these 'futuristic patterns on the desert plains, where soon man's flocks and herds would graze'.[10] The rapid landscape transformation was an impressive display of human technological power, but the clean geometries visible from the air masked a wildlife holocaust on the ground. Millions of reptiles, mammals, baby birds and invertebrates unable to escape the clearing front were crushed, suffocated, entrapped or suffered traumatic injury from falling vegetation, chains or bulldozers. Those unable to escape the subsequent fires were incinerated. The survivors, many in pain or distress, would then suffer and often die as they either returned to the hostile site of their annihilated homes, or faced dehydration, starvation, predation or competition in unfamiliar terrain beyond the clearing.[11]

By the end of 1952, more than sixty thousand acres had been cleared of vegetation and wildlife, and were in various stages of development.[12] Seeding of the first area, near Coonalpyn, began in 1951; activity then moved to the land east of Keith. AMP also looked beyond South Australia; in 1949 Hugh Robinson led a delegation to Western Australia where members were impressed by similarities between the land north of Albany and the Ninety Mile Desert development area.[13] This area was already earmarked for government development, and ultimately the AMP was not involved, but in 1951 the company negotiated with the Victorian government to develop 570,000 acres in the so-called 'tiger' country that extended north of the Western Highway into the Big Desert. Enabling legislation was passed in November 1951 giving AMP a 25-year lease over 240,000 acres. Early the following year the *Age*

---

9 N.S. Tiver, *Desert Conquest: A Review of the Main Events Which Have Contributed to the Development of the Ninety-Mile Desert* (Adelaide: AMP Society, 1986), 4; Fergusson, *Bush Battalion*, 44.

10 Tiver, *Desert Conquest*, 4.

11 In light of such outcomes, in 2017 Australian researchers called for land clearing to be considered as an animal welfare issue: Hugh C. Finn and Nahiid S. Stephens, 'The Invisible Harm: Land Clearing Is an Issue of Animal Welfare', *Wildlife Research* 44, no. 5 (2017): 377–91.

12 Fergusson, *Bush Battalion*, 73.

13 'Albany Zone Land', *West Australian*, 26 May 1949.

reported with excitement that 'the untenanted heath and mallee broom bush terrain ... will shortly be shaken from its calm'.[14]

While the triumphal language of conquest dominated reporting of AMP's South Australian scheme, reservations emerged as early as 1954. Some sub clover pastures had been replaced by barren fescue and bastard barley grass. The *Farmer and Settler* reported that: 'In many instances the establishment of nutritious pastures has not been very successful and the low sandhills present a great wind erosion problem'.[15] Judith Yates, one of the last people recruited for the AMP scheme in South Australia, recalled that in 1957 'the sand just used to blow for miles. They weren't paddocks, just acres and acres of sand, before they all got seeded and if it blew, well the whole country-side shifted'.[16] The sale of farms at private market value was also questioned. Liberal senator for South Australia Keith Laught, visiting the scheme area in 1952, remarked that 'these boys have the glint of private enterprise in their eye. One day they will own this country and they are putting their best into it'.[17] But, when it was revealed that those who had worked on the scheme would have to pay market value for their farms, dissatisfaction arose. Many believed that their commitment and hard work should have entitled them to a reduced rate.[18] Furthermore, any fall in wool prices would make their farms a 'doubtful economic proposition'.[19]

Still the bulldozers and tractors rolled on. By early 1956, 150,000 acres were under development in South Australia, with twenty-seven families already settled on farms. As *Desert Conquest* made plain, the family homes established at the climax of the development process played an important role in the moral economy of the scheme, rewarding men for their hard work and women for their endurance: 'these were real homes; solid, faced with stone. Garden homes in the desert ... with modern kitchens to provide a farmer's meal. All mod cons. No more huts, no more hardships'.[20] While life on the farm was undoubtedly more comfortable than in the temporary settlements, this rhetoric failed to acknowledge the enduring intrusion of an unruly landscape into everyday life. It took Judith Yates two years to get a lawn started

---

14 Redrup, 'Science Tames the Scrub and Desert Land'.
15 John Heney, 'New Problem for A.M.P. Development Scheme', *Farmer and Settler*, 10 December 1954, 1.
16 Dunsford, *The Desert Blooms*, 201.
17 'Progress of A.M.P. Scheme', *Advertiser*, 30 January 1953.
18 Fergusson, *Bush Battalion*, 91.
19 Heney, 'New Problems for A.M.P. Development Scheme', 1.
20 Halliday, *Desert Conquest*.

at her farmhouse, for the wind carried drifting sand over tender shoots, and 'tiny little things attacked everything that went into the soil'.[21]

In 1959 the scheme was lauded for its conversion of '250,000 acres of South Australian Desert into lush grazing land'. Cecil H. Hoskins, chairman of the AMP Principal Board, declared his satisfaction with the scheme's success in contributing not only to the nation's economic development but also to the virtuous objective of peopling the country: 'The men and their families are now producing wool, beef, wheat and children in a very happy and proper way', he said.[22]

While the rhetoric reflected the long-standing yeoman vision, in fact the South Australian government's commitment to closer settlement in the region had waned, such that the AMP was permitted to sell large, minimally developed blocks on the open market, delivering it a 'welcome and unexpected profit'.[23] This pattern continued over the border in Victoria, where the 'tiger' country seemed harsher and more isolated than anything the developers had tackled in South Australia. In the early 1960s AMP made three large sales at Telopea Downs in Victoria, including seventeen thousand acres to a South Australian wool broker, before individual sales were limited to four thousand acres.[24] These limitations ultimately saw the AMP relinquish its option on developing land in the Little Desert. The project was instead pursued by the Victorian government in a move that generated considerable controversy and ultimately resulted in abandonment of the scheme and reform of processes for determining the use of public land (see Chapter 11).

By the time the last AMP property was sold in 1974, the company had at least partially developed seventy-eight farms in South Australia and ninety-one in Victoria.[25] The scheme had also encouraged private investment in land development in the region, fuelled by concessions that turned land development costs into income tax deductions, and made capital gains on the sale of developed property tax exempt. Without such concessions, much of the post-war new land development would probably have been unprofitable.[26] Hugh Robinson left the AMP in 1953 and ran a land development consultancy that would facilitate the development of nearly 100,000 hectares of farmland in South Australia and Victoria, thus providing a model for agribusiness

---

21   Dunsford, *The Desert Blooms*, 204.
22   'A.M.P. Success in Desert Scheme', *Western Herald*, 13 March 1959.
23   Fergusson, *Bush Battalion*, 102–03.
24   Fergusson, *Bush Battalion*, 114–15.
25   Fergusson, *Bush Battalion*, 125–6.
26   'Australia: Trends in Primary Production', *Round Table* 50, no. 197 (1959): 98.

consultancy that would increasingly replace the services provided by the state departments of agriculture.[27]

The pasture systems established on the 'desert' sands were increasingly reliant on lucerne, making them vulnerable to the lucerne aphids that arrived in Australia in 1977. While the aphids were first observed in New South Wales, giving the South Australian farmers a season to prepare for their arrival, the impact in the 'desert' areas was still devastating. One study found that, over two years, aphids reduced the number of lucerne plants in unsprayed pastures by 85 per cent.[28] By this time, prices for wool had fallen and profit margins were minimal, so the main challenge was to find an economic solution. Researchers in the early 1980s found that aphids could be controlled with rotational hard grazing and strategic insecticide use. Their recommendations were not widely adopted, however, because of difficulty monitoring aphid density over the large farm areas, insufficient livestock for hard grazing, concerns that hard grazing was an erosion risk, and the cost of insecticide.[29]

Intensive work on the development of aphid-resistant lucerne began but, in the meantime, a weed called sand fescue (or silver grass, *Vulpia fasciculata*) moved in to fill the gap. Its pointy seeds worried the condition off sheep and caused blindness and skin infections. Salt, too, encroached. In some areas, the deep-rooted lucerne had kept saline groundwater down; in its absence, water tables rose, and the spread of salinity was accelerated. In 1991, a survey found that 75 per cent of farmers in the upper south east of South Australia recognised salinity as a problem in their district, and 50 per cent had undertaken some activity to manage or control salinity on their own farms.[30] Today, productivity is threatened by increasing soil acidity and non-wetting (water-repellent) soils, while market instability has led to stress and financial hardship. Some farmers have made a comfortable living growing irrigated lucerne for seed and hay production, their vibrant green circles prominent on satellite images of the region. Grazing and cropping also continue to provide livelihoods. The desert conquest was, however, never complete.

---

27   David F. Smith, *Natural Gain: In the Grazing Lands of Southern Australia* (Sydney: UNSW Press, 2000), 165; Tiver, *Desert Conquest*, 4.

28   Peter G. Allen, 'The Management of Spotted Alfalfa Aphid, *Therioaphis trifolii* (Monell) F. *maculata*, in Dryland Lucerne Pasture in South Australia' (PhD thesis, University of Adelaide, 1984), i.

29   Allen, 'The Management of Spotted Alfalfa Aphid', 259–60.

30   A. Presser, *Upper South East Salinity Survey 1991: Bakers Range/Marcollat Watercourses* (Adelaide: Department of Agriculture, 1992).

Private Development and Soldier Settlement in Western Australia

In the five years from 1959–60 to 1964–65, Sir David Brand's Western Australian governments released six times more land for agriculture than did South Australian governments.[31] This frenzy was driven by the developmentalism that had become central to the political culture of an isolated state with a small population and deep-seated anxieties over its perceived mendicant status. Agricultural development in this era was driven by local as well as state interests, and its promotion bundled up the old yeoman vision of independent and prosperous families on the land with a populist language of adventure and opportunity. The state's developmentalist commitments saw scientific reservations about the scale and pace of clearing swept aside, including multiple warnings that it would lead to widespread salinity.[32]

An experiment in state-supported private development—similar in some ways to the AMP ventures further east—took place in the Esperance region in far south-eastern Western Australia. While farms had been established in mallee country north of Esperance in the 1910s and 20s, the dry seasons and price collapses of the late 1920s and early 1930s saw the area under cultivation decline from 40,525 acres in 1929–30 to just 6,310 in 1936–37.[33] In the wake of widespread farm abandonment, farms in the region were reconstructed for viability during the 1940s. After the war, many Esperance district farmers looked to the sand-plain country to usher in a new era of prosperity. The state government established a research station on sand-plain country north of Esperance in 1949, which soon demonstrated that pastures could be successfully established with superphosphate and trace elements. Sand-plain land was subsequently released to individual farmers as conditional purchase leases, but, as most applicants had limited capital with which to clear the land and bring it into production, the pace of development was too slow to satisfy local and state ambitions. One answer was private capital, and Bert Hawke's Labor government responded enthusiastically when approached in 1956 by an American syndicate with a development scheme.

---

31 *Western Australian Parliamentary Debates* (*WAPD*), Legislative Assembly (1965), 167, 1659, quoted in Quentin Beresford, 'Developmentalism and its Environmental Legacy: The Western Australian Wheatbelt, 1900–1990s', *Australian Journal of Politics and History* 47, no. 3 (2001): 405.

32 Beresford, 'Developmentalism and its Environmental Legacy'.

33 *Statistical Register of Western Australia* (Perth: Government Printer, 1929/30 and 1935/36).

Led by Allen Chase, Esperance Plains (Australia) Pty Ltd brought together capital from investors including film and television celebrities. Having recently emerged from a failed rice-growing venture at Humpty Doo in the Northern Territory, Chase looked to recoup losses on the Esperance sand plains and, in August 1956, officially approached the minister for lands. Just two months later, cabinet approved an agreement by which the government would make available 1,500,000 acres to be selected by the company for development over five years at four shillings per acre plus up to one shilling per acre for survey costs. The company would clear and establish pasture on at least half of each 2,000-acre holding, along with fencing and buildings, before sale. The scheme failed spectacularly, losing half a million pounds in three years. Undercapitalised for the venture and disparaging of local knowledge, the company ploughed in the heath rather than burning it in an attempt to shorten the establishment phase, with disastrous results. Meanwhile, some of the American investors who took up Esperance land, including radio and TV personality Art Linkletter, took heed of local knowledge and ultimately developed successful farms (see figure 10.2).[34]

In 1960 the government served notice of default on the Esperance Plains company, and Chase assigned its interests to Esperance Land & Development Company, a new partnership representing largely American capital. The new developers, too, had underestimated the expense of developing the Esperance land, and the Brand government, keen to avoid another failure, released the company of some of its obligations. Vast areas of land in the region were developed, although, when the opposition called for a royal commission into the Esperance lands in 1967, evidence of dummying practices and sale of undeveloped land emerged.[35] The 'wilderness' was erased, but the vision of closer settlement was sacrificed in the process.

Another state-sponsored agriculture development venture in the West involved soldier settlement. Commencing shortly after the end of World War II, a Commonwealth-supported soldier settlement scheme saw purchase and redevelopment of 446 individual farms in established areas. After the Land Sales Control Act was rescinded in 1949, prices increased. The government looked to large-scale development projects on Crown land in order to meet

---

34   *WAPD*, Legislative Assembly, 27 September 1960, 1408–13; *WAPD*, Legislative Council, 19 October 1960, 1930–9; Nicole Chalmer, 'Consuming Eden: An Environmental History of Food, Culture and Nature in the Esperance Bioregion' (PhD thesis, University of Western Australia, 2018), 183–5; *Esperance Lands Agreement Act 1960* (Western Australia), Schedule 1; Art Linkletter, *Linkletter Down Under* (New Jersey: Prentice Hall Press, 1968).

35   *WAPD*, Legislative Assembly, 8 November 1967, 1906–22.

Figure 10.2: American TV personality Art Linkletter was part of an American syndicate that made an agreement with the state government in 1956 to develop land near Esperance. While the venture was a spectacular failure, Linkletter persisted with his farm, shown here around 1960, and established a successful enterprise.
Photograph by Harcourt Hilton Long.
(Courtesy State Library of Western Australia 140205PD)

the ongoing strong demand for farms from returned servicemen.[36] One of the largest such war service project areas in Australia was on mallee and sand-plain land at Jerramungup–Gairdner–Corackerup. The government purchased Hassell's Jarramongup sheep station in 1950 on the cusp of the Korean War wool boom, and project supervisor Colin Cameron arrived in early 1953. A big, genial man, Cameron was a former Australian Imperial Force major who got around 'with his 6 gun hanging on his hip and nobody ... argued with him'.[37] He would command what the *West Australian* called the 'big assault on virgin land'.[38]

Cameron described the undeveloped parts of the scheme area as a 'mallee wilderness', while the productivity of the station itself had been destroyed by

---

36   A.R. Barrett, *History of the War Service Land Settlement Scheme, Western Australia* (Perth: A.B. Davies, Government Printer, 1965), 10, 13.

37   Frank Smithson, interviewed by Frank Rijavek for *A Million Acres a Year*, directed by Frank Rijavec (Sydney: Snakewood Films, 2002), video recording.

38   Max Brown, 'Jerramongup ... Big Assault on Virgin Land', *West Australian*, 1 April 1959.

overstocking and rabbits, leading to significant erosion. 'The project would not have been possible without myxomatosis', Cameron admitted.[39] Soon after his arrival, project workers caught and inoculated three thousand rabbits; within a few months 'millions' lay dead. Poisoning and warren ripping were also employed. Like the AMP project, the War Service Land Settlement scheme run out of Jerramungup used heavy marine chain for clearing. Cameron directed the contractors doing the clearing to drive for two hours in one direction, then turn right and drive again for two hours and so on until the entire vast area was flattened.[40] The contractor leading clearing operations, Johnnie Walker, 'roared on day and night', becoming legendary for his speed and endurance. One day, a record 648 hectares of bushland were chained, and by September 1953 16,200 hectares had been flattened.[41] The contractors were spurred by the payment of ten shillings per acre cleared, and endeavoured to tear up as much bushland as possible before the burning season began.

Cameron decided to start burning in January 1954, 'well before the official opening of the Burning Season'.[42] This meant that they would not 'lose a year' if rain started early. Burning on hot, dry days also consumed more of the detritus, keeping 'stickpicking' costs down. They had men and machines available for the work and were isolated from neighbours—though not isolated enough. Farmers from nearby Needilup complained that the summer burning threatened their farms, but Cameron was unmoved: 'we lit our first fires and although much vocal criticism was levelled at us, all of a hostile nature, we never let up until the 40,000 acres were burnt'.[43]

While tractors, chains and fire were powerful tools in the hands of the developers, they did not exhaust the vitality of the mallees. 'Root picking' was always necessary, sometimes before the first ploughing but always after the second. At Jerramungup this work was undertaken by teams of Italian migrants, who pulled out the mallee roots, dragging, stacking and burning them for quick disposal.[44] Often these men subsisted on dried fish and bread, but they also used the wild food around them, cutting dandelion leaves for

---

39   Brown, 'Jerramongup'.
40   Smithson, interview.
41   Colin Cameron, Papers of Colin Cameron, ACC 3441A, J.S. Battye Library, Perth; Terry Spence, *Jerramungup: Soldiers of the Soil* (Perth: T. Spence, 2002), 57–8.
42   Cameron, ACC 3441A (capitalisation as in original).
43   Cameron, ACC 3441A, 7.
44   Greg Norrish, 'Recollections of the War Service Land Settlement Scheme at Jerramungup/Gairdner River', in *Jerramungup 50 Years on: A Celebration of Soldier Settlement Country: 1955–2005* (Jerramungup, WA: 50th Celebration Committee, 2005), n.p.

greens and shooting birds to make a pasta sauce more hearty.[45] While the teams removed many of the roots, the process went on for years, with wives and children often removing deeper roots dislodged over time.

Poison plants, too, withstood the initial onslaught. Box poison (*Gastrolobium parviflorum*) and thickleaf poison (*Gastrolobium crassifolium*) were particularly common in the Jerramungup area. Gastrolobiums regenerate from roots as well as seeds that can remain viable in the soil for years. The poison found in all parts of the plant is the same as in 1080—sodium fluoroacetate. Many native animals in the south west have developed a tolerance for the poison, and ruminants can tolerate small amounts of seedlings among pasture, but just two mouthfuls will quickly kill them; there is no antidote. Pulling poison was a hard job, demanding concentration that became maddening. Workers walked steadily forward over countless acres, their eyes scanning the soil for traces of the characteristic bright green. After a while Gastrolobiums seemed to blend into the mallee regrowth and sprouting clover.[46] Missed plants meant that sheep would die, convulsing in pain.

In a curt memo of 1959, the minister for agriculture asked the chairman of the Land Settlement Board to take action in response to ongoing reports of heavy stock losses from poison at Jerramungup. The Commonwealth War Service Land Settlement Division also intervened with suggestions on how to reduce losses. To mid-1959, contract gangs had covered a staggering 80,491 acres, staring at the ground and pulling the deadly shoots by hand.[47] Still, a census of stock losses revealed that 4,433 beasts, including thirty-four cows, had been lost to poison across the Jerramungup–Corackerup–Gairdner project area since the first farmers arrived in 1955. On some farms, more than 20 sheep perished. Authorities blamed the losses largely on settlers' lack of vigilance, but in May 1960 the Commonwealth government agreed to replace 'abnormal losses' of stock (mainly from poison, though also dogs and flood) during the 'unfortunate period' between January 1959 and April 1960. Some settlers received credits to their working expenses accounts in excess of £1,000. Eradication efforts continued. As losses mounted, settlers complained about the quality of the work done by Italian pickers and asked that they be allowed to select 'half-caste' pickers, who they believed would do a better job.[48]

---

45   Smithson, interview.
46   Spence, *Jerramungup*, 128.
47   'Poison Plants on War Service Land Settlement Blocks—Eradication of', Item 1946/02643 v1, State Records Office of Western Australia (SROWA).
48   'Poison Plants on War Service Land Settlement Blocks'.

The prevalence of poison in the area was one reason why by 1982 only 5 per cent of the land remained uncleared. Not only was remnant bushland widely regarded as unattractive, but it also imposed the additional expense of fencing to prevent stock grazing the poison plants within it.[49] In other areas, where poison plants were more restricted, bushland was routinely fenced off, creating valuable pockets of biodiversity.[50] While the scale and ambition of the soldier settler project marked it out as a thoroughly modern enterprise in which men operating powerful machines transformed a reluctant nature, it was very materially shaped by mallee eucalypts, poison plants, the myxoma virus and the manual labour of itinerant grubbers and pullers.

Water supplies also posed a challenge. The Hassells had never sunk dams, instead taking their sheep in summer across their vast lease to the better-watered coastal areas. There was no potable groundwater for more sedentary grazing, so surface supplies had to be created. Experimentation revealed that efficient catchment areas could be formed by pushing back the sandy surface to expose the clay; these 'roads' led to a drain that fed the dam. However, even efficient dams need rain, and 1954 was the driest year ever recorded. By this time there were three thousand sheep, forty project depot staff and another sixty or so contract workers, plus some horses and milking cows, all requiring water. As Colin Cameron later put it:

> The water problem became serious indeed. Every drop for man and beast had to be carted from wherever we could get it. The nearest dam was at Needilup 12 miles away and it went dry, Ongerup was the next stop 30 miles of corrugated road which proved to be very hard on tanks full of water.[51]

The newly built dams remained empty until a deluge in February 1955 that dumped up to three hundred millimetres on some parts of the project area over four days. As a result, 'Every harmless looking little gully became a river in its own right while the Gairdner [River] became a terrifying torrent'. The flood swept over the sixty thousand cleared acres, washing away millions of rotting rabbits along with the topsoil. The remainder of the year was so wet that the Gairdner project area became a quagmire and work stalled for eight months.[52]

---

49   Robert Twigg, 'The Impact of European Settlement on the Environment of Jerramungup' (research essay, Murdoch University, 1982).
50   Sue Hall, Jan Orr and Anne Rick, interviewed by Andrea Gaynor, Newdegate, 2 December 2015.
51   Cameron, ACC 3441A, 8.
52   Cameron, ACC 3441A, 13–14.

The project's resources enabled them to bring sheep in from South Australia and erect a dingo fence around the entire project area. Each developed farm had a house and sheds, dams and tanks; the cleared area was pastured—in some areas using trace elements—and fenced. The Jerramungup and Corackerup project areas were cleared by 1957; in total forty-one farms were established; of these in 1976 only thirteen farms were still held by the original soldier settlers or their sons; most of the remainder had been sold to farmers from interstate or overseas, or to neighbours expanding their holdings.[53] The scheme did not permanently settle many ex-servicemen on the land, and many settlers struggled with inexperience, advancing age, mental and physical health issues and the rigours of isolation. But the extent of farm development and the financial and technical support given to the settlers, along with the largely favourable seasons and markets, meant that the Jerramungup–Corackerup–Gairdner project largely avoided the eviction and abandonment characteristic of past soldier settler schemes.

A Million Acres a Year

The perceived success of the War Service Land Settlement scheme stimulated the release of conditional purchase (CP) blocks in mallee and mallee heath country on sandy, nutrient-deficient soils in the Albany, Jerramungup, Ravensthorpe, Lake King, Hyden, and Esperance areas in the south, as well as Dandaragan in the northern wheatbelt.[54] The releases commenced under Liberal Premier Sir David Brand in mid-1959. In opening parliament in August 1961 Lieutenant Governor Sir John Dwyer noted with satisfaction that 'In a little over two years the Government has released over two and one quarter million acres in the South-West Land Division and the Esperance district'.[55] In discussion of the Address-In-Reply the member for Narrogin, W.A. Manning, congratulated the government for 'the development of a million acres of land per year', a phrase that subsequently became synonymous with the government's program of large-scale agricultural land release.[56]

---

53 Philip Burns, 'A Short History of War Service Land Settlement in Western Australia: With Particular Emphasis on Three Post–World War II Projects South of the State' (History 340 research essay, University of Western Australia, 1976), 23.

54 Rosemary Jasper, 'An Historical Perspective', in *Diversity or Dust: A Review of the Impact of Agricultural Land Clearance Programmes in South West Australia*, eds K. Bradby, R. Jasper, R. Richards and H. Pearce (Melbourne: Australian Conservation Foundation, 1984), 9.

55 *WAPD*, Legislative Council, 3August 1961, 2.

56 *WAPD*, Legislative Assembly, 22 August 1961, 425.

In this bold and confident new era of technologically facilitated development, the pace of alienation of bushland was frenetic, moving rapidly into areas that had not been thoroughly examined or tested for their suitability for agriculture. Although authorities perceived 'the need for control and proper planning and design', the land and climate—critical to agricultural production—played an inconspicuous role in the administrative process of survey and lease. Fat archival files dealing with each land release show that the schedule was 'dictated by the intensity of interest and local necessity'.[57]

The process often commenced with an inquiry from a local farmer, or a letter from a Farmers' Union branch or shire. These letters reached the Department of Lands and Surveys, where they were considered and filed. Maps would be consulted in carpeted offices, far from the jewel beetles and mallee branches swaying in a crisp autumn breeze. Next, a plan for roads was drawn up. Roads were basic to modern agricultural development. They first enabled prospective applicants to view the land (though many took up blocks sight unseen); later they would facilitate farm development and provide efficient access to town centres. The road survey maps epitomise the state's way of seeing the land, distinguishing different parts only according to purpose and ownership—orderly farms, numbered reserves, and the bleak emptiness of Crown land. Once the road alignments were determined, contracts were let and bulldozers deployed; in at least one case surveyors were paid overtime to supervise road construction, which was proceeding with 'a fair degree of urgency'.[58]

Once the roads were established, a detailed design for the subdivisions was produced. This involved identifying main vegetation types—using aerial photography and sometimes ground checking—as a proxy for soil quality, and thus price. The land was infinitely dissectible and the intricate patchwork of vegetation—mallee, broombrush, tea tree, banksia—was carved up in rectilinear plots according to a rough calculus of agricultural value. By 1964, five years into the large-scale land release era, the Esperance senior surveyor reported that 'it is becoming increasingly apparent that … the Agriculture Department should be more actively included in assessment of the potential of the land under subdivision'.[59] Such involvement, however, never became systematic. In some cases, the Department reported on the potential of the land under subdivision. Soil surveys, if they occurred at all, were perfunctory.

---

57 'Internal. Release of Land at Lake Biddy. Shire of Lake Grace', Item 1964/0202v1, SROWA.
58 'Release of Land at Lake Biddy'.
59 'Release of Land at Lake Biddy'.

Otherwise, the surveyors' land classification was the only assessment of agricultural suitability.

After survey a notice detailing 'land open for selection' appeared in the *Government Gazette* setting out the location, area, and price per acre. The higher quality land—clay or loamy clay—sold for up to three times the price of 'light' land. Prospective farmers received a brochure setting out the available allotments, conditions of the scheme and information about indicative costs, production, topography, public transport, schools and so on. The text is typically riddled with disclaimers: 'No reliable information is available regarding underground water supplies'; 'The government does not guarantee the supply of water either by reticulation or other means to the land'.[60] One 1964 brochure for land within fifteen to fifty miles of Jerramungup declared: 'The area is virgin country and the productiveness has yet to be proved'; poison plants were not mentioned.[61]

Some new land farmers were allocated other land or received act of grace payments because their CP land was unsuitable for farming. Faults included saline soils as well as large areas of rock and 'crabhole' or gilgai country, which were visible if aerial photographs were closely scrutinised. The Kingdons at Ongerup refused to clear a thousand acres of salt-lake country and demanded that they be allocated farmable land. In 1974 the under-secretary for lands, writing to the minister, said of the Kingdons' case:

> it behooves us to be very careful indeed as surveys in 1955 and 1962 show that the used farming land which had become salt affected amounted to 186,000 acres and 305,000 acres respectively. The situation after 12 years will be appreciably worse. Yes, I am most concerned over the precedent, which will be established.[62]

The Kingdons were eventually allocated a block previously held by a CP farmer in default of conditions. Another farmer was eventually paid $500,000 because of the inherent soil salinity of much of his carefully fenced and blade-ploughed farm. A consultant reporting on the case noted that, while the form of salinity appeared anomalous, 'no special effort was put in to check for salt' before the land was released in 1978, even though the divisional surveyor expressed

---

60 'Release of Lands NW and NE of Ravensthorpe', Item 1968/00173, SROWA.
61 Western Australia, Department of Lands and Surveys, 'Serial no.57—Kent Locations within 15 to 50 Miles Radius of Jerramungup', 29 June 1964, private archive.
62 'Conditional Purchase Lease Kent Location 1786. Kingdon, RK, VM, DK, JB. Newnes, MF', Item 1964/0235 v1, SROWA.

concerns about salt.⁶³ The effects of the hasty land release procedures continued to be felt in subsequent decades; as clearing controls were tightened, more farmers on CP blocks found themselves unable to clear salt-susceptible land that they had intended to farm.

The conditions attached to the CP blocks were prescriptive: settlers were required to take up residence on their allotment within three years and stay there for at least five; in each of the first four years they had to clear and cultivate 250 acres or one-tenth of the allotment, whichever was less; and, starting in the third year, for at least three years, they were required to crop or plant to pasture the cleared and cultivated area. However, Geoff Bee, whose family began cropping their farm at Jerramungup in 1966, recalled that: 'If you were dinkum you developed the land a lot faster than that. You had to, to maintain viability and to get ahead'.⁶⁴ The CP lease was for twenty-five to thirty years; leases could be converted to freehold after five years, provided that payments and conditions were met.⁶⁵ Inspectors visited regularly, though some were more zealous than others. Ongerup farmer Kelly O'Neill recalled being pressured by the Department of Lands to clear two hundred acres of remnant bushland on his farm; after a meeting in the Ongerup pub he persuaded the inspector to turn a blind eye, and the bushland remains to this day.⁶⁶

Prospective farmers would lodge applications at the Department of Lands and Surveys. The aims of the scheme were social as well as economic, and applicants from outside a district were preferred, though records reveal that plenty of locals were also able to use the process to expand family holdings in the area. In one 1968 release of land to the north west of Ravensthorpe, there were 230 applications for sixty-three lots; of those successful, around a quarter were local, half were from elsewhere in the Western Australian wheatbelt, and a fifth were from interstate, including several from Arno Bay on the Eyre Peninsula.⁶⁷ While the process was intended to select applicants with sufficient experience and capital, this was not always achieved, particularly in the early years. Settlers arriving in Jacup in the early 1960s, for example,

---

63 Veronica Kingdon in *A Million Acres A Year*; 'Purchases Conditional Purchase Lease Fitzgerald Location 1627 Green FJ, MR, C2633 L2838 CP695', Item 1978-02358-01, SROWA; Ian Archibald Consulting, 'Report to Chief Executive of the Department of Land Administration, 6 June 1995', private archive.

64 Geoff Bee, interview by Andrea Gaynor, Jerramungup, 25 August 2016.

65 Western Australia, Department of Lands and Surveys, 'Serial no.57'.

66 Frank Rijavec, *Malleefowl Believers: Stories of the Malleefowl and its Champions* (Ongerup, WA: Malleefowl Preservation Group, 2009), 9.

67 'Release of Lands NW and NE of Ravensthorpe'. The remaining four applicants were from Perth or other areas outside of the wheatbelt.

included two house painters, an electrician from Estonia, a man who owned the cinema at Broken Hill, and another who had been manager of a ladies' dress shop in Wollongong. As one of them later recalled, 'we just had no idea of what to expect or what to do or anything'. Many inexperienced settlers cleared just part of the land before walking away.[68]

Successful applicants included Jim and Maree Johnson. Jim had grown up in poverty in Sydney and, after leaving home at twelve years of age, became a shearer, then a house painter, a soldier and a policeman; Maree was from a farming family in central-western New South Wales. Although they had read that the land was undeveloped, Jim had 'expected to see a sort of parkland area'. They bought the land in 1961, and in 1963 they drove eight miles off the main road from Esperance to arrive at their block. Maree recalled: 'we proceeded down to the block of course but there was no way we could get on to it, because there was all this timber that was laying down … so we turned around and went into Jerramungup to see if there was somewhere we could park there'.[69] Jim thought 'God, well here we are, we can't go anywhere, we are broke, we had no money so we had to stay and we just kept going'.[70]

While most applicants were Australian, some came from further afield. After the Republic of the Congo achieved independence from Belgium in 1960, many of the Belgian colonists left, and the network of Belgian diplomats began scoping opportunities for them in other settler societies. The Belgian consul general in Canberra saw CP land as an opportunity for these people, and sent information out to many prospective settlers in the ex-Congo Belgian network. When Annie Delhaize's parents arrived at their block west of Grass Patch, they found themselves surrounded by other Belgian families.[71]

Some Aboriginal people, too, were keen to become CP landholders, though, as very few possessed any capital, and in the absence of affirmative action, the barriers to land ownership were usually insurmountable. The Native Welfare Department was empowered to assist Aboriginal farmers and had a policy of seeking land from the Lands Department when new areas of farmland were being released. The Gnowangerup Native Welfare Committee in 1965 wrote to E.H. Lewis, minister for native welfare, urging them to purchase

---

68 Jim Johnson, interviewed by Frank Rijavek for *A Million Acres a Year*, c. 2000, private archive.

69 Maree Johnson, interviewed by Frank Rijavek for *A Million Acres a Year*, c. 2000, private archive.

70 Jim Johnson, interview.

71 Keith Bradby and Annie Delhaize, communication with author, 23 and 28 June 2016; see also *Mallee Schoolday Memories: A History and Memories of Education in the Western Australian Mallee 1917–1988* (Salmon Gums, WA: Mallee Historical Society, 1988), 79.

land for Aboriginal people before all the land was alienated; such people had, the Committee argued, 'a need and a moral right to land—eventually farm land'.[72] Newdegate farm consultant Jim Aly also asked the department how to secure assistance for Aboriginal people to take up blocks of land.[73] The department could provide finance for development but only at the same rate as the Rural & Industries Bank; still the minister argued that such support was costly, and furthermore 'it has yet to be proved that the native is prepared to accept the full responsibility of the management of his own farm'.[74] By 1968 just two Aboriginal farmers were each being assisted to develop eight hundred acres of a 2,000-acre farm at Esperance. It was reported that two other Aboriginal men would be helped to farm at Newdegate on completion of agricultural training there. Such was the suspicion attached to such schemes that the *West Australian* felt compelled to point out that the farmers 'had to work to build up their asset'.[75]

The CP policy resulted in a large expansion in cleared land, sheep numbers and wheat production, although, unlike beneficiaries of the War Service Land Settlement scheme, the CP settlers were left to draw on their own resources in carving farms out of bushland. A promotional film from the time declared: 'The new frontier in Western Australia is a frontier in which people want to be a part of progress. It is not a hardship frontier like the one pushed back by the pioneers of yesteryear, it is a frontier of opportunity'.[76] The reality, as a later opponent of land release put it, was somewhat different: 'nowhere else in Australia was so much land being made available for farming, but neither was there, anywhere in Australia, the opportunity for so many to live in this particular brand of government sponsored poverty and isolation'.[77]

The establishment of a new CP area entailed considerable privation. Jim Johnson recalled that: 'Water had to be carted from Jerramungup, 42kms away … Bathing was done in a half 200L drum supported by mallee roots'.

---

72 Letter from G.E. Shepherdson, Secretary, Gnowangerup Native Welfare Committee, to Minister for Native Welfare E.H.M. Lewis, 30 November 1965, 'Land Settlement for Natives—Policy', Item 1965/0429, SROWA.

73 Letter from Jim Aly to Native Welfare Department, 1 September 1967, 'Land Settlement for Natives—Policy', Item 1965/0429, SROWA.

74 Letter from Minister for Native Welfare E.H.M. Lewis to G.E. Shepherdson, Secretary, Gnowangerup Native Welfare Committee, 6 January 1966, 'Land Settlement for Natives—Policy', Item 1965/0429, SROWA.

75 'Farm Sites Set Aside for Natives', *West Australian*, 1 November 1968, newspaper clipping, AU WA S2030, cons1733, 'Land Settlement for Natives—Policy', Item 1965/0429, SROWA.

76 *A Million Acres a Year*, 17:49.

77 Jasper, 'An Historical Perspective', 9.

Those who could hunt ate well at least, with rabbit, emu and kangaroo being standard fare.[78] Jim painted houses in the local area to get by while the farm was being developed; he got his first stock—twelve sheep—in return for painting a house for a settler who also had no cash.[79]

Cathie Kelly moved from Meckering to a CP block in Newdegate in 1969 as a newly-wed. Her husband Malcolm had taken up the block four years prior. First impressions of her new home were of isolation among the endless mallee. She somewhat reluctantly agreed to live in a transportable, then set up their home with mattresses on the floor and no power, water or phone. When she took a job teaching at Newdegate school, Malcolm rigged up lights to the car battery so that she could prepare lessons at night. While they employed contractors to undertake the clearing, Cathie and Malcolm both undertook the exhausting labour of root picking; Malcolm did the poison grubbing.

Amid the back-breaking work, isolation and privation, some relished the excitement of taking part in a momentous large-scale transformation. Graham Barrett arrived in Jerramungup in 1965; fifty years later he remembered the early days as 'exciting times, when we were all busy clearing, and developing the land. There were plenty of bushfires'.[80] Maree Johnson recalled: 'Oh I loved to burn mallee roots, it was lovely of a night to get up on a hill and look back down and think oh I did all that'; her husband Jim similarly remembered that, after a burn, 'You'd see literally hundreds and hundreds of these little glowing fires, a magic sight'. Cathie Kelly emphasised the sense of community: 'we started off with quite a big contingent of young people and when I look back that was great fun, because we did a lot together', from going to the drive-in cinema to sporting fixtures, church and school associations. In some areas, however, 'newlanders' without family connections felt that it took some time to feel part of the established community.[81]

The newcomers often lived in intimate contact with nature. Wildlife that joined Jim and Maree Johnson's household included Chiller the wedge-tailed eagle and the 'cunning and cheeky' pet crows. The family dog despised the pet emu and chased it away. Pet kangaroos, however, would leave of their own accord once old enough to live in the wild: 'it's a bit sad, you come home

---

78 Jim, Marie and Matt Johnson, in *Jerramungup 50 Years On: A Celebration of Soldier Settlement Country: 1955–2005*, n.p.
79 Jim Johnson, interview.
80 Graham Barrett, in *Jerramungup 50 Years On: A Celebration of Soldier Settlement Country: 1955–2005*, n.p.
81 Maree Johnson, interview; Cathie Kelly, interviewed by Andrea Gaynor, Newdegate, 1 December 2015; Hall, Orr and Rick, interview.

from work and you call your roo and no answer'. This was a landscape in which the boundaries between wild and domesticated were blurred. Animals interacted with people, and each other, with a familiarity alien to many urban dwellers today.

Most settlers found the bush itself an unattractive barrier to progress, though a few sought to protect at least some of it from the onslaught. Kaye Vaux, who took up land with her husband near Ongerup, had low-lying areas of the farm fenced off to preserve the 'natural bush'. Today they are home to an orchid patch and much-loved old-growth mallee, though, at the time, Kaye's husband was incredulous that she might want to 'walk in the bally mallee'.[82] When botanist Anne Rick and her husband took up their Newdegate farm in the early 1980s, she found there was already an energetic group of wildflower enthusiasts around Newdegate.[83] The Bee family retained remnant moort (*E. platypus*) woodland around the house site because of a 'conservation-type attitude.'[84] As he grew older, Geoff photographed the plants and animals around the farm and in the nearby Fitzgerald River National Park, while also using the camera to document the erasure of habitat through chaining, burning and ploughing (see figure 10.3). Many farmers loved the wildflowers, especially, and cleared them with regret; Robbie Smart, farming just north of Fitzgerald River National Park, sometimes ploughed in the regrowth at night to avoid witnessing the destruction.[85]

Like many CP holdings, the Bees' farm was created incrementally, limited by available finance. Seven hundred acres of bush were chained down in 1964; the second round of chaining and burning took place in 1967 (see figure 10.4). Clearing was finally completed in 1975. However, the battle with the mallees continued well after this. A disc plough and root rake removed the surface roots, pulverising the soil as they did so, but the deeply embedded roots tore at machinery, pierced tyres and wrenched ligaments as the farmer struggled to keep control of the steering wheel. Tyres were initially protected by layers of old bomber aircraft tyres; wire armoured tyres were used from the late sixties. No such protection was available for human shoulders, some of which would need surgical reconstruction many years later. Like generations of mallee farmers before them, the Bees also had to try to harvest the grain

---

82 Kaye Vaux, interview by Frank Rijavek for *A Million Acres a Year*, c. 2000, private archive.
83 Hall, Orr and Rick, interview.
84 Bee, interview.
85 Robbie Smart, interviewed by Frank Rijavek for *A Million Acres a Year*, c. 2000, private archive.

before mallee shoots grew tall enough to contaminate it. In the 1980s Geoff bought a multi-tined ripper with steel wheels to dislodge stumps; on part of their property cleared later a blade plough was used. This, Geoff says, was revolutionary in allowing them to farm the country 'in a more sedate manner'.[86]

Figure 10.3: Jacup farmer Geoff Bee photographed the delicate flowers and wildlife on and around his family's Jacup farm, as well as the process of clearing (1970s).
(Photographs by and courtesy of Geoff Bee)

---

86   Bee, interview.

Figure 10.4: Burning after clearing on the Bee family's new land farm at Jacup, 1967. (Photograph by May Bee, courtesy of Geoff Bee)

Rethinking Farming

While there were floods on the south coast in the 1950s and some heavy rains in the 1960s, the seasons during this period of rapid expansion had been largely favourable. Indeed, the 1960s were wet years in Western Australia, and this is reflected in the Soil Conservation Service reporting, which emphasised water erosion and the deployment of contour bank systems. Farmers were starting to tackle soil conservation more proactively; in 1965 the Soil Conservation Service was unable to keep up with demand for visits to farms, local authorities and farmer groups, and their surveying and farm plan services were also in high demand.[87] However, there simply had not been sufficient time for settlers to learn how to farm the new land for the long run. As Rex Edmonson, a new land farmer at Jerramungup, later recalled:

> For one of our CP blocks we got the person from the Department of Agriculture that was the best in the game at the time to plan the property before we cleared it, and we got it horribly wrong. With the

---

87 Western Australia, Department of Agriculture, *Annual Report of the Department of Agriculture for the Year Ended 30th June 1965* (Perth: Department of Agriculture, 1965), 38.

science that was available to us at that stage, we thought we were right on track. Looking at it now, my son says to me … "What the hell did you clear that for?" as he fences it out.[88]

The year of reckoning was 1969, when new land farmers in the process of establishing their holdings first encountered a dry season. Newdegate recorded 234 millimetres of rain; Hyden only 215 millimetres. As farmer Ross Strahan reflected, the expansion to the east of the established agricultural area 'came to a screeching halt, and it all blew away … The dominoes started to fall, people started leaving, and it just got harder'.[89] The expansion scheme was a victim of its own success. Following a record Western Australian wheat harvest of more than three million tonnes, Australian wheat stocks were deemed too high. As overseas demand fell, in 1969 the Western Australian government introduced wheat quotas. This limited the total amount of wheat accepted from each farm, based on a percentage of past production. While new land farmers were granted a concession, often it was too limited to meet their needs. Then wool prices fell dramatically in the 1970–71 season, effectively cutting off that alternative. A Stock Reduction Scheme saw many older sheep simply shot. The Kellys at Newdegate responded by raising pigs, laboriously constructing yards and housing for the animals that would help keep the farm afloat. Don Fenwick left his family on the farm in Jerramungup and worked on a prawn trawler in the north of the state.[90]

When the Commonwealth decided to discontinue the phosphate fertiliser bounty in 1974, the effect of this policy on Western Australia's three thousand new land farms was referred to the Commonwealth Industries Assistance Commission. It found that many new land farmers had a low equity base and limited cash flow and capacity for borrowing, while facing high costs for fertiliser inputs. Their living standards were 'sometimes very low'. The commissioners pinned the blame squarely on the state government:

> Many of the present problems and hardships facing new land farmers could have been avoided at the time blocks were allocated … The Commission has no evidence that the State Government planned

---

[88] Australia, House of Representatives, Standing Committee on Science and Innovation, 'Coordination of the Science to Combat the Nation's Salinity Problem' (12 November 2003), 48, accessed 6 November 2018, http://www.aph.gov.au/binaries/hansard/reps/commttee/r7164.pdf. Thanks to Charlie Nicholson for this reference.
[89] Rijavec, *Malleefowl Believers*, 36.
[90] Don and Jean Fenwick, in *Jerramungup 50 Years On: A Celebration of Soldier Settlement Country: 1955–2005*, n.p.

comprehensively for the financial needs of settlers, and land was released in some areas where development and farming alternatives were unproven.[91]

The new land farmers also faced increasing evidence of land degradation. Following the drought year of 1969, the focus of soil conservation efforts shifted abruptly to wind erosion. One response was grassroots organisation of a kind later formalised and supported under the rubric of Landcare. In 1972 the Soil Conservation Service reported that it was meeting with informal 'soil conservation catchment groups' across the wheatbelt. Groups in mallee country at Lake Grace (Jinarning Gully) and Newdegate (Lake Stubbs) were among the most active.[92] The service declared that 'working with neighbourhood groups can be an effective extension activity' and supported them by providing catchment analysis using interpretation of aerial photographs and field reconnaissance, group meetings, field days, and individual advice.

Another response lay in the development of minimum-till techniques. In the wake of the 1930s dust bowl in the United States, American agronomist Edward Faulkner in 1943 published *Plowman's Folly*, which controversially challenged the need to plough the soil. During and after the war potent herbicides such as atrazine, 2,4-D and paraquat were developed. In the early 1960s a team led by A.E.M. Hood used paraquat—then manufactured by ICI—in research on 'ploughless farming' at ICI's Jealott's Hill Research Station in Berkshire in the UK.[93] Fewer than ten years later, it was estimated that British farmers were using 'direct drill' or 'sod seeding' techniques on 1.3 million hectares.[94] By 1975 the Western Australian Soil Conservation Service was experimenting with minimum cultivation using 'Spray Seed'—a mixture of the herbicides Paraquat and Diquat—to improve the workability of hard-setting clay soils.[95]

---

91 Industries Assistance Commission, *New Land Farms: Assistance to New Land Farms in Western Australia* (Canberra: Australian Government Publishing Service, 1975), ii–iii.

92 Western Australia, Department of Agriculture, *Annual Report of the Department of Agriculture for the Year Ended 30th June 1972* (Perth: Department of Agriculture, 1972), 104.

93 A.E.M. Hood, H.R. Jameson, and R. Cotterell, 'This Technique Involved Destruction of Pastures by Herbicides such as Paraquat as a Substitute for Ploughing', *Nature 197 (1963): 4869*; A.E.M. Hood, 'Ploughless Farming Using Gramoxone', *Outlook on Agriculture* 4, no. 6 (1965): 286–94.

94 Kenneth Blaxter and Noel Robertson, *From Dearth to Plenty: The Modern Revolution in Food Production* (Cambridge: Cambridge University Press, 1995), 59.

95 'Western Australia, Soil Conservation Service Branch Report', in Western Australia, Department of Agriculture, *Annual Report of the Department of Agriculture for the Year Ended 30th June 1975* (Perth: Department of Agriculture, 1975), 5.

While farmers in Western Australian mallee country began to experiment with minimum- or no-till techniques in the 1970s, it was the dry and windy years of the early 1980s that really focused their attention on this approach. In the Jerramungup district alone, forty-six dams were affected by sand drift in 1980, eight of them being completely filled with sand. Erosion of grazing land was widespread over the summer of 1980–81; by winter 1981 over 64,000 hectares remained affected by sandblasting and wind erosion.[96] In February 1983 a particularly severe storm in the Esperance area was reported to have stripped some 260 tonnes of soil per hectare from many paddocks.[97]

Geoff Bee learned about direct drilling in the late 1970s through an ICI-run extension program encouraging the practice. With his brother, Richard, he had bought a 'broad spectrum weed-killing machine' (cultivator bar), but found that it was also:

> a good soil degradation machine ... when we got into the light country, of course, if the wind blew and there wasn't quite enough rain, the stuff took off. We had a 200-acre blow out through the middle of one of our farms ... so we were certainly becoming focused on using herbicides for weed control and then direct drilling.[98]

Geoff's adoption of the new techniques was supported by the Department of Agriculture office in Jerramungup. Staff there worked with several local farmers, including Geoff, to experiment with broadacre adoption of direct drilling. Farmers provided departmental staff with sites for trial plots, and the department loaned their new triple disc drill to farmers. Many farmers disliked using chemicals for weed control, not least as the mixing process was unpleasant and dangerous.[99] Still, around a quarter of the 1982 Western Australian wheat crop was direct drilled—835,000 hectares with Spray Seed and 400,000 hectares without any chemical.[100] While the direct drilling allowed successive cropping of greater areas, some criticised the abandonment of livestock associated with much no-till farming as eliminating 'soil-building elements'.[101]

---

96   Bryan J. Goddard, M.G. Humphry, and D.J. Carter, *Wind Erosion in the Jerramungup Area 1980–1981*, Report 3 (Perth: Department of Agriculture and Food, 1981), 10–12.

97   Agricultural Memo, Western Australian Department of Agriculture Jerramungup Branch, 30 April 1983, private archive.

98   Bee, interview.

99   Goddard, Humphry, and Carter, *Wind Erosion*, 14.

100   Fred Morony, 'Farmers Need to Act Now', *West Australian*, 30 July 1983.

101   Maurice Armstrong, 'Threat Seen to Farming', letter to the editor, *West Australian*, 10 February 1983.

The severe wind erosion experienced in Western Australia in the early 1980s, along with increasing concern over salinity, also saw the old Soil Conservation Act updated. The amendments provided for the establishment of soil conservation district advisory committees, comprising mainly local farmers and empowered to raise funds for projects by a rate collection or from government sources.[102] In light of the growing realisation that land degradation problems required change across the landscape, and their scale was beyond the capacity of government agencies alone to redress, these groups were soon regarded as the principal means to combat the difficulties identified.[103] The Act also made it easier for the commissioner to serve Soil Conservation Notices and increased penalties for non-compliance.

In the early 1980s, amid dramatic media coverage of erosion in the southern wheatbelt, farmers were increasingly coming under fire from the public for clearing new land and leaving no trees in increasingly large paddocks. For their part, farmers often regarded remnant vegetation as an obstruction to the use of ever-larger machinery as well as a haven for vermin. However, district-based officers noticed that 'many' farmers were adopting more conservation-oriented attitudes, leaving shelter belts, fencing off remnant vegetation and planting trees, and even adapting farm machinery for revegetation purposes.[104] Geoff Bee was one of these. Although he felt that tree-planting was wrongly viewed by the public as a panacea for land degradation rather than just one component of a wider set of good land management measures, he collected native plant seeds on his property and developed a system of fluid seeding—inspired by machinery seen on a visit to Ireland—to revegetate five hundred acres of his farms.[105]

Gnowangerup shire president and farmer Ron Brown summed up the feeling among many local farmers in 1981: 'We have won the battle against the mallee but lost the war against nature. We have to learn to live with our environment and stop fighting it'.[106] Yet, from 1980, the government had once more begun to release large areas of land for agriculture, especially to the north and east of Esperance and near Jerramungup. While the new purchase

---

102 Western Australia, Department of Agriculture Division of Resource Management, *Annual Report 1981–82* (Perth: Department of Agriculture, 1982), 1–2.

103 Western Australia, Department of Agriculture Division of Resource Management, *Annual Report 1983–84* (Perth: Department of Agriculture, 1984).

104 Western Australia, Department of Agriculture Division of Resource Management, *Annual Report 1981–82*, 5.

105 Bee, interview.

106 Max Piggott, 'Farmers Beat Mallee but Lose to Nature', *Western Farmer and Grazier*, 12 November 1981.

conditions included retention of some native vegetation for shelter, windbreaks and conservation, the effectiveness of such measures was challenged in light of a lack of controls over clearing on freehold land.[107] The government policy of large-scale release of Crown land for agriculture only ceased in the West in 1985 (see Chapter 11).

Successive state governments, particularly in Western Australia, bear significant responsibility for the social and environmental problems that have arisen from their hubris in marshalling such vast and rapid erasure of existing landscapes for farming. They mobilised powerful forces—science, technology, capital and human desire—and often ignored the unknowns and the voices of caution. Productive farms were created, but so too were salinity, erosion and the death of plants and animals on a staggering scale, along with human isolation and hardship. For their part, the 'desert' farmers, soldier settlers and new land farmers did not come to mallee country because they wanted to destroy it. Some liked the bushland plants and animals that remained, and over time many came to love the land. Encouraged by the official rhetoric of agricultural progress, they chained, burned and ploughed, not to degrade the land or diminish biodiversity but to make a living as well as an inheritance for their children. In this way they were no different from the rest of us, implicated as we all are in exploitation of people and ecologies in the 'shadow places' of the world.[108] And, if we have eaten toast in Melbourne or udon noodles in Tokyo, or downed a Tsingtao beer in Shanghai, then we, too, have played a role in creating, and consuming, the mallee country as it is today.

---

107 Armstrong, 'Threat Seen to Farming'.
108 Val Plumwood, 'Shadow Places and the Politics of Dwelling', *Australian Humanities Review* 44 (March 2008), http://australianhumanitiesreview.org/2008/03/01/shadow-places-and-the-politics-of-dwelling/.

Chapter 11

CONSERVING THE MALLEE

It is December. Under a vast blue sky the mallee is humming to the sound of the harvest. Fire units, harvesters and chaser bins congregate in fields; roadside mallees quiver as passing grain trucks huff and rumble their way to the silos.

Inside the nature reserve, life is moving to a different rhythm. Small birds arc from one unseen shrub to another. A malleefowl appears beside the road, looks around, then stalks back into the bush. Millions of tiny ant feet silently maintain an elaborate network of trails. This is not a wilderness, having been shaped by millennia of changing Aboriginal stewardship. The more recent arrival of dingoes, then rabbits, foxes and cats—and the still more recent poison baits lying in wait for them—further shaped life here, as did the honeybees and mice. These islands in a sea of wheat exist always in relation to the land beyond, rendering them by turns vulnerable and threatening. They are often unruly, a source of fire and marauding animals, yet also crucial for maintaining the region's biodiversity. They are places where wildlife and flora thrive, and are beloved of many scientists, naturalists, artists and nature lovers from the local area and beyond.

In 2014, our mallee regions on average had 10 to 30 per cent of their area set aside for conservation, recreation and wilderness purposes—more than most areas of the country outside the wet tropics and desert heartlands.[1] They include many of the largest reserves in southern Australia (see Map 4). How did this relative natural richness come about in country that state governments so desperately tried to settle, but which seemed to taunt the settlers who aspired to farm it?

From the first visionary reserve declarations more than a hundred years ago, conservation in mallee country grew, quietly at first, then in a gathering crescendo. The movement gathered pace because a growing number challenged the inevitability of development, on scientific and sentimental grounds.

---

1 Australia, Department of the Environment, 'National Reserve System: IBRA Region Protection Level', 2014, accessed 6 November 2018, http://www.environment.gov.au/system/files/pages/3a086119-5ec2-4bf1-9889-136376c5bd25/files/ibra-regions.pdf.

MAP 4:
AUSTRALIAN MALLEE NATIONAL PARKS AND RESERVES

EYRE PENINSULA

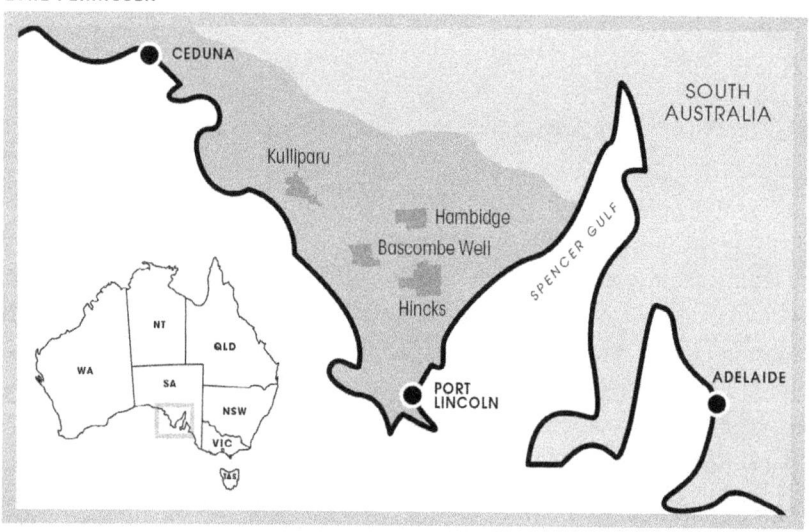

WESTERN AUSTRALIA

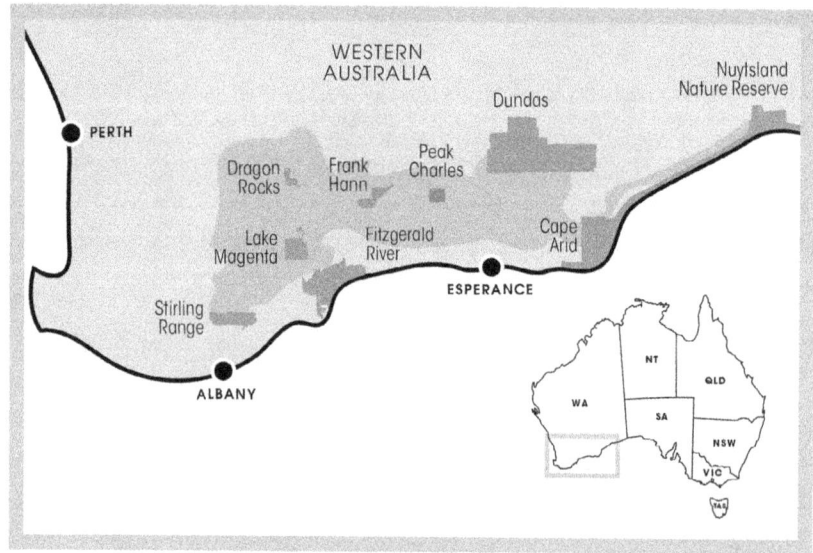

MURRAY AND VICTORIAN MALLEE

They also argued for the growing prospects of economic gain from preserving nature in the mallee, for its isolation and its quietude. Much of the land that was spared the roller or the bulldozer would have resisted it anyway, being too sandy, too rocky, too salty, or otherwise unsuitable for extractive uses. Even so, development has perpetually bayed at the door of conservation, and often it has been fed. The motives of those who advocated for nature have reflected the hopes and anxieties of their time and often been problematic. Conservation advocates grappled with the compatibility of tourism and conservation, proposed multiple scientific benefits of reservation, and until recently subscribed to colonial fantasies that Aboriginal people did not manage the land. Without their advocacy, however, today's mallee country would be less widely valued, and less sustainable.

Worthless Lands?

Two of the earliest reserves in the southern mallee lands were Wyperfeld National Park in the Victorian Mallee, and the Stirling Range National Park in the far south-western corner of Western Australia's mallee country. The networks that would ultimately produce them had their origins in the 1870s, when the world's first national parks were being created as 'natural' areas to be protected from alienation and conserved for public recreation and enjoyment. These early parks by and large confirmed the worthless lands hypothesis, which proposes that national parks (and similar conservation reserves) were only created because there were no alternative economic uses for these places. Even as late as 1979, the historian who developed the worthless lands hypothesis believed that 'national parks must appear worthless, and remain worthless, to survive'.[2] Over time, as economic uses were found, reservations were routinely challenged and their protections undermined, leading prominent American conservationist John Muir to warn in 1910 that 'Nothing dollarable is safe, however guarded'.[3]

In Australia, early reservations were indeed seen by governments as a way to deal with land deemed unsuitable for extractive or agricultural use.[4] In mallee

---

2   Alfred Runte, *National Parks: The American Experience* (Lincoln: University of Nebraska Press, 1979), 183.

3   John Muir, 'The Hetch-Hetchy Valley: A National Question', *American Forestry* 16, no. 5 (1910): 263.

4   C. Michael Hall and Warwick Frost, 'National Parks and the "Worthless Lands Hypothesis" Revisited', in *Tourism and National Parks: International Perspectives on Development, Histories and Change*, eds Warwick Frost and C. Michael Hall (London: Routledge, 2009), 51.

country these decisions were often challenged by farmers seeking more land and local governments seeking more ratepayers, although, as nature-based tourism grew and the importance of conservation was more widely acknowledged, even 'dollarable' land became safer.

'A paradise for nature-lovers and those fond of sight-seeing' was how ornithologist Arthur Mattingley perceived the land between Ouyen and Pinnaroo on his first visit in 1907. Mattingley had 'mentally pictured a howling wilderness, a drought-stricken arid mallee waste' but instead found graceful pines and grass in 'fantastic arrangements'. He was captivated by the abundant bird life, from the raucous gangs of black cockatoos to the emu-wrens that 'hopped saucily through the spinnifex [sic]'. All this paradise needed to make it 'the finest national park', he told readers of the *Argus*, was the addition of some Western Australian orchids and everlasting flowers.[5] The area had previously been included in pastoral leases, though some were never occupied and others abandoned, giving the land suitably 'worthless' credentials.

Figure 11.1: A.J. Mattingley, one of the early advocates for reservation of what would become Wyperfeld National Park, appreciated mallee flora as well as bird life. He photographed these flowers of Sweet Appleberry (*Billardiera cymosa*) in Wyperfeld National Park probably around 1934–35.
(Courtesy Pictures Collection, State Library Victoria)

---

5   Arthur Mattingley, 'National Parks', *Argus*, 31 August 1908.

Mattingley noted that 'in the Mallee thickets the wonderful nesting mounds of the Mallee fowl were numerous'. The malleefowl (*Leipoa ocellata*) looms large in mallee conservation, featuring prominently in arguments for Wyperfeld and many subsequent reserves.[6] A large, ground-dwelling bird with attractive barred and variegated wings, its intriguing nesting habits captured both the public imagination and scientific attention (see Figure 11.2). Males and females usually mate for life, which can be as long as twenty-eight years. In autumn, they begin work on their incubator—a mound made of sand, up to five metres in diameter and a metre in height, in which is buried up to a cubic metre of moist leaf litter. These mounds form distinctive features in open mallee landscapes.

Figure 11.2: Fascination with the malleefowl did not necessarily engender conservation, as in this image from South Australia's Ninety Mile Desert, where the party cleared mallee around the mound then dug out the eggs for the photograph. Photograph by A.J. Waugh, c.1910–20.

(Courtesy Pictures Collection, State Library Victoria)

---

6   Libby Robin, *The Flight of the Emu: A Hundred Years of Australian Ornithology, 1901–2001* (Melbourne: Melbourne University Press, 2001), 88–9.

The female malleefowl lays her eggs inside the mound, starting in spring. While days are still cool the composting litter provides the warmth to incubate the eggs, but later in the season the sun's warmth is also used. The male tests the temperature periodically with his beak, adding or removing litter to maintain the nest at around thirty-three degrees. After about two months of incubation the chicks emerge, struggling through the sand and litter and out into the world, beginning to run and feed independently in a matter of hours.

The malleefowl is highly vulnerable to threats to habitat and food resources posed by clearing, increased fire frequency and introduced herbivores. Once widely distributed across southern Australia, malleefowl numbers plummeted in the wake of the pastoral and agricultural transformation, and, by the early twentieth century, they were seen not only as a curiosity but also as in need of protection.

In May 1909 a deputation from the Victorian National Parks Association took the resolutions of a public meeting to the premier, John Murray. There, Mattingley urged that a mallee reservation be declared to act as a sanatorium and 'one of the lungs of the city'. Such a reserve would also help to preserve the flora and fauna, including that 'wonderful building enigma', the malleefowl. Murray was agreeable, especially as 'the land was not of much value'.[7] A national park in the parishes of Wyperfeld and Ginap was gazetted a few months later. A larger area of sixteen thousand acres was permanently reserved in 1921, with a further 7,680 acres added in early 1922. Naturalists were delighted, though not everyone shared their enthusiasm. The representative of Karkarooc shire (who was also president of the Yaapeet branch of the Victorian Farmers' Union) said that he had been appointed to the park's committee of management 'on the understanding that he was to try to get the Southern portion of the Park cut up'. In July 1922, 220 residents of the Rainbow and Yaapeet districts petitioned the minister for lands to abolish the Wyperfeld National Park as 'a menace to the settlement of the country' that would harbour vermin and noxious weeds and deprive the farmers of timber and duck-shooting. The minister agreed to look into claims that there was valuable land lying idle, but all the experienced surveyors in the mallee were too busy with soldier and other settlement schemes, and the matter lapsed.[8]

With no budget and a large swathe of remote country to oversee, the committee of management, under Sir James Barrett's careful guidance, granted

---

7   'National Parks', *Age*, 6 May 1909.
8   Department of Conservation and Natural Resources—Public Land Administration, Wyperfeld National Park, Part 1, Region code 01, Tenure code 826, file number RS 1128–4254.

leases over the entire park to Hugh O'Sullivan for cattle grazing and Ernest Ey for beekeeping. These were issued on the condition that the lessees become honorary game inspectors and work to preserve the park's flora and fauna. O'Sullivan was also made a Crown lands bailiff, able to impound others' stock found at large in the park. The grazier and the apiarist duly reported on the park's game and bird life, identifying malleefowl nesting locations and opposing permits to destroy kangaroos. O'Sullivan later became the park's caretaker, and when he died in 1929 his son took on the role. The lease funds were used to print notices of park regulations, poison rabbits and produce a 'Travel Folder' to attract and guide visitors.

In the 1930s Barrett reported that the local people were becoming interested in the park and using it as 'a Picnic Resort'. The London-based periodical *Country Life* had also requested information and pictures.[9] This 'worthless land' was already providing some modest livelihoods as well as conservation and recreation. As the value of Wyperfeld National Park—and the difficulty of agriculture in the surrounding land—was increasingly recognised, further additions were made. By the time Barrett died in 1945, Wyperfeld had grown to 138,700 acres, more than fourteen times its original size.

Across the mallee lands to the west, the Stirling Range National Park found its key advocate in José Guillermo Hay. Hay had worked as a draftsman in the NSW Lands Department in the lead-up to the creation of Australia's first national park south of Sydney in 1879. By 1903 he was living in East Perth and had joined the Mueller Botanic Society, then the state's only scientific organisation. No evidence survives that Hay ever visited the range, but he became increasingly captivated by the idea of the region's unique flora and fauna. In 1910, he wrote to the premier to request that a thousand square miles around the range 'be permanently dedicated as a National Park for the Preservation of Native Flora and Fauna, as well as for public health, recreation and enjoyment of future generations as for the present population of Western Australia'.[10]

Like Barrett and many other national parks advocates of the era, Hay saw no conflict between conservation and recreation: nature could be preserved even as growing numbers of visitors came to picnic, play and learn. Drawing on both Australian and American precedents, he happily mixed the progressive languages of public health and recreation and the religious language of

---

9   Department of Conservation and Natural Resources—Public Land Administration, Wyperfeld National Park, Part 1.

10   Joseph Christensen, 'An Early Western Australian Conservationist: The Romantic Figure of Jose Guillermo Hay', *Early Days: Journal and Proceedings of the Royal Western Australian Historical Society* 12, no. 5 (2005): 497.

creation to buttress his argument. Other influential citizens supported the proposal, and in 1910 an 800,000-acre temporary reservation was declared around the Stirling Range.

Pressure to open more land for farming saw the area reduced to 270,000 acres when the Stirling Range was declared an A Class reserve in 1913. Still it would be the largest such reserve in Australia until 1954. In recommending the reservation, the under-secretary for lands, R. Cecil Clifton, noted that it contained 'some of the finest scenery in the state' while being 'quite unsuitable for settlement'. International influences were also significant; Clifton made explicit comparisons with Yellowstone and Yosemite national parks in the USA and referred to remarks made by Dr Eric Mjöberg as leader of the recently concluded Swedish scientific expedition to North-Western Australia.[11] In 1911 Mjöberg had eloquently declared his fear that the state's 'particularly peculiar plant and animal life' was in grave danger of 'dying out' and urged the government to reserve extensive areas for conservation.[12]

Concerns remained, however, that this vast tract of land was lying idle. Proposals to develop roads and accommodation emerged throughout the 1920s, as increasing emphasis was placed on both preserving and developing the state's 'natural beauties' for tourism. At the same time, and in parallel with Wyperfeld, local farmers were agitating politically to open the Stirling Range National Park for agriculture. One, George Williss, even told John Scaddan, MLA for Albany, in 1921: 'Never say die till a dead horse kicks you; so with us, we do not intend to let this drop'.[13] The Lands Department, however, maintained its line that the area was unsuitable for selection and the reserve would remain.

Whereas Wyperfeld was leased for grazing and beekeeping, no such compromises were made in the Stirling Range. In 1926 the district surveyor thought that grazing would be impractical owing to poison plants and dingoes, while Surveyor General John Camm felt that granting grazing rights would be 'a great mistake' because, if one lease were to be granted, soon the entire park would be under leasehold and the native vegetation would be 'totally destroyed'.[14] The 'rugged terrain' of the Stirling Range and its remoteness

---

11 Memo from Under-Secretary for Lands to Minister for Lands, 13 May 1911, 'National Park—Stirling Range', Item 1908/03809, State Records Office of Western Australia (SROWA).
12 'Swedish Scientific Expedition', *Western Mail*, 2 September 1911.
13 Letter from Geo Williss to J. Scaddan, 23 June 1921, 'National Park—Stirling Range', SROWA.
14 'National Park—Stirling Range', f.138.

from major settlements also proved obstacles to mass tourism. Although by the end of the 1940s a trail had been blazed through the bush to the foot of the imposing Bluff Knoll, the lack of water and basic facilities meant that visitor numbers remained low.

In South Australia in the 1920s, prominent naturalists were nurturing an incipient public interest in the creation of reserves for native flora and fauna, at a time when clearing of mallee country was rapidly increasing.[15] In the 1930s, members of the Field Naturalists' section of the Royal Society of South Australia called for the reservation of marginalised ecosystems, including mallee country, as well as reserves especially to preserve the malleefowl. By the late 1930s, in the wake of widespread wind erosion, reserves were being valued for their nature and soil conservation potential. Reservation was increasingly regarded as a way of making 'worthless lands' do conservation work for free. Mallee country, widely regarded as having little scenic value, would not even incur the costs associated with visitor facilities.[16]

In 1938 the Land Board, an advisory section of the South Australian Department of Lands, recommended that an area on deep sand country in the Peebinga region be reserved for flora and fauna. This was marginal farming land in the Murray Mallee, some of which had been abandoned as recently as 1934. J. Neil McGilp, chair of the Land Board, was a keen amateur ornithologist and wanted to see Peebinga reserved as habitat for the rare mallee whipbird. However, the Department of Lands agreed to the reservation only if pharmaceutical company F.H. Faulding was given permission to harvest mallee leaves in the area for the production of eucalyptus oil.[17] Although Faulding lost interest in the scheme, the reserve was dedicated in March 1940 only 'on the understanding that the cutting of mallee leaf on the reserve could later be allowed conditionally and under supervision if the occasion arose'.[18] Peebinga's conservation value did not rule out potential economic uses.

The larger Billiatt reserve, just over ten kilometres west of Peebinga, was declared in 1940 after a farmer from nearby Mannum asked whether the land was available for development. The Soil Conservation Committee advised the Land Board that it should be set aside as a flora and fauna reserve. The

---

15   Colin Harris, 'The National Parks and Reserves of South Australia' (MA thesis, University of Adelaide, 1974), 37–8; see also, for example, 'Native Fauna and Flora', *Mail*, 13 August 1921.
16   Harris, 'The National Parks and Reserves of South Australia', 75.
17   Harris, 'The National Parks and Reserves of South Australia', 60–1.
18   Harris, 'The National Parks and Reserves of South Australia', 61.

Land Board, for its part, assured the director of lands that 'the land is of no economic value for Agricultural or pastoral purposes, and would serve a better purpose if left undeveloped'.[19]

Meanwhile, members of the Flora and Fauna Advisory Committee, established in 1937 to protect South Australia's 'fast fading fauna and flora',[20] were poring over maps of South Australia to look for potential reserves. They identified some large areas of unalienated land on Eyre Peninsula for further investigation and approached the director of agriculture to ask his advisers in the region to report on their potential. The resulting reports reflect the cultural status of mallee vegetation: one area was deemed 'not suitable as a Flora and Fauna Reserve as there are no natural water supplies and the climatic and soil conditions are such that only vegetation of a low order will grow there unless the soil is cultivated'.[21] These areas, which would later become Hambidge and Hincks conservation reserves, were estimated to contain 50 per cent and 10 per cent agricultural land respectively. One adviser therefore recommended that Hambidge not be declared a reserve, while 'The State would not lose anything' if Hincks were reserved. The commissioner of Crown lands subsequently recommended that both be set aside, but on a temporary basis. The Flora and Fauna Advisory Committee decided that insecure reserves were better than no reserves, and accepted this outcome, even if parts of the reserves could be made available 'if and when required for settlement'.[22]

The 1950s saw strong global demand for wheat and wool, as well as the advent of trace element fertilisers that dramatically increased yields on sandy soils. These factors, together with infrastructure improvements, federal support for soldier settlement and tax concessions for agricultural development, created a strong popular demand for release of more Crown land for farming, and governments were willing to oblige. Between 1954 and 1960, 41,768 acres of Hambidge, Hincks, and Peebinga reserves were resumed for farming.[23] The Flora and Fauna Advisory Committee opposed more extensive resumptions, arguing that large areas were essential for sustaining flora and fauna

---

19 Harris, 'The National Parks and Reserves of South Australia', 62, 90.

20 Minutes of the Flora and Fauna Committee, 16 November 1937, GRG81/3, 1939, 1, State Records of South Australia (SRSA).

21 Report by A.D. Adams, Agricultural Advisor, 'Flora and Fauna Reserves on Eyre Peninsula', 23 September 1939, Fisheries and Game 77/1939, SRSA.

22 Harris, 'The National Parks and Reserves of South Australia', 64.

23 Derek Whitelock, *Conquest to Conservation: History of Human Impact on the South Australian Environment* (Adelaide: Wakefield Press, 1985), 133.

conservation. Besides, these areas were a storehouse of plant material with potential for future commercial value, for example in developing medicines.[24]

Some reserves were more secure from agricultural development but might be subject to proposals to develop tourism infrastructure as a way to extract economic benefit from them. In 1949, for example, the state government renewed its efforts to turn Western Australia's Stirling Range National Park into a mountain resort. The proposal attracted praise from the *West Australian*, which declared that 'it should be our constant aim to examine and catalogue all our potential resources with a view to their eventual development in the State's interests'.[25]

Not everyone concurred. In the 1940s educated people with an interest in native flora and fauna were arguing that some areas should be preserved in their 'natural state' as timeless 'primitive areas' with minimal facilities, sufficient only to enable visitors to observe the nature there.[26] This idea had been pioneered by the US Forest Service in 1929 when, responding to public demand for 'wilderness' experiences, it moved to establish 'primitive areas'. These would 'maintain primitive conditions of transportation, subsistence, habitation, and environment to the fullest degree compatible with their highest public use'.[27] The pursuit of wilderness had roots in long-standing settler–colonial masculine anxieties around closing frontiers and the perceived feminising and racially degrading influence of urbanisation. However, by the 1940s it was experienced more as a desire for respite from modern life. In Australia, while ideas of wilderness gained ground in agitation against imprudent development, they disregarded the long history of Aboriginal occupation and management.[28] In presenting an image of an ancient, timeless, self-contained nature, they also encouraged a vision of nature preservation in discrete reserves and a business-as-usual approach elsewhere that would prove increasingly impracticable.

---

24 Harris, 'The National Parks and Reserves of South Australia', 104–05.
25 'Mr Davidson's Quest', *West Australian*, 7 January 1949.
26 See, for example, 'National Parks. Two Opposing Interests', *West Australian*, 14 September 1946.
27 'Parks and Primitive Areas', *Katoomba Daily*, 5 December 1935; see also Forest History Society, '1929: Forest Service L-20 Regulation for Primitive Areas', US Forest Service History Collection, accessed 6 November 2018, https://foresthistory.org/research-explore/us-forest-service-history/policy-and-law/wilderness-national-forests/wilderness-national-forests-timeline/1929-forest-service-l-20-regulation-for-primitive-areas/.
28 Tom Griffiths, *Hunters and Collectors: The Antiquarian Imagination in Australia* (Melbourne: Cambridge University Press, 1996), 263.

Mallee Sublime and Vulnerable

Although appearing as a period of techno-optimism, the immediate postwar era saw growing sympathy for the plight of wildlife in the face of large-scale development schemes and breathtakingly powerful modern technologies. In this context, popular media fed a growing public appetite for natural history and conservation. Legislation, too, reflected the shifting values. Game Acts were replaced by Fauna Protection Acts, starting in New South Wales in 1948. Western Australia followed suit in 1950; South Australia in 1964. Victoria continued with amendments to its Game Act until the Wildlife Act was passed in 1975. Although the New South Wales Act emphasised habitat protection, the ecosystem idea had not yet become pervasive, and anxieties over potential loss were often expressed in terms of iconic species.

By the 1950s the arid interior of Australia had become a modern sublime. Semi-arid mallee landscapes were not then widely regarded as sites of aesthetic redemption, though their unconventional beauty was beginning to be recognised by artists such as Sidney Nolan and Arthur Boyd, and the poet and schoolteacher Flexmore Hudson.

Based for a time at Caliph in the South Australian Murray Mallee, Hudson was aligned with the Jindyworobak school of Australianist poets and writers. Like fellow Jindyworobaks Ian Mudie and Nancy Cato, in the wake of the 1943–45 drought Hudson had written of the blasted desolation of farming landscapes:

> So we waited for rain, till our tamarisk shrivelled
> and blew away with the saltbush and the shells of the paddymelons
> till the eagles had gorged on our cattle'.[29]

However, he also captured the unanticipated appeal of mallee country's nature. 'Mallee in October' conveys the otherworldliness of 'iceplants sheathed in beaded glass / spider orchids and shivery grass'. 'Mallee Dawns', recalling the poet's time as a teacher in the 'drifting Murray Mallee', describes how his irritation at being awoken at dawn by ringneck parrots sliding down his roof would always subside:

---

29 Flexmore Hudson, 'Country of the Modern Heart', in Flexmore Hudson, *Pools of the Cinnabar Range* (Melbourne: Robertson & Mullens, 1959), 10.

> grateful my rusty roof outcoloured
> a coral pool of the Barrier Reef;
> reminded, too, of happy children swarming
> on slippery-dips at the beach.[30]

The move toward cultural and scientific revaluation of mallee vegetation is reflected in the Adelaide Botanic Garden, where a section for 'Mallee Eucalypts' was set aside in 1953 and still exists today.[31]

Mallee country was more widely valued as the home of iconic wildlife. This quality was invoked in an article on malleefowl by R. Aitken, headmaster of Nyabing School in Western Australian mallee country, which appeared in the *Gould League Notes* for 1952–53. Aitken bemoaned the fact that 'Australians are not as "preservation conscious" as the Americans'; otherwise a large national park 'dedicated to the protection of the splendid and harmless bird' would have been already declared. He concluded: 'Too many of our native birds and animals are already thinning out. It's time you and I raised our voices in defence of what is left. Don't you think so?'[32] Aitken's agitation led to a series of events that exemplified many of the issues encountered in nature conservation through reserves across the mallee lands prior to the 1970s.

Aitken also wrote to prominent ornithologist and conservationist Dom Serventy about reserving land north of Nyabing townsite to preserve the malleefowl. Serventy had played a significant role in the foundation of the Western Australian Naturalists' Club in 1924 and edited the organisation's journal from its inauguration until 1980. In 1951 he became officer-in-charge of the Wildlife Survey Section of CSIRO, based in Perth. In 1952, Serventy in turn wrote to the under-secretary for lands, H.E. Smith, requesting reservation of the Nyabing land and was told that, while it was too late to reserve the Nyabing land, it might be possible to reserve some of the unallocated mallee country further east, toward Lake Magenta. Meanwhile, the local road board (local government body, precursor to a shire) had got wind of the proposal for a reserve. In 1953 its members argued that this would represent 'great wastage',

---

30 Hudson, 'Mallee in October' and 'Mallee Dawns', in Hudson, *Pools of the Cinnabar Range*, 17, 28.

31 Richard Aitken, David Jones, and Colleen Morris, *Adelaide Botanic Garden Conservation Study* (Adelaide: Department of Environment and Heritage South Australia, 2006), 137.

32 R. Aitken, 'Mallee Fowl', *Gould League Notes: The Gould League of Bird Lovers of Western Australia* (1952–53): 16.

depriving the area of primary producers and ratepayers.[33] This was typical of conservation conflicts across the mallee lands in the immediate post-war decades, which pitted local government bodies with a clear financial interest in development, against an increasingly diverse range of conservationists.

Conservationists still had to show that reservation of land would produce good outcomes for the state. In early 1953, Serventy inspected the land bordering Lake Magenta and wrote to the under-secretary for lands to confirm the land's suitability for a malleefowl reserve. In doing so, he emphasised its potential utility as 'a centre for mallee research studies'.[34] Serventy also emphasised the way scientific knowledge derived from the reserve might ultimately assist agricultural development and pointed out the reserve's potential value for honey production. His argument for the reserve was therefore threefold, turning on the intrinsic value of the reserve for conservation, its value to science (and application to economic development), and non-agricultural economic uses.

The divisional surveyor, reporting to the surveyor general on the proposal, noted the outcome of a previous soil survey, which had concluded that development on this type of land should not be encouraged until it was being successfully farmed elsewhere, making it presently 'worthless'. Although he considered the reserve large, he acknowledged—with some prescience—'that any reserve for this purpose must be large scale, if it is to be effective'. He supported Serventy's request. Meanwhile, the Kent District Road Board continued to object to the proposal, arguing that it included a considerable area of good land in strong demand, and also that it provided a potential stronghold from which wild dogs, foxes, kangaroos and emus would invade agricultural land. This was clearly a familiar scenario for the under-secretary for lands, who wrote: 'This is another case of farm development versus protection of natural fauna or flora. The Board certainly put up a strong case, but surely the State has every right to try to protect its fauna where it is likely to disappear'.[35] Although these remarks showed concern about economic development, they also demonstrated that the fauna, including iconic mallee species, were valued in a more abstract way, as state assets. While this interest boded well for conservation, it also reflected a settler valuation of nature that disregarded Indigenous values and interests.

---

33   'Reserve for Fauna (Mallee Fowl) North of Nyabing. Roe & Kent CSIRO "Wildlife Sect"', Item 1952/05856 v1, SROWA.
34   'Reserve for Fauna (Mallee Fowl) North of Nyabing', f.14–16.
35   'Reserve for Fauna (Mallee Fowl) North of Nyabing'.

The proposal for the Lake Magenta reserve rolled slowly on through the bureaucracy, attracting support from conservation interests and opposition from agricultural ones. As new techniques made agricultural development of the light and mallee lands in marginal rainfall areas more feasible (see Chapter 10), resistance to the reserve proposal increased. In July 1957, after much circulation of typewritten correspondence on thin paper, the Department of Lands approved a compromise, setting aside an area around two-thirds of the size of the original proposal. All subsequent objections were met with the response that the area of the proposed reserve had been reduced, and the area west of the reserve would be released for selection in due course. As in South Australia, however, the gazettal of the Lake Magenta reserve did not put an end to the matter, and pressure to resume part or all of it for agriculture continued for years. In 1960, the Lower Great Southern Regional Council requested that the reserve be further reduced in size from 232,000 to 30,000 acres. This request was immediately protested by the WA Naturalists' Club whose Secretary, Miss L. Serventy, noted that:

> There has been too great a tendency in the past in Western Australia to regard Natural History Reserves as so much waste land, held in cold storage as it were, until some "useful" purpose can be discovered for them. Sectional interests in every country form pressure groups for the alienation of reserve areas such as National parks, and in most countries, the authorities are out of sympathy with such moves.[36]

Indeed, they were in this case. The minister for fisheries, Ross Hutchinson, refused the request, attaching by way of justification a 'scientific and technical appreciation' of the value of such reserves. This encompassed a list of their 'day-to-day economic value', such as apiculture and recreation, as well as key points derived from the international literature on conservation, including the 'immense value' of primitive reserves to agriculture.[37] Hutchison similarly

---

36 'Reserve for Fauna (Mallee Fowl) North of Nyabing'.
37 'Reserve for Fauna (Mallee Fowl) North of Nyabing'. This justification was also noted in Ian G. Crook and Andrew A. Burbidge, *Lake Magenta Nature Reserve*, WA Nature Reserve Management Plan, No. 4 (Perth: Department of Fisheries and Wildlife, 1980), 13. Certainly, palaeoclimatological studies conducted using *Callitris* gathered from uncleared (though not reserved) land near Lake Tay in the mallee zone of the Great Western Woodlands have usefully suggested multi-decadal variations in rainfall: Louise E. Cullen and Pauline F. Grierson, 'Multi-decadal Scale Variability in Autumn–Winter Rainfall in South-Western Australia since 1655 AD as Reconstructed from Tree Rings of *Callitris columellaris*', *Climate Dynamics* 33 (2009): 433–44.

rejected further requests, adding that: 'The overwhelming opinion is that habitat reserves must be massive in area ... some of the reserves created overseas exceed five million acres'.[38] Both amateur naturalists and the conservation bureaucracy were abreast of international trends in the theory and practice of conservation, and they deployed these understandings strategically.

The late 1950s and early 1960s saw rising advocacy in relation to conservation in Australia. The voracious appetite of a boom economy was consuming forests, bushland and urban heritage across the nation. Political conservatism and the material benefits of 'progress' forestalled mass mobilisations, but voices were raised against the destruction. The Victorian National Parks Association was established in 1952, and the Western Australian Tree Society in 1956. The 1960s also saw environmental discontent captured prominently in print; Robin Boyd's *The Australian Ugliness* (1960) took aim at a nation of arboriphobes, and, although his critique ran largely along aesthetic lines, it incorporated a broader awareness of conservation issues. In 1966, contributors to A.J. Marshall's provocatively titled *The Great Extermination: A Guide to Anglo-Australian Cupidity, Wickedness and Waste* stridently denounced the impact of colonisation and economic development on Australia's vegetation and wildlife, questioning the values that enabled such widespread and relentless destruction. In 1966 Vincent Serventy declared that Australia was *A Continent in Danger*.[39]

Some public servants, too, resisted the zeal for development that characterised this era. Clearly becoming frustrated with the continual pressure to reduce the size of the Lake Magenta reserve, Chief Warden of Fauna A.J. Fraser fulminated in a briefing note to the minister:

> It has come to be generally recognised that tying up land in wilderness areas is as necessary a form of land use as in agricultural development. The fact that a national park, or wilderness area, could be put under production is not a sound reason for its cancellation or amendment.

He continued, pointing to a prized bushland park in the heart of Perth city: 'What if a request were made for King's Park to be subdivided for home or industrial sites?'[40] While Fraser used the language of 'wilderness', the Fauna

---

38 'Nature Reserves–Tenure–Lake Magenta 25113 [WL19550075]', Item 15019F3102, SROWA.

39 Alexander J. Marshall (ed.), *The Great Extermination: A Guide to Anglo-Australian Cupidity, Wickedness and Waste* (London: Heinemann, 1966); Vincent Serventy, *A Continent in Danger* (London: Andre Deutsch, 1966).

40 'Nature Reserves–Tenure–Lake Magenta', f.103.

Protection Advisory Committee that managed the reserve took a more strictly scientific approach. Following a visit to the Lake Magenta reserve, the Committee consented to a road through it but recommended that 'otherwise, this reserve remains exactly as it is at present delineated'. It maintained that the reserve: contained ecosystems not represented elsewhere; posed a risk of salinity if cleared; satisfied the need to include sufficient area for representative ecosystems to be 'self-perpetuating'; and had a compact shape that minimised boundary-related problems such as the invasion of exotic species.[41]

This justification reflected the emergence of a more systematic approach to conservation, involving protection of representative ecosystems. This was pioneered in Australia by the Australian Academy of Science's Committee on National Parks and Reserves established in 1958 and its state subcommittees, which in the early 1960s inquired into the coverage of conservation reserves across Australia with a view to establishing a more 'national' approach.[42] Refined by Australian botanist Ray Specht, this approach would later be codified in the USA as 'gap analysis' using Geographical Information Systems.[43] It viewed each reserve as part of a broader system and sought to use scientific survey data to ensure the conservation of at least one representative example of each ecosystem type. Though appearing somewhat philatelic, as historian Libby Robin notes, this approach represented a rational approach to conservation that enabled 'pragmatic' decision-making and encouraged collaboration between scientists and managers.[44]

Meanwhile, the conservation conflict around the Little Desert in the Wimmera mallee region of Victoria reflected a broader shift in public views of mallee bushland. This area was similar in many respects to the Mallee proper to the north. It was not picturesque in any conventional sense, nor very accessible to metropolitan visitors. In 1968 the Victorian minister for lands (also holding the conservation portfolio), Sir William McDonald, proposed a scheme to subdivide the Little Desert. McDonald was a farmer with property in the region and a staunch belief that, with lime and superphosphate, the yeoman vision of prosperous smallholder settlement could yet be brought to fruition

---

41   'Nature Reserves–Tenure–Lake Magenta', f.151.
42   Libby Robin, 'Nature Conservation as a National Concern: The Role of the Australian Academy of Science', *Historical Records of Australian Science* 10, no. 1 (1994): 1–24.
43   J. Michael Scott *et al.*, 'Gap Analysis: A Geographic Approach to Protection of Biological Diversity', *Wildlife Monographs*, no. 123 (1993): 3–41. See also the discussion of Specht's work in Libby Robin, *Defending the Little Desert: The Rise of Ecological Consciousness in Australia* (Melbourne: Melbourne University Press, 1998), 68.
44   Libby Robin, *How a Continent Created a Nation* (Sydney: UNSW Press, 2007), 164–6.

on these 'idle' lands.[45] The dominant public view, however, was that the land should be set aside as a national park. Some were perplexed by the force of the public campaign; one journalist asked: 'Who on earth would want to preserve this horrid piece of land?'[46] But an increasing number of citizens—most of them urban—regarded the mallee 'wilderness' as vulnerable and valuable, for nature preservation as well as spiritual and recreational reasons.

Growing sympathy for a beleaguered fauna saw an early experiment in private conservation take place in 1968 near Blanchetown in South Australia. An already decimated southern hairy-nosed wombat population was found to be suffering terribly in the drought of 1965–67. Members of the Natural History Society of South Australia living in the region's towns took emaciated wombats into their homes and nursed them back to health, while the Society fed their wild counterparts kangaroo pellets and gave them vitamin injections to sustain them. They also planned to purchase part of Portee Station, then fence and reticulate it for the wombats' long-term survival. A public appeal by the Society in 1968 urged nature and animal lovers to buy an acre of reserve land for $4 and add another $2 to provide fencing and water, receiving in return a commemorative certificate and their name in a book of honour. Hides would be built for viewing the animals, enabling photographers and others to get 'splendid views of one of Australia's unique marsupials in its own home territory'. The wombat was promoted as a deserving recipient of such welfare, being 'a quaint little creature, who would have delighted the eyes of Walt Disney. He has few or no vices, is very easy to tame, very clean in his personal habits and engagingly friendly when tamed'.[47] A campaign involving fetes, exhibitions, flyers and newspaper articles, as well as public talks and TV appearances featuring adorable six-month-old wombat Ernest, saw the appeal over-subscribed, and around two thousand hectares of land was purchased. In an early success for private conservation, by 2001 the wombat population of the Moorunde Wildlife Reserve had increased to three to four times that of its 1968 level.[48]

---

45 Robin, *Defending the Little Desert*, 14–15.
46 Derek Ballantine, *Sun*, 12 August 1971, quoted in Robin, *Defending the Little Desert*, 16.
47 'Moorunde 1968 Public Appeal', Natural History Society of South Australia, 2018, accessed 6 November 2018, http://nhssa.com.au/our-reserves/moorunde/moorunde-1968-public-appeal/; see also 'Haven for the Hairy-Noses', *Canberra Times*, 23 May 1968; Harris, 'The National Parks and Reserves of South Australia', 147–8.
48 Peter Clements, 'The Founding of Moorunde Wildlife Reserve', *Ockham's Razor*, ABC Radio National, 14 October 2001, accessed 6 November 2018, http://nhssa.com.au/our-reserves/moorunde/abc-radio-891-moorunde/.

In 1969, a similar shift in attitudes was evident in Western Australia. The Shire of Nyabing–Pingrup, successor to the road board that had previously so vigorously opposed the Lake Magenta reserve, wrote to the chief warden of fauna proposing that the management of the reserve be changed to enable the development of tourism, with fencing, access roads, and small patches 'cleared and planted for food to bring kangaroos and other animals into the areas where they could be seen and at which water could also be provided'. The shire was willing to assist in any of these measures. However, by this time the Western Australian Wildlife Authority was considering classifying Lake Magenta as a 'prohibited area', meaning that the reserve would 'be treated as a primitive area to maintain its fauna in a completely natural state free from development or exploitation and excluded from tourist and other activities'. Similar applications to open the reserve to tourism were rejected well into the 1970s.[49]

This story reveals the rapid transition among local government bodies from a focus on agricultural development to tourism as the long agricultural development boom came to an end amidst a severe drought and increasingly unprofitable international markets. Unfortunately for the shires, this period also marked an equally rapid transition among the scientists from an acceptance of multipurpose reservation (recreation and apiculture as well as conservation), to reservation for science and conservation only. Lake Magenta Nature Reserve was listed on the Register of the National Estate in 1978. As the only reserve larger than forty thousand hectares within the Western Australian wheatbelt region, it plays a key role in maintaining rare plant and animal species as well as ecosystem processes.[50]

Managing the Mallee

While Sir James Barrett and the early Wyperfeld management committees had understood the necessity of having people on the ground to look after these areas, mallee reserves—like many others—were often regarded as self-maintaining. In a 1959 review of South Australian flora and fauna reserves, the Lands Department prepared a report highlighting the difficulty of exercising 'control and care of the natural Flora and Fauna' in the large areas represented

---

49 'Nature Reserves–Tenure–Lake Magenta'.
50 Australia, Department of the Environment and Energy, 'Lake Magenta Nature Reserve, Newdegate East Rd, Pingrup, WA, Australia', Australian Heritage Database, accessed 6 November 2018, http://www.environment.gov.au/cgi-bin/ahdb/search.pl?mode=place_detail;place_id=9923.

by Hincks and Hambidge. It explicitly identified the problem of reserves being 'in name only', and decried what had 'become a popular practice to "declare" what appeared on the surface to be waste land and pass it over to the Flora and Fauna Committee'. Reserves required funds for fencing as well as control of fire, weeds and feral animals. In South Australia this would lead to a transfer of responsibility for flora and fauna reserve management from the Flora and Fauna Advisory Committee to the commissioners of the National Park and Wildlife Reserves, who had access to funds from the hire of sporting facilities at Belair National Park.[51] Recreation would sponsor conservation management.

Questions also arose over management objectives: conservation, or protection of adjacent landholders? Fire was perceived as a particular threat. Large bushfires swept through the Stirling Range National Park during 1949–50, and by the mid-1950s landholders adjoining the park were letting fires go into the park 'to protect themselves'.[52] Neither the local bush fire brigades nor the National Parks Board possessed the knowledge or the resources to establish fire regimes that met the needs of both the park's ecosystems and the surrounding landholders. Nyungar people still camped within the reserve; however, laws prohibiting burning of Crown land, part of a broader process of dispossession, had long since disrupted any systematic Nyungar fire regimes.[53] In this context, authorities increasingly sought to manage fire in the park for the protection of adjacent properties and their residents. By 1969 the National Parks Board had a policy of burning thousands of acres of the park each year, with a view to cyclically burning the entire park over a four- or five-year period in order to prevent large wildfires that would threaten adjoining properties. Though it is doubtful whether they had the resources to fully implement this policy, some local observers felt the burning was too widespread and frequent, and that it was negatively impacting the flora and fauna.[54]

Conservation reserve managers also struggled to combine the often-competing demands of conservation and recreation. In the Stirling Range as early as 1963 busloads of tourists were visiting the park and taking away posies of wildflowers; visitors also dumped rubbish, shot kangaroos, dug up plants and

---

51   Harris, 'The National Parks and Reserves of South Australia', 112–13.
52   Rev. W.A. Atkins, Extract from State Gardens Board File 1214/2, National Parks Board, 'Fire Control—Stirling Range National Park', Item 1942/1382 V1, SROWA.
53   Report from Ranger to National Parks Board, 3 June 1964, 'Fire Control—Stirling Range National Park'.
54   Western Australian Tourist Development Authority, 'Stirling Ranges—General', Item 1966/117, SROWA.

took stone and gravel. In an area with many endemic species, such uses could have serious consequences. Sheer numbers of even respectful visitors could also impact an area—around three hundred people visited Bluff Knoll on a single Sunday afternoon in 1964.[55] As well as bringing in more people, roads also provided corridors into the park that facilitated the entry of cosmopolitan animals and plants, including foxes, rabbits and weeds. Weeds were pulled by hand, while foxes would later be targeted by aircraft dropping baits containing sodium fluoroacetate (1080) poison. By the early 1970s tyres and boots were carrying mud containing an introduced water mould, *Phytophthora cinnamomi*, through the park. This organism moves independently at a rate of around one metre per year and can be spread over small distances by animals, but in the Stirling Range its principal vector is humans, who can carry it long distances in soil attached to footwear, machinery and tyres. Locally known as 'dieback', it engineers a more favourable soil environment for itself by killing susceptible vegetation. In affected areas, the composition of the park's flora was radically changed.

Figure 11.3: Bluff Knoll in the early 1970s: a site of conflict between conservation and recreation.
(Courtesy Michael Easton)

---

55   'Fire Control—Stirling Range National Park'.

Though it was well known in the 1970s that dieback was established in nearby jarrah forest, no access controls were implemented, and, by the time dieback was formally detected in the Stirling Range in 1974, it was already widespread within the park's boundaries. The opening of gravel pits and road construction within the park—probably with infested gravel—hastened the spread of dieback, as did the increasing number of bushwalkers who were permitted to traverse the highest peaks with no soil hygiene management. By the 1970s the park was also being used for military training; in return, army personnel assisted with park management activities.[56] Army and hiking boots carried dieback to the peaks, then rainfall and gravity spread it down the slopes.

As the impacts were belatedly realised, and as the rise of environmentalism fostered widespread community concern over the loss of biodiversity, access to parts of the park was restricted, dating from 1994. Managers also began a program of spraying phosphite from aircraft over small areas of the park to increase the dieback resistance of rare vegetation communities. Some endangered plants were translocated, and some were caged to protect them from both rabbits and quokkas (a vulnerable native marsupial).[57] Over time, the desire to prevent further loss of biodiversity called for intensified human intervention to counter the effects of dieback.

Meanwhile, in Lake Magenta, a management plan was drafted and in 1981 circulated to interested parties, including adjoining landholders. Many of these people wrote to the Department of Fisheries and Wildlife to express their gratitude at being consulted; one Pingrup farmer said: 'it has been encouraging to know you realize we exist'.[58] Their letters collectively express a love of the reserve and pride in local knowledge of its needs. Many suggested that water be installed in the reserve for the wildlife, as this might not only reduce their inclination to seek water on neighbouring farms but reduce stress in times of drought, when access to the region's few natural freshwater supplies had been cut off by roads and fences. One farmer, Maureen Duncombe, expressed the conflict the farmers felt between livelihood and conservation, noting that while her sons 'would like more land and would be happy to see the Reserve made available' for farming, she had 'spent many relaxing hours out at Warwick Farm observing the beautiful birds and bush. I often told my husband we

---

56 Ian Herford et al., *Stirling Range and Porongorup National Parks Management Plan 1999–2009* (Perth: Department of Conservation and Land Management, 1999), 79.
57 Damien Rathbone et al., 'Battling the Odds', *Landscope* 31, no. 3 (2016): 40–4.
58 'Nature Reserves—Tenure—Lake Magenta'.

would [sic] forget about farming and turn to tourism ... We look upon the Wild Turkeys [malleefowl] as ours and would be upset to see them harmed'.[59]

Yet fire and wildlife made the reserve hard to live with; firebreaks were deemed inadequate, emus and kangaroos trampled crops, and dingoes and eagles attacked livestock. Farmers adapted, for example by shooting kangaroos to keep the eagles fed. However, farmers also suggested extending the reserve and closing roads that enabled recreational 4WD vehicle users and 'so-called sportsmen with guns' to access it illegally. Most supported the prohibition on general access to the reserve, and many volunteered to join a management advisory committee. A 1981 Department of Fisheries and Wildlife briefing note summed up the situation well: 'Early local resistance to the Reserve has turned to support leavened only with concern about the adequacy of "good neighbour" type management provisions'.[60]

In this era of widespread scientific and popular concern over the state of the environment, the slowly dawning realisation that effective conservation might require significant management did nothing to stem the tide of conservation in the mallee lands. The 1970s and early 1980s saw the gazetting of several major reserves in the region. In Western Australia, following the declaration of the vast Cape Arid National Park in 1969, Frank Hann National Park was quietly declared in 1970, with Peak Charles National Park following in 1979 and the massive Dundas Nature Reserve in 1981. These reserves lay across the south of what would later be re-conceived as the 'Great Western Woodlands'. Being outside of the agricultural area, their establishment seems to have attracted little controversy. Not so Dragon Rocks Nature Reserve near Hyden, which a local farmer sought to have reserved through protracted, if low-key, agitation starting in 1966. It was finally declared in 1979.[61] Peak Charles, Dundas and Dragon Rocks were all recommended to cabinet as part of a state-wide systematic process conducted by the Conservation Through Reserves Committee appointed in 1972 by the Western Australian Environmental Protection Authority.[62]

Meanwhile, in South Australia, pressure to rescind Hambidge had receded in the face of a concerted campaign by conservation groups such as the Nature

---

59   'Nature Reserves—Tenure—Lake Magenta'.
60   'Nature Reserves—Tenure—Lake Magenta'.
61   Andrea Gaynor, 'State, Scientists and Citizens: Conserving Lake Magenta and Dragon Rocks, Western Australia', *Historical Records of Australian Science* 25, no. 2 (2014): 212–14.
62   The committee's key task was to review and update the Australian Academy of Science report on National Parks and Nature Reserves.

Conservation Society of South Australia, as well as the imposition of wheat quotas in 1969.[63] Indeed, so far had the pendulum swung that 1970 saw the declaration of the 33,577-hectare Bascombe Well National Park, just south east of Lock.

The early 1970s saw a great deal of action in South Australia on the conservation front: a committee of inquiry into the environment was established, chaired by chemist Denis Jordan; a ministerial portfolio and department for environment and conservation was inaugurated; and a National Parks and Wildlife Act declared. The 'Jordan Report' identified an urgent need for representative samples of 'plant communities, native fauna and scenery' to be protected, in the face of extensive and rapid development.[64] The Nature Conservation Society of South Australia, with the support of the National Parks Commission, had proactively conducted biological surveys of several reserves, including Hincks and Hambidge, and this work helped to gradually change the prevailing opinion in official circles that one conservation reserve was as good as another.[65] As in Western Australia, the basis for state conservation was moving from 'worthless lands' to representative protection.

As development of wheatlands in South Australia continued in the late 1960s, it came up against the 'tiger country' in the northern part of the Ninety Mile Desert. Here, just west of Victoria's Big Desert, the mallee and heath vegetation was easy to clear, but the steep parabolic sand dunes scattered throughout the region—some rising to over thirty metres—presented a formidable erosion hazard. Still, the area was assessed for development in 1967–68 by the Departments of Agriculture and Lands. They recommended that twenty thousand hectares of land be subdivided, with stringent clearing controls to avoid erosion. The establishment of national parks at Scorpion Springs and Mt Shaugh was also recommended. Given the heat being generated by the Little Desert dispute just across the border, the subdivision proposal unsurprisingly provoked immediate opposition from the Nature Conservation

---

63   Whitelock, *Conquest to Conservation*, 138.
64   Denis Oswald Jordan (chair) *et al.*, *The Environment in South Australia: Report of the Committee on Environment* (Adelaide: Committee on Environment in South Australia, 1972), 186.
65   Colin Harris, cited in Whitelock, *Conquest to Conservation*, 135. See also C.W. Bonython and K.A. Preiss, 'Hambidge Wild Life Reserve: A Survey by the Nature Conservation Society of South Australia', *South Australian Naturalist* 42, no. 2 (1967): 35–62; K.A. Preiss and P.M. Thomas, 'Hincks National Park: A Survey of its Natural Values Carried Out by the Nature Conservation Society of South Australia', *South Australian Naturalist* 45, no. 2 (1970): 29–84; and Nature Conservation Society of South Australia, *Hambidge, Hinks and Blesing: An Assessment of Three Areas on the Eyre Peninsula* (Adelaide: Nature Conservation Society of South Australia, 1969).

Society of South Australia. Declining wool prices and an adverse report from the Australian Institute of Agricultural Science sealed the fate of the scheme. Conservation Parks at Scorpion Springs and Mt Shaugh were declared in 1970 and 1971 to preserve the mallee heath.[66]

The Victorian Land Conservation Council

Meanwhile, over the border, in the wake of the Little Desert controversy, the Victorian parliament under the conservative leadership of Henry Bolte passed the *Land Conservation Act 1970*, developed in consultation with conservationists. It established a Land Conservation Council (LCC) to 'carry out investigations and make recommendations to the Minister with respect to the use of public land in order to provide for the balanced use of land in Victoria'.[67] In a process taking some twenty-two years, the LCC systematically surveyed each region of the state. Its approach was balanced, consultative and, overall, very successful. The Mallee area was one of the first to be examined. Following its 1974 Mallee report the LCC developed a set of draft recommendations, which generated considerable controversy.[68] The most contentious proposals were around creation of new parks and enlargement of existing ones, as well as proposals to phase out grazing from some parks.

The arguments against the recommendations pitched local against outsider knowledge, and livelihood against conservation. E.P. and L. Hayer of Underbool wrote angrily to the *North West Express*, arguing that the Mallee had once been overrun with rabbits, a problem controlled only through settlement and cultivation. 'Yet', they continued,

> it is proposed to ignore history and revert the country back into a barren wilderness. How can a band of Government officials, with no experience of the area, have any idea how to tackle such a job? It is a task best performed by the experts—the men on the land—whose very livelihood depends on that land.[69]

---

66   Harris, 'The National Parks and Reserves of South Australia', 179–81; Colin Harris, interviewed by George Lewkowicz for the Don Dunstan Oral History Project, 8 May 2008, Adelaide, accessed 6 November 2018, https://dspace.flinders.edu.au/jspui/bitstream/2328/25086/1/HARRIS_Colin_Cleared.pdf.

67   *Land Conservation Act 1970* (Victoria), s.5.1.a.

68   Land Conservation Council (Vic.), *Report on the Mallee Study Area* (Melbourne: Land Conservation Council (Vic.), 1974); Land Conservation Council (Vic.), *Final Recommendations: Mallee Study Area* (Melbourne: Land Conservation Council (Vic.), 1977), 5.

69   E.P. and L. Hayer, letter to the editor, *North West Express*, 26 May 1976, 'Environment General' file, Ouyen Historical Society.

Other letters suggested that without grazing in the parks the vegetation would rapidly become a fire hazard, parks would harbour pest animals, and that formal reservation would restrict recreational activities at popular sites such as Pine Plains.

Concerns about the management of these vast and remote tracts of public land were understandable; many of the areas earmarked for conservation had been grazed for many years, and, if the graziers were excluded, where would the knowledge and resources to manage the land come from? Grazing licences issued in the Mallee in the 1930s enabled stock owners to depasture their animals on public land for payment of an annual fee. In the 1950s and 60s about forty licensees obtained 21-year grazing leases, and by 1974 around fifty thousand sheep and three thousand cattle were being grazed on fifty thousand hectares of public land in the region.[70]

While mindful of the dependence of some licensees on public land and the utility of grazing as a land management tool, the LCC also carefully assessed the impact of stock and the actual management of licensed areas. Insecurity of tenure had led to minimal investment in fencing and water supply, which concentrated the impact of stock on particular areas. Grazing had prevented regeneration of *Casuarina* and *Callitris* forests, and the intermittent use of public land during drought conditions had contributed to wind erosion. The LCC recommended that the grazing areas should not be extended and grazing should not be permitted in parks or wildlife reserves, and all grazing on uncommitted land and state forest should be overseen by the Department of Crown Lands and Survey, advised by the District Advisory Committees of the Soil Conservation Authority. In doing so, they acknowledged that little research had been conducted on grazing management of public lands in the Mallee and sought to draw on 'the experience of the current grazing lessees and licensees' by including them in the proposed advisory group.[71] Given the variable degrees of stewardship found in the grazing on public lands, however, the LCC regarded state oversight of these activities as essential.

The LCC also dealt with the issue of military use of Crown land, which had attracted 'considerable public concern' due to destruction of vegetation by tracked vehicles and consequent erosion potential. The army had been using the Big Desert and Sunset Country for infantry and armoured-vehicle training for some time. As the LCC pointed out, under Commonwealth law the army was not obliged to obtain permission from state authorities

---

70   Land Conservation Council (Vic.), *Report on the Mallee Study Area*, 126.
71   Land Conservation Council (Vic.), *Final Recommendations: Mallee Study Area*, 29.

to conduct military training on Crown land. The LCC therefore proposed a compromise that would see military exclusion from the large areas of the Big Desert and Sunset country set aside for wilderness and conservation purposes, and army use being subject to access and rehabilitation conditions over the remainder.[72]

The LCC's final recommendations were released in 1977. Over the next two years, Wyperfeld and Hattah Lakes National Parks were enlarged, a new state park was created at Pink Lakes, and regional parks were established at Lake Albacutya and Murray–Kulkyne, along with several smaller reference areas, flora and fauna reserves, wildlife reserves, and bushland reserves. The 114,000-hectare Big Desert Wilderness Area was also declared in 1979.

The long tradition of viewing the Mallee as wilderness, in the sense of a place of desolation and despair, continued until the late twentieth century.[73] In formally designating the Big Desert a 'wilderness', however, the LCC was evoking a different concept that combined elements of the older 'primitive area' idea with a new ecological consciousness. In 1964 the American Wilderness Act created a National Wilderness Preservation System, which over time encompassed many of the Forest Service's 'primitive areas'. It defined wilderness as 'an area where the earth and its community of life are untrammelled by man, where man himself is a visitor and does not remain'.[74] This merged older ideas of timeless, uninhabited places with a rising earth-consciousness.

Similarly, the LCC saw the Australian wilderness experience as one marked by:

> the perception of being part of nature, of an environment unaltered by human intervention, of isolation, and of being exposed to the challenge of the elements. In a wilderness, man should function as a part of the natural systems, and on equal terms with nature.[75]

The significance of wilderness was multiple and contradictory; as a source of 'spiritual refreshment and an awareness of solitude arising from close contact with the uninhabited, undisturbed natural environment' it overlooked prior Aboriginal occupation and removal, just as the 'primitive area' concept had done. This was accompanied by an adversarial, Darwinian vision. One principal

---

72   Land Conservation Council (Vic.), *Final Recommendations: Mallee Study Area*, 71–2.

73   Katie Holmes and Kylie Mirmohamadi, 'Howling Wilderness and Promised Land: Imagining the Victorian Mallee, 1840–1914', *Australian Historical Studies* 46, no. 2 (2015): 191–213.

74   *Wilderness Act 1964*, USA.

75   Land Conservation Council (Vic.), *Final Recommendations: Mallee Study Area*, 14.

appeal of wilderness was said to be the opportunity it presented to pit one's capacity for self-reliance and endurance against the elements. Alternately, it was conceptualised as a negative space, which in bearing no obvious traces of western industrialised culture might provide 'refuge from the pressures, sights, and sounds of modern urban life'.[76] Finally, its utility was both practical and theoretical; the knowledge that such wilderness existed was seen to be a key element of its appeal. The ability to dream of the Big Desert Wilderness, without visiting or perhaps even intending to visit it, was a legitimate reason to exclude vehicles, timber production, grazing and mining.

Figure 11.4: By the 1970s mallee 'wilderness' was increasingly understood as valuable for nature conservation and recreation. This photograph of a track in the Big Desert on the border of South Australia and Victoria, c. 1973, was part of the image collection of the Australian News and Information Bureau, charged with representing Australia abroad.
(Courtesy National Archives of Australia, c. 1973, A6135, K14/3/73/9)

---

76   Land Conservation Council (Vic.), *Final Recommendations: Mallee Study Area*, 14. The sensory dimensions of 'wilderness' and centrality of absence and remoteness to its definition are discussed by Tom Griffiths in *Hunters and Collectors*, 259–60.

In order to fulfil these aims, wilderness areas had to be large and remote, devoid of roads and tracks, and buffered from other land uses. The LCC emphasised that there were probably only two areas in Victoria that would fulfil these requirements: the semi-arid Mallee country and the mountains. It also recommended that to preserve these areas' wilderness qualities the number of people using them at any one time should be controlled. It would be 1989 before the *National Parks Act 1975* was amended to include a separate section for wilderness parks, although this legislation followed the lead provided by the LCC. At that time, the director of national parks was charged with promoting 'the understanding and appreciation of the purpose and significance of wilderness and the proper use of wilderness by the public', as well as ensuring that there were no roads, commercial activity, use of motorised or mechanical transport, use of any non-indigenous animal, or hunting. On the other hand, 'evidence of developments of non-aboriginal origin' could be removed, non-indigenous flora and fauna were to be eradicated, and indigenous fauna controlled if necessary to protect any species.[77] While concealing its cultural origins, the wilderness was to be very much a co-production of nature and culture.

For the LCC, the value of the Big Desert Wilderness area was increased because it adjoined a large area of public land in South Australia that was already reserved or subject to reservation proposals. Having opposed the proposed agricultural development of the area in the late 1960s, the Nature Conservation Society of South Australia had become increasingly concerned in the early 1970s about the activities of beekeepers and trail bike rallies on its 'natural character'. As there was no LCC in South Australia, the Nature Conservation Society conducted its own biological survey, in October 1977, of the area adjacent to the Big Desert. There was considerable support within the South Australian government for the planned conservation area, and it acted quickly, announcing in November 1977 that all of the unallocated Crown land would be reserved. The 200,000-hectare Ngarkat Conservation Park was gazetted in September 1979.[78]

---

[77] *National Parks (Amendment) Act 1989* (Victoria), s.17A.3.b; s.17C.1.a-e; 17A.2.a-d.

[78] Colin Harris, Anne Reeves, and David Symon (eds), *The Ninety Mile Desert of South Australia: A Report of Surveys Carried out by the Nature Conservation Society of South Australia in 1973 and 1977* (Adelaide: Nature Conservation Society of South Australia, 1982), 5, 29.

Land Clearing and Conservation

In 1974 Colin Harris was commissioned to lead an inquiry into land clearing and conservation in South Australia. The subsequent report, which made front-page news in 1977, estimated that only 8.2 per cent of native vegetation cover remained in the Murray Mallee, and recommended offering incentives to encourage farmers across the state to preserve native vegetation.[79] This was met by strong support from some sectors amid increasing environmental and conservation awareness,[80] and vehemently opposed by others who regarded it as effectively proposing a ban on the form of development that had fuelled South Australia's prosperity.

The scheme was launched in 1981 with the slogan 'Now it pays you to protect native vegetation on your land'. As the environment minister responsible for the scheme later pointed out, it represented 'the largest per capita investment in a conservation project of any state or country in the world'.[81] Sam Jericho, a farmer at Rudall on the Eyre Peninsula, was more circumspect, believing that 'the voluntary nature of the legislation only succeeded in obtaining areas held by dedicated conservationists and the scrub clearing in general proceeded at an even greater pace'.[82] Les and John Evans, farmers at Mantung in the Murray Mallee, similarly recalled that 'Putting 1300 hectares under Heritage Agreement rather than clearing it met with a fair bit of local comment. We were fairly unpopular and, I think, we were regarded as fools or misfits!'[83] Doug and Kay Day, farmers at Lameroo in the Murray Mallee, entered into a heritage agreement because of the intrinsic interest of the bushland: 'many people find the mallee boring and drive through it as quickly as they can. You

---

79   Colin Harris, *Vegetation Clearance in South Australia: Report of the Interdepartmental Committee on Vegetation Clearance* (Adelaide: Interdepartmental Committee on Vegetation Clearance in South Australia, 1976); Kym Tilbrook, 'Curb Land Clearance, SA Urged', *Advertiser*, 3 June 1977.

80   See Editorial, *Advertiser*, 6 June 1977.

81   David Wotton, Minister for Environment and Natural Resources, opening address in Tim Dendy and Joan Murray (eds), *From Conflict to Conservation: Native Vegetation Management in Australia: A Focus on the South Australian Program and Other Australian Initiatives, Past Present and Future* (Adelaide: Department of Environment and Natural Resources, 1996), 1.

82   Rudall farmer Sam Jericho, quoted in Geoffrey Bishop and Jocelyn Thomas, *Bushland Heritage: The Heritage Agreement Experience. The South Australian Heritage Agreement Scheme 1980–2002* (Adelaide: National Parks and Wildlife, Department for Environment and Heritage, 2002), 5, accessed 6 November 2018, http://www.pir.sa.gov.au/__data/assets/file/0013/151006/NRM_Hist_HeritageAgreeInside.pdf.

83   Murray Mallee farmer John Evans, quoted in Bishop and Thomas, *Bushland Heritage*, 29.

need to take time to walk around in the mallee and observe—there is lots there of interest once you start looking'.[84] By 2002, a total of 561,802 hectares of bushland across the state was protected under the scheme.

Farmers who did not take the carrot were soon faced with the stick. In May 1983 John Bannon's Labor government, acting to curb the state's 'excessive' land clearing, imposed land clearance regulations with penalties for infringement of up to $10,000.[85] While this was not a ban as such, clearing of native vegetation was only permitted with the consent of the South Australian Planning Commission, and no compensation was to be offered to farmers whose applications were denied. Some farmers argued that the new regulations ignored the ways farmers relied on the bushland. Murray Mallee farmer, Leon Stasinowsky, recalled a frenzy of land clearing around him, as 'many farmers had a lot of uncleared land and relied on wood-cutting and mallee stumps for part of their income'.[86] Others offered more politically oriented criticism: 'The land-clearing controls introduced by this government are typical of bureaucratic, growth inhibiting Socialism. The State's future rests on agriculture ... Our parasitical public sector sucks on its wealth. And now this collection of obsequious individuals wants to limit agriculture's future'.[87]

Following outrage from the farming community, heavy lobbying by the United Farmers and Stockowners Association, and a successful High Court challenge leading to subsequent review of the land clearance controls, from November 1985, farmers whose applications to clear native vegetation were refused were to be compensated, provided the land was then placed under a Heritage Agreement.[88] After initial resistance the government saw compensation 'as an effective long-term investment as it is far more effective to retain remnant bushland than to have to rehabilitate degraded land in the future'.[89] An end to land clearing in the state came with the *Native Vegetation Act 1991*, which included sunset clauses for compensation for farmers unable to clear land and a formal end to broadacre clearing.

---

84 Murray Mallee farmer Doug Day, quoted in Bishop and Thomas, *Bushland Heritage*, 26.
85 Regulations introduced under the *South Australian Planning Act, 1982*, 12 May 1983, requiring landowners to apply for approval to clear native vegetation. See example of government notice, Government of South Australia, 'Native Vegetation Clearance Controls', *Sunday Mail*, 15 May 1983, accessed 6 November 2018, http://www.pir.sa.gov.au/__data/assets/file/0014/151016/NRM_Hist_I8NatVegNotice.pdf.
86 Quoted in Bishop and Thomas, *Bushland Heritage*, 30.
87 Letter to the Editor, *Advertiser*, 3 November 1983, cited in Whitelock, *Conquest to Conservation*, 146.
88 Bishop and Thomas, *Bushland Heritage*, 6.
89 Bishop and Thomas, *Bushland Heritage*, 7.

While the South Australian government was working to preserve native vegetation, across the border in Western Australia Charles Court's conservative coalition government was escalating its destruction. With a degree of economic recovery in the agricultural sector in the late 1970s, allocation of Crown lands to agriculture had been quietly increasing. However, in June 1980 the government announced that up to a hundred thousand hectares would be opened up for agriculture every year, including land outside existing agricultural districts, until 'up to' another 3.1 million hectares of bushland had been replaced by farmland. This was, in effect, a scaled-back continuation of the large-scale 'new land' Conditional Purchase agricultural releases interrupted by the events of 1969. Welcomed by some farmers, this expansionist agenda was opposed by others as well as conservationists and some scientists and public servants.[90]

The decision to embark on this new era of large-scale land release followed a report of a committee of the Rural and Allied Industries Council. Appointed in early September 1979, the committee took public submissions in October and completed its report in November 1979. It concluded that '2,990,000 hectares were considered suitable and available for possible agricultural development', most of which was in two vast swathes of mallee country, north west and north east of Esperance and east of Hyden. Several submissions recommended that if release proceeded then some vegetation should be retained on each farm. However, the committee envisaged total development of alienated land, deeming it 'impractical to retain and administer uncleared land within farm boundaries'.[91]

In response to the announcement, a group of concerned citizens with expertise in biology, botany, sociology, economics and history was formed in July 1980 as the Land Release Study Group.[92] Taking inspiration from developments in South Australia and Victoria, including the Little Desert conflict, the group began a campaign of lobbying and press releases, arguing that the decision was based on a hurried evaluation by agricultural interests. They pointed out that officers of relevant government departments, including Agriculture, Fisheries and Wildlife and Conservation and Environment, had not been consulted, and that the 'three month growing season' line that was

---

90   Rosemary Jasper, 'An Historical Perspective', in *Diversity or Dust: A Review of the Impact of Agricultural Land Clearance Programmes in South West Australia* (Melbourne: Australian Conservation Foundation, 1984), 9–12; 'Introduction', in *Diversity or Dust*, vii–viii; 'Chronology of Important Events', in *Diversity or Dust*, 65–7.

91   Rural and Allied Industries Council, *Rural Land Release Policy in Western Australia* (Perth: Premier's Department, 1979), 1, 77.

92   The core group comprised Ron Richards, Rosemary Jasper, Ken Newbey, Brenda Newbey, Peter Luscombe, Keith Bradby and Heather Pearce.

central to the Rural and Allied Industries Council committee recommendations differed significantly from Bureau of Meteorology and their own data (see Figure 11.5). Erosion and salinity posed real risks in this area, and the biological diversity had been only partially surveyed. The process of land release, the study group claimed, was 'covert and irresponsible', based on financial interests and political favour. What was needed was a careful and impartial evaluation of the use and management of Crown land, such as that provided by the LCC in Victoria.[93] Rather than focusing on a particular piece of land, the study group sought a radical change to policy and process that, in effect, would end agricultural land release in the state. The main battleground would be mallee country.

The Land Release Study Group gained significant press coverage and cultivated concern among public servants, particularly in the light of growing recognition of salinity, erosion and threats to endangered species.

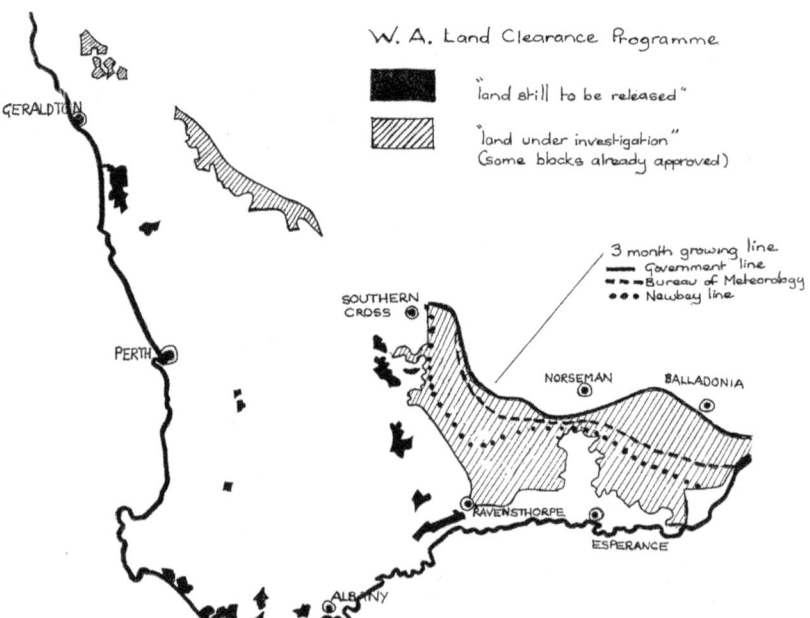

Figure 11.5: This map of the land approved and under investigation for agricultural alienation in Western Australia in the early 1980s was used by the Land Release Study Group in their campaign to stop the release of Crown land for agricultural development.
(Courtesy Keith Bradby)

---

93   Ron Richards, 'Land Releases—New Policy' (typescript), 15 May 1981, Keith Bradby archive.

However, the fiercely pro-development Court government would not countenance a policy change. The study group made unlikely alliances in order to delay the releases. Noticing a newspaper article in which the secretary of the Association for Mining and Exploration Companies called for a halt to agricultural land release because it would 'effectively give away mineral development opportunities and royalties in these areas', the study group arranged a meeting with the mining lobby group. There it was agreed that the next area scheduled for release, at Mt Ridley, would be pegged for mineral exploration, adding an extra layer of complexity that would delay the release process.[94]

As opposition to land release gained traction in the lead-up to the 1983 election, opposition leader Brian Burke announced that, if elected, a Labor government would conduct a review of land release. He made good on this promise in May 1983, when Minister for Lands Ken McIver instigated a review and suspended the release of Crown land for agriculture, with the exception of two areas, including the land north of Fitzgerald River National Park. The Land Release Study Group countered with evidence of a lack of objective assessment of the area and the presence of species at risk. In October 1983 the North Fitzgerald land release was deferred, pending a statewide study of the endangered Western Ground Parrot (*Pezoporus flaviventris*), known to have occurred in the area.[95] The Australian Conservation Foundation supported publication of the Land Release Study Group's analysis of the land release policy, and, together with the Conservation Council of Western Australia, organised a seminar on 'Wheatbelt: Conservation or Dust?' in a wealthy western suburb of Perth.[96] Emboldened public servants undertook additional studies on soil conservation and biological diversity that further complicated the case for land release and confirmed the inadequacies of earlier procedures.[97] The economic tide, too, had turned; it was the unanimous opinion of the Agricultural Land Release Review Committee that 'the current rural economic position supports the indefinite suspension of further land release

---

94 'Mines Man: Halt New-land release,' *West Australian*, 8 November 1982; Keith Bradby, communication with author, 8 February 2018.

95 Doug Watkins for Western Australian Department of Conservation and Land Management, *Report of the RAOU Ground Parrot Survey in Western Australia* (Melbourne: Royal Australasian Ornithologists Union, 1985).

96 *Diversity or Dust*; 'Wheatbelt: Conservation or Dust', poster and press release, Bradby archive.

97 See, for example, G.G.H. Scholz, *Mt Beaumont Land Release Area, Stage II, Final Report* (Perth: Soil Conservation Service Branch, Department of Agriculture, 1984); Mark A. Burgman, 'Spatial Analysis of Vegetation Patterns in Southern Western Australia: Implications for Reserve Design', *Australian Journal of Ecology* 13, no. 4 (1988): 415–29.

except in limited cases where there is a proven need for "build up" of existing farms'.[98] The recommendation was accepted by cabinet in 1985, though the battle to end all land clearing for agriculture goes on. As late as 2014–15, the Goldfields–Esperance Development Commission, Shire of Esperance and local chamber of commerce put forward a proposal that gained significant traction with cabinet, to assess five hundred thousand hectares of unallocated Crown land for potential agricultural development.[99] A Department of Regional Development discussion paper obtained under Freedom of Information indicated that the state government 'would like to see development proceed through the maximisation of private sector involvement with the necessary supports given through approvals facilitation', but warned of the likelihood that any development would likely attract 'large corporates (perhaps foreign entities) rather than mum and dad farmers'.[100] Met with significant resistance from local people and conservation groups, the proposal was quietly set aside, with implementation 'TBC' in the Esperance Region Economic Development Strategy.[101]

Loving Mallee Country

While at first many of the non-Indigenous people who encountered mallee country found it grim and desolate, it appealed to some from the outset; others came to value it over time. They loved its bird life, its harsh beauty, its stillness in contrast to the hustle and bustle of modern urban life. Across the twentieth century the champions of mallee bushland had to argue for its preservation by proclaiming its 'uselessness' for conventional industries while emphasising its value for recreation, tourism and nature conservation. There

---

98   Western Australian Government Cabinet Summary Sheet, 'Agriculture Land Release Review—Final Recommendations', private archive.
99   Brad Thompson, 'Clear Run For New Farmland', *Countryman*, 8 August 2014, accessed 6 November 2018, https://thewest.com.au/countryman/news/clear-run-for-new-farmland-ng-ya-375440; Jake Sturmer, 'Great Western Woodlands: Fears Over Proposal to Release 500,000 Hectares of Reserve for Farming', *ABC News*, 8 December 2014, accessed 6 November 2018, https://www.abc.net.au/news/2014-12-08/fears-over-proposal-to-release-500,000-hectares-of-wa-woodland/5950072.
100 Eugene Carew, 'Esperance Agricultural Precinct: For Discussion Purposes', 21 August 2014, Department of Regional Development document obtained by the Wilderness Society under Freedom of Information, Bradby archive.
101 AEC Group, *Esperance Region Economic Development Strategy* (Kalgoorlie: Goldfields–Esperance Development Commission, *c*. 2015), accessed 6 November 2018, https://www.ecc.esperance.wa.gov.au/sites/default/files/publication/files/publication_-_esperance_region_-_economic_development_strategy_0.pdf.

was always, however, a risk that 'useless' land would be resumed if profitable uses were found. Decisions on the value of different kinds of utility in land have been made by bureaucrats and politicians influenced by state political agendas, anxieties around the decline of flora and fauna, national and international developments in approaches to conservation, and economic contexts. These have led to the establishment of a significant part of the Australian conservation estate in mallee country.

But while large-scale land releases have ended, much undeveloped mallee country remains contested, being subject still in some areas to mining and calls for agricultural development. Management of fire, rabbits, cats and dingoes over large expanses of land remains a challenge in areas that are often sparsely populated. Aboriginal ranger programs represent a promising development in some areas, combining caring for country with livelihood. The bushland helps to maintain the ecological health of landscapes fragmented by agriculture, and, as runaway levels of carbon dioxide are changing global climates, early advocates' claims that undisturbed mallee country could be the 'lungs of the city' take on new meanings. Across its vast expanse, however, the changing climate will sorely test the mallee's native resilience.

Part Four

Living with the Mallee 1983 to the Present

The conflict over agricultural development in Western Australia in the 1980s signalled the end of the long era of large-scale release of mallee land for agriculture. With the days of mass pioneering over, farmers across the region now focused on how to sustain increasingly large and complex enterprises in the face of unstable markets and environmental challenges. At the same time, the ascendency of neoliberalism saw state support for agriculture rolled back. While some services were replaced in the market, farmers and communities also worked together to meet their needs, for example in farmer-led research and development, and in the Landcare movement. While individual and technological adaptation has enabled many mallee farms to prosper, it is unclear whether this kind of response will be sufficient to cope with the dual challenges of climate change and community sustainability.

By the early twenty-first century, mallee communities had increasingly become victims of their farmers' success. Surviving the cost–price squeeze for most meant becoming larger, more capitalised and more efficient. As farm sizes increased, the number of families on the land fell. While this continued a long-term trend in many mallee communities, even those in the more recently settled areas would soon be shrinking. Some residents have sought to meet the challenges by diversifying their enterprises, though the opportunities to do so have been limited in a landscape and with an infrastructure developed almost entirely around mixed grain and sheep farming. But roads that take grain out can also bring people in, and many communities are looking to the arts and heritage as potential income generators. Arguably, however, they have a more important purpose to serve in strengthening local relationships and providing opportunities for collective reflection on the nature of these places. All the while, Aboriginal people have survived in the region, against the odds. As Native Title claims are negotiated or determined, a fragile maturity is emerging in settler approaches to Aboriginal history and heritage.

Chapter 12

SUSTAINING MALLEE FARMS 1983–2018

On Tuesday afternoon 8 February 1983 a dust storm enveloped Melbourne when almost a million tonnes of topsoil blew in from the Mallee and land to its west. Melburnians gained a sense of what a full-scale Mallee dust storm was like. As a huge cloud of red dust over three hundred metres high towered over the city, visibility dropped to a hundred metres, forcing traffic to a standstill and people to huddle in doorways covering their mouths. Airports were closed, powerlines brought down and trees uprooted by the severe winds.

While the storm caused disruption in Melbourne, it bespoke environmental disaster elsewhere. The 1982–83 drought—which broke with heavy rains a month after this dust storm—was one of the most severe on record across mallee lands. Despite decades of work by farmers and soil conservation authorities to reduce soil drift, the drought left paddocks bare and exposed; sheep scoured them for any remaining foliage, pounding the fragile soil to dust as they searched. Smaller dust storms preceded the big blow, dashing hopes that the problem of drift and erosion had been solved. The Soil Conservation Authority estimated that the storm carried 'somewhere between one-quarter and one million tonnes of topsoil containing between 800 and 3000 tonnes of nitrogen and between 8 and 30 tonnes of phosphorus from western areas of the State'.[1] Some landed in the sea. Half of all cropping land and three-quarters of land with sandy topsoils suffered damage, 60 per cent of the latter 'being significantly eroded'.[2] Even Mallee residents, hardened to the ravages wind could inflict on their land, were shocked.

The devastation of the 1982–83 drought drove researchers to seek new ways to tackle wind and water erosion. They worked with farmers to improve soil

---

1   Victoria, Soil Conservation Authority, '24th Annual Report, for the Year Ended 30 June 1983' (Melbourne: F.D. Atkinson, Government Printer, 1983), 10–11.
2   Victoria, Soil Conservation Authority, '24th Annual Report, for the Year Ended 30 June 1983', 10–11.

structure and increase water-use efficiency.³ Meanwhile, in the West, dry years from 1979 to 1982 and the accompanying wind erosion reduced cleared land to 'bare drifting paddocks'.⁴ Perhaps this explains why it was in the West that no-till techniques—the sowing of a crop without disturbing the soil—first significantly arrested drift and soil erosion.

Figure 12.1: Sand drift on North Jerramungup Road, Western Australia, 1982. The extent of drift is evident against the height of the car. The blow forced the closure of the road, with sand needing to be trucked away to allow the school bus to get through.
(Photograph by and courtesy of Keith Bradby)

The decades since the 1982 drought have brought dramatic and on-going challenges to mallee farmers. The first was a cost–price squeeze that economists labelled the 'farm problem'.⁵ This had become urgent in the 1980s as

---

3   R.L. Amor *et al.*, 'Changing Research and Extension Priorities in North-West Victoria as Influenced by Trends in Agricultural Systems', Research Project Series, no. 215 (Victoria: Department of Agriculture and Rural Affairs, August 1985).
4   Keith Bradby and Andrea Gaynor, 'Draft History of WA Landcare' (unpublished manuscript, 2018), 4.
5   L.R. Malcolm and A.G. Lloyd, 'Agriculture in the Economy', in *Agriculture in Victoria*, eds D.J. Connor and D.F. Smith (Melbourne: Australian Institute of Agricultural Science, 1987), 23–5.

wheat growers, including those on mallee country, faced the problem of rising prices for farm inputs, such as capital, labour and materials, in the context of declining prices for farm products. From the late 1960s to the mid-1980s prices received by farmers declined by over one-fifth while the prices they paid increased by over a fifth. Farmers tried to increase productivity. Economists at the Australian Bureau of Agricultural and Resource Economics (ABARES) tracked productivity using data from individual farms and sophisticated econometric modelling. They found a general success story. Across Australia farm productivity grew annually from the late 1970s through to the mid-1990s, with most of this change taking place in the period from 1987 to 1994 owing to greater use of fertilisers, earlier cropping and specialisation in cropping.[6]

The second challenge has been the rise of neoliberal thinking, which emphasises competition and market forces as the rightful drivers of social and economic activity. While in previous decades, economic policies had provided farmers with some protection from significant market fluctuations, market deregulation from the 1980s, along with the privatisation of services, withdrawal of government funding and extension services, and the closure of state-supported research stations—all reflective of neoliberal policies—have left individual farmers to manage on their own. Many have formed or joined 'grower groups', providing a platform for research and information exchange.

The third challenge is climate change, which has increased the variability of an already highly variable climate. These challenges led to changes in farm technology, farming practices and farm sizes, as well as the varying population levels of mallee lands. In the face of such challenges mallee farmers negotiated change, striving to make their farms pay, ever alert to the next problem coming their way.

Farmer-led Research and Development

In the post–World War II period, research and development in agricultural industries was primarily government led with a 'top down transfer of technology from experts to farmers'.[7] Ian McClelland, a third-generation Mallee

---

[6] Neal Hughes, Kenton Lawson, and Haydn Valle, *Farm Performance and Climate: Climate-adjusted Productivity for Broadacre Cropping Farms*, Research Report 17.4 (Canberra:, ABARES, May 2017); Regional figures can be found at: https://public.tableau.com/views/Farmperformanceandclimate/REGION?:embed=y&:display_count=yes&:showVizHome=no.

[7] Beena Anil, Matthew Tonts, and Kadambot Siddique, 'Grower Groups and the Transformation of Agricultural Research and Extension in Australia', *Agroecology and Sustainable Food Systems* 39, no. 10 (26 November 2015): 1105.

farmer from Birchip, recalls that the Department of Agriculture employed researchers and extension officers who talked to farmers face to face: 'This is before consultants, and before things like Landmark and Elders had sold herbicides ... Now the Department of Ag. still have researchers, but they have virtually no extension staff'.[8] John Cass, a third-generation farmer in the South Australian Mallee, remembered a two-way relationship with the Department of Agriculture; farmers learnt from its officers, and the officers learnt from farmers. He added that they were good to listen to provided you did not do everything they said, recalling one officer who suggested John run his farm in a consistent manner, doing the same each year and planning ahead. John was unimpressed and replied:

> But the Mallee's different. If you get a big rain early, and everything looks good, you put in 1,500 acres and if your year looks doubtful you put in less, you know, and you can't spend the same amount each year, because one year you'll get a big harvest and the next year you'll get very little.[9]

Different types of farmer-led research and development groups emerged across Australia and developed a greater reach than government officers, who were unable to move across state boundaries.[10] 'Grower groups' ranged in size, but they shared the ambition of increasing the productivity and financial performance of the farms in their region. Their essential activities involved research trials, finding solutions to local needs, and communicating the results of research.[11] There are more than forty grower groups in Western Australia's mallee wheatlands, two of the most significant being the Kondinin Group and the South East Premium Wheat Growers Association (SEPWA). In the east, important groups include the Birchip Cropping Group, and Mallee Sustainable Farmers.

Most groups had small and localised origins. The Kondinin group began in 1955 with a 'kitchen table meeting' of local farmers. Its initial aim was to test machinery, but it grew substantially in the 1990s in response to the

---

8   Ian McClelland, interviewed by Katie Holmes, in Australia's southern mallee lands oral history project, 24 March 2014, National Library of Australia (NLA), http://nla.gov.au/nla.cat-vn6489414.

9   Jan Cass and John Cass, interviewed by Katie Holmes, in Australia's southern mallee lands oral history project, 12 May 2015, NLA, http://nla.gov.au/nla.cat-vn6858516.

10   Anil, Tonts, and Siddique, 'Grower Groups and the Transformation of Agricultural Research and Extension in Australia', 1107.

11   Anil, Tonts, and Siddique, 'Grower Groups and the Transformation of Agricultural Research and Extension in Australia', 1107.

neoliberal withdrawal of state support, spreading eastwards to become one of the most influential grower groups in the country.[12] SEPWA began as a result of a statement by the Australian Wheat Board that the wheat grown in the Esperance Port Area was of poor quality and had a low rating. The group began once 'a few blokes got together to organise a Wheat Quality and Varieties Seminar in July 1993'.[13]

Other groups had similar beginnings, some with a broader focus than better crop yields. Ian McClelland recalled the Birchip Cropping Group stemmed from a farmers' discussion group in 1989. 'At the first meeting one of the farmers here in the group gave everyone a copy of his financial statements for the last five years, and said, "They're yours, take them home". We were all very interested in how people make their money!' This began a discussion about the future for their farms and families. The group was supported by the Department of Agriculture and became incorporated into the Farm Management 500 scheme, founded in the early 1990s and extending into NSW and South Australia. Members of the Birchip group began trials to overcome the lack of research on their local area and the low performance of its red-brown earth. They raised $50,000 and held a field day that attracted five hundred people. The group employed its first manager in 1993 and became the Birchip Cropping Group. It now employs twenty staff, conducts research, runs field days, expos and extension activities, and seeks to communicate research relevant for its members. Ian McClelland, the group's chairman for two decades, maintained its key motivation was always about the health of the community: 'we wanted our schools to be full, and supermarkets … and we decided that the best way was to get farmers to be prosperous so they could stay on the farm. We didn't want to play tennis on our own'.[14]

The research model of larger grower groups, including the Birchip Cropping Group and Mallee Sustainable Farming, is based on partnerships with researchers from CSIRO, universities, state departments, and also the federally based Grains Research and Development Corporation. The grower groups generally

---

12   Mark Casey and Donald Cameron, 'Understanding the Kondinin Group Phenomenon—A Study of an Innovative Farmer Organisation', in *Proceedings of the 18th International Farm Management Congress*, vol. 1 (Methven, Canterbury, New Zealand: International Farm Management Association, 2011), 442.

13   SEPWA, 'SEPWA's History', accessed 27 April 2018, http://www.sepwa.org.au/about/about-sepwa/history.

14   McClelland, interview.

drive the research, and the traditional research organisations are participants.[15] Field days remain popular grower group extension activities. Farmers value local research performed by high-profile grower organisations above that of major research bodies such as CSIRO.[16] Indeed the desire for research specific to their area was the motivation of those who established the Birchip Cropping Group. These groups are a creative response to the withdrawal of government support but do not conduct (as state-sponsored researchers did) blue sky or pure research, which can produce unexpected and positive outcomes.

Neoliberal ideas underpinned the closure of state-run research facilities. The shutting of the Victorian Mallee Research Station at Walpeup in 2009 ended seventy-seven years of operation. In Western Australia the Newdegate Research Station closed in 2009, while Salmon Gums station had been winding down since 1986. Rolf Meeking from Hyden observed wryly that staff once

Figure 12.2: A group of farmers listen intently at a Birchip Cropping Group's Filling the GAPP program, 2015. GAPP (growth, adoption, production and profit) was an initiative of BCG with the Victorian government to bring together young farmers to explore ways of increasing productivity and profitability through agronomic management.
(Photograph by and courtesy of Linda Walters)

---

15   Rick S. Llewellyn, 'Information Quality and Effectiveness for More Rapid Adoption Decisions by Farmers', *Field Crops Research* 104, no. 1 (1 October 2007): 153.
16   Llewellyn, 'Information Quality and Effectiveness for More Rapid Adoption Decisions by Farmers', 155.

employed by the different state Departments of Agriculture became private consultants charging farmers for advice they formerly gave for free. Younger staff who remained lacked the necessary experience, and their research sometimes failed to meet farmers' needs. Bob Schilling, a third-generation farmer from Rainbow in Victoria, believes the shift from state-funded extension officers to privately employed agronomists has been a positive one. The Department of Agriculture's staff were good 'but it wasn't intense enough'. Agronomists 'cost money but it's worth it because you don't have to make mistakes … I don't believe that any farmer can today understand and know what all the different chemicals are and what they do and everything. It's just so complicated'.[17] George Gum, a third-generation farmer near Pinnaroo in SA, was sanguine about the privatisation of services and the deregulation of the industry. He thought the Walpeup Research Station in particular had been fantastic. Now, in relation to research 'you want it, you pay for it, basically'. He used the example of seed to demonstrate an impact of deregulation. Once you bought your seed from a registered seed grower, sowed it and kept your own seed. Now, you still buy your seed from a grower, 'you plant it and you're allowed to keep your own, but everything you sell from that day onwards, you're paying $1, $2, $3 a ton back to whoever bred it, forever. Forever. Some of them are $3.80 a ton, it's a lot of money'.[18]

Depopulation: Bigger Farms and Smaller Communities

Anxiety around depopulation stalks many rural communities, especially those in semi-arid areas. While there has been a drift to the city for a hundred years, the most significant factor in rural town depopulation has been the growth in farm size. Stephen Hooper and Caroline Levantis from ABARES reported that across the Victorian and South Australian mallee lands the average size of specialist grain farms increased from about 1,750 hectares in the 1980s to 2,375 hectares in the early 2000s.[19] In Victoria, the towns of Hopetoun and

---

17   Bob Schilling and Shirley Schilling, interviewed by Katie Holmes, in Australia's southern mallee lands oral history project, 9 June 2014, NLA, http://nla.gov.au/nla.cat-vn6578385.

18   George Gum, interviewed by Katie Holmes, in Australia's southern mallee lands oral history project, 14 May 2015, NLA, https://nla.gov.au/nla.cat-vn6858657.

19   Stephen Hooper and Caroline Levantis, *Physical and Financial Performance Benchmarks for Grain Producing Farms, South Australia and Victoria Mallee Agroecological Zone: ABARES Report Prepared for the Grains Research and Development Corporation, Canberra, February 2011* (Canberra: ABARES, 2011). These figures are interpolated from chart C, page 9.

Sea Lake declined by 10 per cent while Birchip and Ouyen recorded more steady population growth. Social researcher Neil Barr has drawn on a century of rural population records to estimate that in 'each farmer's working lifetime, the number of farms will halve'.[20] Russell Hilton observed that

> farmers are fundamentally in competition with their neighbor to buy the third neighbour out … So in the long run [the farmer] has to make smarter moves, work harder and grow better crops than his neighbor and if that happens in the long run he'll be the one able to buy his neighbor out … It's sort of a slow motion form of chess.[21]

The same applied to Western Australia. Anne Rick from Newdegate observed wryly that the process of neighbours buying out neighbours 'has been going on forever'. When she and her husband moved onto their new land block in the 1980s there were eight farms. Now there are three.[22] Rolf and Sue Meeking's Hyden farm has doubled in size to eight thousand hectares since 1977. Rolf noted that farm aggregation has 'been an ongoing process since my grandfather was here'.[23] The population of Newdegate and Salmon Gums plummeted by 61 and 76 per cent respectively between 2006 and 2016. Lake Grace and Hyden fared better, with slight population increases in the same period—an example of what is known as the 'sponge city' phenomenon, whereby larger regional centres gain populations at the expense of smaller ones. South Australia's Murray Mallee recorded minor population increases in the towns of Loxton and Lameroo and a slight decline in Pinnaroo.[24]

The causes of increasing farm size, driving depopulation, are multiple, but most significant is the pressure to increase productivity and profit margins in a competitive global market in which commodity prices fluctuate while the cost of 'inputs'—seed, chemicals, fuel, machinery—continue to rise. At the heart of productivity increases are technological innovation and the purchase of bigger machinery for bigger farms. More sophisticated machinery requires less labour, leading to fewer jobs in rural areas. Economies of scale

---

20 Neil Barr, *The House on the Hill: The Transformation of Australia's Farming Communities* (Canberra: Halstead Press, 2009), 11.
21 Russell Hilton, interviewed by Katie Holmes, in Australia's southern mallee lands oral history project, 10 June 2014, NLA, https://nla.gov.au/nla.cat-vn6578387.
22 Anne Rick, interviewed by Andrea Gaynor, Newdegate, 2 December 2015.
23 Rolf and Sue Meeking, interviewed by Andrea Gaynor, Hyden, 3 December 2015.
24 Information taken from Australian Bureau of Statistics 'QuickStats' website, accessed 1 September 2018, http://www.abs.gov.au/websitedbs/D3310114.nsf/Home/2016%20QuickStats. Because the area boundaries used for each location change from census to census, these results are ultimately a rough estimate.

mean that the practice of no-till (discussed below) has been accompanied by a move to larger farms and industrial-scale agriculture. A larger farm justifies bigger machinery and enables a farmer to economise on labour costs. Helen Ballentine, who runs a farm with her husband and sons near Hopetoun in the Victorian Mallee, noted that 'It's a catch 22. If you want bigger acres you need bigger machinery. If you want bigger machinery, you need a bigger income. So therefore, you tend to think that you'll get a bigger income from more acres'.[25] No-till equipment is expensive with the outlay for seeders, headers and sprayers coming close to AUD$1,000,000. Those with larger farms have a greater capacity to borrow money to fund land and machinery purchases and so grow bigger, further squeezing out the smaller farmers. But bigger machinery has an environmental impact; larger machines call for bigger paddocks—meaning fewer windbreaks—more clearing of fencelines, the widening of roads, and clearing along them. It has not been an environmentally benign development.

The challenges and uncertainties of farming dissuade many sons and daughters from a farming future, the next generation opting instead for more stable incomes in urban or regional centres. This exodus began generations ago, and education has increasingly offered children a ticket off the family farm. Some farming couples actively discouraged their offspring from staying on the land, not wishing on them the vicissitudes of a farming life. Sue Meeking remarked: 'It's too hard'. Another farmer laughed, 'if you leave your son a farm he's liable to sue you for child abuse'.[26] For those with offspring who wish to stay, the purchase of additional land helps ensure a viable holding for multiple families. Many of those who remain farm land their great grandfathers selected, their identity firmly built around generations of stories told about their place.

A declining population has precipitated other changes in a dance of cause and effect. Governments have centralised their services and withdrawn public servants from townships. Banks similarly have closed their doors in smaller towns and withdrawn from local community involvement. Residents have exacerbated some of these changes, driving to larger towns to shop. Fewer services mean fewer jobs, fewer families mean dwindling school numbers and the closure of local schools. Local football teams, once the centre of community activity and the focus of intense loyalty and proud inter-town rivalry, merge with teams they once sought to annihilate on the footy field,

---

25 Helen Ballentine, interviewed by Katie Holmes, in Australia's southern mallee lands oral history project, 9 June 9 2014, NLA, http://nla.gov.au/nla.cat-vn6578384.

26 Quoted in *A Million Acres a Year*, directed by Frank Rijavec (Sydney: Snakewood films, 2002), video recording.

a core of the town's identity thus radically altered. As women increasingly take off-farm work to bring in an income to help support their families, the unpaid labour that frequently wove the social fabric of a community together has changed. In a number of towns, the annual agricultural show, another celebration of local identity and the proud display of local productivity and agricultural prowess, has faltered for want of organisers. Ageing residents often lack the health and ability to carry the leadership roles they once held, and many move to larger regional centres.

In 2006 the *Age* newspaper ran an article on the Victorian Mallee town of Patchewollock, known locally as 'Patche'. The population of 150 could no longer support the Easter Sports Meeting, a highlight of the social and sports calendar. Public liability insurance was the nail in the coffin, but resident Brian O'Sullivan also commented that 'the people who were running it were getting older and older, and the few young ones left don't seem to be interested in doing these things any more'. Like other small towns Patche was struggling. Its primary school was closing, and only 'sepia photos' now reminded the town of its football team. But the pub remained. Publican Janet Torney noted that 'Patche's got the same problem as any other small town. Not enough people and not enough to keep them here'.[27] But small towns suit some people. Ash Summerhayes, a fourth-generation farmer from Berriwillock, who attended the town's school until it closed in 1993, observed that small towns like his have certain advantages over larger towns as they have a stronger community spirit. But he envisages a future in which younger farmers live in the larger town of Swan Hill and commute to the farm, a choice increasing numbers are already making.[28]

As populations plummet and house prices fall, so the complexion of townships alters. Attracted by the opportunity to buy a home for a price undreamed of in urban centres, people looking for the security of home ownership, or low rents, have moved in. Some of these, such as Laura O'Dwyer, have brought welcome energy to her chosen town of Quambatook in Victoria, or 'Quamby' as it is locally known. Laura moved in 2006 and has since become actively involved in town activities, including running the Quambatook Silo Cinema, which uses the silos as a screen. The monthly screenings of Australian movies bring people from as far away as South Australia and NSW, inspiring singer John Williamson to declare that he was 'so proud of my dear little birth town

---

27 'Mallee Battlers at Least Can Still Drown Sorrows', *Age*, 17 April 2006, accessed 15 August 2018, https://www.theage.com.au/national/mallee-battlers-at-least-can-still-drown-sorrows-20060417-ge2579.html.

28 Ash Summerhayes, interviewed by Karen Twigg, Berriwillock, 7 May 2018. See also Barr, *House on the Hill*, 126.

of Quambatook'.[29] The role of the arts and culture in sustaining mallee communities is discussed further in Chapter 13. The arrival of Michael White in the tiny South Australian town of Mantung was a substantial boost to its population of seven. Michael bought and is restoring the long-closed general store, preserving a small piece of South Australian Mallee history.[30]

Not all newcomers bring such welcome energy and vision. Social welfare policies and inadequate incomes force families, many of which need care, into failing towns where rents are cheap but support services are unavailable. Some long-term residents express concern that such newcomers will generate social problems. In 2008 Wycheproof, a town on the southern edge of the Victorian Mallee, offered two empty farmhouses for rent at one dollar a week and set up a five-member selection panel to shortlist suitable applicants. They were looking for people prepared to make a long-term commitment to the town.[31] The search for economic diversification is one that characterises many declining mallee communities.

Other developments are shaping population changes. Increasing numbers of farmers are choosing to live closer to schools and services in town, and to 'commute' to their farms, just as Charles Coote had done in the early decades of settlement. And, like Coote, many farmers rely on off-farm investments to carry them over lean years and keep their farming enterprises viable. Corporate ownership of farms is also increasing in mallee country, as in other parts of Australia. Companies such as Lawson Grains, Warakirri and Hassad own large landholdings in Western Australia and Victoria. They are joined by national and international superannuation funds and a number of international agricultural companies with holdings in mallee lands, including Swiss-owned Glencore Grain and Chinese-owned Heilongjiang Feng Agricultural.[32] Such

---

29 ABC Radio, *Australia Wide*, 30 April 2018, accessed 17 August 2018, http://www.abc.net.au/radio/programs/australia-wide/australia-wide-small-rural-towns-are-not-economically-viable/9689790; John Williamson, 'Quambatook Silo Cinema', last modified 10 November 2017, accessed 17 August 2018, http://johnwilliamson.com.au/true-blue-news/quambatook-silo-cinema/.

30 ABC Radio, 'Gone Mallee Part Three: The Mantung Yearbook', *The History Listen—ABC RN*, broadcast 21 August 2018, http://www.abc.net.au/radionational/programs/the-history-listen/gone-mallee-part-three-the-mantung-yearbook/9768044.

31 See Mex Cooper, 'Wycheproof is Hot Property', *Age*, 15 July 2009, accessed 22 October 2018, https://www.smh.com.au/national/wycheproof-is-hot-property-20090715-dl72.html.

32 See *Weekly Times*, 23 May 2018, 4, accessed 22 October 2018, https://www.weeklytimesnow.com.au/agribusiness/who-owns-australias-farms-nations-biggest-landholders-revealed/news-story/e314bb8e11ee4b95ca50e518f0aafef3.

changes reflect a broader story of market deregulation, the privatisation of services and a neoliberal shift that privileges the activity of 'the market' over state- or community-owned enterprises. While such thinking might be the antithesis of what many in rural communities believe or want, the transformations in farming and the rural townships that agricultural industry supports are inescapably enmeshed in such changes.

No-till

The adoption of no-till techniques has revolutionised farming across the mallee lands, some referring to it as the saviour of mallee farming. The term 'no-till' refers to the absence of cultivation to remove weeds and prepare the ground prior to sowing a crop. However, it has assumed a complex set of other meanings, most particularly concerning how up to date farmers may be, their 'responsibility' in farming to control for soil drift, and their willingness to adapt to changing technologies. The no-till system uses chemicals, primarily glyphosate (Roundup), for weed control.

No-till cropping is part of what is known as 'conservation agriculture'. The term itself is value laden, implying that those who do not farm in this way are not interested in soil 'conservation'. The practice of conservation agriculture is dependent on herbicide use, machinery able to sow into undisturbed soil and through mulch residue, and broadleaf rotation crops such as lupins, peas and canola. No-till has brought dramatic changes to farming across the mallee lands, maintaining productivity in the face of declining growing-season rainfall (see further discussion below), and improving soil health. Leaving the stubble of the previous crop in the ground has all but removed soil drift and the dust storms that plagued the mallee lands. The build-up of humus has improved the structure of the soil, the soil retains more moisture and worms have returned.

In mallee lands, cultivating the soil during the summer months outside the growing season was a key strategy of weed control. Widely adopted in the 1920s, the system of bare fallowing involved repeated cultivation of the soil, but by the 1930s it was seen as responsible for the devastating soil drift and dust storms that plagued the eastern mallee. As discussed in Chapter 10, experimentation with no-till began in Western Australia in the 1970s and became widely adopted in the 1980s. Rolf Meeking was amongst the early practitioners. He started 'mucking around' with no-till in the 1980s in an attempt to grow lupins more successfully. He adapted his own machinery and started making good money. Economic factors played their part as well.

Figure 12.3: A field of stubble near Luxton, South Australia, 2015. In the 'no-till' system, stubble from the previous harvest is left and the next crop sown in between the rows. (Photograph by and courtesy of Richard Broome)

Rick Llewellyn remarked that the tipping point for many eastern mallee farmers to adopt no-till was the drop in the price of glyphosate relative to diesel.[33] But some recall other factors. Victorian Mallee farmers travelled to South Australia to look at no-till in action, but it was not until developments in machinery, especially seeders able to cope with the thicker Victorian stubble and different soil types, that they began to adopt no-till techniques. The hard soils of the Victorian Mallee also bent the steel of the American machines; improving the strength of the steel aided the uptake of no-till. Weeds played their part too; the higher summer rainfall in the east made summer weeds such as heliotrope, melons and skeleton weeds a significant problem. Winter weeds such as rye grass and the prostrate brome grass remained an impediment until pre-emergence herbicides such as trifluralin became registered for use. Such developments in machinery and in-crop herbicides made the uptake of no-till techniques more viable.[34]

---

33   Rick S. Llewellyn, Frank H. D'Emden, and Geoff Kuehne, 'Extensive Use of No-Tillage in Grain Growing Regions of Australia', *Field Crops Research* 132 (June 2012): 205.

34   John Cooke, long-term Mallee resident, botanist and deputy chair of the Mallee Catchment Management Authority, in discussion with Katie Holmes, 7 September 2018.

Farmers express relief that no-till has effectively removed the anxiety surrounding drift and feel that they are caring for their soil more adequately than previously. Ian McClelland compares the Federation drought of 1902 when farms 'nearly blew away' to the recent Millennium drought when 'virtually nothing had blown away at all because farmers changed their system'. Bob Schilling concurs; no-till has made a 'fantastic difference to the way we farm, and looking after the soil, that is the main thing'. As Bob notes of the recurring dry years that characterised the Millennium drought, 'these dry years, we know we would not have grown the crops we have without doing it that way'. By using GPS-guided machinery farmers keep their seeders, sprayers and harvesters all travelling the same tracks, reducing the area compacted by the wheels. 'Controlled traffic', as this is called, also enables farmers to deliver fertilisers and herbicides to crops within a two-centimetre degree of accuracy. Farmers use yield maps to determine which area of a paddock is producing well and which areas require more 'inputs' to lift their game.

The widespread uptake of no-till has also marked significant changes in farm management. Most farmers using no-till employ private agronomists to advise on when and what to sow, how much fertiliser to use, and where, when and what to spray. They have ceded a significant amount of knowledge about their farm to external consultants and are now reliant on them for guiding decision-making on the farm. Agronomists have helped farmers re-imagine their farms as businesses rather than a way of life. Bob Schilling reflected on the change:

> they say you've got to run the farm as a business. I s'pose we've always tried to. But in the old days farming was just a way of life 'n you knew nothing else 'n you did it the way you were taught and perhaps improvised a bit on the way and hopefully it worked. Well it did work but it's just so much better now.[35]

Agricultural scientist John Kirkegaard waxed lyrical about the changes brought about through conservation agriculture and 'precision agriculture': the capacity of farmers to manage their fields down to centimetre accuracy, controlled traffic, zone management and in-crop sensing to improve farming systems' efficiency and sustainability.[36] The modernist language of science,

---

35   Bob Schilling, interview.
36   John Kirkegaard, 'From Dust Bowls to Food Bowls: Australia's Conservation Farming Revolution', *The Conversation*, 11 April 2012, accessed 10 December 2017, http://theconversation.com/from-dust-bowls-to-food-bowls-australias-conservation-farming-revolution-6020.

efficiency and progress that the Better Farming Train had carried along its tracks in the 1920s is now being employed to advocate for a very different style of farming. But the belief in science as holding the answers to the challenges of mallee farming remains.

Anne Rick observed that these changes have increased farm work pressures. Increasingly sophisticated, highly mechanised equipment allows farmers to sow and crop through the night. They store their own grain (in mouse-proof storage facilities) and manage its sale. Newdegate farmer Sue Hall reflected: 'We used to be just farmers growing things. Now we've got to market our own grain … you've got to live it and breathe it 24/7'.[37]

The family farm, still prevalent across mallee lands, is notable for the flexible management it enables, allowing farmers to respond quickly to new developments or rapidly changing conditions. Family farms contain generational knowledge but they also include tensions. Generational differences are frequently apparent in attitudes to no-till. Young farmers can be inpatient with the more conservative approach to farming of their parents. Older farmers express concern that their farming sons do not have the same knowledge of or relationship with the soil or the land as they did, that it is now all filtered through scientific language and data. They even fear that the climate-controlled enclosed cabins of the machines remove them from the smell and feel of the soil they work—a relationship important to older farmers who knew the health of the soil through its smell.[38] They worry about the reliance on external experts and the relinquishing of hard-won—often generational—knowledge that it implies. Many also expressed concern about the amount of chemicals used in the no-till regime: 'Are we poisoning the Mallee?' John Cass wondered in an interview.[39] He was not the only one—concern about drift has been replaced by worry over excessive chemical use. Lindsay Slarke from Lake Grace, whose son now farms the land Lindsay's father farmed, observed that chemical farming is 'the only way to go but we all wonder how much chemical we can keep putting in the ground. It's a never-ending question'.[40]

At the same time, older farmers express a sense of wonder at the advances in agriculture that they have witnessed and are all too aware of the pressures

---

37　Sue Hall, interviewed by Andrea Gaynor, Newdegate, 2 December 2015.
38　Twigg, Karen, '"Another Weed Will Come Along": Attitudes to Weeds, Land and Community in the Victorian Mallee', in *Telling Environmental History: Intersections of Memory, Narrative and Environment*, eds Katie Holmes and Heather Goodall (Cham, Switzerland: Palgrave Macmillan, 2017), 220.
39　John Cass, interview.
40　Lindsay Slarke, interviewed by Andrea Gaynor, Lake Grace, 30 November 2015.

under which their children work and the massive debts many carry, even as they shake their heads at the gigantic computer on wheels that the standard farm machine has become. Farmers young and old express other concerns about the no-till regime, in particular the growing awareness of herbicide-resistant weeds. While farmers may employ strategies to reduce the risk of resistant weeds developing, for most it is a constant struggle to stay a step ahead of the ever-evolving and adapting weeds. Ian McClelland is confident that something else will be developed to control resistant weeds: 'there'll be life after herbicides … there'll be something else that will develop. Already people are doing these mechanical things to kill weeds rather than spraying them'. One such mechanical invention is the Harrington Seed Destructor, which pulverises weed seeds during harvesting and can be integrated with headers. Some farmers have trialled the burning of stubble in an attempt to rid their land of the seeds of herbicide-resistant weeds. But returning to burning of stubbles or physically cultivating the soil creates significant environmental concern such as exposing the soil surface to erosion, loss of valuable nutrients, reducing soil organic matter and releasing CO_2.[41]

Organic and Regenerative Farming

A handful of farmers across mallee lands have sought alternatives to chemically charged no-till farming, choosing to employ organic or reduced-chemical techniques and to develop soil health in other ways. Malcolm Kelly and his son Nick, who farm near Newdegate, dislike being 'chained' to a boom spray. Nick commented that 'the more I sprayed the weeds the worse they seemed to get. I realised that we had to change what we were doing to find a better way'. Nick tried to replicate the principles he saw in the natural environment in the paddock: 'I climbed over the fence and saw what was going on there. Saw the huge amount of biomass that was growing there … At the same time I was connected with people from all over the world who were getting the same kind of revelation'. The principles Nick adopted involved keeping

---

41 For the use of burning in weed control, see: Western Australia, Department of Primary Industries and Regional Development, 'Crop Weeds: Reduce Weed Seed Numbers in the Soil', accessed 5 November 2018, https://www.agric.wa.gov.au/grains-research-development/crop-weeds-reduce-weed-seed-numbers-soil?page=0%2C1. Some farmers also choose to burn in the belief that stubble slows down seeding operations: Grains Research and Development Corporation, 'The Burning Issue of Stubble Cover', accessed 5 November 2018, https://grdc.com.au/resources-and-publications/groundcover/ground-cover-supplements/ground-cover-issue-63-growers-sharing-knowledge-supplement/the-burning-issue-of-stubble-cover.

'cover on the ground, all the time, preferably growing. Minimal soil disturbance. Diversity. An understory and diverse things growing all the time. No monocultures. It's rare to find a monoculture in nature'. The Kellys have pioneered the growing of summer cover-crops, with French White Millet as the main species, and are trialling winter perennials. Nick now understands his approach as one of 'regenerative agriculture', drawing on the influential book by Charles Massey, *Call of the Reed Warbler*.[42]

In South Australia at Taplan, south east of Loxton, John and Jenny Schwarz began farming organically in the early 1990s after chemical exposure was creating health problems in the family. They farmed their property organically for twenty years, after which Josh and Peri McIntosh joined them in the enterprise. In their organic system, weeds are a friend rather than a foe, providing nutrients for the soil, nitrogen and carbon build-up, and food for their livestock. With a two-year break between crops, they crop on a three-year rotation, reducing their potential yields, but also reducing their risk.[43] Organic products bring premium prices, a point Justin and Rita Porker make in discussing their organic farm near Marama in South Australia, east of Tailem Bend. Like John Schwarz, Justin believed the health issues he was suffering were due in part to the chemicals he was using on the farm. The Porkers now grow wheat, rye and barley, and produce lamb, duck, geese and chicken.[44]

Across the Victorian border in Murrayville Barry Edwards is also running a 2,250-hectare organic and biodynamic farm with his son Blake. Their philosophy 'is about farming with nature and complementing natural cycles, rather than using chemicals to drive productivity and solve problems ... It's really about trusting what nature does and the natural soil partners'. The Edwards use a system of fallowing but do not have a problem with erosion. Unlike their neighbours who practise no-till farming, the Edwards only crop every second year. Their yields are smaller, but they have half the input

---

42   Malcolm Kelly and Nick Kelly, interviewed by Andrea Gaynor, Newdegate, 1 December 2015. See also NutriSoils podcast, 'Episode 7—Building a Holistic Regenerative Farming System with Nick and Lucy Kelly', posted 11 July 2018, https://nutrisoil.com.au/episode-7-building-a-holistic-regenerative-farming-system-with-nick-and-lucy-kelly/; Charles Massey, *Call of the Reed Warbler: A New Agriculture, a New Earth*, (Brisbane: University of Queensland Press, 2017).

43   Sarah Johnson, 'Organic Farming in the Mallee: Making a Dream Come True', *SANTFA: The Cutting Edge* (Summer 2016): 12–16.

44   Catherine Miller, 'Mallee Lamb Brand Hits Mark', *Stock Journal*, 15 June 2016, accessed 8 September 2018, http://www.stockjournal.com.au/story/3948392/mallee-lamb-brand-hits-mark/.

costs. Like other organic farmers, they carry sheep, although mainly for weed control. Organic farming across mallee lands is the exception rather than the rule, but those who practise it believe passionately in the value of their approach for their own health and that their families and customers, as well as the land they work.[45]

Disappearing Sheep

Mixed farming characterised mallee agriculture for much of the twentieth century. Sheep—sold for wool or as prime lambs—could provide a source of income when wheat yields or prices were low. Ian Wurfels of Brim observed that when the wheat crop failed there was always wool in the shed to sell.[46] But, as organic farmers have realised, sheep have other benefits, including helping to fertilise the soil and control the weeds, frequently eating them right out of existence. However, overall, sheep have played less of a role in mallee farms in the early twenty-first century. By the mid-2000s specialist grain producers cropped over 60 per cent of their holdings, and among the best-performing mixed cropping and livestock farms the area sown increased to about 50 per cent. The result of this was a decline in sheep numbers.[47] In the western mallee lands similar intensification occurred.[48]

The decline in sheep numbers has changed farm management and the configuration of farms. Fences built to keep sheep contained posed an unwelcome restriction to the movement of the ever-larger machines used in no-till farming. The compaction and roughing of the soil that is part and parcel of running sheep was similarly seen as discordant with a no-till farming regime. Increasingly sheep came to be seen as incompatible with no-till. Across mallee lands farmers removed their fences, opened up their paddocks and sold off

---

45   Jacinta Gange, 'Biodynamic Farming in Murrayville', *Mallee Farmer*, Edition 09 (Winter 2015): 6–7, accessed 8 September 2018, https://issuu.com/malleecma/docs/mallee_farmer_edition_09.

46   Ian Wurfels, in conversation with Katie Holmes and Richard Broome, Brim, 25 March 2014.

47   See Hooper and Levantis, *Physical and Financial Performance Benchmarks*, see chart C, pages 10, 11, 12.

48   See Hooper and Levantis, *Physical and Financial Performance Benchmarks*. Long-term sheep numbers are not available from ABARES for the malllee region of Western Australia. In ABARES Northern and Eastern Wheatbelt District sheep numbers have declined by around 40 per cent since 1990. See Australia, Department of Agriculture and Water Resources, ABARES, 'Farm Survey Data', accessed 9 November 2018, http://agriculture.gov.au/abares/research-topics/surveys/farm-survey-data.

their sheep. Unused shearing sheds, water troughs and farms gates remind us that not so long ago this landscape carried other forms of life.

Changing conditions and recent research have, however, led a number of farmers to revisit the compatibility of sheep—or other livestock—with no-till. The Millennium drought in the East, 2010 in the West, and the very dry year of 2015 brought home to farmers their economic vulnerability when crops were their only income. In the context of increasing climate variability, sheep offer some protection against the vicissitudes of the weather. And, as health concerns related to herbicide use and problems with herbicide-resistant weeds increase, sheep offer an alternative, non-chemical, form of weed control. Recent research conducted in collaboration with CSIRO and a number of farmer groups, including the Western Australian No-tillage Farmers Association and the Birchip Cropping Group, suggests that light grazing from sheep has 'no significant effect on the amount of residue, soil properties, soil water, weeds or yield in the following crop. The main effect of grazing was to knock down and scatter the standing crop residues'.[49] The widespread belief that sheep lead to the significant compaction of soil was not upheld, at least not in light grazing conditions. Farmers who have kept their sheep will no doubt welcome such research.

For those who have removed their fences, the development of 'virtual fencing' whereby 'technology uses coordinates, wireless technologies and sensors to control the location of livestock without the need for an actual fence' offers an alternative.[50] With this system, the location of 'virtual fences' is set and a number of animals fitted with collars that send a mild electric shock if they cross the 'fence'. The rest of the mob keep in tow. Whether mallee farmers who have got rid of their sheep decide to reinvest remains to be seen. What is apparent from oral history interviews is that few farmers express much grief about the loss of sheep from their farms; an air-conditioned tractor cab is far more inviting than crutching sheep. Many younger farmers seem to dislike livestock and want to be able to leave their farms over summer—sheep demand on-going labour. It seems a highly personal choice. As Kerry Conway, a former sheep farmer herself, observed: 'You either like sheep or you don't. People will justify their decision

---

49   Grains Research and Development Corporation, 'Study Shows Sheep and No-till Can Coexist', *Ground Cover* (August 2016), accessed 27 April 2018, https://grdc.com.au/resources-and-publications/groundcover/ground-cover-issue-123-julyaugust-2016/study-shows-sheep-and-no-till-can-coexist.

50   CSIRO 'Virtual Fencing', accessed 27 April 2018, https://www.csiro.au/en/Research/AF/Areas/Animal-Science/Animal-Health-Welfare/Virtual-fencing.

to keep or sell them on the basis of so-called evidence, but it comes down to a personal preference'.[51]

Mick Evans likes sheep, and his property near Mantung in South Australia is primarily grazing country, the stony ground unsuited to cropping. He would much prefer to be looking after sheep than spending time sitting on a tractor. Nor does he want the cycle of sustaining maximum debt to achieve maximum profits that the cropping farmers take on, although he admires the farmers who can manage that challenge. Unlike the farmers getting out of sheep, Mick is erecting more fencing and adding watering points to existing paddocks because sheep lose condition if they have to walk too far to get water. Mick balances sheep farming with a strong conservation ethic, a philosophy he inherited from his grandfather, father and uncle, whose vision for the property included preserving uncleared sections for conservation. They were early applicants for heritage protection on a block of their land with remnant bush, ensuring it could not be cleared, grazed or cropped and thereby protecting the resident malleefowl. 'They were SO passionate about it', observed Mick, and they wanted to ensure it would be there for generations to come. Mick Evans's vision is to leave the land in better condition than he found it: 'I want my girls' kids … to be able to come back here and see some of what it used to be like, not just paddocks of nothing … It's more trying to master living with the country not fighting against it'. But, he laughs: 'there's times when you do fight'.[52]

Landcare

Mick Evans's interest in conservation may have been unusual in his grandfather and father's generations, but it became more mainstream in the 1980s with the development of the first formal Landcare initiative. The long-standing concern for soil conservation saw the formation of a number of local groups dedicated to action around pressing conservation issues. Indeed, farmer-led initiatives in the early 1980s in Western Australia (see Chapter 10) prefigured the development of Landcare groups.[53]

Landcare began as a Victorian scheme in 1986, set up by the state's minister for conservation, forests and lands, Joan Kirner, in collaboration with

---

51 Kerry Conway, in discussion with Katie Holmes, Hopetoun, 3 December 2016.
52 Michael Evans and Suzanne Evans, interviewed by Katie Holmes, in Australia's southern mallee lands oral history project, 13 May 2015, https://nla.gov.au/nla.cat-vn6858637.
53 Bradby and Gaynor, 'Draft History of WA Landcare', 10.

the Victorian Farmers Federation. They created a community-based, multi-disciplinary program aimed at reversing the environmental damage evident across the state and developing sustainable practices of land management. The success of the Victorian program sparked federal government interest, and in 1990 Landcare went national. The 'Decade of Landcare' was born, with bipartisan support and $340,000,000 in funding. Landcare became both a government-funded initiative and a community movement. The term refers to both an approach to land management and the numerous groups around the country that practise 'landcare'. The Landcare ethos, or ethic, is summarised as 'an attitude or understanding by people from all backgrounds about everyone being responsible for caring for natural resources—land, water and vegetation—for the long term'.[54]

Landcare developed in the context of increasing national and international concern about the destruction of the natural environment. In Australia land degradation became a particular, and urgent, focus of anxiety. The Australian Broadcasting Commission's TV series *Heartlands* brought the serious nature of land degradation to a national audience. Filmed in early 1983 when the country was still in the grip of major drought, the presenter Dean Graetz, a child of the South Australian Mallee and a CSIRO scientist, had a simple message: only 10 per cent of Australia's land mass was arable land—land needed to feed the nation's population and build its wealth—and poor farming practices were destroying it. This was everyone's concern. Graetz's message echoed that of the 1944 film *Mallee Country Facing Drought*, which forecast the loss of national prosperity if action was not taken to halt the loss of topsoil (see Chapter 7). In *Heartlands*, Graetz crouched on the ground with a handful of top soil and warned: 'This topsoil is all we've got to sustain our dreams. This topsoil is linked to our future. If through indifference or lack of concern we allow that to be lost, then our society will be lost also. That's the choice we have'.[55]

Taking its cue from Western Australia and Victoria, the South Australian government formed a State Management Committee for the Year of Landcare in 1989. Like its neighbouring states, where many of the early Landcare groups were formed by individuals and community groups that had been working on conservation issues for many years, South Australia built on decades of work between government and farmers on soil conservation. This was in keeping with the aims of Landcare, which sought to facilitate community participation,

---

54   Landcare, National Facilitator Project, *Annual Report, 2006–07*, 12.
55   *Heartlands with Dean Graetz, Part 1:Dust*, TV program (Australian Broadcasting Corporation, 1983), accessed 21 August 2018, https://www.youtube.com/watch?v=NzKFpi-okYs.

educate farmers about land management, and instil an ethic of stewardship in their approach to land use.[56]

Landcare brought focus, funding and credibility, not to mention national attention, to a wide range of local conservation issues. With this came a change in attitude. The South Australian publication detailing the history and successes of Landcare, *Signs of Change*, noted: 'People are talking about sustainability without fear of being labelled a "greenie". This change of culture has meant farmers are proud of their landcare activities'.[57] In broadacre farming areas such as mallee country, Landcare groups were instrumental in the 'ten-year revolution' that saw the introduction of conservation farming.[58] The Yeelanna Landcare group on the Eyre Peninsula was involved in a ten-year trial of different management and rotation practices to establish which ones were the most sustainable. Field days, local media and the Agricultural Bureau all helped spread the results of the trials.

In Mantung other issues captured the attention of the local Landcare group. Mike Evans had recently returned to Mantung when the first Landcare-style group formed, and he became its first president. The area had a number of malleefowl sites, which the group was keen to protect. Early work undertaken by the Adelaide Zoo and supported by state government funding was taken over by the Landcare group, which made malleefowl protection its primary focus. Meetings were dominated by discussions of fox baiting and hunting, and rabbit eradication. Evans observes that there is less money available now for these activities, and more red tape, but the group still meets, primarily to organise fox baiting. Mick notes, laughing, that the meetings are sometimes 'a bit like the *Vicar of Dibley*', but they get more things done than the vicar's meetings.[59]

In Victoria the 1993 Mallee Landcare plan set clear priorities for the region, namely soil conservation and salinity.[60] These issues were taken up by Landcare groups across the Mallee. Peter Kelly, who grew up on a dryland farm in the

---

56   For further discussion of the Australian Landcare movement, see Katie Holmes, 'Redeeming Landscapes: Ireland and Australia', in *Exhuming Passions: The Pressure of the Past in Ireland and Australia*, eds Katie Holmes and Stuart Ward (Dublin: Irish Academic Press, 2011), 230–9.

57   Melanie Kitschke (ed.), *Signs of Change: Landcare at Work in SA* (Adelaide: Primary Industries SA, 200-?), 2.

58   Kitschke, *Signs of Change: Landcare at Work in SA*, 4.

59   The *Vicar of Dibley* was a 1990s British sitcom about an English country parish where the vestry meetings took forever and achieved little.

60   Elizabeth Beovich and Scott Jaensch, *Mallee Regional Landcare Plan* (Mildura, Vic.: Landcare Victoria, 1993).

Millewa, became the facilitator of the Millewa–Carwarp Landcare Group, one of the first such groups in the Mallee and with 500 thousand hectares in its range. One of the key activities of the group was the reclamation of 'big blown-out sand hills', which had been so ravaged by wind erosion that no crop would grow on them. About 120 farms and eighty farmers were involved in this rehabilitation work, and the sand dunes now grow crops fence to fence. The group took a 'whole of landscape' approach and was equally concerned with native vegetation loss as a result of soil erosion. Members worked to revegetate public land and brought degraded agricultural land back into production.[61] Rabbit control was another focus, with nineteen action control groups within the larger Landcare cohort. Peter Kelly comments that they were really just neighbours working together; they would have a breakfast or tea to plan their approach, and Peter would invite volunteers from Conservation Volunteers Australia—young women from England and Europe—which was a successful ploy to get young men to come along and fumigate rabbits! Peter's ambition was to make these conservation activities interesting and fun. He held competitions to see who could shoot the most rabbits or foxes, recording the results on a board at the local pub.[62]

Twice a year the group hired a bus to attend field days at Kadina and Lameroo in South Australia to observe their sand-dune management. Then two farmers came up with the idea that they could have a Sunday drive around their own district to see what farmers were doing. In this way local knowledge was extended and used to educate others. Such an approach epitomised one of the key tenets of Landcare: that 'those closest to the action get to direct the action'.[63] This practice worked well in the early years of Landcare, but, as time went on and the government withdrew funding and bureaucratised processes, disenchantment increased.[64] Rolf Meeking recalls that his local Landcare group closed in the mid-2000s because they were sick of the red tape and outside people telling them what to do.

Each Landcare group developed its own mission. In Rainbow, integrated district pest control was a major focus and achievement. At Yaapeet the Landcare

---

61   Kevin Chaplin, 'Happy Birthday Landcare', *Mallee Farmer*, no. 11 (August 2016): 15, accessed 21 August 2018, https://issuu.com/malleecma/docs/full_mallee_farmer_11.

62   Peter Kelly, interviewed by Karen Twigg, Mildura, 23 September 2015.

63   Beovich and Jaensch, *Mallee Regional Landcare Plan*.

64   See: Stewart Lockie and Frank Vanclay (eds), *Critical Landcare*, Key Papers Series 5 (Wagga Wagga, NSW: Charles Sturt University, Centre for Rural Social Research, 1997, 2000); Rob Youl, Sue Marriott and Theo Nabben, *Landcare in Australia* (Wallington, Vic.: SILC and Rob Youl Consulting Pty Ltd, revised ed. 2006).

community created an asset for the area with a town wetland. Murrayville organised a trip to Western Australia in the late 1990s to observe no-till methods and arranged for speakers from other mallee regions to speak to the group. They held field days so that people could see the no-till machinery in action. Glennis McKee from the Murrayville group commented in a special 30-year anniversary tribute to Landcare that these activities 'opened people's eyes and changed farming practices in this district forever'.[65] This sentiment was echoed by the Manangatang group, which also educated members about direct drilling, providing the machinery for farmers to trial without the initial outlay. Salinity was another focus, and members created saltbush plantations to reduce soil salinity in low-lying areas and also undertook considerable revegetation on public land. Lyonel O'Shannassey commented, 'As a group we've done some amazing work as unpaid custodians of a lot of public land. We're very willing but it's very important that it's never taken for granted by the Government'.[66]

Lyonel's point is pertinent. In a neoliberal context Landcare provided a way for the government to harness a huge resource of unpaid labour in order to attend to some significant problems with land degradation, often of former governments' making. In 2008 Landcare became incorporated into a larger federal government approach, 'Caring for our Country'. The move marked a significant reduction in government support for Landcare programs, but the ethos that Landcare espoused, together with the shift in community attitudes it enabled, remains.

Salinity

Landcare groups provided strategies for tackling the growing problem of salinity. This creeping menace, a long-term problem, can take decades to reveal itself and longer to fix. Scientists call salinity the 'Legacy of History', indicating it continues to unfold even as people and governments work to redress it. Dryland salinity across mallee lands has occurred as a result of the clearing of deep-rooted native vegetation, which used most of the rainfall and existed in equilibrium with the water table. Replacement crops with shallow roots use less of the rainfall, causing the water table to rise and with it the underlying salt. In Western Australia the relationship between clearing and salinity was recognised before 1897. Despite this and the establishment of a

---

65   Chaplin, 'Happy Birthday Landcare', 16.
66   Chaplin, 'Happy Birthday Landcare', 17.

'Special Committee on Salinity in Soils' as early as 1924,[67] successive governments vigorously encouraged the clearing of millions of acres of bushland for agricultural development in full knowledge that land and water would become saline (see Chapter 10).

Governments now measure the problem of salinity in terms of productivity. The Western Australian government for example has calculated that the one million hectares of dryland under agriculture severely affected by salinity in the south west of the state has cost 'at least $519 million per year since 2009/10' in lost agricultural production. A further 2.8 to 4.5 million hectares remain under threat.[68]

The cost of salinity can be measured in other ways. The ancient geological history of the land that is exposed as salt rises to the surface reveals the devastating impact that clearing and farming has had on this fragile environment. In the 2002 documentary *A Million Acres a Year*, Keith Bradby observed that 'fifty years of agriculture [undid] three billion years of evolution'. Susanne Dennings, interviewed for the film, commented: 'I look north to dead trees and I look south to dead trees and it's all salinity, they're gradually dying around us'. The problem of salinity points to a massive loss of biodiversity and habitat destruction. It is a problem compounded by struggling farmers who feel compelled to work the land harder in order to try and extract much-needed production from it. The result is country pushed 'until it crashes'.[69] It is not only the country that suffers. Rural infrastructure suffers, along with public and private water resources.[70] Those living in salinity-affected areas have a higher rate of hospitalisation for depression, their mental health perhaps mirroring that of the land around them.[71]

In the 1990s, the Western Australian government began to tackle the salinity problem in a sustained way, developing a Situation Statement and Action Plan. But the political will was short-lived. When the Commonwealth Landcare programs were collapsed into the Rudd government's 'Caring for

---

67   W.E. Wood, 'Increase of Salt in Soil and Streams Following the Destruction of Native Vegetation', *Journal of the Royal Society of Western Australia* 10, no. 7 (1924): 35–47.

68   Western Australia, Department of Primary Industries and Regional Development, 'Dryland Salinity Extent and Impact', accessed 3 September 2018, https://www.agric.wa.gov.au/soil-salinity/dryland-salinity-extent-and-impact.

69   *A Million Acres a Year*, directed by Frank Rijavec.

70   Western Australian Agriculture Authority, *Report Card on Sustainable Natural Resources Use in Agriculture: Status and Trends in the Agricultural Areas of the South-west of Western Australia* (Perth: Western Australia, Department of Agriculture and Food, 2013), 110.

71   Peter C. Speldewinde, Angus Cook, Peter M. Davies and Philip Weinstein, 'A Relationship between Environmental Degradation and Mental Health in Rural Western Australia', *Health & Place* 15, no. 3 (1 September 2009): 880–87.

our Country' program, federal funding for salinity declined steeply, and cooperation between the Western Australian and Commonwealth governments on natural resource management broke down. In Western Australia Colin Barnett's coalition government, elected in 2008, also failed to prioritise salinity, and the old pattern of denial and apathy returned. The magnitude of the salinity problem demands political and community will, and substantial financial investment. Approximately 80 per cent of the south-eastern wheatbelt 'would need to be replanted with deep rooted trees and shrubs to stabilise and lower water tables ... and the current extent of broad scale agriculture would no longer be possible'. A more likely approach, now taken by the government, has been to focus on discrete catchments and attempt to contain the affected areas, thereby protecting critical infrastructure and assets, and leaving the rest.[72] Farmers taking matters into their own hands have had success with other strategies; Geoff Bee planted the deep-rooted perennial lucerne on his Jerramungup property to good effect, while Lake Grace farmer Michael Lloyd has rehabilitated salt-affected land by revegetating with saltbush and deep-rooted perennial grasses and thus trebling its stocking capacity.[73]

The eastern mallee has not been as seriously affected by salinity as the western mallee lands, but it has still been an issue of considerable concern, justifying the 1993 Landcare plan naming it as one of its top priorities. Despite the 1920s evidence from Western Australia that clearing and cropping caused salinity, clearing did not stop. Lower groundwater and intervening clay layers mean that evidence of salinity can take decades to reveal itself; and different soil structures mean there is considerable variability in rates of salinity across the eastern mallee. As the area falls within the Murray–Darling Basin, concerns about the salinity of the Murray River have driven extensive research on the problem and the contribution of dryland salinity to the health of the river. Between 1992 and 2012 some 350 technical and scientific papers on salinity in the Victorian Mallee were published. Since the establishment of the Murray–Darling Basin Authority, plans for dealing with salinity have been reasonably well coordinated across state boundaries, particularly for irrigation-induced salinity.

---

72   Western Australia, Office of the Auditor General, 'Report 8: Management of Salinity, Key Findings', 16 May 2018, accessed 8 September 2018, https://audit.wa.gov.au/reports-and-publications/reports/management-of-salinity/key-findings/.

73   Jenne Brammer, 'Salinity Pioneer Honoured', *West Australian*, 8 May 2015, accessed 22 October 2018, https://thewest.com.au/countryman/news/salinity-pioneer-honoured-ng-ya-389947. See also David Pannell, 'National Economic and Policy Issues in the Productive Use of Salinised Resources', SEA Working Paper 02/05, accessed 22 October 2018, http://dpannell.fnas.uwa.edu.au/dpap0205.htm.

Figure 12.4. Salinity is highly visible across vast areas of the western mallee lands. This image taken near Hyden in 2015 shows its devastating impact on land and vegetation.
(Photograph by and courtesy of Andrea Gaynor)

Concerns in the late 1980s about the extent of the problem have lessened, not least because the increasing number of dry years has reduced the threat salinity poses. Less rainfall means less water reaching the water table, reducing the risk of it rising; drought slows down rates of salinity! Rather than just relying on drought, however, key strategies for managing salinity in the east have included targeting the sandhills and sandhill seepage to reduce the amount of water reaching the water table. Farmers have become much more attuned to 'water use efficiency', meaning they are better at using all the water available in the system. The addition of nitrogen to the soil is crucial to increasing the capacity of crops to use the water available. Inclusion of legumes in crop rotation increases the amount of nitrogen in the soil and has a significant effect on efficiency.[74] The planting of deep-rooted perennials such as lucerne also helps. Researchers continue to warn, however, that the improved management of dryland agriculture can only partially mitigate the problem of salinity; the Legacy of History will ensure that salinity continues to be a challenge into the future.[75]

---

74   Victor O. Sadras and Glenn McDonald, *Water Use Efficiency of Grain Crops in Australia: Principles, Benchmarks and Management* (Adelaide: Grains Research and Development Corporation, 2012), 18.
75   John Fawcett, 'Dryland Salinity Drivers and Processes', in Mallee Catchment Management Authority, *Mallee Salinity Workshop, May 30, 2013*, accessed 24 October 2018, http://www.malleecma.vic.gov.au/resources/salinity.

Climate Change

The year 1990 was especially challenging for farmers as the cost–price squeeze tightened its grip. For George Gum in Pinnaroo, it was worse than drought: 'wool crashed and everything crashed. Grain was worth nothing, wool was worth nothing, sheep—they were shooting them. That was worse than any drought I have ever had, and I don't think it can get worse than that'.[76] By the early 2000s the heroic attempts of farmers to break loose from the cost–price squeeze faced an even more serious hurdle: global warming. Yet its effects were uneven across mallee lands. In the late 1990s the rising trend of improved farming productivity stalled alarmingly. In 2017 Neal Hughes and his colleagues at the Australian Bureau of Agricultural and Resource Economics (ABARES) produced startling estimates of the uneven inter-regional impact of global warming on mallee wheat yields. Their research was based on the long-term collection of individual data from farm surveys going back to the 1970s. As can be seen in more detail in the Appendix, the most critical downturn has been in Victoria. In the Mildura and Buloke Shires, Hughes's team estimated that the long-term effects of climate change have been a decline in wheat yields of around 18 per cent. The Shire of Swan Hill was better placed, but even there the drop was over 12 per cent. The South Australian Mallee has suffered the least. The Murray Mallee has suffered drops in the order of 7 to 10 per cent, while on the Eyre Peninsula the losses have been less than 10 per cent. In the West, the Esperance region has suffered the least, while in other areas rates of decline comparable to Victorian proportions were observed.[77]

Similar results have been found by climate scientists, led by Zvi Hochman at the CSIRO, who have modelled the potential impact of declining rainfall on yields from Australian wheat lands. These scientists have also included the impact of rising CO_2 levels, which have slightly reduced loss of yields but have not negated the impact of changing rainfall patterns.[78] A particular problem

---

76   Gum, interview.
77   Survey data available at http://agriculture.gov.au/abares/research-topics/surveys/farm-survey-data#summary-data-tables, accessed 24 October 2018. See also Hughes, Lawson and Valle, *Farm Performance and Climate: Climate-adjusted Productivity for Broadacre Cropping Farms*.
78   Zvi Hochman, David Gobbett and Heidi Horan, 'Climate Trends Account for Stalled Wheat Yields in Australia since 1990', *Global Change Biology* 23, no. 5 (January 2017): Figure 2.

in Victoria has been the declining intensity of the autumn rain breaks and the delay in the arrival of these breaks.[79]

The capacity of mallee farmers to adapt to this new challenge is a 21st-century iteration of the foundation story. Such understandings shape the ways farmers respond to the challenges of climate change; the narrative of adaptability demands continuing innovation irrespective of ecological limits, albeit with the recognition, as Bob Schilling puts it, that 'if it don't rain, it's not going to grow'.

Climate change calls for renewed efforts to farm more efficiently and in new ways. Some in the eastern mallee, with a climate more variable than the West, see climate change as demanding more of the kind of adaptable farming that good farmers have been demonstrating for decades. The idea of adaptability is yoked to the nature of the Victorian Mallee climate. It is a practice and a mindset that has developed in response to the environment—farmers need to be 'infinitely adaptable' as the *Mildura Cultivator* put it in 1912. The persistence of such an attitude in a neoliberal climate leads to a highly individualised approach to challenges and an expectation that individual farmers will adapt as best they can with minimal government support.

The idea that mallee farmers are more adaptable than most is frequently expressed. George Gum is passionate about the Mallee and its farmers and observes that there are 'not too many places in the world that would try to grow wheat on 300 mls of rain ... we must be some of the best farms in the world! [laughing]'.[80] Russell Hilton, a third-generation farmer near Hopetoun who has retired from farming, argued of Victorian Mallee farmers:

> they are highly responsive ... They've had the acid on them for quite a few years now, so any that are still around are highly responsive. I don't know one farmer who is young and actively farming, who's not really, really good at their job. Adaptation is the key to it.[81]

Mallee agronomist Kate Wilson concurs. In her view Mallee farmers are so adaptable they are a step ahead of climate change. Productivity and profitability will drive adaptability, and farming techniques will evolve to stay ahead. In

---

79 Michael Pook, Shaun Lisson, James Risbey, Caroline C. Ummenhofer, Peter MacIntosh and Melissa Rebbeck, 'The Autumn Break for Cropping in Southeast Australia: Trends, Synoptic Influences and Impacts on Wheat Yield', *International Journal of Climatology* 29, no. 13 (2009): 2012–26.
80 Gum, interview.
81 Hilton, interview.

this understanding, climate change is an extension of an already challenging environment rather than a completely new paradigm.[82]

Ian McClelland is one farmer who thinks that climate change is a paradigm shift, raising difficult questions about the future of farming in the Mallee. The 2002 drought marked a turning point in his thinking about the climate. When we interviewed him in 2014 he had experienced five droughts in seven years, and his growing-season rainfall had fallen from 240 millimetres per year to an average since 1995 of 190 millimetres—a 20 per cent decrease. Many of the farming stories he shared were narratives about the advances science has brought to the Mallee: the new and improved varieties of wheat, and better understanding of soil structure. He has been actively involved in promoting research that will help Mallee farmers adapt to the changing climate. However, while he places great faith in the ability of research to provide answers, he acknowledges that climate change presents serious challenges for scientists and farmers.

Some of those challenges are emotional as well as practical. Anne McClelland is married to Ian and spoke of the strain of dealing with the uncertainties climate change presents. Whereas the Mallee environment had been a source of 'great succour and consolation' for her and others, climate change has made that relationship more difficult. The Victorian Mallee was already marginal country, 'and then climate change, invidiously and insidiously, and almost without our knowing [arrived], then suddenly that was it, and we knew that … something had happened and was happening and would continue to happen and get worse'. Rains became more uncertain, and there was prolonged drought. 'Things died. We felt even less sure that things were going to be alright in the long run. Conversations were more about "are we going to be alright, are we not going to be alright? What's going to happen this year"?'[83]

Climate change does not just mean less and a more variable rainfall or hotter years. Weather patterns will also change. The predictions for the eastern mallee are for wetter summers and drier springs, for earlier and later frosts, and for higher temperatures and 'heat shocks' in September, October and November affecting the quality of the harvest.[84] The expectation is that the

---

82   Kate Wilson, in discussion with Katie Holmes, Woomelang, 3 December 2016.

83   Anne McClelland, interviewed by Katie Holmes, in Australia's southern mallee lands oral history project, 26 March 2014, NLA, http://nla.gov.au/nla.cat-vn6489415.

84   Harm van Rees, B. White, J. Laidlaw and D. McKinley, 'Farming during a Period of Extreme Climate Variability: Consequences and Lessons, Final Report', prepared as part of the Birchip Cropping Group's Project, *Developing Climate Change Resilient*

trend of declining wheat yields will continue as the climate warms.[85] In the southern Victorian Mallee, the area where the McClellands live, the heavier soils are expected to fare worse with lower rainfall than the northern, finer soils. John Cooke, a lifetime Mallee resident, botanist and deputy chair of the Mallee Catchment Authority, suggests that several factors have masked the early impacts of climate change in the eastern mallee. Without the northern Mallee and Wimmera–Mallee pipelines, he estimates, the area would have run out of water two or three times in the last decade. Instead farms have good quality water for house, garden and stock on demand, protecting them from scarcity. Improved tillage techniques have also hidden effects of climate change, and low interest rates have enabled farmers to carry debt levels they otherwise could not afford.[86]

In the western mallee lands farmers have also noticed changes in rainfall patterns. While average rainfall has not changed much, its timing has. Newdegate farmers Helen McDonald and Ron Shalders remarked on the novelty of recent rain before Christmas. Ron observed that the rain 'seems to fall at different times. We seem to get nearly as much through the summer as we do in the growing season, then it peters off late in the year'.[87] Anne Rick, also from Newdegate, agreed but sees farmers adjusting to these new patterns: 'I'm amazed at how quickly farmers adapt to changes. I think because you're your own boss you can make decisions and change very quickly'. Rolf and Sue Meeking from Hyden are not so optimistic. Neither thinks that they will be able to adapt quickly enough to the transformations climate change is bringing. Rolf notes that the climate change models suggest that the 'mulga belt' is moving further south and that their farm may soon be in mulga country rather than mallee country, commenting wryly, 'they don't grow crops in the mulga'.

The types of plants that are growing are also changing: wild oats are being replaced by native grasses; the Pilbara plant nulla-nulla, which never used to grow in the district, now does. In the dry season desert birds come in that are not native to the area.[88] Third-generation Lake Grace farmer Allan

---

Cropping and Mixed Cropping/Grazing Businesses in Australia (Birchip: Birchip Cropping Group, 2011).

85 Hochman, Gobbett and Horan, 'Climate Trends Account for Stalled Wheat Yields in Australia since 1990', 2071–81.

86 John Cooke, conversation with Katie Holmes, 7 September 2018.

87 Helen McDonald and Ron Shalders, interviewed by Andrea Gaynor, Newdegate, 2 December 2015.

88 Rolf and Sue Meeking, interviewed by Andrea Gaynor, Hyden, 3 December 2015.

Marshall believes the sea breezes are not as strong as when he was a child. They no longer get the 'Albany Doctor': 'You used to see it—just about hear it—coming. There was this cloud of dust in front of it and you'd hear the roar and then it would settle down'. He attributes its disappearance to clearing: as the land heats up, it slows the wind.[89]

In the Eyre Peninsula farmers are preparing for a hotter, drier future. In anticipation of the challenges of climate change, and in the absence of leadership at the federal government level, groups from different sectors across the Peninsula in 2010 formed the Eyre Peninsula Integrated Climate Change Agreement Committee (EPICCA). In February 2014 they released the Regional Climate Change Adaptation Plan for the Eyre Peninsula, which sets out the different adaptation options for each industry sector across the region. Using data from the Intergovernmental Panel on Climate Change, the group worked on the assumption of two degrees of warming within the next three decades, and four degrees longer term if no mitigating measures are introduced.[90] Rainfall is predicted to decline by 3.5 per cent by 2030, but with a 7.5 per cent decline during winter and spring. What would this look like for an area that is already marginal cropping country?

The plan noted that current 'leading edge' practices would provide 'some measure of adaptation in the coming 10–20 years', but longer term 'adaptation may require more transformational responses such as adoption of advanced breeding techniques' that require foresight and planning. New crop varieties with improved water use efficiency, salt tolerance and disease resilience would be needed. Better land management techniques to protect the soil from erosion, such as wind breaks, cover crops and stubble retention, were advised. Business management practices that maintain a high equity and thus a greater capacity to 'weather the negative financial impacts of a more inclement climate', and greater diversification of the farming enterprise to protect against 'high risk years' would be necessary to remain viable.[91] Without such strategies, the plan warned, production levels would decline to the point where farms would become unviable and the area would return to

---

89   Allan Marshall, interviewed by Andrea Gaynor, Lake Grace, 30 November 2015.

90   *The Fifth Assessment Report of the Intergovernmental Panel on Climate Change* (Geneva: IPCC, 2014) (commonly known as the IPCC report) was produced for the United Nations and published in 2014, although summaries of the findings had been released in September 2013.

91   Mark Siebentritt, Nicole Halsey, and Mark Stafford Smith, 'Regional Climate Change Adaptation Plan for the Eyre Peninsula' (Prepared for the Eyre Peninsula Integrated Climate Change Agreement Committee, 2014), 15.

a more 'pastoral/forage based grazing system'.[92] The plan noted the 'emerging view' that breeding programs would not be able to deliver new traits in crops fast enough to 'keep up with the speed of a changing climate'. In such a context, genetically modified crops may provide an alternative option, but these would also require changes in public policy and community opinion, both of which would take time.[93]

The EPICAA Plan also noted the impact climate change would have on ecological systems and biodiversity. Refuges and protected areas needed to be identified to protect vulnerable species, of which the malleefowl is a leading example. Migration or translocation of key species may be necessary, including the movement of plants and animals to habitats outside the region. The considerable foresight that the EPICCA Plan reflects points to the scale of changes needed.

The response of farmers to the challenges of climate change across the mallee lands suggests that many already notice significant changes in weather patterns and in ecological systems. While some are optimistic about the capacity of farmers to adapt to these changes, the scale of change forecast threatens not just the systems of farming but the future of farming itself. The historically unprecedented rates of change will also have dramatic impacts on the ecological systems that many mallee residents have come to know and love.

The risk climate change poses to biodiversity threatens those aspects of mallee lands that evoked most feeling among our interviewees. Their emotional connection with the mallee landscape is almost tangible. And it is not the agricultural landscape they speak of, but places of remnant bushland. Ian McClelland reflected: 'I like the beauty of the Mallee. I think it has a raw beauty ... light and dark, a lot of shadow, a lot of diversity'. Russell Hilton spoke of the 'tangible touch of the Mallee ... the trees, the climate, the birds, you know the pleasure of walking out on a frosty morning and then by about 10 o'clock you're like a bird warming your wings'. Sue Meeking referred to the 'deeply familiar' landscape: 'It's just part of us 'cause we grew up here. It's just deeply soothing and very beautiful ... It's very hard to explain what the emotional tie is but it's very strong'. Michelle Slarke from Lake Grace was taught the names of the bush plants by her mother, and she values them all the more because of the loss of so much bushland. She still goes for a walk in the remnant bush every day: 'I go to reconnect I think with myself but also

---

92 Siebentritt, Halsey, and Stafford Smith, 'Regional Climate Change Adaptation Plan', 29.

93 Siebentritt, Halsey, and Stafford Smith, 'Regional Climate Change Adaptation Plan', 30.

with that bush ... It's my sacred space really'.[94] Writer Kerry Conway talked of her feelings for the Mallee: 'it's just a very tough, very delicate, and very beautiful place. And you really do get to love it even if there are times when you just don't want to be here. You know it's just really, it's so resilient, and it's, it seems to be also so responsive'.[95]

If there is some good news from the recent research of Hughes and his colleagues, it is that between 2007–08 and 2013–14 farmers once again increased their productivity and learnt ways to deal with changing climate. When Hughes and his colleagues modelled variations in wheat yields and included controls for climate changes in that period, they found that yields increased largely because of changes in technology. After a slow adoption of no-till farming in the 1970s and 1980s, implementation rose dramatically in the early 2000s.[96] Since 2005–06, however, farmers have further closed the gap between good and bad years by methods that reduce crop sensitivity to dry conditions. 'By 2013–14 climate sensitivity reached a historically low level, such that a 1 in 20 drought year only reduced average productivity by around 26 per cent, compared with 37 per cent in 1979–80.'[97]

But farm size remains critical. In both the ABARES and CSIRO models the impacts of climate change are especially severe in Victoria, where earlier land laws governing the size of properties may have a lingering and detrimental influence on the ability of farmers to deal with climate change. This can be seen by comparing the Victorian Mallee with the Eyre Peninsula. In the Victorian Mallee farm numbers have fallen since the Great Depression—from 5,890 in 1931 to 2,500 in 1951, 2,300 in the mid-sixties, 2,088 in the mid-seventies, 2,142 in 1990 and 1,066 in 2017. Since 1990 farm size has increased from 1,029 to 1,943 hectares. On the Eyre Peninsula the years since the mid-1960s have also seen a decline in the number of farms and an increase in the size of farms. Between 1990 and 2017 the number of farms fell from 1,611 to 973 and the size of farms rose from 1,675 to 3,619 hectares. Eyre Peninsula farms are 86 per cent larger than those in the Victorian Mallee.[98]

---

94   Michelle Slarke, interviewed by Andrea Gaynor, Lake Grace, 30 November 2015.
95   Kerry Conway, interviewed by Katie Holmes, in Australia's southern mallee lands oral history project, 10 June 2014, NLA, http://nla.gov.au/nla.cat-vn6578389.
96   Hughes, Lawson and Valle, *Farm Performance and Climate: Climate-adjusted Productivity for Broadacre Cropping Farms*, 26 (Figure 17).
97   Hughes, Lawson and Valle, *Farm Performance and Climate: Climate-adjusted Productivity for Broadacre Cropping Farms*, 26.
98   The Victorian Mallee figures for 1907 to 1951 are drawn from: the National Archives of Australia; the Australian Bureau of Statistics; Parish Agricultural Statistics, MP570, books 6–7, 20–1, 34–5, 48–9. The figures for the 1960s and 1970s are drawn

On the Eyre Peninsula earlier decisions to permit larger farm sizes have enabled farmers to deal with difficult times more successfully than their counterparts in the Victorian Mallee. Initially settled on smaller blocks, Victorian farmers have been less able to take advantage of the modern technology of seeding and harvesting, which favours broadacre farming. The increase in farm sizes achieved in Victoria has come at the expense of sheep, which have declined in numbers. On the Eyre Peninsula sheep numbers have also declined, but sheep and wool sales have remained a major part of farmers' incomes. In the 1960s wheat yields on the Eyre Peninsula were lower than the Victorian Mallee, but since 2000 this situation has changed in favour of the Eyre Peninsula and 'farm cash incomes' have greatly exceeded those in Victoria.[99] In the Southern and Central Wheatbelt of Western Australia—the ABARES region that includes mallee landscapes but also extends north of the mallee—farmers have enthusiastically adopted the new no-till technology. Since 1990 wheat yields have risen about 15 per cent despite climate change. Driving this is a massive expansion of farms, which by 2017 were three times their 1990 size. At the same time the number of farms has declined by over 40 per cent.[100] The implication for Victoria from the success of both the Eyre Peninsula and Western Australia is that farms will get larger and their numbers will decrease.

The long-term impacts of climate change threaten the capacity of mallee land farmers to keep being responsive and endlessly adaptive in order to manage global markets and climate change. Farmers juggle these challenges, drawing succour from the landscape, while struggling to make their farms on it pay. Many hope they will be the ones able to stay a step ahead, to survive and to prosper. As Ian McClelland reflects, 'It's like the devil you know is better than the devil you don't know'.

---

from Australia, Bureau of Agricultural Economics, *The Australian Wheatgrowing Industry: An Economic Survey, 1964–65 to 1966–67* (Canberra: ABARES, December 1969), 15, 19 and 20; and Australia, Bureau of Agricultural Economics, *Australian Agricultural and Grazing Industries Survey, 1976–77 and 1977–78, Wheat Growing Industry* (Canberra: ABARES, Australian Government Publishing Service, 1983), 1, 6–7 and 14–15. The figures from 1990 can be found at ABARES 'farm survey data', accessed 24 October 2018, http://agriculture.gov.au/abares/research-topics/surveys/farm-survey-data.

99 These figures are based on ABARES farm survey data, accessed 24 October 2018, http://agriculture.gov.au/abares/research-topics/surveys/farm-survey-data.

100 See ABARES farm surveys, accessed 24 October 2018, http://agriculture.gov.au/abares/research-topics/surveys/farm-survey-data.

Chapter 13

REINVENTING THE MALLEE

Without communities, mallee country becomes an agro-industrial wilderness, dominated by machines, peopled only for production. Country that was kin to Aboriginal people and wrested from them—sometimes with violence—was transformed by settlers on an epic scale. Many developed their own tenacious attachment to it, with at least some of the remaining residents seeing themselves as 'custodians of the land', charged with the important task of keeping the country peopled with those who know and love it. They have sought to sustain their settlements socially and culturally, to keep people in the towns and perhaps attract new residents. This not only helps to retain local services such as schools and medical care but also to maintain a sociable environment for people to inhabit. Without strong communities, the mallee lands are vulnerable to being neglected, unliveable, *unknown*.[1] Community life also helps to offset the challenges of living and working in mallee country: heat, uncertainty, isolation.

As the screws of economic efficiency have been tightened to the breaking point of communities, many mallee people have worked hard to refine and adapt conventional farming to the new conditions. However, they have also sought to diversify the region's economic base in various ways, including new kinds of farming—from tree crops to aquaculture—as well as festivals and other forms of tourism. In the process, they have grappled with the limitations and opportunities of a landscape and infrastructure geared almost solely towards the needs of industrial agriculture.

Diversification

One of the new industries centred on the mallees themselves.[2] This was not entirely novel; while most settlers had seen mallees as an execrable pest, by

---

1   Fiona Martin *et al.*, in 'From Pub to Hub: Nyabing Progress Association Community Enterprise', videorecording, 2016, accessed 24 October 2018, https://vimeo.com/channels/nyabing.
2   This section draws on Andrea Gaynor and Yann Toussaint, 'Revaluing Mallees', paper presented at the 'Foreign Bodies, Intimate Ecologies' conference, Sydney, 13

1882 the Eucalyptus Mallee Company led by Joseph Bosisto was extracting oil from mallees—mainly *Eucalyptus dumosa*—on over ten thousand acres at Antwerp in the Wimmera mallee. However, agricultural expansion in the region made subdivision a more lucrative proposition than oil, so this large-scale oil mallee enterprise moved to Euston, NSW, where it failed to compete with independent distillers.[3] While eucalyptus oil remained an important sideline for several mallee farmers into the 1950s, the Australian industry struggled to compete with oil produced from Tasmanian blue gum plantations overseas, and by the early 1980s it held only 3 per cent of the world market.[4]

In the early 1990s, however, as Western Australia's salinity problem became more evident, eucalyptus oil appeared to be a way to make salinity control affordable, and perhaps even profitable. Oil mallees produced a saleable commodity and reduced saline groundwater levels, heralding a new kind of mallee country throughout the wheatbelt. Research into the selection of high-oil-yielding eucalypts from Western Australian species began in the 1980s. The Western Australian Department of Conservation and Land Management (CALM) established nurseries after 1990 to provide mallee seedlings. Between 1988 and 2008, farmers and contractors across the wheatbelt were heavily subsidised to plant more than twenty-five million mallees, mostly subspecies of Western Australian natives *Eucalyptus loxophleba* and *Eucalyptus kochii*.[5] The state's attention was given largely to breeding and planting—rolling out the vision on a large scale. Harvesting, processing and marketing, which would ensure the trees' economic future, were secondary considerations.

From the late 1990s, the focus changed to using mallee biomass for electricity generation. Western Power, the state's power utility, believed greenhouse gas emissions were a significant looming problem that demanded solutions.[6] In 1996 Western Power investigated utilising mallees for renewable electricity generation, and three years later teamed with other organisations in an integrated wood-processing feasibility study at Esperance. This led to a 1 MW demonstration plant at Narrogin that produced renewable electricity,

---

February 2016.

3   Michael Pearson, 'The Good Oil: Eucalyptus Oil Distilleries in Australia', *Australasian Historical Archaeology* 11 (1993): 101.
4   Pearson, 'The Good Oil'.
5   URS Australia, *Oil Mallee Industry Development Plan for Western Australia*, version 3 (Perth: URS Australia, 2009), 30.
6   Adrian Chegwidden, interviewed by Andrea Gaynor, 2000, OH3049, J.S. Battye Library.

activated carbon, and eucalyptus oil. Supported by the Australian Greenhouse Office and AusIndustry, the plant was publicised in 2000, stimulating further mallee plantings. Trials began in 2006.[7] While local farmers with oil mallees benefited, the plant highlighted the difficulty of transporting a bulky fuel source economically. It was mothballed within a year. An earlier project by a Woodside Petroleum subsidiary, which planted one million mallee seedlings in the Esperance region for bioelectricity, failed when the state government extended a gas pipeline from Kalgoorlie to Esperance.[8] Yet another economic potential discovered for mallees centred on their roots, which are extremely efficient carbon-storage devices. This was linked to the development of carbon-trading systems. In 2003 a Japanese power company paid for a thousand hectares of Western Australian wheatbelt farms to be planted to oil mallees as part of alley farming systems, combining crop production with carbon sequestration.[9] In time, they were visible on satellite imagery as patches of parallel lines scratched into the gridwork of paddocks. However, uncertainties over carbon markets stymied this new industry.

The oil mallees provide salinity control, shelter for stock and habitat for some of the more adaptable fauna, but a search for more direct economic uses continues. In 2011 a multinational alliance was formed to develop systems for converting mallee biomass to aviation fuel, and research is ongoing.[10] In 2013 Macco stockfeeds, near Williams, began using mallees in their biomass boiler, saving $450,000 in annual fuel costs. Such small-scale initiatives could provide a future for mallees, though farmers are losing patience; many are bulldozing unproductive mallees in a re-run of earlier destructions.[11]

Other farmers established niche enterprises to supplement conventional farming. In 1969, Michael and Mary Nenke of Kukerin in Western Australian

---

7   Western Power, *Annual Report 2000* (Perth: Western Power Corporation, 2000), 68; Enecon, 'Bioenergy Project Examples', accessed 24 October 2018, http://www.enecon.com.au/bioenergy.php?section=renewable_energy.
8   URS Australia, *Oil Mallee Industry Development Plan*, 26.
9   URS Australia, *Oil Mallee Industry Development Plan*, 29.
10 Chris Pash, 'Fuel Made from Australian Mallee Trees Could Be Powering Aircraft by 2021', *Business Insider Australia*, 21 May 2014, accessed 24 October 2018, http://www.businessinsider.com.au/jet-aircraft-blast-into-the-skies-powered-by-fuel-made-from-australian-mallee-trees-2014-5; Jill Griffiths and Gio Braidotti, 'Tree-Powered Aviation Takes Off in WA's Wheatbelt', *Ground Cover*, no. 96 (2012), accessed 24 October 2018, https://grdc.com.au/Media-Centre/Ground-Cover/Ground-Cover-Issue-96-January-February-2012/Treepowered-aviation-takes-off-in-WAs-wheatbelt.
11 Sean Murphy (reporter), 'Mallee Oil', *Landline*, ABC TV, broadcast 22 June 2014, accessed 24 October 2018, http://www.abc.net.au/tv/programs/landline/old-site/content/2014/s4030485.htm.

mallee country stocked their farm's dams with yabbies, initially as a hobby and for an annual Easter yabby party. However, low grain and wool prices in the late 1980s and high interest rates in the 1990s inspired a more focused effort. The Nenkes established Cambinata Yabbies in 1991 and, by 1993, were exporting the crustaceans. They added value with a function centre in a converted shearing shed, featuring yabbies and other regional produce. At first the work was frenetic. Their children helped to catch, sort, pack and weigh yabbies, or completed homework on the dam bank while Mary fed the yabbies. Deputy Premier Hendy Cowan, a mallee-born man, opened Cambinata's cutting-edge export facility in 1994, its capacity tripling by 1998. One December they filled orders for ten tonnes of yabbies. However, droughts reduced the available dam water and the enterprise slowed, forcing further diversification.

The Nenkes established some off-grid eco-friendly cottage accommodation. Michael Nenke had also worked with bees on and off for decades and sold honey to tourists visiting Cambinata Yabbies. His best honey came from mallee light soils. Michael had cleared six hundred acres of this land in the 1960s but rued that in 2015: 'If I knew what I know now I would never have touched it'. He replanted most of it with mallee, remarking, 'my bees make it worthwhile these days'.[12]

Beekeeping was not novel in mallee country, and was sometimes used as an initial cash crop. In 1899, the Aylmore brothers and their families left farming in the Barossa valley and migrated to Albany by steamer, accompanied by five working horses, twenty-five fowls and forty beehives. Their hives were upset in rough seas and the bees escaped but fortunately were 'persuaded to return to their hives without incident'.[13] The brothers took up land near Tambellup, in the far south west of mallee country. Their bees provided the main source of income, flourishing on the mallee and yate blossoms and the fresh water of nearby Lake Toolbrunup. In a good year the Aylmores sent twelve tons of honey to Albany for sale.[14]

By the 1970s, professional beekeepers in Victoria and South Australia were increasingly utilising mallee country. Greater mobility and mechanisation enabled migratory beekeepers to take advantage of the region's milder weather and winter-flowering species for over-wintering their hives. The

---

12 Mary Nenke and Michael Nenke, interviewed by Andrea Gaynor, Kukerin, 29 November 2015.

13 Margaret Aylmore, 'The Three Aylmore Brothers, Pioneers Corner', *Gnowangerup Star*, 22 April 1965.

14 Aylmore, 'The Three Aylmore Brothers'.

Victorian Land Conservation Council's (LCC) mallee study in 1974 found ninety-two permanent and fifty-five temporary apiary sites on public land.[15] These areas became more important as more private property was cleared, and as agricultural insecticides made beekeeping less compatible with conventional farming. In light of this, the LCC in 1977 permitted the construction of tracks through public land to enable beekeepers to find alternative sites. In 1987 the number of permanent apiary sites was steady at ninety-two, while the temporary sites had grown to 221. By this time the Mallee produced around a third of Victoria's honey.[16] Beekeepers also provided pollination services for irrigated pastures, lucerne crops and horticultural crops along the Murray, almond plantations requiring thousands of hives for pollination.[17]

Beekeeping had been a forceful argument for conservation of native vegetation by making mallee retention pay. However, by the 1980s the LCC recognised that beekeeping was not entirely benign. Honey bees competed with native nectar eaters, including bees, beetles and birds. As honey-bee foraging was less species specific than that of native fauna, these bees also contributed to hybridisation of native plants. Furthermore, feral and managed honey bees were becoming increasingly problematic in summer, when they vigorously sought out water, including from camp supplies. The LCC recommended control of feral bees and relocation of some apiary sites in order to avoid this human–bee conflict.[18]

By the 2010s, beekeepers in mallee country were facing hard times. Several large fires, for example in 2005 in the Eyre Peninsula and 2014 in Ngarkat, 'wiped out' forage sites. Other factors increased pressure on apiarists. Eyre Peninsula apiarist Norm Pope described how declining autumn and spring rains meant that eucalypt flowerings were less frequent and less productive of nectar. Intensification of cropping and declining sheep numbers meant less pasture, which had also provided bee fodder. Finally, cheap imported honey and the retail duopoly put downward pressure on prices, leading more apiarists to pack and market their own honey, and express fears for the future of the industry.[19]

---

15   Land Conservation Council (Vic.), *Report on the Mallee Study Area* (Melbourne: Land Conservation Council (Vic.), 1974), 135.

16   Land Conservation Council (Vic.), *Mallee Area Review: Final Recommendations* (Melbourne: Land Conservation Council (Vic.), 1989), 68.

17   Nelson Nye, *Report on the Mallee Area Review* (Melbourne: Land Conservation Council (Vic.), 1987), 253.

18   Land Conservation Council (Vic.), *Mallee Area Review: Final Recommendations*, 69.

19   Interview with Eyre Peninsula apiarist Norm Pope, *ABC News*, 12 February 2014, accessed 24 October 2018, http://www.abc.net.au/news/rural/2014-02-12/

Another, more extractive, use of public land in the Victorian Mallee was broombush (*Melaleuca uncinata*) harvesting for fencing material. This activity came under closer scrutiny in November 1980, when members of the Wildlife Survey Unit in the northern part of the Big Desert found that broombush removal was operating on a significant scale. One operator was filling a semi-trailer weekly with about eighteen tonnes of broombush.[20] This threatened habitats for rare birds, including the Western Whipbird. Cutters focused on broombush plants over twenty years old that would re-grow and be ready for harvesting in six to ten years. But, by 1986, as broombush fencing became more fashionable, harvesting had increased to 2,756 tonnes per year in South Australia.[21]

Concern over the sustainability of operations grew in both Victoria and South Australia in the 1980s, leading to restrictions, first in South Australia, then Victoria. The Victorian Department of Conservation, Forests and Lands licensed only six operators in 1989 to harvest annually 1,360 tonnes of broombush—principally in the Big Desert—though about 650 tonnes were harvested illegally. The industry employed about three dozen cutters, fencing contractors and processing workers, creating fencing with a retail value of about $1.8 million. The LCC became concerned not just about the industry's sustainability but also about the ecological impact of the proliferating tracks used by cutters. It wanted harvesting limited to five defined areas, and to be subject to 'adequate supervision'. And it recommended that royalties should reflect the cost of supervision and research as well as the market value of the product.[22] By 1991 research projects on broombush plantations were underway, though the economic viability was not promising.[23] By the early 2000s, wild broombrush harvesting on public land was subject to heavy restrictions in three states right across southern mallee country. Wild harvesting continued in NSW, supplying most of the Australian market, but, under pressure from environmental activists, its days

---

rural-sa-norm-pope-1202/5254270; Interview with Tintinara beekeeper Ian Zadow, *ABC News*, 12 February 2014, accessed 24 October 2018, http://www.abc.net.au/news/rural /2014-02-12 /nrn-tintinara-bees-final/5253018.

20   Letter from P. Menkhorst to Officer in Charge, Wildlife Management, 21 November 1980, VPRS 11544/309, Desc 47/4/79, Public Record Office Victoria (PROV).

21   A. Boutland *et al.*, 'Alternative Products from Trees and Shrubs to "The Role of Trees in Sustainable Agriculture" Conference, Albury, September 30th – October 3rd, 1991', *Agroforestry Systems* 20, nos 1–2 (November 1992): 22–58 (47).

22   Land Conservation Council (Vic.), *Mallee Area Review: Final Recommendations*, 127–9, 131. See also the remarkable map of broombush-cutting tracks in Margaret Blakers and Luisa McMillan, *Mallee Conservation in Victoria* (Melbourne: RMIT Faculty of Environmental Design and Construction, 1988), 38.

23   Boutland *et al.*, 'Alternative Products from Trees and Shrubs ...', 47.

there are numbered. This is good news for farmers in Western and South Australia who established broombush plantations as a landcare measure with a view to commercial cropping too.[24]

Meanwhile, mining on mallee lands has grown in significance. A gold mine ten kilometres north west of Lake Grace in the Western Australian mallee operated in the 1980s, but the main focus of mallee mining has been gypsum, salt and mineral sands. In 1977 there were two thousand hectares of gypsum mining leases in the Victorian mallee, and traces of past mining were scattered across the landscape in the form of sterile, unsightly overburden mounds dumped in excavated pits.[25] The LCC recommended more efficient mining and site rehabilitation. Ten years later gypsum leases covered only 1,130 hectares of public land but rehabilitation remained inadequate.[26] Mineral sands operations were established in the Victorian and Murray Mallee after 2010, excavating the ancient beach sands of the Murray Gulf to supply zircon, rutile and titanium to Chinese manufacturers. The mines provide local jobs and offsets toward the National Recovery Plan for Malleefowl, though the rehabilitation of the sites will take decades to play out.

Salt is part of the mallee landscape—a relic of the ancient inland sea in the east, and millions of years of rainfall in the west. Although the word conjures images of rusting fences and dead forests reaching up from waterlogged samphire flats, there is a more positive thread to the salt story. Pink Lake near Dimboola has long been a significant site for the Wotjobaluk people. European settlers extracted salt from the lake from the 1860s, and Aboriginal people from Ebenezer mission and their descendants worked at the salt mine, shouldering heavy sacks in the crystalline glare of the lake in summer. Settlers worked there too. Former salt harvester Mick McDonald, who worked at the mine from age fourteen, recalled that southerly winds made the best salt—'If the wind swung around to the north and you copped a bit of dust it put a layer of dust over your salt'.[27] The Department of Sustainability and Environment cancelled the mining lease in the late 1980s, when the salt was being mechanically mined, but in 2009 the Seymour family—founders

---

24   Frank McKinnell, *Brushwood in Western Australia: Industry Development Plan 2008* (Western Australia: Southern Brook Landcare Group and Wheatbelt Development Commission, 2008).

25   Land Conservation Council (Vic.), *Final Recommendations: Mallee Study Area* (Melbourne: Land Conservation Council (Vic.), 1977), 57.

26   Blakers and Macmillan, *Mallee Conservation in Victoria*, 37.

27   Tim Lee, reporter, 'In the Pink,' *Landline*, ABC TV, broadcast 19 July 2009, accessed 24 October 2018, http://www.abc.net.au/tv/programs/landline/old-site/content/2008/s2630001.htm.

of Mt Zero olives—formed a partnership with the Barengi Gadjin Land Council of Horsham to hand harvest small amounts of the mineral-rich salt for sale as a gourmet product.

Salt was also mined from 1916 at Lake Crosbie in what is now Murray–Sunset National Park until the Pink Lakes state park was created in 1979. Cheetham Salt took up leases at Lake Tyrrell in 1963 and in 1988 commenced operations at Kevin near Ceduna as part of a broader salt-mining portfolio servicing food, stockfeed, hide, pool and industrial needs.[28] From the air, the intricate geometry of the bright white-and-green salt fields that overlay the organic outlines of Lake MacDonnell near Kevin form a striking contrast to the beige-and-olive patchwork of adjacent farmland stretching out in a narrow strip along the coast. But it is an anomaly. At the far western reaches of cultivated South Australian mallee country, broadacre agriculture remains the dominant force shaping the landscape.

Heartlands to Artlands?

Approaching Brim in the Wimmera mallee, lines on the canvas of wheatfields—powerlines, railway, road—point to a small beige-and-white rectangle on the horizon. Roadside mallees break ranks with this linearity, pointing out and up through their broken canopies to the big sky. As you reach the 80-kilometre speed signs the rectangle becomes a cylinder, with something atop it. Following the road as it veers left, you arrive alongside the structure: six concrete wheat silos, the agro-industrial cathedrals you find on the edge of many wheatland towns. These particular silos, however, carry the images of four figures. Thirty metres tall, they are picked out in sepia tones, giving the figures the appearance of emerging organically out of the buff concrete and surrounding land. Three are men, the other—somewhat ambiguously—a woman. All are expressive, inviting viewers to divine their story from expression, demeanour, and body type, shaped by decades of work on the land.

These silos, painted by Brisbane artist Guido van Helten in January 2016, became an overnight sensation, attracting hundreds of visitors and briefly holding the national social media spotlight.[29] The project was coordinated by Melbourne street arts management company Juddy Roller and funded

---

28 'Historical Timeline', *Cheetham Salt*, 2013, accessed 24 October 2018, http://www.cheethamsalt.com.au/LinkClick.aspx?fileticket=kwfa6-CgvbA%3d&tabid=227.

29 See, for example, Danielle Grindlay, 'Brim Silo Artwork: The Tall Tales and Colourful Characters behind Guido van Helten's Paintings', *ABC News*, 7 January

by the Yarriambiack Shire, Regional Arts Victoria and the Brim Active Community Group. Van Helten worked with the Brim community to refine a design. The success of the project inspired a 200-kilometre 'silo art trail' in the Wimmera–Mallee region, funded by state and private backers as well as federal drought-relief money.[30] The Brim silos were followed by a mural by Fintan Magee at Patchewollock, featuring local farmer Nick Hulland, in a chequered flannel shirt, squinting in the bright mallee sun. The imagery here, as at Brim, is iconically rural. A somewhat different approach was taken in the third silo artwork in the series, at Sheep Hills. Street artist Adnate spent several weeks with the Barengi Gadjin Land Council to conceive and plan the mural. Featuring local Aboriginal elders and children, it is one of the few prominent signs of first peoples in mallee landscapes. While the first two silos seek to generate pride—as well as tourism revenue—by celebrating conventional understandings of farming communities, Adnate says that at Sheep Hills he wanted to celebrate young Aboriginal people and their identity.[31] Other silos have subsequently been painted with archetypically (white) rural figures at Lascelles (Rone) and Rosebery (Kaff-eine).[32]

The Brim silos followed a 2015 silo art project in the inner Western Australian wheatbelt town of Northam, which featured the artwork of two international street artists. This was a collaboration between FORM, a metropolitan Perth-based not-for-profit arts organisation, and CBH, the large Western Australian cooperative responsible for storing, handling and marketing grain, which owns the silos. These, too, were the first works in a proposed rural 'art trail', 'where people from the city could take a day's drive to various towns in the wheatbelt and see some internationally-renowned artists' works'.[33]

2016, accessed 24 October 2018, http://www.abc.net.au/news/2016-01-07/brim-grain-silos-guido-van-helten-art-wimmera-victoria/7072768.

30 Erin Witmitz, 'Brim Silos: Artwork to Expand to Five More Towns', *Wimmera Mail–Times*, 9 June 2016, accessed 6 November 2018, http://www.mailtimes.com.au/story/3958130/brim-silo-art-to-continue-to-five-sites/; Ian Royall, 'Silo Art at Brim Germinates into 200km Trail', *Herald Sun*, 9 June 2016, accessed 6 November 2018, http://www.heraldsun.com.au/news/victoria/silo-art-at-brim-germinates-into-200km-trail/news-story/edaf2ade495bf4f9db3c9a31c459750f.

31 'Sheep Hills Silos Biggest Project for Artist Adnate', *Weekly Advertiser*, 23 November 2016, accessed 6 November 2018, http://www.theweeklyadvertiser.com.au/2016/11/23/sheep-hills-silos-largest-project-for-artist-adnate.

32 'Silo Art Trail' website, accessed 6 November 2018, http://siloarttrail.com/home.

33 'International Art Project Sprouts on Side of Grain Silos in WA's Wheatbelt', *ABC News*, 27 March 2015, accessed 6

The next FORM/CBH silo art project was at Ravensthorpe on the southern fringe of mallee country and, at 530 kilometres from Perth, more than a day trip. Here Perth-based artist Amok Island produced a stunning mural featuring the *Banksia baxteri* flowering cycle, along with its main pollinators—the New Holland honeyeater and the honey possum. Just north of the Fitzgerald River National Park, and within the International Biosphere Reserve, this artwork, completed in September 2016, is well placed to attract 'grey nomads'—retirees on extended travels around Australia—as well as European backpackers heading to the clear white sands and crystal waters of Esperance beaches. It was inspired in part by the annual Ravensthorpe wildflower festival, in place since 1983, and energised by increasing tourist interest in the south-west biodiversity hotspot.

Unlike the wildflower festival, the silo project was conceived and managed externally. Despite a lack of community input, the design appears popular among local people, one resident remarking, 'I think it looks beautiful … There are some painted silos in another country town, but ours are the best by far'.[34] The CEO of CBH summarised the positive impact of the artwork in terms of its cultural tourism potential, linked to the company's corporate social responsibility agenda: 'It's fostered a sense of community pride and the opportunity for sustainable cultural tourism in the areas in which CBH operates'.[35]

This spectacular promotion of local biodiversity elides a tension in local attitudes to the bushland. Much of the wealth of the Ravensthorpe community is derived from farms established by clearing highly biodiverse heathlands and mallee—including *Banksia baxteri* lands—for agriculture, with the product stored inside the silos awaiting transport to Esperance for export. Indeed, in the early 1980s, the area just to the north east of Ravensthorpe was the scene of heated conflict over proposals to clear and develop further vast tracts of bushland (see Chapter 10).[36] While pride in the local flora has flourished over the past three decades, and especially since the Ravensthorpe Wildflower Festival was established, agriculture is still paramount. In 2014 the Shire of Ravensthorpe supported proposals to clear another half a million hectares of bushland across the region. Local mallee fauna is also featured in the Western

---

November 2018, http://www.abc.net.au/news/2015-03-27/phlegm-hense-silo-art-transforms-grain-silos-in-wa-wheatbelt/6355030.

34 Debbie Daw, quoted in Victoria Laurie, 'Never Mind Banksy, Here's "Six Stages of Banksia"', *Australian*, 18 October 2016.
35 Andy Crane, quoted in Laurie, 'Never Mind Banksy'.
36 K. Bradby, R. Jasper, R. Richards and H. Pearce (eds), *Diversity or Dust: A Review of the Impact of Agricultural Land Clearance Programmes in South West Australia* (Melbourne: Australian Conservation Foundation, 1984).

Australian silo trail at Newdegate, where the silos are decked out with Brenton See's images of local wildlife: western bearded dragon, spotted-thighed tree frog, red-tailed phascogale, and iconic malleefowl.

The use of local biodiversity in silo art reflects, on the one hand, local attachment to mallee plant and animal life and, on the other, the commodification of nature within increasingly globalised and competitive tourist markets. In an homogenising world, distinctive local flora and fauna become an important point of uniqueness and a marketing tool. Like the 'big things' (the big pineapple, big ram, big lobster and so on) developed by Australian regional towns and businesses as identity statements and tourist attractions in the 1970s and 80s, the silos have the power to 'make us stop at places we would never have dreamt of visiting'.[37] These, and more highbrow large-scale landscape art projects such as the Kelpies (Falkirk, Scotland, 2013) and Antony Gormley's 'Inside Australia' (Lake Ballard, Western Australia, 2003), certainly have the potential to draw tourists, though not necessarily to extract revenue from them. However, tourism brings risks as well as opportunities, and not all locals welcome all kinds of tourist.[38] Yet local responses to the silo art reveal the dominance of the cultural tourism perspective. The mayor of Yarriambiack, Ray Kingston, described the project as an economic boost, with the art 'giving confidence to local retailers by dragging tourists through the area'.[39]

Silo art projects that do not have meaningful local input run the risk of being by and for the city; a spectacle for urban tourists rather than a locally empowering participatory project. In the early 2000s, research into rural cultural development accumulated evidence of the benefit of the arts to community wellbeing.[40] These findings contributed to an increasing emphasis on the role of the arts in strengthening rural community relationships and identities in the face of ongoing decline.[41] Art could help to provide the social

---

37   John Cross, 'Kings of Kitsch: Big Things', *Artlink* 15, no. 4 (1995): 50.

38   Keith Bradby, 'New Challenges in the Bush', in *The Bush Comes to the City: Fitzgerald Biosphere Project: Papers from a Seminar Held at Murdoch University, 25 September 1987* (Jerramungup: Fitzgerald Biosphere Project, 1989), 65.

39   'Brim Silo Art to Expand into "Outdoor Gallery" through Communities in North-west Victoria', *ABC News*, 10 June 2016, accessed 6 November 2018, http://www.abc.net.au/news/2016-06-09/street-artists-to-create-silo-art-trail-in-regional-victoria/7496990.

40   Julia Anwar McHenry, 'My Art has a Secret Mission: The Role of the Arts in Australian Rural, Remote and Indigenous Communities', *International Journal of the Arts in Society* 4, no. 1 (2009): 159.

41   See, for example, 'Background' and 'Cultural Engagement Framework', website of the Australia Council for the Arts, accessed 6 November 2018, http://www.australiacouncil.gov.au/programs-and-resources/cultural-engagement-framework/.

'glue' that makes for strong and capable communities able to work together to solve problems—including the growing number of environmental ones. One example of this approach is provided by the South Australian mallee town of Coonalpyn, where in 2017 Guido van Helten completed a silo mural featuring local schoolchildren, as part of a wider 'Creating Coonalpyn' arts-led rural recovery program (see figure 13.1). This started with the arts group, which sought to revitalise the town by making it a source of beauty and pride. Their works included a garden project, underpass mural, and mosaics, all of which gave a 'buzz' to the town and a sense that decline was not inevitable.[42]

Figure 13.1: Coonalpyn silo art by Guido van Helten, photographed as 'Three Boys' by Michael Coghlan via Flickr (https://bit.ly/2Cu9T3w) CC BY-SA 2.0.
(https://creativecommons.org/licenses/by-sa/2.0/)

---

42   Coorong District Council, 'A Rural Town Transformed through Art: The Creating Coonalpyn Silo Mural Story', accessed 6 November 2018, https://www.youtube.com/watch?v=SVt1lbnL82g&feature=youtube; Coonalpyn has also led the way with the first 'care farm' for early-onset Alzheimers patients—at a snail farm that hopes to supply the Australian gourmet food market: Claire Campbell, 'Snail Farm in South Australia's Mallee Offering "Hope" to Early Onset Dementia Sufferers', *ABC News*, 3 August 2016, accessed 6 November 2018, http://www.abc.net.au/news/2016-08-03/alzheimers-early-onset-dementia-care-farm-snail-farm-sa-mallee/7686358.

Another more participatory and vernacular approach to rural public art is represented by the Tin Horse Highway, on the road between Kulin and Jilakin Rock in Western Australia. The 'Highway' and its complement, the West Kulin Tin Horses, comprise an evolving array of horses mainly constructed out of old fuel and chemical drums and discarded farm machine parts, displayed on farms adjacent to the road. The tin horses started in association with the Kulin Bush Races, inaugurated by the community in 1995 in an effort to restore morale and attract visitors who would provide an economic boost to the area amid the gloom of the early 1990s. By 1998 the horses were becoming a popular attraction in their own right, and a source of friendly local rivalry. Most years there is a Tin Horse competition, with winners announced on race day.[43]

The humour on the Highway and among the West Kulin Tin Horses is irreverent and often dark. One horse sits on a toilet reading *Playhorse* magazine; another erupts from the sunroof of a mini PV with 'Jilakin Pest Eradicators' painted on the side in rough lettering, its rifle sight set on a tin fox on a nearby fence. There are the four horses of the apocalypse, and 'Dead Cert', the skeleton of a feral horse held together with wire, rusty springs, chains and ploughshares. An elegant seahorse fabricated entirely of tillage points stands in a saline gully (see figure 13.2).[44]

Most of the horses are individual or family projects made in farm workshops with local materials and no external funding, though Kulin Arts Council offers advice and support to prospective tin-horse makers. Many reflect family events or histories, and develop their own histories as they are modified, stolen and replaced. Others are motivated by friendly rivalry or the desire for self-expression. Some of the more bawdy offerings represent a resistance to middle-class cultural norms, and a refusal to subscribe to metropolitan notions of good taste. Part of a broader revival that slowed the population decline as the Kulin community pooled resources and worked together to open a bank, buy a large water slide and landscape the town centre, the tin horses have provided a durable sense of identity and belonging, as well as an ongoing opportunity for self-expression.[45]

---

43 *Much More than Metal: Tin Horse Highway, Kulin, Western Australia* (Kulin: Shire of Kulin, n.d.), 35.

44 Some images and a promotional video can be viewed at: 'Tin Horse Highway', website of the Shire of Kulin, accessed 6 November 2018, http://kulin.wa.gov.au/main/tourism/tin-horse-highway.

45 *Much More than Metal*. See also Gary Burke, 'What is it about Kulin?' (RDA Wheatbelt Inc., April 2017), accessed 6 November 2018, https://vimeo.com/215319359.

Figure 13.2: Seen on the tin horse highway between Kulin and Jilakin Rock, 2015.
(Photographs by and courtesy of Andrea Gaynor)

'Farm art', in the form of sculptures welded out of old farm implements, machinery and paraphernalia, embellishes the main streets of many mallee towns. In Hyden a procession of metal figures relate key moments in the district's history; Jimmy Johnson's spherical creations startle visitors to Wycheproof; Nullawil is famous for its 'iron man'. At Piccoli's Spanner Sculptures, on the Boort–Quambatook road in Victoria, retired farmer John Piccoli has a garden with a marlin, a bull, horses and more, all welded out of spanners. Wheelchair-bound John started admitting visitors to cover the cost of buying the spanners, which come from swap meets or the local hardware store, but his passion for sculpting has boosted the local economy by bringing visitors to the nearby town of Boort.[46] This kind of art is not unique to mallee country—Lockhart in the NSW Riverina, for example, runs a national farm-art competition in association with its annual 'Spirit of the Land' festival.[47] But it is an ideal art tradition for mallee country, skilled, quirky and flexible, able to be carried out alone or in a group, using rural skills and materials but not bound to replicate stereotypical images of mallee identity.

Many local art practices have been inspired by the uniqueness of mallee country. At Lake Grace in the 1960s, local women learned to paint by correspondence and workshops in other regional centres. Margaret Carruthers recalled that 'landscape painting made you really *see* the landscape—the detail, and all the colours'.[48] Lake Grace artists, including Margaret, also used local paperbarks to create monochrome collage landscapes. Some did macramé using sheoak nuts instead of beads. Kerrie Argent, who moved to Lake Grace from Kalgoorlie in 1982, practised part time with various art groups. Argent studied art by distance education at Perth's Curtin University, learning how to use the local trees for natural dyes and making this part of her art practice. Another Lake Grace artist, Tania Spencer, as a child scoured the family farm's junk heap for interesting objects. She also learned the domestic crafts of knitting, crochet, embroidery and macramé from her mother, grandmother and the Country Women's Association ladies, and later put the two together, combining textile techniques with industrial agricultural materials in her art practice.[49] Like Kerrie Argent, Tania Spencer holds a fine arts degree from

---

46   Emily Stewart, 'The Spanner Man: Meet One of the World's Most Unusual Artists', *ABC News*, 14 January 2016, accessed 6 November 2018, http://www.abc.net.au/news/2016-01-14/the-spanner-man-one-of-the-world's-most-unusual-artists/7080726.

47   'Spirit of the Land Festival Lockhart', accessed 6 November 2018, https://www.spiritofthelandlockhart.com.au/.

48   Margaret Carruthers, personal communication, 1 December 2015.

49   'Tania Spencer', website of Tania Spencer, accessed 6 November 2018, http://www.taniaspencer.com/about-tania-spencer.

Curtin, and both exhibit at major events including Sculpture by the Sea. While their works are locally inspired, both also engage with wider environmental themes and issues.[50]

In 2003, the Spencer and Argent families bought a former supermarket building in the main street of Lake Grace and established a Regional Artspace as a multi-use arts venue. They believed that 'place-making—the process of developing a public space that attracts people, builds connectivity and creates identity—is at the heart of a strong creative culture'.[51] Lake Grace Regional Artspace hosts annually up to six exhibitions and four skills workshops, and occasionally a large cultural event. The local community values the public art produced, and it is never vandalised. This artspace is linked with other regional arts groups. In 2010 artists from the south-coast Western Australian town of Denmark spent a ten-day residency at Lake Grace in high summer. These artists found the stark landscape, with its dry mallee scrub and salt lakes, quite alien.

Mallee arts are not only visual. Since 2005 Hyden has hosted a music festival, the 'Wave Rock Weekender', which attracts around six hundred visitors as well as bringing together many local residents. Apart from the income generated for local businesses, the event raises the profile of Hyden and nearby towns. Patchewollock's 2012 music festival in the Victorian Mallee was to be a one-off event but has become an annual highlight, popular with the locals as well as metropolitans.

While the vogue for regional music festivals is recent, there is a tradition of cultural festivals in mallee country, starting with Swan Hill's Shakespeare Festival, which ran from 1947 to 1976. It flourished amid a particular brand of post-war regionalism that understood the quality of life in rural towns to be essential to the growth of a strong agricultural sector.[52] Driven initially by Marjorie McLeod, who had arrived in Swan Hill from Melbourne in 1941, the Shakespeare Festival drew in both celebrities and tourists. It spawned spin-off events and underwrote the development of two motels. Importantly, it also fostered widespread community involvement; in the 1950s and 60s, 'everyone

---

50   'The Creative: Sculptor Kerrie Argent', *We Love Perth*, 11 March 2014, accessed 6 November 2018, http://weloveperth.net.au/the-creative-sculptor-kerrie-argent; 'Sculpture by the Sea, Bondi', website of Tania Spencer, accessed 6 November 2018, http://www.taniaspencer.com/group-exhibitions/group-exhibitions-2008/sculpture-by-the-sea,-bondi./.

51   'What We Do', website of the Lake Grace Regional Artspace, archived 13 March 2016, accessed 6 November 2018, https://web.archive.org/web/20160313203756/http://lakegraceartspace.org/what-we-do.

52   This impetus also underpinned an annual theatre festival launched in Birchip in 1952.

could contribute' to the festival. The local branch of the National Theatre acted as a social club while cultivating acting talent; high school children built and decorated floats for the opening parade; local women cooked and catered. Residents from town and farm, men and women, professionals and workers, all participated—though this spirit of inclusivity did not extend to residents of the nearby Aboriginal settlement at Windy Hill. The Festival started to decline in 1964 when McLeod retired, though the rise of television and car ownership were also factors in that they fostered greater self-sufficiency and diversity of entertainment.[53]

Some festivals in mallee country have looked to the mallee itself for inspiration. Ouyen's Mallee Root Festival, inaugurated in March 2017, brings together community and visitors for a free day of music and fun, including mallee-root-themed events such as the mallee root tossing and 'largest mallee root' competitions. Other festivals continue to take their cue from international events. Kulin, for example, is host to the annual 'Blazing Swan' festival, inspired by the 'Burning Man' festival in Nevada. Revolving around principles such as radical inclusion, decommodification, radical self-expression and communal effort, the event features theme camps, mutant vehicles, installations and performances, and other experiments in temporary community. The event grew from 1,400 participants in 2014, to 2,500 in 2017. While participants are mainly metropolitan, the festival gives back to the local community in ways beyond incidental revenue. In 2015, $10 from each ticket was donated to fund an aged care nurse in the town. Kulin was also gifted a three-metre-wide metal egg sculpture, which can be lit up with a gas flame on special occasions.[54]

Mallee country needs communities able and motivated to care for it and to reverse decades of environmental damage to a land occupied and managed by Aboriginal people for up to sixty thousand years. Art has a role to play in not only revealing deep truths about these places and people's relation to them, but also developing capacity and resilience in communities faced with economic pressure, environmental degradation, depopulation and climate change (see Chapter 12). While an externally driven, narrow focus on cultural tourism may provide a marginal increase in hospitality revenue, and perhaps improve

---

53 Kate Darian-Smith, David Nichols and Jane Grant, 'Cultural Progress in a Rural Community: The Swan Hill Shakespeare Festival', in *Cultural Sustainability in Rural Communities: Rethinking Australian Country Towns*, eds Catherine Driscoll, Kate Darian-Smith and David Nichols (Abingdon: Routledge, 2017), 50–60.

54 'Blazing Swan', website for Blazing Swan Inc., accessed 6 November 2018, http://blazingswan.com.au; Karla Arnall, 'Blazing Swan Memento: Kulin's Giant Egg', *ABC, Great Southern WA*, 15 April 2015, accessed 6 November 2018, http://www.abc.net.au/local/stories/2015/04/15/4216972.htm; see also Burke, 'What is it About Kulin?'

cultural opportunities for residents, even better are grassroots and participatory arts projects and events. These strengthen community relationships—both between local people and between city and country—and provide space for reflection, while also giving visitors pleasure. This kind of art is arguably now necessary, if not sufficient, to sustain the mallee lands.

Commodifying, Conserving, Commemorating

In an era of post-industrial metropolitan profusion, in which work has been intensifying and the leisure choices for better-off urban residents have proliferated, the appeal of sparse, quiet mallee landscapes to urbanites has been growing. In this context, in 2016 an article on the Australian *Traveller* website spruiked the virtues of Lake Albacutya: 'It's almost always dry and provides a stunning vista of, well … nothing. Dead trees, cracked earth. It's not often that most of us get to look out on something that bare'.[55]

In 2014, the big skies of Sea Lake in the Victorian Mallee suddenly began to attract Chinese tourists; by 2016 five to six carloads per week, plus buses, were arriving during the winter months. They came to see Lake Tyrrell—just a salt lake to locals but in China known as the 'mirror lake'. In the right light and wind conditions the lake forms perfect reflections, producing a remarkable backdrop for photographs of figures reflected or walking in infinite sky (see figure 13.3).[56] On clear nights, the absence of light pollution renders the sky so bright that the stars are reflected on the surface of the lake: a miraculous vision, not least for visitors from the bright lights and thick air of urban China. Some also appreciate the quiet; one visitor in 2016 remarked 'I like not many people and quiet here', while Melbourne-based tour guide Freddie Huang said that part of the attraction was that 'nothing is man-made. I mean, very, very wild. They've got nothing but flies, the kangaroos … wild nature stuff. There's not many places in the world have these kind of attractions to see'.[57]

---

55   Gabrielle Costa, 'Victoria Hidden Holiday Spots: Eight Stunning Gems that you've Probably Never Heard of', *Traveller*, 26 December 2016, accessed 6 November 2018, http://www.traveller.com.au/victoria-hidden-holiday-spots-eight-stunning-gems-that-youve-probably-never-heard-of-gtg9ni. The article also lauded Rainbow's 'remarkable sense of community'; an implied contrast to the atomisation of the city.

56   See examples at Cayla Dengate, 'Optical Illusion Is Drawing Tourists to Regional Australian Lake', *Huffpost*, Australian edition, 7 September 2016, accessed 6 November 2018, https://www.huffingtonpost.com.au/2016/09/06/optical-illusion-is-drawing-tourists-to-regional-australian-lake_a_21466829/.

57   Quoted in Danielle Grindlay (reporter), 'Sea Lake', *Landline*, ABC TV, broadcast 25 July 2016, accessed 6 November 2018, http://www.abc.net.au/news/2016-07-23/sea-lake/7657426.

Figure 13.3: In the mid-2010s Lake Tyrrell became popular with Chinese tourists keen to post photos of the remarkable reflections of the 'mirror lake' on social media. Photograph by Richard Goh, https://bit.ly/2McIUNh CC BY-SA 4.0. (https://creativecommons.org/licenses/by-sa/4.0/)

The town initially struggled with the cultural and language differences, which elicited 'varied comments from all around the town'.[58] The tourists, for their part, have struggled with the town's limited trading hours and getting their cars bogged in the soft ground around the lake. However, the Sea Lake community soon established a Chinese Tourism Steering Committee that produced bilingual signage and brochures and expanded the town's tourism infrastructure. Like most mallee towns Sea Lake has struggled with declining population and a loss of services and businesses, particularly in drought. The 'quietness' of the town is a selling point but also a liability, for the small community is stretched in its endeavours to both add value to the tourist experience and protect the fragile environment of Lake Tyrrell.

Nobody quite knows exactly how Chinese tourists became aware of Lake Tyrrell, though it appears that a local publican uploaded a photograph of the lake to social media, which was picked up by friends in Melbourne with connections to the Chinese tourism industry.[59] Social media remains a key element of its attraction; the remarkable images taken at the lake are uploaded to Facebook and Instagram, generating social capital for the visitors.

---

58   Grindlay, 'Sea Lake'.
59   'Why are Chinese Tourists Flocking to Sea Lake?', *3AW693 News* Talk, 7 May 2016, accessed 6 November 2018, https://www.3aw.com.au/why-are-chinese-tourists-flocking-to-sea-lake-20160507-gop0nr/.

A similar route from service town to tourist attraction, albeit before the advent of social media, was taken by Hyden in the early 1960s. In 1963, school principal and amateur photographer Jay Hodges photographed Wave Rock and entered it in the Kodak International Colour Picture Competition at the New York World Photography Fair. It won and, shortly afterwards, was featured on the cover of *Walkabout Magazine* and in a major *National Geographic* feature article. In 1965 the *Women's Weekly* published a full-page photograph of Wave Rock observing that it had 'become a tourist attraction and a favourite picnic spot with the completion of a sealed road'. A nearby cave featuring 'aboriginal hand paintings' was another local drawcard.[60] A syndicate of local farmers built a tin-and-asbestos hotel with six rooms, adding twenty-seven more rooms in 1986, with further expansion taking place in 1995. Income from the hotel/motel enabled development of a caravan park, café and shop, a wildlife park and three museums, in addition to other community facilities. The syndicate has diversified its promotions to attract visitors for a longer stay, encompassing the spectacular seasonal wildflowers, Aboriginal and settler heritage, salt and gypsum lakes, and a hypersaline swimming pool. Another syndicate project was to tackle the spreading dryland salinity, which is affecting Wave Rock and some of the other granite features; here tourism and landcare intersect.[61]

Even ants—usually seen as one of the less attractive features of mallee country—have boosted local identity and tourism at one place. In 1931 a specimen later called the 'Dinosaur Ant', *Nothomyrmecia macrops*, was found near Balladonia, north east of Esperance. This new species appeared to be the the closest living relation to the earliest true ants that emerged around 100 million years ago, during the Cretaceous. It provided a valuable model for studying ant evolution from solitary wasps. Dinosaur Ants are nocturnal, timid and unique. Although they live in colonies, there is no evidence they cooperate in hunting, brood care or other tasks as do other ant species. However, efforts to find further living specimens around the original, ill-documented, discovery site failed, and the species soon became the 'Holy Grail of Myrmecology' (ant science).[62]

In 1977, a party of entomologists led by Bob Taylor was en route from Canberra to Balladonia to look again for the elusive ant. Mechanical trouble

---

60 'Beautiful Australia: Wave Rock', *Australian Women's Weekly*, 28 April 1965, 59.
61 Wave Rock Management Pty Ltd, 'Wave Rock 2 Day Experience', accessed 6 November 2018, http://waverock.com.au/wave-rock-management-pty-ltd.
62 Robert Taylor, 'Australian Endangered Species: Dinosaur Ant', *The Conversation*, 9 January 2014, accessed 6 November 2018, https://theconversation.com/australian-endangered-species-dinosaur-ant-21603.

forced a stopover at Poochera on the Eyre Peninsula, leading to an impromptu survey. They were elated to discover the Dinosaur Ant. Astonishingly, the location where the ant was rediscovered was subsequently bulldozed and burnt during the installation of an underground telephone line, wiping out the only known colony. However, other colonies of the ant were soon located nearby on farmland that was then fenced and protected by the owner. It has since been found in other old-growth mallee woodland areas along the Eyre Peninsula.[63] Poochera became a popular international destination for ant scientists and enthusiasts, and the ant now appears throughout the town—in stencils on lamp-posts, signage, and of course a metal sculpture. While the International Union for the Conservation of Nature regards the ant as critically endangered, the federal government currently deems it ineligible for endangered listing due to insufficient information. This reflects an ongoing lack of investment in scientific knowledge of mallee fauna, especially invertebrates.

Mallee flora has attracted more attention. The Western Australian mallee country hosts a vast array of plant species, many of which have showy flowers in spring,. In addition to the Ravensthorpe Wildflower Show, Ongerup has a long-running spring wildflower festival. And people from other local areas have produced resources for visitors, such as Annie Slarke and Elsie Bishop's attractive colour booklet *Flourish: Native Flora of the Lake Grace Shire*.[64] Newdegate resident Sue Hall has described the growing appeal of nature-based tourism in the Western Australian mallee as an extension of wildflower forays out of Perth. With more comfortable vehicles and better roads, tourists are able to travel further. Many simply desire to escape the pressures of the city, attracted by the notion that 'you can just pull up in amongst the bush and you wake up and the birds are chirping … I think people crave that more'.[65]

Indeed, they do. The 1974 Victorian LCC report on the Mallee declared that, even though the mallee scrub and heath could not 'be rated as attractive scenery', the mallee as a whole is a recreational resource, as a cultural landscape with a 'distinctive character'.[66] Not all visitors came for nature's tranquillity. The Sunraysia Desert Rally—Australia's first off-road motor race—began on

---

63   Australia, Department of the Environment and Energy, 'Dinosaur Ant, Fossil Ant (*Nothomyrmecia macrops*),' accessed 6 November 2018, http://www.environment.gov.au/biodiversity/threatened/nominations/ineligible-species/nothomyrmecia-macrops.

64   Annie Slarke and Elsie Bishop, *Flourish: Native Flora of the Lake Grace Shire* (Lake Grace: Shire of Lake Grace, 2010).

65   Sue Hall, Jan Orr and Anne Rick, interviewed by Andrea Gaynor, Newdegate, 2 December 2015.

66   Land Conservation Council (Vic.), *Report on the Mallee Study Area*, 110.

a course in the eastern Sunset country in 1970. It proved highly popular, and in 1973, 390 trail bikes and 4WD vehicles took part. That year the race was joined by the Mallee Desert Rally around Lake Tyrrell, mainly on private land.[67] A growing number of independent trail bike riders and 4WD enthusiasts were drawn to the area. Given the potential for these uses to erode the land and destroy vegetation, the LCC noted that some roads might need to be closed and that suitable sites should be dedicated to motor sports.[68] Hunting was another popular, if increasingly controversial, recreation. In 1974, the LCC estimated that the number of duck hunters in the region, mainly around the Kerang Lakes, would range from four thousand to twenty thousand, with eight thousand in an average season. Around five thousand quail shooters were estimated to use the south-eastern mallee in a good season, while others hunted rabbits, foxes, pigs and goats.[69] In 1989 the LCC acknowledged the important role played by game shooters in wetland conservation; hunting is ongoing in the area.

Most visitors, however, have sought less extractive engagement with the region's nature. Visits to national parks in the mallee were already increasing in the 1960s and 70s. Wyperfeld National Park hosted 6,400 visitor days in 1967–68; only five years later the figure had ballooned to 19,697.[70] The LCC was aware of this growing demand and, in the 1980s, also determined that ongoing grazing was incompatible with nature conservation and likely to exacerbate problems of soil erosion and increased groundwater recharge in the region.[71] In 1989 it recommended increasing the size and number of mallee parks and conservation reserves. The proposals for extensions to Wyperfeld and the establishment of a vast new national park in the far north west in particular were met with anger from graziers who would be excluded from these areas. Some also objected to the minister's choice of an Aboriginal name—Yanga-Nyawi—for the new park.[72] On 6 May 1990, nearly two thousand people marched in protest at Mildura. Victorian Farmers' Federation president Alex Arbuthnot criticised the government's record of public land management, proposing that 'farmers lead the way in conservation and the

---

67   Land Conservation Council (Vic.), *Report on the Mallee Study Area*, 117.
68   Land Conservation Council (Vic.), *Final Recommendations: Mallee Study Area*, 52.
69   Land Conservation Council (Vic.), *Report on the Mallee Study Area*, 116–17.
70   Land Conservation Council (Vic.), *Report on the Mallee Study Area*, 115.
71   Peter Sandell, *Victoria's Rangelands: In Recovery or in Transition?* (Parks Victoria, 2011), 11, accessed 6 November 2018, https://parkweb.vic.gov.au/__data/assets/pdf_file/0020/521417/Rangeland-master_Final-c2.pdf.
72   Sandell, *Victoria's Rangelands*, 22.

government should use their expertise, not cast them aside'.[73] They argued that the region's altered hydrology and rabbit populations would preclude any return to a 'natural' state, so the government should partner with graziers to keep the land healthy. However, one lease had already been terminated in 1982 after an inspection revealed that up to half of it was 'in an advanced state of desertification'; on another lease an area of five thousand acres was found to have been 'bared off totally' such that even weeds and rabbits were absent.[74] In a 1987 review, consultants for the LCC had found that long-term grazing tended to turn the land into 'agricultural grazing land rather than public land in which grazing is a management tool'. Furthermore, although the grazing licences required licensees to control 'vermin and noxious weeds', some of the licensed areas were carrying so many rabbits that it was seen as 'almost inevitable that the urgently required control works will need to be met by the government'.[75]

The new National Park—named Murray–Sunset—was declared in 1991, along with the other reserves and Wyperfeld extensions. All grazing in the new park areas was wound up by the end of 1996.[76] The LCC's 1989 goal was to establish 'a sustainable (although not entirely natural) ecosystem based on the key elements of the original vegetation communities'.[77] This led to a vast program of ecological restoration, based largely on reducing the remaining sources of grazing pressure. An extensive program of rabbit eradication was undertaken, assisted by the escape of Rabbit Haemorrhagic Disease from its Wardang Island field trial and emergence in the Mallee by 1996.[78] Management of water sources, kangaroos and goats—the latter in association with the Sporting Shooters Association of Australia—has helped to stabilise eroding landscapes and allow for some woodland regeneration. The fears of the LCC's opponents have not been realised, though ongoing management intervention is needed.[79]

Promoted by Parks Victoria for its 'vastness and isolation', these features of Murray–Sunset became liabilities when in 2012 a glitch in Apple's Maps app

---

73 Alex Arbuthnot, 'Feelings Run Hot at Mallee Rally', unknown newspaper, 17 May 1990, clipping in 'Environment General' folder, Ouyen Historical Society. See also Leo O'Leary, 'Bush War: Farmers See Red over Green', *Australian Farmer*, May/June 1990, 6–10.
74 Sandell, *Victoria's Rangelands*, 15–17.
75 Nye, *Report on the Mallee Area Review*, 242.
76 Sandell, *Victoria's Rangelands*, 11.
77 Land Conservation Council (Vic.), *Mallee Area Review: Final Recommendations*, 60.
78 Sandell, *Victoria's Rangelands*, 12, 40.
79 Sandell, *Victoria's Rangelands*, 35–77, 92.

wrongly located Mildura around seventy kilometres away in Murray–Sunset, leaving several unprepared travellers bogged among 'dangerous sandhills' and having to walk long distances to find phone reception for emergency calls.[80] The size and isolation of the growing number of mallee reserves also posed challenges for the agencies charged with park management and maintenance, particularly as the rise of neoliberal ideology saw funding for conservation reduced. In this context, some conservation tasks have been picked up by private conservation initiatives. In 2002, for example, the Trust for Nature purchased Ned's Corner Station—thirty thousand hectares adjoining Murray–Sunset along the Murray River—then immediately destocked it and commenced management for restoration.[81]

A group established to coordinate opposition to the LCC's recommendations called itself the 'Mallee Heritage Committee' in an effort to capitalise on the claims to a traditional livelihood among the region's farmers.[82] This title also drew on a rising interest in the post-war decades in Australia's colonial past and folk traditions, associated with an increasing separation from Britain, growing economic confidence, and a new sense of national identity. Rural communities invested extensive effort in collecting and documenting their local histories, publishing books and brochures, and establishing museums and heritage trails.[83] Many created displays along main thoroughfares of the implements and machinery used in agricultural development. One of the most monumental is 'Big Lizzie', a 45-tonne iron tractor used to clear mallee and scrub around Red Cliffs in the 1920s, and now displayed as a 'fitting tribute' to the region's pioneers. The Village—Historic Loxton was established in 1970 and remains an important Murray Mallee heritage site, maintained by fifty volunteers.

An influential initiative was the Swan Hill Folk Museum, established in 1963 after town clerk Bob Pugsley and town engineer Noel Scofield heard from Eric Westbrook, director of the National Gallery of Victoria, about his recent visit to the folk museum in Skansen, Norway. Buildings were salvaged and relocated to the Swan Hill site to give visitors an experience of life in early Mallee towns. Soon renamed the Pioneer Settlement, it became

---

80   Stuart Rintoul, 'Victoria Police Say Apple has Half-Fixed Troubled Maps App', *Australian*, 11 December 2012, accessed 6 November 2018, http://www.theaustralian.com.au/business/technology/victoria-police-say-apple-has-half-fixed-troubled-maps-app/news-story/2558a95788764de5c38ebf30c8d4c92d.
81   Sandell, *Victoria's Rangelands*, 13.
82   *Victorian Parliamentary Debates*, Legislative Assembly, 5 April 1990, 761.
83   Darian-Smith, Nichols, and Grant, 'Cultural Progress in a Rural Community', 60.

a popular open-air museum and entertainment precinct, with the number of visitors rising rapidly from 170,000 in 1969–70 to 300,000 in 1972–73. About 80 per cent of visitors were from southern Victoria.[84] The enthusiasm for local tradition eclipsed the less proximate tradition of the Shakespeare festival, which wound up shortly after two failed attempts to merge it with a pioneer festival.[85]

Most mallee museums and pioneer villages seek to invoke admiration and respect for the early settler arrivals in a district, paying tribute to their ingenuity and resilience in the face of daily hardship. The evolution of technology is an important theme, with machinery museums creating a satisfying trajectory of improvement over time. Many come with a hefty dose of nostalgia—the bad old days of living without a town water supply or air conditioning amid the dust and heat were also the good old days of the local brass band and big spring picnics. The rolling and burning of the mallee are presented as mute facts, while it takes some effort to read the rise of global capitalism in the array of objects and photographs assembled. These sites operate resolutely at the level of family and community—though Aboriginal families and communities are not often well represented. There is no sense, as began to emerge for example in Western Australian wheatbelt literature of the 1940s, that the obliteration of bushland on such an enormous scale might be 'a crime of human pride against the order of nature'.[86] They are—as are all museums—sites of forgetting as well as remembering.

In recent years, some mallee museums and pioneer villages have continued to act as repositories of local artefacts and stories, limited in their ability to attract tourists due to the scarcity of volunteer labour. Others have garnered sufficient resources to upgrade and differentiate their displays in order to generate more regional tourism. The Mallee Tourist and Heritage Centre at Pinnaroo, inaugurated in 1999, brought together the Gum family Farm Machinery Museum, established in 1969, with the more recent D.A. Wurfel Grain Collection (1983) and the Heritage and Printing Museums (1984 and 1988) to provide several interpretative displays, including one on the role of women in the development of Pinnaroo and the mallee region.[87] The

---

84 Land Conservation Council (Vic.), *Report on the Mallee Study Area*, 111.
85 Darian-Smith, Nichols, and Grant, 'Cultural Progress in a Rural Community', 60.
86 Tony Hughes-d'Aeth, *Like Nothing on this Earth: A Literary History of the Wheatbelt* (Perth: UWA Publishing, 2017), 209.
87 'Mallee Tourist and Heritage Centre', website of South Australian Community History, accessed 6 November 2018, http://community.history.sa.gov.au/mallee-tourist-and-heritage-centre#about.

Warracknabeal Wheatlands Agricultural Machinery Museum, established in 1963, in 2017 received a $100,000 upgrade from the state government's Drought Support Package, in the hope of seeing 'thousands of people flock to Warracknabeal for a piece of agricultural history'.[88] Swan Hill Pioneer Settlement added an award-winning laser show—'Heartbeat of the Murray'—to its attractions. New institutions and installations are emerging to cover different episodes in mallee history. The Bush Engineers Tractor Museum in Lake King, completed in 2016, features six tractors built by local farmers from parts of other machinery in the 1970s and 80s. Visitors can read about how and why the tractors were fabricated, and hear recordings of their engines.[89] Nearby Varley capitalised on its proximity to the rabbit-proof fence with a quirky rabbit cemetery, dedicated 'in Memory of all the Rabbits who lost their lives at the Rabbit Proof Fence'. While many of these institutions are oriented largely toward visitors, some also offer opportunities for local pride and reflection.

Iconic native species still provide rallying points for communities, and a potential source of tourist revenue. The malleefowl became an important focus of community conservation and citizen science efforts prior to the 1980s, and this has continued in recent decades. Biologist Joe Benshemesh established sites for monitoring malleefowl in Victoria in 1987, and local volunteers emerged to help check on and conserve malleefowl. Rod Smith offered courses on malleefowl at the Eyre Bird Observatory in 1989, participants searching the area for mounds.[90] The Friends of Riverland Parks began monitoring a large malleefowl grid in Pooginook Conservation Park in 1990.[91] By 1998 the Ouyen Malleefowlers—later the Victorian Malleefowl Recovery Group—had more

---

88 'Wheatlands Agricultural Machinery Museum Upgraded', website of the Premier of Victoria, 16 April 2017, accessed 6 November 2018, https://www.premier.vic.gov.au/wheatlands-agricultual-machinery-museum-upgraded. At the time of writing, Warracknabeal's most famous son—Nick Cave—was yet to be memorialised in the town, though a film screening of *Distant Sky: Nick Cave and the Bad Seeds Live in Copenhagen* was screened in the Warracknabeal town hall on 22 September 2018 to mark the singer's 61st birthday.

89 'Unique, Homemade Tractors Have New Home in Purpose-built Museum in Western Australia's Great Southern', *ABC News*, 26 October 2017, accessed 6 November 2018, http://www.abc.net.au/news/rural/2017-10-26/lake-king-tractor-museum-shows-farmer-ingenuity/9081872.

90 Stephen Davies, 'Malleefowl at Eyre Bird Observatory, WA', *Around the Mounds: Newsletter of the National Malleefowl Recovery Team*, no. 1 (April 2012): 1, accessed 6 November 2018, http://www.nationalmalleefowl.com.au/uploads/news/id2/ART%202012%20Autumn.pdf.

91 Kevin Smith, 'Friends of Riverland Parks, SA,' *Around the Mounds: Newsletter of the National Malleefowl Recovery Team*, no. 1 (April 2012): 3.

than fifty members; the Malleefowl Preservation Group was established in the West in 1992.[92]

While most of these groups maintained a focus on citizen science and conservation work, the Malleefowl Preservation Group and Ongerup Community Development Group began in 2000 to plan for an Australian Malleefowl Centre. It obtained $1.3 million in funding from government, business and community sources. The Centre opened in 2007 with a café, displays on the malleefowl and its historical context, and a large aviary allowing visitors to see the birds in natural bushland habitat. Despite great volunteer enthusiasm the crucial establishment phase was difficult, with cash-flow projections proving overly optimistic. The relocation of the Ongerup District Telecentre to Yongergnow in 2008 enabled both organisations to survive by sharing staff and resources. The centre continued to grow. In 2009 local Nyungar people established the Bush Tucker Garden with support from Western Power and Colgate University (USA), and in 2010 Yongergnow started captive raising malleefowl for release at sites where the birds had previously existed. Another aviary was added and a five-hectare predator-proof sanctuary established on adjacent land. The first malleefowl chicks bred in captivity at the centre hatched early in 2016.

The history told at Yongergnow is somewhat different from that related in most pioneer and local museums. It starts seventy million years ago with the early rainforests of Gondwana and follows the development of mallee landscapes through deep time. It encompasses traditional Nyungar life, as well as survival into the twentieth century, amid the dramatic rupture caused by pastoral and farming development. The inescapable fact demonstrated here is that the arrival of white settlers and their animals have been the main cause of the malleefowl's demise. This is treated with sensitivity, using quotations, poetry and images, to highlight the growing realisation among farmers that the over-zealous nature of farming development played a major role in the bird's current predicament. Hope is offered in panels depicting the active involvement of the local community in conservation and landcare efforts, while one panel shows the annual activities of farmers and malleefowl side by side, fostering a sense of shared dwelling in place.

---

92   Editorial, *Lowan Behold: The Journal of the Ouyen Malleefowlers* 1, no. 1 (August 1998): 1, accessed 6 November 2018, http://www.malleefowlvictoria.org.au/documents/lowanbehold/Volume%201/Page%201.jpg.

The Aboriginal Imprint

There is also an emerging, if fragile, maturity in approaches to Aboriginal history and heritage. While some settler families have denied that there was ever a significant Aboriginal presence in parts of mallee country, the silence is lifting, old traditions are being recovered and wounds are healing. Aboriginal heritage at Mulka's Cave near Hyden in Western Australia has moved from early appropriation to a more collaborative approach. Visitors can see rock art (mostly hand stencils) and learn about the oral tradition of Mulka—a cautionary tale about wrong-way marriage and the dangers of young children straying from camp that also illuminates the Nyungar connections between Hyden and other parts of the south west. A nearby heritage trail introduces visitors to a gnamma hole as well as plants and animals used by Nyungar people. The interpretive signage acknowledges the Nyungar people as custodians and recognises their continuing connection to these places.

While such sites tend to gloss over the realities of colonisation, a memorial at Kukenarup, west of Ravensthorpe, marks the violence of the 1870s and 80s when settler John Dunn was speared and many Nyungar people were killed. The Yarramoup Aboriginal Corporation and Ravensthorpe Historical Society collaborated on the project, and the memorial was dedicated at a moving ceremony in 2015. The entry is marked by two wings, symbolising the *walitj* (wedge-tailed eagle), on which are inscribed complementary settler and Nyungar commentaries on the site (see figure 13.4). Both acknowledge the long Nyungar occupation of the site as well as their role in recent economic development. While the violence is mentioned, the emphasis is on reconciliation and healing, and the development and dedication of the memorial played an important role in these processes. In 2017, the local council at Elliston on the Eyre Peninsula erected a similar reconciliation memorial to the victims of a massacre that occurred at Waterloo Bay in 1849. It is unclear how many Aboriginal people died and in exactly what circumstances, but Wirangu oral tradition and some historical evidence exists about a violent incident there following the killing of several settlers. However, this memorial has been subject to considerable local controversy over the use of the word 'massacre'. Reconciliation is always a fragile entity.[93]

---

93   Damien Cave, 'Where These Killings a "Massacre"? And Who Gets to Decide?' https://www.nytimes.com/2018/12/04/world/australia/aboriginal-massacres-elliston-memorial.html.

Figure 13.4: Entry to Kukenarup memorial near Ravensthorpe, 2018.
The two wings, symbolising the *walitj* (wedge-tailed eagle), bear Nyungar and settler commentaries on this site of past violence and present reconciliation.
(Photograph by and courtesy of Andrea Gaynor)

Aboriginal attempts to regain land in mallee country that is laid out in freehold farms is still extremely difficult, even after the Mabo case and the subsequent *Native Title Act 1993*. Non-freehold land is claimable but only under strict tests of traditional connection described by Patrick Wolfe as 'repressive authenticity'.[94] The Yorta Yorta on the Murray just east of the Victorian Mallee suffered such repressiveness. The Federal Court ruled that the 'tide of history' had washed away traditional connections and native title rights, a judgment confirmed a decade later by the High Court of Australia.

The Wotjobaluk in the Victorian Mallee proper followed the path of negotiation not litigation. Wotjobaluk groups and the Victorian Labor government in 2002 agreed to: a grant of non-exclusive native title rights to hunt, fish and camp along the Wimmera River (similar to rights enjoyed by the public); an advisory role in managing national parks and Crown lands in certain areas; and freehold title to forty-five hectares at the old Ebenezer Mission and the Antwerp Reserve. The Wotjobaluk were recognised as the Mallee's Traditional Owners but relinquished exclusive native title rights to 98 per cent of the land claimed in order to bring certainty to land use in the region. In November

---

94   Patrick Wolfe, 'Nation and MiscegeNation: Discursive Continuity in the Post-Mabo Era', *Social Analysis*, no. 36 (October 1994): 93–152.

2003 the federal government backed the deal, making the Wotjobaluk the first acknowledged native title holders in Victoria. A spokesperson for the group, Jennifer Beer, declared it would be the first stage in rehabilitating Wotjobaluk law, customs and language.[95]

The Barengi Gadjin Land Council in Horsham now exists as the prescribed body corporate with the legal authority to work on behalf of Wotjobaluk Traditional Owners. It represents five umbrella clan groups descended from seven apical ancestors registered in the Native Title determination, the first named people recorded as being on country when the dispossession began.[96] The benefits of native title are disputed within Aboriginal groups, but it has created more community awareness and respect for the aspirations of Traditional Owners, especially their desire to create a sustainable connection to country. The old Ebenezer Mission site is now in Wotjobaluk hands, the church, outbuildings still white against the blue mallee sky and parched grasses. However, the site needs a viable plan for the adaptive re-use and preservation of its buildings, lest they go the way of other buildings in the mallee and fall into ruin.

By 2018, native title determinations by the Native Title Tribunal over other parts of mallee country are either in process or finalised with mixed outcomes. In the South Australian Murray Mallee, non-exclusive native title exists along the Murray River from the Victorian/South Australian border to Morgan. On the Eyre Peninsula coastal areas are under claim, but inland on the Peninsula native title has been found not to exist. However, claimants gained non-exclusive title over some conservation parks, such as the Barngala title to Hincks and Hambidge Wilderness Protection Areas. In the West, much of the south west is subject to the Noongar Native Title Settlement, but determinations have been made by the Native Title Tribunal over mallee country from Ravensthorpe to five hundred kilometres eastward. Along the coast, native title has been extinguished or found not to exist. However, over much of the remainder of this area, recognition has been given as non-exclusive native title and, in some areas, an exclusive form of native title.[97] The Ngadju have exclusive title to some undeveloped mallee country in a band

---

95 *Age*, 4 November 2002; 15 October and 21 November 2003.
96 'Welcome to Barengi Gadjin Land Council', website of the Barengi Gadjin Land Council, accessed 15 January 2017, http://www.bglc.com.au.
97 See 'Native Title Determinations and Claimant Applications: Schedule of Native Title Determination Applications: As at 31 December 2016', website of the National Native Title Tribunal, accessed 10 April 2017, http://www.nntt.gov.au/Maps/Schedule_and_Determinations_map.pdf.

to the north of Esperance. In 2018 the federal government granted over half a million dollars to establish the Ngadju Indigenous Protected Area of 4.4 million hectares.[98]

Determinations are slow, held up by legal processes and numerous challenges from non-Aboriginal objectors and Aboriginal counter-claimants. Outcomes are often unfair on people in mallee country, where reserve and assimilation policies shifted people around. It is difficult to prove in court traditional and continuous connections to land. The claims, however, reveal ongoing Aboriginal adherence to traditional clan lands and their boundaries as a supreme value, and the desire to gain respect and recognition as Traditional Owners. Native title can do much to erode the humiliations and heartbreak over the loss of land in the European takeover of mallee country.[99]

In the context of a wider, global neoliberal denial of community, there has been a growing realisation that country needs people who care for it, especially Traditional Owners, and that the past tight focus on agricultural production was insufficient to sustain healthy rural communities. In the early twenty-first century, several mallee communities have joined together to invest in basic services and facilities to sustain their communities, including the community-owned pubs and social hubs at Loxton, Nyabing and Hopetoun. Attempts at economic diversification have often struggled with a geography developed around the demands of broadacre grain and sheep, but roads constitute multipurpose infrastructure that has facilitated growth in tourism. Local communities have energetically promoted and developed mallee places as ideal destinations for visitors seeking nature, rural tradition, or even just sparse backdrops to their own aesthetic ambitions. Aboriginal heritage is increasingly a part of that.

However, rural arts, nature, heritage—Aboriginal and European—are arguably even more important for sustaining local communities than attracting visitors. They now play a critical role in developing community relationships, a sense of place, and landscapes for livelihood. The growing attention being

---

98 Melissa Price, MP, '$2.5 Million Investment for New Indigenous Protected Areas', media release, website of the Australian Government: Department of the Environment and Energy, 30 May 2018, accessed 6 November 2018, http://www.environment.gov.au/minister/price/media-releases/mr20180530.html; 'Native Title Determinations Maps and Regional Maps', website of the National Native Title Tribunal, accessed 6 November 2018, http://www.nntt.gov.au/assistance/Geospatial/Pages/Maps.aspx.

99 Richard Broome, *Aboriginal Victorians: A History Since 1800* (Sydney: Allen & Unwin, 2005), 379–85.

paid by business and government to cultural sustainability, particularly through the arts, reflects a revived comprehension of the need to foster positive community relationships and pride in order to maintain rural populations that are able to carry on agricultural production.

There is also a dawning recognition that mallee country needs strong and motivated communities with the capacity to repair and sustain local ecologies. The arts can play a role in encouraging—and indeed reflecting—a deep identification with local nature, while providing an attractive and interesting place in which to live. But there is yet much cultural work to do in reconciling settler and Indigenous interests, knowledges and histories. The way forward is unclear, for the mallee lands remain inextricably tied into regional and global circulations of capital, people and ideas. As such, the future will lie with metropolitan culture and politics and international markets, as well as changing climates and local resilience.

EPILOGUE

We must prepare the land for a difficult sowing,
a long and hazardous growth of a strange bread
that our sons' sons may harvest and be fed

Judith Wright, 1945[1]

Over millennia, the flora and fauna of mallee country became exquisitely adapted to the semi-arid climate and variable seasons, enduring and even thriving in the wind, sand and heat. Attachment and mobility sustained Indigenous peoples' leisured mastery of their mallee homelands. Arriving in mallee country from the mid-nineteenth century, settlers reliant on non-indigenous plants and animals have had less time to adapt to the unique conditions. While they developed enterprising strategies for maintaining production, the climate has remained challenging and will become more so in the future.

The year in which we finished this book, 2018, was a difficult one globally, due to extreme weather. Record high summer temperatures seared across Europe into Russia, causing unprecedented wildfires in Greece. Wildfires affected the United States in November, including the worst in a century in Butte County, California, which killed eighty-six people and thousands of stock, and destroyed fourteen thousand homes and five thousand other structures, altogether costing several billion dollars. In Australia extreme drought in Queensland and NSW was followed in late November by unprecedented high temperatures and low humidity. Such conditions fostered 130 fires in north and central Queensland, some rated for the first time as 'catastrophic'. On the same day a 'super storm' dumped 120 millimetres on the Sydney region, much of it over several hours, the highest single November day's total in Sydney since 1984.

Three key climate reports were issued as this book was completed. In October the Intergovernmental Panel on Climate Change released its most challenging report yet on the impacts of global warming of 1.5 degrees Celsius above pre-industrial levels, which on current trends will be reached

---

1   Judith Wright, 'Dust', *Meanjin Papers* 4, no. 1 (1945): 20.

between 2030 and 2050. To prevent overshoot beyond 1.5 degrees Celsius will require, the panel reported, 'rapid and far-reaching transitions in energy, land, urban and infrastructure (including transport and buildings) and industrial systems. These systems transitions are unprecedented in terms of scale'.[2] In November, a federally mandated report in the United States, backed by thirteen key agencies including Defence, Energy, NASA and the Smithsonian Institute, warned that: 'Earth's climate is now changing faster than at any point in the history of modern civilization, primarily as a result of human activities ... The assumption that current and future climate conditions will resemble the recent past is no longer valid'. It also concluded that current actions by governments are of inadequate scale to avoid substantial damage to the economy, environment and human health.[3] Also in November 2018, the ninth annual United Nations Emissions Gap Report tracking progress towards current global agreements to keep emissions under 2 degrees Celsius, and ideally below 1.5 degrees Celsius, reported dismal progress, with global CO_2 emissions rising in 2017. The report warned that if G20 countries did not raise their target ambitions before 2030, 'exceeding the 1.5°C goal can no longer be avoided'. Indeed, current targets 'imply global warming of 3°C by 2100, with warming continuing afterwards'.[4]

In Australia, between 1910, when the national observational data sets began, and the end of 2018, the average temperature has risen by 1.1 degrees Celsius. Most of the recorded rise has taken place since 1950, and human action is accepted as the major cause of the rise by the vast majority of scientists. Recent scientific research using natural, documentary and instrumental sources to study the climate of eastern Australia over the last thousand years has clearly identified the impact of human-induced climate change since the industrial revolution. While the regional climate is naturally—notoriously—variable, evidence relating to drought, snow, fire, flood and sea level rise all clearly show change beyond the range of natural variability.[5]

---

2   Intergovernmental Panel on Climate Change, 'Global Warming of 1.5°C. Summary for Policy Makers', A1, C2, accessed 7 November 2018, http://report.ipcc.ch/sr15/pdf/sr15_spm_final.pdf.

3   US Global Change Research Program, *Fourth National Climate Assessment, Vol. 2, Impacts, Risks, and Adaptations in the United States*, Overview, 1–3, accessed 25 November 2018, https://nca2018.globalchange.gov.

4   United Nations Environment Programme, *Emissions Gap Report 2018*, Executive Summary, 4, accessed 28 November 2018, https://www.unenvironment.org/resources/emissions-gap-report-2018.

5   Joëlle Gergis, *Sunburnt Country: The History and Future of Climate Change in Australia* (Melbourne: Melbourne University Press, 2018), 187. See especially chapters 27–29.

At the close of 2018, nine of the ten hottest years recorded in Australia had occurred since 2005, while worldwide all ten hottest years had happened since 1998, the last four being the hottest. Despite the absence of an El Niño effect, 2018 was the third-warmest year on record in Australia. Its average maximum temperatures were second highest, and its minimum temperatures the eleventh warmest. Rainfall over the south-east quarter of the continent was the seventh lowest ever recorded.[6] The number of extreme heat days is increasing while cold weather extreme days are decreasing.[7] The long-term decline in rainfall observed in south-western Australia since the 1970s, and south-eastern Australia since the mid-1990s, can only be explained by models that include increased levels of carbon dioxide in the atmosphere due to human activities.[8]

The natural processes driving climate variation from year to year, including the El Niño and La Niña systems in the Pacific and the Indian Ocean Dipole in the West, still influence our weather, but the climate is getting hotter and drier as anthropogenic carbon emissions rise. Mallee farmers will increasingly contend with more challenging farming conditions. Challenges are of course not new. Farmers have used technology to farm better and smarter since the first use of the stump jump plough to manage the mallee lignotubers. Machinery evolved from simple horse-drawn implements to powerful computerised mechanical behemoths. Over a century, wise mallee farmers learnt that survival required larger farms and scaled-up machinery. Scientists helped farmers on mallee country by experimentation on wheat types and cropping techniques, on fertilisers and trace elements, and on ways to arrest drifting soil and do battle with rabbits. Recently, pipelines in Victoria's Mallee and aquifers in parts of the Murray Mallee of South Australia have ameliorated some of the risks of low or variable rainfall. Science and technology have helped to develop resilience against hotter and drier years, but where will the limits to such resilience be found?

At present, technology continues to offer hope if not a sustainable solution to the problem of climate change. Plant genetics and breeding are important focus areas, as warming climates are reducing wheat yields. After thirteen years of effort by the International Wheat Genome Sequencing Consortium,

---

6   'Annual Climate Statement 2018', Australia, Bureau of Meteorology, accessed 10 January 2019, http://www.bom.gov.au/climate/current/annual/aus/?utm_source=tw&utm_medium=org&utm_campaign=sm-004-0002&utm_content=vid.
7   Gergis, *Sunburnt Country*, 183–4.
8   'Rainfall. Climate 2016', Australia, State of the Climate, accessed 31 January 2019, https://soe.environment.gov.au/theme/climate/topic/2016/rainfall.

the team of over two hundred scientists announced in the journal *Science* in August 2018 that it had achieved what was previously considered almost impossible. The genome of bread wheat, five times larger and more complex than the human genome, had been mapped. Consortium team member Dr Catherine Feuillet remarked: 'we have a high-quality reference sequence that can be used to accelerate wheat research and breeding'.[9] Also in 2018, Professor Roger Parish and Dr Song Li of La Trobe University, in conjunction with Dr Rudy Dolferus at CSIRO, were researching heat stress in bread wheat. Field trials revealed a single high-temperature day during flowering can reduce yields by 25 per cent. Their research into the genetic dimensions of pollen development aims to provide useful tools for plant breeders to rapidly develop heat-tolerant strains of wheat.[10]

Hope is also growing for socially driven responses. Australians increasingly believe that human-caused climate change is a reality, and farmers' beliefs are shifting too. In recent years over half of all Australians have come to believe that climate change is occurring, and in 2018 a poll by the Australian Institute revealed that 76 per cent, a 5 per cent increase over the previous year, believe climate change is happening.[11] Farmers' attitudes have been slower to shift, but this is changing. A survey of a thousand irrigators in the Murray–Darling Basin was carried out in 2015–16 by two agricultural researchers, Sarah Ann Wheeler, professor of Water Economics at the University of Adelaide, and Céline Nauges, research director of the French National Institute for Agricultural Research. In their survey, 43 per cent of farmers in this key region accepted that climate change was a risk, up from 32 per cent in their 2010–11 survey. However, even in 2016 a majority of those surveyed still denied climate change was occurring. The researchers were not convinced that the farmers' conservatism fully explained their scepticism or denial, and suggested psychological factors also played a role. Respondents might not have wished to acknowledge a more uncertain future, or worse still, that they would leave a farm to the next generation

---

9   Melissa Davey, 'Scientists Sequence Wheat Genome in Breakthrough once Thought "Impossible"', *Guardian*, 17 August 2018, accessed 6 November 2018, https://www.theguardian.com/science/2018/aug/16/scientists-sequence-wheat-genome-in-breakthrough-once-thought-impossible.

10 Grain Research Development Corporation, 'Heat-tolerance Genes in Sight for Wheat', accessed 18 January 2019, https://grdc.com.au/resources-and-publications/groundcover/groundcover-138-january-february-2019/heat-tolerance-genes-in-sight-for-wheat.

11 Ebony Bennett, *Climate of the Nation 2018: Tracking Australia's Attitudes towards Climate Change and Energy*, The Australian Institute, accessed 6 November 2018, http://www.tai.org.au/content/climate-nation-2018.

that was going to be less productive, not more so, than when they inherited it.[12] Their faith in progress was being threatened and their stewardship of the land questioned. However, farmers' groups for climate action now exist, and in 2018 the National Farmers' Federation president, Fiona Simson, declared that 'people on the land' had 'turned a corner', being no longer able to ignore the evidence of climate change on their farms. Simson acknowledged that the changes were exacerbating the 'already unpredictable impacts of drought' and called for action to reduce carbon emissions.[13]

Those living in mallee environments have proved resilient. Many farmers have hung on through difficult droughts and tough market conditions, as this book has revealed. Despite population loss resulting from farms needing to expand to survive, some people—including small groups of refugee families—are moving into mallee towns and, in the process, slowing or arresting population loss. The Mildura Local Government Area, for example, was declared a Refugee Welcome Zone in 2002, and refugees are increasingly making their homes there. Some of these groups are also farming, using labour-intensive and traditional techniques to make idle farmland productive again—initiatives that also build community relationships and resilience.[14]

Many mallee plant and wildlife species have hung on in conservation areas, remarkably in some cases, although their habitats have been vastly reduced and fragmented. New initiatives bring hope. Connectivity conservation organisations Gondwana Link (south-western Australia), WildEyre (Eyre Peninsula), and Habitat 141 (Murray Mallee and Wimmera) are pursuing visions for restoring and maintaining biodiversity and ecosystem function in reserves and across farmland on a vast scale—millions of hectares—including mallee country.[15] These groups work through cohesive processes involv-

---

12 Sarah Ann Wheeler and Céline Nauges, 'Farmer's Climate Denial Begins to Wane as Reality Bites', *The Conversation*, 12 October 2018, accessed 6 November 2018, https://theconversation.com/farmers-climate-denial-begins-to-wane-as-reality-bites-103906.

13 Mark Ludlow, 'Farmers Must Tackle Climate Change: NFF', accessed 6 November 2018, https://www.afr.com/news/politics/farmers-need-to-do-more-to-tackle-climate-change-says-nff-20180828-h14nme; Katharine Murphy, '"We've Turned a Corner": Farmers Shift on Climate Change and Want a Say on Energy', *Guardian*, 30 June 2018, accessed 6 November 2018, https://www.theguardian.com/australia-news/2018/jun/30/weve-turned-a-corner-farmers-shift-on-climate-change-and-want-a-say-on-energy.

14 Olivia Dun, Deborah Bogenhuber, Lesley Head, Joselyne Kadahari, Natascha Klocker, John Niyera and Joel Sindayigaya, 'Bringing Together Landless Farmers and Unused Farmland: The Sunraysia Burundian Garden and Food Next Door Initiative', in *Reclaiming the Urban Commons: The Past, Present and Future of Urban Food Production*, eds Nick Rose and Andrea Gaynor (Perth: UWA Publishing, 2018), 39–52.

15 See http://www.gondwanalink.org/; http://www.habitat141.org.au/; http://wildeyre.com.au. All accessed 6 November 2018.

ing local Indigenous people and government agencies as well as community organisations, private landholders and philanthropists, and through taking a holistic approach to conservation and restoration. In less than two decades they have achieved some remarkable results. For example, by 2018 groups involved in Gondwana Link had secured private funding to purchase 16,000 hectares of rural property in key habitat gaps and restored 6,500 hectares of marginal farmland to bushland. They had also supported the Ngadju people to develop a ranger program extending over 4.4 million hectares, and worked with Curtin University and Nyungar elders to establish a Bush University campus that delivers education informed by Nyungar culture on country, on one of the properties secured for Gondwana Link.[16]

Avifauna also provide some hopeful stories. While some mallee bird species are endangered or vulnerable, one of the smallest mallee birds, the tiny Mallee Emu-wren, has survived against the odds. This 15-centimetre-high wren with reddish head feathers, a white feathered throat and weighing only five grams is a feisty bird. But by 2014 it was found in only four mallee country conservation areas. Bushfires in that year killed the Mallee Emu-wrens in Ngarkat and Billiatt Conservation Parks in South Australia, but a healthy colony persisted in the Murray–Sunset National Park. In the winter of 2018 forty of those birds were translocated to Ngarkat to colonise the regenerating *Triodia* razor grasses and, it is hoped, provide for the survival of the species.[17] This is one of six birds, including the malleefowl and regent parrot, that are the focus of a Mallee Birds Conservation Action Plan promoted by four governments, two zoos, two universities and Birdlife Australia.[18]

This book began with the land and must end with it. Mallee landscapes have been changed from natural to cultural ones over the last fifty thousand years or more. The country that emerged over millions of years in the East and tens of millions of years in the West is now vastly altered. At first it was shaped by fire managed by Indigenous people over many millennia. Then, from the late-nineteenth century, came a rapid and dramatic transformation wrought by settler farmers, many of whom paid with their mental, financial and physical health. In just over a hundred years, three-quarters of mallee country was flattened, burnt and cleared. Mallee nature was not easy to subdue,

---

16   Gondwana Link, 'Overview', accessed 6 November 2018, http://www.gondwanalink.org/aboutus/wherewework.aspx.
17   Liam Mannix, 'A Passion for Angry Birds and Smart Phones Finally Pays Off', *Age*, 23 July 2018.
18   'Threatened Mallee Birds Conservation Action Plan', accessed 8 November 2018, http://www.birdlife.org.au/projects/threatened-mallee-birds.

and countless hours of back-breaking labour as well as technical ingenuity were devoted to its eradication. As we have shown, the environmental cost of this transformation has been immense.

As the twenty-first century unfolds, the remnants of mallee nature that remain relatively unscathed, as well as the farms that settlers carved out of it, are both vulnerable to climate breakdown and the drying and fires accompanying it. How each will survive remains to be seen, but, just as humans have wrought dramatic and destructive changes to mallee country in the past, they are now demonstrating a capacity to apply their energies and initiative to secure the future of this ancient land and the preservation of its exquisite biota.

APPENDIX

Regional decline in wheat yields and Total Factor Productivity under climate conditions experienced from 2001–01 to 2014–15 compared with what would have been achieved under average climate conditions from 1915 to 2015

Region	Average Annual Decline in Wheat Yield %	Average Annual Decline in Total Factor Productivity %
Victorian Mallee		
Mildura	-17.18	-9.55
Buloke	-18.70	-9.22
Swan Hill	-12.03	-6.21
South Australian Mallee		
Murray Mallee		
Southern Mallee	-10.45	-7.71
Loxton-Waikerie	-7.17	-1.18
Karoonda-East Murray	-4.04	-1.58
Eyre Peninsula		
Wuddinna	-4.11	-0.05
Kimba	-1.40	0.69
Cleve	-7.02	-3.49
Elliston	-2.59	0.17
Western Australia		
Esperance	-4.94	-1.45
Lake Grace	-15.25	-8.67
Ravensthorpe	-10.47	-5.17
Kondinin	-13.92	-7.64
Kulin	-14.36	-7.85
Kent	-16.78	-8.62

This table is drawn from data published by ABARES.[1] The table is derived from data that ABARES have collected from their annual surveys of sampled farms from 1978 to 2015. The aim of the ABARES project was to measure the impact of climate change on the productivity of wheat farms. Total Factor Productivity is a term used by economists to measure the output of farms (the value of what they produce such as wheat and wool) relative to inputs (the cost of machinery, chemicals and seed etc.). ABARES also examined the impact of climate on wheat yields. Farming in Australia, and particularly in much of the mallee landscapes explored in this book, is subject to highly variable climate conditions. Sharp fluctuations in wet and dry years can cause 'short run noise' in estimates of productivity, and with climate changing over time it becomes difficult to interpret productivity trends. To overcome these problems economists at ABARES have developed computer models to 'control for climate' and to predict what would happen under alternative climate conditions. The performance of farms under recent climate conditions is compared, or modelled, with the performance they would have experienced under a 'counterfactual climate' of the average climate conditions from 1915 to 2015. Of the two measures, wheat yield is more sensitive to climate conditions than productivity. Both, however, show that climate change has had a profound impact on mallee farms. To stay ahead of climate change farmers have had to adopt new technology and new farming management practices.

---

[1] The data can be found at https://public.tableau.com/views/Farmperformanceandclimate/HOME?:embed=y&:display_count=yes&:showVizHome=no

NOTE ON MEASUREMENTS

At the time of European colonisation of Australia, the Imperial system of weights and measures was in use. The system continued almost unchanged until the gradual introduction of metric units from 1970 onwards. Throughout this volume, weights and measures have been expressed in terms that would have been understood by contemporaries.

Amounts of money have been expressed as they would have been at the time. The British pound was the basic currency in Australia and equivalent in value until a devaluation of the Australian pound to 80 per cent of the English pound in the 1930s Great Depression. In 1966 Australia moved to decimal currency and £1 became $2. The 20 shillings in each pound became 200 cents; the 12 pence in each shilling became 10 cents; the sixpence became 5 cents; but there was no exact equivalence for 3 pence and a penny, although the two cent and one cent coins were respectively approximate to those two coins. Given inflation over long periods of time, it is less helpful to make direct comparisons of imperial and decimal currency than to consider the relative purchasing power of money. In this volume, money values are linked on occasion to workers' weekly or annual wages, or an item of consumption such as a loaf of bread.

A bag of wheat before 1908 contained about four bushels (240 lbs or 108 kgs) and thereafter three bushels (180 lbs or 81 kgs). A bushel of wheat at 13.5 per cent moisture content was 60 lbs or 27.22 kgs.

Conversion Table

Imperial to Metric	Metric to Imperial
Inch = 2.54 cm	Centimetre = 0.39 in
Foot = 30.00 cm	Metre = 3.28 ft
Yard = 91.00 cm	Kilometre = 0.62 mile
Acre = 0.41 ha	Hectare = 2.47 acre
Mile = 1.60 km	Gram = 0.04 oz
Ounce = 28.30 gm	Kilogram = 2.20 lbs
Pound = 4.54 gm	Tonne = 0.98 ton
Ton = 1.02 tonne	Millilitre = 0.35 fl oz
Pint = 568 ml	Litre = 1.76 pint
Quart = 1.14 l	
Gallon = 4.55 l	

ACKNOWLEDGEMENTS

This project was conceived in 2010. A pilot data survey undertaken by David Harris and funded by La Trobe University confirmed its viability. The team, led by Katie Holmes and including Ruth Ford, won an Australian Research Council grant in 2012 (DP130102169), which was essential for the project's implementation and successful completion. La Trobe University and the University of Western Australia, where members of the team are based, gave significant financial and research infrastructure support to the project. For this institutional support we are extremely thankful.

From the moment of grant writing onwards this was a collaborative project that was both enjoyable and immensely challenging. We all contributed to the framing of the research and book over a myriad of email discussions across a continent and four face-to-face discussions in Melbourne, each of one or two days' duration. We also held a conference in Melbourne to present and discuss our initial findings, gave papers to national and international conferences, and published a special issue on mallee country for the American journal *Agricultural History* in 2017. When we proceeded to work on the manuscript, Richard Broome led the writing of chapters 1 to 4 and 8, Charles Fahey of chapters 6 and 9, Andrea Gaynor of chapters 10, 11 and 13, and Katie Holmes of chapters 5, 7 and 12. We all contributed ideas, feedback, and words to each part of the book. Richard Broome also led the writing of the prologue and epilogue as well as undertaking invaluable project management work: coordinating the production of maps, compiling front matter, collating final versions of chapters and part introductions, and liaising with the publisher.

The project was assisted by several excellent research assistants who added enormous research power to this project and without whom this book could not have been written. They are: Janette Bailey, Jane Davis, Kate Laing, Kerriann Larsen, Kylie Mirmohamardi, Katrina Stats, Yann Toussaint and Karen Twigg. Sadly, Janette Bailey suffered a massive and fatal brain haemorrhage in 2016, and we dedicate this volume to her memory. The significant and expert help of these researchers enabled us to cover a vast amount of material that was loaded onto a shared database called Zotero, and there sorted, catalogued and managed by Karen Twigg.

Many colleagues too numerous to name attended conferences, seminars and community events where we presented, and they always gave generous and invaluable feedback. Several people kindly read and gave pertinent comments on our penultimate draft, and we thank them for their significant help and considerable time commitment to our project, namely: Kerry Conway, Russell Hilton, Anne McClelland, and John Cooke. We are also grateful to Melbourne Life Writers and to Keith Bradby for invaluable detailed feedback on several chapters. Liz Downes and Elizabeth Gralton gave meticulous help in wrangling footnotes into a coherent and consistent format. Judith Smart provided thorough copyediting and proofreading to bring four authors into a coherent whole.

The School of History at the Australian National University provided space and support to Andrea Gaynor while she conducted research at the university's library while on sabbatical in 2016. In thinking and writing on this project, Andrea also benefited from the stimulating environment and intellectual generosity found at the Rachel Carson Center for Environment and Society, Ludwig-Maximilians-Universität München (Munich). We also thank Kerry Conway and Russell Hilton of Hopetoun for their kindness in providing accommodation over several nights for two of our team, and those who provided lunch or invaluable mallee experiences, including Ian and Anne McClelland of Birchip, George and Pat Gum of Pinnaroo, the Slarke family of Lake Grace, and Ron and Gwyn Wiseman of Hopetoun.

The following institutions provided access to and assistance to use their archives: the National Archives of Australia (Canberra and Melbourne offices); the University of Melbourne Archives; Public Record Office Victoria; and the State Records Office of Western Australia. Libraries that provided access to their collections included: the J.S. Battye Library of West Australian History; the Borchardt Library, La Trobe University; Loxton Public Library; Mildura Library; the State Library of South Australia; State Library Victoria; Swan Hill Regional Library; the Mitchell Library, State Library of New South Wales; ANU Libraries; and the National Library of Australia. The following generously provided access to their picture collections: the Haddon Library of Archaeology and Anthropology, University of Cambridge; the Lester Marks Harradine Collection, Horsham; the National Gallery of Victoria; the National Library of Australia; the State Library of South Australia; the State Library of Western Australia; and State Library Victoria. We are also grateful to those individuals who generously assisted by providing access to their private archives and collections, including: Geoff Bee, Albany/Jacup; Keith Bradby, Albany; and Gwyn and Ron Wiseman, Hopetoun. We thank Meredith McKinney for permission to reproduce the extract from Judith Wright's poem, 'Dust'.

Historical societies provided important help, including: Birchip, Dimboola, Hopetoun, Mildura, Murrayville, Ouyen, Rainbow, the Royal Historical Society of Victoria, and the Royal Western Australian Historical Society. We are also grateful for the assistance of the Barengi Gadjin Land Council (Horsham); Birchip Cropping Group; Hyden Community Resource Centre; Lake Grace Visitor Centre; Mallee District Aboriginal Services; Mallee Tourist and Heritage Centre, Pinnaroo; Newdegate Pioneer Museum; Varley and Districts Museum; Wave Rock Visitor Centre; the Millewa Pioneer Park (Meringur), and the Wimmera Mallee Pioneer Museum, Jeparit.

The following advisers and colleagues greatly assisted the project: Kerrie Argent, Lake Grace Regional Artspace; Trudy Bell, Wamba Wamba Elder, Swan Hill; Wendy Brabham, Wamba Wamba Elder, Swan Hill; Keith Bradby, historian and CEO Gondwana Link, Albany; John Burch, historian; Nicole Chalmers, historian, Esperance; Sheenagh Collins, Hyden; Dale Conroy, historian, Dimboola; John Cooke, botanist; Abby Cooper, archaeologist, Horsham; Annie Delhaize, Albany; Ruth Ford, historian, La Trobe University; Bill Gammage, historian, Canberra; Tom Gara, historian, Adelaide; Michael Gilby, Victorian Fisheries Authority Officer, Mildura; Mark Grist, archaeologist and Nyeri Nyeri Elder, Mildura; Sharon Harrup, mapmaker; Steve Howell, librarian, J.S. Battye Library, Perth; Tony Hughes-d'Aeth, literary scholar, University of Western Australia; Rosemary Jasper, Ravensthorpe; Jim Johnson, Albany; Rebecca Jones, historian; Alf Lane, Hyden; Glenace Meyer, Albany; Myles Mitchell, archaeologist, Denmark; Brett Moir, Perth; Mina Muhlen, historian, Melbourne; Charlie Nicholson, Fremantle; Mandy Paull, historian, Adelaide; Damien Rathbone, ecologist, Albany; Jayne Regan, historian, Australian National University; Ron Richards, Ravensthorpe; Ted Ryan, historian, Nullawil; Michael Stewart, manager Barengi Gadjin Land Council, Horsham; Malcolm Traill, historian, Albany; University of Western Australia history writing group members; Gwyn and Ron Wiseman, Hopetoun; Rohan Walker, Charles William Coote's grandson; Enid and Max Wurfels, Pinnaroo.

Several colleagues took the time to attend our symposium on mallee histories, held at La Trobe University in 2014. We thank Nicole Chalmer, Matthew Churchward, Lisa Dale-Hallett, Liz Downes, Don Garden, Tom Griffiths, David Harris, Sue Janson, Sara Maroske, Malcolm McKinnon, Ruth Morgan, Libby Robin, Lauren Rickards, Kathryn Schneider, Mike Stevens, and Sharon Willoughby for their insightful feedback and ideas.

Our history of mallee country would have been colourless without the many mallee residents who agreed to take a risk, generously share their stories and

Acknowledgements

be interviewed by our team. In alphabetical order they are: Helen Ballantyne, Hopetoun; Geoff Bee, Albany; John Cass, Loxton; Jan Cass, Loxton; Kerry Conway, Hopetoun; Mick Evans, Mantung; Suzi Evans, Mantung; Merv Gladigau, Loxton; Raelene Gladigau, Loxton; George Gum, Pinnaroo; Sue Hall, Newdegate; Gail Harradine Wotjobaluk artist, Horsham; Brett Harrison, Wotjobaluk Cultural Officer, Barengi Gadjin, Horsham; Nancy Harrison, Wotjobaluk Elder, Dimboola; Russell Hilton, Hopetoun; Bev Hyde, Varley Museum; Cathie Kelly, Newdegate; Malcolm Kelly, Newdegate; Nick Kelly, Newdegate; Peter Kelly, Mildura; Jack Larkin, Spring Gully; Neil Mcfarlane, Vinefera; Ron Marks, Wotjobaluk Elder, Horsham; Allan Marshall, Lake Grace; Graham Mann, Bendigo (formerly Quambatook); Geoffrey Marshall, Hyden; Ian McClelland, Birchip; Anne McClelland, Birchip; Helen McDonald, Newdegate; Adrian Meehan, farmer, Pine Plains; Rolf Meeking, Hyden; Sue Meeking, Hyden; Mary Nenke, Kukerin; Michael Nenke, Kukerin; Jan Orr, Newdegate; Dawn Petschel, Rainbow; Anne Rick, Newdegate; Winsome Roberts, Melbourne; Ivan Roll, Rainbow; Bob Schilling, Rainbow; Shirley Schilling, Rainbow; Annie Slarke, Lake Grace; Lindsay Slarke, Lake Grace; Michelle Slarke, Lake Grace; Ron Shalders, Newdegate; Ken Stewart, Indigenous Facilitator at the Mallee Catchment Management Authority (CMA), Mildura; Barry Wait, Swan Hill; and Ian Wurfels, Brim.

Last of all we must thank our families for living with this mallee country project for so long and for the endless encouragement they provided to us all along the way.

SELECT PUBLISHED SOURCES

This select list focuses on major published sources about mallee lands in southern Australia. It does not include sources that are very general in nature, or specific items such as single newspaper articles or archival files, individual interviews (see the Acknowledgements for a list of these) or web news sources. These are fully referenced in footnotes throughout the book. In addition, valuable farm diaries have been used extensively, particularly those of Charles William Coote (1896–1955), William Alfred Joseph Pearse, and William Henry Lane, and these are also fully referenced in footnotes.

Books, Book Chapters and Journal Articles

Allen, Harry (ed.), *Australia: William Blandowski's Illustrated Encyclopedia of Aboriginal Australia*, first published by Blandowski in 1862 under the title *Australien* (Canberra: Aboriginal Studies Press, 2010).

Andrews, John, 'The Emergence of the Wheat Belt in Southeastern Australia to 1830', in *Frontiers and Men: A Volume in Memory of Griffith Taylor, 1880–1963*, ed. John Andrews (Melbourne: F.W. Cheshire, 1967).

Bailey, Janette-Susan, *Dust Bowl: Depression American to World War Two Australia*, Palgrave Studies in World Environmental History (Cham, Switzerland: Palgrave Macmillan, 2016).

Barr, Neil, *The House on the Hill: The Transformation of Australia's Farming Communities* (Canberra: Halstead Press, 2009).

Barrett, A.R., *History of the War Service Land Settlement Scheme, Western Australia* (Perth: A.B. Davies, Government Printer, 1965).

Beaton, Florence, *A Woman's Work: The Story of a Mallee Farmer's Wife from 1913* (Red Cliffs, Vic.: Sunnyland Press, 1985).

Beer, Carl, *Amongst the Last of the Pioneers: A Story of the Pioneering Days of the Mallee and Millewa* (Mildura: Larena Media Services, 1986).

Beveridge, Peter. *The Aborigines of Victoria and Riverine as Seen by Peter Beveridge*, first published 1889 (Donvale: Lowden Publishing, 2008).

Birch, A.R. and Blencowe, J.P., 'The Badly Drifting Farm: Report of the Murray Mallee District Soil Conservation Board, 1948–1952' (Murray Bridge: Murray Mallee District Soil Conservation Board, 1952).

Blakers, Margaret and McMillan, Luisa, *Mallee Conservation in Victoria* (Melbourne: RMIT Faculty of Environmental Design and Construction, 1988).

Blandowski, William, 'Recent Discoveries in Natural History on the Lower Murray', *Transactions of the Philosophical Institute of Victoria* 2 (1857): 124–37.

Bonython, C.W. and Preiss, K.A., 'Hambidge Wild Life Reserve: A Survey by the Nature Conservation Society of South Australia', *South Australian Naturalist* 42, no. 2 (1967): 35–62.

Bowler, J.M., Kotsonis, A., and Lawrence, C.R., 'Environmental Evolution of the Mallee Region, Western Murray Basin', *Proceedings of the Royal Society of Victoria* 118, no. 2 (2006): 161–202.

Bradby, K., Jasper, R., Richards, R., and Pearce, H., *Diversity or Dust: A Review of the Impact of Agricultural Land Clearance Programmes in South West Australia* (Melbourne: Australian Conservation Foundation, 1984).

Brock, Peggy and Kartinyeri, Doreen, *Poonindie: The Rise and Destruction of an Aboriginal Community* (Adelaide: South Australian Government Printer and Aboriginal Heritage Branch, Department of Environment and Planning South Australia, 1989).

Broome, Richard, 'Murray Mallee: A Riverine Geography of Aboriginal Labor', in *Agricultural History* 91, no. 2 (Spring 2017): 150–70.

Burch, John, *Returning the Kulkyne* (Melbourne: John Burch, 2017).

Burvill, G.H., 'The Development of Light Lands', and 'The Last Fifty Years, 1929–1979', in *Agriculture in Western Australia: 150 Years of Development and Achievement 1829–1979*, ed. G.H. Burvill (Perth: University of Western Australia Press, 1979).

Callaghan, A.R. and Millington, A.J., *The Wheat Industry in Australia* (Sydney: Angus & Robertson, 1956).

Christensen, Joseph, 'An Early Western Australian Conservationist: The Romantic Figure of Jose Guillermo Hay', *Early Days: Journal and Proceedings of the Royal Western Australian Historical Society* 12, no. 5 (2005): 488–505.

Crook Ian G. and Burbidge, Andrew A., *Lake Magenta Nature Reserve*, W.A. Nature Reserve Management Plan, No. 4 (Perth: Department of Fisheries and Wildlife, 1980).

Dunsdorfs, Edgars, *The Australian Wheat-growing Industry, 1788–1948* (Melbourne: Melbourne University Press, 1956).

Dunsford, Adair (ed.), *The Desert Blooms: Stories of the Women of the AMP Society Land Development Scheme* (Adelaide: Wakefield Press, 1995).

Edwards, Milton, *To the Mallee Born* (Adelaide: M. Edwards, 1993).

Eggleston, Deryck J., *Kondinin, Page by Page: Frank Eggleston's Letters 1925–1932* (Perth: Deryck J. Eggleston, 2010).

Everard, George, 'Pioneering Days: Journal of George Everard' (Horsham, Victoria: *Horsham Times* Print, 1892, reprinted April 1977).

Eyre, Edward John, *Journals of Expeditions of Discovery into Central Australia and Overland from Adelaide to King George's Sound*, two volumes (London: T. & W. Boone, 1845).

Fahey, Charles, 'Agricultural Settlement in Victoria's Last Frontier: The Mallee, 1890–1951, *Agricultural History* 91, no. 2 (Spring 2017): 187–214.

Fenner, Charles, 'The Murray River Basin', *Geographical Review: American Geographical Society of New York* 24, no. 1 (January 1934): 79–91.

Fergusson, June, *Bush Battalion: The AMP Society's Ninety Mile Desert Development in South Australia* (Sydney: Australian Mutual Provident Society, 1984).

Ford, Ruth, '"The Wattles Are in Bloom … Crops Are Looking Wonderfully Well": Settler Women in the Victorian Mallee, 1920–30s', in *Outside Country: Histories of Inland Australia*, eds Alan Mayne and Stephen Atkinson (Adelaide: Wakefield Press, 2011).

Forrest, R. and Crowe, S., *Yarra-mo-up: Place of the Tall Yate Trees: A Report on the Noongar Social History of the Jerramungup Region* (Canberra: Australian Government Publication Service, 1996).

Gaynor, Andrea, 'State, Scientists and Citizens: Conserving Lake Magenta and Dragon Rocks, Western Australia', *Historical Records of Australian Science* 25, no. 2 (2014): 212–14.

Gaynor, Andrea, 'Self-Sown Crops, Modernity and the Making of Mallee Agricultural Landscapes', *Agricultural History* 91, no. 2 (Spring 2017): 171–86.

George, Ivan, *From London to Willah 1926–49* (Mildura, Vic.: Ivan George, 1990).
Gergis, Joëlle, *Sunburnt Country: The History and Future of Climate Change in Australia* (Melbourne: Melbourne University Press, 2018).
Glynn, Sean. *Government Policy and Agricultural Development: A Study of the Role of Government in the Development of the Western Australian Wheat Belt, 1900–1930* (Perth: University of Western Australia Press, 1975).
Greble, William E., *A Bold Yeomanry: Social Change in a Wheat Belt District: Kulin 1848–1970* (Perth: Creative Research, 1979).
Grey, George, *Journals of Two Expeditions of Discovery in North-West and Western Australia: During the Years 1837, 38, and 39, under the Authority of Her Majesty's Government: Describing many Newly Discovered, Important, and Fertile Districts, With Observations of the Moral and Physical Condition of the Aboriginal Inhabitants, &c. &c.* (London: T. & W. Boone, 1841).
Haebich, Anna, *For Their Own Good: Aborigines and Government in the Southwest of Western Australia, 1900–1940* (Perth: University of Western Australia Press, 1988).
Hall, Michael C. and Frost, Warwick, 'National Parks and the "Worthless Lands Hypothesis" Revisited', in *Tourism and National Parks: International Perspectives on Development, Histories and Change*, eds Frost, Warwick and Michael Hall, C. (London: Routledge, 2009).
Hallam, S.J., *Fire and Hearth: A Study of Aboriginal Usage and European Usurpation in South-western Australia* (Canberra: Australian Institute of Aboriginal Studies, 1975).
Harris, Colin, Reeves, Anne, and Symon, David (eds), *The Ninety Mile Desert of South Australia: A Report of Surveys Carried out by the Nature Conservation Society of South Australia in 1973 and 1977* (Adelaide: Nature Conservation Society of South Australia, 1982).
Harris, Colin, *Vegetation Clearance in South Australia: Report of the Interdepartmental Committee on Vegetation Clearance* (Adelaide: Interdepartmental Committee on Vegetation Clearance in South Australia, 1976).
Hassell, Ethel, *My Dusky Friends: Aboriginal Life, Customs and Legends and Glimpses of Station Life at Jarramungup in the 1880's* (East Fremantle: C.W. Hassell, 1975).
Hercock, Mason (ed.), *The Western Australian Explorations of John Septimus Roe 1829–1849* (Perth: Hesperian Press, 2014).
Herford, Ian et al., *Stirling Range and Porongurup National Parks Management Plan 1999–2009* (Perth: Department of Conservation and Land Management, 1999).
Hofmaier, Keith C., *Mallee Memories: Some Folk History of Beulah and District* (Warracknabeal: *Warracknabeal Herald*, 1976).
Hogan, Hazel V., *The Story of Kulwin* (Kulwin, Vic.: CWA of Victoria, Kulwin Branch, 1948).
Holmes, Katie, 'Redeeming Landscapes: Ireland and Australia', in *Exhuming Passions: The Pressure of the Past in Ireland and Australia*, eds Katie Holmes and Stuart Ward (Dublin: Irish Academic Press, 2011), 230–9.
Holmes, Katie and Mirmohamadi, Kylie, 'Howling Wilderness and Promised Land: Imagining the Victorian Mallee, 1840–1914', *Australian Historical Studies* 46, no. 2 (2015): 191–213.
Holmes, Katie and Mirmohamadi, Kylie, 'All Aboard for Modernity: The Better Farming Train', *Journal of Agricultural History* 91, no. 2 (Spring 2017): 215–38.
Holt, Alan J., *Wheat Farms of Victoria: A Sociological Survey* (Melbourne: School of Agriculture, University of Melbourne, 1946).

Hooper, Stephen and Levantis, Caroline, *Physical and Financial Performance Benchmarks for Grain Producing Farms, South Australia and Victoria Mallee Agroecological Zone: ABARES Report Prepared for the Grains Research and Development Corporation, Canberra, February 2011* (Canberra: ABARES, 2011).

Hopper, S.D. and Gioia, P., 'The Southwest Australian Floristic Region: Evolution and Conservation of a Global Hot Spot of Biodiversity', *Annual Review of Ecology, Evolution and Systematics* 35, no. 1 (2004): 623–50.

Hughes-d'Aeth, Tony, *Like Nothing on this Earth: A Literary History of the Wheatbelt* (Perth: UWA Publishing, 2017).

Hughes, Neal, Lawson, Kenton, and Valle, Haydn, *Farm Performance and Climate: Climate-adjusted Productivity for Broadacre Cropping Farms'*, Research Report 17.4 (Canberra: ABARES, May 2017).

Johnson, Sarah, 'Organic Farming in the Mallee: Making a Dream Come True', *SANTFA: The Cutting Edge* (Summer 2016): 12–16.

Jones, Rebecca, *Slow Catastrophes: Living with Drought in Australia* (Melbourne: Monash University Publishing, 2017).

Jordan, Denis Oswald (chair) et al., *The Environment in South Australia: Report of the Committee on Environment* (Adelaide: Committee on Environment in South Australia, 1972).

Kenyon, Alfred S., *The Story of the Mallee: A History of the Victorian Mallee Read before the Historical Society of Victoria, 18 March 1912* (Melbourne: Wilke & Co., 1982). Originally published in *Victorian Historical Magazine* 4, nos 1, 2, 3, 4 (September and December 1914, March and June 1915).

Kirby, James, *Old Times in the Bush of Australia: Trials and Experiences of Early Bush Life in Victoria during the Forties* (Melbourne: Geo Robertson and Co., n.d.).

Kitschke, Melanie (ed.), *Signs of Change: Landcare at Work in SA* (Adelaide: Primary Industries SA, 200 ?).

Krefft, Gerard, 'On the Manners and Customs of the Aborigines of the Lower Darling and Murray', *Transactions of the Philosophical Society of NSW* (1862–65), read 2 August 1865, 357–74.

Lack, John and Fahey, Charles, 'Harvester Wars: The Global Struggle between H.V. McKay, Massey–Harris and International Harvester', *Ontario History* 46, no. 1 (Spring 2004): 9–40.

Lake, Marilyn, *The Limits of Hope: Soldier Settlement in Victoria, 1915–38* (Melbourne: Oxford University Press, 1987).

Lindner, Jocelyn, *Flora and Fauna of the Victorian and South Australian Mallee* (Ouyen: Jocelyn Lindner, 2015).

Low, Tim, *Where Song Began: Australia's Birds and how they Changed the World* (Melbourne: Penguin, 2017).

The Mallee Country of Victoria and its Wonderful Resources with Maps and Illustrations (Prahran: Alfred Drakard, under instructions from E.H. Lascelles Esq., Prahran and St Kilda Chronicle Offices, 1893).

Mallee Schoolday Memories: A History and Memories of Education in the Western Australian Mallee 1917–1988 (Salmon Gums, WA: Mallee Historical Society, 1988).

Mann, James, *Mallee Pioneer: The Recollections of James Barrett Mann, Founder of Morningquest* (Swan Hill: B.R. Mann, 1981).

Massola, Aldo, 'The History of the Yelta Mission Station', *Victorian Historical Magazine* 33, no. 1 (August 1962): 251–61.

Massola, Aldo, 'Aborigines of the Mallee', *Proceedings of the Royal Society of Victoria* 79 (new series), part 2 (1966): 267–74.

Massola, Aldo, 'Aboriginal Campsites on Wyperfeld National Park and Pine Plains Station', *Victorian Naturalist* 86 (March 1969): 71–6.
May, P. and Fullagar, R.L.K., 'Aboriginal Exploitation of the Southern Mallee', *Records of the Victorian Archaeological Survey* 10 (June 1980): 152–71.
McClelland, Anne, *Strong Hands, Strong Hearts: Kaneira–Culgoa, 1890–1980* (Culgoa, Vic.: A. McClelland, 1980).
McCormick, Andrew, 'Closer Settlement in the Mallee: Dust Followed the Plough: The Millewa in the 1930s and 1940s' (MA thesis, La Trobe University, 2010), http://hdl.handle.net/1959.9/520929.
McLennan, Jennifer A., *Time, Tide and the Tyrrell: A History of the Shire of Wycheproof* (Melbourne: Hargreen Publishing, 1994).
Mitchell, T.L., *Three Expeditions into the Interior of Eastern Australia; with Descriptions of the Recently Explored Region of Australia Felix, and of the Present Colony of New South Wales* (London: T. & W. Boone, 1839), two volumes, 4 June 1836, Project Gutenberg Australia, http://gutenberg.net.au/ebooks/e00036.html.
Nature Conservation Society of South Australia, *Hambidge, Hinks and Blesing: An Assessment of Three Areas on the Eyre Peninsula* (Adelaide: Nature Conservation Society of South Australia, 1969).
Pook, Michael, Lisson, Shaun, Risbey, James, Ummenhofer, Caroline C., MacIntosh, Peter, and Rebbeck, Melissa, 'The Autumn Break for Cropping in Southeast Australia: Trends, Synoptic Influences and Impacts on Wheat Yield', *International Journal of Climatology* 29, no. 13 (2009): 2012–26.
Powell, J.M., *The Public Lands of Australia Felix and Land Appraisal in Victoria 1834–91 with Special Reference to the Western Plains* (Melbourne: Oxford University Press, 1970).
Preiss, K.A. and Thomas, P.M., 'Hincks National Park: A Survey of its Natural Values Carried Out by the Nature Conservation Society of South Australia', *South Australian Naturalist* 45, no. 2 (1970): 29–84.
Rijavec, Frank, *Malleefowl Believers: Stories of the Malleefowl and its Champions* (Ongerup WA: Malleefowl Preservation Group, 2009).
Robin, Libby, *Defending the Little Desert: The Rise of Ecological Consciousness in Australia* (Melbourne: Melbourne University Press, 1998).
Sadras, Victor O. and McDonald, Glenn, *Water Use Efficiency of Grain Crops in Australia: Principles, Benchmarks and Management* (Adelaide: Grains Research and Development Corporation, 2012).
Schürmann, C.W., *The Aboriginal Tribes of Port Lincoln in South Australia: Their Mode of Life, Manners, Customs, etc.* (Adelaide: George Dehane, 1846).
Senyard, June E. (ed.), *Birchip—Essays on a Shire* (Birchip: Shire of Birchip, 1970).
Siebentritt, Mark, Halsey, Nicole, and Stafford Smith, Mark, 'Regional Climate Change Adaptation Plan for the Eyre Peninsula' (Prepared for the Eyre Peninsula Integrated Climate Change Agreement Committee, 2014).
Shaw Neilson, John, *The Autobiography of John Shaw Neilson* (Canberra: National Library of Australia, 1978).
Smith, David F., *Natural Gain: In the Grazing Lands of Southern Australia* (Sydney: UNSW Press, 2000).
Speldewinde, Peter C., Cook, Angus, Davies, Peter M., and Weinstein, Philip, 'A Relationship between Environmental Degradation and Mental Health in Rural Western Australia', *Health & Place* 15, no. 3 (1 September 2009): 880–87.
Spence, Terry, *Jerramungup: Soldiers of the Soil* (Maylands, WA: T. Spence, 2002).
Statham Drew, Pamela. 'Sandalwood: Western Australia's Sometime Saviour', *Journal of the Fremantle Historical Society* 5 (2007): 87–105.

Stone, A.C., 'The Aborigines of Lake Boga, Victoria', *Proceedings of the Royal Society of Victoria* XXIII (new series), part 2 (March 1911): 433–68. Sturt, Charles, *Two Expeditions into the Interior of Southern Australia: During the Years 1828, 1829, 1830 and 1831: With Observations on the Soil, Climate and General Resources of the Colony of New South Wales*, two volumes (London: Smith, Elder and Co., 1833).

Taylor, Phil, *Karkarooc: A Mallee Shire History 1896–1995* (Warracknabeal: Yarriambiack Shire Council, 1996).

Thompson, George T., *A Brief History of Soil Conservation in Victoria, 1834–1961* (Melbourne: Soil Conservation Authority, 1979).

Tiver, N.S., *Desert Conquest: A Review of the Main Events Which Have Contributed to the Development of the Ninety-Mile Desert* (Adelaide: AMP Society, 1986).

Twigg, Karen, '"Another Weed Will Come Along": Attitudes to Weeds, Land and Community in the Victorian Mallee', in *Telling Environmental History: Intersections of Memory, Narrative and Environment*, eds Katie Holmes and Heather Goodall (Cham, Switzerland: Palgrave Macmillan, 2017), 213–40.

White, Matt, D., 'The Mallee Vegetation of North Western Victoria', *Proceedings of the Royal Society of Victoria* 118, no. 2 (2006): 239–43.

Whitelock, Derek, *Conquest to Conservation: History of Human Impact on the South Australian Environment* (Adelaide: Wakefield Press, 1985).

Whitwell, Gregory and Sydenham, Diane, *A Shared Harvest: The Australian Wheat Industry, 1939–1989* (Melbourne: Macmillan, 1991).

Williams, Michael, *The Making of the South Australian Landscape: A Study in the Historical Geography of Australia* (London and New York: Academic Press, 1974).

Government Publications

Australia, Bureau of Agricultural Economics, *The Australian Wheatgrowing Industry, An Economic Survey, 1964–65 to 1966–67* (Canberra: Bureau of Agricultural Economics, December 1969).

Australia, Bureau of Agricultural Economics, *Australian Agricultural and Grazing Industries Survey, 1976–77 and 1977–78, Wheat Growing Industry* (Canberra: ABARES, Australian Government Publishing Service, 1983).

Journal of Agriculture, Western Australia, 1951–1984.

Journal of Agriculture, South Australia, 1958–1976.

Journal of the Department of Agriculture of South Australia, 1905–1958.

Journal of the Department of Agriculture of Victoria, 1902–1955.

Journal of Agriculture, Victoria, 1955–1968.

Land Conservation Council (Vic.), *Report on the Mallee Study Area* (Melbourne: Land Conservation Council (Vic.), 1974).

Land Conservation Council (Vic.), *Final Recommendations: Mallee Study Area* (Melbourne: Land Conservation Council (Vic.), 1977).

Land Conservation Council (Vic.), *Mallee Area Review: Final Recommendations* (Melbourne: Land Conservation Council (Vic.), 1989).

Victoria, Crown Lands Commission of Inquiry, 'Minutes of Evidence Taken Before the Royal Commission Appointed to Inquire into the Progress of Settlement under the Land Act of 1869; also to Suggest Such Amendments Therein as may Appear to be Necessary; and Further to Report upon the Steps Necessary to Meet the Requirements of the Country on the Termination of the Pastoral Tenure at the Close of the Year 1880', *Victorian Parliamentary Papers* 1879–80, vol. 3, paper no. 72.

Victoria, Crown Lands Commission of Inquiry, 'Report of the Crown Lands Commission of Inquiry on both the Agricultural and Pastoral Occupation of the Public Lands to be Instituted on the Expiration of the Present Land Act at the Close of 1880', *Victorian Parliamentary Papers*, 1879–80, vol. 3, paper no. 73.

Victoria, Royal Commission on Soldier Settlement, 'Report of the Royal Commission on Soldier Settlement: Together with Appendices', *Victorian Parliamentary Papers*, 1925, vol. 2, paper no. 32.

Victoria, Royal Commission on Migrant Land Settlement, 'Report of the Royal Commission on Migrant Land Settlement: Together with Schedule', *Victorian Parliamentary Papers*, 1933, paper no. 3.

Victoria, Parliament, Standing Committee on Railways, 'Final Report from the Parliamentary Standing Committee on Railways on the Question of Mallee Water Supply: Together with the Appendices and Minutes of Evidence' (Melbourne: Robt S. Brain, Government Printer, 1902).

Western Australia, 'Report of the Royal Commission on the Mallee Belt and Esperance Lands', *Votes and Proceeding of the Parliament of Western Australia*, 1917, paper no. 5.

Western Australia, 'Report of the Agricultural Bank Royal Commission', *Votes and Proceedings of the Parliament of Western Australia*, 1934, paper no. 1.

Western Australia, Rural and Allied Industries Council, *Rural Land Release Policy in Western Australia* (Perth: Premier's Department, 1979).

Western Australia, Department of Parks and Wildlife, *Florabase: Database of the Western Australian Flora*, https://florabase.dpaw.wa.gov.au.

Films

Desert Conquest, directed by Lex Halliday, produced by Australian Mutual Provident Society (Australian Instructional Films, 1954), http://www.slsa.sa.gov.au/site/page.cfm?u=991&c=44290.

Mallee Country Facing Drought, Cinesound Review No. 0682 (Cinesound Productions, 1944).

Murray Darling Association, *1956 Murray Darling Floods—Part 1* (Apricot Film & Television, 2006), https://www.youtube.com/watch?time_continue=278&v=oLqAPICdvhc.

Murray Darling Association, *1956 Murray Darling Floods—Part 2* (Apricot Film & Television, 2006), https://www.youtube.com/watch?time_continue=527&v=BYaTZBzzRKU.

Rijavec, Frank (director), *A Million Acres A Year* (Snakewood Films, 2002), video recording.

INDEX

1080 poison 219, 227, 254, 292
ABARES *see* Australian Bureau of Agricultural and Resource Economics
Abbott, William 164–5
Aboriginal astronomy 11–12
Aboriginal farm workers 67, 81–4, 97, 192, 196–7, 202, 204
Aboriginal farmers, Western Australia 201–2
Aboriginal Fellowship Group 194
Aboriginal groups, in mallee country *see also names of specific groups, e.g.* Nyungar people, Wotjobaluk people 15–16, 24–5, 374–5
   Mitchell's relations with 51–3
   Sturt's relations with 47–50
Aboriginal labour 32–3, 35, 192, 193, 195, 196–7, 198, 202
Aboriginal missions 85–8
Aboriginal myths 196
Aboriginal people, and conditional purchase scheme 260–1
   custodianship of country 11–45. 282, 298, 307, 372
   eel farming 15
   exchange cycles 33–5
   food gathering 200, 203, 204–5
   forced relocation in WA 203
   history and heritage 373–6
   and mallee lands 190–206, 310
   and overlanders 67–70
   removal from Victorian Mallee 104, 191
   and silo art 354
Aboriginal women workers 198
Aborigines Protection Act 1886 (Vic) 87, 191
Aborigines Uplift Society 194, 195
Adamthwaite, Alfred 156
Adelaide Botanic Garden 284
Adnate 354
aerial spraying, of insecticides 181–2
Agricultural Bank (WA) 143, 144, 217
agricultural economics 312–3, 318–9
agricultural infrastructure, Millewa 159–60
   Ninety Mile Desert 243

Agricultural Land Release Review Committee (WA) 305–6
agricultural machinery *see also types of machinery, e.g.* disc ploughs; levellers; mallee roller; tractors; stump jump plough 244, 323, 324
   as art materials 360
   heritage displays 369, 370–1
   shortage 213, 224
agricultural policy, criticism 210
   Western Australia 142–3
agricultural productivity 312–3, 318–9, 338, 385–6
agricultural publications 170, 171, 177
agricultural research and development 313–7, 380–1
agriculture, as civilising endeavour 106
agronomists, reliance on 324
Aitken, R. 284
all-Father, Aboriginal concept 16–17
Aly, Jim 261
Amok Island 355
AMP *see* Australian Mutual Provident Society
Angas, George French 49
Anthropocene period 9–10
ants *see also* Dinosaur ants viii
Antwerp 190–201, 347, 374
aquifers xii, 122, 380
Ardipithicus ramidis 4
Argent, Kerrie 360–1
arsenic baiting, of locusts 180
artists, and mallee country 37, 283, 353–63
assisted immigrant schemes 158–9
Association for Mining and Exploration Companies 305
AusIndustry 348
'Australia Felix' 53, 54
Australian Aborigines Mission 203, 204–5
Australian Academy of Science Committee on National Parks and Reserves 288
Australian Bureau of Agricultural and Resource Economics 313, 338, 344, 385–6

Australian Conservation Foundation 305
Australian Greenhouse Office 348
Australian Institute 381
Australian Malleefowl Centre 372
Australian Mutual Provident Society 45, 208, 242–8
Australian ringneck parrots viii
Australian Wheat Board 213, 239
Australopithecus afarensis 4
avifauna *see* birdlife
Avoca River 74
Aylmore brothers 349

Bailey, Janette 185
Baird, Colin 166–8
Baird, Frank 165–7
Baird, Mary 166–8, 175
Balladonia 365–6
Ballentine, Helen 319
Balranald 51
bare fallowing *see* fallowing
Barengi Gadjin Land Council 353, 354, 375
Barngala title 375
Barr, Neil 318
barrel medic 225–6, 232
Barrett, Graham 262
Barrett, Sir James 277, 278, 290
Barrett, James W. 181
Bascombe Well National Park 295
Baxter, John 57
Beaton, Clara 176, 177
Beaton, Florence 176
Bee, Geoff 259, 263–5, 268, 269, 336
beekeeping 349–50
  in national parks 278
Beer, Carl 183–4
Beer, Jennifer 375
Beilby, John Wood 21, 37, 75
  search for pastoral country 62–4, 70, 83
Belgian colonists, as settlers 260
Benshemesh, Joe 371
Berriwillock 239, 320
Better Farming Train 171–4, 325
Beveridge, Andrew 69
Beveridge, Peter 28, 29, 32, 37–8, 45
Big Desert 6, 246–7, 297–8, 351
Big Desert Wilderness Area 298, 299, 300

Billiatt reserve 280–1, 383
Birchip 154, 177, 248, 318
Birchip Cropping Group 314–5, 316, 329
birdlife *see also specific birds, e.g.* malleefowl; regent parrots ix, 275
  conservation 383
Birdlife Australia 383
Bishop, Elsie 366
black-eared miner 22
Blanchetown 289
Blandowski, William 27–8, 29, 30, 32, 35
Blazing Swan Festival 362
blue lupins 228
Bluff Knoll 280, 292
Bob (Aboriginal guide) 58, 59, 60
Bogdish, P. 191
Bolte, Henry 220, 296
Bolton, Geoffrey 98
Bond, W.H. 195
Booroung people 11–12
Boort 153, 360
bore drilling 122
Bosisto, Joseph 95–6, 347
Bowler, Jim 13
Boyd, Arthur 283
Boyd, Robin. *The Australian Ugliness* 287
Bradby, Keith 335
Brand, Sir David 256
Brand, Harry 88
Brim Active Community Group 354
Brim station 89, 91, 92, 328, 353
British government intervention 161–2
British people, immigration scheme 158–63, 170
British Settlers League 160
broombush, as fencing material 351–2
Brown, Ron 269
Bruce, Stanley 161
Buandik people 18
Budj Bim 15
Bulga 112, 123
Bull family 194
bullocks, use of 137
bulrush root *see* kumpung
Bumbang station 89
Burch, John 70, 84, 89
Burdeu, Arthur 194, 195
Bureau of Agricultural Economics 210, 230

Index

Burke, Brian 305
Burnett (Aboriginal guide) 50, 51, 52
burning, and land clearing 45, 103, 113, 244, 245, 253, 262, 265
Bush Engineers Tractor Museum 371
bush hospitality 80, 91
Bush Tucker Garden 372
bushfires, and nature reserves 291, 383
bushland regeneration 368
Buttfield, Monty 243

Cadell, Francis 77, 78
Cambinata Yabbies 349
Cameron, Blanche 191–2
Cameron, Colin 252–3, 255
Cameron, Pelham 191–2, 198, 200
Camm, John 279
canoes 36
Cape Arid National Park 294
Cape Riche 58, 60–1
carbon dioxide emissions 379, 380
Caring for our Country program 334, 335–6
Carpobrotus glaucescens see pigface
Carrolup 203
Carruthers, Margaret 360
Carwarp 176, 177
Casey, R.G. 243
Cass, John 314, 325
cattle, effect on land 98
Cay, Robert 37
Central Board for the Protection of Aborigines (Vic) 192, 193
cereal rye 222, 225
chaff cutting 139, 140
Chaffey's Landing 27–8, 30
Chalka Creek 26
Chandos District Wheat Crop Competition 178
Chase, Allen 251
Cheetham Salt 353
Chevalier, Nicholas 37
child-rearing, instruction 174
Chinese tourists 363–4
Chisholm, Alec viii, 180–1
Clarke, Emma 197
Clarke, Eric 193, 197
Clarke, Michael F. 22
Clarke, Thomas 197, 198
Clifton, R. Cecil 278

climate change 4, 378–9
 and agriculture 313, 338–45, 380–2, 386
climate oscillations 5, 8, 380
closer settlement 102, 104, 105, 120, 124, 147, 158, 185, 215, 251
Closer Settlement Act 1912 (Vic) 148
Closer Settlement Board 148–9, 150, 151–2, 156, 164–8
clover 219–20, 225
Clow, James Maxwell 74
coal deposits, southwestern Australia 60
compung see kumpung
cobalt 227–8
conditional purchase scheme, Western Australia 256–65
conservation see nature conservation; soil conservation
conservation agriculture 322, 324
Conservation Council of Western Australia 305
Conservation Volunteers Australia 333
Conway, Kerry 329–30, 344
Cooke, John 341
Coombes, Albert 191
Coombs, John George 67, 84
Coonalpyn 44, 246, 357
Cooper, Duncan 54, 55
Coote, Ada 130, 140, 142, 153, 211–2
Coote, Charles 111–2, 115, 117–9, 129–31, 132, 137–40, 152–3, 177, 213, 321
 and 1944–45 drought 185–6
 and farm consolidation 146
 farm income 231–2
 and Federation drought 125
 and mice plague 133
 Quambatook home 211–2
 and rabbit eradication 218
 and rural politics 156
 and the wheat pool 135
Coote family 111–2
copper 228
Coppock, John 79
Corackerup 252–6
corporate ownership, of farms 321–2
Correll (Aboriginal guide) 97
Correll brothers 136
cost–price squeeze 312–3, 338
Coucill, Jacqueline 152

Council for Scientific and Industrial Research 227–8
cover crops 224–6, 327
Crawford, Sir John 213
Crook, Arthur Roy 151
crop rotation *see* ley farming
cropping competitions 170, 171, 178
Crosby, Alfred 65
Crown land, SA release 281
   WA release 208, 251–2, 256–9, 269–70, 303–5
Crown Lands Commission Inquiry (Vic) 90, 93–4
Crutzen, Paul 9
CSIR *see* Council for Scientific and Industrial Research
CSIRO, climate change research 338, 344
   wheat research 381
cumpung *see* kumpung
Curtin University 383

D.A. Wurfel Grain Collection 136, 370
dairy cows 141
dam building 89–90, 91, 188, 255
Darling River 48, 50
   pastoralists 77–8
Dattuck 167–8
Davis Plains station 91
Day, Doug 301–2
Day, Kay 301–2
debt relief 178, 215, 216, 217
Deep Time 3–10
Delhaize, Annie 260
Dempster, Andrew 97–8
Dempster, Charles 97–8
Dennings, Susanne 335
Desert Conquest (film) 45, 242, 245, 246, 247
Development and Migration Commission 160–161, 162
Devil's Lair, WA 12
dieback 292–3
Dimboola 191, 193, 196, 198
dingo fences, South Australia 94–5
   Western Australia 256
dingoes 76–7, 92–3
Dinosaur ants 365–6
direct drilling 267, 268
disc ploughs 244, 263

Discharged Soldiers Settlement Act 1917 (Vic) 147, 148
Dixon, Samuel 76
Dolferus, Rudy 381
domestic instruction *see* farmhouse management
Doran, Jack 110
Dragon Rocks Nature Reserve 294
drainage flows 5
drought *see also* Federation drought; Millennium drought 23, 120–8
   1860s 88
   1870s 87
   1914 125–6, 129
   1944–45 185–8, 210, 220
   1967–68 237–9
   1969 267
   1982–83 240, 311
Drummond, James 60
dry farming methods 135–40, 145, 178
dry scrub country 36–45
dryland salinity *see* salinity
duck trapping 33
Duncombe, Margaret 293–4
Dundas Nature Reserve 294
dune formation 6
Dunn, John 373
dust bowl phenomenon 185, 267
dust storms 6, 126–8, 173, 176, 182–9, 240
   1983 311

Ebenezer Mission 83, 87, 96, 191–2, 352, 374, 375
echidnas viii
eco-friendly tourist accommodation 349
Edmonson, Rex 265–6
educational facilities, in rural communities 212
Edwards, Ada *see* Coote, Ada
Edwards, Barry 327–8
Edwards, Blake 327–8
Edwards, Milton 182
Eggleton, G.B. 110
El Niño Southern Oscillation 120
electricity generation 347–8
Eleftheriou, Krista 237
Elliston memorial 373
Empire Settlement Scheme 158–63, 170, 186

Index

emu eggs 37
EPICCA *see* Eyre Peninsula Integrated Climate Change Agreement
Esperance 60, 98, 228–9, 250–1, 269
Esperance Land & Development Company 251
Esperance Plains (Australia) Pty Ltd 251
eucalypts, flowering times viii
Eucalyptus dumosa xi, 51, 96, 347
Eucalyptus kochii 347
Eucalyptus loxophleba 347
Eucalyptus Mallee Company 96, 346–7
eucalyptus oil industry 95–6, 214–5, 280, 347
Eureka (barge) 77
Evans, John 301
Evans, Len 301
Evans, Mick 330, 332
Everard, George 75, 78, 79–81, 88, 93, 105
Everard, Joseph 81
extreme weather conditions 378, 380
Ey, Ernest 278
Eyre, Edward John 42–4, 54–7, 66
Eyre Bird Observatory 371
Eyre Peninsula 41, 55, 56, 57, 70–1, 74, 75, 76, 85, 281, 314–5
  land settlement 114–5, 144
Eyre Peninsula Integrated Climate Change Agreement 342–3

F.H. Faulding (pharmaceutical company) 214–5, 280
fallowing 135–6, 137, 140, 145, 172, 219, 224, 327
  and dust storms 128, 173
  reduced use 178
family farms, generational conflict 325
farm art 360
farm consolidation 179, 208, 216, 217, 230
farm failure *see* farms, abandonment of
farm labourers 157, 192, 196–7, 202, 213
Farm Management 500 scheme 315
farm mechanisation 229–30, 232
farm numbers, decline in 178–9
farm reconstruction 215–7, 250
farm rehabilitation 333
farm size 142–3, 145–6, 210, 234, 240, 310, 317–9, 344–5
  Victorian Mallee 89, 91, 105, 111, 137

farm training, of Aboriginal boys 85, 201
farmer education 170–4, 177–8, 220–1
farmhouse management, instruction 173–4
farmhouses, standard of 211–2
farming xiii–xiv
  and Aboriginal impoverishment 202
  annual cycle 137–40
  improved methods *see also* fallowing; fertiliser use; pasture, improvement *etc*. 159, 170–1, 177–8, 232–5
farms, abandonment of, Victorian Mallee 150, 165, 168, 169, 170, 183, 184
  Western Australia 144, 163, 250, 260
Farr, Frank 213, 218, 232
Fauldings *see* F.H. Faulding
Faulkner, Edward 267
fauna, and land clearing 246
  protection legislation 283
Fauna Protection Advisory Committee (WA) 287–8
Federation drought 121–5, 191, 324
fences, removal 328, 329
Ferguson System 229–30
Ferguson tractors *see* tractors
fertiliser use 136, 145, 171, 220, 222, 235, 238
  New Mallee 178
  South Australia 113
  Victorian Mallee 213
  Western Australia 228, 266
Feuillet, Catherine 381
fibre plants, uses 28–32
fibre rush 30
Field, Henry 68
field days 171, 221, 228, 315, 316, 334
Filmer, J.F. 227–8
fire, Aboriginal use 9, 10, 18–22
First World War *see* World War I
fishing 200
  and Murray River peoples 27–9
Fitzgerald River National Park 263
Flatchen, Max 236
floods 235–7, 255
flora, southwestern Australia 7, 366
Flora and Fauna Advisory Committee (SA) 281, 291
food supply, in rural communities 212
Ford, Ruth 175–7

403

FORM/CBH collaboration 354–5
Forsyth, W.D. 170
Fowlers Bay 57
Frank Hann National Park 294
Fraser, A.J. 287–8
Fraser, L.J. 225
Fraser Ranges 98
freehold land, and native title 374
French White Millet 327
Friends of Riverland Parks 371
Frost, Lionel 136
fuel, from mallee biomass 348
Fullagar, R.L.K. 36

Gairdner 252–6
Gairdner River, 1955 flood 255
Gammage, Bill. *The Biggest Estate on Earth* 19–20, 21
Gastrolobiums 97, 227, 254
Gawler Ranges 55, 56
generational differences, on family farms 325–6
George family 186
Gepp, Herbert 161, 162
giant mallow 30
Gill, S.T. 66–7
glacial activity 4, 5, 8
global warming *see* climate change
glyphosate 322, 323
gnamma holes 39–40, 59
Gnowangerup 203–5, 228
Gnowangerup Native Welfare Committee 260–1
gold mining 352
gold-rush, and farm labour 84
Gondwana 3–4, 6
Gondwana Link 382, 383
Goodman, David 106
Goodwin, J.H. 86–7
Goreng people 202
Gott, Beth 20, 32
Gourrmjanyuk people 26
government agricultural assistance schemes 208, 209
Goyder, George 103
Goyder's line 103, 115, 144
Graetz, Dean 331
grain, Quambatook store 153, 156
  storage 239
  transporting 112

granite country, southwestern Australia 26, 39–40, 58–9
grass tree root, as food 42
Gray, John 115–6
grazing, licences 297, 368
  in national parks 278, 368
Great Ancestors, Aboriginal concept 16, 18, 69
Great Australian Bight 57, 58
Great Depression 157, 209
Great Southern Region, Aboriginal population 201, 203
Grey, George 22, 66, 68
group settlement scheme 243–4
grower groups 314–5
Gum, George 317, 338, 339
gypsum mining 352

Habitat 141 382
Haebich, Anna 201, 202, 206
Hagenauer, Reverend 87
Haigh, John Frederick 74
Hale, Mathew 85
Half-Caste Act (Vic) *see* Aborigines Protection Act
Hall, Sue 325, 366
Hallam, Sylvia 19, 70
Hambidge reserve 281, 290–1, 294–5, 375
Hanslow Cup competition 221, 225
Harnett, Benjamin 98
Harradine, Gail 198, 200
Harradine, Leila 198
Harradine, Lester Marks 193
Harrington Seed Destructor 326
Harris, Colin R. 42, 301
Harrison, Athol 195, 198
Harrison, Margaret 195
Harrison, Nancy 191, 195, 196, 198
Harrison, Samuel 200–1
Harrison family 193, 194–5, 196, 197
Hassell, Edith 17–18, 20, 39–40, 41
Hassell family 97
Hattah Lakes National Park 298
Hawdon, John 69
Hawson, Henry 70
Hay, José Guillermo 278–9
header harvesters 241
Heartlands (TV series) 331
herbicide use 235, 267, 322, 323

INDEX

Hillsea station 81–2
Hilton, Russell 237, 238–9, 318, 339, 343
Hincks reserve 281, 290–1, 295, 375
Hochman, Zvi 338
Hodges, Jay 365
Hogan, Hazel 175, 188–9
Holding brothers 118
Holocene period 8
Holt, Alan J. 211–2
Homesteads Act 1893 (WA) 142
hominids 4
honey production *see* beekeeping
honeyeaters viii
Hopetoun 107–8, 134, 154, 177, 317–8, 376
horses 98–9, 117–9, 138, 139, 140
    replaced by tractors 137, 224, 229
    replaced by trucks 153
Hoskins, Cecil H. 248
Howitt, A.W. 16, 17
Hudson, Flexmore 283–4
Hughes, Neal 338, 344
human migration, from Africa 8
hunting 367, 368
Hutchinson, Ross 286–7
Hutchinson, William 192
Hyden 318, 337, 341, 365
Hyden Rock 39

Inman, Henry 68
insecticides 180–1
insects viii
Insignia (wheat variety) 238
International Wheat Genome Sequencing Consortium 380–1

Jacup 259–60, 263–4
Jamieson, Hugh 79, 83, 84
Jari Jari people 27–8, 33, 38
Jarikari people 84
Jarramongup station 17, 20, 39, 252
Jericho, Sam 301
Jerramungup 58, 97, 252–6, 259, 262, 265–6, 269, 336
    Italian migrants 253–4
    as trade centre 40–41
jewel beetles viii
Jindyworobaks 283
Johnson, Jim 260, 261–3

Johnson, Jimmy (artist) 360
Johnson, Maree 260, 262–3
Jones, Rebecca 123, 125
Jordan, Denis 295
Juddy Roller (company) 353
Junginginyook *see* Kennedy, Richard

kangaroo hunting 201
Kaniera 111
karkalla see pigface
Karoonda 126, 232, 233
Katanning 202–3
Kelly, A.W. 179
Kelly, Cathie 262, 266
Kelly, Malcolm 262, 266, 326
Kelly, Nick 326–7
Kelly, Peter 332–3
Kennedy, Patrick 200–1
Kennedy, Richard 191, 195
Kennedy family 197
Kenny, Robert 87
Kenyon, Alfred xii, 88–9, 111, 190
Kerang Lakes 367
Kevin 353
Kimber, Dick 44, 45
King, Alf 195
King, Truby 174
Kingdon family 258
Kinnear family 194
Kirby, James 28, 29, 32
Kirkegaard, John 324
Kirner, Joan 330
Kondinin, dust storm 182
Kondinin Group 314–5
Koonibba 86
Krefft, Johann 28, 30, 32, 33, 34
Kukenarup memorial 373, 374
Kulin 358–9, 362
Kulkyne station 38, 84, 89, 91
Kulwin 149–52, 154, 166, 175, 178–9, 230
kumpung 28, 30, 32

La Trobe University 381
labour, shortages 213
    on pastoral runs 78–84, 97
Ladjiladji people 84
Lady Augusta (steamboat) 77, 78
Lake, Marilyn 151
Lake Agnes 35, 36

Lake Albacutya 26, 35, 74, 78, 79, 83, 196, 363
Lake Albacutya Regional Park 298
Lake Benanee 51
Lake Boga 26, 53, 74, 86
Lake Bonney 68
Lake Buloke 6
Lake Bungunnia 5, 6, 9
Lake Corrong station 89, 90–91, 92, 107
Lake Crosbie 353
Lake Dundas 26
Lake Gillies 55
Lake Grace xii, 26, 97, 188, 228, 318, 336, 341–2, 352, 360–1
Lake Grace Regional Artspace 361
Lake Hamilton 81
Lake Hattah 26
Lake Hindmarsh 15, 16, 26, 35, 54, 64, 74, 75, 93, 196
Lake Hindmarsh Act 1904 (Vic) 87
Lake King 26, 58, 371
Lake MacDonnell 353
Lake Magenta 26, 58
Lake Magenta Nature Reserve 284–8, 290, 293–4
Lake Mungo 13
Lake Nitchie 13
Lake Torrens 55
Lake Tyers 191
Lake Tyrrell 6, 11, 14, 26, 353, 363–4, 367
Lake Victoria 74
Lake Wirrengren 6, 74
Lake Wonga 74
L'Albert station 89
Lamb, George Hamilton 194
Lambert, Cecil Ralph 209–10
Lameroo 154, 177, 318
Lampard, Clarice 162
Land Act 1898 (WA) 143
Land Board (SA) 280–1
land clearing 103–12, 113, 115–9, 208
  and conservation 301–6
  control of 223, 302
  Ninety-Mile Desert 243–6
  Victorian Mallee 137, 150, 166
  Western Australia 202, 204, 253, 262, 263, 269–70
Land Conservation Act 1970 (Vic) 296
Land Conservation Council (Vic) 208, 296–300, 304, 350, 351, 352, 367–8

land degradation 267, 269
Land Release Study Group (WA) 303–5
land settlement, South Australia 103, 113–5
  Western Australia 143
Land Settlement (Development Leases) Act 1949 (SA) 243
Landcare 267, 310, 330–4
landscape painting 360
Lane, Maud 141, 142, 152
Lane, William 141, 149–52, 179, 217
Lascelles 354
Lascelles, Edward 91, 93, 107–8
Last Glacial Maximum 8, 12–13, 14
Laught, Keith 247
Lay, John 69
lead arsenate spraying 180
Leichhardt, Ludwig 19
Leipoa ocellata see malleefowl
lerp viii, 37–8
levellers 244
Lewis, E.H. 260
ley farming 219–20, 224
Li, Song 381
lignotuber *see* mallee root
Linkletter, Art 251, 252
Little Desert 6, 196, 200, 248
Little Desert National Park 288–9
Little Swamp 70
lizards viii
Llewellyn, Rick 323
Lloyd, Michael 336
loan *see* malleefowl
Lock, Annie 203
Lockhardt 360
locusts 179–82
Lowaldie 154
lowan *see* malleefowl
Loxton 237, 318, 369, 376
lucerne 249, 336, 337
  aphids 249
Lutheran farming community 86

Macfarlane, J. 88, 90
Magarey, Alexander 43
Magee, Fintan 354
mallee, etymology ix–x
mallee biomass, conversion to fuel 348
  and electricity generation 347–8

Index

Mallee Birds Conservation Action Plan 383
Mallee Catchment Authority 341
Mallee Country Facing Drought (film) 184, 331
mallee country, Aboriginal custodianship xiii, 2, 11–45, 307
  climate xii
  diversification 346–77
  European colonisation xiii–xiv, 2, 9, 46–64
  exploration 46–64
  extent ix–x, xi
  and human occupation xiii, 8–10
  place names 72–3
  population decline 310, 317–22
Mallee Desert Rally 367
Mallee emu-wrens 383
mallee eucalypts xi, 7, 22
Mallee Heritage Committee 369
Mallee Landcare plan 1993 (Vic) 332–3, 336
mallee lands, clearance xi, 51
  ecology x–xii, 23
  flora vii, 275, 366
  soil conditions vii, xiii, 104
  southeastern Australia vii, xii, 4–6, 12–15
  southwestern Australia vii, xii, 6–7, 9, 12, 39–41
Mallee Pastoral Leases Act 1883 (Vic) 94, 96, 104
Mallee Research Station 220, 224, 225–6, 316, 317
mallee roller 103–4, 105, 108, 109, 115–6
mallee root xi, 244, 254
  as food 44
Mallee Root Festival 362
mallee roots, removal 116–7, 119, 137, 150, 151, 166, 177, 204, 253–4, 263–4
Mallee Soil Drift Control competition *see* Hanslow Cup competition
Mallee Sustainable Farming 314, 315
Mallee Tourist and Heritage Centre 136, 370
mallee whipbird 280, 351
malleefowl viii–ix, 22, 276–7, 284
  eggs 37
  protection 332, 352, 371–2, 383

Malleefowl Preservation Group 372
Manangatang Landcare group 334
Mandeville, Arthur 91, 92
manganese 227, 228
Mann, Bob 122
Mann, James 106, 122–3, 127, 156
Manning, W.A. 256
Mannum 236
Manorina melanotis see black-eared miner
Mantung 321, 330, 332
Marama 327
Maraura people 68
marginal farms, reclamation 215–7, 232, 233–4
Marks, Clara 198–9
Marks, Norman 196
Marks, Ron 196, 197, 200
Marks, William Thomas 200
Marks family 193, 194, 197
Marshall, A.J. *The Great Extermination* 287
Marshall, Allan 341–2
marsupials viii
Martindale family 198–9
Mary Anne (steamboat) 77
massacres, of Aboriginal people 67–8, 69, 71, 373
Massey, Charles. *Call of the Reed Warbler* 327
Massola, Aldo 35–6, 43
Mattingley, Arthur 275, 276, 277
May, P. 36
McBryde, Isabel 34–5
McClelland, Anne 340
McClelland, Ian 313–4, 315, 324, 326, 340, 343
McCredie, Thomas 89–90, 91, 92
McDonald, Helen 341
McDonald, Mick 352
McFarlane, Neil 223
McGilp, J. Neil 280
McIntosh, Josh 327
McIntosh, Peri 327
McKee, Glennis 334
McLeay, George 47, 49
McLennon, John 91, 92
McLeod, Marjorie 361–2
McNeil, J.R. 9
medical facilities, in rural communities 212

Meehan, Adrian 36
Meeking, Rolf 316, 318, 322, 333, 341
Meeking, Sue 318, 319, 343
Melaleuca uncinata see broombush
Melbourne, 1983 dust storm 311
Melbourne–Kerang railway 112
Melville, Donald 108
Menzies, James 192
mice plagues 132–4, 239
Mildura 382
  Sturt's description of 46–7
military training, in national parks 293, 297–8
Millennium drought 324, 329, 340
Miller, Henry 'Money' 89, 90
Miller, John 75, 89, 91, 92
Millewa *see also* Murray River 159–60, 183, 186
  settlers' grievances 160–2
Millewa–Carwarp Landcare Group 333
A Million Acres a Year (documentary) 335
Milloo *see* Murray River
mineral sands extraction 352
minimum-till techniques 267–8
mining, and mallee country 352
Miocene period 4
Mitchell, Thomas 18, 26, 27, 32, 69, 126
  exploration of NSW inland rivers 50–4
Mjöberg, Eric 279
Mondellimin *see* Chaffey's Landing
Monkey, account of massacre 67–8
Moore family 194
Moore River 203
Moorhouse, Matthew 68
Moorna station 84
Moorunde Wildlife Reserve 289
moral education, and Better Farming Train 172–4
Moravian missions 86, 87
Morey, Edmund 68, 74, 76–7, 83
Morgan 236
Morton, William Lockhart 81
motor racing 366–7
motor vehicles, effect on rural townships 157
Mt Dispersion 52, 53, 69
Mt Ney 59

Mt Ridley 59
Mt Shaugh Conservation Park 295–6
Mt William 15
Mueller Botanic Society 278
Muir, John 274
Mulka's Cave 40, 373
mullenising *see* land clearing
Mungo Man 13
Mungo Woman 13
Murphy, James F. 209
Murray Gulf, extent 4–5, 7, 9
Murray Mallee, cropping competition 178
  land settlement 114, 144
  pastoral crisis 88–97
  rainfall 113
  remnant vegetation 301
  usage x
Murray Mallee District Soil Conservation Board 222
Murray pines ix
Murray River 13–14, 20, 23, 26–32, 1956 flood 236–7
  Aboriginal populations 83, 84, 86
  course 5
  flow rate 5, 74
  Mitchell's exploration 50–3
  pastoral runs 71
  pastoralists 78
  steamboats 77
  Sturt's exploration 46–7
Murray–Darling junction 86
Murray–Darling Basin, 1956 flood 235–6
  climate change survey 381
Murray–Darling Basin Authority, and salinity 336
Murray–Darling system 5, 23
Murray–Kulkyne Regional Park 298
Murray–Sunset National Park 353, 367–9, 383
Murray, Jack 192–3
Murray, John 277
Murrayville 327
Murrayville Landcare group 334
mus domesticus see mice
museums 369–71
music festivals 361
Muthi Muthi people 13
myxomatosis 218–9, 229, 253

Naou people 41–2, 43, 70, 88
Narrogin 347
National Park and Wildlife Reserves (SA) 291
national parks 272–3, 274–80
    opposition to 277, 279, 281, 284–7, 288–9, 296–7, 367–8
National Parks (Amendment) Act 1989 (Vic) 300
National Parks and Wildlife Act (SA) 295
National Parks Association of Victoria 277
National Parks Board (WA) 291
National Soil Conservation Program 223
native bees viii
native fauna, and silo art 356
native flora, and silo art 355–6
native grasses 75–6, 341
Native Title Act 1993 374
Native Title Tribunal 375
Native Vegetation Act 1991 (SA) 302
Natural History Society of South Australia 289
nature conservation 208, 271–307, 382–3
    advocacy 271–4, 275, 277, 278–9, 280, 284, 287, 301 2, 303–4, 306–7
    incentives 301–2
        opposition to 301, 369
    private initiatives 289
Nature Conservation Society of South Australia 294–6, 300
nature reserves 271–3
Nauges, Céline 381
Ned's Corner station 369
Neilson, John Shaw 119
Nenke, Mary 348–9
Nenke, Michael 348–9
neoliberalism, and agriculture 310, 313, 316, 322
    and Landcare 334
Neumayer, George 84
Neville, A.O. 203
New Mallee 146, 147, 148, 242–70
New Norcia Mission 201
Newdegate 262, 263, 318, 341, 356
Newdegate Research Station 229, 316
Ngadju Indigenous Protected Area 375–6
Ngadju people 383

Nganguraki people 12
Ngargad people 15–16, 42, 44
Ngarkat Conservation Park 300, 383
Ngarkat people *see* Ngargad people
Ngyiampaa people 13
Ninety Mile Desert 228, 242–6, 276, 295
Nitschke, Carl 191
no-till techniques 312, 319, 322–6, 328, 329, 334, 344
Nobby (Aboriginal shepherd) 83
noisy miners viii
Nolan, Sidney 283
Noongar Native Title Settlement 375
Norris, Ray 11
North Brighton station 79
Northam 354
Norton's Market Garden 193
Nothomyrmecia macrops see Dinosaur ants
nulla-nulla 341
Nullan station 91
Nullarbor Plain 7, 12, 99
Nullawil 360
nutrient-deficient soils 227
Nyabing 284, 376
Nyungar people 12, 40, 61, 201, 204, 206, 291, 372, 373, 383

oats 131, 140, 224
O'Dwyer, Laura 320
oil mallees, and salinity control 348
Olmstead, Alan L. 229–30
O'Neill, Kelly 259
Ongerup 258, 259, 263, 366
Ongerup Community Development Group 372
organic farming 326–8
O'Shannassey, Lyonel 334
O'Sullivan, Hugh 278
Outlet Creek 15, 35, 64, 74
Ouyen 152, 154, 318, 362
Ouyen Malleefowlers *see* Victorian Malleefowl Recovery Group
over-expansion, of mallee farms 142–6, 209
overgrazing 76
overlanders 66–70
Overseas Mallee Settlers' Association 161
overstocking 76

409

ownership, Aboriginal concepts of 16, 17, 69

Paakantji people 13
Pallinup River 58
Pangkala people 88
Pardoe, Colin 14
Parilla Sands 5, 6
Parish, Roger 381
parrots viii
pastoral licences 69, 71, 89, 93
pastoral runs, establishing 70–8, 97
pastoralism 65, 80
   southwestern Australia 71, 97–9
pastoralists 2
   ideological opposition to 93
   relations with Aboriginal people 82–3
pasture, improvement 219–26
   seeding 244
Patchewollock 320, 354, 361
Patton, C.T. 238
Peak Charles 58, 59
Peak Charles National Park 294
Peak Eleanora 58
Pearse, Alfred 141
Pearse, William 112, 115, 123–4, 125–6, 131
Peebinga reserve 280
Pental Island 89
Pepper, Nathanael 87
Perkins, Arthur 142, 144, 145
Phytophthora cinnamomi see dieback
Piangil station 89
Piccoli, John 360
pig-farming 266
pigface 29, 42
pigs, effect on land 98
Pine Plains 15, 36, 64, 74, 75, 78, 81, 89
Pink Lakes saltworks 198, 352
Pink Lakes State Park 298, 353
Pinnaroo 136, 144, 154, 177, 318, 370
   land settlement 114
Pioneer Settlement, Swan Hill 369–70, 371
pioneer villages 369–71
Piper (Aboriginal guide) 50, 51, 52, 53
plant genetics 380–1
plants poisonous to livestock 97, 227, 254–5, 258
Pleistocene period 8

ploughing competitions 85
poets, and mallee country 283–4
poisonous plants *see* plants poisonous to livestock
pollinators vii–viii
Poochera 365–6
Pooginook Conservation Park 371
Poonindie Mission 85, 88
Porker, Justin 327
Porker, Rita 327
Port Lincoln 56, 57
possum hunting 30, 83, 201
post-war boom 231–5
prickly grass 51
primeval continents 3
private development, Esperance 250–1
private investment, in land development 242–50
privatisation, of agricultural services 316–7, 322
Provisional Allotment Scheme (SA) 232
Pugsley, Bob 369
pygmy possums viii
Pyne, Stephen 18–19
Pyramid Hill 53

Quambatook 106, 111, 127, 138, 152–3, 154–7, 211, 320

RAAF *see* Royal Australian Air Force
Raak Plains 15, 38
rabbit fences, South Australia 94–5
Rabbit Haemorrhagic Disease 368
rabbit-proof fences, Victoria 94
   Western Australia 99, 371
rabbits, effect on pastoral runs 91–2, 95, 99
   eradication 107, 168, 217–9, 253, 333, 368
railway construction 87, 112, 114, 115, 124, 144, 149, 153, 159, 161
railway workers 157
Rainbow Landcare group 333
rainfall 113, 145, 237–8, 266, 339, 341, 342, 380
   effect on salinity 337
Randell, William 77
Ravensthorpe 259, 355
Ravensthorpe Historical Society 373
Ravensthorpe Range 103, 113

Ravensthorpe Wildflower Show 366
red sands, coloration 6
Redcliffs 236
reduced-chemical techniques 326
reed beds 28
refugees, and rural communities 382
regenerative farming 326–8
regent parrots viii, 383
Regional Arts Victoria 354
remnant vegetation 263, 269, 330, 343
Renmark 236
returned servicemen *see* soldier settlement schemes
revegetation 269, 336
Rhode, Paul 229–30
Riceman, David 228, 242
Richardson, A.E.V. 158, 219
Rick, Anne 263, 318, 325, 341
road construction, Western Australia 257
Robin, Libby 9–10, 288
Robinson, George Augustus 75
Robinson, Hugh 243, 246, 248
rock art 12, 40, 373
Roe, John Septimus 21
  survey of WA mallee 58–61
root rakes 263
Rosebery 354
rotation cycles 178, 224–5, 231, 327
Royal Australian Air Force 181–2
Royal Commission on Australian Wheat Industry 1934 215
Royal Commission on Light Lands and Poison-Infested Lands (WA) 227
Royal Commission on Migrant Land Settlement 1933 162–3
Royal Commission on the Mallee Belt and Esperance Lands (WA) 143
Royal Society of South Australia 280
Rufus River massacre 67–8
Rural and Allied Industries Council (WA) 303, 304
rural communities, ageing population 320
  and refugees 382
  sustainability 376–7
  withdrawal of services 319–20
rural life, research 210, 211–2
Rural Reconstruction Commission 208–12, 215, 219

Russell Ranges 59
Rutherglen Research Station 219
rutile 352

Sahlins, Marshall 35
salinity 249, 258–9, 269, 304, 334–7
  control, Western Australia 222–3, 335–6, 348
Salmon Gums 318
salmon gums xii
salt country, in mallee lands 7, 39
salt lakes xii–xiii, 26, 56, 258
  and water birds ix
salt mining 352–3
salt pans 55
sand drift *see* soil drift
sand fescue 249
sandalwood, southwestern Australia 61
Santalum spicatum see sandalwood
scarred trees 36
Schell, J.T. 74, 76
Schilling, Bob 238, 240, 317, 324, 339
Schulz, Reverend 194
Schürmann, C.W. 41, 43
Schwarz, Jenny 327
Schwarz, John 327
scientific farming, belief in 158, 159, 171, 172, 325
Scofield, Noel 369
Scorpion Springs Conservation Park 295–6
Scown, Alan 237
Scrub Lands Act 1866 (SA) 103
sculptures, of agricultural machinery 360
Sea Lake 318, 363–4
sea-level changes, southeastern Australia 4–5
Second World War *see* World War II
See, Brenton 356
SEPWA *see* South East Premium Wheat Growers Association
Serventy, Dom 284–5
Serventy, Vincent. *A Continent in Danger* 287
Seymour family 353
Shakespeare Festival 361–2, 370
Shalders, Ron 341
Shaw, Flora 105, 106, 107
shearers 78, 80, 81–2

sheep, adapting to mallee lands 65
  and damage to land 95, 98, 329
  numbers 89, 90, 91, 92, 95, 136, 234, 328–9
  and organic farming 328
  and wheat farming 136, 140, 145, 151, 178, 220, 233, 328–30
Sheep Hills 354
sheep farming 2, 79–81, 88–96, 97–9, 214
shepherds 80–1, 83
silo art 353–7
Simson, Fiona 382
Skene, A.J. 93–4
Slarke, Annie 366
Slarke, Lindsay 325
Slarke, Michelle 343
smallpox epidemics 27, 44–5, 69
Smart, Eric 228
Smart, Robbie 263
Smith, Charles 70
Smith, Rod 371
Soil and Land Conservation Act 1945 (WA) 223
soil conditions 104, 113
soil conservation 219–26, 265, 267–9
Soil Conservation Service (WA) 223, 265, 267
soil drift 183–5, 188, 221, 240, 247, 268, 269, 304, 311–2
soil erosion, control strategies 220–2, 311–2, 322, 333, 368
soldier settlement schemes 146–52, 164–70
  Western Australia 251–5
Solomon, John 85
Sonchus oleraceus see sow thistles
South Australia, Eyre's surveys 55–7
  mapping 103
South East Premium Wheat Growers Association 314–5
sow thistles 79
Specht, Ray 288
Special Committee on Salinity in Soils 1924 (WA) 335
species migration, and climate change 341–2, 343
Speedway pamphlet 159, 161, 162
Spencer, Tania 360–1
Spieseke, Reverend 86, 87

Sporting Shooters Association of Australia 368
Stanbridge, William Edward 11
Stasinowsky, Leon 302
steamboats, Murray River 77
Stirling Range 6, 7
Stirling Range National Park 208, 274, 278–9, 282, 291–3
stock losses, to poison plants 254
Stock Reduction Scheme (WA) 266
stock routes 66–70
stock tax 91
Stone, A.C. 26
stone artefacts, in mallee country 190
Strahan, Ross 266
Strangways Act 1869 (SA) 103
Streaky Bay 55, 56, 57
stripper 103–4, 138
stripper-harvester 136, 138
stripper-thresher 137
stubble grazing 224–6
stump-jump plough 103–4, 105, 108, 109, 117
Sturt, Charles 26–7, 46–50, 69
Summerhayes, Ash 320
Sunraysia Desert Rally 366–7
Sunset country 297–8, 366–7
Sunset Desert 6
superphosphate see fertiliser use
sustainability, of agriculture 310
  of rural communities 376–7
Swan Hill 361–2
Swan Hill Folk Museum 369–70

taarp see lerp
Taeger, Reverend 86
Tambellup 349
tanks see dam building
Taplan 327
Taylor, Bob 365–6
Teakle, L.J.H. 228
tectonic movements 5–6
Telopea Downs 248
Thompson, Charley 38
Thomson, Donald 35
Tilki 53
Tin Horse Highway (WA) 358–9
titanium 352
Titybong station 89
Tjaltjraak Native Title Corporation 16

Index

Tonts, Matthew 142
Torney, Janet 320
totemic relations 17–18
totems 200
tourism, in mallee country 363–72
   and nature reserves 274, 275, 279, 280, 282, 290, 291–2, 294
   and silo art 355–6
towns, in mallee country 152–7
trace elements 227–9, 242
tractors, and agricultural productivity 208, 229–30, 231, 240
   and flood defence 236
   heritage displays 371
trade routes, southwestern Australia 40–1
trading systems *see* Aboriginal people, exchange cycles
Traditional Owners, recognition of 374–6
Trimble, J.J. 221
Triodia scariosa vii
Trust for Nature 369
Typha muellera see kumpung
typha reed *see also* reed beds 20, 32

underground water *see* aquifers
Underwood, E.J. 227–8
United Aborigines Mission *see* Australian Aborigines Mission
United Farmers and Stockowners Association 302
University of Newcastle massacre map 69, 70–1

van Helten, Guido 353–4, 357
Varley 371
Vaux, Kaye 263
vegetation, and climate change 341–2
Victoria, the Speedway to Rural Prosperity see Speedway pamphlet
Victorian Farmers Federation 331, 367–8
Victorian mallee *see Eucalyptus dumosa*
Victorian Mallee, Aboriginal artefacts 190
   Aboriginal people 190–201
   and climate change 339–41
   land subdivision 104, 105, 107, 108, 147
   mapping 105
   pastoral runs 71, 74

population decline 185, 188
reimagining 107–8
soldier settlement 147–52, 164–70
standard of living 211
women's accounts of 175–7
Victorian Malleefowl Recovery Group 371–2
Victorian National Parks Association 287
Victorian Soil Conservation Authority 222, 311
The Village–Historic Loxton 369
virtual fencing 329
Vulpia fasciculata see sand fescue

Wade, Henry, survey of Vic–SA border 54, 61
Wadham, Samuel Macmahon 209–10, 212
Wadi Wadi people 29, 37
Wagant 149–52, 230
Waite Agricultural Research Institute 227
walk-offs *see* farms, abandonment of
Walker, Johnnie 253
Walpeup Research Station *see* Mallee Research Station
War Service Land Settlement Scheme (WA) 251–3, 254, 256
Warracknabeal Wheatlands Agricultural Machinery Museum 371
water, finding in dry country 42–3, 56, 61–2, 75, 122
   shortage 74–5, 120
   supply 380
      Victorian Mallee 120, 121, 123, 124, 125–6, 187, 211, 232, 341
      Western Australia 188, 255, 261
   tanks 125
water birds ix
Waterloo Bay massacre 373
Watson, Ernest William 149–50
Wave Rock 365
Wave Rock Weekender 361
Webb, Stephen 29–30
weedicides *see* herbicide use
weeds *see also* sand fescue 323
   control 322, 326–8
Weekly Times, women's letters to 175–7
Welfare, Mary *see* Baird, Mary
wells, sinking of 75

Wemba Wemba people ix, 26, 46, 86
Wentworth 236
Wergia people 16, 36
Western Australia Department of Lands and Surveys 257, 259
Western Australian Department of Agriculture 227–8, 257
Western Australian Naturalists' Club 284, 286
Western Australian No-tillage Farmers Association 329
Western Australian Tree Society 287
Western Australian Wildlife Authority 290
Western Ground Parrot 305
Western Power 347, 372
wheat, carting 138–9
  decline in demand 266
  exports 129, 132
  genome mapping 380–1
  global overproduction 239
  harvesting 110–1, 137–8
    technology 136–7, 231, 240, 241
  importing 129–30
  planting restrictions 213
  prices 160, 213, 231
    1930 collapse 168, 178, 183, 208, 209, 215
  quotas 208, 239, 266, 295
  sowing 139
  stubble burning 139, 224, 226, 326
  varieties *see also* Insignia 139
    heat-tolerant 381
    introduction of new 139, 171, 178, 234–5
  yields 142, 144, 234, 327, 338, 344, 345, 380, 385–6
Wheat Board 134
wheat farmers, standard of living 266–7
wheat farming 103–56
  decline 230
  profitability 234
wheat pool, and guaranteed minimum price 135, 144
wheat stabilisation scheme 213
Wheeler, Sarah Ann 381
Wheelman people *see* Wiilman people
White, Edward Riggs, survey of Victorian Mallee 61–2, 70
White, Michael 321
White, Richard 22–3
Wiilman people 18, 41
wild dogs *see* dingoes
wilderness areas, concept of 282, 298–300
WildEyre 382
Wilguldy (Aboriginal guide) 57
Willandra Lakes 6, 8, 13
Williams, Jack 204–6
Williams, Leonard *see* Williams, Jack
Williamson, John 320
Williss, George 279
Wilson, Doss 237
Wilson, Gloria 237
Wimmera, farming success 105
Wimmera–Mallee open channel system 187
Wimmera River 15, 23, 35–6, 54, 75, 79–80, 87
  Aboriginal presence 192, 193, 196, 197, 374
  Eyre's exploration 54
wind erosion *see* soil erosion
winnowing 110, 136–37
Wiradjuri people 48
Wirangu people 86, 373
Wirrengren–Kulkyne path 70, 90
Wirrengren Plain 15, 35–6, 64
Wise, Frank 209
Wolfe, Patrick 374
wombats, hunting 30, 31
  protection 289
women, and Better Farming Train 173–4
  and farming 140–2
  and rural isolation 212
  and the settlement endeavour 175–7
Woods, Alma 205
Woods, Robert 75
wool, demand for 65
  prices 231, 249, 266
  production 214
  transporting 77–8
Woolridge, A.G. 232–3
World War I 129, 135
World War II 157, 181, 209, 213–4
Wotjobaluk people 16, 35, 36, 70, 81, 87, 191–2, 196–201, 374–5
Wowinda, Fred 87
Wurfel Grain Collection *see* D.A. Wurfel Grain Collection

Wurfels, Ian 328
Wycheproof 321, 360
Wylie (Aboriginal guide) 55, 57
Wyperfeld Lakes 15
Wyperfeld National Park viii, 36, 208, 274, 275, 277–8, 290, 298, 367

Yaapeet Landcare group 333–4
yabby farming 349
yam cultivation 22
Yarramoup Aboriginal Corporation 373
Yarriambiack Shire 354, 356
Yates, Judith 247–8

Yeelanna Landcare group 332
yellow-throated miners viii
Yelta Mission 86–7
yeoman farmer concept 104–6, 110, 142, 146–7, 158, 170, 179, 185, 248
Yerre Yerre station 79, 83
Yongergnow 372
Yorke Peninsula 103
Yorta Yorta people 374
Young, Sir Henry 77

zinc 228
zircon 352

ABOUT THE AUTHORS

Richard Broome is Emeritus Professor in History at La Trobe University and President of the Royal Historical Society of Victoria. He is the author of 14 books on Indigenous and Australian History, his most recent being *A Naga Odyssey: Visier's Long Way Home* (2017) with Visier Sanyü, and *Aboriginal Australians: A History Since 1788* (2019, 5th edition).

Charles Fahey taught history at La Trobe University, Melbourne until his retirement in 2018. His research explores Australian Labor, rural and mining History. With Alan Mayne he published *Gold Tailings: Forgotten Histories of Family and Community on the Central Victorian Goldfields* (2010).

Andrea Gaynor is Associate Professor of History, Chair of the History Discipline Group and Director of the Centre for Western Australian History at the University of Western Australia. An environmental historian, she seeks to use the contextualising and narrative power of history to help address environmental problems.

Katie Holmes is Professor of History and Director of the Centre for the Study of the Inland at La Trobe University, Melbourne. Her work integrates environmental, gender and oral history, and seeks to understand the experience of Australian settlement. Her most recent book is *Between the Leaves: Stories of Australian Women, Writing and Gardens* (2011).

CPSIA information can be obtained
at www.ICGtesting.com
Printed in the USA
BVHW031344040320
574022BV00003B/72